Lecture Notes in Computer Science 12770

More information about this subseries at http://www.springer.com/series/7409

Jessie Y. C. Chen · Gino Fragomeni (Eds.)

Virtual, Augmented and Mixed Reality

13th International Conference, VAMR 2021
Held as Part of the 23rd HCI International Conference, HCII 2021
Virtual Event, July 24–29, 2021
Proceedings

Springer

Editors
Jessie Y. C. Chen
U.S. Army Research Laboratory
Aberdeen Proving Ground, MD, USA

Gino Fragomeni
U.S. Army Combat Capabilities
Development Command Soldier Center
Orlando, FL, USA

ISSN 0302-9743   ISSN 1611-3349   (electronic)
Lecture Notes in Computer Science
ISBN 978-3-030-77598-8   ISBN 978-3-030-77599-5   (eBook)
https://doi.org/10.1007/978-3-030-77599-5

LNCS Sublibrary: SL3 – Information Systems and Applications, incl. Internet/Web, and HCI

This Springer imprint is published by the registered company Springer Nature Switzerland AG
The registered company address is: Gewerbestrasse 11, 6330 Cham, Switzerland

Foreword

Human-Computer Interaction (HCI) is acquiring an ever-increasing scientific and industrial importance, and having more impact on people's everyday life, as an ever-growing number of human activities are progressively moving from the physical to the digital world. This process, which has been ongoing for some time now, has been dramatically accelerated by the COVID-19 pandemic. The HCI International (HCII) conference series, held yearly, aims to respond to the compelling need to advance the exchange of knowledge and research and development efforts on the human aspects of design and use of computing systems.

The 23rd International Conference on Human-Computer Interaction, HCI International 2021 (HCII 2021), was planned to be held at the Washington Hilton Hotel, Washington DC, USA, during July 24–29, 2021. Due to the COVID-19 pandemic and with everyone's health and safety in mind, HCII 2021 was organized and run as a virtual conference. It incorporated the 21 thematic areas and affiliated conferences listed on the following page.

A total of 5222 individuals from academia, research institutes, industry, and governmental agencies from 81 countries submitted contributions, and 1276 papers and 241 posters were included in the proceedings to appear just before the start of the conference. The contributions thoroughly cover the entire field of HCI, addressing major advances in knowledge and effective use of computers in a variety of application areas. These papers provide academics, researchers, engineers, scientists, practitioners, and students with state-of-the-art information on the most recent advances in HCI. The volumes constituting the set of proceedings to appear before the start of the conference are listed in the following pages.

The HCI International (HCII) conference also offers the option of 'Late Breaking Work' which applies both for papers and posters, and the corresponding volume(s) of the proceedings will appear after the conference. Full papers will be included in the 'HCII 2021 - Late Breaking Papers' volumes of the proceedings to be published in the Springer LNCS series, while 'Poster Extended Abstracts' will be included as short research papers in the 'HCII 2021 - Late Breaking Posters' volumes to be published in the Springer CCIS series.

The present volume contains papers submitted and presented in the context of the 13th International Conference on Virtual, Augmented and Mixed Reality (VAMR 2021) affiliated conference to HCII 2021. I would like to thank the Co-chairs, Jessie Y. C. Chen and Gino Fragomeni, for their invaluable contribution in its organization and the preparation of the Proceedings, as well as the members of the program board for their contributions and support. This year, the VAMR affiliated conference has focused on topics related to designing and evaluating VAMR environments, multimodal and natural interaction in VAMR, interaction using head-mounted displays and VR glasses, and applications of VAMR in learning, culture, design, the industry and the military.

I would also like to thank the Program Board Chairs and the members of the Program Boards of all thematic areas and affiliated conferences for their contribution towards the highest scientific quality and overall success of the HCI International 2021 conference.

This conference would not have been possible without the continuous and unwavering support and advice of Gavriel Salvendy, founder, General Chair Emeritus, and Scientific Advisor. For his outstanding efforts, I would like to express my appreciation to Abbas Moallem, Communications Chair and Editor of HCI International News.

July 2021   Constantine Stephanidis

HCI International 2021 Thematic Areas and Affiliated Conferences

Thematic Areas

- HCI: Human-Computer Interaction
- HIMI: Human Interface and the Management of Information

Affiliated Conferences

- EPCE: 18th International Conference on Engineering Psychology and Cognitive Ergonomics
- UAHCI: 15th International Conference on Universal Access in Human-Computer Interaction
- VAMR: 13th International Conference on Virtual, Augmented and Mixed Reality
- CCD: 13th International Conference on Cross-Cultural Design
- SCSM: 13th International Conference on Social Computing and Social Media
- AC: 15th International Conference on Augmented Cognition
- DHM: 12th International Conference on Digital Human Modeling and Applications in Health, Safety, Ergonomics and Risk Management
- DUXU: 10th International Conference on Design, User Experience, and Usability
- DAPI: 9th International Conference on Distributed, Ambient and Pervasive Interactions
- HCIBGO: 8th International Conference on HCI in Business, Government and Organizations
- LCT: 8th International Conference on Learning and Collaboration Technologies
- ITAP: 7th International Conference on Human Aspects of IT for the Aged Population
- HCI-CPT: 3rd International Conference on HCI for Cybersecurity, Privacy and Trust
- HCI-Games: 3rd International Conference on HCI in Games
- MobiTAS: 3rd International Conference on HCI in Mobility, Transport and Automotive Systems
- AIS: 3rd International Conference on Adaptive Instructional Systems
- C&C: 9th International Conference on Culture and Computing
- MOBILE: 2nd International Conference on Design, Operation and Evaluation of Mobile Communications
- AI-HCI: 2nd International Conference on Artificial Intelligence in HCI

List of Conference Proceedings Volumes Appearing Before the Conference

1. LNCS 12762, Human-Computer Interaction: Theory, Methods and Tools (Part I), edited by Masaaki Kurosu
2. LNCS 12763, Human-Computer Interaction: Interaction Techniques and Novel Applications (Part II), edited by Masaaki Kurosu
3. LNCS 12764, Human-Computer Interaction: Design and User Experience Case Studies (Part III), edited by Masaaki Kurosu
4. LNCS 12765, Human Interface and the Management of Information: Information Presentation and Visualization (Part I), edited by Sakae Yamamoto and Hirohiko Mori
5. LNCS 12766, Human Interface and the Management of Information: Information-rich and Intelligent Environments (Part II), edited by Sakae Yamamoto and Hirohiko Mori
6. LNAI 12767, Engineering Psychology and Cognitive Ergonomics, edited by Don Harris and Wen-Chin Li
7. LNCS 12768, Universal Access in Human-Computer Interaction: Design Methods and User Experience (Part I), edited by Margherita Antona and Constantine Stephanidis
8. LNCS 12769, Universal Access in Human-Computer Interaction: Access to Media, Learning and Assistive Environments (Part II), edited by Margherita Antona and Constantine Stephanidis
9. LNCS 12770, Virtual, Augmented and Mixed Reality, edited by Jessic Y. C. Chen and Gino Fragomeni
10. LNCS 12771, Cross-Cultural Design: Experience and Product Design Across Cultures (Part I), edited by P. L. Patrick Rau
11. LNCS 12772, Cross-Cultural Design: Applications in Arts, Learning, Well-being, and Social Development (Part II), edited by P. L. Patrick Rau
12. LNCS 12773, Cross-Cultural Design: Applications in Cultural Heritage, Tourism, Autonomous Vehicles, and Intelligent Agents (Part III), edited by P. L. Patrick Rau
13. LNCS 12774, Social Computing and Social Media: Experience Design and Social Network Analysis (Part I), edited by Gabriele Meiselwitz
14. LNCS 12775, Social Computing and Social Media: Applications in Marketing, Learning, and Health (Part II), edited by Gabriele Meiselwitz
15. LNAI 12776, Augmented Cognition, edited by Dylan D. Schmorrow and Cali M. Fidopiastis
16. LNCS 12777, Digital Human Modeling and Applications in Health, Safety, Ergonomics and Risk Management: Human Body, Motion and Behavior (Part I), edited by Vincent G. Duffy
17. LNCS 12778, Digital Human Modeling and Applications in Health, Safety, Ergonomics and Risk Management: AI, Product and Service (Part II), edited by Vincent G. Duffy

http://2021.hci.international/proceedings

13th International Conference on Virtual, Augmented and Mixed Reality (VAMR 2021)

Program Board Chairs: **Jessie Y. C. Chen,** *U.S. Army Research Laboratory, USA,* **and Gino Fragomeni,** *U.S. Army Combat Capabilities Development Command Soldier Center, USA*

- Shih-Yi Chien, Taiwan
- Jeff Hansberger, USA
- Fotis Liarokapis, Cyprus
- Phillip Mangos, USA
- Crystal Maraj, USA
- Rafael Radkowski, USA
- Jose San Martin, Spain
- Andreas Schreiber, Germany
- Peter Smith, USA
- Simon Su, USA
- Denny Yu, USA

The full list with the Program Board Chairs and the members of the Program Boards of all thematic areas and affiliated conferences is available online at:

http://www.hci.international/board-members-2021.php

HCI International 2022

The 24th International Conference on Human-Computer Interaction, HCI International 2022, will be held jointly with the affiliated conferences at the Gothia Towers Hotel and Swedish Exhibition & Congress Centre, Gothenburg, Sweden, June 26 – July 1, 2022. It will cover a broad spectrum of themes related to Human-Computer Interaction, including theoretical issues, methods, tools, processes, and case studies in HCI design, as well as novel interaction techniques, interfaces, and applications. The proceedings will be published by Springer. More information will be available on the conference website: http://2022.hci.international/:

General Chair
Prof. Constantine Stephanidis
University of Crete and ICS-FORTH
Heraklion, Crete, Greece
Email: general_chair@hcii2022.org

http://2022.hci.international/

Contents

Multimodal and Natural Interaction in VAMR

Head-Mounted Displays and VR Glasses

VAMR Applications in Design, the Industry and the Military

VAMR in Learning and Culture

Designing and Evaluating VAMR Environments

Narrative Cognition in Mixed Reality Systems: Towards an Empirical Framework

Luis Emilio Bruni[1]([⊠]), Hossein Dini[1], and Aline Simonetti[1,2]

[1] The Augmented Cognition Lab, Aalborg University, 2450 Copenhagen, Denmark
{leb,hdi}@create.aau.dk
[2] Department of Market and Marketing Research, University of Valencia, 46022 Valencia, Spain
aline.simonetti@uv.es

Abstract. In this paper, we propose an interdisciplinary theoretical and empirical framework to investigate the particular faculties related to human "narrative cognition", in general, and in relation to MRT in particular. In order to contextualize our approach, we shortly review the cognitive turn in narratology, as well as state of the art in different domains that have undertaken psychophysiological studies that either characterize aspects that are relevant to narrative cognition, or which investigate mixed reality experiences. The idea is to bring together knowledge and insights from narratology, different branches of semiotics and cognitive sciences, with empirical strategies that bridge the gap between first-person phenomenological approaches and psychophysiological and behavioural methods. We propose a rationale in order to combine tools and techniques from MRT/VR/AR, interactive digital narratives and storytelling, with a suite of integrated psychophysiological methods (such as EEG, HR, GSR and eye tracking) and phenomenological-subjective approaches.

Keywords: Narrative cognition · Mixed reality technologies · Psychophysiology · VR · Electroencephalogram (EEG) · Phenomenology · Interactive narratives

1 Introduction

With the rapid development of mixed reality technologies (MRT) in different domains, there is an increase usage of narratives and interactive digital storytelling (IDS) techniques as immersive or rhetorical devices for engagement and persuasion (e.g., in advertisement, marketing, pedagogics, cultural heritage, social work, sustainability, health, motivational strategies, etc.). On the front line we can see trends in the development of narrative-based technologies for many different purposes (e.g.: communicational, pedagogical, educational, persuasive, therapeutic, entertaining, or artistic). This can be seen, for example, in emerging fields such as computational narratives [1–4], narrative logic [5, 6], interactive narratives and digital storytelling [7–9], edutainment [10–12], ambient intelligence [3, 13], and cybermedicine [14, 15], for instance.

© Springer Nature Switzerland AG 2021
J. Y. C. Chen and G. Fragomeni (Eds.): HCII 2021, LNCS 12770, pp. 3–17, 2021.
https://doi.org/10.1007/978-3-030-77599-5_1

On the other hand, in the last four decades, the "narrative mode" has been widely recognized as a fundamental human cognitive faculty to make sense out of reality [16–19].

In this paper, we propose an interdisciplinary framework to advance our understanding of the particular faculties related to human "narrative cognition", in general, and in relation to MRT in particular. Before presenting our own perspective, we review the state of the art in different disciplines and related domains, considering the interdisciplinary intersections necessary to narrow down the research area. For this purpose, we present a critical review of a number of psychophysiological studies that fall within two main categories:

1) Psychophysiological studies that directly or indirectly characterise aspects of narrative experience.
2) Psychophysiological studies that investigate mixed reality experiences with or without narrative considerations.

Our review of related work is not meant to be exhaustive. Rather, it is intended for gathering best practices, ideas, and useful techniques. From it, we can also infer that the cognitive aspect of narrative involvement in mixed reality systems has been very little investigated, which makes it pertinent to start filling the gap. In our perspective, "storifying" our experience implies grasping together and integrating into a whole what would otherwise be perceived as multiple and scattered events. This entails bringing together and exploring goals, causes, characters, events, and objects within the temporal unit of a whole and complete action during our journey through the virtual environment.

2   The Cognitive Turn in Narratology

In the last three decades the so-called "cognitive turn" has also gained prominence in the study of narrative communication. This can be seen in the proliferation of disciplines, paradigms and fields of inquiry that are interested in, or have as focus, the relation between cognition and narratives [20–23]. For example, cognitive narratology, as a new development that sprung from classical narratology, has emerged as a new field in the last two decades [24–26]. We can also see interest in the cognitive aspects of involvement with narratives in the fields of cognitive semiotics [27–30] and biosemiotics [26, 31, 32], which pay attention to the embedded levels of analysis in narrative cognition, from the physiological to the phenomenological level.

Ryan [33] has addressed the "problematic" relation between narratology and cognitive science and has distinguished three realms in which this relation is gaining attention, namely the study of the minds of characters, inquiries on the cognitive and interpretative processes of target audiences, and research on narrative as a mode of thinking and apprehending the world. An example of this last realm was the "Narrative Networks" research project by the US Defense Advanced Research Project Agency (DARPA). This project was aiming at understanding the psychological, behavioural, and neurobiological impact of narratives to support the development of innovative approaches that would enable advances in narrative science, devices, and/or systems. It promoted empirical and neurophysiological studies that would aid the discovery of neural networks involved in narrative comprehension and persuasion in order to understand factors that influence political radicalization and violence across cultures, and apply those findings to international security contexts, conflict prevention and resolution, effective communication strategies and novel approaches to treat post-traumatic-stress-disorder, etc. [34].

It remains an open challenge bridging the gap between bottom- up approaches measuring physiology (sometimes risking to become excessively reductionist) and top-down approaches that consider the phenomenological aspects (but face the empirical challenge of assessing subjective experience in real time) [35]. This is especially the case when dealing with the kind of higher-level cognitive processes and affective states involved in narrative intelligibility, closure and related "lower level" cognitive processes – such as, for example, episodic memory, categorical perception, semantic congruence, expectancy, arousal, etc., for instance.

Ryan [33] has been critical of such experimental approaches claiming that they focus almost exclusively in the most automatic and unconscious of mental operations, which are often indistinguishable from the processing of language. Part of the criticism is that results obtained in this manner may end up being common-sense truism already known to literary theorists and narratologists, which just become "scientifically confirmed". A difference between literary studies and cognitive neuroscience scholars may be the focus of their interests. The concern of cognitive and psychological approaches to narrative has often not been much the elucidation of important aspects of narratives but rather the investigation of higher order cognitive processes elicited by narratives. In other words, the narratives are just stimuli for the investigation of e.g. understanding (particularly in brain-imaging experiments for localizing brain areas, see for example [36–39].

The challenge remains the attempt to bridge the gap without renouncing a scientific empirical approach on the one hand, and without disregarding the irreducibility of subjective phenomenological experience on the other. Therefore, further research and theory is needed in order to identify and characterize the cognitive processes, features and parameters in the interaction with narrative systems that are amenable to be investigated with such empirical methods.

3   Towards the Psychophysiology of Narrative Experience

Since the late 1980's there has been a growing interest in what we could retrospectively call "the psychophysiology of narrative experience" [35]. However, in many cases these works were only indirectly related to narrative cognition, or their use of narratives was instrumental to investigate other cognitive processes or faculties such as, for example, language comprehension, attention, empathy, emotions, etc. In these cases, the narrative faculties were not the central focus but were somehow implied. In any case, these studies constitute a rich body of knowledge and techniques that may serve as "primitives" for a more systematic study of narrative cognition.

For instance, many psychophysiological studies on attention have used stories as a way for presenting stimuli without having a central interest in what we may call narrative faculties. This is the case, for example, of studies that focus on the auditory sense by using auditory stories or narratives in environments with concurrent auditory stimuli. The majority of them analyse event-related potentials (ERPs) of the electroencephalogram (EEG) signals to understand selective attention processes in attending two or three stories simultaneously (e.g., [40–42]). Using a different technique, Jaeger et al. [43], analysed the individual decoding performance over time and linked it to behavioural performance as well as subjective ratings of listening effort, motivation, and fatigue. This kind of assessment of attentional resources and capacity to focus on one or the other story could be developed into a metric for engagement with the target story. Future research could explore how environmental distractors impact on our perceptions and reactions toward a narrative.

To know which narrative moments lead to higher engagement is crucial for understanding narrative success. A study conducted by Stuldreher et al. [44] employed a multimodal approach to explore physiological synchrony (i.e., inter-subject correlations) in EEG, galvanic skin response (GSR), and heart rate (HR; ECG – electrocardiogram) signals. The authors found that multimodal signal similarity between participants helps on detecting attentionally engaging events over time. Moreover, they also provided useful insights of each metric in separate. EEG was recommended for "well for well-timed effortful cognitive stimuli", HR for emotional stimuli, and GSR for both stimuli types. Finally, they point that "as the relation between physiological synchrony and engagement is dependent on event type and physiological measure, (…) when the stimulus type is unknown, a multimodal metric is most robust" [44, p. 1].

Using an immersive VR tool, Shavit-Cohen and Zion Golumbic [45] investigated attention and speech comprehension in an audio-visual environment. As in the previous studies, participants had to attend to the narrative of a target speaker, whereas concurrent speakers served as distractors. The authors employed eye-tracking to monitor participants' gaze behaviour. They found that while part of them remained focused on the target, others shifted gaze to other stimuli/elements, and those shifts impaired speech comprehension.

In this direction, numerous cognitive scientific approaches to language have sometimes brought knowledge about narrative cognition even if narrative was not the central focus, as many studies that refer to narrative qualities are actually interested in language in general. For example, Liberto et al. [46] investigated language learning acquisition in participants who listened to children's stories. By measuring EEG temporal response functions to language features, including semantic features, the authors found that language proficiency affects linguistic encoding. From these kinds of studies, we can draw valuable metrics and correlates for important cognitive processes that underlie "higher" level narrative faculties.

Narratives have also been used for investigating other processes besides auditory attention and speech comprehension. Empathy mechanisms, specifically experience sharing and mentalizing, were investigated using autobiographical stories [47]. Self-reported and physiological metrics (i.e., HR) were obtained from narrators and listeners. This may be of interest to narrative cognition as empathy is an important factor in emotional involvement with a story. Also, VR combined with eye-tracking was used to explore the concentration locus of eye gaze in predetermined story frames [48].

A significant contribution towards establishing the relation between narrative and cognition is the work of Sanford and Emmott [21], where the authors aim to examine the psychological and neuroscientific evidence for the mechanisms which underlie narrative comprehension. The authors explore the scientific developments, which demonstrate the importance of attention, counterfactuals, depth of processing, perspective, and embodiment in these processes. This interdisciplinary work provides an integrated account of the research which links psychological mechanisms of language comprehension to humanities work on narrative and style. They provide an interesting review of experimental methods utilizing EEG and ERP, which provide cues for identifying potential "markers" (i.e., related cognitive processes) of what we define as narrative intelligibility and closure [49]. As a matter of fact, ERP techniques have been a useful tool to characterize different verbal and non-verbal communication modalities [50–63].

More directly related to narrative cognition, few studies have been in relation to interactive narratives [64–69]. To our knowledge there are a few studies explicitly investigating narrative cognition with continuous EEG. A group of studies evaluated narrative cognition using the Inter-Subject Correlation method [70, 71], which investigate shared brain activity among subjects. We also found a study using Power Spectrum Density to directly investigate aspects of narrative cognition, specifically discerning between narrative and non-narrative modes [72].

On the other hand, there have been studies using other physiological measurements such as GSR, ECG, and eye-tracking to directly investigate narrative features, such as, for example, degree of suspense [73–75].

Even though in many brain-imaging experiments the narratives have just been stimuli for the investigation of complex cognitive processes (such as "understanding", e.g., [36–39]) or "empathy" (e.g., [64]), an extensive review of neuroimaging studies using naturalistic stimuli (i.e., movies and narratives) concluded that these kinds of stimuli contributed extensively to the cognitive research area [76]. Specifically, the authors emphasize their importance for understanding language, attention, memory, emotions, and social cognition. Moreover, neuroimaging techniques allowed the investigation of how the brain default-mode network is related to narrative-processing. However, the authors state that although narratives and movies are naturalistic stimuli, they still differ from real-life. Therefore, they suggest the use of virtual reality settings to turn the subject from a passive listener and/or viewer to an active decision-making agent. In their words: "virtual reality setups would allow circumventing this limitation that pertains to research on memory, attention, language, emotions and social cognition, and might indeed be the next step in this exciting area of research" [76, p. 224].

4 Towards the Psychophysiology of Mixed Reality Experiences

With the gain in popularity of immersive technologies, several studies have started to analyse user experience in cinematic virtual reality (CVR) using psychophysiological methods. The cinematic material is usually mediated through a head-mounted display (HMD), which provides users the freedom to direct their gaze to any scene area. However, this flexibility also implies that users might lose important details of the story. Thus, analytical tools using viewers' dynamic eye-tracking data are being developed, ultimately aiming to guide users attention [77]. Furthermore, CVR allows a certain level of user interactivity. Therefore, researchers are creating eyes- and head-based methods to provide more natural user-movie interaction forms [78, 79]. CVR has been found to potentially produce stronger emotional reactions in the viewers than traditional movies. This may be the case due to the influence of specific factors such as: (i) the sense of presence in the VR environment, (ii) its wide viewpoint, (iii) the novelty of the format, and (iv) the first-person viewpoint [80]. For example, Ding et al. [80] used a combination of self-reported instruments and physiological signals (skin temperature, ECG, respiration, and photoplethysmography) to assess emotional differences between CVR and 2D movies. They found that both sets of metrics demonstrated a stronger emotional effect of CVR compared to traditional movies, mainly for excitement, nervousness, hostility, and jitteriness. Moreover, they posit that "the design of the VR environment in CVR, which is as important as the narrative, has an important influence on the emotional experience of the audience" [80, p. 7].

In immersive VR environments, it is sometimes necessary to create scene changes to improve a story progression or sustain a narrative arc. However, the user cannot be aware of those changes. Marwecki et al. [81] used eye-tracking data provided by the VR headset, such as gaze point, saccades, and pupillometry to assess users' attention and cognitive load to manipulate environmental cues or scene changes. The authors tested their software for several applications, including story-user interaction. They concluded that changes can be successfully hidden from user's perception when eye gaze data is combined with masking techniques. Furthermore, just as it happens with VR, videos in 360° are already being used in cultural heritage sites. Škola et al. [82] combined EEG measurements with subjective metrics to evaluate how those story-based videos are perceived when embedded in an immersive VR application. Their findings demonstrated that users felt high levels of presence, immersion, and engagement. In this context, an increase in the EEG beta band was attributed to the active engagement reported by the users. The increase in alpha and theta band were considered normal for VR experiences.

Even though mixed reality technologies, including VR, CVR and AR may be media "for stories", so far these kinds of investigations have not been so much interested in the ways we interact cognitively with stories, as they are interested in analysing ways of cognitive interaction with the medium. The focus is not on the effects of the narratives on the emotional-cognitive system, but on the differences in emotional involvement elicited by different platforms.

However, we can now advert an incipient interest in investigating aspects of narrative cognition by combining psychophysiological measurements and virtual environments. For example, Tiffany et al. [83] aimed to investigate the effect of adaptive gaze guided narratives on tourism experience compared to traditional methods. They designed a virtual environment to introduce participants to panoramic scenes of three cities. Then, they compared the virtual environment results with the results of participant's experiencing real scenes. In the middle of the experiment, they provided some stories on each scene in an interactive way. Their results revealed that the Gaze-Guided Narratives system obtained better user experience, lower cognitive load, and better performance in a mapping task compared to a classic audio guide. Previously, Bee et al. [84] designed an interactive Eye-Gaze Model while the participants were interacting with a virtual character. They evaluated the subjects' eye-gaze and emotions while interacting with virtual characters using eye tracker and speech analyser. The findings showed that there was a significant difference between interactive and non-interactive mode considering the social presence and rapport with character ratings. Moreover, by comparing participant's eyes gazes in the experimental environment with real human-human interaction, they found that participants looked significantly more at the virtual character's eyes compared to a real human while listening.

5   An Interdisciplinary Approach to Narrative Cognition in MRT

Our approach aims to develop a mixed empirical strategy that bridges the gap between first-person subjective perspectives and psychophysiological methods and techniques. Therefore, our framework grows by combining tools and techniques from MRT/VR/AR, interactive digital narratives and storytelling, with a suite of integrated psychophysiological methods (such as EEG, HR, GSR and eye-tracking) and phenomenological-subjective approaches, in order to study key cognitive processes and affective states elicited by narrative and rhetorical devices in immersive technologies. The relation is bi-directional: MRTs constitute a privileged tool for investigating narrative cognition – especially with the emerging possibilities of combining MRT with advanced biometric signals processing – and, on the other hand, interactive digital storytelling techniques and narrative constructs are becoming an important aspect of mixed reality experiences.

For this purpose, let us define "narrative cognition" as a field of inquiry that studies the cognitive and affective processes, faculties, attributes or features that are implicated and which enable the generation and/or the intelligibility of recognizable narrative patterns [32, 35]. Therefore, when considering narrative cognition in relation to mixed reality systems, we consider the following two aspects:

1) Narrative cognition as a fundamental human cognitive mode for organizing experience.
2) The pervasiveness and multifarious uses of narratives in MRT and transmedia platforms.

In this sense, we are using interactive digital narratives and storytelling (IDN/IDS) in different platforms as a tool to investigate different cognitive processes that are germane to a subject's situatedness in a narrative trajectory, either as a spectator or as an active agent. For example, we have been looking at intelligibility, closure, suspense, surprise, suspension of disbelief, narrative hindsight/foresight, emplotting (i.e.: causal-inference-making), decision-making, among others (e.g., [55, 85]). In relation to MRT, we are looking at the use of narratives as rhetorical devices (e.g.: in advertising, marketing, pedagogics, politics, sustainability, motivational strategies, etc.), through our participation in the European project RHUMBO [86].

Our work progresses by developing an interdisciplinary framework that interconnects knowledge and insights from narratology, different branches of semiotics and cognitive sciences, with empirical strategies that bridge the gap between first-person phenomenological approaches and psychophysiological and behavioural methods.

Aware of the scepticism and critic that this kind of endeavour have elicited in narratologists and humanists, we pursue an empirical strategy that consciously accounts for an "educated reduction" considering three necessary correlational steps when building the theoretical framework for a particular experimental design:

1) Identify what are the "features" or "parameters" in an (interactive) narrative experience that are of interest (e.g., narrative intelligibility, closure, surprise, suspense, hindsight/foresight, emplotting, suspension of disbelief, emotional immersion, etc.).
2) Investigate and make the theoretical connections between the cognitive and affective processes, faculties or tasks that underlie or relate to the narrative features that have been chosen as relevant (e.g., episodic memory, categorical perception, semantic congruence, expectancy, arousal, etc.)
3) Select the psychophysiological correlates, which have been found to have some degrees of correlation with the given processes, and hence develop the appropriate metrics.

These three steps should be integrated in a cohesive theoretical framework to guide hypothesis formulation and data analysis. Between such "higher-level" features of "user experience" and the actual psychophysiological correlates (e.g., HR, GSR, EEG), there are a myriad of embedded and related processes, which can in turn be linked to many physiological and cognitive processes. We recognize that there is no direct bottom-up lineal pathway from the "low level" physiological processes to the "high level" psychological constructs. Therefore, we pay attention to the increase in indeterminacy that goes from the physiological correlates, the observable causal outcomes and the phenomenological accounts of the subject. In other words, the embedded physiological, cognitive, and sociocultural processes gain in "semiotic freedom" [31, 87, 88], i.e., there is an increase in indeterminacy when the aggregated processes (and the underlying structures) go from neural correlates to the very human sophisticated capacity for narrative intelligibility and interpretation. Between these extremes there are a myriad of embedded semiotic processes that have to do with many forms of pattern-recognition, categorical and multimodal perception, integration and semantic congruency, and many other related physiological and cognitive processes, which can be found either as "prototypic" forms with lower levels of indeterminacy or as more developed manifestations with increasing levels of semiotic freedom, as manifested in the open and creative instantiations of narrative communication. Narrative cognition on top of language and symbolic capacity affords humans with the highest levels of semiotic freedom - enabling narrative identity, temporal development, imagination, virtual and storyworlds, scenario prospecting, long term anticipation, historical awareness, etc.

Even though definitions of what constitutes a narrative have been debated extensively for decades there is still no consensus on the matter [89–93]. The discussion is now revived by the innovative possibilities afforded by new interactive and digital media. Therefore, in our framework we do not take for granted what is to be considered a narrative, as this may have crucial implications for any empirical endeavour in the field. According to Ryan, the dilution of the concept can only be prevented by broadening it beyond the classical literary definitions [16–19, 94–97], but at the same time compensating by a semantic narrowing down so that not all contents of all media end up being considered as narratives: "The property of 'being a narrative' can be predicated of any semiotic object produced with the intent to evoke a story to the mind of the audience" [23, p. 11]. Therefore, for us it is important to develop our designs considering narrativity as a scalar property that can be defined and characterized along a continuum rather than defining narrative as an either/or phenomena. In this direction we have taken inspiration in Ryan's "semi-parametric" set of criteria for defining narrativity as a scalar property [23]. We use this kind of modelling to establish testable criteria for selecting and classifying communication forms in their degrees of narrativity, in order to relate different "thresholds of narrativity" to relevant cognitive functions. In this sense we work to ground our model in a cognitive characterization of narrative experience which considers perceptual, affective, cognitive, and phenomenological aspects.

6 Conclusions

With the rise in availability of different immersive platforms and networked media that the advent of digital culture has brought, the use of the narrative mode of communication has been extended into many domains that go from education to advertisement, and even to cases of indoctrination and manipulation. Our perspective proposes an interdisciplinary theoretical and empirical framework to investigate what are the key cognitive aspects involved in our ways of processing narratives so we can use this knowledge to identify and analyse the intentional and unintentional, beneficial and deleterious, uses of narrative. We combine novel methodologies and measurement tools to characterize the cognitive aspects of the way people are experiencing narratives. These methods could aid the development of communication strategies to effectively use the narrative mode for its potential beneficial applications, or to detect or counteract its unsustainable uses in digital culture.

In particular, we are interested in key aspects of narrative cognition that may have an implicit influence in decision-making processes when story elements are mediated through MRT with the purpose of advising, prompting or persuading subjects into particular courses of action, choices and decisions. These could include for example decision-making processes that may be affected by conditions such as (but not limited to) lack of hindsight, faulty foresight, causal inferences, emotional involvement, ambiguity, uncertainty, moral dilemmas, or paradoxes.

As previously mentioned, the challenge and our ambition remain the attempt to bridge the gap without renouncing a scientific empirical approach on the one hand, and without disregarding the irreducibility of subjective phenomenological experience, on the other. Therefore, further research and theory is needed in order to identify and characterize the cognitive processes, features and parameters in the interaction with narrative systems that are amenable to be investigated with such empirical methods.

Even though there has been a rich history of alternative theoretical frameworks and models of cognition in the last 30 years, very seldom have these innovations been included in the more practical implementations of knowledge for the development of representational technologies or for the characterization of involvement with narratives. For example, the enactive paradigm [98] and its phenomenological variants, with all its increasing influence in studies of cognition, has not been considered in the main fields that intend to assess "user-experience" within new media and representational technology and could provide lots of insights in our search for new methodologies for the investigation of narrative cognition and its multifarious implications.

Acknowledgments. The authors acknowledge the financial support of Rhumbo (European Union's Horizon 2020 research and innovation program under the Marie Skłodowska-Curie Grant Agreement No 813234).

References

1. Broniatowski, D.A., Reyna, V.F.: Gist and verbatim in narrative memory. In: Finlayson, M.A., Fisseni, B., Löwe, B., Meister, J.C. (eds.) 2013 Workshop on Computational Models of Narrative, pp. 43–51. Schloss Dagstuhl--Leibniz-Zentrum fuer Informatik, Dagstuhl (2013). https://doi.org/10.4230/OASIcs.CMN.2013.43
2. Bolioli, A., Casu, M., Lana, M., Roda, R.: Exploring the betrothed lovers. In: Finlayson, M.A., Fisseni, B., Löwe, B., Meister, J.C. (eds.) 2013 Workshop on Computational Models of Narrative, pp. 30–35. Schloss Dagstuhl--Leibniz-Zentrum fuer Informatik, Dagstuhl (2013). https://doi.org/10.4230/OASIcs.CMN.2013.30
3. Bhatt, M., Suchan, J., Schultz, C.: Cognitive interpretation of everyday activities: toward perceptual narrative based visuo-spatial scene interpretation. In: Workshop on Computational Models of Narrative, pp. 24–29. Leibniz-Zentrum für Informatik (2013). https://doi.org/10.4230/OASIcs.CMN.2013.24
4. Damiano, R., Lieto, A.: Ontological representations of narratives: a case study on stories and actions. In: Proceedings of 2013 Workshop on Computational Models of Narrative, pp. 76–93 (2013). https://doi.org/10.4230/OASIcs.CMN.2013.76
5. Dumas, J.E., Szilas, N., Richle, U., Boggini, T.: Interactive simulations to help teenagers cope when a parent has a traumatic brain injury. Comput. Entertain. **8**, 1–3 (2011). https://doi.org/10.1145/1899687.1899692
6. Szilas, N.: Interactive drama on computer: beyond linear narrative. In: AAAI Fall Symposium on Narrative Intelligence, pp. 150–156 (1999)
7. Schoenau-Fog, H., Bruni, L.E., Khalil, F.F., Faizi, J.: First person victim: developing a 3D interactive dramatic experience. In: Aylett, R., Lim, M.Y., Louchart, S., Petta, P., Riedl, M. (eds) Interactive Storytelling, ICIDS 2010, Lecture Notes in Computer Science, vol. 6432. Springer, Heidelberg (2010). https://doi.org/10.1007/978-3-642-16638-9_32
8. Baceviciute, S., Rützou Albæk, K.R., Arsovski, A., Bruni, L.E.: Digital interactive narrative tools for facilitating communication with children during counseling: a case for audiology. In: Oyarzun, D., Peinado, F., Young, R.M., Elizalde, A., Méndez, G. (eds) Interactive Storytelling, ICIDS 2012, Lecture Notes in Computer Science, vol. 7648. Springer, Heidelberg (2012). https://doi.org/10.1007/978-3-642-34851-8_5
9. Mulholland, P., Wolff, A., Zdrahal, Z., Li, N., Corneli, J.: Constructing and connecting storylines to tell museum stories. In: Koenitz, H., Sezen, T.I., Ferri, G., Haahr, M., Sezen, D., Çatak, G. (eds) Interactive Storytelling, ICIDS 2013, Lecture Notes in Computer Science, vol. 8230. Springer, Cham (2013). https://doi.org/10.1007/978-3-319-02756-2_14
10. Kalogeras, S.: Media-education convergence: applying transmedia storytelling edutainment in e-learning environments. Int. J. Inf. Commun. Technol. Educ. **9**, 1–11 (2013)
11. Marsh, T., Nickole, L.Z., Klopfer, E., Xuejin, C., Osterweil, S., Haas, J.: Fun and learning: blending design and development dimensions in serious games through narrative and characters. In: Ma, M., Oikonomou, A., Jain, L. (eds.) Serious Games and Edutainment Applications. Springer, London (2011). https://doi.org/10.1007/978-1-4471-2161-9_14

12. Heiden, W., Räder, M., Fassbender, E.: Interactive storytelling in academic teaching. In: Aylett, R., Lim, M.Y., Louchart, S., Petta, P., Riedl, M. (eds.) Interactive Storytelling, pp. 216–221. Springer, Heidelberg (2010). https://doi.org/10.1007/978-3-642-16638-9_27
13. Guger, C., Holzner, C., Grönegress, C., Edlinger, G., Slater, M.: Control of a Smart Home with a Brain-Computer Interface (2008)
14. Si, M., Marsella, S., Miller, L.: Interactive stories for health interventions. In: Aylett, R., Lim, M.Y., Louchart, S., Petta, P., Riedl, M. (eds.) Interactive Storytelling, pp. 291–292. Springer, Heidelberg (2010). https://doi.org/10.1007/978-3-642-16638-9_46
15. Szilas, N., Richle, U., Boggini, T., Dumas, J.: Using highly interactive drama to help young people cope with traumatic situations. In: Aylett, R., Lim, M.Y., Louchart, S., Petta, P., Riedl, M. (eds.) Interactive Storytelling, pp. 279–282. Springer, Heidelberg (2010). https://doi.org/10.1007/978-3-642-16638-9_42
16. Barthes, R., Duisit, L.: An introduction to the structural analysis of narrative. New Lit. Hist. **6**, 237 (1975). https://doi.org/10.2307/468419
17. Bruner, J.: Acts of Meaning. Harvard University Press, Cambridge (1990)
18. Polkinghorne, D.E.: Narrative Knowing and the Human Sciences. Suny Press, Albany (1988)
19. Ricoeur, P.: Time and Narrative. University of Chicago Press, Chicago (1984)
20. Finlayson, M.A., et al.: Workshop on computational models of narrative. In: CMN 2013, Saarbrücken/WadernSchloss Dagstuhl-Leibniz-Zentrum für Informatik, Hamburg (2013)
21. Sanford, A.J., Emmott, C.: Mind, Brain and Narrative. Cambridge University Press, Cambridge (2012)
22. Ryan, M.-L.: Narrative as Virtual Reality: Immersion and Interactivity in Literature and Electronic Media. Johns Hopkins University Press, Baltimore (2001)
23. Ryan, M.-L.: Avatars of Story. U of Minnesota Press, Minneapolis (2006)
24. Herman, D.: Cognitive narratology. In: Handbook of Narratology, pp. 46–64. de Gruyter, Berlin (2009)
25. Jahn, M.: Frames, preferences, and the reading of third-person narratives: towards a cognitive narratology. Poet. Today. **18**, 441 (1997). https://doi.org/10.2307/1773182
26. Cobley, P.: Narrative. Routledge, London (2014)
27. Zlatev, J.: Cognitive semiotics: an emerging field for the transdisciplinary study of meaning. Public J. Semiot. **4**, 2–24 (2012). https://doi.org/10.37693/pjos.2012.4.8837
28. Ranta, M.: Stories in pictures (and non-pictorial objects): a narratological and cognitive psychological approach. Contemp. Aesthetics **9**, 6 (2011)
29. Matuk, C.F.: Narratives in mind and media: a cognitive semiotic account of novices interpreting visual science media (2010)
30. Lee, Y.: Narrative cognition and modeling in new media communication from Peirce's semiotic perspective. Semiotica **2012**, 181–195 (2012). https://doi.org/10.1515/sem-2012-0029
31. Bruni, L.E.: Heterarchical semiosis: from signal transduction to narrative intelligibility. In: Trifonas, P.P. (ed.) International Handbook of Semiotics, pp. 1079–1097. Springer, Netherlands (2015). https://doi.org/10.1007/978-94-017-9404-6_49
32. Bruni, L.E., Baceviciute, S.: On the embedded cognition of non-verbal narratives. Sign. Syst. Stud. **42**, 359–375 (2014). https://doi.org/10.12697/SSS.2014.42.2-3.09
33. Ryan, M.L.: Narratology and cognitive science: a problematic relation. Style. **44**, 469–495 (2010)
34. Defense Advanced Research Projects Agency: Narrative Networks. https://www.darpa.mil/program/narrative-networks. Accessed 10 Feburary 2020
35. Bruni, L.E., Baceviciute, S., Arief, M.: Narrative cognition in interactive systems: suspense-surprise and the P300 ERP component. In: Mitchell, A., Fernández-Vara, C., Thue, D. (eds.) Lecture Notes in Computer Science, pp. 164–175. Springer International Publishing, Cham (2014). https://doi.org/10.1007/978-3-319-12337-0_17

36. Speer, N.K., Reynolds, J.R., Swallow, K.M., Zacks, J.M.: Reading stories activates neural representations of visual and motor experiences. Psychol. Sci. **20**, 989–999 (2009). https://doi.org/10.1111/j.1467-9280.2009.02397.x
37. Yarkoni, T., Speer, N.K., Zacks, J.M.: Neural substrates of narrative comprehension and memory. Neuroimage **41**, 1408–1425 (2008). https://doi.org/10.1016/j.neuroimage.2008.03.062
38. Mar, R.A.: The neuropsychology of narrative: story comprehension, story production and their interrelation. Neuropsychologia **42**, 1414–1434 (2004). https://doi.org/10.1016/j.neuropsychologia.2003.12.016
39. Zacks, J.M., Speer, N.K., Swallow, K.M., Maley, C.J.: The brain's cutting-room floor: segmentation of narrative cinema. Front. Hum. Neurosci. 4 (2010). https://doi.org/10.3389/fnhum.2010.00168
40. Lambrecht, J., Spring, D.K., Münte, T.F.: The focus of attention at the virtual cocktail party—electrophysiological evidence. Neurosci. Lett. **489**, 53–56 (2011). https://doi.org/10.1016/j.neulet.2010.11.066
41. Münte, T.F., Spring, D.K., Szycik, G.R., Noesselt, T.: Electrophysiological attention effects in a virtual cocktail-party setting. Brain Res. **1307**, 78–88 (2010). https://doi.org/10.1016/j.brainres.2009.10.044
42. Nager, W., Dethlefsen, C., Münte, T.F.: Attention to human speakers in a virtual auditory environment: Brain potential evidence. Brain Res. **1220**, 164–170 (2008). https://doi.org/10.1016/j.brainres.2008.02.058
43. Jaeger, M., Mirkovic, B., Bleichner, M.G., Debener, S.: Decoding the attended speaker from EEG using adaptive evaluation intervals captures fluctuations in attentional listening. Front. Neurosci. **14**, 1–16 (2020). https://doi.org/10.3389/fnins.2020.00603
44. Stuldreher, I.V., Thammasan, N., van Erp, J.B.F., Brouwer, A.-M.: Physiological synchrony in EEG, electrodermal activity and heart rate detects attentionally relevant events in time. Front. Neurosci. **14**, 1–11 (2020). https://doi.org/10.3389/fnins.2020.575521
45. Shavit-Cohen, K., Zion Golumbic, E.: The dynamics of attention shifts among concurrent speech in a naturalistic multi-speaker virtual environment. Front. Hum. Neurosci. 13, 1–12 (2019). https://doi.org/10.3389/fnhum.2019.00386
46. Di Liberto, G.M., Nie, J., Yeaton, J., Khalighinejad, B., Shamma, S.A., Mesgarani, N.: Neural representation of linguistic feature hierarchy reflects second-language proficiency. Neuroimage **227**, 117586 (2021). https://doi.org/10.1016/j.neuroimage.2020.117586
47. Jospe, K., Genzer, S., Klein Selle, N., Ong, D., Zaki, J., Perry, A.: The contribution of linguistic and visual cues to physiological synchrony and empathic accuracy. Cortex. 132, 296–308 (2020). https://doi.org/10.1016/j.cortex.2020.09.001
48. Ju, Y.S., Hwang, J.S., Kim, S.J., Suk, H.J.: Study of eye gaze and presence effect in virtual reality. In: Communications in Computer and Information Science, pp. 446–449. Springer International Publishing, Heidelberg (2019). https://doi.org/10.1007/978-3-030-23528-4_60
49. Bruni, L.E., Baceviciute, S.: Narrative intelligibility and closure in interactive systems. In: Koenitz, H., Sezen, T.I., Ferri, G., Haahr, M., Sezen, D., Çatak, G. (eds.) Interactive Storytelling, pp. 13–24. Springer International Publishing, Cham (2013). https://doi.org/10.1007/978-3-319-02756-2_2
50. Duncan, C.C., et al.: Event-related potentials in clinical research: guidelines for eliciting, recording, and quantifying mismatch negativity, P300, and N400. Clin. Neurophysiol. **120**, 1883–1908 (2009). https://doi.org/10.1016/j.clinph.2009.07.045
51. McPherson, W.B., Holcomb, P.J.: An electrophysiological investigation of semantic priming with pictures of real objects. Psychophysiology **36**, 53–65 (1999). https://doi.org/10.1017/S0048577299971196

52. West, W.C., Holcomb, P.J.: Event-related potentials during discourse-level semantic integration of complex pictures. Cogn. Brain Res. **13**, 363–375 (2002). https://doi.org/10.1016/S0926-6410(01)00129-X

53. Proverbio, A.M., Riva, F.: RP and N400 ERP components reflect semantic violations in visual processing of human actions. Neurosci. Lett. **459**, 142–146 (2009). https://doi.org/10.1016/j.neulet.2009.05.012

54. Sitnikova, T., Holcomb, P.J., Kiyonaga, K.A., Kuperberg, G.R.: Two neurocognitive mechanisms of semantic integration during the comprehension of visual real-world events. J. Cogn. Neurosci. **20**, 2037–2057 (2008). https://doi.org/10.1162/jocn.2008.20143

55. Hein, G., Doehrmann, O., Muller, N.G., Kaiser, J., Muckli, L., Naumer, M.J.: Object familiarity and semantic congruency modulate responses in cortical audiovisual integration areas. J. Neurosci. **27**, 7881–7887 (2007). https://doi.org/10.1523/JNEUROSCI.1740-07.2007

56. Federmeier, K.: Picture the difference: electrophysiological investigations of picture processing in the two cerebral hemispheres. Neuropsychologia **40**, 730–747 (2002). https://doi.org/10.1016/S0028-3932(01)00193-2

57. Wu, Y.C., Coulson, S.: Meaningful gestures: electrophysiological indices of iconic gesture comprehension. Psychophysiology **42**, 654–667 (2005). https://doi.org/10.1111/j.1469-8986.2005.00356.x

58. Sitnikova, T., Kuperberg, G., Holcomb, P.J.: Semantic integration in videos of real–world events: an electrophysiological investigation. Psychophysiology **40**, 160–164 (2003). https://doi.org/10.1111/1469-8986.00016

59. Chao, L.L., Nielsen-Bohlman, L., Knight, R.T.: Auditory event-related potentials dissociate early and late memory processes. Electroencephalogr. Clin. Neurophysiol. Potentials Sect. **96**, 157–168 (1995). https://doi.org/10.1016/0168-5597(94)00256-E.

60. Cohn, N., Paczynski, M., Holcomb, P., Jackendoff, R., Kuperberg, G.: Comics on the brain: structure and meaning in sequential image comprehension. In: Proceedings of the Annual Meeting of the Cognitive Science Society (2011)

61. Cohn, N., Paczynski, M., Jackendoff, R., Holcomb, P.J., Kuperberg, G.R.: (Pea)nuts and bolts of visual narrative: structure and meaning in sequential image comprehension. Cogn. Psychol. **65**, 1–38 (2012). https://doi.org/10.1016/j.cogpsych.2012.01.003

62. Barrett, S.E., Rugg, M.D.: Event-related potentials and the semantic matching of pictures. Brain Cogn. **14**, 201–212 (1990). https://doi.org/10.1016/0278-2626(90)90029-N

63. Hamm, J.P., Johnson, B.W., Kirk, I.J.: Comparison of the N300 and N400 ERPs to picture stimuli in congruent and incongruent contexts. Clin. Neurophysiol. **113**, 1339–1350 (2002). https://doi.org/10.1016/S1388-2457(02)00161-X

64. Gilroy, S.W., et al.: A brain-computer interface to a plan-based narrative. In: Proceedings of the Twenty-Third International Joint Conference on Artificial Intelligence, pp. 1997–2005. AAAI Press (2013)

65. Ekman, I., et al.: Review on psychophysiological methods in game research. In: Proceedings of the 2010 International DiGRA Nordic Conference: Experiencing Games: Games, Play, and Players, DiGRA Nordic 2010 (2010)

66. Nijholt, A.: BCI for games: a 'state of the art' survey. In: Stevens, S.M., Saldamarco, S.J. (eds.) Lecture Notes in Computer Science, pp. 225–228. Springer, Heidelberg (2008). https://doi.org/10.1007/978-3-540-89222-9_29

67. Gjøl, B.A., Jørgensen, N.V., Thomsen, M.R., Bruni, L.E.: Predictability and plausibility in interactive narrative constructs: a case for an ERP study. In: Rouse, R., Koenitz, H., Haahr, M. (eds.) Interactive Storytelling, pp. 121–133. Springer International Publishing, Cham (2018). https://doi.org/10.1007/978-3-030-04028-4_9

68. Coderre, E.L., O'Donnell, E., O'Rourke, E., Cohn, N.: Predictability modulates neurocognitive semantic processing of non-verbal narratives. Sci. Rep. **10**, 10326 (2020). https://doi.org/10.1038/s41598-020-66814-z

69. Coco, M.I., Araujo, S., Petersson, K.M.: Disentangling stimulus plausibility and contextual congruency: electro-physiological evidence for differential cognitive dynamics. Neuropsychologia **96**, 150–163 (2017). https://doi.org/10.1016/j.neuropsychologia.2016.12.008
70. Ki, J.J., Kelly, S.P., Parra, L.C.: Attention strongly modulates reliability of neural responses to naturalistic narrative stimuli. J. Neurosci. **36**, 3092–3101 (2016). https://doi.org/10.1523/JNEUROSCI.2942-15.2016
71. Cohen, S.S., Parra, L.C.: Memorable audiovisual narratives synchronize sensory and supramodal neural responses. Eneuro. 3, ENEURO.0203–16.2016 (2016). https://doi.org/10.1523/ENEURO.0203-16.2016
72. Wang, R.W.Y., Chang, Y.-C., Chuang, S.-W.: EEG spectral dynamics of video commercials: impact of the narrative on the branding product preference. Sci. Rep. **6**, 36487 (2016). https://doi.org/10.1038/srep36487
73. Chun, C., Park, B., Shi, C.: Re-living suspense: emotional and cognitive responses during repeated exposure to suspenseful film. Front. Psychol. **11**, 2786 (2020). https://doi.org/10.3389/fpsyg.2020.558234
74. Foulsham, T., Wybrow, D., Cohn, N.: Reading without words: eye movements in the comprehension of comic strips. Appl. Cogn. Psychol. **30**, 566–579 (2016). https://doi.org/10.1002/acp.3229
75. Barraza, J.A., Alexander, V., Beavin, L.E., Terris, E.T., Zak, P.J.: The heart of the story: peripheral physiology during narrative exposure predicts charitable giving. Biol. Psychol. **105**, 138–143 (2015). https://doi.org/10.1016/j.biopsycho.2015.01.008
76. Jääskeläinen, I.P., Sams, M., Glerean, E., Ahveninen, J.: Movies and narratives as naturalistic stimuli in neuroimaging. Neuroimage **224**, 117445 (2021). https://doi.org/10.1016/j.neuroimage.2020.117445
77. Rothe, S., Hollerer, T., Hubmann, H.: CVR-analyzer: a tool for analyzing cinematic virtual reality viewing patterns. In: 2018 IEEE International Symposium on Mixed and Augmented Reality Adjunct (ISMAR-Adjunct), pp. 403–404. IEEE (2018). https://doi.org/10.1109/ISMAR-Adjunct.2018.00117
78. Rothe, S., Pothmann, P., Drewe, H., Hussmann, H.: Interaction techniques for cinematic virtual reality. In: 2019 IEEE Conference on Virtual Reality and 3D User Interfaces (VR), pp. 1733–1737. IEEE (2019). https://doi.org/10.1109/VR.2019.8798189
79. Rothe, S., L. Chuang, L.: Implications of eye tracking research to cinematic virtual reality. In: Symposium on Eye Tracking Research and Applications, pp. 1–3. ACM, New York (2020). https://doi.org/10.1145/3379157.3391658
80. Ding, N., Zhou, W., Fung, A.Y.H.: Emotional effect of cinematic VR compared with traditional 2D film. Telematics Inform. **35**, 1572–1579 (2018). https://doi.org/10.1016/j.tele.2018.04.003
81. Marwecki, S., Wilson, A.D., Ofek, E., Gonzalez Franco, M., Holz, C.: Mise-unseen: using eye-tracking to hide virtual reality scene changes in plain sight. In: Proceedings of the 32nd Annual ACM Symposium on User Interface Software and Technology, pp. 777–789. ACM, New York (2019). https://doi.org/10.1145/3332165.3347919
82. Škola, F., et al.: Virtual reality with 360-video storytelling in cultural heritage: study of presence, engagement, and immersion. Sensors. **20**, 5851 (2020). https://doi.org/10.3390/s20205851
83. Kwok, T.C.K., Kiefer, P., Schinazi, V.R., Adams, B., Raubal, M.: Gaze-guided narratives. In: Proceedings of the 2019 CHI Conference on Human Factors in Computing Systems, pp. 1–12. ACM, New York (2019). https://doi.org/10.1145/3290605.3300721
84. Bee, N., et al.: Discovering eye gaze behavior during human-agent conversation in an interactive storytelling application. In: International Conference on Multimodal Interfaces and the Workshop on Machine Learning for Multimodal Interaction on - ICMI-MLMI 2010, p. 1. ACM Press, New York (2010). https://doi.org/10.1145/1891903.1891915

85. Gere, C.: Digital Culture. Reaktion Books, London (2009)
86. Rhumbo. http://rhumbo.eu/webs/rhumbo/. Accessed 01 Feburary 2021
87. Bruni, L.E.: Hierarchical categorical perception in sensing and cognitive processes. Biosemiotics **1**, 113–130 (2008). https://doi.org/10.1007/s12304-008-9001-9
88. Bruni, L.E.: Semiotic freedom: emergence and teleology in biological and cognitive interfaces. Am. J. Semiot. **24**, 57–73 (2008). https://doi.org/10.5840/ajs2008241/35
89. Vincent, D., Perrin, L.: On the narrative vs non-narrative functions of reported speech: a socio-pragmatic study. J. Socioling. **3**, 291–313 (1999). https://doi.org/10.1111/1467-9481. 00080
90. Goodman, N.: Twisted tales: story, study and symphony. In: Mitchell, W.J.T. (ed.) Narrative, Chicago (1981)
91. Hutto, D.D.: Narrative and understanding persons. R. Inst. Philos. Suppl. **60**, 1–16 (2007). https://doi.org/10.1017/S135824610700001X
92. Strawson, G.: Against narrativity. Ratio **17**, 428–452 (2004). https://doi.org/10.1111/j.1467-9329.2004.00264.x
93. Herman, D.: Basic Elements of Narrative. Wiley, New York (2009)
94. Goodson, I., Gill, S.R.: Narrative Pedagogy: Life History and Learning. Peter Lang, Bern (2011)
95. White, M., Wijaya, M., White, M.K., Epston, D.: Narrative Means to Therapeutic Ends. WW Norton & Company, New York (1990)
96. Kleinreesink, E., Moelker, R., Richardson, R.: Books and Bikes. Amsterdam University Press, Amsterdam (2012)
97. Corman, S.R.: Narrating the Exit from Afghanistan. Tempe: Center for Strategic Communication (2013)
98. Varela, F.J., Rosch, E., Thompson, E.: The Embodied Mind. MIT Press, Cambridge (1993)

Exploratory Study on the Use of Augmentation for Behavioural Control in Shared Spaces

Vinu Kamalasanan[1], Frederik Schewe[2(✉)], Monika Sester[1(✉)], and Mark Vollrath[2(✉)]

[1] Institute of Cartography and Geoinformatics, Leibniz University Hannover, Appelstraße 9a, 30167 Hannover, Germany
{vinu.kamalasanan,monika.sester}@ikg.uni-hannover.de
[2] Engineering and Traffic Psychology, Technische Universität Braunschweig, Gaußstr. 23, 38106 Braunschweig, Germany
f.schewe@tu-braunschweig.de, mark.vollrath@tu-bs.de

Abstract. Shared spaces are regulation free, mixed traffic environments supporting social interactions between pedestrian, cyclist and vehicles. Even when these spaces are designed to foster safety supported by reduced traffic speeds, unforeseen collisions and priority conflicts are always an open question. While AR can be used to realise virtual pedestrian lanes and traffic signals, the change in pedestrian motion dynamics using such approaches needs to be understood. This work highlights an exploratory study to evaluate how speed and path of pedestrians are impacted when using an augmented reality based virtual traffic light interface to control collisions in pedestrian motion. To achieve this objective we analyse the motion information from controlled experiments, replicating pedestrian motion on a lane supported by a stop and go interface and including scenarios such as confronting a crossing pedestrian. Our statistical and quantitative analysis gives some early insights on pedestrian control using body worn AR systems

Keywords: Augmented control · Pedestrian safety · Shared spaces

1   Introduction

Shared space design [5] has drawn significant attention recently as an alternative to conventional regulated traffic designs. In shared spaces, heterogeneous road users such as pedestrians, cars and cyclists share the same space. The idea is that unclear situations and a mix of all traffic participants leads to reductions in speed and this results in everybody being more cautious. While the safety behind such designs has always been under debate due to fewer or no road signs, signals

© Springer Nature Switzerland AG 2021
J. Y. C. Chen and G. Fragomeni (Eds.): HCII 2021, LNCS 12770, pp. 18–31, 2021.
https://doi.org/10.1007/978-3-030-77599-5_2

and lane marking [6], such spaces have continued to gain acceptance. There are a growing number of such spaces, e.g. in London, Bohmte, Norrköping, and Drachten.

Shared spaces however have also been a subject for criticism and debate for many reasons. Among traffic participants, many pedestrians feel less safe, due to the lack of vertical separation between pedestrian and vehicle movement regions. They also are vulnerable from cyclist attributed from the lack of separate cyclist lanes and the increased possibility of cyclist collision with walking pedestrians. While collisions are essentially a safety issue, priority confusion in such unregulated spaces are equally dangerous. This, for example, can prove fatal to a tourist with little or no knowledge of the local traffic rules while navigating such spaces with vehicular drivers who would continue to react to interactions based on priority.

Pedestrian infrastructure can reduce pedestrian exposure to vehicular traffic and reduce vehicle speeds [10–14]. Specific engineering measures that reduce traffic volumes and pedestrian exposure to vehicular traffic include approaches that support sidewalks and footpaths, marked crossings, overpasses and underpasses, and mass transport routes [9]. Including the existing knowledge from conventional traffic designing to complement shared spaces with virtual pedestrian infrastructure would bundle the benefits of both street design approaches while reducing costs and improving safety.

Augmented Reality (AR) with its power of visualisation can be used to visualize virtual lanes and control traffic participants using traffic signals in mixed traffic [15]. Such large AR deployments will help pedestrians safety move in outdoor spaces [16], while avoiding collisions and also mediate participants to avoid priority confusion. This could enable behavioural change interventions in traffic using AR.

While walking in virtual lanes spaces people usually cross paths with other traffic participants. Existing research around pedestrian motion in free space considering collisions avoidance relates to the adjustment of the path and speed of motion as two of the most important parameters. In scenarios considered for motion towards a goal or target destination, adjusting the speed is more favourable amongst both. This is supported based on findings that speed adjustments help with keeping the intended path avoiding re-planning of the motion trajectory. Braking on the other hand seems to be favored when the field of view is restricted [1], in small areas, or crowded places [2], and when the environment or the obstacle's behavior is uncertain [3]. However when a pedestrian motion happens in a spatially constrained and temporally restricted setting like for example a pedestrian walking in an AR guided virtual lane, signaled to stop by a virtual traffic signal at an intersection, braking is the expected and favoured option [4].

The situational factors and environmental factors can also affect the motion dynamics. Situational factors (in other words, those that characterise the particular context in which a pedestrian finds himself or herself, but which are not 'fixed' from one outing to the next) may also help explain differences in recorded walking speeds between studies. It is well known, for example, that the prevailing density of other pedestrians has a significant effect on individuals' walking speeds: indeed, the speed flow relationship of pedestrian movement patterns is well documented (for example, [18]). Early reports have suggested that people prefer to maintain a buffer zone of around 0.45 m between themselves and the edges of buildings [18], a smaller distance (approximately 0.1 m) to stationary items of street furniture [19] and a larger distance (around 0.8 to 0.9 m) between themselves and other pedestrians [20]. One report also suggested that people like to maintain a distance of around 0.75 m between themselves and their companion(s) when walking [21]. When a pedestrian motion happens in a virtual infrastructure controlled with a virtual traffic signal, these factors could still be accountable.

Fig. 1. Stop and go interface for pedestrian motion control

The goal of this study is to explore how an AR guided collision control interface affects the dynamics of interaction between pedestrians whose paths cross with each other. For a fair comparison, we have used the existing knowledge and understanding in research on crossing collision avoidance to evaluate the AR guidance approach. We compare the impact in terms control, safety and user feedback while using the interface with both a crossing and non crossing constellations of pedestrian motion. We focus on the diversity of the interactions captured and map them to scenarios when these interactions are mediated with an AR based virtual pedestrian traffic control system.

2   Experimental Setup and Procedure

2.1   Participants

Six participants (2 females and 4 males) with a mean age of 25.5 took part in the study. All the participants had normal mobility, normal vision or corrected to normal vision. Two confederates taking turns volunteered in the experiment.

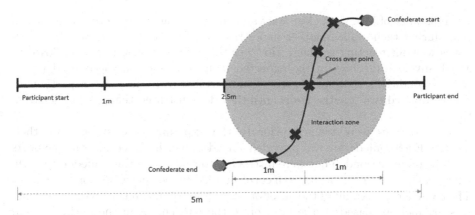

Fig. 2. Experimental scene: The pedestrian start and stop positions are marked with standardised crossing marking for confederate

2.2 Interface Design

A traffic light based 3D AR interface was designed using Unity (Fig. 1) with a Stop and Go (S&GI) trigger activating the corresponding transitions in control. The S&GI was positioned at a fixed height from the ground and tested with the Hololens. An external trigger was developed which communicated to the Hololens AR signalling interface over WiFi network. This S&GI transition trigger was controlled by a volunteer who observed interactions in the experiment.

2.3 Experimental Setup

Floor markings were made to support a visual path of motion (Fig. 2) for both the participant and confederate. While the participant markings were directed to propel him to walk on a straight line from the start to the end, the markings for the confederate were designed to intersect the participant starting with a motion at an obtuse angle (180°) and later intersecting at right angles at the cross over point. We have defined the cross over point as the point where the confederate crosses the path with the participant and is positioned at the center of the interaction zone. This is also the point where the collision would happen if the participant would not react to the motion of confederate. This path was chosen to account for complete visibility of the confederate and to enable complex interaction and have been detailed in the paper. The experiment was conducted with a static camera overlooking the scene, capturing video frames at 30 frames per second. The tracked scene was 6 × 3 m in a well lit indoor lab setting for clear augmented visualisation. The camera was focused to cover foot movements. A local WIFI network connection was set up in the experimental arena for remote control of AR interfaces.

Before the start of the experiment, the participants were explained the procedure and introduced to the HoloLens device. The participants had to walk a total distance of 5 m, with clear start and end marking. They were also informed that during their walk, another pedestrian (confederate) would possibly cross paths without reacting to them. However this information was not disclosed to avoid any learning bias in the expected behaviour and this accounted in the total 4 conditions that were tested (herein called scenarios). Each participant also completed two practise trails until they demonstrated that they understood the task.

Confederates were trained prior to the experiment to standardise their motion. Each confederate was provided a headset which played metronome beats at 70 beats per second. They were instructed to walk along the confederate path, where each cross mark on the path corresponded to foot positions for every beat. The confederate estimated the onset of interaction (point in time where they had to start motion) based on the position of the participant in the initial 1m and the entry of the participant to the interaction zone and was expected to walk not reacting to the participant motion even in the event of near collision. The behaviour of the confederate changed in a few scenarios as detailed:

Scenario I - No Interface - No Interaction (No Interaction Motion Baseline). The participant moved from the start to the end position wearing the Hololens but with no S&GI control. The confederate was expected to remain stationary at the confederate start position during the experiment.

Scenario II - No interface - Interaction (No Interface Interaction Baseline). The participant moved from the start to the end position wearing the Hololens but with no S&GI control. The confederate moved along the confederate path with motion directed to create a conflict at the cross over point (Fig. 2).

Scenario III - Interface - No interaction (AR Interface Guided Motion). The participant moved from the start to the end position wearing the Hololens but was motion controlled with S&GI control. A green indication was triggered by the external volunteer to signal the participant to "go" and the participant followed the control. The confederate was expected to remain stationary at the confederates start position during the experiment.

Scenario IV - Interface - Interaction (AR Interface Guided Interaction). The participant moved from the start to the end position wearing the Hololens but with motion controlled with S&GI control. The confederate moved along the confederate path with motion directed to create a conflict at the cross over point. A green indication was trigger by external volunteer to signal the participant to "go". As the participant approached the interaction zone and confederate motion approached the cross over point, the external volunteer trigger the interface transition from green to red signalling the participant to "stop". Once the confederate stepped away from the cross over point, the AR trigger was transitioned to green allowing the participant to continue motion.

Prior to each experiment, the first trail was used to familiarise the participant with the different scenarios. For each of the participant, the ordering of scenarios were randomised to avoid any learning bias. Once the experiment was completed, a questionnaire was handed over after each scenario for a user feedback of their experience.

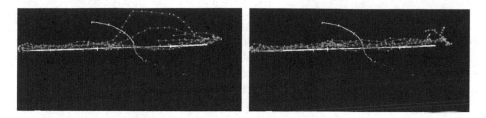

Fig. 3. The left shows the participant trajectories interacting in Scenario II (No Interface Interaction Baseline) while the picture on the right shows the interaction in Scenario IV (AR Interface Guided Interaction)

3 Data Processing

3.1 Camera Based Position Information

Location information of both the participant and confederate was extracted using the deep learning based image detection approach Yolo [29]. The frames were processed at 30 fps and the pedestrians in each frame were tracked with DeepSORT [28] tracking to extract the individual trajectories. The foot of the pedestrian in each pedestrian frame was used to find the position of the participant. The position information from the image coordinate frame were transformed to world coordinate frame using the size of know landmarks in the images. A projective transformation was used to transform the location information to a birds eye view. The position information from the camera was further down-sampled to 5 frames per second. The trajectory position was further smoothed with a sliding window with a filter size of three.

4 Results and Discussion

For all the 6 participants, the dynamics of the participant path and velocity profiles across different scenarios have been compared.

To account for the change in positional information of the participant, the instantaneous tangential velocity of the body was computed according to the formula

$$V(t) = \sqrt{\dot{x}(t)^2 + \dot{y}(t)^2}$$

In order to measure the variability of the velocity profile among the different participants and scenarios, we computed the mean speed and the corresponding SD and this information has been used give statistical insights on different scenarios.

The time to collision (TTC) was calculated using the position information of the participant when the confederate is at the cross over point

$$TTC = \frac{d}{V_f - V_l}$$

where d is distance between the participant and confederate and V_f and V_l correspond to the speed of the participant between consecutive frames.

As it can be shown by the results (Table 1), the stop and go interface has significantly improved the distance between the participant and confederate (GAP) and the TTC as opposed to the no interface scenarios.

Table 1. Response comparing Scenario II (No Interface Interaction Baseline) with Scenario IV (AR Interface Guided Interaction)

Participant	Scenario	GAP (cm)	TTC (sec)
P1	No interface	77.05	2.5
	AR interface	106.01	3.5
P2	No interface	111.01	3.7
	AR interface	132.6	4.42
P3	No interface	59	0.65
	AR interface	104	3.4
P4	No interface	32	0.36
	AR interface	67	2.23
P5	No interface	70.29	0.39
	AR interface	95.18	3.17
P6	No interface	72.11	0.48
	AR interface	100.12	3.37

To further evaluate the user acceptance of the interface, we analysed the questionnaire data. The acceptance was measured using the Van der Laan scale and the results for the responses for 5 participants are shown in Table 2.

Table 2. User satisfaction user feedback

Scenarios	Satisfaction		Usefulness	
	Mean	SD	Mean	SD
Scenario I	−0.7	0.65	−0.84	0.512
Scenario II	−0.3	1.19	−0.56	1.29
Scenario III	0.9	0.64	1.28	0.51
Scenario IV	0.95	0.748	1.4	0.619

To measure how exhaustive the speed regulation effort was, participant rated their experience over a SMEQ scale [31] with a value of 220 corresponding to extremely demanding. The participants rated to have felt the need for more effort using the interface (Table 3) than scenarios without the interface. However more experiments need to be done to verify the same. Future designs for AR based interaction support systems should take this into account.

Table 3. Scale measurement based on SMEQ

Iteration	Mean	Variance
Scenario I	39.33	70.67
Scenario 2	43.3	69.76
Scenario 3	49.2	44.9
Scenario 4	50.67	41.31

The exploratory study focused on evaluating the impact of the AR based control on both motion path and speed dynamics. Furthermore we have focused on the following research questions to better understand the change in behaviours enabled with the interface.

Q1. How does the general walking speed of the participant change using a body worn control system?

From the speed profile information of the participants while comparing (Table 4) the participant motion in Scenario I (No Interaction Motion Baseline) with Scenario III (AR Interface Guided Motion) gives a fair comparison. While most of the participants maintained more controlled pedestrian motion exhibiting lower average speeds and lower speed variations (low SD), one in six participants exhibited increased average speed supported with low speed variations during walking reflecting in more confidence in using AR controlled interface. This has been reflected in the speed for the participant for other scenarios too, throughout the experiment.

All participants showed controlled speed motion dynamics (low SD in speed) when using the interface. This however is in contrary to the observations made in vehicular traffic studies for virtual traffic interface [26] where the drivers have shown to exhibit only lower speeds at traffic intersections. The low speeds for pedestrians could be attributed to the level of attention given continuously as exemplified from the speed information while using AR based navigation applications [27].

Q2. How does the behaviour of the participant change with the interface to strategies to adjust walking path to accommodate for static confederate in the scene?

26   V. Kamalasanan et al.

Table 4. Walking speed variations for different participants comparing motion based scenarios

Participant	Scenario I		Scenario III	
	Mean speed (m/s)	SD	Mean speed (m/s)	SD
P1	0.79	0.46	0.53	0.277
P2	0.85	0.56	0.50	0.37
P3	0.60	0.30	0.43	0.21
P4	0.57	0.23	0.62	0.18
P5	0.53	0.37	0.55	0.25
P6	0.56	0.23	0.47	0.202

During human locomotion in goal-oriented tasks, they pursue a planning and/or control strategy for the spatially oriented task [23]. These strategies also include steering, obstacle avoidance and route selection and depends on the appearance of the obstacle [24].

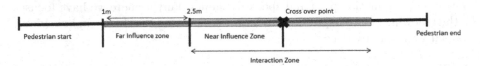

Fig. 4. Spatial zones identified to account for the influence of confederate on participant motion.

Recent pedestrian simulation models have also accounted for it at a microscopic level. In these models, the collision avoidance pattern stems automatically from a combination of the velocity vector of the other pedestrians and the density parameter. An individual tries to keep a minimum distance from the others ("territorial effect"). In the social force model for example, this pattern is described by repulsive social forces.

To evaluate the impact of the static confederate in the scene, we identified spatially separated Far Influence Zone and Near Influence Zone and observed the speed variations in Scenario I (No Interface Motion Baseline) and Scenario III (AR Interface Guided Motion) for the participants in these zones. Two (P3 and P4) in six participants approached the intersection cautiously without an interface and later increased the pace of motion once no interactions were predicted.

All participants reacted equally in Scenario III (AR Interface Guided Motion) showing significant impact of the interface to counter the effects of external forces. Figure 5 shows how P4 speed variation in the near influence zone.

Q3. How abrupt is the stopping motion for participants using the interface?

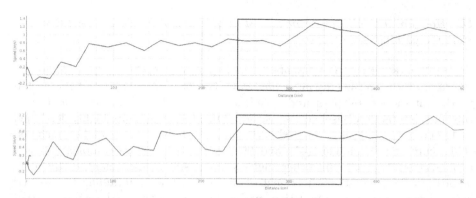

Fig. 5. The figure on the top shows the participant speed vs distance variation for near influence zone (Fig. 4) for Scenario I (No Interface Motion Baseline) while the bottom shows no speed adjustments accounted by the participant in Scenario III (AR Interface Guided Motion)

The motion data pointed that P3 participant reacted cautiously by reducing speed in the near influence zone, as the confederate approached closer to the cross over point. P3 continued to show significant speed variations and exhibited backward motion (Fig. 6) while stopping in the interaction zone when encountering the crossing pedestrian at the cross point in Scenario II (No Interface Interaction Baseline).

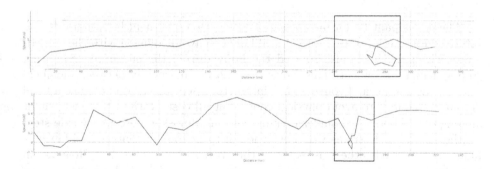

Fig. 6. The figure above shows the response of participant P3 stopping abruptly while the figure below shows same participant reacting to interface instructions more smoothly when mediating the interaction.

When using the interface in Scenario IV (AR Interface Guided Interaction) participant P3 continued to react cautiously in the near influence zone coupled with lower speeds of motion and backward motion. Thus the cautious pedestrian reacted with less backward motion and lower window of reaction while using the interface.

Q4. How are the collision avoidance strategies mapping when mediated with a stop and go interface?

While most of the participants in the experiment preferred to brake giving the right of way to the crossing confederate, two participants P4 and P5 reacted to the interaction by path and speed adjustment (Fig. 7) in Scenario II (No Interface Interaction Baseline). These adjustment strategies are highly depended on the crossing angle as accounted in the finding [25] wherein it can be concluded that acute crossing angles (45° and 90°) account for more complex collision avoidance strategies. While other angles support speed adjustment, really small angles (45°) support the adjustment of the path while maintaining the desired speed. However in these interactions pedestrians can optimise the smoothness of trajectories by implementing braking, thereby avoiding big changes in walking paths.

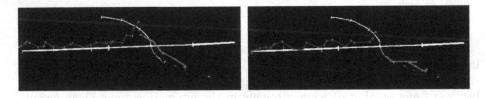

Fig. 7. The left shows participant P4 exhibits path adjustment as the collision avoidance strategy while encountering the confederate, while P5 exhibits a combination of both path and speed adjustment to counter the crossing confederate.

The participant P4 for instance applied a path adjustment in Scenario II (No Interface Interaction Baseline) but still failed to avoid collision with the confederate. The participant also rotated the body during the encounter exhibiting step-and-slide movement. This movement [22] occurs mostly between members of the same gender and conveys that interacting pedestrians do not take a total detour or attempt to avoid physical contact at all cost. Rather, there is a slight angling of the body, a shoulder turning, and an almost imperceptible side step. Neither of the pedestrians will move enough to guarantee contact avoidance or bumping into each other, unless the other pedestrian cooperates. However in Scenario IV (AR Interface Guided Interaction) the participant P4 accounted for more controlled interaction when augmented with the stop and go interface and this is reflected in the results from the calculated time to collision.

A combination of both speed adjustment and path adjustment strategy for P5 help steer pass the crossing confederate, where the speed of motion was increased. P5 however exhibited controlled motion in the interaction in Scenario IV (AR Interface Guided Interaction).

The current study investigated the influence of AR virtual traffic interface with respect to walking and interaction dynamics of pedestrians. The results indicate body worn control systems are successful in averting collisions and influencing motion. When we take the mean speed and its SD in No Interaction Motion

Baseline, it is observed that participants move at their desired speed but are also influenced by the presence of other pedestrians in the environment. It also seems that this influence is based on the distance of the crossing pedestrian. When the participants are augmented with virtual control for motion, we observed that they preferred to walk at lower speeds with lower speed variations and were less impacted by the influence of nearby pedestrians.

We urge that the increase in TTC in interaction involving AR interfaces might be due to a combination of factors. While the standardised trigger to stop is significant, other factors like the increased attention of the participant to the control interfaces in the event of a conflict is equally significant. However we are unable to back this claim with technical data but urge that the user acceptance ratings evaluating it as a useful system as a strong indicate of this.

While significant efforts have been made to standardize the motions in our work. It should also be noted that the experiments did not simulate a real shared space, since the simulated setting was unable to mimic the motion dynamics of all other agents in a mixed traffic scene. In addition visual clues to indicate the confederate foot positions were visible to all the participants during the experiment. Understanding how the participants would behave while moving in virtual lanes with virtual traffic interfaces would be equally interesting.

To give a summary of the findings: We investigated on how AR can mediate collision avoidance along the pedestrian path. By introducing AR, we reduce the impact of other participants by instructing them to stop or go whenever they are hesitant on whether they should keep going, reducing the more diverse and less predictive behaviours which might include stopping and moving back, changing trajectory or speeding up. This will also make shared spaces more predictable and reduce the impact of other pedestrians or other traffic participants on the walking behaviour of subjects. We also observe that the control element introduces the fear of not obeying rules recommended to them (e.g.: stop when a red signal is shown). This is an indicative of how these interfaces can resolve conflicts

The results of the study give some insights on the dynamics involved in human interface controlled motion. Several domains could benefit from the findings. Firstly it contributes to how people would walk in virtual infrastructure junctions and this could be useful traffic planners and traffic designers. On the other hand the learning's could also be valuable to transportation engineers on understanding how interactions would differ between pedestrians and other agents like autonomous vehicles when using AR based interfaces to avoid collisions in shared spaces. Finally it could also be interesting to researchers on how pedestrians would be accommodated as traffic agents in lane-free vehicular traffic [30].

5   Conclusion

We have investigated how different free space collision avoidance interactions in pedestrians differ when the interactions are supported by a central collision avoidance traffic infrastructure for pedestrians. On this basis we conclude that spatiotemporal restrictions imposed via augmented reality can enable collision avoidance by braking and enable controlled motion dynamics in pedestrians. Furthermore we compare how pedestrians with different levels of tolerance to safety react to virtual safety systems. We conclude that AR based pedestrian control systems are effective in increasing the Time to Collision (TTC) and resolving conflicts.

While the first results of this proof-of-concept experiments have been promising, there is still room for improvement. The study currently has focused only on a small number of participants with limited scenarios and hence the conclusions are more biased along the observations on this small group. As a shared space would include more traffic participants and a wider interaction landscape, user studies including more participants and open spaces would give more insights and is a direction for future works. While safety of pedestrians is important factor being considered, the scalabilty of such systems when considering cyclist and vehicles still remains an open question which needs to be addressed.

References

1. Jansen, S.E.M., Toet, A., Werkhoven, P.J.: Human locomotion through a multiple obstacle environment: strategy changes as a result of visual field limitation. Exp. Brain Res. **212**(3), 449–456 (2011)
2. Moussaïd, M., Helbing, D., Theraulaz, G.: How simple rules determine pedestrian behavior and crowd disasters. Proc. Nat. Acad. Sci. **108**(17), 6884–6888 (2011)
3. Basili, P., et al.: Strategies of locomotor collision avoidance. Gait Post. **37**(3), 385–390 (2013)
4. Cinelli, M.E., Patla, A.E.: Task-specific modulations of locomotor action parameters based on on-line visual information during collision avoidance with moving objects. Hum. Mov. Sci. **27**(3), 513–531 (2008)
5. Clarke, E.: Shared Space-the alternative approach to calming traffic. Traffic Eng. Control **47**(8), 290–292 (2006)
6. Hamilton-Baillie, B.: Shared space: reconciling people, places and traffic. Built Environ. **34**(2), 161–181 (2008)
7. Koorey, G.: The 'On-again/Off-again' debate about cycle facilities. In: 5th NZ Cycling Conference (2005)
8. Peitso, L.E., Michael, J.B.: The promise of interactive shared augmented reality. Computer **53**(1), 45–52 (2020)
9. Stoker, P., et al.: Pedestrian safety and the built environment: a review of the risk factors. J. Plan. Liter. **30**(4), 377–392 (2015)
10. Lonero, L.P., Clinton, K.M., Sleet, D.A.: Behavior change interventions in road safety. Injury Viol. Prev. Behav. Sci. Theories Methods Appl. 213–233 (2006)
11. Zegeer, C.V., et al.: Guidance for implementation of the AASHTO strategic highway safety plan. Volume 10: A Guide for Reducing Collisions Involving Pedestrians. No. Project G17–18 (3) (2004)
12. Retting, R.A., Ferguson, S.A., McCartt, A.T.: A review of evidence-based traffic engineering measures designed to reduce pedestrian-motor vehicle crashes. Am. J. Public Health **93**(9), 1456–1463 (2003)
13. Zegeer, C.V., Bushell, M.: Pedestrian crash trends and potential countermeasures from around the world. Accid. Anal. Prev. **44**(1), 3–11 (2012)

14. Pedestrian Safety: A Road Safety Manual for Decision-makers and Practitioners. World Health Organization. http://www.who.int/roadsafety/projects/manuals/pedestrian/en/. Accessed 25 Aug 2013
15. Kamalasanan, V., Sester, M.: Behaviour control with augmented reality systems for shared spaces. Int. Arch. Photogram. Remote Sens. Spat. Inf. Sci. **43**, 591–598 (2020)
16. Damien Constantine, R., et al.: Towards large scale high fidelity collaborative augmented reality (2019)
17. Franek, M., Penickova, S., Ondracek, L., Brandysky, P.: Influence of urban vegetation on the walking speed of pedestrians. Ceskoslovenska Psychologie **52**(6), 597–608 (2008)
18. Fruin, J.J.: Designing for pedestrians: A level-of-service concept. No. HS-011 999 (1971)
19. Habicht, A.T., Braaksma, J.P.: Effective width of pedestrian corridors. J. Transp. Eng. **110**(1), 80–93 (1984)
20. Dabbs Jr, J.M., Stokes III, N.A.: Beauty is power: the use of space on the sidewalk. Sociometry 551–557 (1975)
21. Burgess, J.W.: Interpersonal spacing behavior between surrounding nearest neighbors reflects both familiarity and environmental density. Ethol. Sociobiol. **4**(1), 11–17 (1983)
22. Wolff, M.: Notes on the behaviour of pedestrians. In: People in Places: The Sociology of the Familiar. Praeger, New York, pp. 35–48 (1973)
23. Hicheur, H., et al.: The formation of trajectories during goal-oriented locomotion in humans. I. A stereotyped behaviour. Eur. J. Neurosci. **26**(8), 2376–2390 (2007)
24. Fajen, B., Warren, W.H.: Behavioral dynamics of steering, obstacle avoidance, and route selection. J. Exp. Psychol. Hum. Percept. Perform. **29**(2), 343 (2003)
25. Huber, M., et al.: Adjustments of speed and path when avoiding collisions with another pedestrian. PloS one **9**(2), e89589 (2014)
26. Olaverri-Monreal, C., et al.: In-vehicle virtual traffic lights: a graphical user interface. In: 7th Iberian Conference on Information Systems and Technologies (CISTI 2012). IEEE (2012)
27. Tang, L., Zhou, J.: Usability assessment of augmented reality-based pedestrian navigation aid. In: Duffy, V.G. (ed.) HCII 2020. LNCS, vol. 12198, pp. 581–591. Springer, Cham (2020). https://doi.org/10.1007/978-3-030-49904-4_43
28. Wojke, N., Bewley, A., Paulus, D.: Simple online and real time tracking with a deep association metric. In: 2017 IEEE international conference on image processing (ICIP). IEEE (2017)
29. Bochkovskiy, A., Wang, C.-Y., Liao, H.-Y.M.: Yolov4: optimal speed and accuracy of object detection. arXiv preprint arXiv:2004.10934 (2020)
30. Papageorgiou, M., et al.: Lane-free artificial-fluid concept for vehicular traffic. Proc. IEEE **109**(2), 114–121 (2021)
31. Zijlstra, F.R.H.: University of Technology, Van Doorn. The construction of a scale to measure perceived effort (1985)

Pose Estimation and Video Annotation Approaches for Understanding Individual and Team Interaction During Augmented Reality-Enabled Mission Planning

Sue Kase[✉], Vincent Perry, Heather Roy, Katherine Cox, and Simon Su

DEVCOM Army Research Laboratory, Aberdeen Proving Ground, Aberdeen, MD 21005, USA
{sue.e.kase.civ,vincent.p.perry7.civ,heather.e.roy2.civ,
katherine.r.cox11.civ,simon.m.su.civ}@mail.mil

Abstract. Two video analysis approaches (pose estimation and manual annotation) were applied to video recordings of two-person teams performing a mission planning task in a shared augmented reality (AR) environment. The analysis approaches calculated the distance relations between team members and annotated observed behaviors during the collaborative task. The 2D pose estimation algorithm lacked scene depth processing; therefore, we found some inconsistencies with the manual annotation. Although integration of the two analysis approaches was not possible, each approach by itself produced several insights on team behavior. The manual annotation analysis found four common team behaviors as well as behavior variations unique to particular teams and temporal situations. Comparing a behavior-based time on task percentage indicated behavior-type connections and some possible exclusions. The pose estimation analysis found the majority of the teams moved around the 3D scene at a similar distance apart on average with similar variation in fluctuation around a common distance range between team members. Outlying team behavior was detected by both analysis approaches and included: periods of very low distance relations, infrequent but very high distance relation spikes, significant task time spent adjusting the HoloLens device during wearing, and exceptionally long task time with gaps in pose estimation data processing.

Keywords: Augmented reality · Mission planning · Pose estimation

1 Introduction

The proliferation of immersive technologies (augmented reality (AR) and virtual reality (VR) systems) has accentuated their potential utilization across a wide range of operational situations from strategic planning to the tactical edge. However, little is known about individual performance and especially team collaboration associated with using immersive technologies. Researchers at DEVCOM Army Research Laboratory (ARL) have been using Microsoft HoloLens devices to investigate AR technology for supporting collaborative mission planning. Shared AR spaces, such as simulated operational

J. Y. C. Chen and G. Fragomeni (Eds.): HCII 2021, LNCS 12770, pp. 32–46, 2021.
https://doi.org/10.1007/978-3-030-77599-5_3

terrains, have the potential to provide command staff with a common virtual battlespace for collaborative decision making. As a starting point, we investigated the shared visualization of an operational terrain using HoloLens devices to aid team performance in a simple mission planning task. Two-person teams (called dyads) conducted a mission planning scenario using the HoloLens by interactively manipulating a small subset of military symbology to plan a mission route for retrieving a repository of intelligence documents located within enemy-held territory. While planning the mission each team member could change the 3D scene by rotating, dragging, and resizing the terrain. Each team member's HoloLens interface allowed for pointing to objects and marking symbols and paths on the terrain. Additionally, the collocated team members could verbally communicate and physically move around the holographic terrain while planning their mission.

Previous reports on the experimental outcomes of this investigation as a whole have focused on several different topic areas: framing the mission planning task within the military decision making process (MDMP) for improving collaborative course of action planning using a 3D visualization approach [1]; developing a sensor data fusion framework allowing multiple HoloLens users to view a shared holographic scene with minimal object registration error [2]; developing a new survey instrument for capturing shared AR experience based on Witmer and Singer's [3] factors of presence [4]; comparing mission-based time metrics and a learning effect when using 2D versus 3D visualization technologies [5]; analyzing team efficacy, performance and workload across path-related and time-related metrics [6]; and incorporating this study into a broader vision of adapting advanced visualization technologies for use in data-intensive workflows [7].

This portion of the study focuses on two video analysis approaches for identifying common team member behaviors and the *distance relations* between team members while using the HoloLens to complete the task. We define distance relations as the physical proximity of one device wearer to another while interacting with the holographic scene. Kase et al. [1] initially detected a variety of team member physical configurations and their potential connection with establishing an individual-based and team-based understanding of the terrain. We anticipated a preliminary analysis of the video recordings would reveal a set of interactive behaviors and distance distributions between team members during the task. Outcomes of the two approaches for video analysis could contribute to a better understanding of how individuals and teams build situational awareness using AR technology in operational and decision making contexts.

The reminder of the paper is organized as follows. The next section overviews the collaborative AR mission planning experiment in which dyads were video recorded while planning their mission. Section 3 describes the two approaches for analyzing the video data collected during the experiment. Preliminary analysis results from both approaches are highlighted and interpreted in Sect. 4. Section 5 discusses several limitations of the video analysis approaches and possible future next steps. Section 6 concludes the paper.

2 Experiment Overview

A mission planning scenario was developed for dyads to investigate collaboration within a shared AR environment. Each dyad played the role of command staff in planning and rehearsing a simulated mission to retrieve a repository of intelligence documents located within enemy-held territory. AR devices offer the capability to superimpose a 3D model on the actual physical environment of HoloLens users. Team members co-located in physical laboratory space could walk around the holographic terrain and interactively manipulated symbols and path makers to create their mission route.

Figure 1 shows the holographic mission terrain as viewed through a team member's HoloLens. In Fig. 1, the vertical blue arrow in the center of the building model estimates the location of the targeted document repository. The blue lines are example mission routes planned by the team members to retrieve the documents and reach an extraction point on the waterfront. The black squares to the left of the building function as an operational menu for mission-level modes and route planning features. Su et al. [8] describes the 3D multi-user interface facilitating the mission planning task in the AR environment.

Fig. 1. 3D holographic image of the mission terrain viewed from a HoloLens device

The full experiment was a two-condition within-subjects design where each dyad used two different technologies to plan the mission—Microsoft HoloLens and a multi-touch Samsung SUR40 Surface table. The Surface table, in a tabletop horizontal viewing position, displayed a more traditional static 2D representation of the mission terrain characteristic of paper maps or sandboxes used in command centers or out in the field. Team members completed a battery of questionnaires pre- and post-technology use. Basic performance metrics were captured throughout the mission planning task on both technologies and categorized as either path-related or time-related metrics. Analyses were conducted at the dyad level to focus on teaming-related aspects such as perceived team efficacy, team performance, and workload. Roy et al. [6] offers additional details on the study design comparing the two technologies and preliminary results from the questionnaires.

In the next section, we describe the two approaches for analyzing the video recordings of the dyads using the HoloLens to plan their mission. Participants for 12 dyads were recruited and all but one dyad successfully planned a mission route and captured the targeted intelligence documents. One dyad's route (dyad 11) did not cross exactly over the target location; therefore, this mission didn't result in a capture per se. The video recordings for this dyad and dyad 6 contained formatting errors. The video analysis approaches and results described in the remainder of the paper apply to 10 of the 12 dyads participating in the experiment.

3 Video Analysis Approaches

Supplemental to collecting path- and time-related performance metrics, team members were recorded on video using an external camera attached to the ceiling of the laboratory overlooking the physical space in which the holographic terrain scene was displayed. Also during the HoloLens condition, the field of vision through each team member's HoloLens device was recorded capturing their interaction with the holographic mission terrain. For example, Fig. 2 shows the HoloLens views of each team member (left side) and their corresponding physical position while viewing the terrain as captured by the external camera (right side).

Fig. 2. HoloLens views of each dyad member with the turquoise Gaze disc indicating their current focus (left side). Corresponding video capture from the external camera showing the physical position of each dyad member while viewing the 3D mission terrain (right side)

During mission planning the distance or proximity of team members to each other and what actions they were performing constantly changed. Each team member moved around the scene in order to view terrain features such as buildings and natural obstacles from different perspectives. Although the 3D scene could be manipulated using finger controls and menu selections, team members appeared to prefer physical movement and changing posture when interacting with the scene. For example, physically pointing to a specific location on the terrain appeared to trigger discussion and coordination on a particular topic. Figure 2 (right side) shows one team member stooping to gain a lower perspective of building access points.

We used two approaches for analyzing the video data collected during the HoloLens condition of experiment: a manual approach similar to labeling or annotating video for human movement patterns; and a machine learning-based pose estimation approach.

3.1 Manual Annotation Approach

Typically, the goal of video annotation is to assign predefined concepts to video segments based on their semantic and visual content [9]. While the social sciences have a long history of annotating human behavior [10], semi-automated and automated video annotation tools using computer vision and machine learning methods have been recently developed and applied to large scale visual datasets [11–13]. The small number of videos and their relatively short time length in this study enabled application of a traditional manual annotation approach in addition to the opportunity of employing a more state-of-the-art machine learning based approach.

In the first video analysis approach, the VLC media player and framework by the VideoLAN organization was used to view the video recordings. VideoLAN [14] produces open source software for multimedia released under the General Public License. A timeline for each video was divided into cells each corresponding to 1 frame per second (fps) in the video. Initially, a list defining a basic set of behaviors of interest was developed for labeling. After more detailed reviewing of the videos, the cells were labeled indicating the presence of specific team member behavior in corresponding frames. Table 1 lists the behavior labels for the most commonly found behaviors (first row) and behavior labels which tended to be more unique to specific dyads and temporal situations (second row).

Table 1. Behavior labels used for manual annotation of the videos: common behaviors across dyads (first row); and behavior variations unique to dyads and temporal situations (second row)

Behavior labels common across teams	Verbal communication	Moving	Pointing	Adjust HoloLens
Behavior variations	1 team member speaking	Shuffling feet	1 team member pointing	2 handed adjustment
		Side stepping		
	Both team members speaking at the same time	Change of posture	Both team members pointing at the same time	1 handed adjustment
	Giving a command		Double-arm pointing	Extending holding of device
	Shout of success		Raising both arms	
			Giving 'high five'	
			Varioushand and arm gestures	

3.2   Pose Estimation Approach

Pose estimation has been a long studied area in computer vision research. It is oftentimes a preprocessing step for many more complex problems. For example, machine learning algorithms can be trained to estimate the position of human limbs to support smart surveillance, detect abnormal behavior, and even to control animated 3D model motion.

The second analysis approach applied a realtime multi-person 2D pose estimation system called OpenPose [15, 16] to the video recordings. Human pose estimation is a critical component in enabling machines to visually understand and interpret humans and their interactions [16]. OpenPose uses Part Affinity Fields, a set of 2D vector fields that encode the location and orientation of limbs, to learn to associate body parts with individuals in images and videos [15]. OpenPose has the capability to estimate the pose of multiple socially engaged individuals by detecting body, foot, hand, and facial keypoints. OpenPose is widely used for many research topics involving human analysis, and is available open source and included in the OpenCV library [17].

We installed OpenPose on a laptop running Windows 10. For this study, we selected OpenPose runtime choices of video input, the set of algorithms for the body, and output as JSON files with the keypoints in the format of body part locations (x, y) and confidence scores (z). Keypoints are ordered by body part (Fig. 3) As an initial attempt using OpenPose to study team member distance relations, we focused on keypoint #1 in the BODY_25 pose output format which is located at the base of the neck at the intersection of the arms.

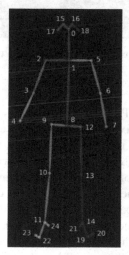

Fig. 3. OpenPose output of JSON files consists of a set of 25 body keypoints ordered by pose output format BODY_25. https://cmu-perceptual-computing-lab.github.io/openpose/web/html/doc/md_doc_02_output.html

Figure 4 shows four examples of OpenPose output captured as static images with the BODY_25 keypoints overlaid on the team members while performing mission planning. The upper left and lower right images show the team members positioned at opposite ends of the holographic terrain. In both these images one of the team members is pointing at a specific location on the terrain while the other team member appears to be physically moving around the terrain model. The upper right and lower left images show the team members positioned adjacent to each other both viewing a specific area of the terrain. In the upper right image, both team members are in a slightly stooped position leaning over the terrain for a closer viewing perspective. Additionally, one team member is pointing to an area of interest on the terrain.

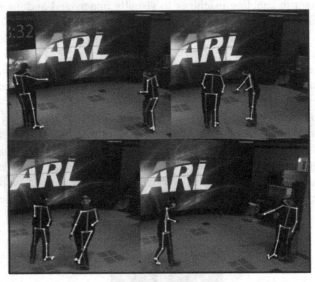

Fig. 4. Example images of OpenPose BODY_25 keypoints overlaid on team members while performing mission planning

We post-processed the OpenPose JSON output files by extracting the video frame number and the x,y positions in pixels of keypoint #1 for each team member in the scene. The difference between the team members' keypoint #1 values gave us an approximate distance metric for the team member positions in relation to each other. We were initially interested in the distance relations between team members when they were nearest and furthest apart from each other. These near and far distance values and associated frames could assist us when indexing specific segments of the video files during manual annotation. However, the distance values derived from the OpenPose keypoints were not as accurate as expected which is discussed in a later section. Therefore, the manual annotation approach of the videos was performed unaided by the OpenPose distance relations analysis.

In the next section, we present preliminary results from the two video analysis approaches. Manually annotating the video recordings produced a set of common dyad behaviors associated with total time on task percentages for each behavior. The pose estimation analysis of the video recordings produced distance distributions generated by OpenPose keypoint #1 tracking of both team members across time on task.

4 Video Analysis Results

Using the HoloLens team members could inspect the holographic scene and click menu buttons controlling different operational modes of the mission simulation while positioned at a static location in reference to the holographic terrain. The AR technology itself allowed for more interesting team member behaviors such as physically moving around the terrain, changing posture for different viewing perspectives, verbally communicating with a team member, and using various arm and hand gestures. Sometimes these behaviors occurred while team members were positioned close to each other supporting team coordination and shared situational awareness, while other times the behaviors occurred when team members were far apart, for example at opposite ends of the terrain model supporting more individual level reflection and perception of the environment.

4.1 Manual Annotation Results

The manual annotation effort of the videos produced some understanding of how team members interacted as they used the HoloLens as a resource or tool in the process of accomplishing the collaborative task of mission planning. There were several basic behaviors commonly identified across dyads in addition to some uniqueness exhibited by each dyad. Table 1 provides a list of annotated behaviors with the top-level annotation labels characterizing common dyad behaviors (e.g., communicating, moving, pointing). The more descriptive second-level annotation labels were applied to unique behaviors of particular dyads and team members and sometimes were triggered by a mission-related outcome (e.g., a side-step and shuffle, the double-point, a high five, a celebratory shout).

Table 2 shows the results of applying the top-level annotation labels to each dyad's video recording. The values represent the percentage of total task time of the observed behavior. For example, dyad 4 team members verbally communicated 77.7% of the time during mission planning from start to end of the task which was the highest communication percentage across dyads. Team members in dyad 4 also spent the greatest percentage of time using a pointing gesture (29%) compared to other dyads. Dyad 12 had the second highest percentages for both time spent verbally communicating (70.5%) and pointing (24.5%); comparatively a decrease of 7.2% for communicating and 4.5% for pointing from dyad 4's times. However, dyad 12 spent the lowest amount of time moving around the terrain compared to the other dyads. There appears to be a connection between time spent communicating and pointing gestures supported by dyad 10's third highest times for both. Dyad 2 showed the 4th highest pointing time, but unfortunately, the trend ends with the technical malfunction of dyad 2's audio recording listed as 0% for verbal communication in Table 2.

The percentage of times engaged in each behavior can be visualized with the bar charts in Fig. 5. For example, time spent physically moving around the 3D terrain (Fig. 5, upper right) was greatest for dyad 1 (58.5%) followed by dyad 5 (51.8%) and then dyad 8 (43%) a decrease of 8.8% of the task time from dyad 5 and a substantial decrease of 15.5% from dyad 1.

The behavior of adjusting the HoloLens device while wearing it, either using one or both hands, is shown in the lower right chart of Fig. 5. Six out of the 10 dyads exhibited some evidence of device adjustment behavior. For two of those six dyads,

Table 2. Percentage of task time associated with the four most common behaviors observed during manual annotation of the video recordings of the ten dyads performing the mission planning task. *Note dyad 2 lost audio recording and thus verbal communication appears as zero*

Dyad	Verbal communication	Moving	Pointing	Adjust HoloLens
D1	49.0	58.5	2.5	3.5
D2	0	26.6	19.3	4.3
D3	29.8	33.3	18.9	0.7
D4	77.7	34.3	29.0	0
D5	37.2	51.8	2.5	0
D7	50.0	31.7	17.0	0
D8	37.0	43.0	10.0	0
D9	56.2	29.7	10.9	36.4
D10	57.1	27.7	20.5	0.3
D11	70.5	24.0	24.5	3.6

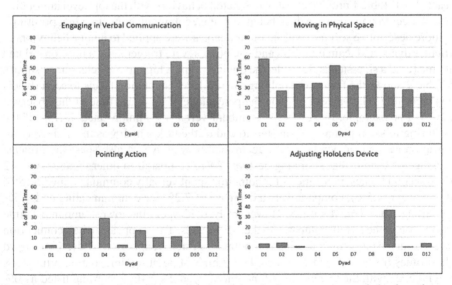

Fig. 5. Percentage of task time bar graphs visualizing the four most common behaviors observed in the video recordings of the ten dyads (x-axis) performing the mission planning task. *Note dyad 2 lost audio recording and thus verbal communication appears as zero*

the amount of time was minimal (0.7% for dyad 3, 0.3% for dyad 10). This equated to approximately 1 and 3 s of a team member's task time. Two other dyads had device adjustment behavior times in the single digits (3.5% for dyad 1, 4.3% for dyad 2) which equated to approximately 7 and 18 s of task time. With nine out of ten dyads spending no to very little time adjusting their device, we can assume the fit and comfort of wearing the HoloLens for relatively short periods of time was acceptable.

Dyad 9 was the exception with one team member spending 36.4% of task time adjusting the HoloLens device or holding on to the device while planning the mission. Visual inspection of the video showed the device adjustment behavior started approximately 3 min into the task and continued for two minutes until the HoloLens lost its network connection. At that point, the device had to be removed and reset. After the team member put the HoloLens back on to continue the task, no additional device adjustment behaviors were observed. This instance appeared to be a one-off occurrence of device discomfort possibly caused by the device not fitting comfortably from the start, and the behavior of holding onto the device could be related to the limited field of view.

The manual annotation of the videos identified four behaviors common across most of the teams. A percentage of total task time spent on each behavior was calculated and compared. Three of the four behaviors (verbal communication, moving, and pointing) appeared to support team interaction, coordination, and collaboration in the AR environment. The infrequently observed HoloLens device adjustment behavior most likely detracted from team performance especially in the case of dyad 9 where one team member spent over a third of the total task time fiddling with the device.

We can make several generalizations based on the percentage of behavior time values. Oftentimes two different types of behavior were exhibited in parallel such as verbally communicating with a team member while pointing to a specific location or object on the terrain. For three dyads (4, 10, and 12), high verbal communication times were associated with more pointing actions. Inversely, one type of behavior can restrict or limit another type of behavior. For example, dyads spending more time communicating appeared to spend less time physically moving around the scene; and dyads that communicated less spent more time moving around the scene (dyads 4 and 12 compared to dyads 5 and 8). The role of two or more concurrent behaviors and how these behavior combinations might influence teaming is interesting and requires further investigation.

4.2 Pose Estimation Results

The OpenPose analysis results of the dyad videos increased understanding of the distance distributions between team members while they were collaboratively performing the mission planning task. We were particularly interested in the distance relation or proximity of team members and the corresponding time intervals when they were positioned close to each other versus far apart from each other.

OpenPose calculated a 2D pose estimation outputted in the form of a distance metric for each frame in the video sequence. Using 30 fps, we averaged the distance metrics for each 30-frame sequence representing one second of video feed. This provided a single distance or proximity value for each second of a dyad's performance. Unfortunately, we did find several seconds of video recordings that were not captured by the OpenPose software.

Table 3 shows descriptive statistics for each dyad's distance metrics averaged per second of video feed. In the table, eight of the ten dyad mean distances are within the range of 200 to 300, with dyads 3 and 12 averaging 337 (highest distance) and 181 (lowest distance), respectively. The standard deviations appear to be consistent across dyads as well as the minimum, maximum, median, and quartile values. To aid interpretation of the summary statistics in Table 3, Fig. 6 visualizes the statistics using multiple boxplots. The boxplot shapes appear to be relatively consistent across dyads with the exception of dyad 4 which has the largest number of outliers and greatest range of distance values.

Table 3 Descriptive statistics for dyad distance metrics calculated by OpenPose and averaged per second of video feed

	Dist_D1	Dist_D2	Dist_D3	Dist_D4	Dist_D5	Dist_D7	Dist_D8	Dist_D9	Dist_D10	Dist_D12
Count	204.00	434.00	451.00	471.00	209.00	478.00	235.00	586.00	374.00	459.00
Mean	243.55	252.83	336.88	259.21	257.54	214.22	276.86	230.10	270.96	181.08
std	83.49	87.78	114.11	177.78	122.57	90.15	105.88	77.16	119.57	92.87
min	106.57	69.81	79.84	46.72	74.97	61.06	79.53	75.93	87.38	56.57
25%	168.22	196.78	233.75	134.47	142.76	146.63	206.06	177.69	187.95	110.92
50%	222.15	241.30	320.01	220.61	234.22	192.37	276.63	221.66	252.95	155.41
75%	313.82	296.27	415.93	333.63	373.45	274.75	322.00	276.30	305.89	212.50
max	494.72	637.11	642.40	1145.40	513.04	572.48	660.79	474.39	716.89	510.49

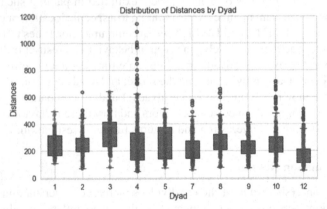

Fig. 6. Dyad boxplots compare the distribution of distances for each dyad's interquartile with median and outliers

Figure 7 visualizes the OpenPose data from a time series perspective with the average distance between dyad members (y-axis) plotted across seconds of the video feed (x-axis). The data from all 10 dyads included in the Fig. 7 plot somewhat overlap making interpretation difficult; however, two observations are clearly evident. First, dyad 12's mission planning time of 864 secs is approximately 53% longer than the next longest dyad time (456 s). In the plot, dyad 12 is represented by a brown-colored line that extends well past the stop times of the other dyads. Also, the breaks in the dyad 12 timeline show time segments where OpenPose did not capture a distance metric. The second observation pertains to the high spikes in dyad 4's distance metrics. Dyad 4 is represented by the red-colored line that shows the greatest range of distance between team members from a minimum of 46.7 to a maximum of 1145.4. This corresponds to the outlying distance values at the high end shown in the dyad 4 boxplot (see Fig. 6).

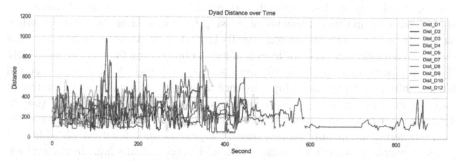

Fig. 7. Time series plot visualizing distance metrics across task time for all dyads. Legend labels for distance value plot lines are color-coded by dyad number (Color figure online)

The time series plot in Fig. 8 focuses on only three of the 10 dyads: dyad 4 (red line) with the highest distance value spikes, dyad 3 (green line) with the highest interquartile value, and dyad 7 (cyan line) which appears to have the lowest interquartile value (refer to Table 3). This visualization of the three dyads' distance measures allows us to compare the variations of the values across time. A visual inspection reveals that dyad 4 has extended segments of low distance values showing lack of team member physical movement near the start and end of the task compared to dyads 3 and 7 that show relatively consistent variation in distance values across the task time. Dyad 3 has slightly higher distance spikes than dyad 7 while dyad 7 has more low distance values contributing to its low interquartile value.

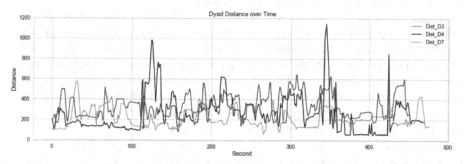

Fig. 8. Time series plot comparing distance value plot lines for only dyads 3, 4, and 7 (Color figure online)

By analyzing the OpenPose generated output from the video recordings of the dyads performing the mission planning task, several observations can be made. All dyad-calculated distance metrics displayed a normal distribution with rightward skew towards the larger distance values. Dyad team members moved around the 3D scene while planning their mission mostly staying a similar distance apart from each other. Eight of the ten dyad distance values appear similar in variation with fluctuation around a common distance range between team members as they moved closer and further apart while inspecting the virtual mission planning environment.

More specifically, we have noted the extended length of time dyad 12 required to complete the task and time segments of missing OpenPose data. We have identified dyad 4 as an outlier in regards to exceptionally large distance spikes which means team members were positioned at opposite ends of the terrain viewing the scene from entirely different perspectives at those specific time periods. Although this behavior occurred relatively infrequently, Dyad 4's high distance value spikes should be analyzed more closely by referring back to the associated time segments in the video recording to potentially identify any anomalous behavior of the team members while performing the task. Considering the identification of missing OpenPose data for dyad 12, additional OpenPose inaccuracies might be the cause of dyad 4's exceptionally high distance values.

5 Discussion

As part of an AR collaborative mission planning experiment, video recordings captured dyads using the HoloLens to plan a mission route on a holographic terrain. Two different video analysis approaches, manually annotation and pose estimation, were used to identify common human behaviors and distance distributions of the team members while performing the task.

The initial strategy for using two analysis approaches employed OpenPose output as a proximity guide for identifying specific video segments of interest calling for an in-depth manual annotation approach. For example, if we were specifically interested in HoloLens wearer discomfort the OpenPose keypoint formatting structure could detect specific poses resembling attempts to adjust the device while on the wearer's head. In this case, keypoints 7 and/or 14 representing the hands would be overlapping some of the keypoints located on the head (0, 15 to 18, see Fig. 3).

Unfortunately, our decision to use a 2D pose estimation algorithm such as OpenPose limited the integration of the two analysis approaches. When OpenPose is applied to a video, it only records lateral distances between the humans in the environment not the depth in the environment. Not accounting for depth decreased the usefulness of the OpenPose output for application of manual video annotations. For example, if both team members were in line with the camera but positioned at opposite ends of the terrain (i.e., far apart from each other) the OpenPose output would indicate the team members were very close to each other or even overlapping in 2D space.

Repeating the analysis using a 3D human pose estimation method [18–20] would be a good next step. Incorporating a third type of analysis on the gaze from each team members' HoloLens view (Fig. 2, left side) begins to offer multimodal data opportunities—mutual gaze, gaze oriented to objects— combined with body postures, common behaviors, and team member distance distributions. Another future direction is to leverage our previously published results (e.g., path and time-based metrics; measures of team efficacy, team performance, and workload; subjective feelings of presence, and preferred visualization technology) by conceptualizing how these embodied features could be incorporated into a framework for recording and analyzing patterns of team member collaboration in shared AR environments.

6 Conclusion

The paper presented two different video analysis approaches for analyzing video recordings of dyads performing a mission planning task in a shared AR environment. Team members were co-located and each wearing a HoloLens with synchronized views of the mission terrain. The analyses focused on the distance or proximity of team members to each other and what behaviors or actions the team members were performing at the time. A manual approach similar to labeling or annotating video for human movement patterns and a machine learning-based pose estimation approach were used to analyze the videos. Applying a 2D pose estimation algorithm to the videos was a limiting factor because of lack of depth processing of the scene; therefore, the analysis approaches could not be integrated as planned. However, each analysis approach separately produced several insights on dyad behavior as well as detected anomalies in distance relations between team members and unique individual and dyad behavior during the collaborative task.

Acknowledgements. This work was supported in part by the DOD High Performance Computing Modernization Program at DEVCOM Army Research Laboratory (ARL), Department of Defense Supercomputing Resource Center (DSRC).

References

1. Kase, S.E., Su, S.M., Perry, V.P., Durkee, A.C.: Observations of individual and team understanding in augmented reality mission planning. In: Proceedings of the 22nd International Command and Control Research and Technology Symposium (ICCRTS), Los Angeles, CA (2017)
2. Su, S., Perry, V., Guan, Q., Durkee, A., Neigel, A.R., Kase, S.: Sensor data fusion framework to improve holographic object registration accuracy for a shared augmented reality mission planning scenario. In: Chen, J.Y.C., Fragomeni, G. (eds.) Virtual, Augmented and Mixed Reality (VAMR) HCII 2018. LNCS, vol. 10909, pp. 202–214. Springer, Cham (2018). https://doi.org/10.1007/978-3-319-91581-4_15
3. Witmer, B.G., Singer, M.J.: Measuring presence in virtual environments. ARI Technical Report 1014. U.S. Army Research Institute. Alexandria, VA (1994)
4. Kase, S., Su, S., Perry, V., Roy, H., Gamble, K.: An augmented reality shared mission planning scenario: observations on shared experience. In: Chen, J.Y.C., Fragomeni, G. (eds.) Virtual, Augmented and Mixed Reality (VAMR) HCII 2019. LNCS, vol. 11575, pp. 490–503. Springer, Cham (2019). https://doi.org/10.1007/978-3-030-21565-1_33
5. Kase, S., Perry, V., Roy, H., Cox, K., Su, S.: Comparative analysis of mission planning and execution times between the Microsoft HoloLens and the Surface Touch Table. In: Chen, J.Y.C., Fragomeni, G. (eds.) Virtual, Augmented and Mixed Reality (VAMR) HCII 2020. LNCS, vol. 12190, pp. 478–492. Springer, Cham (2020). https://doi.org/10.1007/978-3-030-49695-1_32
6. Roy, H., Cox, K.R., Fink, I., Perry, V., Su, S., Kase, S.E.: Tools for enabling teaming during mission planning and rehearsal. In: Proceedings of the SPIE Defense + Commercial Sensing Symposium 11426. Virtual, Augmented, and Mixed Reality (XR) Technology for Multi-Domain Operations, 114260A (2020)
7. Su, S., Perry, V., Bravo, L., Kase, S., Roy, H., Cox, H.: Virtual and augmented reality applications to support data analysis and assessment of science and engineering. Comput. Sci. Eng. **22**(3), 27–29 (2020)

8. Su, S., Perry, V., Roy, H., Gamble, K., Kase, S.: 3D user interface for a multi-user augmented reality mission planning application. In: Cassenti, D.N. (ed.) Advances in Human Factors and Simulation, vol. 958, pp. 120–131. Springer International Publishing, Cham (2020). https://doi.org/10.1007/978-3-030-20148-7_12

9. Wang, J., Yang, J., Yu, K., Lv, F., Huang, T., Gong, Y.: Locality-constrained linear coding for image classification. In: Proceedings of the IEEE Conference on Computer Vision and Pattern Recognition, pp: 3360–3367, San Francisco, CA (2010)

10. Saldana, J.: The Coding Manual for Qualitative Researchers, pp. 1–42. SAGE Publications Ltd., Thousand Oaks (2016)

11. Bianco, S., Ciocca, G., Napoletano, P., Schettini, R.: An interactive tool for manual, semi-automatic and automatic video annotation. Comput. Vis. Image Underst. **131**, 88–99 (2015)

12. Chamasemani, F.F., Affendey, L.S., Mustapha, N., Khalid, F.: Automatic video annotation framework using concept detectors. J. Appl. Sci. **15**, 256–263 (2015)

13. Manikandan, N., Ganesan, K.: Deep learning based automatic video annotation tool for self-driving car. arXiv preprint arXiv: https://arxiv.org/abs/1904.12618 (2015)

14. VideoLan. VLC media player (2006). https://www.videolan.org/vlc/index.html

15. Cao, Z., Simon, T., Wei, S. -E., Sheikh, Y.: Realtime multi-person 2D pose estimation using part affinity fields. In: Proceedings of the IEEE Conference Computer Vision Pattern Recognition, pp. 1302–1310 (2017)

16. Cao, Z., Hidalgo, G., Simon, T., Wei, S.-E., Sheikh, Y.: OpenPose: realtime multi-person 2D pose estimation using part affinity fields. Proc. IEEE Trans. Pattern Anal. Mach. Intell. **43**(1), 172–186 (2021)

17. Hidalgo, G., Cao, Z., Simon, T., Wei, S.-E., Joo, H., Sheikh, Y.: OpenPose library. https://github.com/CMU-Perceptual-Computing-Lab/openpose

18. Haque, A., Peng, B., Luo, Z., Alahi, A., Yeung, S., Fei-Fei, L.: Towards viewpoint invariant 3D human pose estimation. In: Leibe, B., Matas, J., Sebe, N., Welling, M. (eds) Proceedings of the European Conference on Computer Vision, vol. 9905, pp. 160–177 (2016). https://doi.org/10.1007/978-3-319-46448-0_10

19. Moon, G., Yong Chang, J., Mu Lee, K.: V2V-PoseNet: Voxel-to-voxel prediction network for accurate 3D hand and human pose estimation from a single depth map. In: Proceedings of the IEEE Conference on Computer Vision and Pattern Recognition, pp. 5079–5088 (2018)

20. Wang, K., Zhai, S., Cheng, H., Liang, X., Lin, L.: Human pose estimation from depth images via inference embedded multi-task learning. In: Proceedings of the 24th ACM International Conference on Multimedia, pp. 1227–1236 (2016)

GazeXR: A General Eye-Tracking System Enabling Invariable Gaze Data in Virtual Environment

Chris Lenart, Yuxin Yang, Zhiqing Gu, Cheng-Chang Lu, Karl Kosko, Richard Ferdig, and Qiang Guan[✉]

Kent State University, Kent, OH 44240, USA
{clenart4,yyang45,zgu1,cclu,kkosko,rferdig,qguan}@kent.edu

Abstract. Controlling and standardizing experiments is imperative for quantitative research methods. With the increase in the availability and quantity of low-cost eye-tracking devices, gaze data are considered as an important user input for quantitative analysis in many social science research areas, especially incorporating with virtual reality (VR) and augmented reality (AR) technologies. This poses new challenges in providing a default interface for gaze data in a common method. This paper propose GazeXR, which focuses on designing a general eye-tracking system interfacing two eye-tracking devices and creating a hardware independent virtual environment. We apply GazeXR to the in-class teaching experience analysis use case using external eye-tracking hardware to collect the gaze data for the gaze track analysis.

Keywords: Virtual reality · Eye-tracking · Human-Computer Interaction · Education technology

1 Introduction

Eye-tracking methodologies have existed since the late 1970s [20,29], significant progress, was established with the addition of the eye-mind hypothesis (EMH). The EMH attempts to establish a correlation with fixation and cognition [12]. While the premise of the EMH theory has not implicitly been proven, eye-tracking technology is based on its premise. One particular issue is covert attention, as attention was shown be independent of where a user is looking [18]. However, it has been shown that the movement of the attention will substantially move the eyes [4,9]. While eye-tracking data may not be bijective, it has been shown to give valuable information for domain-specific applications such as geometry [24].

Being a domain-specific application, virtual reality (VR) stands to benefit from eye-tracking. The first to utilize this technology was aircraft training [6]. Unlike typical, non-free movement, eye-tracking devices; virtual reality provides a 3D space for gazing. This virtual environment is consistent and a well-controlled state, unlike the world. Controlled virtual environments allows for

© Springer Nature Switzerland AG 2021
J. Y. C. Chen and G. Fragomeni (Eds.): HCII 2021, LNCS 12770, pp. 47–58, 2021.
https://doi.org/10.1007/978-3-030-77599-5_4

researchers to know what exists in at a given time. Knowing this information, a well crafted training experience can be utilized and annotated. While not unique to Virtual Reality, eye-tracking can show expertise through visual understanding. Like chess [21], this is particularly apparent for environments that are information-rich and dynamic [11]. With the fine grain control of environments, virtual reality and eye-tracking can provide keen insights for discerning expertise.

While eye-tacking has given virtual reality an additional layer of information, through the 3rd dimension of space, it does not come without its issues:

- **Head movement.** Traditional methods of eye-tracking, such as Pupil Center Corneal Reflection (PCCR), are error prone when head movements are introduced [31]. Fortunately, eye-tracking solutions such as Pupil Lab utilize a model-based solution that allows for free head movements [15]. This problem, in-directly, has lead to different adaptions in the gaze estimation process.
- **Lack of open standards.** Eye-tracking suffers from the lack of open standards in interfacing with these devices. With the increase of availability and quantity of eye-tracking devices [7], this issue will continue to grow. From calibrating the device, structuring of gaze data, and interfacing methodologies, eye-tracking devices differ from manufacturer to manufacturer.

The nature of our study is interdisciplinary, being that it aims to improve existing computer science methodologies; while yielding beneficiary to educational professional development.

- **Computer Scientist's Perspective.** This paper aims to improve the methodology of interfacing with multiple eye-tracking devices to unify the collection of gaze data. Creating an unique solution and method for standardization of gaze estimation pipeline.
- **Educator's Perspective.** This papers provides educators with a consistent solution for gaze datum interpretation. Which allows educators to correctly analyze and critique professional skills through behavioral and observable methods.

The paper is organized as follows. The introduction presents a logical stepping-stone for eye-tracking technology into virtual reality and establishes two clear problems in the field. The background provides the reader with research in the area and discusses key terminology that will be used throughout the paper. The system overview describes the architecture of the project and steps taken to solve any challenge. The case study section provides readers with results of our work and the performance overview. Finally, the conclusion section provides a detailed summary of solutions solved, with future works providing the next steps in the project.

2   Background

2.1   Gaze Mapping

Eye-tracking methodologies have existed since the late 1970s [20,29]. The movement of the eye is often broken down into two categories: saccadic and visual fixations [19]. Raw eye movement is tracked through IR cameras, segmenting the pupil and other eye features. Once process of gaze estimation finishes, it returns a gaze-vector and a confidence based on the given eye image. Traditional methods of mapping gaze become more complex in virtual reality. As eye-tracking adds an additional dimensional to gaze data, known as depth. Using ray casts from the user's head to the gazed object, depth information can be computed [2]. However, with flat videos such as that used in a skybox, the depth is constant. As the depth value is computed when the two dimensional video is mapped into 3D space.

2.2   Head and Eye-Tracking

Ordinary methods of eye-tracking, like Pupil Center Corneal Reflection (PCCR), could result in errors with angled movement of one degree [31]. Some solutions, like that of Pupil Lab's Core uses a model-based approach [15], rendering an eye in 3D space fitting the pupil to an eclipse [28], to allow for free movement. This new free movement, allows for an additional layer of head tracking to be added. One method of measuring head movement is through the use of an inertial measurement unit (IMU). This method is what allows observer head control for virtual reality headsets.

2.3   Eye-Tracking Issues

Modern eye-tracking headsets can utilize different calibration methods for gaze-vector prediction. This can be problematic, when attempting to interface with multiple eye-trackering devices. While appearance-based deep convolutional neural networks (CNNs) can solve auto-calibrate [14,27,30]. Leading to removal of the overhead of platform specific calibration methods, it would require consumer products to have support from manufactures.

2.4   Visualizing Gaze Data

Gaze data provides spatial-temporal attention details for a given subjects. This means that data can be represented in terms of both space and/or time. There exist two scopes of data:

- **Local Data.** Restricted to a range, such a time restriction
- **Global Data.** Representative of the whole, such as, a collection of sessions or a whole video session.

Each sequence of data can utilize a probability density function (PDF) to understand Areas-of-Interests (AOI). Statistical likelihood can be visualized in terms of a heatmap; this can directly overlay video frames to determine the objects that peaked the user's attention and gaze [17]. Displaying an unwrapped video, can provide context such as field of view (FOV) [16]. Another aspect of gaze data is fixation, which typically within the threshold of 100–200 ms [23], usually represented as a path.

3   System Overview

3.1   GazeXR Architecture

For the Pupil Lab's Core device, our approach utilizes the hmd-eyes Unity plugin[1] to communicate with the Pupil Capture service through the ZMQ protocol over the network [13]. This can be useful if the HMD device is not directly connected to the eye tacking device, resulting in an additional communication layer. For our setup, we used an Oculus Rift S[2], tethered to a host machine, that ran the Pupil Lab's Capture service. Utilizing the host machine as middleware, the host can ingress gaze data and time synchronize the request with that of the headset. The middleware server serves as the hub for content and storing data. It's broken into two part, web-server and data management. The web-server provides a route to list the existing videos and is the broker for video streaming. While the data management part accepts all event logs and session gaze data ad-hoc or post-session. This process allows for the host machine to take a detached approach in collecting gaze data. Implicitly, the data will be piped from the eye-tracker, to the host machine.

Handling this data, there are two coexistent approaches. The first being the direct storage of raw pupil source frame, gray-scale to keep a minimal data storage. Saving raw source data would allow for the user to process the eye later in a gaze estimation pipeline, resulting in better data as models improve. But this method would require more space to store the image and time writing to disk over the network. Since the gaze estimation methods of some eye-trackers are private, the output of gaze vector may be the only output. In this case, the only approach is to let gaze estimation pipeline handle the process and receive its values. Resulting in the pupil data being estimated into gaze data, make storage easy and removing the need for post-posting.

The same approach works for standalone devices, like the Pico Neo 2 Eye, which was able to handle both the eye-tracking and application running from within the device. Once a gaze event happens, the hook of the custom "Gaze Manager plugin" (see Fig. 1) would fire, resulting in a request to get the head-tracking position from the headsets IMU. Based on Pupil Lab's white paper, "the average gaze estimation, from tracking pipeline to network output, was 0.124 s" [13]. Being that these values don't need to be displayed in real-time, these values can be queued for later processing. Previous head positional values must be kept in memory, temporarily, to be correctly paired with proper gaze

---

[1] https://github.com/pupil-labs/hmd-eyes.

[2] https://www.oculus.com/rift-s/.

data. Being that the speeds of 348 ± 92 degrees per second are peak for healthy individuals [22], this is suitable base-line for sampling. Meaning that for a latency less than one second, no more than 440 head position values will need to be kept in memory. Once the head position values are found in memory, they can be grouped together with the queued gaze data. Returning both the gaze and head position together at a specific time of gaze. This provides a fair annotation data point for a given gaze event.

3.2   Interfacing Multiple Devices

When handling multiple Virtual Reality headsets, it is important to keep an agnostics approach to handle multi-platform support. This approach allows for a singular monolithic codebase to handle the functionality, allowing for consistent experience, despite the platform. A multiple component system can be utilized to break up the platform's code where functionality differs. This solution attempts to generalize both Virtual Reality functionalities and Eye-tracking solutions, in order to, interface and record the appropriate data. There exists a plethora of SDK solutions to manage interfacing with virtual reality devices such as OpenVR and Unity XR. These solutions provide a way to communicate with multiple native interfaces, for a single subsystem to handle. Allowing for Inputs devices such as controllers, IMU sensors, and displays to be controlled by a software interface.

Unlike interfacing with a virtual reality device, no general interface exists to handle eye-tracking by default. Eye-tracking devices can be broken down into two categories: built-in eye-tracking and external eye-tracking devices. Built-in eye-tracking can be implemented through features within a manufacturer's native SDK, such as that in the Pico Neo 2 Eye[3]. External eye-tracking hardware from the HMD device, like a Pupil Core[4] devices requires an extra communication level of abstraction to handle gaze data. To generically handle multiple devices, an additional level of abstraction is required to handle gaze data. Being limited to two eye-tracking devices, one built-in eye-tracking device and one external eye-tracking device. Our approach was generalized to attempt to handle the addition of future devices. Given the constraints, our solution provides a custom Unity plugin to create a gaze event hook. This method will take the multiple sources of gaze data and generalize it so that it becomes generic and consistent implementation. Allowing for universal functions to be created despite the data source.

---

[3] https://www.pico-interactive.com/us/neo2.html.
[4] https://pupil-labs.com/products/vr-ar/.

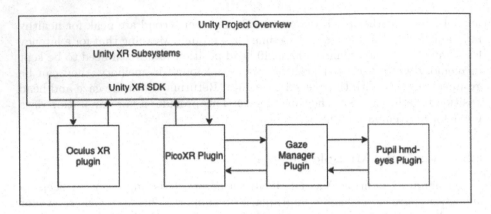

Fig. 1. The Gaze Manager Plugin is a default interfaces with PicoXR and Pupil Lab's hdm-eye plugin. Allowing for a direct communications for managing gaze datum.

3.3   Video's Role in Gaze Data

Being that our research targets gaze events that exist within a video, a more few parameters must be considered to be able to properly recreate the experience. One important property is the video frame number, the still image number at the time of gaze. Much like obtaining head position, the video frame must take into account latency from the gaze event. Unlike the head position, this value can be computed since it is time dependent. This is done by taking the current frame, $f_{current}$, and subtracting the frames from since that time. The amount of frames since latency is the product of the video's frames per second, fps, and the latency time, $Time_{current}$. Where f_x is targeted frame in the video.

$$F_x = F_{current} - (fps * Time_{current}) \tag{1}$$

Being that f_x is reliant on several variable, the equation is built to be devices agnostic. As video formats can change the frame-rate based on the device, this information can be pulled from the video's meta-data.

3.4   Data Management

Once, this frame has been calculated, the all the required properties are computed for the gaze event. Meaning that the gaze event data can be saved as a JSON object (see the Fig. 2 for format) and queued to be added to the database. Interfacing with a NoSQL database means no structures, that the JSON structure can directly be pushed as it comes in. Collections can be made for each of the 3 structures: videos, videoSessions, and gazeEvents.

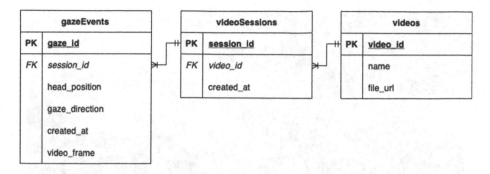

Fig. 2. The data relationship model for gaze events

3.5   Creating a Virtual Environment

Given a 360° equirectangular video, there are two classical approaches for video mapping: equirectangular projection (ERP) [25] and cubic mapping (CMP) [8]. Projecting is the process of taking a 2D video and projecting it onto a geometric object. Where an observer, the VR users, stands in the middle of said object. Giving the video the appearance of depth, creating a virtual environment. A panoramic video can be converted from its longitude and latitude layout and mapped to a UV texture. Then this texture that can be used as a skybox, resulting in a similar appearance of a CMP (see Fig. 3). This means that the projection gains all the benefits that come with CMP such as visual quality improves due to texel density. Since the resulting video is projected, the same calculations and shader functions can be used to transform the 2D gaze data into the needed its spot in 3D space.

Due to the large size of panoramic videos and ambisonic audio, it can be difficult for a standalone virtual reality headset to save to disk. To combat this issue, a hosting external machine, running a web-server and a database can aid. As seen in Fig. 2, a collection of videos and there name can be pulled from the web-server by a HTTP request. Then when a video is requested to be played on a headset, the video is sent by MPEG-DASH (DASH) to be streamed. Using DASH allows for content to be streamed over the network in segments [26]. Since the Pico Neo 2 is running a version of Android, and the support for DASH isn't full-supported yet [5], the web-server will serve the content as a progressive stream as a fallback. If paired with a tile based method and a hexaface sphere-mapping, it can save up to 72% bandwidth [10].

3.6   User Event Handling

Many things can go wrong physically when it comes to a VR headset. The cables could tangle, the controller's batteries could die, the headset could slip-off the users, or a software related issue could exist. Slipping, can cause an issue with the data collected during an experiment. It's even recommended to readjust the headset and re-calibrate the eye-trackers every five to ten minute [1]. It is

Fig. 3. This frame is the front facing cube texture, or positive X, of the skybox video projection. The video is streamed to the application through DASH.

more important to be able to stop recording data when things go wrong. For this reason, a event-driven architecture (EDA) was chosen, as it is important to send events asynchronous and tie them to state. Two current states exist for this architecture: recording and video player state. Given the possible failure, it is critical to pause before data become unusable. On the other spectrum, being that users are in a virtual space, being able to pause and to take a further look is important too. This allows for a more data to be collected on an area-of-interest (AOI). Including the additional data produced by the event logs, an additional layer of information such as time of pause and gaze points during pause. Since the frame of video is recorded on a gaze event, pausing will still record gaze data for the proper video context. Along with this, data that exists over-multiple frames; while the time of gaze from the system's clock increases, can be used to sequentially build paused video segments of a session.

3.7   Results

With gaze visualization methods, gaze can be projected into virtual classrooms. Using gaze data, fixations can be determined and plotted to a heatmap which displays clear AOIs in the classroom (as seen in Fig. 4A). Through the visualization of gaze vectors and binding perspective to be the top view, or positive Z-axis, rotational data be show where users stopped turned. In the case of Fig. 4D, the user spent most of the time in the front and didn't even turn around.

4   Discussion

With the high resolution video being sent through the network, it can lead to performance bottleneck for networks that exceed its bandwidth. We profile the network traffic shown in Fig. 5, while downloading the 360 video into VR headset.

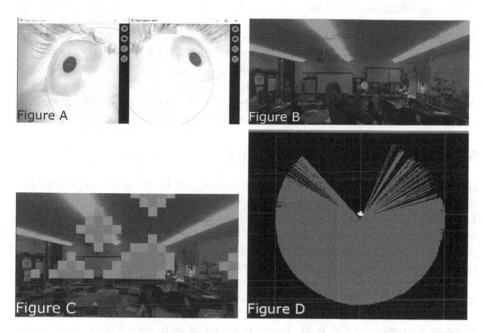

Fig. 4. The figure A provides is Pupil Lab's Capture program, which is tracking the pupil and passing it through the gaze estimation. The remaining figures [B-D], shows gaze in a virtual environment: through fixation markers, heatmaps, or gaze vectors.

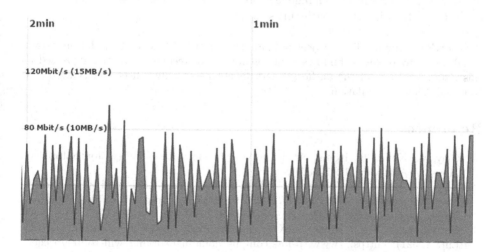

Fig. 5. The bandwidth of a 2.94 GB equirectangular video being streamed over Pico Neo 2 for 3 min, through http progressive streaming. The blue represents the inbound traffic, peaking at 97.39 Mbit/s or 12.17 MB/s. (Color figure online)

With standalone headsets, like Pico Neo 2, sending data through the WiFi is the only networking method. Networking standards like WiFi 4, or IEEE 802.11n-2009, might struggled if interfaced with multiple devices due to 600Mbit/s theoretical limit. However, more durable solutions like WiFi 5, IEEE 802.11ac-2013, or WiFi 6, IEEE 802.11ax, can handle 866 Mbit/s and 1201 Mbit/s respectively [3]. Local-storage can solve this solution, but isn't applicable on all standalone devices. As these videos can take up significant file-storage space. With moderation, sending videos over the network can be successful.

5   Conclusion and Future Work

In this paper, we present GazeXR, which is designed for projecting eye-tracking data into virtual reality headsets. Utilizing the Gaze Manager plugin, both Pupil Lab's Core Device and Pico Neo 2 Eye are able to interface with the virtual realty based in-class teaching experience analysis application on their respective platforms. GazeXR provides a customs platform for handling gaze events that can be managed and analyzed by researchers.

In future work, we plan to collect research data through systematic trials. to provide a way of computing insight for social science researchers utilizing gaze data in any virtual environment applications. GazeXR can help to compute a score of expertise in the field, through gazed objects recognizing from video frames. Using machine learning (ML), objects can be detected and classified. An expert in the field then can be introduced to input a baseline knowledge to determine important actions. To determine if a user fixates on an object, a bounding-boxes or image segmentation can be used to see if the user's gaze collides, which may result in a change in score. Along with this, a mobile application could be built to interface with this system.

Acknowledgement. This project is funded by National Science Foundation, Grant #1908159. Any opinions, findings, and conclusions or recommendations expressed in this paper are those of the author(s) and do not necessarily reflect the views of the National Science Foundation.

References

1. Clay, V., König, P., König, S.U.: Eye tracking in virtual reality. Journal of Eye Movement Research **12**(1), (2019)
2. Clay, V., König, P., König, S.U.: Eye tracking in virtual reality. Journal of Eye Movement Research 12(1) (Apr 2019). https://doi.org/10.16910/jemr.12.1.3, https://bop.unibe.ch/JEMR/article/view/4332-Clay-final-sub
3. Corporation, T.L.: Archer AX10 — AX1500 Wi-Fi 6 Router — TP-Lin (2021), https://www.tp-link.com/us/home-networking/wifi-router/archer-ax10/#specifications, accessed on 02.09.2021
4. Deubel, H., Schneider, W.X.: Saccade target selection and object recognition: Evidence for a common attentional mechanism. Vision Research **36**(12), 1827–1837 (Jun 1996). https://doi.org/10.1016/0042-6989(95)00294-4, https://doi.org/10.1016/0042-6989(95)00294-4

5. Developers, G.: Supported media formats | Android Developers (2021), https://developer.android.com/guide/topics/media/media-formats.html# recommendations, accessed on 02.09.2021
6. Duchowski, A., Shivashankaraiah, V., Rawls, T., Gramopadhye, A., Melloy, B., Kanki, B.: Binocular eye tracking in virtual reality for inspection training. In: ETRA (2000)
7. Ferhat, O., Vilariño, F.: Low cost eye tracking: The current panorama. Computational Intelligence and Neuroscience **2016**, 1–14 (2016). https://doi.org/10.1155/2016/8680541, https://doi.org/10.1155/2016/8680541
8. Greene, N.: Environment mapping and other applications of world projections. IEEE Computer Graphics and Applications **6**(11), 21–29 (Nov 1986). https://doi.org/10.1109/mcg.1986.276658,https://doi.org/10.1109/mcg.1986.276658
9. Hoffman, J.E., Subramaniam, B.: The role of visual attention in saccadic eye movements. Perception & Psychophysics **57**(6), 787–795 (Jan 1995). https://doi.org/10.3758/bf03206794,https://doi.org/10.3758/bf03206794
10. Hosseini, M., Swaminathan, V.: Adaptive 360 VR video streaming: Divide and conquer. In: 2016 IEEE International Symposium on Multimedia (ISM). IEEE (Dec 2016). https://doi.org/10.1109/ism.2016.0028, https://doi.org/10.1109/ism.2016.0028
11. Jarodzka, H., Holmqvist, K., Gruber, H.: Eye tracking in educational science: Theoretical frameworks and research agendas 10 (01 2017). https://doi.org/10.16910/jemr.10.1.3
12. Just, M., Carpenter, P.: A theory of reading: from eye fixations to comprehension. Psychological review **87**(4), 329–54 (1980)
13. Kassner, M., Patera, W., Bulling, A.: Pupil. In: Proceedings of the 2014 ACM International Joint Conference on Pervasive and Ubiquitous Computing: Adjunct Publication. ACM (Sep 2014). https://doi.org/10.1145/2638728.2641695, https://doi.org/10.1145/2638728.2641695
14. Krafka, K., Khosla, A., Kellnhofer, P., Kannan, H., Bhandarkar, S., Matusik, W., Torralba, A.: Eye tracking for everyone. In: 2016 IEEE Conference on Computer Vision and Pattern Recognition (CVPR). IEEE (Jun 2016). https://doi.org/10.1109/cvpr.2016.239, https://doi.org/10.1109/cvpr.2016.239
15. Lab, P.: Pupil Lab's Pupil Capture (2021), https://docs.pupil-labs.com/core/software/pupil-capture/#pupil-detection, accessed on 02.09.2021
16. Löwe, T., Stengel, M., Förster, E.C., Grogorick, S., Magnor, M.: Gaze visualization for immersive video. In: Burch, M., Chuang, L., Fisher, B., Schmidt, A., Weiskopf, D. (eds.) Eye Tracking and Visualization, pp. 57–71. Springer International Publishing, Cham (2017)
17. Masse, B., Lathuiliere, S., Mesejo, P., Horaud, R.: Extended gaze following: Detecting objects in videos beyond the camera field of view. In: 2019 14th IEEE International Conference on Automatic Face & Gesture Recognition (FG 2019). IEEE (May 2019). https://doi.org/10.1109/fg.2019.8756555, https://doi.org/10.1109/fg.2019.8756555
18. Posner, M.I.: Orienting of attention. Quarterly Journal of Experimental Psychology **32**(1), 3–25 (1980). https://doi.org/10.1080/00335558008248231, https://doi.org/10.1080/00335558008248231
19. Purves, D., Augustine, G., Fitzpatrick, D., Katz, L., LaMantia, A., McNamara, J., Williams, S.: Neuroscience 2nd edition. sunderland (ma) sinauer associates. Types of Eye Movements and Their Functions (2001)

20. Rayner, K.: Eye movements in reading and information processing: 20 years of research. Psychological Bulletin **124**(3), 372–422 (1998). https://doi.org/10.1037/0033-2909.124.3.372, https://doi.org/10.1037/0033-2909.124.3.372

21. Reingold, E., Sheridan, H.: Eye movements and visual expertise in chess and medicine, vol. 528–550, pp. 528–550 (08 2011). https://doi.org/10.1093/oxfordhb/9780199539789.013.0029

22. Röijezon, U., Djupsjöbacka, M., Björklund, M., Häger-Ross, C., Grip, H., Liebermann, D.G.: Kinematics of fast cervical rotations in persons with chronic neck pain: a cross-sectional and reliability study. BMC Musculoskeletal Disorders 11(1) (Sep 2010). https://doi.org/10.1186/1471-2474-11-222, https://doi.org/10.1186/1471-2474-11-222

23. Salvucci, D.D., Goldberg, J.H.: Identifying fixations and saccades in eye-tracking protocols. In: Proceedings of the symposium on Eye tracking research & applications - ETRA '00. ACM Press (2000). https://doi.org/10.1145/355017.355028, https://doi.org/10.1145/355017.355028

24. Schindler, Maike, Lilienthal, Achim J.: Domain-specific interpretation of eye tracking data: towards a refined use of the eye-mind hypothesis for the field of geometry. Educational Studies in Mathematics **101**(1), 123–139 (2019). https://doi.org/10.1007/s10649-019-9878-z

25. Snyder, J.P.: Flattening the earth: two thousand years of map projections. University of Chicago Press (1997)

26. Sodagar, I.: The MPEG-DASH standard for multimedia streaming over the internet. IEEE Multimedia **18**(4), 62–67 (Apr 2011). https://doi.org/10.1109/mmul.2011.71, https://doi.org/10.1109/mmul.2011.71

27. Sugano, Y., Matsushita, Y., Sato, Y.: Learning-by-synthesis for appearance-based 3d gaze estimation. In: Proceedings of the IEEE Conference on Computer Vision and Pattern Recognition. pp. 1821–1828 (2014)

28. Swirski, L., Dodgson, N.: A fully-automatic, temporal approach to single camera, glint-free 3d eye model fitting. Proc. PETMEI pp. 1–11 (2013)

29. Ten Kate, J., Frietman, E.E., Willems, W., Romeny, B.T.H., Tenkink, E.: Eye-switch controlled communication aids. In: Proceedings of the 12th International Conference on Medical & Biological Engineering. pp. 19–20 (1979)

30. Zhang, X., Sugano, Y., Fritz, M., Bulling, A.: Appearance-based gaze estimation in the wild. In: 2015 IEEE Conference on Computer Vision and Pattern Recognition (CVPR). IEEE (Jun 2015). https://doi.org/10.1109/cvpr.2015.7299081, https://doi.org/10.1109/cvpr.2015.7299081

31. Zhu, Z., Ji, Q.: Novel eye gaze tracking techniques under natural head movement. IEEE Transactions on biomedical engineering **54**(12), 2246–2260 (2007)

SpatialViewer: A Remote Work Sharing Tool that Considers Intimacy Among Workers

Sicheng Li[(✉)], Yudai Makioka, Kyousuke Kobayashi, Haoran Xie[iD], and Kentaro Takashima[(✉)][iD]

Japan Advanced Institute of Science and Technology, Kanazawa, Ishikawa, Japan
{lisicheng,ktaka}@jaist.ac.jp

Abstract. Due to the influence of the new coronavirus disease (COVID-19), teleworking has been expanding rapidly. Although existing interactive remote working systems are convenient, they do not allow users to adjust their spatial distance to team members at will, and they ignore the discomfort caused by different levels of intimacy. To solve this issue, we propose a telework support system using spatial augmented reality technology. This system calibrates the space in which videos are projected with real space and adjusts the spatial distance between users by changing the position of projections. Users can switch the projection position of the video using hand-wave gestures. We also synchronize audio according to distance to further emphasize the sense of space within the remote interaction: the distance between projection position and user is inversely proportional to the audio volume. We conducted a telework experiment and a questionnaire survey to evaluate our system. The results show that the system enables users to adjust distance according to intimacy and thus improve the users' comfort.

Keywords: Telework system · Awareness sharing · Spatial Augmented Reality · Personal space

1 Introduction

Currently, new coronavirus disease (COVID-19) infections are exploding. To prevent and control infections, the normal offline working environment has been inhibited in a growing number of companies. Teleworking from home is a burgeoning way of working in many industries. Teleworking has the advantages of creating a comfortable working environment and reducing interruption and distractibility, while having the disadvantages of impeding communication with colleagues and causing a sense of loneliness. Various applications have been proposed to encourage communication in teleworking, including commercial applications such as Zoom [1] and Cisco Webex [2] for remote meetings and Slack [3]

Supported by Seiwa Business Co., Ltd. and Workscape Lab.

© Springer Nature Switzerland AG 2021
J. Y. C. Chen and G. Fragomeni (Eds.): HCII 2021, LNCS 12770, pp. 59–70, 2021.
https://doi.org/10.1007/978-3-030-77599-5_5

and Microsoft Teams [4] for collaboration and business contact. These applications satisfy the formal communication needs of the business operations, which is the primary demand for teleworking, but not the only demand.

It is still challenging to realize a teleworking environment that resembles a real office using these applications. It is difficult to remain aware of each other's state, listen to surrounding sounds, or occasionally consult with colleagues. In general, users launch these applications only when they need to hold a meeting or business conversation. Existing remote video-conferencing tools can certainly be used to remain aware of team members' current situations if they are used continually. However, these applications do not consider the different levels of intimacy among team members. These applications do not allow remote workers to adjust the strength of their awareness of different partners.

When remote workers connect to these regular teleworking support platforms to share their daily situations, all workers on a large team or in a department are displayed on one screen and mute themselves on group calls until they need to speak. Workers might feel oppressed and become tired when facing team members with whom they are unfamiliar. Workers sometimes want to share news only with more intimate colleagues and may be reluctant to share with others. In real life, people have a sense of interpersonal distance. In an office environment, personal space is secured by adjusting the distance between people according to their relationships. If remote workers could make such adjustments virtually, they would be able to remain more comfortable while teleworking.

This study proposes a novel telework support system called SpatialViewer that considers the different levels of intimacy among users. SpatialViewer allows remote workers to adjust interpersonal distances and audio volumes during mutual video connections (See Fig. 1). The system achieves video and audio spatialization by integrating with a prototype of a video chat system. The proposed system projects videos of colleagues onto items in the user's actual desk environment using Spatial Augmented Reality(SAR). SpatialViewer enables users to adjust the distance of the projected items from themselves and to continue teleworking comfortably for a long time. Besides, it allows users focus on the colleagues who users needed to share information and support smooth communication.

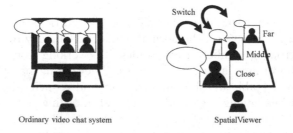

Ordinary video chat system   SpatialViewer

Fig. 1. Our proposal

The main contributions of the proposed SpatialViewer system are as follows:

- We pay attention to the influence of interpersonal distances among team members and try to replicate these interpersonal distances in remote interactions.
- We propose a novel teleworking system that allows users to arrange the video and audio of team members according to the desired spatial intimacy.
- We develop a user interface that supports gesture control to switch the location of each video flexibly.

2   Related Works

In recent years, SAR technology has been widely used in the field of human-computer interaction (HCI). It realizes to transfer a virtual user interface into real space. Many studies have focused on developing HCI based on Augmented Reality (AR) [5–7]. Other research has worked on situation sharing and communication support in a distributed environment, using SAR and virtual reality (VR) technology [8,9] and to visualize the working environment constantly, thus facilitating remote communication [10].

For example, Pesja et al. [11] proposed a telepresence system that makes remote conversation feel more immediate by projecting the image of the interlocutor in real space. In their research, the experience of a face-to-face conversation is realized by projecting a full-scale image of a remote interlocutor onto an assigned location. Yao et al. [12] proposed a system that supports coordination among coworkers for collaborative teleworking and improves educational experiences by visualizing the sight lines of collaborative users. Hoppe et al. [13] proposed a collaborative system that enables multiple users to interact face-to-face simultaneously by moving users' avatars between different locations, so they can each share their perspective.

In addition, some works have visualized remote communicators by reproducing them as avatars. For example, some works proposed methods by which users in remote locations can perceive themselves to be sharing space using VR, mixed reality (MR) devices, and robots [9,14]. Misawa et al. [8] proposed a telepresence method using a robot equipped with a simulated human face to act as the avatar of remote users in support of nonverbal communication. In addition, Piumsomboon et al. [15] developed a remote collaboration system that visualizes the gaze direction and body gestures of a remote user wearing a VR headset; using avatar representation, the size and orientation of the remote user avatar are changed to stay in the AR user's field of sight. Ruvimova et al. proposed a platform that aims to improve business performance by building a virtual environment away from the office using virtual reality (VR) [16].

However, it was a challenging for previous studies to adjust the degree of the information sharing and intimacy among team members. In the physical environment, the degree of presence and the amount of information shared with other people are regulated mainly by interpersonal distance. Interpersonal distances include close distances (0–45 cm) for close relationships, individual distances

(45–120 cm) for private communication, social distances (1.2–3.6 m) for formal information sharing, and public distances (more than 3.6 m) where no personal interaction takes place [17]. As interpersonal distance decreases, the other person's presence and influence increase. With a close interpersonal distance to other users, one's situation is shared and the probability of communication increases. It is important for users to adjust their interpersonal distance with coworkers according to their relationship and communication situation. Even within a virtual space, people have been reported to perform adaptive behaviors to maintain an individual distance when interacting with agents in the virtual space on the screen [18].

3   Proposed System

3.1   System Overview

In this research, we propose a novel teleworking system that allows users to adjust their distance to each team member according to their interpersonal relationships. The system overview is shown in Fig. 2. The system projects the video images of remote team members onto pre-set items placed in the teleworkers' desk environments. Users can customize the location of each item and place it nearby (i.e. close to the display of the working PC) or far away (i.e. on a partition above the desk that is out of sight), depending on their intimacy and the need for information sharing with each team member. Users can also switch the location of team members' video images while the system is in use by gesture control. The volume of each team member's audio is changed automatically according to the projection distance.

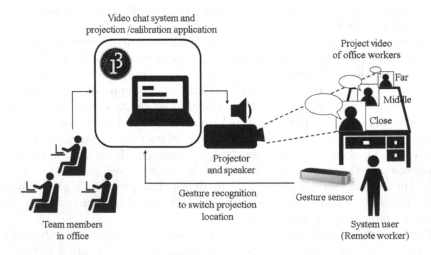

Fig. 2. Overview of the proposed SpatialViewer system

3.2   System Functions

Video and Audio Connection. To realize the video and audio connection among team members, we built a video chat system that provides multi-user mutual video and audio streaming connection (Fig. 3). This system provides similar function as with ordinary video chat system (e.g. Zoom) but can receive commands from a gesture sensor to control the position and volume of each video.

Fig. 3. Web chat system with ordinary video chat interface

Video Projection and Calibration. We determined three projection positions for team members' video images on the user's teleworking desk environment. The closest projection position is on the desk, the middle one is on a shelf, and the farthest is on the opposite wall. Three sticky notes were attached to the corresponding positions, and team members' videos were projected onto these notes. The work setup used with our system is shown in Fig. 4.

To project video images onto a real desk environment, it is necessary to calibrate the projection space with the real space. A video image of each team member who is using the video chat system was captured and transformed to fit onto the projection planes.

Gesture Control. We developed the function of moving video images among the projected items, which also changes the corresponding audio volumes. To offer users more interactivity and freedom of manipulation, we used a gesture sensor to capture user input. Users can switch the projection locations by interacting with the sensor using hand-wave gestures.

Volume Adjustment. We developed the function of automatically adjusting the audio volume when a video's position is changed. The volume increases

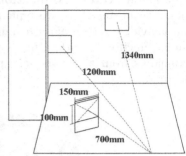

Fig. 4. Working scene with SpatialViewer system

or decreases when a video projection moves nearer or farther. The volume of farthest video is 0.1 times that of the nearest video, and the volume of middle-distance video is a quarter the volume of the nearest video.

4 Implementation of the System Prototype

We implemented a prototype of the proposed system. We developed a web browser-based video chat system with JavaScript and SkyWay API [19]. We also developed a Processing application to transform video images for calibration and projection. We used Keystone Library in the Processing application to adjust the shape and position of the projection planes for calibration. This library enabled us to move and distort video images by dragging the pins on the corner of images (see Fig. 5). The Processing application and video chat system were run on a laptop PC. The audio was played by an external speaker connected to the laptop. To project the images, we places a laser 4k projector to the back and the left of the user's seat.

Before calibration
(images from video chat system)

During calibration

Fig. 5. Calibration process for multiple video frames

To achieve gesture control, we used the Leap Motion gesture sensor. Leap Motion can send commands to the video chat system via the Processing application to switch projection positions. The WebSocket module was installed to realize a two-way real-time connection between the Processing application and the video chat system. To adjust the volume along with the projected distance, the Processing application kept recording the projection position of each video image. Each time the positions were switched, the video chat system was notified of the new position to control the audio volume.

5 User Study

In this section, we first explain the experimental design and setting and then present the questionnaire design.

5.1 Experimental Setting

We attempted to simulate a team collaboration teleworking environment. We recruited 11 participants for our experiment, six male and five female. Nine are master's students in their 20 s attending the author's institute and two are professors in their 30 s. We organized three experimental groups consisting of four participants. Each group included one professor and three students (one of the professors was included in two groups.)

Each participant took part in experiment for a total of nine hours. Each participant tried SpacialViewer (see Fig. 4) alone for three hours and connected to the other members using our developed video chat interface (see Fig. 3) for six hours. All three students in each group shifted roles of SAR system user and video chat interface partner during a group of experience. After using the system, the students were asked to fill out the questionnaire, which asked them to evaluate the proposed system and ordinary video chat interface and record intimacy among every group members. The professors were an experimental variable to diversify group members' relationships, so they did not answer the questionnaire.

5.2 Questionnaire Design

To achieve a valid evaluation, we asked several five-point Likert scale-style questions. The questions are listed below:

- Questions about SpatialViewer experience
  - Q1: Were you interested in the situations of the projected participants?
  - Q2: Did you want to talk to the projected participants?
  - Q3: Did you want to switch the location of projections during the experiment?
  - Q4: Could you feel the sense of space via the system?
  - Q5: Did you think the system enabled you to place projections according to intimacy?

- Q6: Was the system useful for you compared with other teleworking applications you have used?
- Q7: Did you think the system provided a relaxing, comfortable teleworking environment?
- Questions about ordinary video chat interface experience
  - Q2': Did you want to talk to the participants?
  - Q5': Did you think the system enabled you to place images according to intimacy?
  - Q7': Did you think the video chat interface provided a comfortable teleworking environment?

The evaluation items included the users' interaction experience (Q1 and Q2); the interactivity enabled by this system (Q3); the improvement of the sense of space (Q4); the ability to adjust projection distance according to intimacy (Q5); and the overall usefulness and comfort (Q6 and Q7) of our system. Considering compare the aspects we are most concerned about, we also asked questions analogous to Q2, Q5, and Q7 about the traditional ordinary video chat interface for comparison analysis (Q2', Q5', and Q7'). We also asked users about their sequence of intimacy (close-middle-far) to their group members and recorded the sequence of projection distance (close-middle-far) maintained the longest by participants when using the system. We then evaluated the results by analyzing the relationship between intimacy and distance.

6   Results and Analysis

We analyzed the results of questionnaire to verify whether our system allowed users to adjust projection distance and provided comfort. We aggregated the scores of the questionnaire, calculated the average score of each question (see Fig. 6), and conducted observation analysis of the experimental scene. Data visualization shows the positive evaluations of our system, with average scores for all questions above 3. A comparison between our projection system and a traditional video chat interface shows that our system made is easier for users to adjust distance according to intimacy (see Q5 in Fig. 6) and provided a more comfortable teleworking environment (see Q7 in Fig. 6). Through observing the experiment, we found that users were interested in using the interactive function provided by the gesture sensor. They used this function to adjust the projection locations to create a comfortable interaction environment.

The results also show that the individual initiative of communication did not change between SpatialViewer and ordinary video chat interface (see Q2 in Fig. 6), which is consistent with the result of observation analysis. Most users conducted some daily conversations rather than talking about their work and worked silently most of the time. This might be because group members were not actually working on the same project during the experiment, which means that the need for communication was insufficient. Although the participants did not communicate much, they tended to place the projection of their communication

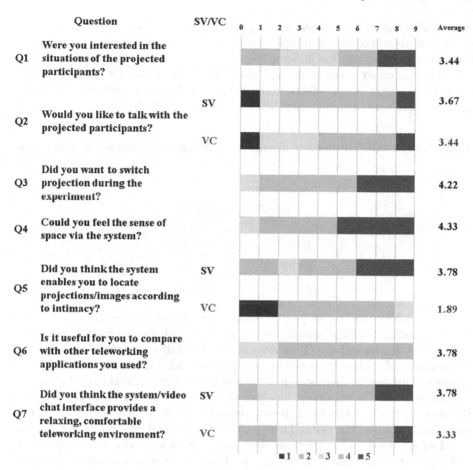

Fig. 6. Score results of the questionnaire questions. (SV: SpatialViewer, VC: Ordinary video chat interface)

target closer to them during the conversation, which shows that the system realized the spatial sense of communication.

Participants could freely control interpersonal distances during the experiment. Table 1 shows a matrix of the relationship between projection distance and degree of intimacy of users. Seven of the nine experimental results conformed to the ideal matrix distribution (diagonal distribution), which indicates that the projection distance was positively correlated with intimacy. For instance, many users chose to put the professor farther away, and most users had the most distant relationship with the professor. This proves that, even when teleworking, interpersonal distance is affected by intimacy.

However, some results did not conform to expectations. We interviewed each participant and received some valuable feedback. For instance, they told us that they cared more about how the member's appearance in the video made them feel than intimacy. They preferred to place the image of a group member with good posture and a moderate distance from the camera closest to themselves. If another member was too close to the camera or put the camera in the wrong position, this could cause stress and discomfort. The interviews indicated that there is no single factor affecting the projection locating preference of users; intimacy and visual comfort may be other influencing factors.

Table 1. Cross tabulation matrix of projection distance and intimacy of group members.

Dist.	Intim.		
	Close	Middle	Far
Close	7	1	1
Middle	0	8	1
Farther	2	0	7

In the interviews, many participants reported that our system provided a novel way of teleworking, and they felt it would be valuable to them (see also Q6 in Fig. 6). A convenient use of the system was the ability to move the projections of members who they were talking to. Another advantage was the ability to adjust the projection distance, in accordance with our original expectations.

We also asked users about any concerns with or desired improvements for the system. Most of the participants' recommendations focused on interaction and communication functions. Three participants wished the interactive function could adjust the size of projections. Two participants wanted a device promoting willingness to communicate, and one participant wanted a method of private communication to talk with specific group members without being heard by the others. These advises show that our system is weak in motivating interaction and communication.

7 Conclusion

In this work, we proposed a remote work sharing system that takes into consideration the levels of intimacy among workers. Users can customize the location of the projected videos and audio volume corresponding to each team member. We conducted an experiment to evaluate the system. The questionnaire results show that the system allowed users to adjust projection distances according to intimacy, provided a sense of space, and thus improved users' comfort with remote work compared with a traditional video chat interface.

We developed a prototype system for use in experiments and laboratory demonstrations. According to the feedback received from participants, the system needs to be improved in terms of interactivity and convenience. Also, we will improve the user interface and append more functions like controlling projection position at any place in user's desk environment in the future. The experiment setting will also be reconsidered. The system should be evaluated under actual working conditions and compared with other applications proposed in previous studies.

References

1. Zoom Video Communications Inc: Zoom. https://zoom.us/
2. Cisco Webex: Cisco Webex. https://www.webex.com/
3. Slack Technologies Inc: Slack. https://slack.com/
4. Microsoft Corporation: Microsoft Teams. https://www.microsoft.com/
5. Peng, Y., Mishima, Y., Igarashi, Y., Miyauchi, R., Okawa, M., Xie, H., Miyata, K.: Sketch2domino: interactive chain reaction design and guidance. In: 2020 Nicograph International (NicoInt), pp. 32–38 (2020)
6. Ajisaka, S., et al.: Learning rubik's cube through user operation history. In: 2020 Nicograph International (NicoInt), pp. 43–46 (2020)
7. He, Z., Xie, H., Miyata, K.: Interactive projection system for calligraphy practice. In: 2020 Nicograph International (NicoInt), pp. 55–61 (2020)
8. Misawa, K., Ishiguro, Y., Rekimoto, J.: Livemask: a telepresence surrogate system with a face-shaped screen for supporting nonverbal communication. J. Inf. Process. **21**(2), 295–303 (2013)
9. Murata, N., Suga, S., Takaya, E., Ueno, S., Kiyota, Y., Kurihara, S.: Proposition of VR-MR hybrid system for sharing living-in-room. In: Proceedings of the 2018 ACM Workshop on Multimedia for Real Estate Tech, RETech 2018, New York, NY, USA, pp. 22–26. Association for Computing Machinery (2018). https://doi.org/10.1145/3210499.3210527
10. Morrison-Smith, S., Chilton, L.B., Ruiz, J.: Facilitating team awareness through ambient displays, August 2020. https://www.microsoft.com/en-us/research/publication/facilitating-team-awareness-through-ambient-displays/
11. Pejsa, T., Kantor, J., Benko, H., Ofek, E., Wilson, A.: Room2room: Enabling life-size telepresence in a projected augmented reality environment. In: Proceedings of the 19th ACM Conference on Computer-Supported Cooperative Work & Social Computing, CSCW 2016, New York, NY, USA, pp. 1716–1725. Association for Computing Machinery (2016). https://doi.org/10.1145/2818048.2819965
12. Yao, N., Brewer, J., D'Angelo, S., Horn, M., Gergle, D.: Visualizing gaze information from multiple students to support remote instruction. In: Extended Abstracts of the 2018 CHI Conference on Human Factors in Computing Systems, CHI EA 2018, New York, NY, USA, pp. 1–6. Association for Computing Machinery (2018). https://doi.org/10.1145/3170427.3188453
13. Hoppe, A.H., van de Camp, F., Stiefelhagen, R.: Shisha: enabling shared perspective with face-to-face collaboration using redirected avatars in virtual reality. In: Proceedings of the ACM on Human-Computer Interaction 4(CSCW3), January 2021. https://doi.org/10.1145/3432950
14. Jones, B., Zhang, Y., Wong, P.N.Y., Rintel, S.: Vroom: virtual robot overlay for online meetings. In: Extended Abstracts of the 2020 CHI Conference on Human Factors in Computing Systems, CHI EA 2020, New York, NY, USA, pp. 1–10. Association for Computing Machinery (2020). https://doi.org/10.1145/3334480.3382820

15. Piumsomboon, T., et al.: Mini-me: an adaptive avatar for mixed reality remote collaboration, pp. 1–13. Association for Computing Machinery, New York, NY, USA (2018). https://doi.org/10.1145/3173574.3173620
16. Ruvimova, A., Kim, J., Fritz, T., Hancock, M., Shepherd, D.C.: "Transport me away": fostering flow in open offices through virtual reality. In: Proceedings of the 2020 CHI Conference on Human Factors in Computing Systems, CHI 2020, New York, NY, USA, pp. 1–14. Association for Computing Machinery (2020). https://doi.org/10.1145/3313831.3376724
17. Spencer, R.E.: Book reviews : The hidden dimension by edward t. hall. New York: Doubleday and company, inc., 1966. pp. xii + 193. Educational and Psychological Measurement **26**(4), 1118–1119 (1966). https://doi.org/10.1177/001316446602600462
18. Rapuano, M., Sbordone, F.L., Borrelli, L.O., Ruggiero, G., Iachini, T.: The effect of facial expressions on interpersonal space: a gender study in immersive virtual reality, pp. 477–486. Springer, Singapore(2021). https://doi.org/10.1007/978-981-15-5093-5_40
19. NTT Communications Corporation: Skyway. https://webrtc.ecl.ntt.com/

A Review of Virtual Therapists in Anxiety and Phobias Alleviating Applications

Oana Mitruț[1]([✉]), Alin Moldoveanu[1], Livia Petrescu[2], Cătălin Petrescu[1], and Florica Moldoveanu[1]

[1] Faculty of Automatic Control and Computers, University Politehnica of Bucharest, 060042 Bucharest, Romania
oana.balan@cs.pub.ro
[2] Faculty of Biology, University of Bucharest, 050095 Bucharest, Romania

Abstract. As more and more people suffer from anxiety disorders, new means of clinical and therapeutical interventions are required. For instance, virtual agents or embodied conversational agents, enriched with human-like appearance and verbal and non-verbal behavior have emerged in recent years. They simulate the real-world therapist, communicate with the patient and convey motivating messages. This paper presents an overview of virtual therapists that have been applied for relieving anxiety and phobias symptoms. It discusses aspects such as: whether the agents have been used for home-based or clinical-based therapy, their physical appearance, verbal and non-verbal behavior, attitude towards the patient, efficacy and results obtained in clinical trials. The field is characterized by a large complexity of models, ideas and study designs. The virtual agents, although many of them are in pilot phase, have been appreciated by the patients as a new and modern approach to traditional therapy, fact that is highly promising in the context of developing new and attractive modalities for relieving emotional distress.

Keywords: Virtual agent · Anxiety · Phobias

1 Introduction

Anxiety disorders are affecting around 275 million people, which accounts for 4% of the world's population [1]. Phobias, the debilitating fear of objects, places or situations, is the most common type of anxiety disorder. Phobias' therapy includes desensitization by in-vivo gradual exposure to the stimuli causing anxiety, cognitive-behavioral therapy, counselling or medication. Virtual reality has emerged in recent years due to the technological advancements and has provided new modalities for treating phobias by controlled exposure in the virtual environment in the presence of the therapist.

Robots are increasingly used in all fields of human activity, not only in the industrial area. An assistive robot was defined as a robot which performs a physical task for the well-being of a person with a disability. Also, it is seen as a device which can receive information through sensors and perform actions to help people with disabilities or old people [2].

© Springer Nature Switzerland AG 2021
J. Y. C. Chen and G. Fragomeni (Eds.): HCII 2021, LNCS 12770, pp. 71–79, 2021.
https://doi.org/10.1007/978-3-030-77599-5_6

In [3], Feil-Seifer and Matarić proposed three categories of virtual agents: assistive robots (AR) which can be seen as an aid or a support for people, socially interactive robots (SIR) with a form of interaction as the main task and socially assistive robotics (SAR) which serve human users through social interaction. The goal of a SAR is to create close and effective interaction with a human user for the purpose of giving assistance and achieving measurable progress in convalescence, rehabilitation or learning [3]. The interactions between a SAR and the human users can be performed through various ways including speech, gestures or direct input by using for example the mouse or the keyboard [3].

Social assistive robots offer a variety of services: tutoring, physical therapy, daily life assistance, emotional expression, rehabilitation, education and motivation [3–5]. SARs have been used as therapeutic assistants in rehabilitation, mental healthcare or physical disabilities treatment [4–6].

Robot Therapy (RT) is defined as a non-pharmacological intervention that promotes social contact, as well as cognitive and physical stimulation [7]. By using the heart rate data acquired from users, the authors proposed in [7] an adaptive robot called Eva that offers support for therapeutic interventions in a geriatric residence and to help people with sleep disorders. Eva has features such as speech capabilities and emotions expression.

Smart virtual agents are adaptive and standalone programs used to create software products that solve certain tasks on behalf of a particular user, based on explicit or implicit instructions from him. Virtual agents operate with pre-established or learned knowledge to perform specific or repetitive activities for an individual user, a business process or a software application.

Intelligent agents can optimize human activity by:

- masking the complexity of difficult work tasks;
- performing laborious actions or work tasks;
- conducting transactions on behalf of the user;
- training;
- stimulating collaborative interactions;
- monitoring processes and diagnosing errors that may occur;
- creating remedial contexts and providing feedback.

In some applications, the psychologist or the clinician is replaced by a virtual therapist or a virtual coach that guides the patients through the steps of the therapy. The virtual health agent also provides motivation, encouragement and has an empathic behavior. Another functionality is to explain to the patients their psychological condition, to give information about their progress or to interpret the biophysical data collected during the therapy sessions, all in the comfort and safety of their own homes [8].

This paper proposes a review of applications and research pursuits that introduced virtual therapists in anxiety and phobias therapy.

In a previous paper published at HCII 2020, we described e-Ther [9], a prototype of an assistive virtual agent for acrophobia therapy that provides support and encouragement to the patients by changing its voice parameters according to the user's emotional state. We are currently working in a project that aims to develop a system for phobia therapy that can be used in both clinical settings and at home. The virtual assistive agent becomes an important part of the home-based therapy, as it is aimed to replace the human therapist and to play various roles such as: interpret user input, communicate verbally and non-verbally with the patient, drive the therapy towards its goal, provide reassurance during the course of a task, restructure the patient's irrational thoughts by incorporating cognitive behavioral therapy principles [10], conduct a short psycho-education session in which it explains the relationship between anxious thoughts and physiological reactions [11], come up with alternatives, exhibit an empathic behavior.

The virtual agents possess various advantages: full-time availability, the anonymity of the virtual character increases self-disclosure by patients [12], dialog and contact result in more patients completing the treatment [13], visual and auditory instructions improve adherence and alliance (the relationship established between the patient and the therapist) [14]. Moreover, the sensation of being with another in the virtual environment enhances social presence [15].

The virtual agent can be represented as a human avatar [16] or as an animated character [17]. It is autonomous and automatically reacts to the user's input based on a predefined artificial intelligence model or algorithm.

We have identified various research questions to which we sought to find answers in the papers we studied, such as: the physical appearance of the virtual therapist, its verbal and non-verbal capabilities, behavior and efficacy in user experiments. They are presented in the following sections of the paper.

2 Home-Based or Clinical-Based Virtual Agents

The Memphis system [8] is a home-based virtual reality exposure therapy (VRET) system dedicated to the treatment of social anxiety disorders, that includes 19 exposure scenarios presenting situations such as meeting an old friend or strangers, giving a speech in front of an audience that changes its behavior, visiting a doctor etc. The communication is ensured through free speech with the virtual characters that can respond either positively or negatively. The therapist can set the treatment plan that will be followed by the virtual therapist and monitor the progress remotely by using a dedicated application where the information is encrypted and decrypted. The patient's performance is evaluated in terms of anxiety measures, calculated based on the collected Subjective Units of Discomfort (SUD) and heart rate.

In [12], the virtual coach participates remotely in the therapy. SPARX [18] uses a virtual therapist in a fantasy world where the patient plays the role of a hero who saves the world for treating depression in young adolescents. The modified version, Rainbow SPARX is dedicated to the young sexual minorities battling with trauma and depression. The virtual therapist Ellie [16] was preferred by the participants in two situations: when it operated autonomously and when it was manipulated by a clinician. The least favorite situation was when they participated in face-to-face interviews.

3 The Physical Appearance of the Virtual Therapist

In Hartanto et al. [8], a female avatar describes the monitoring data, while a male virtual agent gives instructions on how to use the head-mounted display. Angela is a 3D animated embodied conversational agent that uses cognitive-behavioral therapy (CBT) to help presenters overcome the fear of public speaking [10].

In [19], the virtual therapist has a physical embodiment by means of a holographic image that moves while speaking. Here, the voice of a male avatar delivers instructions and the voice of a female acts as a biology spider expert in a spider phobia alleviation application.

Effie is a female virtual therapist that practices a healing method called the Emotional Freedom Technique (EFT). Effie's dialogues are based on pre-recorded voice [20]. Another female avatar has been used in [21] and in [12], in an application dedicated to people suffering from post-traumatic stress disorder, with voices generated by text-to-speech systems. The virtual agent can also have the appearance of the clinician's photograph [22] or of a fantasy character [23].

For relieving depression symptoms using CBT, the virtual therapist took the appearance of a fantasy character that guided the patient in a serious game [23] and even the photograph of the real therapist was embodied in a Web-based application [24]. Virtual animal characters helped children overcome performance anxiety [25].

4 Verbal and Non-verbal Capabilities

Embodied conversational agents (ECAs) are autonomous or semi-autonomous intelligent entities that can have verbal and non-verbal behavior, being able to simulate human-like gestures. The embodiments can be human characters or robots and the communication is done either via natural language (speech and synchronized non-verbal behavior [26, 27]) or written messages [14]. Self-disclosure is a method in which people talk about their problems openly in front of a virtual counselor [26, 27]. Health communication with a virtual avatar in a serious game is an effective method for reducing depression symptoms [28].

Ontologies have been created so that the virtual agent can pose appropriate and personalized questions in trauma recollection therapies [12], as it considered that the virtual agents should have knowledge about the traumatic experience and should also pay attention to the meaning of the questions they ask [29, 30]. In [10], the virtual coach Angela can move its eyebrows, display facial expressions, direct the gaze, nod the head, shift its posture and make various hand gestures. A corpus of negative examples has been collected with the help of a psychologist and natural language generation techniques have been used to compute replacement thoughts that the virtual therapist transmitted to the patient. In SPARX [18], the virtual therapist explains how the game can be useful in real-world situations. In [19], voiceover commentaries accompanied the therapy sessions.

The study of Ring et al. [21] presents a conversational agent that has both verbal and non-verbal animated abilities for depression therapy. The dialogue is facilitated by a text-to-speech engine, while the non-verbal behavior includes facial and hand gestures, as well as posture shifts. The user interacts with the system by selecting his response from a list of responses, using speech or by interacting with a touch screen display. The virtual agent Effie [20] uses predefined recorded dialogue sequences and not text-to-speech, as the latter is more artificial and difficult to be understood.

5 Behavior - Motivation, Encouragement, Empathy

The virtual agents provide motivation, interactive psycho-education sessions, interpretation of the monitoring data and information about the treatment's progress [8]. They can also be used to deliver cognitive behavioral therapy to people suffering from anxieties [31], such as fear of public speaking. The virtual coach asks questions and helps the patient to deal with irrational thoughts. The users express their thoughts and then the virtual coach explains why these thoughts are senseless, starts a dialogue and challenges the irrational feelings [10].

Empathy implies understanding one's emotions, willing to help others and placing yourself in another one's position [32]. It was shown that the connection between the user and the therapist is higher when the therapist resembles in appearance with the user [33] and that empathic agents are preferred over the neutral ones [34]. Bickmore [35] named as "relational agent" an empathic agent who is caring, trustworthy and interested in improving rapport - mutual interaction and a warm connection. A virtual nurse which possesses relational dialogue was considered more caring than a non-relational one [35]. Similarly, a virtual exercise advisor called Laura, enriched with positive feedback and facial expressions was more appreciated than its neutral version [36]. Ranj et al. [20] introduced two virtual therapists, one who shows an empathic behavior through verbal communication and a neutral one. The results have shown that the higher the emotional distress, the higher is the rapport established with the empathic virtual agent.

Empathic behavior has been provided by a virtual coach in [37] and motivation was given using a 2D animated avatar called Tara running on a mobile application [38]. In [19], the virtual agent provided feedback according to the patient's Subjective Units of Distress (SUD) ratings – positive encouragements if the SUDs were high and advice if they were low. Pontier et al. [39] present a virtual agent that guides the user through filling in the Beck Depression Inventory (BDI) questionnaire, which measures the intensity of depression. The virtual agent shows either happiness or sadness (empathy), depending on the user's responses, accompanied by characteristic facial expressions.

ECAs in CBT-based interventions should be trustworthy and empathic, as it has been shown that the empathic virtual agents are preferred over the non-empathic ones [24]. The relationship established between the patient and the virtual therapist is as solid as the one established with the human therapist [27]. Anonymity is a highly appreciated characteristic of the virtual therapist [26], along with adaptability and configurability [40].

The embodied conversational agent for depression therapy described in [21] provides utterances such as reflections and empathic messages. Some empathic messages imitate empathic listening, by rephasing the user's statements. The user's speech is passed through an affect detection system which classifies the emotion as happy, neutral and sad. When the subjects did not interact via speech, their facial expressions have been classified on the 3-dimensional valence scale.

6 Efficacy and User Feedback

The ontology-based system facilitated memory recollection for people suffering from post-traumatic stress disorder. It has been shown that the ontology-based system increases the time spent in the therapeutic procedure and enhances the patients' ability to use descriptive terms to characterize their inner feelings in more detail, compared to non-ontology, non-personalized systems [12].

Cognitive-behavioral therapy employing virtual agents has been efficiently used for alleviating psychological symptoms in the therapy of mental disorders [41], depression [21] and anxiety [31], where college students reduced their anxiety levels after 2 weeks of practice, assisted by a virtual agent which communicated via text messages. The virtual therapist had a significant role in reducing public speaking anxiety and increased confidence for non-native English speakers [42]. Other virtual coaches significantly improved the quality of the presentation [43] and interviewing performance [44]. The virtual agent Angela [10] reduced the incidence of maladaptive thoughts associated with anxiety and nervousness, even if the therapy session was shorter. The authors claim that virtual therapy is effective also for presenters with moderate and high confidence.

The Virtual Therapist Alliance Scale (VTAS) collects information about the relationship between the patient and the virtual therapist. In a virtual reality experiment for spider phobia alleviation, it has been found that alliance, the relationship between the patient and the therapist, is a significant predictor of treatment outcome [19].

28 participants completed the BDI questionnaire, accompanied by the virtual agent [39]. They evaluated the virtual agent as friendly, trustworthy and kind. 81% of the subjects preferred to fill in the questionnaire in the presence of the virtual agent, an experience they considered to be more attractive and entertaining, adding value to the self-help therapy and reducing the drop-out rate. As recommendations, the participants suggested that the voice of the virtual agent should be more friendly and that the agent should offer feedback for each answer provided.

The embodied conversational agent for depression therapy [21] has been tested in a pilot study with 10 participants (5 male and 5 female) who validated that the agent understood their emotions and responded accordingly, especially by offering pauses during the dialogue whenever they felt sad.

7 Conclusions

This paper provided an overview of technological possibilities for virtual agents employed in the context of therapeutic applications. Although the field is new, many studies covered a large variety of aspects in their study design and virtual agent embodiment with promising results.

The use of assistive robots in psychotherapeutic applications is an innovative approach, with effective interventions both as a mediator of the therapist and as standalone applications. Given the relatively small number of studies that provide quantitative data on the use of virtual assistive robots in anxiety and phobias, large-scale clinical trials and longitudinal studies are required in the future.

A very useful approach would be real-time quantitative measures related to patient stress and anxiety, extracting his emotions and changing the therapeutic behavior of the virtual agent depending on the feedback received.

Pilot testing should be extended in order to prove that the use of conversational agents is safe and reliable for anxiety disorders therapy.

One of the directions in which assistive robots can be used with great success is working with children and adolescents, because it makes them more approachable for therapy and improves the effectiveness of the therapeutic process.

Acknowledgement. This work was supported by a grant of the Romanian Ministery of Research and Innovation, CCCDI - UEFISCDI, project number 43PTE/2020, "PhoVR - Tratarea Imersiva a Fobiilor prin Realitate Virtuala Adaptiva si Biofeedback" / "PhoVR - Immersive Treatment of Phobias through Adaptive Virtual Reality and Biofeedback", within PNCDI III, UEFISCDI proiect 1/2018 and UPB CRC Research Grant 2017.

References

1. Fleming, S.: This is the world's biggest mental health problem - and you might not have heard of it (2019). https://www.weforum.org/agenda/2019/01/this-is-the-worlds-biggest-mental-health-problem. Accessed 21 Jan 2021
2. Jaffe, D.L., Nelson, D., Thiemer, J.: Perspectives in assistive technology (2012). https://web.stanford.edu/class/engr110/2012/04b-Jaffe.pdf. Accessed 21 Jan 2021
3. Feil-Seifer, D., Mataric, M.J.: Defining socially assistive robotics. In 9th International Conference on Rehabilitation Robotics, ICORR 2005, Chicago, IL, 2005, pp. 465–468 (2005). https://doi.org/10.1109/ICORR.2005.1501143
4. Malik, N.A., Hanapiah, F.A., Rahman, R.A.A., Yussof, H.: Emergence of socially assistive robotics in rehabilitation for children with cerebral palsy: a review. Int. J. Adv. Rob. Syst. 13(3), 135 (2016)
5. Rabbitt, S.M., Kazdin, A.E., Scassellati, B.: Integrating socially assistive robotics into mental healthcare interventions: applications and recommendations for expanded use. Clin. Psychol. Rev. 35, 35–46 (2015)
6. Fasola, J., Mataric, M.J.: Robot motivator: Improving user performance on a physical/mental task. In: Proceedings of the 4th ACM/IEEE International Conference on Human Robot Interaction - HRI 2009. ACM Press, New York (2009)
7. Cruz-Sandoval, D., Favela, J., Parra, M., Hernandez, N.: Towards an adaptive conversational robot using biosignals. In: Proceedings of the 7th Mexican Conference on Human-Computer Interaction. ACM, New York (2018)
8. Hartanto, D., Brinkman, W.-P., Kampmann, I. L., Morina, N., Emmelkamp, P. G. M., Neerincx, M. A.: Design and implementation of home-based virtual reality exposure therapy system with a virtual eCoach. In: Brinkman, W.-P., Broekens, J., Heylen, D. (eds.) IVA 2015. LNCS (LNAI), vol. 9238, pp. 287–291. Springer, Cham (2015). https://doi.org/10.1007/978-3-319-21996-7_31
9. Bălan, O., Cristea, Ş, Moise, G., Petrescu, L., Ivaşcu, S., Moldoveanu, A., Moldoveanu, F., Leordeanu, M.: ETher – an assistive virtual agent for acrophobia therapy in virtual reality. In: Stephanidis, C., Chen, J. Y. C., Fragomeni, G. (eds.) HCII 2020. LNCS, vol. 12428, pp. 12–25. Springer, Cham (2020). https://doi.org/10.1007/978-3-030-59990-4_2
10. Kimani, E., Bickmore, T., Trinh, H., Pedrelli, P.: You'll be great: virtual agent-based cognitive restructuring to reduce public speaking anxiety. In: 2019 8th International Conference on Affective Computing and Intelligent Interaction (ACII). IEEE (2019)
11. Hope, D.A., Heimberg, R.G., Turk, C.L.: Managing Social Anxiety, Therapist Guide: A Cognitive-Behavioral Therapy Approach. Oxford University Press, Oxford (2019)

12. Tielman, M., van Meggelen, M., Neerincx, M. A., Brinkman, W.-P.: An ontology-based question system for a virtual coach assisting in trauma recollection. In: Brinkman, W.-P., Broekens, J., Heylen, D. (eds.) IVA 2015. LNCS (LNAI), vol. 9238, pp. 17–27. Springer, Cham (2015). https://doi.org/10.1007/978-3-319-21996-7_2

13. Kelders, S.M., Kok, R.N., Ossebaard, H.C., Van Gemert-Pijnen, J.E.W.C.: Persuasive system design does matter: a systematic review of adherence to web-based interventions. J. Med. Internet Res. 14(6), e152 (2012)

14. Provoost, S., Lau, H.M., Ruwaard, J., Riper, H.: Embodied conversational agents in clinical psychology: a scoping review. J. Med. Internet Res. 19(5), e151 (2017)

15. Oh, C.S., Bailenson, J.N., Welch, G.F.: A systematic review of social presence: definition, antecedents, and implications. Front. Robot. AI 5, 114 (2018)

16. Rizzo, A., Shilling, R., Forbell, E., Scherer, S., Gratch, J., Morency, L.-P.: Autonomous virtual human agents for healthcare information support and clinical interviewing. In: Artificial Intelligence in Behavioral and Mental Health Care, pp. 53–79. Elsevier (2016)

17. Bickmore, T.W., Mitchell, S.E., Jack, B.W., Paasche-Orlow, M.K., Pfeifer, L.M., Odonnell, J.: Response to a relational agent by hospital patients with depressive symptoms. Interact. Comput. 22(4), 289–298 (2010)

18. Merry, S.N., Stasiak, K., Shepherd, M., Frampton, C., Fleming, T., Lucassen, M.F.G.: The effectiveness of SPARX, a computerised self help intervention for adolescents seeking help for depression: randomised controlled non-inferiority trial. BMJ (Clin. Res. Ed.) 344(apr183), e2598 (2012)

19. Miloff, A., Carlbring, P., Hamilton, W., Andersson, G., Reuterskiöld, L., Lindner, P.: Measuring alliance toward embodied virtual therapists in the era of automated treatments with the Virtual Therapist Alliance Scale (VTAS): development and psychometric evaluation. J. Med. Internet Res. 22(3), e16660 (2020)

20. Ranjbartabar, H., Richards, D., Bilgin, A., Kutay, C.: First impressions count! The role of the human's emotional state on rapport established with an empathic versus neutral virtual therapist. IEEE Trans. Affect. Comput., 1–1 (2019)

21. Ring, L., Bickmore, T., Pedrelli, P.: An affectively aware virtual therapist for depression counseling. In: Conference on Human Factors in Computing Systems (CHI) Workshop on Computing and Mental Health ACM SIGCHI (2016)

22. Kelders, S. M.: Involvement as a working mechanism for persuasive technology. In: MacTavish, T., Basapur, S. (eds.) PERSUASIVE 2015. LNCS, vol. 9072, pp. 3–14. Springer, Cham (2015). https://doi.org/10.1007/978-3-319-20306-5_1

23. Cheek, C., et al.: Views of young people in rural Australia on SPARX, a fantasy world developed for New Zealand youth with depression. JMIR Serious Games 2(1), e3 (2014)

24. Martínez-Miranda, J., Bresó, A., García-Gómez, J. M.: Look on the bright side: A model of cognitive change in virtual agents. In: Bickmore, T., Marsella, S., Sidner, Candace (eds.) IVA 2014. LNCS (LNAI), vol. 8637, pp. 285–294. Springer, Cham (2014). https://doi.org/10.1007/978-3-319-09767-1_37

25. Schmidt, R., Eifler, P., Masuch, M.: Playfully conquering performance anxiety. In: Schouten, B., Fedtke, S., Bekker, T., Schijven, M., Gekker, A. (eds.) Games for Health, pp. 267–279. Springer, Wiesbaden (2013). https://doi.org/10.1007/978-3-658-02897-8_21

26. Swartout, W., et al.: Virtual humans for learning. AI Mag. 34(4), 13–30 (2013)

27. DeVault, D., et al.: SimSensei Kiosk: a virtual human interviewer for healthcare decision support. In: Proceedings of the 2014 International Conference on Autonomous Agents and Multi-Agent Systems, pp. 1061–1068 (2014)

28. Pinto, M.D., Greenblatt, A.M., Hickman, R.L., Rice, H.M., Thomas, T.L., Clochesy, J.M.: Assessing the critical parameters of eSMART-MH: a promising avatar-based digital therapeutic intervention to reduce depressive symptoms. Perspect. Psychiatr. Care 52(3), 157–168 (2016)

29. Bickmore, T., Schulman, D., Sidner, C.: A reusable framework for health counseling dialogue systems based on a behavioral medicine ontology. J. Biomed. Inform. **44**, 183–197 (2011)
30. Rizzo, A., et al.: An intelligent virtual human system for providing healthcare information and support. Med. Meets Virtual Reality **18**, 503–509 (2011)
31. Fitzpatrick, K.K., Darcy, A., Vierhile, M.: Delivering cognitive behavior therapy to young adults with symptoms of depression and anxiety using a fully automated conversational agent (Woebot): a randomized controlled trial. JMIR Mental Health **4**(2), e19 (2017)
32. Hodges, S.D., Klein, K.J.K.: Regulating the costs of empathy: the price of being human. J. Socio-Econ. **30**(5), 437–452 (2001)
33. Hall, L., Woods, S., Aylett, R., Newall, L., Paiva, A.: Empathic interaction with synthetic characters: the importance of similarity. In: Encyclopaedia of Human Computer Interaction (2005)
34. Brave, S.B.: Agents that care: investigating the effects of orientation of emotion exhibited by an embodied computer agent. Dissertation Abstracts International, 64(5-B), 2437 (UMI No.2003–95022–206) (2003)
35. Bickmore, T.W., Pfeifer, L.M., Jack, B.W.: Taking the time to care: empowering low health literacy hospital patients with virtual nurse agents. In: Proceedings of the 27th International Conference on Human Factors in Computing Systems - CHI 09. ACM Press, New York (2009)
36. Bickmore, T.W., Picard, R.W.: Towards caring machines. In: Extended Abstracts of the 2004 Conference on Human Factors and Computing Systems - CHI 2004. ACM Press, New York (2004)
37. Freeman, D., et al.: Automated psychological therapy using immersive virtual reality for treatment of fear of heights: a single-blind, parallel-group, randomised controlled trial. Lancet. Psychiatry **5**(8), 625–632 (2018)
38. Donker, T., et al.: Effectiveness of self-guided app-based virtual reality cognitive behavior therapy for acrophobia: a randomized clinical trial. JAMA Psychiatry **76**(7), 682–690 (2019)
39. Pontier, M., Siddiqui, G. F.: A virtual therapist that responds empathically to your answers. In: Prendinger, H., Lester, J., Ishizuka, M. (eds.) IVA 2008. LNCS (LNAI), vol. 5208, pp. 417–425. Springer, Heidelberg (2008). https://doi.org/10.1007/978-3-540-85483-8_42
40. Pagliari, C., et al.: Psychosocial implications of avatar use in supporting therapy for depression. Stud. Health Technol. Inform. **181**, 329–333 (2012)
41. Suganuma, S., Sakamoto, D., Shimoyama, H.: An embodied conversational agent for unguided internet-based cognitive behavior therapy in preventative mental health: feasibility and acceptability pilot trial. JMIR Mental Health **5**(3), e10454 (2018)
42. Trinh, H., Ring, L., Bickmore, T.: DynamicDuo: co-presenting with virtual agents. In: Proceedings of the 33rd Annual ACM Conference on Human Factors in Computing Systems - CHI 2015. ACM Press, New York (2015)
43. Trinh, H., Asadi, R., Edge, D., Bickmore, T.: RoboCOP: a robotic coach for oral presentations. Proc. ACM Interact. Mobile Wearable Ubiquit. Technol. **1**(2), 1–24 (2017)
44. Hoque, M. (ehsan), Courgeon, M., Martin, J.-C., Mutlu, B., Picard, R.W.: MACH: my automated conversation coach. In: Proceedings of the 2013 ACM International Joint Conference on Pervasive and Ubiquitous Computing - UbiComp 2013. ACM Press, New York (2013)

Designing Limitless Path in Virtual Reality Environment

Raghav Mittal[✉], Sai Anirudh Karre[✉], and Y. Raghu Reddy[✉]

Software Engineering Research Center, IIIT Hyderabad, Hyderabad, India
{raghav.mittal,saianirudh.karri}@research.iiit.ac.in,
raghu.reddy@iiit.ac.in

Abstract. Walking in a Virtual Environment is a bounded task. It is challenging for a subject to navigate a large virtual environment designed in a limited physical space. External hardware support may be required to achieve such an act in a concise physical area without compromising navigation and virtual scene rendering quality. This paper proposes an algorithmic approach to let a subject navigate a limitless virtual environment within a limited physical space with no additional external hardware support apart from the regular Head-Mounted-Device (HMD) itself. As part of our work, we developed a Virtual Art Gallery as a use-case to validate our algorithm. We conducted a simple user-study to gather feedback from the participants to evaluate the ease of locomotion of the application. The results showed that our algorithm could generate limitless paths of our use-case under predefined conditions and can be extended to other use-cases.

Keywords: Limitless paths · Bounded virtual environment · Virtual reality products

1 Motivation

Virtual Reality (VR) environments are designed from a participant's perspective. In HMDs, participant is considered to be the center of the VR scene and the environment is oriented around the participant. This idea of centrality helps define the boundary of the VR environment for a given scene. VR practitioners normally design a full-scale scene to orient the participant within a fixed bounded environment rather than building a dynamic bounded environment due to various reasons. Some of the reasons like HMD limitations, physical space limits, dependency on additional hardware support, poor scene baking, poor frame rate, etc. influence the VR practitioners to build navigation controls through hand-held devices by letting the participant stay stationary. This contradicts the idea of creating realness in VR scene as the participant is forced to navigate the scene through hand-held controllers but in reality s(he) is stationary. To help address this issue, we developed an approach to let the participant navigate beyond the control of a hand-held device by taking into account the following two factors:

© Springer Nature Switzerland AG 2021
J. Y. C. Chen and G. Fragomeni (Eds.): HCII 2021, LNCS 12770, pp. 80–95, 2021.
https://doi.org/10.1007/978-3-030-77599-5_7

- let the participant physically navigate in the VR environment without the influence of external haptic hardware.
- let the participant navigate seamlessly with a limitless path in a limited virtual play area.

The above two factors can be addressed by considering the underlying technical aspects

- As part of the predefined constraints, physical environment and virtual environment ratio must be maintained
- An algorithm needs to be built to generate a limitless path with no obstruction for the participant to navigate in a virtual environment setup in a limited room space.
- VR environment assets need to be generated based on the path and orientation of the participant in the virtual environment
- VR environment should appear infinite to the participant. However, physically the participant will still be navigating in a limited predefined space.

In this work, we use the term *'Limitless Path'* in the context of obstruction-free navigation in a VR environment within a limited physical environment. We define limitless path as a programmatically generated never ending path in a VR scene. This path is limitless and unbounded in terms of length. The progress of the path is automatic and the scene assets are generated inline with the generated path. For illustration consider Fig. 1, person A - standing in a 10 ft × 10 ft physical grid wearing a HMD and another person B outside this physical grid. Person A loads a VR scene with the support of limitless path implementation and infinitely walks in this limited space. Person A experiences an endless walk in the VR scene. For person B, person A appears to be walking within a 10 ft × 10 ft physical grid area continuously in a random path within the limited physical area.

The rest of the paper is structured as follows: In Sect. 2, we detail our approach towards designing and implementing path generation and boundary detection in a VR environment. In Sect. 3, we present the user study on a small set of participants. In Sect. 4, we discuss the threats to validity. In Sect. 5, we present some related work in this area and finally in Sect. 6 we present some conclusions.

2   Our Approach

Continuous walking within the specified area (with in the scope of a VR scene or a physical area) is a critical aspect of path generation, as any generated path must be within the specified boundaries of the VR scene. Thus, path generation and boundary detection plays a key role in the progress of the participant along the limitless path. As part of our work, we designed and implemented both the path generation and boundary detection algorithms in a virtual environment.

Consider a use-case where a path has to be presented to the participant in a particular VR context. At the time of the VR scene generation, we are aware

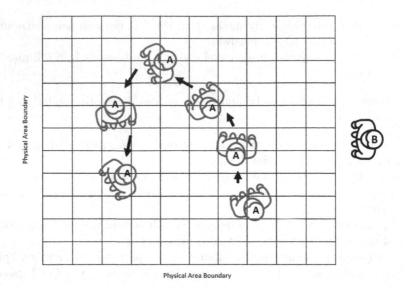

Fig. 1. Person A experiencing limitless path in a finite physical environment

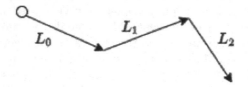

Fig. 2. Path generated on start of system. L_0 starts from player's position.

of the start position of the participant with in a virtual environment. As the participant walks forward, the path is generated by addition and removal of line segments in the path to create a perception of continuity. This path generation system outputs the path as a line made of multiple connected line segments, as shown in Fig. 2. The designed system will generate 3 successive line segments (shown in Fig. 2 as L_0, L_1, and L_2) from the starting point. When the player reaches the end of L_1, the first segment L_0 is removed, and a new segment L_3 is added to the end of L_2 as shown in Fig. 3. This process keeps repeating until the participant terminates the program.

Each generated path line segment forms an obtuse angle with the previous line segment in most cases. This is done to ensure comfortable locomotion to the participant by avoiding sharp turns. It also reduces the possibility of the path intersection or path override when a new line segment is added to the path.

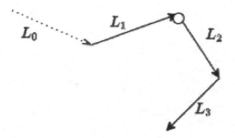

Fig. 3. L_0 is removed and L_3 is added when the player reached to the end of L_1.

2.1 Palling - Path Generation

In this section, we provide step-by-step details of our path generation algorithm. We term *'Palling'* as a user action to move forward in the virtual environment for ease of terms. *1 Pal* unit is equal to 1 unit distance taken by the user in the virtual environment. For purposes of simplicity, we assume the dimension of the rectangular bounded area from $D(0,0)$ to $D(x,z)$. If the user starts at $(0,0)$, the user can take z *Pal* units to reach $(0,z)$ and x *Pal* units to reach $(x,0)$. In order to generate a path, below are the necessary inputs:

- Player's starting position P_0 and head-yaw β_0 at that position.
- Dimensions of the boundary $D(x,z)$, here x and z are the limits of the boundary in a plane along x-axis and z-axis.
- Path properties include segment length l and path width w i.e. the perpendicular distance between parallel boundaries representing the width of the path in virtual environment.

As shown in Fig. 4, upon start of the application, the first line segment L_0 has a starting point P_0 and terminal point P_1 i.e. it is represented as $L_0 = \overline{P_0 P_1}$. Similarly, for L_1, P_1 and P_2 are starting and terminal points respectively. Equation 1 generalizes this for L_i. Currently the length is considered to be a constant value and provided as a necessary input. We plan on computing this automatically depending on the boundary area in future.

$$L_i = \overline{P_i P_{i+1}} \tag{1}$$

In the given play area, the coordinates of position P_{i+1} are calculated as shown in following Eqs. 2 and 3, where $0 <= i <$ total number of segments generated since the start of the application. Here β_0 is head-yaw (HMD's orientation along y-axis in virtual environment) of the user.

$$P_{i+1}(x) = l * \sin \beta_i + P_i(x) \tag{2}$$

$$P_{i+1}(z) = l * \cos \beta_i + P_i(z) \tag{3}$$

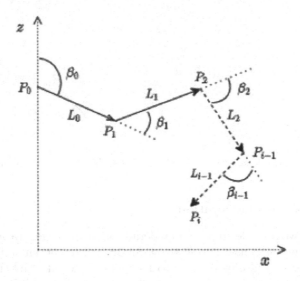

Fig. 4. Locomotion of a participant in the play area

When we recursively run Eqs. 2 and 3, we generate a limitless path in a defined boundary of $D(x, z)$. The generated path is instantaneous, nonlinear, and limited by certain Pal units due to the bounded area. The upcoming P_i needs to be generated by detecting the proximity of P_{i-1} to the boundary. When P_{i-1} is not close to the boundary, β_i is set to a random value in range $\{\beta_{i-1} - \pi/2, \beta_{i-1} + \pi/2\}$. The procedure of generating the next line segment L_i for a given position P_i at a boundary is defined on β_i value.

2.2 Pragging - Boundary Detection

In this section, we detail our boundary detection algorithm. For ease of terms, we refer to a user instance on detecting a boundary or hitting a boundary as '*Pragging*'. 1 *Prag* unit is equal to one hit at a boundary.

To ensure that the player doesn't cross the boundary of the given application, the generated path must not span beyond the bounded-area. To achieve this, the bounded-area is enclosed into wall-like colliders. We define 'j' as a value that equally divides a 180° range into multiple possible rays as shown in Fig. 5. Whenever a new point P_{i+1} has to be generated, $j+1$ number of rays are projected in multiple directions with certain angles called as γ where k is in range $\{0, j\}$ and $j > 0$. The range of angle here is $\beta_{i-1} - \pi/2, \beta_{i-1} + \pi/2$

$$\gamma_j = \beta_{i-1} - \pi/2 + ((\pi/j) * k) \tag{4}$$

If the value of j $= 4$, we have j $+ 1$ rays i.e. 5 rays at equal angles between $\beta_{i-1} - \pi/2, \beta_{i-1} + \pi/2$ are called $\gamma_0, \gamma_1, \gamma_2, \gamma_3, \gamma_4$ as shown in Fig. 5. Here the source of the rays is P_i and length is equal to *path_length + path_width/2*

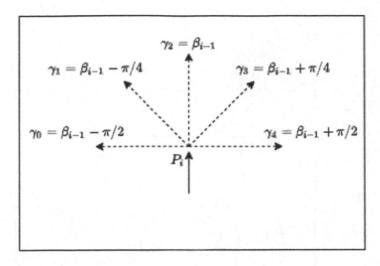

Fig. 5. Dashed lines represent rays, solid line represents the direction of the line segment L_{i-1} of the existing path. Here $j = 4$.

If a ray collides with the play area boundary, we term it as 1 Prag unit. If $j = a$, we have $a + 1$ rays generated. Out of these $a + 1$ rays, one of the γ_i direction is chosen to generate a path L_i. Below are the possible cases in which the generated rays can collide with a boundary:

- If $\gamma = a + 1$ *Prag* units, i.e. all generated rays hit the boundary as shown in Fig. 6. This means that the P_i is at the corner of the bounded area. In this case, $\pm 135°$ is the way to go away from the boundary. Two more rays are shot in directions $\gamma_0^* = \beta_{i-1} - 3\pi/4$ and $\gamma_1^* = \beta_{i-1} + 3\pi/4$ to avoid corner as an escape strategy. The ray which don't hit the boundary is chosen as the direction for L_i. If P_i is equidistant from boundaries then one of the ray from γ_0^* and γ_1^* is chosen randomly.
- If $1 \le \gamma \le a$ *Prag units* i.e. not all but atleast one ray hits the boundary as shown in Fig. 7 and anyone of the non-hitting rays can be used to generate L_i.
- If $\gamma = 0$ *Prag* units, i.e. none of the rays hit any of the boundaries. Here the path is free from boundaries as shown in Fig. 5. Then the β_i is randomly chosen from range $\beta_{i-1} - \pi/2, \beta_{i-1} + \pi/2$ for generating the upcoming L_i.

2.3 PragPal Algorithm

As part of our work, we conduct pragging and palling simultaneously to generate a limitless path for a user in a virtual environment. Algorithm 1 provides the pseudo-code of our concept, which is used in the simulation[1].

---

[1] https://github.com/raghavmittal101/path_gen_sys/.

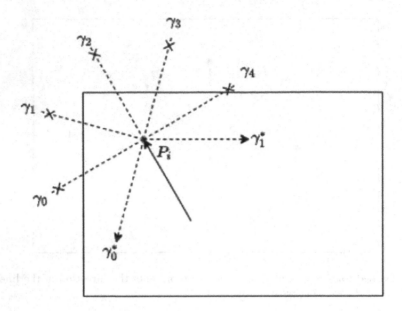

Fig. 6. When all the rays $\gamma_0....\gamma_{j+1}$ hit the boundaries then two more rays are generated to decide the direction of L_i.

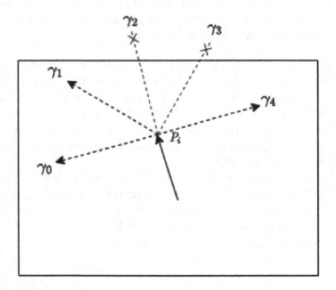

Fig. 7. The γ for next L_i will be chosen from γ_0, γ_1, γ_4.

Algorithm 1: PragPal Algorithm Overview

Input: user position, head yaw, line segment length, path width
Output: List of 2D points x,z which represent a path

1 **Function** GeneratePoint_Pal(*beta, point*):
2 $point.x = segment\_length * \sin(beta) + point.x$
3 $point.z = segment\_length * \cos(beta) + point.z$
4 **return** point
5 **Function** GenerateBeta_Prag(*beta, point*):
6 $j = 4$ // can be any value greater than 1
7 valid_directions = []
8 for k in range (0, j+1): // k = 0, 1, 2, 3, 4
9   ray_direction = $beta - \pi/2 + (\pi/j) * k$
10   ray = Generate ray in direction ray_direction from *point*
11   if ray do not hit boundary:
12   valid_directions.push(ray_direction)
13 if valid_directions.size<0:
14   beta = randomly pick element from valid_directions
15 else:
16   beta = randomly choose from range $\{beta - \pi/2, beta + \pi/2\}$
17 **return** beta
18 **Function** Main:
19 point = current position of player: [x, z]
20 beta = current head-yaw of player in radians
21 points_list = [] // points represent the shape of current path
22 points_list.Append(point)
23 **OnSceneStart:** // called only on initialization of the scene
24   for i in range(4):
25   point = GeneratePoint_Pal(beta, point)
26   points_list.Append(point)
27   beta = GenerateBeta_Prag(beta, point)
28 **OnSceneUpdate:** // called whenever player reaches end of segment
29   points_list.pop() // removes first element
30   point = GeneratePoint_Pal(beta, point)
31   beta = GenerateBeta_Prag(beta, point)
32   points_list.Append(point)
33 **return**

2.4 Prototype Implementation of Virtual Art Gallery

To understand our work's effectiveness, we implemented the algorithm to build a VR based 'Virtual Art Gallery'. It is an endless corridor composed of two walls running parallel to each other. The user can walk through the gallery to explore the art items displayed on these walls. When the user progresses in the forward direction, i.e., palls forward, using the tracked Pal units, the path generation logic updates the upcoming path and auto-generates the corridor with relevant assets in the VR environment.

The corridor consists of two wall-like 2D mesh structures positioned parallel to the path. Whenever the new path is updated, the assets related to the corridor are also updated. In our example application, a set of royalty-free floral drawing images are displayed in the gallery. As the user navigates in the scene, Prag units are simultaneously tracked to detect boundaries to generate the possible paths. A collider trigger placed at the end of each line segment in the current path captures the Prag units. Whenever the user reaches a turn, this method is triggered. Thus generating an infinite limitless path for the participant in VR.

Fig. 8. Inside view the virtual art gallery.

We developed this use-case in Unity3D 2019 LTS, and tested it using Oculus Quest 2019 HMD. The images in the scene are placed at the player's standing height. This is to provide a comfortable view of the player during locomotion. Dimensions of each image are set to 0.5 × 0.5 units in Unity3D (50 cm x 50 cm). A margin of 0.1 units was given on both sides of each image to keep the walls less cluttered as shown in 8. The number of images placed on each wall varied because all the walls cannot necessarily be of the same length, as shown in Fig. 9. Here, the maximum perpendicular distance between the walls called *path_width* is always maintained. This was set to 1.2 m to have enough space for comfortable locomotion. The maximum length of a segment *segment_length* of path was set to 1.3 m. Physical space availability is an important factor to consider while deciding the values of path_width and segment_length. A larger space can accommodate a broader and longer corridor.

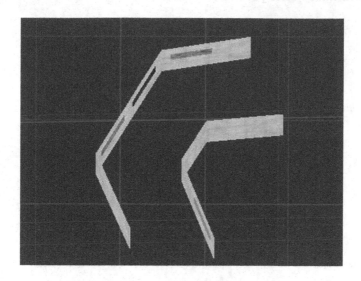

Fig. 9. Top view of the virtual art gallery.

2.5   Corridor Generation

The Pragpal algorithm generates P_i, P_{i+1}, P_{i+2} ..... and so on. It outputs points that can form a line to be used by a participant to traverse the limitless path in a virtual environment. In order to generate a corridor for walking, as shown in Fig. 8 and Fig. 9, we generate points Pr_i and Pl_i on right and left side of each point P_i respectively. These two new points Pr_i and Pl_i are equidistant from P_i and the distance between P_i and Pr_i or Pl_i is half the path width (*path_width*). In the current version of our approach, the *path_width* is a static value defined by the programmer and is set as a default width of the visible or imaginary corridor. However, the path width may be changed depending the size of the boundary and future iterations of our work shall accomodate dynamic generation of path-width based on the VR scene and bounded area size. As P_i, P_{i+1} are generated by PragPal algorithm, the red arrow in Fig. 10 from P_i is normal vector to Pr_i and Pl_i towards P_{i+1}. Once we reach P_{i+1}, we move towards P_{i+2} along the red arrow. However, to position Pr_{i+1} and Pl_{i+1}, we generate a average vector (shown as green dotted arrow) of $\overrightarrow{P_{i+1} - P_i}$ vector and $\overrightarrow{P_{i+2} - P_{i+1}}$. The resultant average vector is dotted green arrow. Using this average vector, we generate Pr_{i+1} and Pl_{i+1}. Similarly, Pr_{i+2} and Pl_{i+2} and Pr_{i+3} and Pl_{i+3} so on will be created along with PragPal points. Joining all Pr_i's and Pl_i's points will provide us the corridor path required for our virtual art gallery. The code-implementation of this corridor generation[2] is included as part of our virtual art gallery scene. Using this corridor generation method, we generate boundary to the path width for better path visualization.

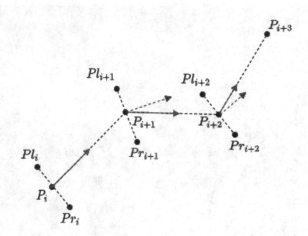

Fig. 10. Placement of left and right points for corridor generation. (Color figure online)

This use-case is a simple instance of validating the limitless path approach. Our approach can be applied to various other use-cases or domains like entertainment, scientific research, studying spatial cognition, education, etc. to validate limitless paths.

3   User Experience Study

This section contains details about the user experience study conducted to understand our implementation's caveats, immersion, and ease-of-locomotion. Our use-case simulation is available on GitHub for practitioners for further experimentation [3] along with its visualization for practitioners' analysis [8].

Experiment Setup - We have set up a physical room with a scale of 24 ft × 17 ft at our university campus to run the virtual art gallery use-case. We used Oculus Quest HMD, a standalone virtual reality headset with inside-out tracking capability. It helps determine the subject's position and orientation with no additional hardware apart from the HMD itself. Its technical specifications include a display resolution of 1440 × 1600 pixels per eye, 72 Hz refresh rate, Qualcomm Snapdragon 835 processor, and 4 GB RAM. As part of our VR scene, a set of 20 images are presented in the virtual art gallery. For test purposes, these images

---

[2] https://github.com/SebLague/Curve-Editor/tree/master/Episode%2006.
[3] https://github.com/raghavmittal101/path_gen_sys/.

are set to be repeated till the termination of the environment. Due to the Coronavirus pandemic, we conducted our tests under COVID-19 protocol and limited the number of users who participated in the study. Special care was taken to sanitize the apparatus after each trial and follow. VR face-masks were provided to the participants to avoid direct face contact with the HMD headset.

Participants - All the subjects who participated in this study were university students/staff recruited randomly. Among the participants, there were six males and four females. The mean age was 24.5 years. Before undergoing the study, we asked them a few questions to understand their prior exposure to VR. We observed that 35% of the participants had used video/computer games regularly, and 29% had prior VR experience.

Tasks - After obtaining participant consent and educating them about VR induced sickness, we asked them to complete the following tasks in the given order:

- **Demographic Survey**[4]: Participants were asked fill out data regarding Age, Sex, Gaming experience, and VR experience.
- **Exploration Task**: Participants had to locomote in the virtual art gallery VR Scene for about 5 min at their will. Post 5 min, the scene was terminated externally by the experimenter by alerting the participant verbally.
- **Questionnaires**: Participants were requested to fill Simulator Sickness Questionnaire(SSQ) [4] to understand simulation sickness while navigating the algorithm generated path, Igroup Presence Questionnaire (IPQ) [1] to understand the participant presence experience in the scene generated by the algorithm.

Table 1. Mean and weighted % of user experience of virtual art gallery

Factors	Mean	% Weighted response
Nausea	1.3	6.19%
Oculomotor	3.2	15.2%
Disorientation	2.8	13.3%
Sense of being	5.2	74.2%
Spatial presence	25.9	74%
Involvement	18.7	66%
Experienced realism	14.8	52%
Presence	64.6	65%

Results and Observations - Table 1 provides the results of our survey study. We observe that the subject has a good understanding of spatial presence and

---

[4] https://forms.gle/CW5kAWjAz7oTsyb26.

sense of being in the virtual reality scene despite automatically generating the subject's path in the virtual environment. The subjects experienced some disorientation and minor Nausea levels while being part of our VR scene automated path generation. There is a reasonable amount of involvement of participant while navigating in the VR scene.

4   Threats to Validity

Internal Validity - We conducted a controlled experiment of our approach using a limited setup. We incrementally recorded the experiment's updates and conducted a minimal study in an optimal setup consisting of a rectangular physcial room. We reviewed the study design with fellow researchers and gathered feedback. Our physical experiment results match the results of simulation studies conducted through automated means. However, given the covid restrictions, the interactions were fairly limited and virtual in nature. A more realistic in-person review of the study design could have yielded better insights.

External Validity - We made every attempt to conduct a simplified study of a use-case among the few participants. Our results show that our approach can be easily extended to a large population. However, a serious user-study with a large sample size is required to understand the underlying challenges of our approach. Additionally, creating different types of rooms in a iterative manner could have provided a different set of results.

Construct Validity - We coined Palling and Pragging as units to determine the motion and halt of a user in the virtual environment for ease of terms. It helped us establish the distance traveled versus the number of times the user hit the boundary. Using these two new units, we could ascertain the user's course and progress in a virtual environment.

Conclusion Validity - In our study, we don't claim our approach as optimal compared to existing methods. There is a possibility of more effective ways of limitless path generation. A comparative study among all available methods is essential to determine the statistical significance of our approach over others.

5   Related Work

Williams et al. conducted experiments on understanding the differences between locomotion in virtual environments using Joystick and locomotion through physical turning [15]. Their work is oriented towards understanding the spatial limitations through the different means of locomotion only. They found that large physical spaces are required for comfortable locomotion. A small space limits the length of the generated path. Such a problem can be solved by scaling up the translational gain or developing alternate methods of locomotion. Darken et al. [2] are the first to develop an omnidirectional treadmill, and Souman et al. have extended it to a Cyberwalk Omnidirectional treadmill to enable infinite locomotion in a finite space [11]. This setup requires external haptic hardware support and may not provide the appropriate end user experience in the virtual environment for locomotion. Juyoung et al. have discussed the differences in treadmill based Walk-in-place methods, and Non-treadmill based Walk-in-place methods [5]. Griffin et al. compare the locomotion techniques, which require a hand-held device for locomotion. For instance, teleportation versus the hands-free techniques like walk-in-place [3]. They observed that hands-free techniques offer a higher presence than hand-busy techniques.

Sun et al. proposed a saccadic redirected walking technique, which worked based on eye-tracking. It allows infinite walking in a room-scale environment without the need for hardware like ODTs. However, one of the major downsides of it was that it required HMD with eye-tracker and high processing resources. [13]. Matsumoto et al. employed a visual-haptic approach to let the user walk on an unlimited virtual straight line. Their method required installing a circular ring-like structure around which the user was required to walk while feeling the boundary with one hand [7]. Such setup makes the overall HMD setup immobile, expensive and less adaptable to the masses. Vasylevska et al. proposed flexible spaces technique in which the environment consisted of 4 rooms with partially overlapping areas, but the overlap was not visible to the user. Such an environment creates a perception of limitlessness because the user cannot see beyond the wall of their current room [14]. Such an approach can be tweaked to provide multiple path options to the participants. Suma et al. extended this work with an argument of maximizing walking in a limited space. Their algorithm dynamically modifies the layout of the scene, which consists of two overlapping rooms. Their overlapping is dynamically modified throughout the game-play to create an illusion of infiniteness, but not a true space [12].

Rietzler et al. proposed a redirection approach in which the user walks in a radius of 1.5 m. They tried to address the motion sickness caused due to the mismatch between vestibular and visual inputs. According to their work, when walking in a circular path of radius more than or equal to 1.5 m, the users cannot differentiate between walking in a circular path, or a straight line [9]. This was a unique observation and can be used for future advancements on non-haptic-based walking in the VR environment. Conventionally, teleportation methods do not require the user to walk, and hence it is not good for presence. However, Liu et al. presented a teleportation method in which a portal to a location is generated when the user points towards a location to teleport. The user has to walk and step into the portal to teleport. Here the portals are defined in a single room-scale boundary [6]. Thus providing limitless locomotion through teleportation.

Ruddle et al. compared the performance of participants in an object searching task done in 4 different conditions. They include search in the real-world, search in the virtual environment through a screen display, search in VE through an HMD with controllers and search in VE with real locomotion. They found the performance to be the most accurate in VE with real locomotion when compared with real-world performance [10]. They observed that the natural locomotion interface is the most suitable interface for locomotion in virtual environments because it provides translational and rotational body-based information. Most of these studies are either haptic based or illusion based to achieve a limitless path.

6 Conclusion

In this paper, we presented an approach to implement limitless path generation in Virtual environments using our PragPal Algorithm. We discussed path generation and boundary detection methods used as part of the algorithm. We implemented the algorithm on a Virtual Art Gallery use-case to understand the robustness through simulation. We also conducted a small user study to capture feedback from real-world participants. Our results and observations are promising and provide reasonable motivation to proceed with our planned work. We are currently working on a comparative study through a systematic literature review to understand the merits and demerits of all available locomotion methods in regards to limitlessness.

As part of future work, we plan to conduct a large scale use-study to understand presence, accommodation, and ease of use experiences from real-world participants to make our algorithm flexible for other implementations. We plan to tweak our algorithm to enable flexibility with the input parameters, for example, length of the line segment, boundary size, width of the path, etc.

In the current approach, only a single path is generated. The participant has to take that path and can only move in the forward direction. Given that the prior line segments are removed in the process of forward movement, retracing the steps is not possible. We plan on extending the algorithm to facilitate create of a multi-path environment. This will have its own set of challenges, especially from a rendering and overlaying perspective when the participant can move either forward in different directions or retrace their steps to a certain point. We also plan to introduce assets in the use cases that involve interaction between the participant and the asset. This will facilitate development of more use-cases towards realizing limitless path navigation for recreation, phobia studies, banking and other education related applications that involve interaction for task completion.

References

1. Igroup presence questionnaire. http://www.igroup.org/pq/ipq/. Accessed 04 Feb 2021
2. Darken, R.P., Cockayne, W.R., Carmein, D.: The omni-directional treadmill: a locomotion device for virtual worlds. In: Proceedings of the 10th Annual ACM Symposium on User Interface Software and Technology, pp. 213–221 (1997)
3. Griffin, N.N., Liu, J., Folmer, E.: Evaluation of handsbusy vs handsfree virtual locomotion. In: Proceedings of the 2018 Annual Symposium on Computer-Human Interaction in Play, New York, NY, USA, pp. 211–219. CHI PLAY 2018, Association for Computing Machinery (2018). https://doi.org/10.1145/3242671.3242707

4. Kennedy, R.S., Lane, N.E., Berbaum, K.S., Lilienthal, M.G.: Simulator sickness questionnaire: an enhanced method for quantifying simulator sickness. Int. J. Aviat. Psychol. **3**(3), 203–220 (1993). https://doi.org/10.1207/s15327108ijap0303_3

5. Lee, J., Hwang, J.I.: Walk-in-place navigation in VR. In: Proceedings of the 2019 ACM International Conference on Interactive Surfaces and Spaces, New York, NY, USA, pp. 427–430. ISS 2019, Association for Computing Machinery (2019). https://doi.org/10.1145/3343055.3361926

6. Liu, J., Parekh, H., Al-Zayer, M., Folmer, E.: Increasing walking in VR using redirected teleportation. In: Proceedings of the 31st Annual ACM Symposium on User Interface Software and Technology, UIST 2018, New York, NY, USA, pp. 521–529. Association for Computing Machinery (2018). https://doi.org/10.1145/3242587.3242601

7. Matsumoto, K., Narumi, T., Ban, Y., Yanase, Y., Tanikawa, T., Hirose, M.: Unlimited corridor: a visuo-haptic redirection system. In: The 17th International Conference on Virtual-Reality Continuum and Its Applications in Industry, VRCAI 2019, New York, NY, USA. Association for Computing Machinery (2019). https://doi.org/10.1145/3359997.3365705

8. Mittal, R.: Limitless path project (2021). https://serc.iiit.ac.in/resources/projects/limit

9. Rietzler, M., Deubzer, M., Dreja, T., Rukzio, E.: Telewalk: towards free and endless walking in room-scale virtual reality. In: Proceedings of the 2020 CHI Conference on Human Factors in Computing Systems, CHI 2020, New York, NY, USA, pp. 1–9. Association for Computing Machinery (2020). https://doi.org/10.1145/3313831.3376821

10. Ruddle, R.A., Lessels, S.: The benefits of using a walking interface to navigate virtual environments. ACM Trans. Comput. Hum. Interact. **16**(1) (2009). https://doi.org/10.1145/1502800.1502805

11. Souman, J.L., et al.: Cyberwalk: enabling unconstrained omnidirectional walking through virtual environments. ACM Trans. Appl. Percept. **8**(4) (2008). https://doi.org/10.1145/2043603.2043607

12. Suma, E.A., Lipps, Z., Finkelstein, S., Krum, D.M., Bolas, M.: Impossible spaces: maximizing natural walking in virtual environments with self-overlapping architecture. IEEE Trans. Visual Comput. Graphics **18**(4), 555–564 (2012). https://doi.org/10.1109/TVCG.2012.47

13. Sun, Q., et al.: Towards virtual reality infinite walking: dynamic saccadic redirection. ACM Trans. Graph. **37**(4) (2018). https://doi.org/10.1145/3197517.3201294

14. Vasylevska, K., Kaufmann, H., Bolas, M., Suma Rosenberg, E.: Flexible spaces: dynamic layout generation for infinite walking in virtual environments. In: IEEE Symposium on 3D User Interface 2013, 3DUI 2013 - Proceedings. pp. 39–42. IEEE Symposium on 3D User Interface 2013, 3DUI 2013 - Proceedings (2013). https://doi.org/10.1109/3DUI.2013.6550194. 8th IEEE International Symposium on 3D User Interfaces, 3DUI 2013; Conference date: 16-03-2013 Through 17-03-2013

15. Williams, B., Narasimham, G., McNamara, T.P., Carr, T.H., Rieser, J.J., Bodenheimer, B.: Updating orientation in large virtual environments using scaled translational gain. In: Proceedings of the 3rd Symposium on Applied Perception in Graphics and Visualization, APGV 2006, New York, NY, USA, pp. 21–28. Association for Computing Machiner (2006). https://doi.org/10.1145/1140491.1140495

A Comparative Study of Conversational Proxemics for Virtual Agents

David Novick[(✉)] and Aaron E. Rodriguez

The University of Texas at El Paso, El Paso, TX 79968, USA
novick@utep.edu, aerodriguez14@miners.utep.edu

Abstract. This paper explores proxemics—interpersonal distances—in conversations with virtual agents in virtual reality. While the real-world proxemics of human-human interaction have been well studied, the virtual-world proxemics of human-agent interaction are less well understood. We review research related to proxemics in virtual reality, noting that the previous research has not addressed proxemics with actual conversation, describe an empirical methodology for addressing our research questions, and present our results. The study used a repeated-measures, within-subjects design and had 23 participants. In the study, participants approached and conversed with a virtual agent in three conditions: no crowd, small crowd, and large crowd. The participant's distance from the agent with whom they conversed was recorded at 60 frames/second by VAIF's proxemics tool. Our results suggest that humans in a virtual world tend to position themselves closer to virtual agents than they would relative to humans in the physical world. However, the presence of other virtual agents did not appear to cause participants to change their proxemics.

Keywords: Embodied conversational agents · Initiative management · Multiparty interaction

1 Introduction

This paper explores proxemics—interpersonal distances—in conversations with virtual agents in virtual reality. While the real-world proxemics of human-human interaction have been well studied, the virtual-world proxemics of human-agent interaction are less well understood. Do dyadic conversational proxemics in virtual reality resemble dyadic conversational proxemics in the physical world? Does the presence of other virtual agents in the environment affect people's proxemic behaviors? The answers to these questions can inform the development of virtual-reality applications with human-agent interactions that feel more realistic and more fluid. For example, a model of how an agent should react when a human enters the room [1] could be augmented with better timing. And any virtual-reality application where an agent initiates a conversation when a human approaches (e.g., [2, 3]) could be improved through timing of the initiation that provides human-agent proxemics at a socially appropriate distance. Initiating the conversation too early would lead to a greater-than-appropriate distance, likely leading

© Springer Nature Switzerland AG 2021
J. Y. C. Chen and G. Fragomeni (Eds.): HCII 2021, LNCS 12770, pp. 96–105, 2021.
https://doi.org/10.1007/978-3-030-77599-5_8

the human conversant to think the agent is, literally, standoffish. And initiating the conversation too late would lead to a less-than-appropriate distance, likely leading the human conversant to feel uncomfortable about the closeness. Developers of human-agent interaction applications in virtual-reality application face these issues on a practical basis. For example, the virtual-reality application shown in Fig. 1 involves multiple conversations with different agents, plus dozens of non-speaking agents in the scene.

Fig. 1. User's view of a scene in [1], in which the user is conversing with the foreground character. In this application, the user converses with seven different agents, in both indoor and outdoor settings. The presence of other agents in the scene may provide the user with guidance on appropriate proxemics. Reproduced with permission.

To address these issues, we review research related to proxemics in virtual reality, noting that the previous research has not addressed proxemics with actual conversation, describe an empirical methodology for addressing our research questions, and present our results. Our study suggests that humans in a virtual world tend to position themselves closer to virtual agents than they would relative to humans in the physical world. However, the presence of other virtual agents did not appear to cause participants to change their proxemics.

2 Review of Related Research

The research literature for proxemics among humans is extensive (e.g., [4–6]); see [7] for a review of the foundational work. In general, observational research has indicated that people have preferred interpersonal distances for conversation and that these distances vary as function of culture and of the relationship between the conversants. According to Hall et al., [4], typical distances for conversations ("personal space") range from 0.46 to 1.2 m. This range is roughly consistent with the cultural variation observed by Herrera, Novick, Jan, and Traum [6], who observed mean interpersonal distances in dyadic conversation to vary across cultures from 1.09 to 1.66 m.

With respect to proxemics in virtual rather than real worlds, the literature is more limited. At least two studies have conducted observational experiments in which participants judge the appropriateness of proxemics of groups of virtual agents. These studies sought to determine perceptually plausible proxemics in virtual worlds for cultural training [8] (see Fig. 2) and for video gaming [9].

Fig. 2. Example animation of North American proxemics model used as stimulus in [5]. Reproduced with permission.

But do humans carry over their proxemics behaviors and values from the real world to virtual worlds? Other studies have addressed proxemics more directly, with first-person interaction by human participants with virtual agents. These studies were conducted for various reasons (e.g., male vs. female, screen vs. immersive) and reported varying results. Where the human and the agent had mutual gaze (or similar), results ranged from 0.4 m [10] to 1.76 m [11]. Some studies (e.g., [12]) tended to confirm that virtual proxemics were similar to real-world proxemics, while others did not. Table 1 summarizes these findings. We note that there are inconsistencies across the reported results, with some studies reporting mean minimum distance and others mean distance.

Table 1. Human-agent proxemics results.

Study	Result (meters)	Notes
Bailenson et al., 2001	0.40	Mean minimum distance
Bailenson et al., 2003	0.54	Male mean minimum distance
Iachini et al., 2014	0.61	Mean stopping distance
Zibrek et al., 2017	1.76	Mean distance
Peters et al., 2018	1.23	Mean stopping distance

In some studies, the human walked up to (and sometimes around) the agent. In others, the agent walked toward the human. But in all of these studies, though, the human and the agent did not interact conversationally. Thus, here we address the open question of whether virtual-world proxemics, in the context of actual conversation, resemble real-world proxemics. Additionally, at least one of the observational proxemics studies [8] reflects an assumption that people will adapt their proxemics behaviors to the proxemics context. That is, people will stand more closely to their conversational partner if there are more people around and these people are closer together. Is this true? Thus, this paper addresses two related issues: The correspondence of virtual to real-world proxemics for conversational interaction and the effects of the whether other agents are nearby.

3 Methodology

To address these issues, we formed three hypotheses:

1. The mean distance between the participant and the ECA with which they are conversing, when only the ECA is present, will be the same as the mean distance between human conversants in a social context.
2. The standard error of the distance between the participant and the ECA with which they are conversing, when only the ECA is present, will be the same as the standard error of the distance between human conversants in a social context.
3. Participants will stand closer to the ECA with which they are conversing when the number of nearby ECAs increases.
   To test the hypotheses, we conducted a within-subjects experiment with three conditions:
1. The participant and the virtual agent are alone.
2. The participant and the virtual agent have a few agents, with relatively distant proxemics, nearby.
3. The participant and the virtual agent have more agents, with relatively closer proxemics, nearby.

Twenty-three participants participated in the study, all of whom were undergraduate students at a public R1 university. Seventeen of the participants were male and five were female. Two of the participants had previously interacted with an embodied conversational agent. In the study, participants interacted with a female agent, and any surrounding agents, in a virtual world created with VAIF [13] and Unity, viewed with an HTC Vive headset. VAIF is both an authoring system for human-ECA interaction and a run-time system for executing these interactions, all built within Unity. The human-agent interactions in this study were entirely automated.

An earlier proxemics study with avatars [14] used a virtual world in which there were both boundaries and room to move (see Fig. 3), and the virtual world we used for this study used a similar layout (see Fig. 4).

Following our research protocol, we briefed the participants on the consent form and asked to read and sign the form, the participants completed a pre-interaction questionnaire on demographic information and then used the HTC Vive headset with a

Fig. 3. Virtual world used by Cafaro et al. [14] in an avatar-based study of proxemics. Reproduced with permission.

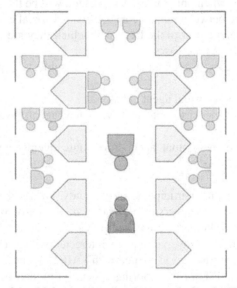

Fig. 4. Layout of virtual world for conversational proxemics study. The agent, shown in red, remains stationary. The human, shown in blue, enters from the bottom of the layout and walks toward the agent. Other agents, shown in green and non-speaking, represent the "large crowd" condition.

microphone headset to participate in three trials, balanced for order across subjects, corresponding to the experimental conditions listed above. Each trial had a different conversation, also balanced for order across subjects and experimental condition. The conversations, which were fully automated using VAIF, dealt with food, movies, and vacations. For example, Fig. 5 presents the beginning of the conversation about movies.

Agent: I love watching movies in my free time. Have you seen any movies lately?
User: Yes, I think so, of course?
    Agent: That's awesome.
          (OR) No, I don't think so, no I don't, I doubt it, ...
    Agent: It's okay.
Agent: I was planning on having a movie night later today. But I do not know which movie to watch. Are there any movies you would recommend?
User: [*wildcard*]
Agent: I have heard that the new Spiderman movie is really good! Have you heard about it before?
User: Yes, I have, ...
    Agent: Oh cool!
          (OR) No, I have not, not really
    Agent: Oh ok.
Agent: I saw the first Spiderman movie in the Galaxy theatre. I love watching movies at the theatre because I get to eat popcorn and drink icees. Where do you like watching movies?

Fig. 5. Beginning of conversation about movies. The *wildcard* notation indicates that any utterance from the user is accepted.

Each participant's distance from the agent with whom they were conversing was continuously recorded at 60 frames/second by VAIF's proxemics tool [15], measured between the center of the agent's head and the center of the participant's head. We confirmed the accuracy of the proxemic tool's measurements by physically verifying that the reported distance matched the actual distance; the largest disparity was 2 cm in a one-meter distance. The agent was triggered to begin speaking one second after the participant came near the agent. The trigger-distance varied as a function of the condition: 2 m in the no-crowd condition, 1.5 m in the small-crowd condition, and 1 m in the large-crowd condition. However, in all cases, the participants stopped moving before the agent began to speak, which means that the trigger distances did not affect the study's results.

For analysis purposes, we measured both minimum distance, to enable comparison with the results in [10] and [16], and mean distance. In the case of mean distance, we calculated this for the each third of each participant's interactions, and for our results we look at the middle third. Figures 6, 7, and 8 show representative images of the participant's view in the no-crowd, small-crowd, and large-crowd conditions, respectively.

Fig. 6. Participant's view in the no-crowd condition

Fig. 7. Participant's view in the small-crowd condition

Fig. 8. Participant's view in the large-crowd condition

4   Results

This study examined two main issues: the correspondence of virtual to real-world proxemics for conversational interaction and the effects of having other agents nearby. Our results suggest that people interacting conversationally with agents in virtual worlds exhibit proxemics that are much closer than those for real-world interaction but that the presence of other agents nearby has little or no effect on people's conversational proxemics.

Our first hypothesis was that the mean distance between the participant and the ECA with which they are conversing, when only the ECA is present, would be the same as the mean distance between human conversants in a social context. The proxemics for dyadic conversations of speakers of American English, reported in [6] had a mean of 1.66 m and a standard error of 0.05. In contrast, the participants in our study produced proxemics values that were much closer, as indicated in Table 2. These values are roughly in line with those in the study report in [17], which involved non-conversational interaction. The values appear larger than those reported in [10], which we expect is due to two factors. First, as with the other previous studies, the interaction in [10] was non-conversational. Second, and probably more significant, the participants' tasks in [10] involved reading text—the agent's name and a number—from patches on the front and back, respectively of the agent. This meant that the participant, as a result of the task, would necessarily have to approach closely to the agent. This effect was likely enhanced by the agent's standing still, rather than interacting, even physically, with the participant. In short, conversational proxemics in virtual worlds appear to be closer than in the real world, but not as close as non-conversational proxemics in the virtual world.

Table 2. Mean average proxemics in meters, by experimental condition and time divisions.

Condition	No crowd	Small crowd	Large crowd
Mean (1st third)	0.810	0.817	0.827
Mean (2d third)	0.835	0.821	0.854
Mean (3d third)	0.814	0.847	0.847

Our second hypothesis was that the standard error of the distance between the participant and the ECA with which they are conversing, when only the ECA is present, would be the same as the standard error of the distance between human conversants in a social context. For the mean dyadic conversational proxemics reported in [3] of 1.66 m, the standard error was 0.05. In our study, for the minimum proxemics (following Bailenson et al., 2001), the mean was 0.713 m, and the standard error was 0.042. This suggests that the range of variation in proxemics among the participants in the virtual conversations in our study is roughly the same as the range of variation in proxemics in the physical face-to-face conversation in [6].

Our third hypothesis was that participants will stand closer to the ECA with which they are conversing when the number of nearby ECAs increases. We expected that both the presence of additional agents and these agents' modeling of proxemics would affect the participant's behavior. However, our results suggest that this hypothesis is not true, at least in the experimental conditions of this study. Looking at the case where the difference in proxemics should be most pronounced, no crowd vs. large crowd, the mean minimum proxemics are 0.713 (stdev 0.20) and 0.695 (stdev 0.23) m, respectively. This difference is not significant (two-tailed paired t-test: $p > 0.45$). Cohen's d was 0.08435, indicating that the effect size is between small and very small. It is unlikely that the lack of statistical significance was due to a small sample size; given these results, even for N = 400 the statistical power would be only 20%.

5 Conclusion

In this paper, we reviewed research related to proxemics in virtual reality. We observed that prior studies of human-agent proxemics did not involve conversational interaction. Accordingly, we designed and conducted a study to examine correspondence of virtual to real-world proxemics for conversational interaction and the effects of whether other agents are nearby. In the study, participants approached and conversed with a virtual agent in three conditions: no crowd, small crowd, and large crowd. Our results suggest that humans in a virtual world tend to position themselves closer to virtual agents than they would relative to humans in the physical world. However, the presence of other virtual agents did not appear to cause participants to change their proxemics.

This study is subject to a number of possible limitations, although it appears that a low N is not one of these, as discussed above. Rather, the first limitation is that the "crowd" agents may not have been sufficiently salient due to their distance from the conversing agent and, possibly, due to the structures in the environment. Second, there may be familiarization effects across the three trials that we did not detect. Consequently, we plan future work with (1) a set-up more faithfully resembling that in [14] so that the area has only external walls rather than interior structures and (2) "crowd" agents that are more numerous and closer to the conversing agent. Indeed, this point could inspire future work determining the circumstances (number of agents, proximity to the participant) in which crowd size and proxemics begin to affect the participant's own proxemics.

References

1. Novick, D., et al.: The Boston Massacre history experience. In: Proceedings of 19th ACM International Conference on Multimodal Interaction, 13–17 November 2017, Glasgow, Scotland, pp. 499–500 (2017)
2. Novick, D., Hinojos, L.J., Rodriguez, A.E., Camacho, A., Afravi, M.: Conversational interaction with multiple agents initiated via proxemics and gaze. In: 6th Annual International Conference on Human-Agent Interaction (HAI 2018), 15–18 December 2018, Southampton, UK (2018)
3. Novick, D., Adoneth, G., Manuel, D., Grís, I.: When the conversation starts: an empirical analysis. In: Joint Proceedings of the IVA 2012 Workshops. Otto von Guericke University Magdeburg, Santa Cruz, USA, pp. 67–74 (2012)
4. Hall, E.T., Birdwhistell, R.L., Bock, B., Bohannan, P., Diebold, A.R., Jr., et al.: Proxemics [and comments and replies]. Curr. Anthropol. 9(2/3), 83–108 (1968)

5. Kendon, A.: Spacing and orientation in co-present interaction. In: Esposito, A., Campbell, N., Vogel, C., Hussain, A., Nijholt, A. (eds.) Development of Multimodal Interfaces: Active Listening and Synchrony. LNCS, vol. 5967, pp. 1–15. Springer, Heidelberg (2010). https://doi.org/10.1007/978-3-642-12397-9_1

6. Herrera, D., Novick, D., Jan, D., Traum, D.: Dialog behaviors across culture and group size. In: Stephanidis, C. (ed.) UAHCI 2011. LNCS, vol. 6766, pp. 450–459. Springer, Heidelberg (2011). https://doi.org/10.1007/978-3-642-21663-3_48

7. Altmann, I., Vinsel, A.M., Altmann, J., Wohlwill, J.F.: Personal space, an analysis of ET Hall's proxemic framework. Hum. Behav. Environ., 181–259 (1977)

8. Jan, D., Herrera, D., Martinovski, B., Novick, D., Traum, D.: A computational model of culture-specific conversational behavior. In: Pelachaud, C., Martin, J.-C., André, E., Chollet, G., Karpouzis, K., Pelé, D. (eds.) IVA 2007. LNCS (LNAI), vol. 4722, pp. 45–56. Springer, Heidelberg (2007). https://doi.org/10.1007/978-3-540-74997-4_5

9. Ennis, C., O'Sullivan, C.: Perceptually plausible formations for virtual conversers. Comput. Anim. Virtual Worlds 23(3–4), 321–329 (2012)

10. Bailenson, J.N., Blascovich, J., Beall, A.C., Loomis, J.M.: Equilibrium theory revisited: mutual gaze and personal space in virtual environments. Presence: Teleoperators Virtual Environ. 10(6), 583–598 (2001)

11. Zibrek, K., Kokkinara, E., McDonnell, R.: Don't stand so close to me: investigating the effect of control on the appeal of virtual humans using immersion and a proximity-based behavioral task. In: Proceedings of the ACM Symposium on Applied Perception, pp. 1–11. ACM, New York (2017)

12. Peters, C., Li, C., Yang, F., Avramova, V., Skantze, G.: Investigating social distances between humans, virtual humans and virtual robots in mixed reality. In: Proceedings of the 17th International Conference on Autonomous Agents and MultiAgent Systems. International Foundation for Autonomous Agents and Multiagent Systems, pp. 2247–2249 (2018)

13. Gris, I., Novick, D.: Virtual agent interaction framework (VAIF): a tool for rapid development of social agents. In: Proceedings of the 17th International Conference on Autonomous Agents and MultiAgent Systems, pp. 2230–2232. Springer, Berlin (2018)

14. Cafaro, A., Ravenet, B., Ochs, M., Vilhjálmsson, H.H., Pelachaud, C.: The effects of interpersonal attitude of a group of agents on user's presence and proxemics behavior. ACM Trans. Interact. Intell. Syst. (TiiS) 6(2), 1–33 (2016)

15. Rodriguez, A.E., Camacho, A., Hinojos, L.J., Afravi, M., Novick, D.: A proxemics measurement tool integrated into VAIF and unity. In: 2019 International Conference on Multimodal Interaction, pp. 508–509. Springer, Berlin (2019)

16. Bailenson, J.N., Blascovich, J., Beall, A.C., Loomis, J.M.: Interpersonal distance in immersive virtual environments. Pers. Soc. Psychol. Bull. 29(7), 819–833 (2003)

17. Iachini, T., Coello, Y., Frassinetti, F., Ruggiero, G.: Body space in social interactions: a comparison of reaching and comfort distance in immersive virtual reality. PLoS ONE 9, 11 (2014)

Real-Time Data Analytics of COVID Pandemic Using Virtual Reality

Sharad Sharma$^{(\boxtimes)}$ (iD), Sri Teja Bodempudi, and Aishwarya Reehl

Department of Computer Science, Bowie State University, Bowie, MD, USA
{ssharma,sbodempudi}@bowiestate.edu,
reehla0924@students.bowiestate.edu

Abstract. Visualizing data effectively is critical for the discovery process in the age of big data. We are exploring the use of immersive virtual reality platforms for scientific data visualization for COVID-19 pandemic. We are interested in finding ways to better understand, perceive and interact with multidimensional data in the field of cognition technology and human-computer interaction. Immersive visualization leads to a better understanding and perception of relationships in the data. This paper presents a data visualization tool for immersive data visualizations based on the Unity development platform. The data visualization tool is capable of visualizing the real-time COVID pandemic data for the fifty states in the USA. Immersion provides a better understanding of the data than traditional desktop visualization tools and leads to more human-centric situational awareness insights. This research effort aims to identify how graphical objects like charts and bar graphs depicted in Virtual Reality tools, developed in accordance with an analyst's mental model can enhance an analyst's situation awareness. Our results also suggest that users feel more satisfied when using immersive virtual reality data visualization tools and thus demonstrate the potential of immersive data analytics.

Keywords: Virtual reality · Immersive VR · Data analytics · Data visualization

1 Introduction

Data visualization is an interdisciplinary field that deals with the graphic representation of data. It is an efficient way of communicating when the data is big as for example COVID-19 [1]. Data Visualization techniques are extremely effective in communicating graphical data around COVID-19 to major audiences like policymakers, scientists, healthcare providers, and the general public. Data visualization in an immersive environment can take the concept a step further by using techniques to immerse the user in the environment. The charts and graphs can be presented for detailed analysis and interactivity. Graphical representations of data are fundamental for the understanding of scientific knowledge [2]. Visualization always plays a key role in exploring data especially when the data sets are large. Decision making increasingly relies on data, which comes at us with an overwhelming velocity, and volume, that we cannot comprehend it without adding some layer of abstraction to it. Without visualization, detecting the inefficiencies hidden

© Springer Nature Switzerland AG 2021
J. Y. C. Chen and G. Fragomeni (Eds.): HCII 2021, LNCS 12770, pp. 106–116, 2021.
https://doi.org/10.1007/978-3-030-77599-5_9

in the data, patterns, and anomalies of that data would be impossible to find [3]. Data visualization fills this gap and gives the user the user flexibility to visualize and analyze the data in a better way.

An immersive environment is an artificial, interactive, computer created world to engage the user. It creates a perception of "being there" in a physical environment. This perception is created by encompassing the user of the VR system with images, sound or other visual effects to provide an engrossing environment. An immersive experience pulls a person into a new enhanced environment with more engagement. With an immersive environment, the end-user can respond to issues more rapidly and they can explore for more insights – perceive data differently, more imaginatively. It promotes creative data exploration. Data Visualization in an immersive environment allows for a more human-centric approach for visualizing data. The user can find new relationships and hidden patterns that one cannot find otherwise. The concept of using bar graphs and charts to understand data has been around for centuries, however data visualization in 2D vs 3D provides an immense impact on how the data is perceived. It helps in analyzing the data more accurately. COVID-19 cases have been on a rise and are increasing rapidly. We have developed an immersive environment for data visualization of COVID-19 data as shown in Fig. 1.

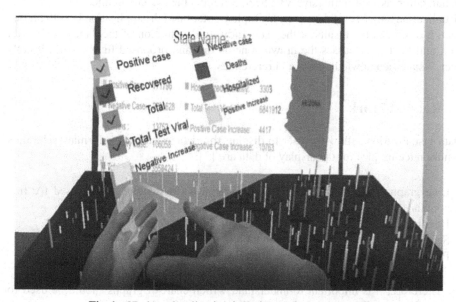

Fig. 1. 3D data visualization in an immersive environment

Our proposed data visualization tool focuses on immersive data visualization of the COVID-19 data on top of a geographical map, to give the user a better understanding of the pandemic data in the USA. We have tested the data visualization tool in an immersive and mobile environment for enhancement and decision-making process. The data visualization tool was developed using unity 3D gaming engine. As a result, the tools can be easily exported to an immersive environment using Oculus Rift S or a mobile environment using smartphones. Our proposed environment in Fig. 1 shows a table with a USA map showing the fifty states. On top of the map, 3D bar graphs are displayed for different variables related to the COVID-19 pandemic. The use of the Oculus controller provides a true hand-based input for virtual reality, which provides a way to interact with data on the map. The map displays nine different variables related to COVID data for each state such as

- Positive Cases
- Negative Cases
- Deaths
- Recovery Cases
- Total Cases
- Hospitalized Currently
- Total Tests Viral
- Positive Cases Increase
- Negative Case Increase

The rest of the paper is organized as follows: Sect. 2 discusses the related work in data visualization as well immersive VR; Sect. 3 details the system architecture of the data visualization tool; Sect. 4 describes the implementation of the application in both phases; Sect. 5 describes the results of the user study and evaluation of the data visualization tool, and Sect. 6 discusses the drawn conclusions and proposed future work. Finally, Sect. 7 states acknowledgments and references.

2   Related Work

Data visualizations allow the user to display the data in numerous formats. The most common techniques for the display of data are [4]:

- Line graph: This shows the relationship between items and can be used for time comparison.
- Bar chart: This is used to compare different quantities
- Scatter plot: This is a two-dimensional plot showing variations.
- Pie chart: This is used to compare the pieces to the whole data.

Therefore, it is important to understand which chart of graphs should be used for data exploration. Prior work in 3D visualizations in virtual reality environments shows the clear mapping between a mental model of the data that is expected to be reviewed, and the manner the data is depicted in the visualization [5]. Perl et al. [6] have documented analyst's mental models to guide the development of 3D visualizations. Data visualization is also important during evacuations for emergency response and decision making. Sharma et al. have conducted virtual evacuation drills in an immersive environment for an aircraft evacuation [7], a building evacuation [8], a subway evacuation [9], a university campus evacuation [10], and a virtual city [11]. Real-time data visualization for location-based navigation in multilevel spaces by generating ARI visualizations for evacuation have also been explored [12–14].

Livnat et al. [15] have discussed that situational awareness is the continuous extraction of environmental information, its integration with previous knowledge to form a coherent mental picture, and the use of that picture in anticipating future events. Situational awareness involves the continuous extraction of environmental information with its integration with previous knowledge to form a coherent mental picture [16]. Data visualization is an evolving field and its advancements in technology and healthcare systems are increasing at a rapid rate [17]. Bryson [18] has defined virtual reality as human-computer interface for creating interactive objects that provide a three-dimensional presence. On the other hand, data visualization researchers have suggested that virtual reality's three-dimensional presence adds value for analyzing scientific data, and will enable more natural and quicker exploration of large data sets [19]. Our proposed work is based on a VR visualization by Brunhart-Lupo et al. [20]

3 System Architecture

Data collecting techniques have improved a lot in the past decade. With the data collection techniques, a large amount of data has been collected. To analyze and understand this data, the old techniques are insufficient because sometimes human intervention is needed to find the new relationships and patterns. One needs a new way of analyzing and visualizing the data. In this paper, we present an immersive 3D data visualization tool to visualize COVID data. We have implemented this tool for Oculus, which gives an immersive feeling to the users.

With the advent of COVID 19, there is a lot of data accumulated in the databases. To visualize this kind of data in 2D with so many variables is a challenging task. Also, understanding that representation requires a certain level of knowledge on the 2D charts. In our proposed data visualization tool, the data is represented as 3D bar charts.

Figure 2 describes the system architecture of our proposed 3D data visualization tool. We have also used the COVID-19 tracking API to get the real-time COVID-19 data. Our proposed data visualization tool extracts COVID-19 data from the real-time API for analyzing the data which can be helpful in predictive analysis. This data is pulled from the database with the help of API calls. When the 3D data visualization application is launched the API call extracts the updated data automatically. For getting the live data updates, we are using an open source Database (DB). This is being updated from time to time with different variables. We are getting our data from this Database by sending API calls from time to time. For the data visualization tool, we focus on nine different factors or variables (i.e. Positive Cases, Negative Cases, Deaths, Recovery Cases, Total Cases, Hospitalized Currently, Total Tests Viral, Positive Cases Increase, Negative Case Increase). To display all these nine variables for individual states, we chose bar graphs as the data visualization medium. The bar graphs are displayed on top of the USA map where each state contains nine bar graphs with different colors. The color coding is maintained consistently for all states so that color code can be used to identify each variable.

A control panel is implemented to provide control to the user for toggling on/off the nine variables on the map. This is implemented with aid of checkboxes. The check boxes

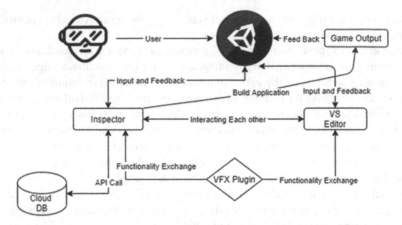

Fig. 2. System architecture diagram for CVE using photon networking asset tool in Unity 3D.

for every nine variables are used to enable and disable the bars on the graph. This allows the user to compare a particular variable such as Positive COVID Cases across all fifty states by just looking at bar graphs. To get the exact numbers, a screen is arranged on the wall in the virtual environment. The screen is configured to display all nine variables for each state, that is selected by the user. If the user selects any state by clicking on that state on the map, the information related to that particular state is populated on the screen. With the help of C# script, the API call is made. This call happens when the application is launched to get updated data. Through this API call, Visual Studio loads with raw data. Based on the filter conditions the data is extracted for all fifty states. This extracted data helps to populate the bar graphs on the map. Based on the user selection the data visualization tool will control the rendering of data on the wall-mounted screen. The visual effects have been implemented for achieving special animations through the use of custom Visual Studio code attached to the objects in the environment.

4   3D Data Visualization Tool

This paper presents the 3D data visualization tool for representing nine COVID variables on the USA map. In this paper, we are introducing a new way of visualizing the COVID data with help of oculus HMD and controllers. It allows a more human-centric approach in analyzing the data in 3D space. Our proposed work shows that virtual reality can be used as a data visualization platform. The oculus integration allows human-centric situational awareness and visualization that is needed for analyzing big data.

The 3D Data Visualization tool is developed for both mobile and Oculus devices using the Unity3D gaming engine. Initially, all asserts like USA map, Hands, Texture, etc. are loaded in Unity 3D. A reasonable scene is created after placing all objects in the environment. The environment includes a room with a table in the center to represent the USA map. Objects such as tables, desks, boards, chairs, and computers are added to create realism. The map helps the user to differentiate and visualize neighboring state data. To display the different factors of the COVID data, we have chosen to display the bar graphs on the map. All these bar graphs are integrated with C# code. This code is responsible to maintain the height of the bar based on the values received for that variable. Figure 3 and Fig. 4 show the 3D Data visualization tool in a non-immersive environment and mobile environment respectively.

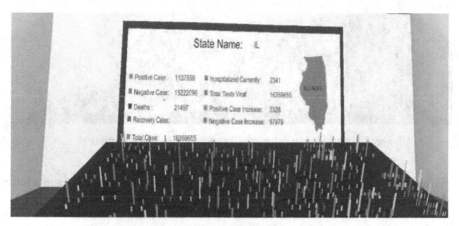

Fig. 3. 3D data visualization in non-immersive environment

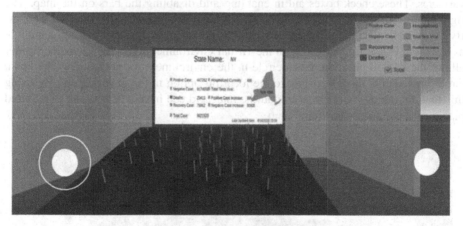

Fig. 4. 3D data visualization in a mobile environment

For each state on the USA map, interactive nonvisible buttons are implemented. This allows the user to select a particular state on the map by clicking on the map. For interaction in the immersive environment, two hands are implemented. These two hands are the two Oculus controllers visible as left and right hands, as shown in Fig. 5.

One of the buttons on the left-hand controllers triggers a canvas. This canvas is capable of displaying all nine-variable data for the selected state along with the last updated date. A C# script written to extract the data from the cloud database through an API call.

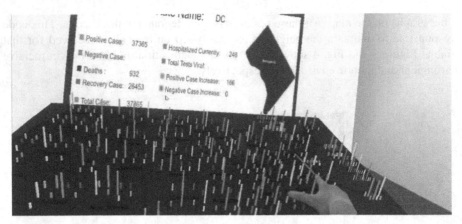

Fig. 5. Interacting with the map through Oculus touch controllers.

After mapping all the variables with proper oculus controller scripts the application is deployed into the Oculus Rift S. When the application is launched, the user is able to see two hands. The two oculus controllers are represented in the environment as the user's hands. In the left hand, the menu panel appears, as shown in Fig. 1 earlier. This panel contains nine check boxes for selecting and deselecting the nine COVID -19 variables. These check boxes aid in enabling and disabling the bars on the map. The right hand controller also triggers a laser beam that helps in selecting the check boxes. By deselecting all boxes, all the bars on the map disappear. The user has a green circle as shown in Fig. 6 for navigating in the virtual environment. The right hand controller allows the user to place the green circle in the environment for navigation. The green circle implements the teleporting to the location option in the environment. By using this feature, the user can move around the map and can have a better look at required places on the map, as shown in Fig. 6.

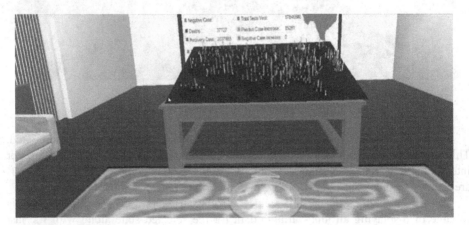

Fig. 6. Navigation in the immersive environment through oculus touch controllers

The 3D visualization tool is also implemented for the mobile devices to reach out to the audience who are not having access to the Oculus Rift S. Unity allows the application to be deployed to an android device, by changing interactive controllers to touch controllers. Instead of hands, two-controller joysticks are implemented for the mobile application as shown in Fig. 4. Using these two controllers, the user can navigate in the environment. When the user touches any state on the map, the information regarding that state is displayed on the wall screen. After these changes were implemented, the APK (Android Package) file was generated. The APK file can be used by anyone to install the 3d Visualization application on their mobile device. For better results we suggest using the immersive environment. In the immersive environment, the user will see a bigger model, so that it will be easy to read the data. Whereas in mobile devices, the screen size is limited and it becomes difficult to observe the data. For testing the Samsung S9 device was used. The specifications of the device include OS: Android 9.0, CPU: Octa-Core, GPU: Mali-G7, RAM: 4 GB [21].

5 Simulation and Results

A limited user study was conducted for evaluating the effectiveness of the 3D visualization tool. The study involved 10 participants and evaluated the two versions of the 3D visualization application namely the mobile version, and the Oculus (immersive) version. The user study was composed of 80% male participants and 20% female participants. The results were collected from the user study, with the help of a questioner. Initially, the participants were shown how to use the 3D visualization application for the phone and oculus. Then, each participant was allowed to use each device independently to visualize the COVID data for different states. Then, they were given a satisfaction questionnaire about their overall experience.

The above chart is the summary of the test results. By observing these results shown in Fig. 7, one can say more participants were able to understand the data in oculus as compared to mobile devices. People were more comfortable using the oculus and were able to interact in the virtual environment better than in the mobile environment. The majority (60%) of the users felt that the oculus was more suitable for visualization than the mobile phone version of the application.

The implementation of User Interaction (UI) is the main difference between the Oculus version and the Mobile version of the data visualization tool. In Oculus version, the user has the menu option attached to the left-hand controller. The right-hand controller triggers the laser beam for selecting and clicking the checkboxes. The menu attached to the left hand is responsible for enabling and disabling the bars on the graph as shown in Fig. 7(a). Whereas in the mobile version, all these options are replaced with touch interaction. On the right top corner of the screen the menu is arranged, which is responsible for enabling and disabling the bars on the graph, as shown in Fig. 7(b). All interactions in the mobile version happen through touch interaction, whereas in the Oculus version, the user can interact using two oculus controllers (Fig. 8).

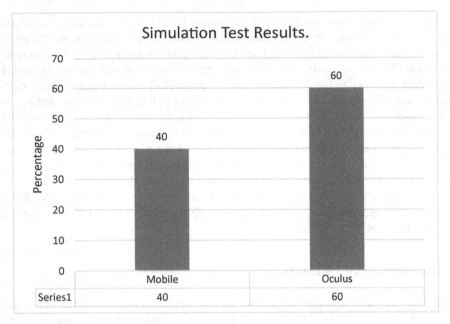

Fig. 7. Device suitability and effectiveness.

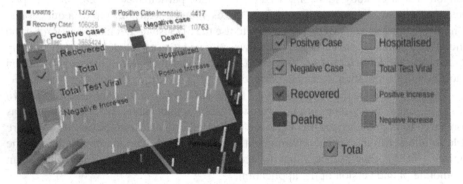

Fig. 8. Oculus and mobile version UI interaction

6 Conclusions

In conclusion, this paper presents a data visualization tool for 3D data visualization developed using Unity gaming engine for an immersive and mobile environment. The data visualization tool can visualize the COVID-19 pandemic data for the fifty states in the USA. This data is pulled from the database in real-time with the help of API calls. Immersion provides a better understanding of the data and leads to more human-centric situational awareness insights. Oculus controllers were used to creating a hand input to help the user immerse in the environment and provide more user engagement through the use of a laser pointer. We believe the data visualization tool enables the user to make human-centric insights by engaging with data in an immersive environment.

Our findings so far should be interpreted with appropriate consideration of the small sample size in our initial limited study. We aim to expand our investigation in our ongoing work, evaluating the visualizations with more participants and incorporating a more detailed analysis of insights. We also plan to enable user interaction and improve usability. We are also interested in adapting our VR visualization tools to enable multi-user data exploration capability and to explore the impact of VR on collaborative analytics tasks.

Acknowledgments. This work is funded in part by the NSF award #1923986, NSF Award number 2032344, and NSF Award Number: 2026412.

References

1. Grainger, S., Mao, F., Buytaert, W.: Environmental data visualization for non-scientific contexts: literature review and design framework. Environ. Model Softw. **85**, 299–318 (2016)
2. Kumar, O., Goyal, A.: Visualization: a novel approach for big data analytics. In: Proceedings of the Second International Conference on Computational Intelligence & Communication Technology, pp. 121–124 (2016)
3. Brigham, T.J.: Feast for the eyes: an introduction to data visualization. Med. Ref. Serv. Quart. **35**(2), 215–223 (2016)
4. Wolfe, J.: Teaching students to focus on the data in data visualization. J. Bus. Techn. Commun. **29**(3), 344–359 (2015)
5. Ehrenstein, W.H., Spillmann, L. Sarris, V.: Gestalt, "Issues in modern neuroscience", Axiomathes **13**, 433–458 (2003)
6. Perl, S.J., Young, R.O.: A cognitive study of incident handling expertise. In: 27th Annual FIRST Conference, Berlin (2015)
7. Sharma, S., Otunba, S.: Collaborative virtual environment to study aircraft evacuation for training and education. In: Proceedings of IEEE, International Workshop on Collaboration in Virtual Environments (CoVE - 2012), as Part of The International Conference on Collaboration Technologies and Systems (CTS 2012), Denver, Colorado, USA, pp. 569–574, 21–25 May (2012)
8. Sharma, S., Vadali, H.: Simulation and modeling of a virtual library for navigation and evacuation. In: MSV 2008 - The International Conference on Modeling, Simulation and Visualization Methods, Monte Carlo Resort, Las Vegas, Nevada, USA, 14–17 July (2008)
9. Sharma, S., Jerripothula, S., Mackey, S., Soumare, O.: Immersive virtual reality environment of a subway evacuation on a cloud for disaster preparedness and response training. In: Proceedings of IEEE Symposium Series on Computational Intelligence (IEEE SSCI), Orlando, Florida, USA, 9–12 December, pp. 1–6 (2014). https://doi.org/10.1109/cihli.2014.7013380
10. Sharma, S., Jerripothula, P., Devreaux, P.: An immersive collaborative virtual environment of a university campus for performing virtual campus evacuation drills and tours for campus safety. In: Proceedings of IEEE International Conference on Collaboration Technologies and Systems (CTS), Atlanta, Georgia, USA, pp. 84–89, 01–05 June (2015). https://doi.org/10.1109/cts.2015.7210404
11. Sharma, S.: A collaborative virtual environment for safe driving in a virtual city by obeying traffic laws. J. Traff. Logist. Eng. JTLE **5**(2), 84–91 (2017). https://doi.org/10.18178/jtle.5.2.84-91. (ISSN: 2301-3680)

12. Sharma, S., Stigall, S.J., Bodempudi, S.T.: Situational awareness-based Augmented Reality Instructional (ARI) module for building evacuation. In: Proceedings of the 27th IEEE Conference on Virtual Reality and 3D User Interfaces, Training XR Workshop, Atlanta, GA, USA, pp. 70–78, 22–26 March (2020)
13. Stigall, J., Sharma, S.: Evaluation of mobile augmented reality application for building evacuation. In: Proceedings of ISCA 28th International Conference on Software Engineering and Data Engineering in San Diego, CA, USA, vol 64, pp. 109–118 (2019)
14. Stigall, J., Sharma, S.: Mobile augmented reality application for building evacuation using intelligent signs. In: Proceedings of ISCA 26th International Conference on Software Engineering and Data Engineering (SEDE-2017), 2–4 October, pp. 19–24, San Diego (2017)
15. Livnat, Y., Agutter, J., Moon, S., Foresti, S.: Visual correlation for situational awareness. In: IEEE Symposium on Information Visualization, INFOVIS 2005, Minneapolis, MN, pp. 95–102 (2005). https://doi.org/10.1109/infvis.2005.1532134
16. Endsley, M.R.: Toward a theory of situation awareness in dynamic systems. Hum. Fact. J. **37**(1), 32–64 (1995)
17. Goceri, E.: Future healthcare: will digital data lead to better care? In: New Trends and Issues Proceedings on Advances in Pure and Applied Sciences (2017). https://doi.org/10.18844/gja pas.v0i8.2781. https://sproc.org/ojs/index.php/paas/article/view/2781
18. Bryson, S.: Virtual reality in scientific visualization. Commun. ACM **39**(5), 62–71 (1996)
19. Van Dam, A., Forsberg, A.S., Laidlaw, D.H., LaViola, J.J., Simpson, R.M.: Immersive VR for scientific visualization: a progress report. IEEE Comput. Graph. Appl. **20**(6), 26–52 (2000)
20. Brunhart-Lupo, N., Bush, B.W., Gruchalla, K., Smith, S.: Simulation exploration through immersive parallel planes. In: 2016 Workshop on Immersive Analytics (IA), pp. 19–24. IEEE (2016)
21. Samsung: https://www.samsung.com/uk/smartphones/galaxy-s9/specs/. Accessed Feb 2021

Design Considerations for Interacting and Navigating with 2 Dimensional and 3 Dimensional Medical Images in Virtual, Augmented and Mixed Reality Medical Applications

Jennifer N. Avari Silva[1,2,3](✉) [iD], Michael K. Southworth[3] [iD],
Christopher M. Andrews[3] [iD], Mary Beth Privitera[4] [iD], Alexander B. Henry[3] [iD],
and Jonathan R. Silva[2,3] [iD]

[1] Department of Pediatrics, Cardiology, Washington University in St Louis, School of Medicine, St Louis, MO, USA
jennifersilva@wustl.edu
[2] Department of Biomedical Engineering, Washington University in St Louis, McKelvey School of Engineering, St Louis, MO, USA
[3] SentiAR, Inc, St Louis, MO, USA
[4] HS Design, Gladstone, NJ, USA

Abstract. The extended realities, including virtual, augmented, and mixed realities (VAMR) have recently experienced significant hardware improvement resulting in an expansion in medical applications. These applications can be classified by the target end user (for instance, classifying applications as patient-centric, physician-centric, or both) or by use case (for instance educational, diagnostic tools, therapeutic tools, or some combination). When developing medical applications in VAMR, careful consideration of both the target end user and use case must heavily influence design considerations, particularly methods and tools for interaction and navigation. Medical imaging consists of both 2-dimensional and 3-dimensional medical imaging which impacts design, interaction, and navigation. Additionally, medical applications need to comply with regulatory considerations which will also influence interaction and design considerations. In this manuscript, the authors explore these considerations using three VAMR tools being developed for cardiac electrophysiology procedures.

Keywords: Extended reality · Mixed reality · Medical applications · Cardiac electrophysiology · Ultrasound · Medical device

1 Introduction

Rigorous standards have been developed for the design and evaluation of software on medical devices for clinical viability on increasingly complex hardware form factors and user input modalities, but have largely relied on fixed 2-dimensional (2D) displays or 3-dimensional (3D) workstations. When the performance of a medical device is combined

J. Y. C. Chen and G. Fragomeni (Eds.): HCII 2021, LNCS 12770, pp. 117–133, 2021.
https://doi.org/10.1007/978-3-030-77599-5_10

with the capabilities virtual, augmented and mixed reality (VAMR) platforms, the complexity in evaluation is dramatically increased, because novel assessment of the medical device is required in the context of novel VAMR hardware. Despite these challenges, there has been an increase in the number and complexity of medical devices that utilize the promise of VAMR technology to meet the needs of the user. Each user group has specific context, experience, and requirements of VAMR integrated medical devices. Classification by target end user, use case and use environment are critical for designing optimal navigation and interaction tools for VAMR medical applications.

Medical imaging can be generalized into 2D data, such as x-rays, patient vitals, and ultrasonography, or 3D data, such as CT scans and MRIs, which require different image interpretation modalities. Both types of medical imaging have roles in clinical practice. Successful integration of both 2D and 3D medical data in VAMR has the potential to enhance the ability to interpret and navigate these data in medical applications. Designing medical applications with meaningful interaction and navigation tools for 2D and 3D medical platforms have unique considerations.

To date, the authors have developed a mixed reality (MxR) solution to empower physicians who perform minimally invasive cardiac procedures. The Enhanced ELectrophysiology Visualization and Interaction System (ELVIS, now being marketed as the CommandEP™ System) has been developed to address the unmet needs in the cardiac electrophysiology (EP) laboratory, by displaying interactive images of the patient-specific cardiac anatomy along with real-time catheter locations in 3D [1–3]. These 3D data allow the physician to visualize the intracardiac geometry and electrical propagation across it with respect to therapeutic catheters that are used to treat cardiac arrhythmia [4]. Additionally, the authors are developing a MxR based ultrasound tool which displays the ultrasound image sector in 2D at it's true 3D location in space (from the tip of the ultrasound probe) and has the additional functionality of medical tool tip tracking to deploy this tool in interventional ultrasound procedures, such as vascular access. Lastly, the authors are developing a MxR tool to make measurements on medical images to assist in medical decision making—the initial use case for these measurements is in the cardiac EP laboratory, where measurements are made to determine the site of abnormal electrical activation to target for ablation.

In this manuscript, we will explore various interaction and navigation tools for medical VAMR applications using the 3 applications mentioned above, with a focus on the varying considerations between 2D and 3D medical imaging.

2 Overview of the Extended Realities

The extended realities currently include virtual, augmented, and mixed realities with the acknowledgement that future developments may further extend or subdivide this continuum. Fully immersive Virtual reality (VR) has important applications in both physician-centric and patient-centric applications spanning education, training, rehabilitation, and therapy. The primary tradeoff of VR hinges on the completely immersive experience, which allows complete control of the user experience of the environment, while simultaneously isolating or mediating the user's current, natural environment. For those use cases and environmental conditions that require meaningful interactions with the natural environment, VR may be prohibitive, but augmented and mixed reality technologies may be well suited [1, 4]. Augmented reality (AR) allows for the user to maintain their view of the natural environment and simply post, or augment, digital images into their environment. Mixed reality (MxR) blends digital augmentation with the natural environment by allowing the user to have meaningful interactions with those digital images, for instance, placing, rotating, zooming, or clipping, in their natural surroundings. A new generation of head mounted displays (HMDs) merged, or pass-through the surroundings into an extended reality, blending virtual and mixed reality in a fully occlusive display. To date, most clinical applications have targeted AR and MxR HMDs to maintain a minimally obstructed view through the HMD into the natural environment, providing the benefits of the platform while allowing the user to create eye contact and maintain peripheral vision in the natural environment. As hardware technologies advance, the distinctions and compromises between the extended realities will continue to diminish, expanding their respective applications for appropriate use cases.

The types of interactions that the end user requires with 2D medical data are distinct from what is required for 3D data. Medical professionals working with 3D medical data require more flexible 3D navigational tools with the ability to move, rotate, zoom, and slice into the data, where this functionality is not strictly required for the 2D counterparts. However, maintaining and expanding capabilities in 2D remain critical, such as the ability to measure and the ability to understand how 3D objects relate to and interact with a 2D image.

3   Developing and Developed Medical Applications in VAMR

Fig. 1. The **Electrophysiology Laboratory** at St. Louis Children's Hospital. 4 systems are required (from left to right): fluoroscopy, electrograms, electroanatomic mapping, and vital signs.

To date, the authors have been developing 3 unique medical applications in VAMR to assist physicians who perform cardiac electrophysiology (EP) procedures [2]. These minimally invasive procedures are performed in patients with heart rhythm abnormalities using flexible catheters that are carefully threaded through larger vessels in the body, leading to the heart. The catheters are electromagnetically tracked and the positions they visit during spatial sweeps are used to create volumes that represent the endocardial surfaces of the heart in electroanatomic mapping systems (EAMS). After these geometries are created, the electrical data that is collected by the tip of the probe is overlayed on the geometry, creating an electroanatomic map. Using these maps, coupled with the direct electrical data signals from the distal tips of the catheters, the physician determines the location of the abnormal electrical activity and then targets it for ablation. These decisions require an understanding of both the cardiac anatomy and electrical system. Currently, these procedures are completed using several distinct systems (see Fig. 1) and require the user to selectively process the data from each system at the appropriate time.

These solutions are intended for use by cardiac electrophysiologists (end users) performing electroanatomic mapping procedures (use cases) in the cardiac electrophysiology laboratory (use environment), with some tools under active development and others having received FDA-clearance. Here we will describe each of the proposed uses, and how the user needs, and environmental factors impact the design.

3.1 Command EP System

The CommandEP™ system creates digital, real-time patient-specific 3D cardiac geometries during minimally invasive cardiac electrophysiology procedures. The system collects data obtained from commercially available EAMS and displays a real-time 3D patient-specific geometry of the heart (or chamber of the heart) with real-time catheter locations (see Fig. 2) [5].

In this system, physicians have a gaze-dwell, hands-free, sterile interaction method with the 3D object (see Sect. 4. Interaction). Currently, visualization of catheter position within the heart is accomplished with 2D screens that present biplane fluoroscopy or electroanatomic mapping to the interventionalist via orthogonal projections (see Fig. 1). The skill to mentally relate these images to the 3D cardiac anatomy remains a key challenge impacting patient

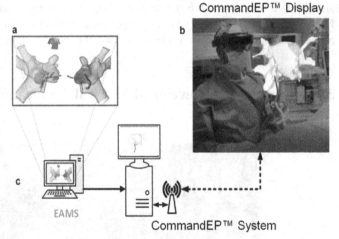

CommandEP™ Display

CommandEP™ System

Fig. 2. CommandEP™ **System.** Data from commercially electroanatomic mapping systems can be wirelessly transmitted to the SentiAR Engine, which is loaded onto the Microsoft HoloLens HMD, and then display the electroanatomic maps with real-time catheter location in 3D.

outcomes, training of future cardiac electrophysiologists and intra-procedural collaboration. This visualization is particularly relevant for anatomic ablations, where the target is predetermined based on patient's anatomy.

Traditionally, manipulation of images requires relaying commands from the proceduralist to a nurse or technician, stationed at the EAMS workstation. If the proceduralist and proxy do not have a strong working background, communication may break down, requiring the proceduralist to instruct the proxy more directly from the computer console or break sterility to control the display themselves [3, 6].

3.2 Mixed Reality-Ultrasound (SentUS) System

At the start of each EP procedure, the electrophysiologist must obtain vascular access and leave a sheath in the vessel. The sheath is similar to a large bore intravenous access site with a hemostatic valve to prevent bleeding and allows the physicians to place catheters through the sheath directly into the vessel. The addition of ultrasound to guide vascular access has improved the efficiency and reduced the mechanical and infectious complications of vascular access [7, 8] However, the practical implementation of using ultrasound to guide vascular access is challenging. To start, this is a bimanual technique with the operator usually holding the probe in one hand (usually the nondominant hand) and the syringe/needle apparatus in the other hand (usually the dominant hand) allowing for fine manipulation for advancing the needle, hold-

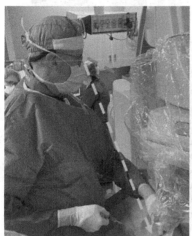

Fig. 3. Obtaining **Vascular Access using Ultrasound in the Electrophysiology Laboratory**. The operator is obtaining access in the right internal jugular vein using ultrasound. In the left panel, the operator is looking at the ultrasound screen (red arrow) while holding the ultrasound probe and needle/syringe apparatus with his hands to understand where the vessel is and where to puncture the skin. In the right panel, the operator is now looking at his hands (green arrow) rather than at the ultrasound screen (red arrow) while manipulating the needle to enter the vessel. (Color figure online)

ing back-pressure on the syringe plunger, and adjusting the angle of entry to the body. Simultaneously, the operator is looking at the ultrasound screen, often placing the target vessel in the center of the screen (see Fig. 3).

Given the location constraints of where access is being obtained, the user frequently must look away from their hands to see the ultrasound machine resulting in the divergence between where they are looking and how they are moving their hands. This multisystem eye-hand-hand coordination can be very difficult to learn, particularly since it has been well described that the eyes play a pivotal role in the guiding of hand movements during actions that require eye-hand coordination [9, 10]. Additionally, ultrasound images do not often visualize the needle itself and therefore requires environmental cues to inform the physician of how close or far the needle tip is to the target structure.

We have created a mixed reality ultrasound system that addresses these issues (see Fig. 4). Using a mixed reality headset, this system has the advantage of placing a "billboard" image of the ultrasound image in the user's field of view in such a way that they can perform this bimanual task and be oriented to be facing their hands. Compared to a conventional ultrasound device

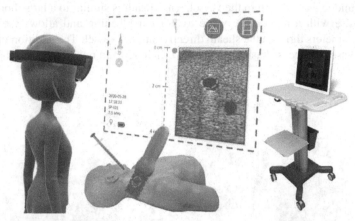

Fig. 4. Schematic **of SentUS Prototype**. Using this system, the user wears a HoloLens 2 head mounted display and is able to visualize the ultrasound data from the tip of the ultrasound probe to see the image in true 3D space, as well as a "billboard" display for the user to see the same data in a larger, ergonomically friendly space. Additionally, there is the ability to assess the position and location of the needle within the ultrasound sector (see Sect. 6. Early Lessons).

screen, the holographic display allows the user to position the display without being restricted by physical space constraints, resize the display to any desired size, and have the display orientation automatically adjust to the user's position throughout the procedure. In addition, the device features a second visualization of the ultrasound image directly projected from the tip of the ultrasound probe over the body, as though providing a cross-sectional X-ray view into the body. Integrated into the mixed reality display is a needle tracking system to allow the user to intuitively understand the trajectory of the needle relative to the target. This allows users to understand the relationship of the needle to the intended target and assess if the needle tip is close to the plane of the target, has gone past the plane, or is approaching the target.

In this system, the presented ultrasound images are 2D images and offer no 3D imaging to the user. However, the needle tracking module provides an inference of 3D data by graphically displaying the anticipated trajectory of the needle.

3.3 Mixed Reality-Electrogram (SentEGM) System

During minimally invasive procedures, physicians obtain data and make measurements on those data to make decisions that are critical to the success of the intervention. During electrophysiology (EP) procedures, the gold standard for identification of tissue for ablation is through live electrogram (EGM) data. Performance

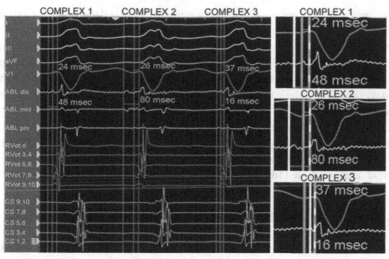

Fig. 5. EGMs from a recent ventricular tachycardia ablation. Caliper measurements are demonstrated for complex 1, 2 and 3 and zoomed in to the right comparing an expert EP (yellow) to a technician (blue) with overlapping lines marked as the yellow-blue dotted line. In complexes 1 and 2, the expert reading (yellow) is markedly longer as it includes the early, low amplitude signals on the white ablation-distal signal. In complex 3, the expert reader notes that the early portion of the signal is noise, rather than abnormal activity and excludes it from the measurement resulting in a shorter measurement than the technician. Radiofrequency lesions placed at the catheter location of complex 3 were not successful due to the misreading of the signals. However, lesions placed at the catheter location of complex 2, identified by re-reading by the expert were successful, resulting in arrhythmia termination. (Color figure online)

of measurements during these interventional procedures is currently hampered by technologies available in these laboratories with current workflows requiring either a second operator or technician to make these crucial measurements or the operating physician to break the sterile field to make measurements themselves, introducing inefficiencies and potential errors at a critical decision point during the procedure (see Fig. 5). Currently, the authors are developing the SentEGM system that will enable operating physicians to take real-time measurements in the operating room while maintaining the sterile field via a gaze-based mixed reality interface (see Fig. 6). This display will combine 3 screens into a single integrated, physician-controlled system, improving efficiency, reducing errors, and easing personnel requirements. Allowing performing physicians to make their own measurements with a hands-free interface has the potential to positively impact patient outcomes in multiple interventional specialties.

Fig. 6. SentEGM **System.** In this prototype of the SentEGM system, the user wears a Microsoft HoloLens HMD and is able to see the electrogram data alongside the CommandEP map data.

However, hands-free measurement and navigation of this data is highly challenging, as these fine types of hands-free, MxR human-computer interaction are nascent. In the CommandEP™ system, we designed a gaze-based interface on the Microsoft HoloLens 1 head mounted display (HMD) that allowed physicians to manipulate a patient-specific cardiac hologram. Physicians could rotate, zoom, and alter the opacity to best understand how to navigate. This gaze-based interface was successfully deployed to perform these big, coarser movements. The SentEGM system will hinge on the fine granularity for measurements, where changes in milliseconds and millimeters can cause significant changes in clinical outcome. Additionally, the development of "smart calipers" will supply a first measurement which can then be micro-adjusted using the gaze-based display and then confirmed likely using multiple navigation tools as described above.

4 Interacting in VAMR

Interactions in VAMR are the methods by which users select and control their virtual environment. Methods of interaction include gesture, gaze, voice, and eye tracking, though these discrete methods may be combined for more complex interactions. As these methods are being increasingly used and tested, optimal interactions will likely result in a method of selection followed by an alternate and secondary method for confirmation. Selecting the optimal method(s) of interaction requires a clear understanding of the end user, use case, use environment, and existing uses of the input mechanism that may drive interactional modalities. Often, clearly defining the end user and use case will make preferred methods apparent. Conversely, certain user needs and use cases may render some interaction methods unusable. For instance, a VAMR tool which is used by physicians to plan procedures may use an intuitive gesture dominant method, allowing for the end users to make both large movements and micro-movements to chart the preferred path during the procedure. This method often requires less training and is easily discoverable for the user. Tools which are used during sterile procedures and operations, however, must rely on methods that allow the physician to have their hands free to perform the procedure, and use gaze, voice or eye tracking (see Table 1). Training simulations using VAMR will also try to need to align with simulation environment as well as the intended use environment.

Table 1. Interaction modes and use cases in medical applications.

	Gesture	Gaze	Voice	Eye tracking
Patient-facing applications (including therapy and rehabilitation)	X			
Medical education	X	X		
Pre-procedural planning	X	X		
Intra-procedural use		X	X	X

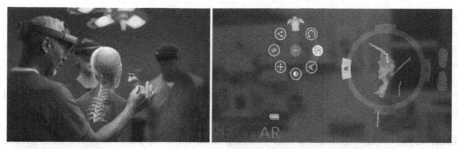

Fig. 7. Interaction **paradigms** in mixed reality (MxR) applications. Gesture interfaces (left) can enable users to grab holograms to reposition, resize, and rotate them. Because users primarily operate gesture interfaces using their hands, they are intuitive and natural to use but can be difficult to operate during clinical interventions when users may need to manipulate surgical tools. Gaze interfaces such as the CommandEP interface (right) can enable hands-free interaction during sterile interventions. Left image depicts the Microsoft HoloLens 2. Used with permission from Microsoft. Original Source: https://news.microsoft.com/hololens2_healthcare2/.

Early in development, creators of medical applications must understand the intended environmental conditions and how this can positively or negatively influence modes of interaction. For instance, developing interaction experiences in VAMR in outpatient, clinic-based, non-sterile environments allows for more flexibility and variation in interaction modes to maximize the user experience. Ambient noise levels tend to be fairly low and use of medical jargon is more limited. In contrast, interactions in VAMR in sterile, procedural environments, such as the operating room, will have stringent user requirements and increased risk levels, resulting in more constrained interaction methods—in these use environments, interactions must consider maintenance of the "sterile field" which directly affects patient safety. Additionally, in these procedural environments there is often frequent use of medical jargon, higher ambient noise levels and tonal normal function sounds and alarms generated by various equipment. Reliability of interaction methods should also be considered when developing VAMR medical applications. In higher-risk environments, inadvertent triggering of features may be distracting to the physician and in the high-risk scenarios can possibly negatively affect a patient outcome. For this reason, reconfirmation of activation may be more widely used in future development.

4.1   Methods of Interaction in VAMR

Gesture. The use of hand motions, or gestures, to interact in VAMR to activate (or select) is an important and intuitive interaction method due to the familiarity of users with hand-based interaction (Fig. 7). The use of hands allows the user to immediately feel comfortable using the system and provides a sense of intuitiveness to the system. However, given the current hardware options available, the types of gestures are still limited in accuracy and reliability, vary by platform and implementation, and ultimately require some degree of training to use effectively. These methods of interaction can be quite useful for pre-procedural planning, or for patient-facing use cases (particularly rehabilitation) as they require larger, more deliberate movements for activation. Optimal use environments for this type of interaction will have open spaces where the end user can move their arms and hands without disturbing other equipment. Other systems use hand-held controllers to support more accurate or reliable hand-based input interactions and can replace or reduce the magnitude of arm movement. The use intra-procedural use cases that we have targeted do not lend themselves well to gesture control as physicians are often using their hands to perform the procedure and are working in a constrained sterile environment.

Gaze. Gaze control allows the user to make head movements to navigate through the digital images in the extended reality. Conceptually, gaze may be considered analogous to operating a pointer such as a mouse cursor in a 2D interface, but considerations must be made to match design with intuitive gaze-based actions. Further, design considerations that inform mouse-driven interfaces can be applied to gaze interfaces as well. In general, gaze controls become easier to activate when the size of the controls is increased and the angular distance the gaze cursor must travel to the controls is decreased. This balance between distance to and size of the target, which is described by Fitts's law [11], must be considered against making software interfaces overly dense or cluttered. Cluttering is critical in MxR interfaces since crowded interfaces can obstruct the users' ability to interact with their physical surroundings and can increase incidence of inadvertent activation. When using gaze, a secondary method is required for activation or selection of an item, akin to a mouse click. In the case of the CommandEP™ system, we implemented a gaze-dwell system, allowing the user to hover over a menu item to select/activate it. Dwell times ranged from short to long dwell times (in the range of 300–1000 ms) depending on the kind of activation. During human factors testing, physician end users commented that they preferred shorter dwell times and interface adjustments were made accordingly, due to the new mapping of head direction to cursor input. Other potential secondary methods that can be used with gaze, such as voice or eye-based confirmation may be important adjunctive methods to confirm navigational commands.

Voice Control. Although voice is an intuitive command and input modality, the technical and design challenges of voice control are not limited to VAMR. Although navigating through the extended realities using voice can be done but should often be implemented alongside other navigation tools in medical applications. Proper understanding of the use environment, including typical words and vocabulary used in the environment are critical when defining "wake" words to reliably activate the system while avoiding accidental activations. Additionally, a unique challenge of voice control is the discoverability of commands, requiring users to either have visual reminders of possible commands or recall commands from memory. Advances and expansions in accents and natural language have made voice control a more tractable navigational tool. Ongoing developments are underway to explore the use of voice control and transcription during intra-procedural use cases.

Eye Tracking. The HoloLens 2 (Microsoft, Redmond, WA) has brought integrated eye tracking technology to a broad audience, and recent development efforts have demonstrated eye tracking to be an intuitive navigational adjunct. In contrast to gaze, eye tracking as an input is unfamiliar and straining for cursor control but is intuitive for communicating focus. Eye tracking can be used to determine what VAMR buttons or objects the user is looking at and respond accordingly, without requiring head motion from the user. While eye tracking may seem to offer superior ease of use to gaze, designs incorporating eye tracking should consider that users may need to look away from buttons or controls when using them. For example, users rotating a 3D model with a hands-free interface need to look at the model during rotation to determine when the desired view has been reached. In this instance, gaze controls are a better choice than eye tracking. Conversely, eye tracking on its own might result in inadvertent selections of buttons as users look across the display or as users learn the interface, though design considerations will be important in interface development and testing to ensure inadvertent activation is avoided. In the future, implementations will be similar to voice control in that eye tracking can be used as an adjunct to gaze or gesture. Using eye tracking as a confirmatory action will likely be of benefit in the future. For example, if a user's gaze cursor hovers over a button, but the user is not looking at the button, an inadvertent selection can be avoided. Eye tracking will also provide developers with opportunities to understand how end users are using and exploring their VAMRs, and may over time allow for an intention-based design where, after collecting and analyzing numerous procedures, the user is presented with the most relevant data they will need at that point in the procedure. This type of intelligent design will also allow for development of clinical decision support tools to aid physicians performing increasingly complex procedures. It is anticipated that these sorts of tools will have a significant impact in medically underserved areas.

5   Navigating in VAMR

Navigation of medical applications in VAMR environments is highly dependent on the type of extended reality and digital images in the virtual environment. Display in VAMR may be either 2D (or "flat") or truly 3D data projected in the extended reality—the dimensionality of the data is of critical significance for how the end user will navigate and interact in the VAMR environment. For those virtual screens, or 2D data posted in the VAMR space, interactions for navigating these images will be specific to the data displayed but is often limited to changes in location and size. For true 3D data in virtual environment, the navigation of the object can be much richer, including rotation and clipping, which can improve both the visualization and the comprehension for the end user.

5.1   Navigating 3-Dimensional Data in VAMR

Navigating 3-dimensional medical data in VAMR allows the user to have a more comprehensive understanding of the anatomy. From the ability to rotate to familiar fixed angles and projections to recreate mental models of anatomic structures, to the ability to freely rotate a structure and analyze the anatomy in a way previously not seen, navigating medical 3D images in VAMR provides the user the ability to understand individual, patient specific, anatomies in ways previously inaccessible. During the Cardiac

Augmented Reality (CARE) Study, where cardiac electrophysiologists were presented with patient specific 3D cardiac anatomies during interventional procedures, 87% of respondents felt that use of the system allowed them "to discover something new about the anatomy."

5.2 Navigating 2-Dimensional Data in VAMR

The types of interactions that are required to navigate and interact with 2-dimensional images are potentially more limited and may have established input patterns. Allowing the end user to alter the size, location, and contrast of the 2D image with VAMR is of fundamental importance but assessing the navigational needs in the context of the overall use is valuable. Making measurements on these 2D images are an important consideration for medical applications, and additional context from 3D annotations (such as 3D anatomical reference) on 2D data can improve navigation and interpretation. Intra-procedural mixed reality allows for the development of a medical device to address this problem.

5.3 Intention Based Design

The design of an intuitive and useful interface requires that the most critical data and controls be the easiest to access by the user. However, discerning user preferences and needs is highly challenging and quite individualized. Users can struggle to communicate the prioritization of tools or data, and the result is that many of their interactions are intuitive and subconscious.

The high-speed eye-tracking from the next generation HMDs, such as the Microsoft HoloLens 2, will allow for evaluation of intent and focus during human factors (HF) evaluation and system use. These intent data will quantify the time spent viewing various data streams from the first-person perspective. This information, which would be unique to this platform can then be fed back into the design process to improve the interface and overall workflow integration.

6 Development and Early Lessons

Through the development, bench testing, contextual inquiries, human factors and clinical testing, there have been many early lessons learned. These early lessons will serve as the base on which more data should be generated for optimal design for medical VAMR applications.

6.1 Command EP System

The improvement in visualization provided by the CommandEP™ System is the most immediately tangible value-add to the electrophysiologist. In the CommandEP™ system, we designed a gaze-based interface on the Microsoft HoloLens 1 HMD that allowed physicians to manipulate a patient-specific cardiac hologram, empowering the physician to rotate, zoom, and alter the

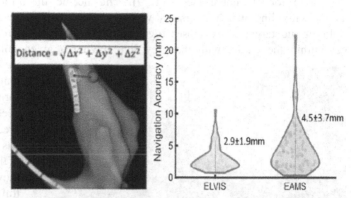

Fig. 8. Clinical **Assessment of Accuracy**. Left: Physician decides whether they are on target. Blue dot is physician's navigation point, red dot is the target. Right: Accuracy data from 150-point navigation tasks using the SentiAR system versus EAMS. Adapted from Avari Silva, J.N., et al., First-In-Human Use of a Mixed Reality Display During Cardiac Ablation Procedures. JACC Clin Electrophysiol, 2020. **6**(8): p. 1023-1025.

opacity to best understand how to navigate. Post-procedure surveys demonstrated that 83% of physicians found manipulation of the hologram to be the most valuable feature with 87% of physicians discovering something new about the anatomy [3]. Considerable resources were devoted to developing an intuitive, hands-free interface for CommandEP™ via iterative human factors testing that allowed the physician to control EAMS data.

In the Cardiac Augmented Reality (CARE) Study, there were additional study tasks the physicians were asked to complete during the post-ablation waiting phase of the procedure. These tasks included the generation of a cardiac geometry followed by sequential navigation to 5 discrete points within the geometry using the current standard of care versus CommandEP™. The data demonstrated that the interface led to clearer care team communication [3], and improved navigational accuracy [12] (see Fig. 8).

6.2 Mixed Reality-Ultrasound (SentUS) System

This system is slated for early formative human factors testing for iterative improvement in the user experience design and user interface design in Spring 2021. The interface has the unique challenge of displaying the 2D ultrasound image plane, and additionally interpolating how a needle will intersect with the desired target in the image. This combination of 2D and 3D imaging has proven challenging.

Currently, the needle tracking tool allows the user to place the target within the circle for alignment (see Fig. 9). The needle tip information is displayed as the gray line which intersects with the target. The chevrons to the left and right of the target move closer together as the needle approaches the given target within the circle, with the grey line having a green color. Once the needle is at the target, the lateral chevrons intersect to form an "X" with the needle shaft remaining green. Once the needle has gone past the plane of the target, the chevrons move away from the central target, with the directionality pointing outwards, and the shaft of the needle becoming a red color, giving a graphical representation to the user that they are past the target, a situation that can lead to procedural complications.

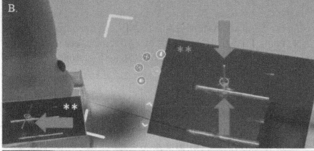
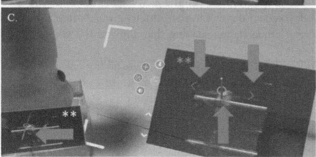

Given the data from the CARE study and the demonstrable improvement in accuracy, we have designed an early feasibility, pre-clinical study to assess this tool using vascular access phantom models. The hypothesis is that the SentUS system will improve accuracy and efficiency as compared to conventional ultrasound vascular access techniques. To test this hypothesis, users will be asked to obtain vascular access in 2 separate phantoms. Assessing accuracy will involve

Fig. 9. SentUS **Prototype**. The SentUS prototype imaging a vascular access phantom is shown above. In these images, the ultrasound probe is in the left side of the image with the ultrasound image displayed at the tip of the probe (yellow asterisks). The "billboard" display (blue asterisks) is to the right of the ultrasound probe. In these images, the interface for the needle tracking, or tool tracking, is shown as displayed by the grey line (see red arrow) with the chevrons denoting directionality (purple arrows). (Color figure online)

measuring the distance of the vessel puncture site to the center of the vessel. To assess efficiency, we will measure the time it takes to complete the task (in seconds). Additionally, the number of access attempts (a predictor of complications) will be recorded as well as the number of needle adjustments.

6.3   Mixed Reality-Electrogram (SentEGM) System

After > 100 interactions with end users evaluating CommandEP™, the majority identified EGMs as essential to their procedural practice and requested integration of these data into the MxR display. During formal ELVIS human factors (HF) validation, 2/8 physicians reported that their "eyes deviate because I'm looking at my electrograms on a different screen" and 3/8 physicians expressed that displaying EGM data alongside the EAMS in MxR "would be huge." This feedback suggests real-time EGM access during the electrophysiology (EP) study to enable physicians to watch for certain EGM characteristics during the procedure would be of value to the end user.

However, making measurements in MxR will prove to be a difficult hurdle, as these micro movements will be laborious, time-intensive and may cause frustration for the end user. As such, the development of "smart calipers" will supply a first, coarse measurement which can then be micro-adjusted using the gaze-based display and then confirmed—likely using multiple navigation tools as described above. Integration of EGM visualization and interaction will require significant development and novel approaches to allow performing physicians to measure accurately and efficiently, while maintaining sterility. Smart Caliper development will greatly facilitate this effort. Developing an interface to allow physicians to obtain intra-procedural measurements will have applications beyond cardiac electrophysiology, including interventional cardiology and interventional radiology.

7   Regulatory Considerations

Medical applications have additional regulatory considerations that influence interaction and navigation design considerations. Highly predictable interfaces that consider medical use environments and users, which will promote positive patient outcomes and not introduce substantial error or risk that may negatively impact patient outcomes are preferred. Understanding medical extended reality applications has been a recent focus of the US Food and Drug Administration (FDA), and this enhanced understanding will likely result in more regulatory guidance for medical applications. In February 2020, the FDA hosted a public workshop entitled "Mixed Extended Reality: Toward Best Evaluation Practices for Virtual and Augmented Reality in Medicine." The participants in this workshop included hardware developers, medical software developers, scientists and clinicians with an interest in medical VAMR to start openly discussing the difficulties of developing these technologies and how the FDA can partner and regulate to safely bring these novel technologies through the regulatory process. It is anticipated that a white paper from this workshop will soon be published and provide an initial review of the discussion.

8 Future Directions

Currently, each system in the EP lab has its own monitor that displays a fixed data stream regardless of procedure phase. The integration of multiple systems allows the display of data as it is needed in a format that the physician can readily interpret and interact with. Thus, while the physician is measuring EGMs or delivering an ablation, the EGM signals from key electrodes that the physician requires for an effective ablation are displayed. Conversely, while the physician is gaining access, only EGMs from the catheter being placed are shown.

The design of an intuitive and useful interface requires that the most critical data and controls be most easily accessible to the user. However, discerning user preferences and needs is highly challenging. Users struggle to communicate the prioritization of tools or data, because their intuition and interactions are often subconscious. The high-speed eye-tracking from next generation HMDs, will allow evaluation of interaction intent and focus during HF evaluation and system use. This intent data will quantify the time spent viewing different data streams within the device. This information, unique to this platform, will then be fed back into the design process to improve the interface and overall workflow integration.

9 Conclusion

In conclusion, critical understanding of the end user and use case are the primary drivers for development of interactions and navigation tools for medical applications in VAMR. Understanding the type of medical imaging presented to the ended user, the use case and environment and intended use will all impact the interaction and navigation methods deployed. New hardware developments coupled with regulatory considerations will influence future applications to help improve patient outcomes.

References

1. Silva, J.N.A., et al.: Emerging applications of virtual reality in cardiovascular medicine. JACC Basic Transl. Sci. **3**(3), 420–430 (2018)
2. Silva, J., Silva, J.: System and method for virtual reality data integration and visualization for 3D imaging and instrument position data. Google Patents (2019)
3. Avari Silva, Jennifer N., Privitera, M.B., Southworth, Michael K., Silva, Jonathan R.: Development and human factors considerations for extended reality applications in medicine: the enhanced electrophysiology visualization and interaction system (ĒLVIS). In: Chen, Jessie Y.C., Fragomeni, G. (eds.) HCII 2020. LNCS, vol. 12191, pp. 341–356. Springer, Cham (2020). https://doi.org/10.1007/978-3-030-49698-2_23
4. Southworth, M.K., Silva, J.R., Silva, J.N.A.: Use of extended realities in cardiology. Trends Cardiovasc. Med. **30**(3), 143–148 (2020)
5. Southworth, M.K., et al.: Performance Evaluation of Mixed Reality Display for Guidance During Transcatheter Cardiac Mapping and ablation. IEEE J. Transl. Eng. Health Med. **8**, 1900810 (2020)
6. Gratzel, C., et al.: A non-contact mouse for surgeon-computer interaction. Technol. Health Care **12**(3), 245–57 (2004)

7. Kornbau, C., et al.: Central line complications. Int. J. Crit. Illn. Inj. Sci. **5**(3), 170–8 (2015)
8. Franco-Sadud, R., et al.: Recommendations on the use of ultrasound guidance for central and peripheral vascular access in adults: a position statement of the society of hospital medicine. J. Hosp. Med. **14**, E1–E22 (2019)
9. Land, M., Mennie, N., Rusted, J.: The roles of vision and eye movements in the control of activities of daily living. Perception **28**(11), 1311–28 (1999)
10. Battaglia-Mayer, A., Caminiti, R.: Parieto-frontal networks for eye-hand coordination and movements. In: Vallar G, C.H. (ed.) Handbook of Clinical Neurology, Elsevier B.V. (2018)
11. Fitts, P.M.: The information capacity of the human motor system in controlling the amplitude of movement. J. Exp. Psychol. **47**(6), 381–91 (1954)
12. Avari Silva, J.N., et al.: First-in-human use of a mixed reality display during cardiac ablation procedures. JACC Clin. Electrophysiol. **6**(8), 1023–1025 (2020)

Virtual Reality Sickness Evaluation in Exergames for Older Hypertensive Patients: A Comparative Study of Training Methods in a Virtual Environment

Oskar Stamm$^{(\boxtimes)}$ ⓘ and Susan Vorwerg ⓘ

Department of Geriatrics and Medical Gerontology, Charité – Universitätsmedizin Berlin,
corporate member of Freie Universität Berlin and Humboldt-Universität zu Berlin,
Reinickendorfer Straße 61, 13347 Berlin, Germany
{oskar.stamm,susan.vorwerg}@charite.de

Abstract. Virtual Reality (VR) sickness is an exclusive problem in immersive VR. However, the target group of hypertensive patients is a particularly vulnerable group that could be more sensitive to such a phenomenon. Therefore, the aim of this study was to determine whether there are differences in the symptoms of the VR sickness between a strength endurance-based and an endurance-based VR exergame. Participants over 65 years old with diagnosed essential hypertension were included. An assessment of cognitive status and an assessment of risk of falling were performed as inclusion criteria. All participants tested two VR exergames (strength endurance and endurance training) on two visits. The Simulator Sickness Questionnaire (SSQ) was used after the task-based application. The endurance exergame tended to have higher scores in the scales than the strength endurance exergame. The increased movement in space could be a cause for this. Significant differences were shown only for the scale "oculomotor". Descriptively, more symptoms were found in women and participants without VR experience and participants over 76 years of age. There were no relevant self-reported cases of VR sickness in the sample. For the target group of older hypertensive patients an exergame, which is arranged as a frontal personal training and requires less movement through the room, could cause less VR sickness and be more appealing.

Keywords: VR sickness · SSQ · Gaming · Older adults

1 Introduction

Performing moderate-intensity endurance and strength endurance exercises almost every day per week is recommended for older adults with hypertension to lower the blood pressure (BP). According to guidelines of the European Society of Cardiology and the European Society of Hypertension (ESC/ESH), hypertensive patients should be advised to perform at least 30 min of dynamic aerobic exercise of moderate intensity (e.g. walking, jogging or cycling) on 5–7 days per week and adjuvant resistance exercise 2–3 days per week may also be recommended [1]. In the age group of people over 60 years old

J. Y. C. Chen and G. Fragomeni (Eds.): HCII 2021, LNCS 12770, pp. 134–146, 2021.
https://doi.org/10.1007/978-3-030-77599-5_11

with training duration ranging from 8 to 78 weeks the average reduction of the diastolic BP was 7.6 mmHg and of the systolic BP 8.8 mmHg [2]. From a clinical standpoint, this is significant as a reduction of 5 mmHg is expected to reduce mortality associated with stroke by 14% and coronary heart disease by 9% [3]. However, long-term adherence in exercises can be low. Common barriers for continuing, such as resistance exercises, are lack of time, being more interested in other physical activities, seasonal reasons and financial cost [4].

Exergames can encourage older adults who lack motivation and exercise adherence to be more physically active. Furthermore, they offer location and time-independent options for individualized training concepts. Previous studies showed that Nintendo Wii exergames have positive effects on increasing light to moderate intensity physical activity, cognitive stimulation, socialization, and motivation to exercise [5–7]. Interactive exergames used as a complementary tool to a conventional cardiac rehabilitation have demonstrated in first pilot studies improvements in ergometry, metabolic equivalents (METS), resistance to fatigue and health-related quality of life with excellent adherence by patients with cardiovascular diseases [8]. The advance of immersive technologies with head-mounted displays (HMD) opens up new possibilities of creating exergames in this field. Virtual Reality (VR) HMD exergames could increase motivation and adherence for long-term training, but are still too understudied [9].

However, the value of head-mounted immersive VR for health care and rehabilitation could be limited by the phenomenon called virtual reality sickness. VR sickness is an exclusive problem in immersive VR resulting from the discrepancy between the simulated movement and the sense of movement derived from the vestibular system. The term "cybersickness" was originally used in connection with virtual environments (VR Cave) whereas "VR sickness" has been used in studies using HMD. Nevertheless the terminology is often used interchangeably in the literature [10]. When comparing the user experience of exergames in immersive VR and on a 50-in. TV, immersive VR was found to be more likely to have higher levels of VR sickness in young adults [11].

Besides the property of the system, such as resolution, type of display screen, field of view and frame rate of HMDs, the content can also influence the risk of VR sickness [12, 13]. Gaming content generated the highest total score of the Simulator Sickness Questionnaire (SSQ) compared to 360 videos, minimalist content and scenic content [10]. However, the majority of immersive VR studies with older adults had a low VR sickness incidence [14–16]. In the meta-analysis of Saredakis et al. four samples were included with a mean age $\geq$ 35 years (n = 64), which report lower total SSQ scores for older samples compared to younger samples [10]. Results on the motion sickness susceptibility indicate that women had higher susceptibility than men and also that the susceptibility decreased with age in healthy subjects and vestibular patients [17].

The target group of hypertension patients is a particularly vulnerable group that could be more sensitive to VR sickness, compared with studies already conducted in older adults. In addition, various training methods in exergame could provoke VR sickness differently. Therefore, the aim of this study was to determine whether there are differences in the symptoms of the VR sickness between a strength endurance-based and an endurance-based VR exergame.

2 Methods

In the pilot study, we applied a task-based application included the testing of two VR exergames recently developed. In order to answer the hypotheses, participants over 65 years old with diagnosed essential hypertension were included. An assessment of cognitive status (TICS ≥ 33) and an assessment of risk of falling (Tinetti mobility test ≥ 24) were performed as inclusion criteria [5, 6]. Participants who did not complete neither the first nor the second training session had to be excluded. All participants gave their written consent and the Ethics Committee of the Charité – Universitätsmedizin Berlin approved the study (No. EA1/019/20).

2.1 Procedure

The pilot study was conducted in a virtual reality setting in a mobile laboratory truck called VITALAB.mobile in 2020 (see Fig. 1). During the study, the ViTALAB.mobile was placed on the campus of the Evangelisches Geriatriezentrum Berlin.

Fig. 1. The mobile laboratory truck VITALAB.mobile

All participants were recruited via the internal sample database of the senior research group or by flyers. During the study, the participants tested two VR exergames (strength endurance and endurance training) on two visits. In total, one game lasted 20 to 25 min. Warm-up and cool-down remained identical in both games and lasted one minute each. However, the VR exergames differed in the main part of the training methods. Exergame strength endurance (SE) was a virtual personal training including strength endurance-based exercises. The participants performed five exercises (squat, overhead press, diagonal pull, leg raise, toe stance) during which they remained in a static position in the virtual environment (see Fig. 2). Each exercise was repeated up to 20 times per set in two sets. An active break for one minute was taken between sets.

Fig. 2. Five exercises (squat, overhead press, diagonal pull, leg raise, toe stance) during strength endurance VR training.

Exergame endurance (E) included three endurance-based exercises (ball game, high five and hustle dance) (see Fig. 3). In contrast to exergame SE, the participants had to move dynamically in the virtual environment. The mini-exergame ball game and high five lasted for about 2 to 3 min. The hustle dance was practiced and danced for about 12 min. All participants tested exergame SE on the first visit and exergame E on the second visit. In both visits, the Simulator Sickness Questionnaire (SSQ) was used briefly after the VR training.

Fig. 3. Three exercises (ball game, high five and hustle dance) during endurance VR training.

2.2 Materials

HTC Vive Pro. In the present study, an HTC Vive Pro was used as the VR HMD headset. The display of the headset has a resolution of 1440 × 1600 pixels per eye. The screen diagonal of the dual screen is 3.5". The refresh rate of the screen is 90 Hz. With a field of view of 110°, it is one of the headsets with a higher field of view on the market. In addition to the headset use, trackers were attached to the hands of the users and on training objects (dumbbells and a chair) in the exergame SE to allow interactivity. Valve Index controllers were used in the exergame E to enable finger tracking and thus grasping, releasing, and throwing. The HTC Vive Pro requires lighthouse base stations for use. We used Valve Index Base Stations 2.0, which were positioned diagonally to each other under the ceiling in the truck.

SSQ. The original purpose of the SSQ developed by Kennedy et al. [18] was to measure motion sickness in flight simulators. The SSQ is still widely used to measure motion sickness in virtual environments and systems [19–21]. The SSQ consists of 16 items representing various symptoms. These symptoms are grouped in three categories (subscales): nausea, oculomotor, and disorientation and can be summed in a total score. Each SSQ item can have a score between 0 and 3 depending on the severity of participant's symptoms.

2.3 Data Analysis

The SSQ was evaluated with SPSS 26 using the scales "Nausea", "Oculomotor", "Disorientation" and "Total Score" as comparison between training methods and as group comparison. The normal distribution was examined using the Shapiro-Wilk test. In the absence of a normal distribution of the sample's result values, the Wilcoxon signed-rank test and the Mann-Whitney U test were used.

3 Results

3.1 Participants

The sample consisted of 22 participants with essential hypertension. Two people had to be subsequently excluded because VR sickness symptoms appeared after a short time in the virtual environment. Accordingly, the training could not be continued. Among the 22 participants, 13 were female and 9 male. The average age was 75.4 ± 3.6 years. The included participants had no increased risk of falling (Tinetti test: 27.6 ± 0.8 points) and had no cognitive impairments (TICS: 37.3 ± 2.6). One participant reported suffering from occasional dizziness (in everyday life). About half of the participants already had experience with VR applications at the time of testing. On average, the participants practiced sports 2–3 times a week, mostly as part of a group training.

3.2 SSQ

Participants tended to have higher scores during exergame E in the scales "Total Score" and "Oculomotor" than during exergame SE. In exergame SE, the most frequent symptoms of the scale were "Nausea" (68.2%), followed by "Disorientation" (54.5%) and "Oculomotor" (40.9%). In exergame E, on the other hand, symptoms of the scale "Oculomotor" (77.7%) appeared most frequently. Symptoms of the scale "Nausea" and "Disorientation" occurred in 54.5% and 59.1% of the participants. Consequently, a statistical comparison between the two games only indicated significant results for the scale "Oculomotor" (exergame SE $\bar{x} = 8.96 \pm 13.36$; exergame E $\bar{x} = 14.47 \pm 15.85$; Wilcoxon test p $= 0.031$). The scales "Nausea" (exergame SE $\bar{x} = 13.01 \pm 13.02$; exergame E $\bar{x}$ $= 12.58 \pm 15.96$; Wilcoxon test p $= 0.609$), "Disorientation" (exergame SE $\bar{x} = 22.15$ ± 32.90; exergame E $\bar{x} = 21.51 \pm 26.73$; Wilcoxon test p $= 0.832$) and "Total Score" (exergame SE $\bar{x} = 15.47 \pm 18.69$; exergame E $\bar{x} = 17.85 \pm 19.55$; Wilcoxon test p $= 0.867$) remained without significance (Fig. 4).

Although no significant differences between men and women were found (Table 1), it was descriptively determined that women had higher VR sickness symptoms than men for E and SE on all scales. Higher descriptive differences between men and women could be observed for endurance based exergame (Fig. 5 and Fig. 6).

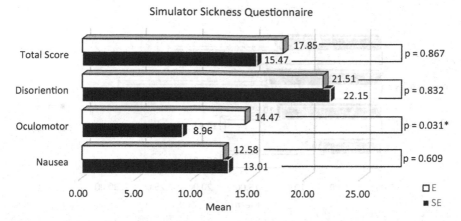

Fig. 4. Comparison between mean values for exergame E and SE within the subscales of the SSQ.

Table 1. P-values for comparison between male and female.

Subscale	Exergame SE	Exergame E
Total Score	p = 0.695	p = 0.209
Disorientation	p = 0.393	p = 0.292
Oculomotor	p = 0.695	p = 0.357
Nausea	p = 0.794	p = 0.209

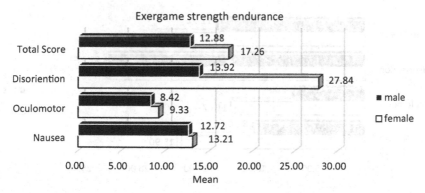

Fig. 5. Comparison between male and female mean values for exergame SE within the subscales of the SSQ.

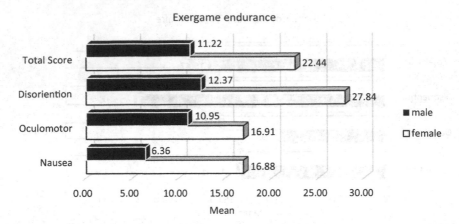

Fig. 6. Comparison between male and female mean values for exergame SE within the subscales of the SSQ.

In a comparison between participants with and without VR experience, persons without VR experience were more likely to show symptoms than persons with VR experience (Fig. 7 and Fig. 8). An exception concerned the scale "Disorientation" at the exergame SE. Participants achieved almost identical mean values in this scale. Overall, there were no statistically provable differences, except for the exergame SE's "Total Score" (Table 2).

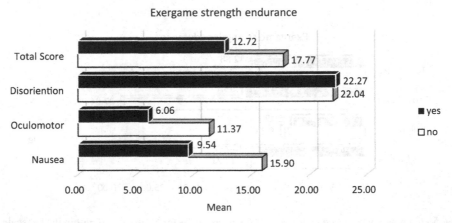

Fig. 7. Mean values when comparing people with and without VR experience for exergame SE within the subscales of the SSQ.

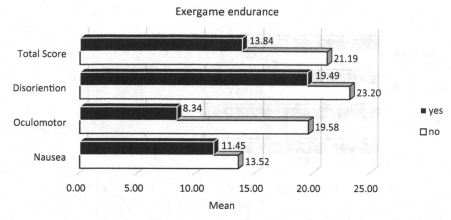

Fig. 8. Mean values when comparing people with and without VR experience for exergame E within the subscales of the SSQ.

Table 2. P-values for comparison between participants with and without VR experience.

Subscale	Exergame SE	Exergame E
Total Score	p = 0.043*	p = 0.228
Disorientation	p = 0.228	p = 0.314
Oculomotor	p = 0.418	p = 0.093
Nausea	p = 0.080	p = 0.771
* p < 0.05		

When distinguishing between younger (65 to 75 years of age) and older (76 to 80 years of age) seniors, VR symptoms were found to be more prevalent in the group over 76 years of age (Fig. 9 and Fig. 10). Despite noticeable descriptive differences, no significant results were determined between the two age groups (Table 3).

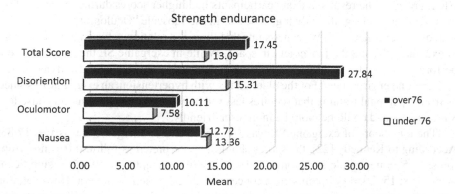

Fig. 9. Mean values when comparing people under and over 76 years of age for Exergame SE within the subscales of the SSQ.

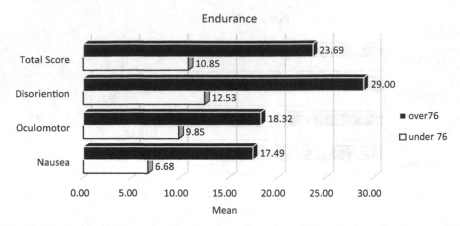

Fig. 10. Mean values when comparing people under and over 76 years of age for Exergame SE within the subscales of the SSQ.

Table 3. P-values for comparison between participants under and over 76 years of age.

Subscale	Exergame SE	Exergame E
Total Score	p = 0.923	p = 0.346
Disorientation	p = 0.582	p = 0.228
Oculomotor	p = 0.872	p = 0.539
Nausea	p = 0.628	p = 0.180

4 Discussion

The primary goal of this paper was to determine the differences in the symptoms of the VR sickness between a strength endurance-based exergame and an endurance-based VR exergame. The results indicate participants had higher scores during exergame E in the total score and significantly higher scores in the subscale "Oculomotor" (p = 0.031) than during exergame SE. We can assume that there is a relation between the lower score in exergame SE and the movement in space. While in exergame SE the exercises were performed in a static position, in exergame E the participants had to move dynamically in the virtual environment. For the older adults with hypertension, an exergame designed as frontal personal training that requires less movement through space might cause less VR sickness and could be more be more user-friendly.

The total score of exergame SE was $\bar{x} = 15.47$ and of exergame E was $\bar{x} = 17.85$. According to Kennedy [22], the scores should be interpreted as follows: 0 = no symptoms; < 5 = negligible symptoms; 5–10 = minimal symptoms; 10–15 = significant symptoms; 15–20 = symptoms are a concern; > 20 a problem simulator. However, this strict categorization of symptoms was based on central tendencies using military aviation personnel in each simulator. The SSQ scores tend to be higher in virtual environments compared to flight simulators [22, 23]. According to the strict categories, the results of the total score would be interpreted as: "symptoms are a concern". Bimber et al. [24] stated that scores above 20 should not automatically be attributed to a bad simulator and future work should determine refined cut-off values based on general population. The interpretation of Kennedy contradicts our observations, in which no anomalies or significant symptoms regarding VR sickness were reported by the participants. Saredakis et al. [10] considered game content in their meta-analysis where SSQ scores indicated a total SSQ mean of 34.26. The total scores in our study were lower than the reference value. Compared to the evaluation of older samples in meta-analysis by Saredakis et al. [10], our values were similar ($\bar{x} = 14.30$). Their study considered samples with a mean age ≥ 35 years (n = 64). In terms of age, we examined the difference in SSQ between 65- to 75-year-old and 76- to 80-year-old seniors. VR sickness symptoms were found to be more common in the group over 76 years of age. This shows that in older seniors (over 76 years), an increase in symptoms can occur, which would contradict a linear decrease in VR sickness symptoms with increasing age or could set a threshold. However, further research with more subjects is needed regarding VR sickness in older adults.

Concerning the gender, no significant differences were found between men and women. However, women had higher VR sickness symptoms than men for E and SE on all scales. This results were consistent with the literature, which also indicates that women had higher motion sickness susceptibility than men [17]. Nevertheless, Chang et al. [25] showed that inconsistent results are reported for gender differences in VR.

Participants without VR experience were more likely to show symptoms than persons with VR experience. Duzmanska et al. [26] found out that some people may adapt over time in multiple sessions to VR sickness. Due to lack of information on the time interval to the last VR session in our study, we cannot accurately track these parameters. Since the strength endurance training always took place first and had a lower total score in the SSQ, it contradicts the theory regarding 2 sessions, however, it may be possible that an adaptation would occur after several sessions.

In our study conducted, a small dropout rate of 8.33% was found compared to the mean dropout rate of 15.6% due to VR sickness reported across 46 experiments in the meta-analysis of Saredakis et al. [10].

The ACSM's exercise prescription for adults with hypertension recommends moderate intensity (40%–59% of $-VO_{2R}$ or 12–13 on the borg scale from 6 to 20 level of physical exertion or an intensity that causes noticeable increases in heart rate and breathing) [27]. Regarding the comparability to prescribed training, in the present study, the exergame SE subjects reported 12.1 and in the exergame E 10.8 on average as Received Perception of Exertion Score on the borg scale, which is almost the same as the conditions for a prescribed training. It cannot be presumed that the training intensity was too high and thus we do not assume that an influence on the VR sickness occurred.

4.1 Limitations

Due to the limitation of the ceiling height in the truck, the installation of the lighthouse base stations was only possible at a limited height. A loss of tracking occurred above a certain height of the trackers or headset, which could have intensified the symptoms. Another challenge was the interpretation of the SSQ score, which is not adapted to HMD headsets. There are two variants of the SSQ the CSQ (Cybersickness Questionnaire) [28] and the VRSQ (Virtual Reality Sickness Questionnaire) [29], which might have been an alternative assessment as they offer better indicators of validity for VR sickness. However, there is a lack of sufficient reference data compared to the SSQ. Due to the small sample size in our study, only few significances could be shown. Further research is needed to determine VR sickness in various training concepts within exergames.

5 Conclusion

The participants showed more symptoms of VR sickness in the endurance-based exergame than in the strength endurance exergame. The increased movement in space could be a cause for this. For the target group of older hypertensive patients an exergame, which is arranged as a frontal personal training and requires less movement through the room, could cause less VR sickness and be more appealing.

References

1. Williams, B., Mancia, G., Spiering, W., Agabiti Rosei, E., Azizi, M.: 2018 ESC/ESH guidelines for the management of arterial hypertension. Eur. Heart J. **39**, 3021–3104 (2018). https://doi.org/10.1093/eurheartj/ehy339
2. Hagberg, J.M., Park, J.-J., Brown, M.D.: The role of exercise training in the treatment of hypertension. Sports Med. **30**, 193–206 (2000). https://doi.org/10.2165/00007256-200030030-00004
3. Carpio-Rivera, E., Moncada-Jiménez, J., Salazar-Rojas, W., Solera-Herrera, A.: Acute effects of exercise on blood pressure: a meta-analytic investigation. Arq. Bras. Cardiol. **106**, 422–433 (2016). https://doi.org/10.5935/abc.20160064
4. Roie, E.V., Bautmans, I., Coudyzer, W., Boen, F., Delecluse, C.: Low- and high-resistance exercise: long-term adherence and motivation among older adults. GER **61**, 551–560 (2015). https://doi.org/10.1159/000381473
5. Chao, Y.-Y., Scherer, Y.K., Montgomery, C.A.: Effects of using Nintendo Wii^{TM} exergames in older adults: a review of the literature. J. Aging Health **27**, 379–402 (2015). https://doi.org/10.1177/0898264314551171
6. Graves, L.E.F., Ridgers, N.D., Williams, K., Stratton, G., Atkinson, G., Cable, N.T.: The physiological cost and enjoyment of Wii Fit in adolescents, young adults, and older adults. J. Phys. Act. Health **7**, 393–401 (2010). https://doi.org/10.1123/jpah.7.3.393
7. Skjæret, N., Nawaz, A., Morat, T., Schoene, D., Helbostad, J.L., Vereijken, B.: Exercise and rehabilitation delivered through exergames in older adults: an integrative review of technologies, safety and efficacy. Int. J. Med. Inform. **85**, 1–16 (2016). https://doi.org/10.1016/j.ijmedinf.2015.10.008
8. García-Bravo, S., et al.: Virtual reality and video games in cardiac rehabilitation programs. A systematic review. Disabil. Rehabil. 1–10 (2019). https://doi.org/10.1080/09638288.2019.1631892
9. Szpak, A., Michalski, S.C., Loetscher, T.: Exergaming with beat saber: an investigation of virtual reality aftereffects. J. Med. Internet Res. **22**, (2020). https://doi.org/10.2196/19840
10. Saredakis, D., Szpak, A., Birckhead, B., Keage, H.A.D., Rizzo, A., Loetscher, T.: Factors associated with virtual reality sickness in head-mounted displays: a systematic review and meta-analysis. Front. Hum. Neurosci. **14** (2020). https://doi.org/10.3389/fnhum.2020.00096

11. Xu, W., Liang, H.-N., Zhang, Z., Baghaei, N.: Studying the effect of display type and viewing perspective on user experience in virtual reality exergames. Games Health J. **9**, 405–414 (2020). https://doi.org/10.1089/g4h.2019.0102
12. Fernandes, A.S., Feiner, S.K.: Combating VR sickness through subtle dynamic field-of-view modification. In: 2016 IEEE Symposium on 3D User Interfaces (3DUI), pp. 201–210 (2016). https://doi.org/10.1109/3DUI.2016.7460053
13. Kourtesis, P., Collina, S., Doumas, L.A.A., MacPherson, S.E.: Technological competence is a pre-condition for effective implementation of virtual reality head mounted displays in human neuroscience: a technological review and meta-analysis. Front. Hum. Neurosci. **13** (2019). https://doi.org/10.3389/fnhum.2019.00342
14. Huygelier, H., Schraepen, B., van Ee, R., Vanden Abeele, V., Gillebert, C.R.: Acceptance of immersive head-mounted virtual reality in older adults. Sci. Rep. **9**, 4519 (2019). https://doi.org/10.1038/s41598-019-41200-6
15. Bauer, A.C.M., Andringa, G.: The potential of immersive virtual reality for cognitive training in elderly. GER **66**, 614–623 (2020). https://doi.org/10.1159/000509830
16. Benham, S., Kang, M., Grampurohit, N.: Immersive virtual reality for the management of pain in community-dwelling older adults. OTJR Occup. Part. Health **39**, 90–96 (2019). https://doi.org/10.1177/1539449218817291
17. Paillard, A.C., Quarck, G., Paolino, F., Denise, P., Paolino, M., Golding, J.F., Ghulyan-Bedikian, V.: Motion sickness susceptibility in healthy subjects and vestibular patients: effects of gender, age and trait-anxiety. J. Vestib. Res. **23**, 203–209 (2013). https://doi.org/10.3233/VES-130501
18. Kennedy, R.S., Lane, N.E., Berbaum, K.S., Lilienthal, M.G.: Simulator sickness questionnaire: an enhanced method for quantifying simulator sickness. Int. J. Aviat. Psychol. **3**, 203–220 (1993). https://doi.org/10.1207/s15327108ijap0303_3
19. Balk, S.A., Bertola, D.B., Inman, V.W.: Simulator sickness questionnaire: twenty years later. Driv. Assess. Conf. **7**, 257–263 (2013)
20. Guna, J., Geršak, G., Humar, I., Song, J., Drnovšek, J., Pogačnik, M.: Influence of video content type on users' virtual reality sickness perception and physiological response. Future Gener. Comput. Syst. **91**, 263–276 (2019). https://doi.org/10.1016/j.future.2018.08.049
21. Rupp, M.A., Odette, K.L., Kozachuk, J., Michaelis, J.R., Smither, J.A., McConnell, D.S.: Investigating learning outcomes and subjective experiences in 360-degree videos. Comput. Educ. **128**, 256–268 (2019). https://doi.org/10.1016/j.compedu.2018.09.015
22. Kennedy, R.S., Drexler, J.M., Compton, D.E., Stanney, K.M., Lanham, D.S., Harm, D.L.: Configural scoring of simulator sickness, cybersickness, and space adaptation syndrome: Similarities and differences. In: Virtual and adaptive environments: Applications, implications, and human performance issues, pp. 247–278. Lawrence Erlbaum Associates Publishers, Mahwah (2003). https://doi.org/10.1201/9781410608888.ch12
23. Stanney, K.M., Kennedy, R.S.: The psychometrics of cybersickness. Commun. ACM **40**, 66–68 (1997). https://doi.org/10.1145/257874.257889
24. Bimberg, P., Weißker, T., Kulik, A.: On the usage of the simulator sickness questionnaire for virtual reality research. In: 2020 IEEE Conference on Virtual Reality and 3D User Interfaces Abstracts and Workshops (VRW) (2020). https://doi.org/10.1109/VRW50115.2020.00098
25. Chang, E., Kim, H.T., Yoo, B.: Virtual reality sickness: a review of causes and measurements. Int. J. Hum. Comput. Interact. **36**, 1658–1682 (2020). https://doi.org/10.1080/10447318.2020.1778351
26. Dużmańska, N., Strojny, P., Strojny, A.: Can simulator sickness be avoided? a review on temporal aspects of simulator sickness. Front. Psychol. **9** (2018). https://doi.org/10.3389/fpsyg.2018.02132
27. Ferguson, B.: ACSM's guidelines for exercise testing and prescription 9th Ed. 2014. J. Can. Chiropr Assoc. **58**, 328 (2014)

28. Stone III, W.B.: Psychometric evaluation of the simulator sickness questionnaire as a measure of cybersickness (2017). https://lib.dr.iastate.edu/etd/15429/. https://doi.org/10.31274/etd-180810-5050
29. Kim, H.K., Park, J., Choi, Y., Choe, M.: Virtual reality sickness questionnaire (VRSQ): Motion sickness measurement index in a virtual reality environment. Appl. Ergon. **69**, 66–73 (2018). https://doi.org/10.1016/j.apergo.2017.12.016

Consistency in Multi-device Service Including VR: A Case Study

Tian Xie[1], Zhifeng Jin[2], Zhejun Liu[1]([⊠]), and Entang He[1]

[1] Tongji University, Shanghai, People's Republic of China
{1933641,wingeddreamer,1933635}@tongji.edu.cn
[2] Shanghai Academy of Spaceflight Technology, 3888 Yuanjiang Road, Shanghai 201109, People's Republic of China

Abstract. Nowadays, we have entered a world of multi-device experiences. This phenomenon poses a significant challenge because we have to deploy applications to different platforms, with a consistent UX for each targeted device preferably. Consistency provides users with a stable framework in similar contexts and helps to improve multi-device usability. Many previous studies focus on maintaining consistency among traditional platforms like smartphones apps and websites. However, with the rapid development of VR, it is crucial to add it to the spectrum because the design for VR differs from that for traditional 2D screens a lot. Therefore, this paper proposes a series of design principles to ensure the consistency across multiple devices including HMD-VR, along with four dimensions of consistency worth considering. We use *Virtual Experiment of Film Language*, a multi-device serious game as an example. Twelve participants were recruited to experience the VR and WebGL versions of the game to spot inconsistency issues. After that, the game was modified according to the survey results and evaluated by the participants again. The evaluation result showed that consistency was improved. We proposed three consistency design principles based on our findings. They can help multi-device applications improve consistency across devices so as to enhance inter-usability and user experience.

Keywords: Consistency · Multi-device · Virtual reality

1 Introduction

Nowadays, we are surrounded by all kinds of digital devices, from smartwatches, smartphones, tablets, PCs to the rapid developing VR devices like HTC VIVE and Oculus Rift. According to Cisco's report, global mobile devices and connections grew to 8.6 billion in 2017, and will grow to 12.3 billion by 2022 [1]. We have entered a world of multi-device experiences and our lives are full of interactions with them, which leads to an ecosystem of connected devices.

The diversity of consumer computing platforms has become an everyday fact nowadays. It is not rare to see users performing their tasks across various devices with various multi-modal interaction resources. This phenomenon poses a significant challenge

J. Y. C. Chen and G. Fragomeni (Eds.): HCII 2021, LNCS 12770, pp. 147–159, 2021.
https://doi.org/10.1007/978-3-030-77599-5_12

because we have to deploy applications to different platforms with suitable UX for each target device. Individuals react to objects and events based on previous experience from similar situations. Thus, it is important to maintain consistency across multiple platforms for the sake of user experience. This study focuses on the multi-device environment, the service aims at sequential (asynchronous) use and cross-platform, as defined in [2], which means that a single application can be experienced on multiple devices and each device has complete functionality and is able to offer the entire experience on its own. Meanwhile, users only use one device at a time and do not switch between different devices frequently. This study follows the consistency design approach defined by Levin [3]: the same basic experience is replicated between devices, keeping the content, flow, structure, and core feature set consistent across the ecosystem.

Consistency is important because it reduces the learning cost, helps to eliminate confusion, and also reduces development cost. It provides users with a stable framework in similar contexts and can help to improve multi-device usability. Nevertheless, maintaining consistency across various devices is an open issue. Some studies show that consistency is a crucial factor for multi-device experience. Many of them focus on common digital media like smartphone apps and websites, but with the rapid development of VR, it's important to take it into consideration.

Virtual Reality offers an immersive experience that closes out the physical world in which users can be transported into various virtual worlds rich in content. Stereoscopic vision, spatial sound, haptic feedback are all fundamental factors to consider while designing the VR experience, which differs from designing for 2D screens considerably. Thanks to her unique advantages, VR plays a vital role in the field of education [4]. For example, the VR version of *Virtual Experiment of Film Language* [5], a serious game that allows users to learn film language in VR, provides an immersive and efficient learning experience, but not everyone can access VR devices at any time. Therefore, it is valuable to propose a systematic solution featuring a multi-device experience. In this way, learners can enjoy a similarly immersive and efficient learning process whenever and wherever needed.

This paper proposes a series of general design principles to ensure the consistency of multi-device experience. We specifically care about how to maintain design consistency between HMD VR and desktop applications. The content is organized as follows: We reviewed various state-of-the-art studies in in Sect. 2 and brought forward four dimensions of consistency in Sect. 3. And then in Sect. 4, we describe the case study and our proposed consistency design principles. Finally, in Sect. 5, we discuss the achieved work and provide some suggestions for future work.

2   Related Work

2.1   Concepts of VR and Serious Games

Nowadays, VR technology has been widely recognized and used in many industries to support decision making and enable innovation [6]. Design for VR is difficult due to the lack of concrete design guidelines and examples [7] mainly because VR has many features that differ from traditional platforms. Many VR devices include optical or ultrasonic tracking systems to calculate physical objects' position and orientation in real-time, which makes gesture-based interaction in VR possible [8, 9]. Most VR devices also have handheld controllers that allow users to navigate and manipulate objects in the virtual world [10]. Force feedback and vibration are provided by haptic devices [11]. Audio in VR is usually supported by a fully surround sound system which enables sound localization.

A serious game is one designed for a primary purpose other than pure entertainment. There has been much research combining VR and serious games with some success [12–14]. Henrikson et al. proposed a workflow, specific to the needs of professionals creating storyboards for VR film, and presented a multi-device (tablet and head-mounted display) storyboard tool supporting this workflow [15]. Moreover, it is worth noting that they try to ensure consistency by making the tablet and the VR system display the same FOV(90°) and let both interfaces contain a ground plane represented by a radial grid and a degree scale wrapped around the environment for orientation. Vara et al. found that the type of device could be an important variable in serious game efficacy [13]. Furthermore, Longo et al. presented an innovative multi-device application based on the concept of intelligent serious games and studied the usability and sense of presence provided by different devices [14].

2.2 Multi-device Consistency

One challenge for interaction designers is to meet the requirements of consistency and continuity across these platforms to ensure the inter-usability of the system, namely the usability and user experience across the different user interfaces of a given system [16]. However, the "design-once-run-everywhere" strategy [17] does not apply for the current market.

Many previous studies focused on how to maintain consistency among traditional platforms like smartphone apps and websites. Lee et al. found that consistency showed a more significant effect on usability and credibility [18]. Sun et al. argued that there were three key object-based beliefs about consistency, namely information consistency, system consistency and service consistency [19], and investigated the standardization–adaptation paradox during the web–mobile service transition [20]. Majrashi et al. found that inconsistency was a principal factor affecting task continuity when participants switched from and to mobile native applications and mobile websites [21], especially when task complexity was sufficiently high [22]. Segerståhl and Oinas-Kukkonen found that the symbols, terms and interaction logic should be as consistent as possible between interaction devices to improve the semantic coherence, which contributed to user experience [23].

Oliveira and Rocha proposed consistency priorities to support multi-device interface design, and they suggested applying consistency on multi-device contexts using the following priorities: *Task Perception*, *Task Execution* and *Task Personalization* [24]. Dong and Wan presented a systematic method for the consistent design of user interaction which focusing on the consistency of logical interaction rather than physical or visual interfaces [25]. Hajdukiewicz et al. argued that content critical to task completion, performance, and behaviour-shaping constraints that users attuned to needed to be consistent in form across platforms, while secondary and supporting information not critical to shaping behaviours did not need to be consistent (but certainly could be if appropriate) [26].

Denis and Karsenty argued that seamless transitions between devices required both knowledge continuity and task continuity, which required inter-device consistency addressed on four levels: *Perceptual, Lexical, Syntactical, Semantic* [27]. Wäljas et al. proposed a framework in which consistency could be leveraged through *perceptual* (look and feel), *semantic* (symbols and terminology) and *syntactic* (interaction logic) consistency [28]. Sànchez-Adame et al. presented their five design guidelines to maintain consistency in multi-device systems include *Honesty, Functional Cores, Multimodality, Usability Limitations, Traceability* [29].

All these works show that consistency in multi-device service is a significant field with many open issues to explore. Although there is a lot of existing research on keeping user experience consistent, there is a lack of theoretical framework. Moreover, the devices considered in the consistency research only include traditional platforms like cell phones and PCs, the latest VR devices are not considered, so there is an urgent need for further exploration.

3   Dimensions of Consistency

Basing on the review of various works on consistency, we present four dimensions of consistency to consider when designing multi-device applications:

- Semantic consistency: multi-device applications shall have the same core content and functionalities across devices. Services provided shall be similar across devices by the definition of the consistency design approach.
- Syntactical consistency (interaction logic consistency): to complete a given task, the same set of operations or steps shall be required across devices; the user can achieve the same result regardless of input and output modalities.
- Perceptual consistency: the overall visual appearance, basic information structure and organization shall be consistent; multi-device applications shall look and feel similar on different devices.
- Lexical consistency: multi-device applications shall use the same set of vocabulary and symbols across devices.

Of course, the most important consistency is about user expectations [30]. The more important an element is in a multi-device application, the more consistent it shall be with users' expectation.

4   Case Study

This section describes a case study to put the proposed consistency dimensions into practical use to spot inconsistency issues and guide the modification of an existing application to enhance its consistency and usability. Preliminary consistency principles for multi-device application development were concluded as the outcome.

4.1 Introduction to the Test Material and Experiment Procedures

The test material we used was *Virtual Experiment of Film Language*, a multi-device serious game that allows users to learn film language in virtual space and provides an immersive and efficient learning experience. It has two different versions: a desktop version embedded in a webpage as a WebGL program(see Fig. 1), and an HMD VR version running on HTC Vive Cosmos (see Fig. 2). We focused on the shooting and editing stage of this serious game because it is the most complex part of the whole learning process, which involves a lot of interaction. In the shooting stage, the user can freely shoot in the virtual environment by using the Vive controllers as a virtual camera in the VR version. Correspondingly, a user may fall back on keyboard and mouse to translate or rotate the virtual camera in the desktop version. In the editing stage, the user can go to the playback mode at any time to review what has been recorded and reshoot the unsatisfying parts. The main differences between the two versions are listed in Table 1.

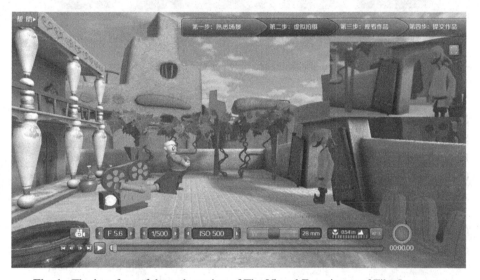

Fig. 1. The interface of the web version of The Virtual Experiment of Film Language

12 participants were recruited to experience them and report how they thought about the consistency issue between two versions individually. We informed them to pay attention to the consistency dimensions mentioned above to provide them with a structure of thinking and to prevent them from being distracted by other design aspects. We chose the participants with backgrounds in HCI and interaction design because of their acquaintance with our research topic. Many of them reported inconsistency issues in the four dimensions after they used both of them for the first time.

Then, this serious game was redesigned by us with the knowledge of their feedback and the theories on consistency. On completion of the modification, we asked the participants to evaluate the revised version again. The general feedback was more positive, showing that both consistency and usability improved.

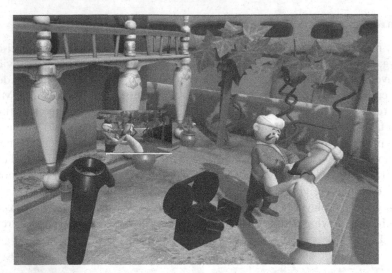

Fig. 2. The VR version of Virtual Experiment of Film Language

Table 1. The main difference between the web and VR version

Main difference	WebGL version	VR version
Move camera	Use gizmo or keyboard	Move one' s body and right hand
Start shooting	Click the red button	Keep pressing the right trigger
Pause shooting	Click the red button	Loosen the right trigger
Check camera view	Click the camera view button	Press the right trigger
Adjust the focal length	Drag the slide bar	Push the left joystick up or down to adjust FOV
Change camera mode	N/A	Click the right joystick
Change current time	Click on a point on the timeline	Press the left trigger and use right joystick and trigger to manipulate timeline
Call for help	Click the help button	Voice help at the beginning
Initial position	Same height as avatar	Same height as the second floor

4.2 Issues and Solutions

According to our participants' feedback, this multi-device serious game's consistency is good enough concerning semantic and lexical consistency. The participants are clear about the purpose and content of the game. As for semantic consistency, they know what they need to do and what they can expect in the game. In terms of lexical consistency, in general it is OK. The only exception is the terminological difference between the two versions: the *focal distance* as called in the desktop version was measured using FOV in the VR version. We fixed this by changing the VR version and using focal distance in both of them.

Syntactical Consistency. One of the most frequently mentioned issue of inconsistency is that the feeling of film shooting differed a lot between the desktop and VR versions. The desktop version felt like creating a movie clip in DCC software such as *blender* or *Maya* in which one has to use a gizmo to translate and rotate the camera from time to time. In contrast, the VR version's shooting felt more natural and realistic because the camera movement is bind to one's right hand's movement. We thought the inconsistency arose from the different level of operation directness between desktop and VR experience. Some participants reported that they were fond of the FPS-game-like control of the camera which allowed them to control its movement directly (see Fig. 3). In contrast, others claimed that to move and rotate the camera with a gizmo gave them more accuracy, so they prefer using the gizmo. So we decided to keep both of them and make the FPS control scheme as the default one in the desktop version. There might be other control scheme capable of offering higher level of directness for desktop applications, say using data from the sensors of a mobile phone for camera control. But since we hoped that the desktop version kept simple and easy to use, these complex schemes were not implemented in this study.

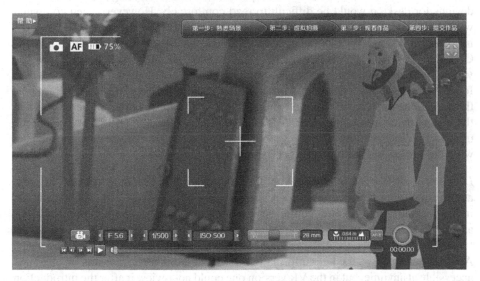

Fig. 3. The first-person view of the web version

Another inconsistency problem arose from the inconvenient timeline controls in the VR version, which was more serious because it changed our participants' behaviour patterns a lot. Many participants were found to move back and forth on the timeline a lot using the desktop version to remake some shots. However, as for the VR version, they tended not to enter playback mode to use the timeline due to the inconvenience of switching between two interfaces. Consistent elements should work in the same way between devices. The solution was that we enlarged the VR version's camera view to 160% and thus the timeline was more visible and could act as an indicator of the progress of the shooting. Furthermore, we allowed the user to manipulate the timeline directly by pushing the joystick on the controller to the left to step back by a frame and to the right to step forward by a frame. In this way, the timeline manipulation in VR was more direct and more consistent with the desktop version subjectively.

Sometimes the control method is a compromise between directness and accuracy. The desktop version was more straightforward and convenient as far as timeline operations were concerned, while the VR version was more straightforward regarding camera movement. Nevertheless, through careful thinking and innovative design, we can minimize the gap to an unnoticeable extent.

Perceptual Consistency. The most significant inconsistent issue was that the information provided by these two versions was different in quantity and modality. The VR version did not use a GUI to provide information or functions while the desktop version relies heavily on many UI elements on the screen to provide functionality. The VR version did not use a GUI because we hoped to reduce the learning cost as much as possible by making the interface minimal, Also, we did not want users to be distracted by GUI. Another reason was that the resolution of contemporary HMD displays, for instance the HTC Vive Cosmos we used in our experiment, was not very high and normal GUI designs for desktop would be difficult to read comfortably. However, when compared with the desktop version the inconsistency of the VR version's lack of GUI and the inconvenience caused by it became unneglectable to many users. As shown in Fig. 1, the GUI in the desktop version not only indicated the progress of the game but also provide various functions including help, zooming in and out, start and stop recording and so forth. In contrast VR version kept a user informed of the progress with vocal instructions, the operations were explained once using figures shown at the center of the viewport at the beginning, there was no other GUI elements except for a small LCD screen at the upper left corner with a tiny progress bar attached at the bottom, to showing the user what the camera was seeing during the shooting.

Different Amount of Information. One of the inconsistency issues came from the different amount of information accessible to a user at the same stage in two versions. For example, in the desktop version, a user could check and change all the important parameters of a real-world camera in the shooting stage, such as aperture size, ISO value and the focal length. However, the VR version hided all these from the user in the same stage. Another example was the help information. In the desktop version, it was detailed and accessible at anytime, but in the VR version one could not review it after the introduction at the beginning. These differences made participants feel inconsistent, especially if they experience the desktop version first and the VR version later.

Our solution to this problem was to add a world space UI to the VR version that kept floating around the camera and showed all the important parameters in it. Users might change these parameters with their right hand controller easily. Moreover, we designed a camera space UI which the user could call out at any time by pressing the grip button (see Fig. 4). This solution improved not only consistency but also usability of the VR version according to our interviewees.

Fig. 4. The help menu UI, enlarged camera view and camera information UI

Modalities. Another problem related to the previous one was that some information, like the operation instructions, was sent to the user via different modalities in the two versions. Many participants reported that they could not remember the vocal instructions well in the VR version, and they preferred the desktop version which conveyed the help information.

We assume that the effectiveness of different modalities affects consistency here. Therefore, important and complicated information shall be delivered to the user in the same way or in a similarly effective approach. We turned most of the vocal instructions that taught a user how to shoot into visual information in camera space GUI as described above. However, for simple information, modality consistency seemed less important. For example, in the desktop version, we used on-screen label to let a user know whether he/she was shooting, editing or reviewing the film while this information was delivered using a vocal reminder playing only once. However, no participant complained about this inconsistency because this information was clearly understandable and straightforward so it did not matter whether it was received by seeing or hearing.

Interestingly, we spotted several inconsistency issues that may not need to be addressed according to the survey. For example, the actions to start shooting were different: in the desktop version, a user needed to click the big red button on the right bottom of the screen, while in the VR version one had to keep pressing the right-hand trigger button. Although many participants tried to press the trigger button once shortly to start shooting because of the mental model affected by the desktop version, but they would soon find out the correct way of operation by themselves and began to love this feature only found in VR as it allowed more accurate control on timing and made users feel like they were really shooting a film. In this case, the consistency rule was altered but not broke. It was a compromise because it obviously unwise to force a user to press and hold down the record button in the desktop version to shoot continuously, which would undoubtedly lead to clumsy operations and worse user experience.

4.3 Design Principles

After the experiments were completed, we summarized three design principles based on our findings to guide future design practice of multi-device applications including VR:

- Interactive operations in different media shall be similar as far as logic and procedure are concerned. Under this premise, we shall design them to be as direct and easy to use as possible.
- The amount of information or content obtained from a given task/stage should be as equal as possible, especially for the important information critical to task completion, performance, and behaviour-shaping.
- System output should be independent from input modalities and platforms. For important outputs critical to shaping crucial behaviours, the output modalities shall be same or at least same in effectiveness. Secondary or auxiliary outputs do not need to have the same modality across different devices.

These principles place emphasis mainly on syntactical and perceptual consistency rather than semantic or lexical consistency. The first principle is specially suitable for VR interaction by taking into account the fact that some operations in VR are more straightforward. We see no reason to give up the advantage of this fact in the case of VR for the sake of consistency. The benefits of VR should be maintained while interaction for other devices should be devised carefully to be as direct and easy to use as possible. The second and third principles are a bit more general but also very helpful to consistency. If a user cannot have equally easy access to the same amounts of information at a given step, he will feel confused and fail to feel or benefit from the consistency between them.

5 Conclusions and Discussion

The main contribution of this paper is a series of design principles for the sake of consistency across different devices including VR HMDs. It also brought forward four dimension of consistency to be use as a guideline for consideration.

The four dimensions of consistency need to be further addressed. Some of our findings suggested that we shall pay more attention to the consistency of logical interaction rather than that of physical or visual interfaces. However, other findings suggested that same look and feel (perceptual consistency) is critical because it determined the user's first impression of the application. More research is needed to clarify the meaning of consistency and the user mental model so that the four dimensions of consistency can be sorted according to their significance.

As mentioned above, we found that the modifications we made according to these principles not only improved consistency but also enhanced usability. Besides obtaining benefits directly from improved consistency, a reasonable assumption is that the process of considering how to maintain multi-device consistency itself prompted us to think about our design from more perspectives. For example, we inspected many different input and output modalities while we were reviewing the original design. In this way, our mindset broadened and thus the overall design quality improved as a result.

We hope that the proposed consistency design principles, for UX designers, will reduce the complexity of designing multi-device applications, and for users, it will contribute to with the availability of products of great consistency and usability, easier to learn and to use.

In the future, the proposed design principles are subject to further revision while we redesign the user experience of this serious game for more kinds of digital devices such as mobile phones, tablets and other kinds of XR devices. Besides, more applications ought to be measured and more practice shall be carried out under the guidance of these consistency principles so as to validate them with prototypes. Secondly, a consistency assessment method should be developed to evaluate the level of consistency quantitatively so that the conclusions will be more objective. It will also help us to have a better understanding of how these factors contribute to each other. Thirdly, we encourage you to conduct a comparative study between our proposed design principles and another set of similar principles to determine its value based on their actual performance in design practice.

There is still much more research to be done in the area of multi-device consistency. Hopefully, our work may serve as a pilot explorative study in this field.

References

1. Forecast, G.M.D.T.: Cisco visual networking index: global mobile data traffic forecast update, 2017–2022 (2019)
2. Brudy, F., et al.: Cross-device taxonomy. In: Proceedings of the 2019 CHI Conference on Human Factors in Computing Systems (2019). https://doi.org/10.1145/3290605.3300792
3. Levin, M.: Designing multi-device experiences: an ecosystem approach to user experiences across devices. O'Reilly Media, Inc. (2014)
4. Radianti, J., Majchrzak, T.A., Fromm, J., Wohlgenannt, I.: A systematic review of immersive virtual reality applications for higher education: design elements, lessons learned, and research agenda. Comput. Educ. **147**, (2020). https://doi.org/10.1016/j.compedu.2019.103778
5. Qiao, X., Liu, Z., Jin, Y.: A VRLE Design Scheme for the Learning of Film Making. In: Zaphiris, P., Ioannou, A. (eds.) HCII 2019. LNCS, vol. 11591, pp. 204–219. Springer, Cham (2019). https://doi.org/10.1007/978-3-030-21817-1_16
6. Berg, L.P., Vance, J.M.: Industry use of virtual reality in product design and manufacturing: a survey. Virt. Real. **21**(1), 1–17 (2016). https://doi.org/10.1007/s10055-016-0293-9
7. Ashtari, N., Bunt, A., McGrenere, J., Nebeling, M., Chilana, P.K.: Creating augmented and virtual reality applications: current practices, challenges, and opportunities. In: Proceedings of the 2020 CHI Conference on Human Factors in Computing Systems (2020). https://doi.org/10.1145/3313831.3376722
8. Mitra, S., Acharya, T.: Gesture recognition: a survey. IEEE Trans. Syst. Man Cybern. Part C (Appl. Rev.) **37**(3), 311–324 (2007)
9. Yang, L.I., Huang, J., Feng, T.I.A.N., Hong-An, W.A.N.G., Guo-Zhong, D.A.I.: Gesture interaction in virtual reality. Virt. Real. Intel. Hardw. **1**(1), 84–112 (2019)
10. Bowman, D.A., et al.: 3D user interfaces: new directions and perspectives. IEEE Comput. Graph. Appl. **28**(6), 20–36 (2008). https://doi.org/10.1109/mcg.2008.109

11. Laycock, S.D., Day, A.M.: A survey of haptic rendering techniques. Comput. Graph. Forum **26**(1), 50–65 (2007). https://doi.org/10.1111/j.1467-8659.2007.00945.x

12. Rodriguez, A., et al.: A VR-based serious game for studying emotional regulation in adolescents. IEEE Comput. Graph. Appl. **35**(1), 65–73 (2015). https://doi.org/10.1109/mcg. 2015.8

13. Dolores Vara, M., et al.: A VR-based serious game to regulate joy in adolescents: a comparison of different devices. eHealth **360°**, 135–142 (2016). https://doi.org/10.1007/978-3-319-49655-9_18

14. Padovano, A., Vetrano, M., Longo, F., Nicoletti, L.: An intelligent serious game for a multi-device cultural heritage experience. Int. J. Simul. Process Model. **12**(6), 498 (2017). https:// doi.org/10.1504/ijspm.2017.10010589

15. Henrikson, R., Araujo, B., Chevalier, F., Singh, K., Balakrishnan, R.: Multi-device storyboards for cinematic narratives in VR. In: Proceedings of the 29th Annual Symposium on User Interface Software and Technology (2016). https://doi.org/10.1145/2984511.2984539

16. Antila, V., Lui, A.: Challenges in designing inter-usable systems. In: Campos, P., Graham, N., Jorge, J., Nunes, N., Palanque, P., Winckler, M. (eds.) INTERACT 2011. LNCS, vol. 6946, pp. 396–403. Springer, Heidelberg (2011). https://doi.org/10.1007/978-3-642-23774-4_33

17. van Welie, M., de Groot, B.: Consistent multi-device design using device categories. In: Paternò, F. (ed.) Mobile HCI 2002. LNCS, vol. 2411, pp. 315–318. Springer, Heidelberg (2002). https://doi.org/10.1007/3-540-45756-9_30

18. Lee, J., Lee, D., Moon, J., Park, M.-C.: Factors affecting the perceived usability of the mobile web portal services: comparing simplicity with consistency. Inf. Technol. Manage. **14**(1), 43–57 (2012). https://doi.org/10.1007/s10799-012-0143-8

19. Sun, Y., Shen, X.-L., Wang, N.: Understanding the role of consistency during web–mobile service transition: dimensions and boundary conditions. Int. J. Inf. Manage. **34**(4), 465–473 (2014). https://doi.org/10.1016/j.ijinfomgt.2014.04.008

20. Sun, Y., Shen, X.L., Wang, N.: Standardization or adaptation during the web-mobile service transition: understanding the moderating role of gender. J. Electron. Commerc. Res. **17**(3), 266 (2016)

21. Majrashi, K., Hamilton, M., Uitdenbogerd, A.L.: Task continuity and mobile user interfaces. In: Proceedings of the 17th International Conference on Mobile and Ubiquitous Multimedia (2018). https://doi.org/10.1145/3282894.3289742

22. Mendel, J., Pak, R., Drum, J.E.: Designing for consistency: can interface consistency reduce workload in dual-task situations? PsycEXTRA Dataset (2011). https://doi.org/10.1037/e57 8902012-426

23. Segerståhl, K., Oinas-Kukkonen, H.: Distributed user experience in persuasive technology environments. In: de Kort, Y., IJsselsteijn, W., Midden, C., Eggen, B., Fogg, B.J. (eds.) PERSUASIVE 2007. LNCS, vol. 4744, pp. 80–91. Springer, Heidelberg (2007). https://doi. org/10.1007/978-3-540-77006-0_10

24. de Oliveira, R., da Rocha, H.V.: Consistency priorities for multi-device design. In: Baranauskas, C., Palanque, P., Abascal, J., Barbosa, S.D.J. (eds.) INTERACT 2007. LNCS, vol. 4662, pp. 426–429. Springer, Heidelberg (2007). https://doi.org/10.1007/978-3-540-74796-3_40

25. Kim, D.S., Yoon, W.C.: A method for consistent design of user interaction with multifunction devices. In: Kurosu, M. (ed.) HCD 2009. LNCS, vol. 5619, pp. 202–211. Springer, Heidelberg (2009). https://doi.org/10.1007/978-3-642-02806-9_24

26. Hajdukiewicz, J.: 6 Interaction Momentum–Industrial Application Design and Consistency Across Platforms (2006)

27. Denis, C., Karsenty, L.: Inter-usability of multi-device systems - a conceptual framework. Multiple User Interfaces, 373–385 (2005). https://doi.org/10.1002/0470091703.ch17

28. Wäljas, M., Segerståhl, K., Väänänen-Vainio-Mattila, K., Oinas-Kukkonen, H.: Cross-platform service user experience. In: Proceedings of the 12th International Conference on Human Computer Interaction with Mobile Devices and Services - MobileHCI 2010 (2010). https://doi.org/10.1145/1851600.1851637
29. Sánchez-Adame, L.M., Mendoza, S., Viveros, A.M., Rodríguez, J.: Consistency in multi-device environments: a case study. Intell. Comput. 232–242 (2019). https://doi.org/10.1007/978-3-030-22871-2_17
30. Tognazzini, B.: Interaction design solutions for the real world, 5 November 2005

Multimodal and Natural Interaction in VAMR

The Effect of Body-Based Haptic Feedback on Player Experience During VR Gaming

Michael Carroll[1] and Caglar Yildirim[2]([⊠]) [iD]

[1] State University of New York at Oswego, Oswego, NY 13126, USA
michael.carroll@oswego.edu
[2] Northeastern University, Boston, MA 02151, USA
c.yildirim@northeastern.edu

Abstract. As the interest in virtual reality (VR) technology as a game console has rapidly grown over the past few years, many new technologies are also being developed to further enhance the VR gaming experience. One of these technologies is haptic feedback vests, which are beginning to hit the market with claims of elevating the player experience (PX). Since the use of haptic vests during gameplay is still in its early stages, their influence on the PX during VR gaming is understudied. Accordingly, the current study investigated the effect of providing body-based haptic feedback on players' sense of presence and overall PX during VR gaming. Participants played a VR-based rhythm game both with and without a haptic feedback vest and provided self-reported ratings of their sense of presence and PX. Results revealed that there was no significant difference between playing with a haptic vest and without a haptic vest in terms of players' sense of presence and PX during the gameplay. As a whole, these results indicate that providing body-based haptic feedback using a haptic vest may not always increase sense of presence and PX levels when playing a rhythm game in VR.

Keywords: VR gaming · Haptics · Haptic feedback · Haptic vest · Player experience

1 Introduction

Innovation is key when it comes to a user's experience in gaming. Often the most successful ideas are the most inventive and create new opportunities for developers. Virtual reality (VR) has opened new possibilities in the realm of gaming, giving users a new way to immerse themselves in the game world. While VR can be used in other areas, the game industry has arguably seen the biggest impact, as evidenced by the increasing number of VR-compatible video games on Steam, a popular game distribution platform [1]. Along with VR, however, other technologies, such as haptic vests and gloves, have been developed to help enhance the gaming experience even further. The goal of these technologies is to provide players with a greater connection to the game world, which is, in turn, purported to enhance their player experience (PX).

VR involves the use of computer-generated imagery in a three-dimensional space that allows the user to interact with a simulation in a more natural way. These simulations are

© Springer Nature Switzerland AG 2021
J. Y. C. Chen and G. Fragomeni (Eds.): HCII 2021, LNCS 12770, pp. 163–171, 2021.
https://doi.org/10.1007/978-3-030-77599-5_13

often referred to as virtual environments (VE). This interaction creates a more immersive feeling when done correctly by allowing the user to traverse through and interact with a VE in a way similar to which they would in the real world [2].

VR gaming continues to grow in popularity as new, more immersive headsets and technologies become available to consumers and as developers create new and innovative ways to play [2, 3]. One of the affordances of immersive gaming technologies is haptic feedback, which can be provided in the form of full-body feedback through a haptic vest and/or in the form of interactive feedback through the use of VR controllers. While the latter has received a great deal of interest from both academic researchers and practitioners [3, 4], the former has been rather understudied. More specifically, little empirical data are available on how providing body-based haptic feedback through a haptic vest affects the PX while users are playing a video game in VR. To address this issue, we conducted a pilot user study in which participants played a VR-based rhythm game, Beat Saber, both with and without a haptic vest. Participants then provided self-reported ratings on their sense of presence and overall PX. Results revealed no statistically significant differences between the haptic vest and no-haptic vest conditions. These results indicate that providing body-based haptic feedback using a haptic vest did not lead to substantial increases in sense of presence and PX, which is a finding incongruent with our initial prediction.

The main contribution of our pilot study is a user study providing an empirical investigation into the effect of body-based haptic feedback through a haptic vest on VR gaming experience, which is an understudied area of research within the VR gaming literature. Thus, it is hoped the findings from the current study will provide an impetus for further research into this emerging domain. In the following sections, we provide a review of related work and a detailed description of our user study, along with the results and discussion.

2 Related Work

2.1 Presence and Player Experience

Virtual reality has enhanced the immersive nature of video games leading to greater levels of presence. Witmer and Singer describe immersion as a psychological state in which oneself is enveloped by and views themselves as integrated with a VE that provides the user with continuous stimulation [8]. The intent of VR is to create an immersive experience for a user with the ideal outcome of achieving a high level of presence. Presence can be summarized as the experience of being in an environment, even though one is physically situated in another [5]. Presence can be measured through two self-observed factors. First, the player should be able to self-report their own level of presence in the game [6]. Additionally, the player should be able to experience a sense of being elsewhere during their gaming experience [6].

Presence and immersion are important elements to consider for game developers because they have a direct connection with the PX, which refers to the player's overall experience with the game and is directly associated with their enjoyment of the game [7]. PX can be considered one of the most important factors contributing to a game's success. The reason is that most games are meant to either exist as a service in which they are playable for years after release, or simply excel to the status of critically acclaimed games. By allowing players to feel immersed and present in a VE, developers stand the chance of creating a great PX.

2.2 Haptic Feedback and Player Experience

The emergence of haptic vests is a relatively new concept in the gaming industry. Just as with VR headsets, haptic vests are starting to enter the consumer market, thus making it more accessible to a larger audience. While some haptic controllers have previously been available to consumers, recently technological improvements have allowed for haptic vests to be developed. The use of haptics can enhance the PX as it helps to provide tactile feedback based on in-game objects [7]. In fact, Kim et al. argue that without the use of haptic responses, VEs can result in a disconnect between the real world and a virtual world [8]. This means that the use of haptic feedback can breathe new life into VEs.

The utility of providing such body-based haptic feedback is to enhance the mean-ingful involvement of multiple senses during the gameplay, which can lead a greater sense of presence inside the VE. To the best of our knowledge, no empirical evidence is available on the effect of providing body-based haptic feedback through a haptic vest on PX during VR gaming. That said, it has already been shown that just the use of haptic controllers can increase a player's sense of presence [8, 9]. With this is mind, providing body-based haptic feedback using a haptic vest can potentially lead to a more immersive experience and further the level of presence experienced by the player while playing a game. Accordingly, the purpose of the current study was to investigate the effect of providing body-based haptic feedback on both sense of presence and PX during VR Gaming. The hypotheses of the current study were:

H1: Compared to no body-based haptic feedback, providing body-based haptic feedback would invoke a greater sense of presence in the VE.

H2: Compared to no body-based haptic feedback, providing body-based haptic feedback would lead to a greater PX.

3 Method

To test these hypotheses, we conducted an experiment in which participants played a VR game with and without body based haptic feedback. The independent variable was the existence of body-based haptic feedback (haptic vest vs. no haptic vest). The independent variable was manipulated within-subjects, so participants took part in both conditions. The dependent variables were the sense of presence, as measure by the Pres-ence Scale, and PX, which was measured using the Game User Experience Satisfaction Scale (GUESS), as described below.

3.1 Participants

The participants in this study were recruited using an email announcement sent to the student population at the university where this study was conducted. In total there were 30 participants, with 18 females and 12 males. The average age of the participants was 21.1 ($SD = 2.6$).

3.2 Materials

Game User Experience Satisfaction Scale. The Game User Experience Satisfaction Scale (GUESS) is a multidimensional scale designed to measure a player's PX during the gameplay [10]. The GUESS has a total of 9 dimensions for the different facets of the PX. These include Usability/Playability, Narratives, Play Engrossment, Enjoyment, Creative Freedom, Audio Aesthetics, Personal Gratification, Social Connectivity, and Visual Aesthetics [10]. Since the game used in this study was a single player rhythm game, the Social connectivity and Narratives dimensions were excluded from the questionnaire presented to participants. Thus, the modified GUESS questionnaire included 44 of items corresponding to the remaining seven dimensions. A total GUESS score quantifying the PX was calculated for each participant in each condition. Greater GUESS scores indicate greater PX.

Presence Scale. The Presence scale is a self-reported measure focused on determining the level of sense of presence an individual experiences in a VE [5]. The presence scale includes a total of eight items rated on a 7-point Likert scale. A total presence is scored by averaging the responses to all items. A higher score on the presence scale indicates a player feeling a greater sense of presence during the gameplay.

Gaming Platform. We used the Oculus Rift CV1 (the Rift) headset for this study [11]. The Rift makes use of an HMD that tracks the user's head movement and position within a VE and includes both a gyroscope and accelerometer to replicate the user's head movement within the VE. The HMD also supports 1080×1200 resolution in each eye with each display having a refresh rate of 90 Hz and sporting a 110-degree field of view (FOV) [12, 13]. Participants also used the Oculus Touch controllers while playing the game.

Body-Based Haptic Feedback. To provide body-based haptic feedback during the VR gameplay, we used a haptic vest, specifically the Tactot vest and Tactosy arm sleeves by bHaptics [14] (Fig. 1). The vest utilizes 40 different vibration points around the user's torso [14]. As for the arm sleeves, they include 6 vibration points for each arm [14]. These vibration points are designed to mimic sensation of touch. In the current study, the sensors were used to convert the rhythm of the sounds within the game into vibrations, mimicking the rhythm of the sound through body-based haptic feedback. Participants put on both the vest and arm sleeves in the haptic feedback condition.

VR Game. This study used a popular VR-based rhythm game called Beat Saber [15]. Beat Saber is a rhythm game where the player must slash blocks as they pass in accordance with the rhythm of the song being played. The song that was used in this study was Country Roads (Sqeepo Remix) by Jaroslav Beck and Kings & Folk. Participants played this song on easy mode and the options for a no-fail mode and a no-obstacle mode were turned on (Fig. 2).

Fig. 1. An image of Tactot vest for torso and Tactosy arm sleeves taken from https://www.bha ptics.com/tactsuit/ [14]

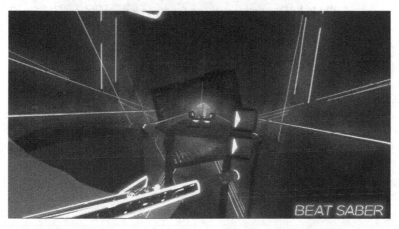

Fig. 2. A screenshot of the Beat Saber game, taken from https://beatsaber.com/ [15].

3.3 Procedure

When participants first arrived, they were greeted and instructed to review the informed consent form. While the form was being completed the participant was assigned a random starting condition, which involved starting with or without the haptic vest. This was done due to the within-subjects manipulation of the independent variable in which participants were to participate in both the no-haptic feedback vs. haptic feedback conditions. Once the consent form was completed, the participant played the tutorial available within the game. After completing the tutorial, the participant played the song (meaning that they played the VR game while the song was being played in the background). Depending on their assigned starting condition, participants put on the haptic vest and arm sleeves as well. Upon the song's conclusion the participant was directed to the questionnaire containing the study measures. After the first completion of the first condition, participants took a short break between the conditions, while the experimenter prepared the next part of the experiment. After the break participants then completed the same song for the other condition. If they started out with the haptic feedback condition, then they did not put on the vest and arm sleeves in this second condition, and vice versa. Following the completion of the second condition, participants were directed to the questionnaire for a second round of measurements. At the end, participants were debriefed and afforded the opportunity to ask any questions. The entire experiment was completed in about 30 min.

3.4 Results

Before hypothesis testing, we explored the data from the experiment (see Table 1 for descriptive statistics) and checked for assumptions. The assumption of normality was not met for a paired samples t test. Therefore, the nonparametric alternative, Wilcoxon Signed Rank Test, was conducted instead (see Table 2 for inferential statistics).

Table 1. Descriptive statistics for dependent variables.

	M (SD)	Mdn
Sense of presence		
No haptic feedback	5.18 (1.56)	5.63
Haptic feedback	4.99 (1.56)	5.13
Player experience		
No haptic feedback	42.37 (3.43)	42.74
Haptic feedback	42.75 (3.21)	41.92

M: mean, SD: standard deviation, Mdn: median

Table 2. Results of hypothesis testing.

	W	Mdn	M_diff	95% CI	d
Sense of presence	208	.656	.125	[−.312, .625]	.125
Player experience	154	.173	−.646	[−1.51, .290]	.146

Mdn: median, Mdiff: mean difference, 95% CI: 95% confidence intervals, d: Cohen's d as effect size measure

A Wilcoxon signed rank was conducted to determine if there were differences in both presence scores and PX scores between the use of a haptic vest and no haptics. Results indicated that presence scores (Hypothesis 1) were not statistically significantly different between the no haptic feedback ($Mdn = 5.63, M = 5.18, SD = 1.56$) and haptic feedback conditions ($Mdn = 5.13, M = 4.99, SD = 1.56$), $W = 208, p = .656, 95\%$ CI $[-.312, .625]$, Cohen's $d = .125$. Figure 3 represents the presence level scores as a function of haptic feedback.

As for the effect of haptic feedback on PX (Hypothesis 2), results revealed no statistically significantly differences between no haptic feedback ($Mdn = 42.74, M = 42.37, SD = 3.43$) and haptic feedback conditions ($Mdn = 41.92, M = 42.75, SD = 3.21$), $W =$

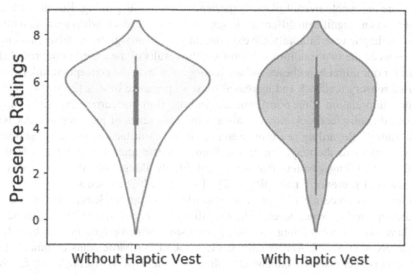

Fig. 3. Sense of presence levels. The violin plot displays the box plot for each condition along with the kernel density estimate for the distribution of scores in each condition.

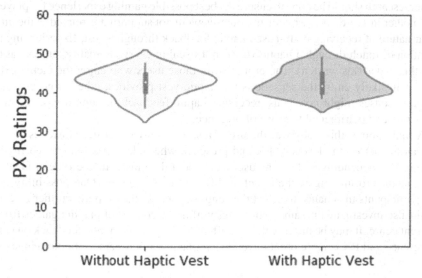

Fig. 4. PX ratings as a function of haptic feedback. The violin plot displays the box plot for each condition along with the kernel density estimate for the distribution of scores in each condition.

$154, p = .173, 95\%$ CI $[-1.514, .290], d = -.146$. Figure 4 represents the PX scores as a function of haptic feedback.

3.5 Discussion

The purpose of this study was to investigate the effect of body-based haptic feedback on sense of presence and PX levels during VR gaming. We hypothesized that providing body-based haptic feedback using a haptic vest would invoke a greater sense of presence and a more enjoyable overall player experience during VR gaming. Results indicated that there was no significant difference in sense of presence levels when gaming with and without the haptic vest. Similarly, the experiment yielded no significant differences in PX levels between the two conditions. Therefore, the results of the experiment provided no support for our initial hypotheses and are incongruent with the conceptual link between increased sensory feedback and increased sense of presence in VEs [2, 3].

One interpretation of the nonsignificant findings from the current experiment is that body-based haptic feedback may not always increase sense of presence and PX levels in VR gaming. Regarding sense of presence, it is a multifaceted construct and while the involvement of the player in an experience is essential, it is not the sole factor [2]. Witmer and Singer believe that perceptual fidelity along with other sensory factors affect levels of presence for the player [2]. However, while a good sensory experience can enhance presence for a player, it is also likely that an unpleasant experience can decrease reported presence levels. The overall experience provided by the haptic vest could have been overwhelming for some participants, which might, in turn, have led to lower levels of presence. Anecdotally, while some of our participants commented that their gaming experience was enhanced by the vest, others found that the haptic feedback through the vest was distracting their attention away from the main experience. As the VR experience continues to develop and the simulations provided become more realistic, further research should be done to ensure the best possible gaming experience for players.

Another interpretation why the hypotheses were not supported is related to the unfamiliar nature of receiving body-based haptic feedback through a vest. Experiencing the sensation of touch through a haptic vest is not usual in everyday reality (at least at the time this paper was written). Therefore, while those users who enjoy the tactile experience will likely enjoy the sensations the haptic vest provides, others who primarily use other senses might not. Thus, receiving haptic feedback through a vest might be distracting and detrimental to sense of presence.

A limitation of this study was the use of a single genre of music. Music taste could have an impact on the levels of PX and presence when playing a song-based rhythm game in VR, depending on how the user feels about the music. It would be prudent for future studies to investigate the effect of different music genres. One possibility is to give participants the chance to select the song they would like to play. Further research should also investigate the same hypotheses within the context of playing games from a different genre. It may be the case that the effect of body-based haptic feedback on sense of presence and PX is more pronounced when playing a first-person shooter game.

References

1. Shelstad, W. J., Smith, D. C., Chaparro, B. S.: Gaming on the rift: how virtual reality affects game user satisfaction. In: Proceedings of the Human Factors and Ergonomics Society Annual Meeting 2017, vol. 61, pp. 2072–2076 (2017)
2. Yildirim, C.: Cybersickness during VR gaming undermines game enjoyment: a mediation model. Displays **59**(1), 35–43 (2019)
3. Hufnal, D., Osborne, E., Johnson, T., Yildirim, C.: The impact of controller type on video game user experience in virtual reality. In: Proceedings of the IEEE Games, Entertainment, and Media Conference 2019, pp. 1–9 (2019)
4. Carroll, M., Osborne, E., Yildirim, C.: Effects of VR gaming and game genre on player experience. In: Proceedings of the IEEE Games, Entertainment, and Media Conference 2019, pp. 1–9 (2019)
5. Witmer, B.G., Singer, M.J.: Measuring presence in virtual environments: a presence questionnaire. Presence **7**(3), 225–240 (1998)
6. Slater, M., Usoh, M.: Presence in immersive virtual environments. In: Proceedings of the IEEE Annual Virtual Reality International Symposium 1993, pp. 90–96 (1993)
7. Eid, M., El Issawi, A., El Saddik, A.: Slingshot 3D: a synchronous haptic-audio-video game. Multimedia Tools Appl. **71**(3), 1635–1649 (2012). https://doi.org/10.1007/s11042-012-1297-4
8. Kim, M., Jeon, C., Kim, J.: A study on immersion and presence of a portable hand haptic system for immersive virtual reality. Sensors **17**(5), 1141 (2017)
9. Jin, S.A.: Effects of 3D virtual haptics force feedback on brand personality perception: the mediating role of physical presence in advergames. Cyberpsychol. Behav. Soc. Netw. **13**(3), 307–311 (2010)
10. Phan, M.H., Keebler, J.R., Chaparro, B.S.: The development and validation of the Game User Experience Satisfaction Scale (GUESS). Hum. Factors **58**(8), 1217–1247 (2016)
11. Oculus Rift: VR Headset for VR Ready PCs|Oculus (2019). https://www.oculus.com/rift/
12. Buy Oculus Rift + Touch - Microsoft Store (2019). https://www.microsoft.com/en-us/p/oculus-rift-touch/8mt5ws8lgbwl?activetab=pivot:techspecstab
13. Oculus Rift Specs (2019). https://www.cnet.com/products/oculus-rift/specs/
14. Tactsuit, full body haptic vest for VR (2019). https://www.bhaptics.com/tactsuit
15. Beat Games: Beat Saber. Steam (2018). https://store.steampowered.com/app/620980/Beat_Saber/

User Defined Walking-In-Place Gestures for Intuitive Locomotion in Virtual Reality

Woojoo Kim[1], Eunsik Shin[2], and Shuping Xiong[1(✉)]

[1] Human Factors and Ergonomics Lab, Department of Industrial and Systems Engineering, Korea Advanced Institute of Science and Technology (KAIST), 291 Daehak-ro, Yuseong-gu, Daejeon 34141, Republic of Korea
{xml1324,shupingx}@kaist.ac.kr
[2] Department of Industrial Engineering, College of Engineering, Inha University, 100 Inha-ro, Michuhol-gu, Incheon 22212, Republic of Korea
12160559@inha.edu

Abstract. Locomotion is one of the fundamental interactions in virtual reality (VR). As a simple yet naturalistic way to enable VR locomotion, walking-in-place (WIP) techniques have been actively developed. Even though various WIP gestures have been proposed, they were adopted or designed from the perspective of developers, not the users. This limits the benefits of WIP as unnatural gestures may result in a higher cognitive load to learn and memorize, worse presence, and increased sensory conflict. Therefore, this study elicited natural WIP gestures for forward, sideways, and backward walking directions from users. Twenty participants experienced the movement while wearing the VR headset and elicited the WIP gesture for 8 walking directions. The grouping results showed that Turn body + Stepping-in-place (SIP) and Step one foot + SIP/Rock/Stay were four promising WIP gesture sets for VR locomotion. A comparison between elicited and existing gestures revealed that elicited gestures have the potential to outperform existing gestures due to easier to perform, less fatigue, and higher presence. The generated WIP gesture sets could be used in gesture-based VR applications to provide a better user experience and greater movement options in VR locomotion.

Keywords: Walking-in-place · Gesture elicitation · VR locomotion

1 Introduction

Virtual Reality (VR) has been around for decades, but users and researchers have recently begun to show increasing interest as VR becomes much more commercially available. The VR markets are growing rapidly, with a total global demand estimated to hit 98.4 million sales by 2023, with 168 million units and a worldwide population penetration of 2% installed [1]. Past human-computer interaction approaches forced human behavior to suit the capabilities of the computer; however, VR interactions are different, since the computer should simulate the real world in order to make the experience as realistic as possible. Because of this interaction close to the real world, interaction strategies that

© Springer Nature Switzerland AG 2021
J. Y. C. Chen and G. Fragomeni (Eds.): HCII 2021, LNCS 12770, pp. 172–182, 2021.
https://doi.org/10.1007/978-3-030-77599-5_14

are common to humans, such as gestures that humans regularly use to communicate with the physical world, are considered promising.

Virtual travel is one of the most popular and universal interactions in VR; however, the methods currently available for VR locomotion depend heavily on the use of the game controller to travel and teleport, or on real walking in a small physical room, neglecting the proliferating demands of the method of navigating limitless virtual space by actually moving the user's feet. A device based on walking-in-place (WIP) techniques has been actively developed [2–6] as a relatively quick and simple method for implementing VR locomotion without the use of bulky and costly mechanical treadmills [7–9].

While WIP lacks some benefits compared to real walking or controller-based methods, WIP needs a very small physical space to travel across endless virtual space, unlike real walking where the same amount of physical space is needed. Moreover, it is not only hands-free in most situations, but also offers greater immersion and spatial awareness compared to conventional joystick interfaces by offering vestibular and proprioceptive signals comparable to real walking [10–13], and less motion-sickness by managing sensory conflict [14, 15].

Table 1. Existing walking-in-place (WIP) gestures proposed by earlier studies

Direction	Refs.	Description
Forward	[16]	Alternately lift the feet upward (commonly referred to as Stepping-in-place (SIP))
	[17]	Alternately lift the heels while having the ball of feet contact the ground or alternately move the feet backward like wiping the floor while bending the moving leg's knee
	[18]	Alternately either step with one foot towards the corresponding direction to move or to bend their knees
	[19]	Alternately swing the arms like when they walk but while keeping their legs still
	[12]	Alternately lift the heels while having the ball of feet contact the ground
	[20]	Alternately lift one leg to make the body lean naturally to one side
Sideways/backward	[2]	*Sideways:* Swing one leg sideways and nominally lift and drop the alternate foot; *Backward:* Alternately swing the feet to the back while the knees are relatively stationary
	[21]	Tilt the head to the side or back while performing WIP to move toward the direction that the head is tilted

As shown in Table 1, developers have adopted or designed new WIP gestures, but they failed to elicit gestures from the perspective of the users. Those proposed gestures could be unnatural for users, consequently result in not only a higher cognitive load to learn and memorize [22], but also worse presence and increased sensory conflict, failing to provide a better experience in VR [23]. Only a few studies have attempted to elicit gestures for VR locomotion. Felberbaum and Lanir [24] elicited foot gestures for GUI and avatar actions, but referents were for controlling an avatar in a monitor display, not for locomotion of the user in the immersive head-mounted display-based VR [24]. In the study of Ganapathi and Sorathia [25], gestures were elicited for VR locomotion but while in a sitting position only [25]. To the best of our knowledge, no studies have elicited WIP gestures for VR locomotion while standing, especially including directions other than forward. Therefore, this study aims to elicit natural WIP gestures covering whole walking directions including forward, sideways, and backward from the users. We collected gestures using the gesture elicitation methodology [26], and subjectively assessed elicited and existing gestures.

2   Methods

2.1   Participants and Experimental Settings

20 Korean young adults with a mean age of 24.0 (SD = 5.8) participated in the experiment. 17 participants had an experience of using a PC-based commercial VR headset, but only a single participant had prior experience in using WIP for VR locomotion thus most participants were light VR users and were free from the legacy bias. All participants gave consent for the protocol approved by the University Institutional Review Board (IRB NO.: KH2020–069).

8 referents, representing 8 different walking directions were selected for the elicitation. 8 directions included forward ($0°$), forward diagonal left/right ($-45°/45°$), left/rightward ($-90°/90°$), backward diagonal left/right ($-135°/135°$), and backward ($180°$). Here, all referents indicated walking in the virtual space towards the corresponding direction while the head always faces forward.

In this study, we limited the scope of the gesture to the lower extremity only, considering technical challenges in full-body tracking and benefits of unrestrictedness of hands and head in practical use cases. By excluding gestures with the use of other body parts and considering evaluation results from previous studies, 10 existing WIP gestures: 3 gestures [12, 17, 20] for forward and 7 gestures (1 gesture for each direction) [2] for other directions were selected for the evaluation.

The experiment was conducted with the Oculus Quest VR headset (resolution: 1440 × 1600 per eye; refresh rate: 72 Hz) while connected to the PC through Oculus Link with a USB 3.0 cable. The PC was equipped with an Intel Core i7–7700 CPU, 16 GB of RAM, and an NVIDIA GeForce GTX 1080 Ti GPU. The RGB video of elicited gestures was recorded by Microsoft Kinect v2 placed at 2.5 m apart from the participant and 1.0 m apart from the ground. The participant was located inside an ordinary room covered by achromatic-colored walls in VR, developed based on Unity 2018.4.0f1. Figure 1 shows the experimental settings.

2.2   Experimental Procedure

First, participants were asked to hold the VR headset in front of their chest and walk 3 steps towards each of 8 directions twice, and their walking speed at the second trial

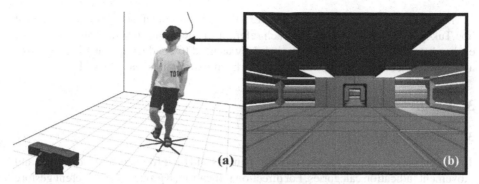

Fig. 1. Experimental settings: (a) real environment and (b) virtual environment

was measured by the VR headset with inside-out positional tracking. Then, participants equipped the VR headset and experienced each of 8 referents for 3 s in randomized order. The walking speed was set to the speed measured earlier to provide the natural feeling when eliciting gestures. After experiencing each referent, participants were asked to elicit a single most appropriate WIP gesture for each referent, and the elicited gesture was recorded with a verbal explanation about the reason for their design (Think-aloud). No hints were provided to participants during the elicitation process to avoid legacy bias.

Lastly, participants were asked to perform each of the elicited and existing gestures for 3–4 walking cycles two times while the referent is being displayed by the experimenter (Wizard of Oz). Right after performing each gesture, participants were asked to give ratings on a 7-point Likert scale (1 = strongly disagree, 7 = strongly agree) for four subjective evaluation items: goodness of fit ('The gesture I picked is a good match for its intended purpose'), ease of use ('The gesture I picked is easy to perform'), perceived fatigue ('The gesture I picked induces high fatigue'), and presence ('I feel like I exist inside the VR space'). These items have been commonly used in gesture elicitation studies [25, 27].

2.3 Data Analysis

Elicited gestures were first decomposed into two components: direction and movement indication, and were grouped through the video analysis based on motion characteristics of gestures and verbal explanations of participants. Then, the agreement rate (AR) was calculated for each referent (Eq. 1) [26] to evaluate the degree of agreement among gestures elicited from different participants:

$$\text{AR(r)} = \frac{\sum_{P_i \subseteq P} \frac{1}{2}|P_i|(|P_i| - 1)}{\frac{1}{2}|P|(|P| - 1)} = \frac{|P|}{|P| - 1}\sum_{P_i \subseteq P}\left(\left|\frac{P_i}{P}\right|\right)^2 - \frac{1}{|P| - 1} \quad (1)$$

where P stands for the total number of elicited gestures for a referent r, and P_i stands for the number of a subset i of identical gestures from P. Qualitative interpretations for AR are as follows [26]: a low agreement when AR ≤ 0.100, a moderate agreement when $0.100 < \text{AR} \leq 0.300$, a high agreement when $0.300 < \text{AR} \leq 0.500$, and a very high agreement when AR > 0.500.

For comparison between elicited and existing gestures, analysis of variance and post hoc Tukey tests were conducted in each referent to check the statistical significance of each subjective evaluation item. Minitab 19 was used to conduct all statistical analyses at a significance level of 0.05. The variation from participants was blocked.

3 Results and Discussion

3.1 Grouping Results

Table 2 shows the user elicited gesture components and their frequencies by direction and movement indication categories. For direction indication, 8 groups with different gesture components were formed. 'Turn body' and 'Step one foot' were two components that were elicited dominantly more than others across all directions with average frequencies of 8.4 and 7.6 out of 20 respectively, which means that participants either turned their body or stepped one foot towards the corresponding direction in most cases (80% of all cases). Participants tended to turn body more instead of stepping one foot at forward and backward directions, and vice versa for sideways ($\pm 45°$, $\pm 90°$, and $\pm 135°$) directions. An exception was found at 90°, where more participants lifted closer foot first and higher to indicate direction instead of turning their body. This is because turning the body 90° is identical to turning the neck 90° to the opposite direction. A normal healthy young adult can only rotate his/her neck up to around 80° [28], and keeping maximum neck rotation delivers severe load on the neck, thereby it is natural to avoid such conditions. For directions above 90° (135°, −135°, and 180°), participants turned their body towards the opposite direction at (−45°, 45°, and 0°, respectively) and conducted the gesture representing backward walking due to the same reason.

For movement indication, 14 groups were formed, representing 'SIP' as the most dominant gesture component with an average frequency of 8.2, followed by 'Rock' (3.2) and 'Stay' (2.0). The dominant elicitation of the SIP gesture (41% of all cases) was expected considering its wide-spread usage and popularity among common users and researchers [2–6], which is consistent with the result of the previous study [24]. It is worth noting that participants tended to elicit the equivalent or variants of the SIP gesture even in non-forward directions. This is because participants generally try to transfer their prior knowledge and experience when they design new gestures [29]. This principle was also reflected in applying the same design standard at designing WIP gestures for different walking directions. 9 out of 20 (45%) participants applied the same standard in all directions, while 7 out of 20 (35%) of participants applied the same standard in sideways but not in forward and backward directions. For the left and right directions, all 20 (100%) participants elicited symmetrical gestures, which is in line with the findings from previous studies where participants adopted reversible gestures for dichotomous tasks [27, 30, 31].

For direction indication, a very high agreement was found at 0° (AR = 0.532), a high agreement was found at ±135° (AR = 0.337) and 180° (AR = 0.437), and a medium agreement was found at ± 45° (AR = 0.300) and ±90° (AR = 0.184). For movement indication, a high agreement was found at 0° (AR = 0.358), a medium agreement was found at ±45° (AR = 0.232), ±90° (AR = 0.232), and ±135° (AR = 0.126), and a low agreement was found at 180° (AR = 0.079). In both indication categories, AR was the

Table 2. Frequency of user-elicited gesture components by direction and movement indication category. For (±)45°, (±)90°, and (±)135°, all elicited gestures were symmetrical for the left and right directions thereby result in the identical grouping result.

Indication	Gesture components	Direction					Average (%)
		0°	45°	90°	135°	180°	
Direction	Turn body	14	6	3	8	11	8.4(42%)
	Step one foot	5	9	7	9	8	7.6(38%)
	Turn one foot	0	4	2	1	0	1.4(6%)
	Walk one step	1	1	1	1	1	1(5%)
	Lift closer foot first and higher	0	0	5	0	0	1(5%)
	Slide one foot to opposite	0	0	1	0	0	0.2(1%)
	Lean body	0	0	1	0	0	0.2(1%)
	Swing one foot	0	0	0	1	0	0.2(1%)
Movement	SIP	12	9	9	6	5	8.2(41%)
	Rock	2	4	4	4	2	3.2(16%)
	Stay	2	2	2	2	2	2(10%)
	Stamp one foot	1	2	2	2	2	1.8(9%)
	Step back and forth	1	1	1	1	1	1(5%)
	Tapping-in-place	1	1	0	1	1	0.8(4%)
	Slide in place	1	1	1	1	0	0.8(4%)
	Swing lower legs	0	0	0	2	2	0.8(4%)
	Swing legs to opposite	0	0	0	0	2	0.4(2%)
	Slide one foot to opposite	0	0	1	0	0	0.2(1%)
	Swing the closer leg	0	0	0	1	0	0.2(1%)
	Draw vertical circles with feet	0	0	0	0	1	0.2(1%)
	Draw horizontal circles with feet	0	0	0	0	1	0.2(1%)
	Step back and forth in place	0	0	0	0	1	0.2(1%)

highest at 0°, which was influenced by the dominant elicitation of the SIP gesture for the forward walking. Participants were less familiar and had less prior knowledge for walking towards non-forward directions, thus came up with more creative and unique gestures. AR for direction indication was the lowest at 90° due to the variation derived from the inconvenience of the body turning. On the other hand, AR for movement indication was the lowest at 180° due to the attempt to avoid the overlap with the common SIP gesture generally assigned for 0°.

Gestures proposed by equal to or more than two participants on average were chosen [27] to generate the recommended gesture set. Those included top 2 components: 'Turn body' and 'Step one foot' for direction indication, and top 3 components: 'SIP', 'Rock', and 'Stay' for movement indication, ultimately forming four gesture sets: Turn body + SIP, Step one foot + SIP/Rock/Stay by combining two components (Fig. 2). As the body cannot be rocked without stepping one foot and staying without stepping one foot is indistinguishable from the neutral standing posture, combinations of Turn body + Rock/Stay were excluded.

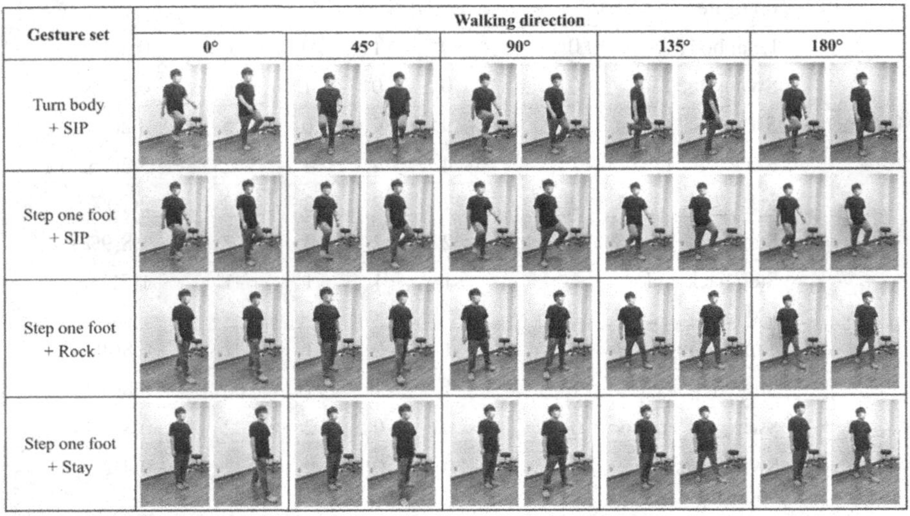

Fig. 2. Generated four WIP gesture sets. For 45°, 90°, and 135°, gestures are symmetrical for the left and right directions. A video demonstration can be seen from https://vimeo.com/472452739.

3.2 Comparison Between Elicited and Existing Gestures

Figure 3 shows the rating for subjective evaluation on elicited and existing WIP gestures in each referent. Here, elicited gestures represent an aggregation of various gestures elicited by all participants. For 0°, elicited gestures and the Tapping-in-place [17] gesture outperformed Jogging-in-place [12] and Swing-in-place [20] gestures in terms of goodness of fit ($p < .001$), ease of use ($p = .001$), and perceived fatigue ($p < .001$). As in 0°, elicited gestures always had significantly higher or at least similar ratings compared to the Gaiter gesture [2] in other directions. For 45°, elicited gestures induced better goodness of fit ($p < .001$), ease of use ($p = .004$), and presence ($p < .001$), whereas elicited gestures surpassed in terms of goodness of fit (p < .001) and presence (p < .001) for 90°. For 135°, the significant outperformance by elicited gestures was found in all subjective evaluation items: goodness of fit (p < .001), ease of use (p < .001), perceived fatigue (p = .045), and presence (p < .001), while only presence showed a significant difference (p = .017) for 180°. In general, participants felt gestures they elicited were more appropriate for VR locomotion, easier to perform, and induced less fatigue and higher presence when compared to gestures proposed by researchers from earlier studies.

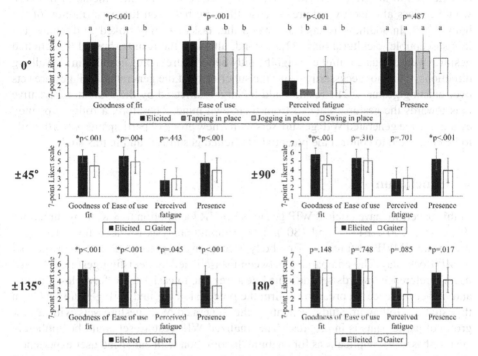

Fig. 3. Mean rating (+SD) for subjective evaluation on elicited and existing WIP gestures in each referent. For 45°, 90°, and 135°, data for left and right directions were grouped because all elicited gestures were symmetrical.

3.3 Application of User Elicited Gestures

The grouping among user elicited gestures revealed four promising user-centered WIP gesture sets for intuitive locomotion in VR. The experimental comparison between self-elicited and existing gestures showed users' preference towards self-designed gestures over existing gestures proposed by the researchers. Generated gesture sets from this study could be applied in gesture-based VR applications for enabling locomotion with enhanced user experience. It is expected that movement options on non-forward directions can enable prompt movement to the side or back by removing unnecessary body rotation, which can be considered especially useful for applications like the VR shooting game where you need to quickly react and move to non-forward directions frequently [21].

3.4 Limitations and Future Work

This study has some limitations. First, studies have shown the presence of a cultural bias on free-hand gesture interaction [29, 32], so it is not known if our findings can be extended to non-Koreans. However, it is assumed that the movements of the WIP would be less affected by culture because they are based on the basic motion of the human gait. In addition, it has been stated that tasks strongly linked to direction are less susceptible to cultural bias [32]. Second, although the results showed that elicited gestures were evaluated similar or significantly better than existing gestures in all walking directions, it did not necessarily prove the superiority of the generated WIP gesture sets over existing gestures. The result could be largely affected by the evaluators' positive bias towards the gestures elicited from their own mind. Therefore, a follow-up study evaluating the generated WIP gesture sets with a new group of participants is worthwhile to be conducted to confirm the potential of elicited gestures found in this study.

4   Conclusion

In this paper, we have elicited WIP gestures for VR locomotion to 8 walking directions ($0°$, $±45°$, $±90°$, $±135°$, and $180°$). The grouping analysis revealed four promising user-centered WIP gesture sets: Turn body + Stepping-in-place (SIP) and Step one foot + SIP/Rock/Stay. The comparison between user-elicited and existing gestures showed users' preference towards self-designed gestures due to easier to perform, less fatigue, and higher presence. In order to confirm the potential of elicited WIP gesture sets from this study, a follow-up study evaluating the generated WIP gesture sets with a new group of participants is in progress. The finalized WIP gesture set could be applied in gesture-based VR applications for enabling locomotion with enhanced user experience.

Acknowledgments. This work was funded by The Basic Science Research Program through the National Research Foundation of Korea (NRF-2020R1F1A1048510).

References

1. Rogers, S.: The year virtual reality gets real (2019). https://www.forbes.com/sites/solrogers/2019/06/21/2019-the-year-virtual-reality-gets-real/. Accessed 03 Jan 2021.
2. Templeman, J.N., Denbrook, P.S., Sibert, L.E.: Virtual locomotion: walking in place through virtual environments. Presence Teleoper. Virtual Environ. **8**, 598–617 (1999). https://doi.org/10.1162/105474699566512
3. Feasel, J., Whitton, M.C., Wendt, J.D.: LLCM-WIP: low-latency, continuous-motion walking-in-place. In: 2008 IEEE Symposium on 3D User Interfaces, pp. 97–104. IEEE (2008). https://doi.org/10.1109/3DUI.2008.4476598.

4. Wendt, J.D., Whitton, M.C., Brooks, F.P.: GUD WIP: Gait-understanding-driven walking-in-place. In: 2010 IEEE Virtual Reality Conference (VR), pp. 51–58. IEEE (2010). https://doi.org/10.1109/VR.2010.5444812.

5. Wilson, P.T., Nguyen, K., Harris, A., Williams, B.: Walking in place using the Microsoft Kinect to explore a large VE. In: Proceedings of the 13th ACM SIGGRAPH International Conference on Virtual-Reality Continuum and its Applications in Industry - VRCAI '14, pp. 27–33. ACM Press, New York, New York, USA (2014). https://doi.org/10.1145/2670473.2670492.

6. Bruno, L., Sousa, M., Ferreira, A., Pereira, J.M., Jorge, J.: Hip-directed walking-in-place using a single depth camera. Int. J. Hum. Comput. Stud. **105**, 1–11 (2017). https://doi.org/10.1016/j.ijhcs.2017.03.006

7. Souman, J.L., et al.: CyberWalk: Enabling unconstrained omnidirectional walking through virtual environments. ACM Trans. Appl. Percept. **8**, 1–22 (2011). https://doi.org/10.1145/2043603.2043607

8. Cakmak, T., Hager, H.: Cyberith virtualizer: a locomotion device for virtual reality. In: ACM SIGGRAPH 2014 Emerging Technologies, SIGGRAPH 2014 (2014). https://doi.org/10.1145/2614066.2614105.

9. Darken, R.P., Cockayne, W.R., Carmein, D.: The omni-directional treadmill: a locomotion device for virtual worlds. In: Proceedings of the 10th Annual ACM Symposium on User Interface Software and Technology - UIST '97, pp. 213–221. ACM Press, New York, New York, USA (1997). https://doi.org/10.1145/263407.263550.

10. Usoh, M., Arthur, K., Whitton, M.C., Bastos, R., Steed, A., Slater, M., Brooks, F.P.: Walking > walking-in-place > flying, in virtual environments. In: Proceedings of the 26th Annual Conference on Computer Graphics and Interactive Techniques - SIGGRAPH '99, pp. 359–364. ACM Press, New York, New York, USA (1999). https://doi.org/10.1145/311535.311589.

11. Williams, B., Bailey, S., Narasimham, G., Li, M., Bodenheimer, B.: Evaluation of walking in place on a Wii balance board to explore a virtual environment. ACM Trans. Appl. Percept. **8**, 1–14 (2011). https://doi.org/10.1145/2010325.2010329

12. Tregillus, S., Folmer, E.: VR-STEP: walking-in-place using inertial sensing for hands free navigation in mobile VR environments. In: Proceedings of the 2016 CHI Conference on Human Factors in Computing Systems, pp. 1250–1255. ACM, New York, NY, USA (2016). https://doi.org/10.1145/2858036.2858084.

13. Bhandari, J., Tregillus, S., Folmer, E.: Legomotion: scalable walking-based virtual locomotion. In: Proceedings of the 23rd ACM Symposium on Virtual Reality Software and Technology, pp. 1–8. ACM, New York, NY, USA (2017). https://doi.org/10.1145/3139131.3139133.

14. Jaeger, B.K., Mourant, R.R.: Comparison of simulator sickness using static and dynamic walking simulators. Proc. Hum. Factors Ergon. Soc. Annu. Meet. **45**, 1896–1900 (2001). https://doi.org/10.1177/154193120104502709.

15. Cherni, H., Métayer, N., Souliman, N.: Literature review of locomotion techniques in virtual reality. Int. J. Virtual Real. **20**, 1–20 (2020). https://doi.org/10.20870/IJVR.2020.20.1.3183.

16. Slater, M., Steed, A., Usoh, M.: The virtual treadmill: a naturalistic metaphor for navigation in immersive virtual environments. In: Göbel, M. (ed.) Virtual Environments '95. Eurographics, pp. 135–148. Springer, Vienna, Austria (1995). https://doi.org/10.1007/978-3-7091-9433-1_.

17. Nilsson, N.C., Serafin, S., Laursen, M.H., Pedersen, K.S., Sikstrom, E., Nordahl, R.: Tapping-In-Place: increasing the naturalness of immersive walking-in-place locomotion through novel gestural input. In: 2013 IEEE Symposium on 3D User Interfaces (3DUI), pp. 31–38. IEEE (2013). https://doi.org/10.1109/3DUI.2013.6550193.

18. Guy, E., Punpongsanon, P., Iwai, D., Sato, K., Boubekeur, T.: LazyNav: 3D ground navigation with non-critical body parts. In: 2015 IEEE Symposium on 3D User Interfaces (3DUI), pp. 43–50. IEEE (2015). https://doi.org/10.1109/3DUI.2015.7131725.

19. McCullough, M., et al.: Myo arm: swinging to explore a VE. In: Proceedings of the ACM SIGGRAPH Symposium on Applied Perception - SAP '15, pp. 107–113. ACM Press, New York, New York, USA (2015). https://doi.org/10.1145/2804408.2804416.

20. Ang, Y., Sulaiman, P.S., Rahmat, R.W.O.K., Mohd Norowi, N.: Swing-in-place (SIP): a less fatigue walking-in-place method with side-viewing functionality for mobile virtual reality. IEEE Access. 7, 183985–183995 (2019). https://doi.org/10.1109/ACCESS.2019.2960409.

21. Lee, J., Kim, G.J., Chul Ahn, S., Hwang, J.-I.: MIP-VR: an omnidirectional navigation and jumping method for VR shooting game using IMU. In: 2019 IEEE International Conference on Consumer Electronics (ICCE), pp. 1–3. IEEE (2019). https://doi.org/10.1109/ICCE.2019. 8661906.

22. Norman, D.A.: Natural user interfaces are not natural. Interactions 17, 6 (2010). https://doi. org/10.1145/1744161.1744163

23. Wu, H., et al.: Understanding freehand gestures: a study of freehand gestural interaction for immersive VR shopping applications. HCIS 9(1), 1–26 (2019). https://doi.org/10.1186/s13 673-019-0204-7

24. Felberbaum, Y., Lanir, J.: Better understanding of foot gestures: an elicitation study. In: Proceedings of the 2018 CHI Conference on Human Factors in Computing Systems - CHI '18, pp. 1–12. ACM Press, New York, New York, USA (2018). https://doi.org/10.1145/317 3574.3173908.

25. Ganapathi, P., Sorathia, K.: Elicitation study of body gestures for locomotion in HMD-VR interfaces in a sitting-position. In: Motion, Interaction and Games on - MIG '19, pp. 1–10. ACM Press, New York, New York, USA (2019). https://doi.org/10.1145/3359566.3360059.

26. Vatavu, R.-D., Wobbrock, J.O.: Formalizing agreement analysis for elicitation studies: new measures, significance test, and toolkit. In: Proceedings of the 33rd Annual ACM Conference on Human Factors in Computing Systems - CHI '15, pp. 1325–1334. ACM Press, New York, New York, USA (2015). https://doi.org/10.1145/2702123.2702223.

27. Chen, Z., et al.: User-defined gestures for gestural interaction: extending from hands to other body parts. Int. J. Hum.-Comput. Interact. 34, 238–250 (2018). https://doi.org/10.1080/104 47318.2017.1342943

28. Ferrario, V.F., Sforza, C., Serrao, G., Grassi, G., Mossi, E.: Active range of motion of the head and cervical spine: a three-dimensional investigation in healthy young adults. J. Orthop. Res. 20, 122–129 (2002). https://doi.org/10.1016/S0736-0266(01)00079-1

29. Wu, H., Zhang, S., Liu, J., Qiu, J., Zhang, X.: (Luke): The gesture disagreement problem in free-hand gesture interaction. Int. J. Hum.-Comput. Interact. 35, 1102–1114 (2019). https:// doi.org/10.1080/10447318.2018.1510607

30. Wobbrock, J.O., Morris, M.R., Wilson, A.D.: User-defined gestures for surface computing. In: Proceedings of the 27th International Conference on Human Factors in Computing Systems - CHI 09, p. 1083. ACM Press, New York, New York, USA (2009). https://doi.org/10.1145/ 1518701.1518866.

31. Wu, H., Wang, J.: User-defined body gestures for TV-based applications. In: 2012 Fourth International Conference on Digital Home, pp. 415–420. IEEE (2012). https://doi.org/10. 1109/ICDH.2012.23.

32. Wu, H., et al.: Influence of cultural factors on freehand gesture design. Int. J. Hum. Comput. Stud. 143, 102502 (2020). https://doi.org/10.1016/j.ijhcs.2020.102502

Exploring Human-to-Human Telepresence and the Use of Vibro-Tactile Commands to Guide Human Streamers

Kevin P. Pfeil[✉], Katelynn A. Kapalo, Seng Lee Koh, Pamela Wisniewski, and Joseph J. LaViola Jr.

University of Central Florida, Orlando, FL, USA
kevin.pfeil@knights.ucf.edu

Abstract. Human-to-human telepresence is rising to mainstream use, and there is opportunity to provide rich experiences through novel interactions. While previous systems are geared towards situations where two users are previously acquainted, or provide channels for verbal communication, our work focuses on situations where audio is not desirable or available, by incorporating vibro-tactile commands into a telepresence setup. We present results from a lab-based study regarding a human-to-human telepresence system which enables one person to remotely control another through these vibro-tactile cues. We conducted a study with 8 participants to solicit their feedback when acting as a Streamer, 8 additional participants to solicit feedback as a Viewer, and 30 bystanders, through surveys and debriefing sessions. While our participants generally found the application favorable, we did find mixed feelings towards vibro-tactile devices, and much room for improvement for the whole interaction. We discuss the implications of our findings and provide design guidelines for future telepresence developers.

Keywords: Telepresence · Vibro-tactile interface · 360° Video

1 Introduction

Telepresence is the ability to perceive and/or interact with a remote environment, as if actually there. Originally conceived by Minsky in 1980, it has been hypothesized that telecommunications can provide an avenue for a worker to perform a task from across the globe using a natural, egocentric point of view [31]. While this ultimate telepresence experience has not yet been fully realized, we have seen immense technological advances in that direction. For instance, the combination of 360° cameras and virtual reality (VR) head-mounted displays (HMDs) allow an individual to explore a remote environment with a greater sense of *immersion*, or a sense of being enveloped in an interaction (see [45,52]), than ever before. To facilitate mobile exploration, the robotics field has brought forth wheeled platforms which can be piloted through a simple graphical user

© Springer Nature Switzerland AG 2021
J. Y. C. Chen and G. Fragomeni (Eds.): HCII 2021, LNCS 12770, pp. 183–202, 2021.
https://doi.org/10.1007/978-3-030-77599-5_15

interface (GUI) [26]. However, these robots are typically constrained to a particular, pre-planned environment such as conference venues [36], hospitals [9], and
sidewalks [12], as they still have problems in navigating difficult terrain.

To circumvent this difficulty, and to provide a more interpersonal experience, some researchers have hypothesized that the robot can be replaced with
another human (called Streamer). This concept of human-to-human telepresence
has recently emerged, and the HCI community is examining its benefits and detri-
ments. However, we have still seen the implementation of human-to-human telepresence in the wake of the recent COVID-19 pandemic, which has forced world-
wide communities to practice social distancing. For instance, the Faroe Islands
conducted telepresence experiences by having a Streamer walk about the islands
while remote users directed them where to go [15]. Additionally, some researchers
suggest that we might even see this concept provide a new avenue for job creation;
one person could perform tasks while being directed by a remote user. Misawa and
Rekimoto describe a "physical body marketplace" [33], where the Streamer's role
is equivalent to ride-sharing drivers (e.g. Uber and Lyft).

It is this style of interaction that thus influences our research interests. While
numerous previous works have focused on the user experience for the Viewer
(the person watching the video stream), we note that the user experience for
the Streamer has been woefully understudied. One consideration is the Viewer
may not have the ability to pick their partner, or perhaps they will share a
Streamer's service with other Viewers simultaneously. As such, verbal guidance
might not be desirable, or even possible. To help tackle this problem, we draw
from Teleguidance literature, in which researchers evaluated vibro-tactile devices
(in this paper, we use the shortened term VibTac). These devices use feedback
in the form of vibrations to convey information (such as directional commands),
and they have been shown to succeed for guidance and navigation as primary
or auxiliary communication channels [8,19,28,30]. We suspect that they are
suitable for use in human-to-human telepresence as well.

Therefore, in this paper, we explore this concept with a lab-based study with
which we gather feedback from 16 participants regarding a telepresence setting
using VibTac devices. We describe a prototypical interactive system that allows
a Streamer to give a live-streamed tour to a Viewer, who in turn can provide
navigational commands in the form of tactile cues through a VibTac belt or hat.
Additionally, we surveyed 30 other observers to help understand their how the
third-party perceives this style of interaction. Our primary research questions
include the following:

- RQ1: What types of VibTac devices are preferred by Streamers?
- RQ2: How do third-party members perceive human-to-human telepresence
  interaction?
- RQ3: What scenarios would benefit from human-to-human telepresence?

We found that our participants did not have a particular preference between
our VibTac devices, though the navigational commands were more strongly felt
with our developed hat. Additionally, our participants responded that, although
they were comfortable acting as a Streamer, they were not particularly energized

to be one. Lastly, observers were somewhat comfortable being collocated with a Streamer, although they felt a greater sense of trust in the Streamer than they did in the remote Viewer.

2   Related Work

Telepresence Streamers have been leveraged in a variety of projects, but we have yet to understand how humans truly regard this role. In this section, we review the relevant literature at the intersection of Human-to-Human Telepresence and VibTac interfaces, and discuss our unique contributions to the telepresence community.

2.1   Human-to-Human Telepresence

Human-to-human Telepresence is a fairly new concept, as the technology and infrastructure to support this kind of interaction has just recently emerged; but, we have seen many projects that in part help to realize this concept. The JackIn system by Kasahara et al. shows how the use of omni-directional video cameras worn on the head by Streamers can give Viewers an immersive avenue to explore remote environments [16–18]. Here, the Viewer typically utilizes a VR HMD, granting the ability to explore the environment through natural head rotations. Pfeil et al. investigated how high a camera could be placed, and found that camera height is not a significant factor to consider for telepresence design [39,40]; thus, this interaction could be enjoyed by broad audiences. Even a simple live-streaming device, such as a mobile phone, can provide an adequate view, as with the Polly system which is mounted on a Streamer's shoulder [21,23, 24]. Here, though the Viewer does not wear a VR HMD, they can change the viewpoint by controlling a gimbal that holds the camera, through a GUI. Between these two projects, the Viewer has either a first-person or third-person point of view in relation to the Streamer. The latter allows for a more personable connection between the two users, but this may or may not be desirable, as the Streamer could be a friend or family member, but they could be a stranger.

Some researchers have explored *who* can be a Streamer. Ishak et al. deployed a technology probe to the university classroom [14]. Here, the authors found that students would be interested in having their friends act as live Streamers, but there were reservations in having strangers be these proxies. This concern was in part addressed through works by Misawa and Rekimoto, where Streamers wore a tablet on their head, to display the face of the Viewer [32,33]. Here, the Streamer did not interact with the environment, except as instructed by the Viewer's audible instructions. In this way, there was an illusion that the Viewer was actually in the remote environment. The authors suggest that the optimal Streamer would be someone known to the Viewer, and someone who has similar physical traits, so to enhance the illusion.

One of the problems in the human-to-human telepresence literature is the common finding that the Streamers feel socially awkward when other people see them using this technology [20,38,42]. In all of the above examples, the devices are clearly identifiable by third-party users, resulting in this awkward feeling. It is thus important to find a way to balance user experience for both members. Baishya and Neustaedter envisioned a way for long distance couples to increase their togetherness using always-on video chat [3]. Here, a smartphone was placed in the shirt pocket of both users, with the camera facing out. In this way, it was inconspicuous to third party observers, although the opportunity to explore the remote environment is stymied because of where the camera is placed. As such, there is work that must be performed to reach an acceptable balance of user experience between all parties involved.

In our paper, we extend prior work by letting a Viewer command a Streamer through the use of VibTac devices. Our work is similar to that of Misawa and Rekimoto, in that the Streamer is asked to follow specific commands given by the Viewer [32,33], and our technology probe is not unlike that of the Faroe Islands remote tourism application [15]. However, our prototype devices were designed to be inconspicuous, by embedding them into clothing. Our work contributes to the telepresence literature by providing an understanding of Streamer's perception of human-to-human telepresence devices, and to understand how comfortable they are with the general interaction style.

2.2   Vibro-Tactile Interfaces

VibTac interfaces have been studied in the past, commonly in the form of belts [28,46,49,50]; but there have also been others in the form of vests [29], helmets [35], head bands [6], caps [19], and even socks and shoes [30]. They have been integrated into user interfaces to support the visually impaired; for instance, McDaniel et al. described their belt prototype in an effort to convey where other people were, in both direction and proximity [28], and Wang et al. developed a belt that provided directional commands to help users navigate around obstacles without a cane [51]. In these implementations, computer vision techniques are used to identify detect people and obstacles, and to calculate a route around them.

However, algorithms do not operate at 100% accuracy. It is sometimes recommended to have a human-in-the-loop (HITL) interaction, so to leverage human expertise and correct problems when algorithms make mistakes. Scheggi et al. proposed an HITL system in which a remote expert could view the surroundings of a visually impaired person, and provide real-time feedback in the form of vibrations [43]. Our work is inspired by this prior work, to help understand if VibTac devices can be used for general telepresence use. There is not a wide range of consumer-grade VibTac wearables, so we developed two simple devices; one is a belt similar to Tsukada's ActiveBelt [49], and the other is a hat based on a reduction of Kaul's HapticHead device [19]. Literature does not seem to point to optimal tactor configurations, so iterative development helped direct our design of these devices. In this paper, we elicit Streamer feedback to the VibTac belt and hat, to understand which provides the clearest set of instructions.

3 Prototype System Design

We developed a custom live-streaming application in Unity3D; Unity's multi-player service allowed us to easily transmit data over the network. To provide visuals, we used the Ricoh Theta S 360° camera, which supports live streaming. The camera was mounted to a backpack rig, giving an overhead view of the Streamer, similar to the work by Tang et al. [48]. We modified FFPLAY[1] code and used it as a DLL in Unity. A script decoded the live, equirectangluar video frames, turned them into RGB values, and mapped them into a spherical image. We were able to achieve a streaming rate of 30 frames per second with approximately 1 s of latency. Using a virtual reality head-mounted display (HMD), or by simply click-and-dragging with a mouse, a Viewer could manipulate the viewpoint to any desired angle. See Fig. 1 for a visual of the hardware worn by the Streamer; this consisted of a backpack rig, the pole-mounted camera, a VibTac device, and a laptop to send and receive data over the network. The total weight was approximately 20lbs (9.1 kg).

The VibTac devices we developed were a belt and a hat (see left section of Fig. 1). Each utilized four coin vibration motors that were sewn into the clothing and interfaced with an Arduino Uno, which was programmed to read serial port data. The Uno was plugged into the Streamer's computer via USB, and Unity's multiplayer service allowed us to easily transmit commands. When activating the motors, we used 3.3V (output of the digital pins), as we found 5V to burn the motors. The motors did not make direct contact with the body, and were veiled behind a layer of fabric. This is in accordance with the findings by Kaul and Rohs, that direct contact could cause marks on the skin of the user [19]. Our navigational commands were similar to those used by the Faroe Islands remote tourism [15]; we simply needed our devices to convey four commands - *Go Forward*, *Go Backward*, *Turn Left*, and *Turn Right*.

For the belt, the mounted motors were sewn into an elastic band that used a belt buckle for fastening. Our final design called for motors contacting the belly, the back, and each hip. Activating the belly motor indicated *Go Forward*, activating the right hip motor meant *Turn Right*, and so forth. For the hat, the motors were sewn into the fabric - our final design consisted of two placed near the temples, and two placed near the sides of the neck. Activating the front motors indicated *Go Forward*, activating the two right motors meant *Turn Right*, and so forth.

When a Viewer pressed a navigation button, a command was sent to the Streamer's laptop, activating the appropriate motors. Latency from button press to motor activation was less than 1 s. For our study, we utilized two Viewer conditions. The first condition used the HTC Vive VR headset, where the built-in head tracking allowed the user to change viewpoints while watching the 360° camera feed. The second condition used a flat laptop screen, and by click-and-dragging a mouse pointer, the omnidirectional video feed could be manipulated in real-time.

---

[1] https://ffmpeg.org.

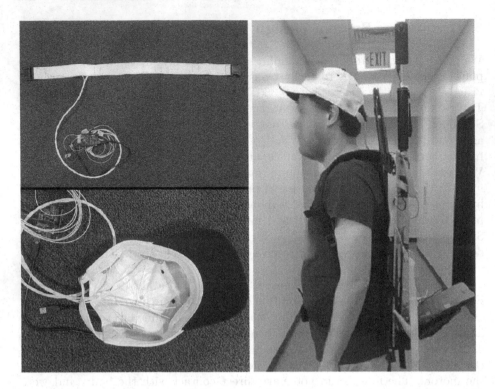

Fig. 1. Left: The developed tactile belt (top) and hat (bottom). Each utilized a 4-tactor design in order to provide feedback to the Streamer. The motors were controlled by an Arduino Uno. **Right**: A user wearing the backpack rig, which consisted of a 360 camera for livestreaming, a vibro-tactile device for feedback, and a laptop.

4   User Study

We conducted a lab-based study at the University of Central Florida with IRB approval. The study aimed at garnering user feedback from Streamers, Viewers, and other third-party members who were not part of the interaction.

4.1   Study Design

We conducted a 2×2 mixed-design study; participants were split into 2 groups - one group consisted of the Streamers, in which the VibTac device selection was a within-subjects variable. The other group consisted of Viewers, in which the Viewing Mode was a within-subjects variable. Per group, condition order was counter-balanced. In addition, we conducted a short survey with non-participants. Our dependent variables aimed at measuring the perceived value of this kind of human-to-human telepresence, effectiveness of VibTac devices as a primary communication channel, and perception of the Viewer-Streamer relationship.

4.2   Subjects and Apparatus

We recruited eight participants to act as a Viewer. These participants consisted of 4 males and 4 females, and their age ranged between 18 and 26 (M = 21.8; SD = 3.20). On a 5-point Likert scale where 1 means Never and 5 means Always, the participants very rarely watched 360° videos (M = 1.75; SD = 0.46). They again very rarely used VR (M = 1.89; SD = 0.64). They very rarely drove robots (M = 1.89; SD = 0.64), and they rarely played first-person video games (M = 2.25; SD = 1.04).

We recruited eight participants to act as a Streamer. These participants consisted of 6 males and 2 females, and their age ranged between 18 and 38 (M = 24.4; SD = 6.30). Only 1 of our participants had experience with a wearable device (such as an Apple Watch or Fitbit). On a 5-point Likert scale where 1 means Never and 5 means Always, the participants exercised somewhat often (M = 3.5; SD = 0.76). They sometimes felt phantom vibrations regarding their cell phone (M = 2.88, SD = 0.83).

We surveyed an additional 30 university students (17 female) to understand their thoughts regarding the concept of human-to-human telepresence. All of our participants were recruited from the University of Central Florida.

4.3   Procedure

Viewers and Streamers. Our recruited participants reported to our lab, where they reviewed an informed consent form. After agreeing to participate, they were given a demographics survey, followed by a brief description of the telepresence setup. We explained how the VibTac interfaces worked, and how the controls were akin to a computer game (WASD keys). After introducing the hardware, our participants moved to their assigned position.

At any given time, a participant was accompanied by an experimenter, and we did not have interaction between participants. During Streamer trials, an experimenter provided the navigational commands. During Viewer trials, an experimenter served as the Streamer. As such, each participant only interacted with authors.

The Streamer was guided through a building on our university campus. The building layout consists of multiple hallways and corridors, which allowed us to take advantage of all VibTac commands. When controlling a Streamer participant, we held down the commands such that the vibration effect was constant. The *Stop Moving* command was issued when no vibrations were activated. We did this to ensure our Streamers had ample interaction time with the VibTac interfaces.

The navigational route was randomized and kept secret from the Streamer. As such, they had to rely on the VibTac devices to complete the trial; Streamers were asked to walk at a comfortable pace, and not run. After a Streamer completed a route, they changed VibTac devices and was then navigated through a different route. After a Viewer participant completed a route, they changed viewing modes and then performed navigation through a different route. In total, a Streamer participant was navigated twice; similarly, a Viewer participant conducted navigation twice. After each condition, a questionnaire was administered to elicit feedback regarding that particular condition. After both trials were complete, a final questionnaire was administered to garner feedback in terms of preference. Between participants, we cleaned the HMD and hat instruments with rubbing alcohol to ensure sanitation. The study took approximately 30 min to complete, and participants were paid $5 for their time. This study was conducted prior to the COVID-19 pandemic.

Survey Respondents. Survey respondents were approached in public and asked if they would like to provide their comments regarding human-to-human telepresence. One author wore the backpack rig, and we described the concept. Feedback was received in the form of a questionnaire and verbal communication. Respondents were not compensated.

4.4   Soliciting User Feedback

We administered quantitative measures to help understand user feedback, in terms of enjoyment and comfort, as well as social and economic aspects; see Table 1 for a list of questions asked to our participants and respondents. All closed-ended questions were given on a 7-pt Likert scale where 1 meant "Strongly Disagree" and 7 meant "Strongly Agree". Open-ended questions were given as free-response prompts.

For the Viewer participants, we also asked simple questions to see if there was a preference in Viewing Mode, but we were more interested in their thoughts regarding the concept of controlling another human. For our Streamer participants, we were also interested in understanding VibTac device preference. We asked questions to understand how well the devices conveyed instructions and how comfortable they were.

4.5   Data Analysis Approach

As we did not have enough power to run statistical tests within the Streamer and Viewer groups, we report our results using descriptive statistics. To determine the overall effectiveness of each VibTac device, we averaged the 4 directional command responses into an index, per device. For the responses garnered from the final questionnaire, we report descriptive statistics and also discuss the positive/negative aspects as indicated by our users.

Table 1. Questions administered to participants. The Group column indicates which set of participants received the question: V = Viewers; S = Streamers; R = Survey Respondents. Asterisks (*) denote questions were given for multiple conditions.

Question	Group
I felt comfortable knowing I was controlling another human	V
I liked having control over the Streamer	V
I trusted the Streamer to go where I wanted them to go	V
I would feel comfortable navigating the Streamer into a private place, such as a restroom	V
I felt comfortable knowing I was being controlled by another human	S
I liked being controlled by the Viewer	S
I trusted the Viewer to give me good directions	S
I would feel comfortable being navigated into a private place, such as a restroom	S
It was easy to understand the Viewer's directions	*S
I could easily feel the *Move Forward* command	*S
I could easily feel the *Move Backward* command	*S
I could easily feel the *Turn Left* command	*S
I could easily feel the *Turn Right* command	*S
Assuming the Streamer did a good job, I would consider paying for a live virtual tour	V, R
How many dollars (USD) would you pay for a live virtual tour?	V, R
Assuming I would be adequately compensated, I would consider being a Streamer as a job	S, R
How many dollars (USD) would you expect to receive, to be a Streamer?	S, R
I would trust the Streamer to do the right thing	R
I would trust the Viewer to do the right thing	R
I think it would be fun to be a Streamer	R
I think it would be fun to be a Viewer	R
I would be comfortable knowing a Streamer is near me in a public place	R
I would be comfortable knowing a Streamer is near me in a private place	R
What did you like about the system?	V, S
What did you dislike about the system?	V, S
What changes would you make to improve the overall experience?	V, S
What scenarios would you use this system for?	V, S, R

5   Results

In this section we report the results of our study, split by the different roles. We begin with the Viewer participants, followed by the Streamer participants, and finish with the survey respondents.

5.1 Viewer Considerations

Overall, our Viewers liked using the system and they had no major discomforts with either Viewing Mode. Six participants were most comfortable with the flat screen, while only two were more comfortable with the HMD. However, five indicated that they preferred the HMD to the flat screen.

Our Viewer participants felt comfortable controlling the Streamer ($M = 5.5$, $SD = 2.1$) and typically liked the interaction ($M = 5.4$, $SD = 2.1$). Only one participant responded negatively, as they were afraid that they would cause harm to the Streamer: *"Controlling people scared me half to death! The building is new to me and I was extremely scared I was going to run the Streamer off a ledge"*. This participant was the only one to express consideration for the Streamer.

Generally, our participants had great trust that the Streamer would follow the commands accurately ($M = 6.6$, $SD = 0.5$). However, the participants were very apprehensive about the idea of sending a Streamer into a private place; see Fig. 4, with only one participant feeling comfortable regarding that situation. Considering the concept as a whole, participants responded that they would be likely to hire a Streamer for a tour ($M = 5.5$, $SD = 1.6$). The range of value was very broad, however; the smallest sum of money participants were willing to pay was \$5, and the most was \$25 (see Fig. 3).

Our open-ended questions revealed that the most negative features of our telepresence setup was the latency; half of our participants complained about lag. From button press to motor activation, approximately 1 s elapsed; but, there was additional overhead time from motor activation to Streamer response, followed by another second of video lag. As such, there were many times where

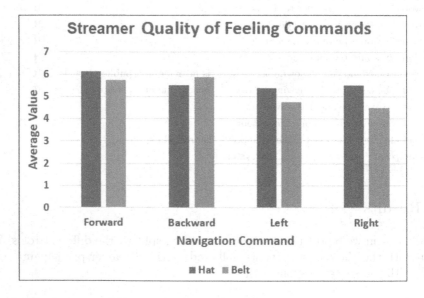

Fig. 2. The commands from both VibTac devices were perceived well, but the Hat device was slightly more conducive to feeling the vibrations.

the Streamer walked too far down a hallway, or missed a turn. In addition to better visuals, some of our participants indicated that they would prefer to hear and speak to the Streamer. Usage scenarios for human-to-human telepresence included campus orientation for new or prospective students, playing augmented reality games, virtual tourism, and remote shopping.

5.2   Streamer Considerations

Our participants generally had no issue with either VibTac device. Comfort was comparable between the Belt ($M = 5.4$, $SD = 1.3$) and the Hat ($M = 5.4$, $SD = 1.2$); likewise, users felt only slightly embarrassed when wearing either device (Belt: $M = 2.3$, $SD = 1.5$; Hat: $M = 2.6$, $SD = 1.8$). Regarding the quality of VibTac commands, there was only a slight difference in the ability to detect them (Belt: $M = 5.2$, $SD = 1.5$; Hat: $M = 5.6$, $SD = 1.0$), and regardless of device, participants felt that they understood where they were being directed to go (Belt: $M = 5.3$, $SD = 1.7$; Hat: $M = 5.8$, $SD = 1.0$). Our participants indicated that they generally felt the belt vibrations with ease, but the hat vibrations were more distinct (see Fig. 2). As such, device preference was not in favor of one over the other; three users preferred the belt, and five preferred the hat.

Participants indicated that they enjoyed the novelty of our system, and we suspect that this novelty may have impacted participant Likert-scale responses. However, open-ended questions did help to reveal weaknesses of our devices. Five of our participants indicated that while the vibrations were enough to complete the walking task, they could have been better. For example, the commands from the belt were perceived as having different strengths. One user informed us that they needed to put their hands on the belt in order to recognize the vibrations. On the other hand, while perception towards the hat was comparable to the belt, users indicated that the vibrations caused a tickling sensation, or were more distracting. This is due to the motors being close to the users' forehead and ears, so the vibrations were more distinct and audible. One user suggested that they were able to hear the motors vibrating near their ears, but this helped them to determine which direction was requested.

5.3   Survey Respondents

Our survey respondents, who were third-party bystanders, had mixed feelings regarding this concept. While they had general trust in a Streamer ($M = 5.3$, $SD = 1.1$), they were much less trusting in the Viewer ($M = 4.4$, $SD = 1.7$). A Wilcoxon Signed Rank Test revealed a significant difference in who they would trust ($Z = -2.964, p < .005$). This is because they are able to see and perhaps identify the local user, but they have no indication as to who is on the other end of the interaction. As such, they were somewhat comfortable with the idea of a Streamer being nearby in a public place ($M = 4.9$, $SD = 1.3$), but were far less enthused with the idea of a Streamer being collocated in a private area ($M = 3.3$, $SD = 1.6$). A Wilcoxon Signed Rank Test reveals a significant difference in the comfort of these scenarios ($Z = -4.168, p < .001$). Although they did

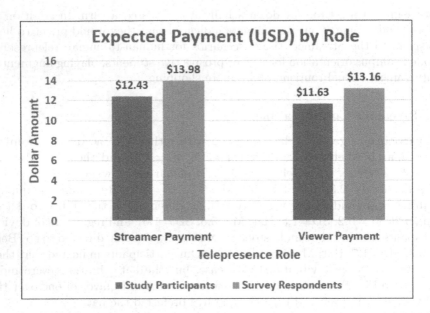

Fig. 3. Expected payment (USD) per telepresence role. Participants and survey respondents both indicated that the Streamer would garner more compensation than Viewers should pay.

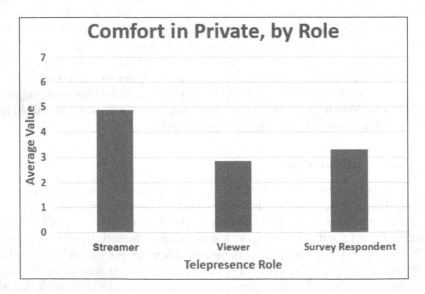

Fig. 4. Average response to comfort of telepresence in a private setting. Interestingly, the Streamers had little issue with the concept, whereas the Viewers and survey respondents were much less enthused.

not see a telepresence scenario taking place, the respondents thought it would be somewhat fun to be a viewer (M = 5.8, SD = 1.4), and less fun to be a Streamer (M = 5.2, SD = 1.6). A Wilcoxon Signed Rank Test revealed a significant difference between these sentiments ($Z = -2.056, p < .05$). Interestingly, however, they responded with slight interest in being a Streamer for payment (M = 5.0, SD = 1.8), and were less interested in paying for a live tour (M = 4.4, SD = 1.6). A Wilcoxon Signed Rank Test revealed a significant difference of interest for these roles ($Z = -2.024, p < .05$). The range of expected dollars-per-hour payment for being a Streamer was broad; the smallest rate was $7, and the largest was $30 (M = 13.98, SD = 5.80). The dollars-per-hour range for being a viewer was from $4 to $20 (M = 13.15, SD = 7.15). Thus, the respondents felt that a Streamer would warrant more compensation than a viewer would need to pay. See Fig. 3 for illustration. The respondents had many scenarios in mind for human-to-human telepresence, including tele-health physical therapy, remote exploration of live events like concerts, housing and campus tours, vlogging, tourism, military missions where talking is prohibited, and giving directions.

6   Discussion

In this section, we unpack the findings which emerged from our study, to address our research questions. We begin with how all parties view each other; next we discuss the perceived value of the interaction; third we describe the potential scenarios pondered by our users; and last we discuss VibTac device efficiency.

6.1   RQ1: Towards Better Telepresence VibTac Devices

Although our Streamer participants responded (with bias) in favor of the VibTac devices, we learned from them that there is room for improvement. First, there are benefits and drawbacks for each device. The belt was not as conducive as the hat in terms of interpreting the commands. McDaniel et al. found users to easily localize the vibrations emitted from their 7-tactor belt [28], but our participants had a measure of uncertainty in simply feeling the vibrations. Although ours and their tactors each vibrated on 3V, theirs were felt more strongly. While we cannot confirm, we believe that this difference stems from the distinct procedures between our studies. While their participants were standing still, ours were engaged in a walking task. As such, our participants had more distractions as they navigated their route. To overcome this problem, we plan on reiterating our belt with the use of motors which can withstand greater voltage ratings.

The hat allowed our participants to recognize the commands more strongly than the belt, but it was not perceived to be perfect. First, the constant vibration of the motors against the cranium caused a tickling sensation to some, a result also found by Kaul and Rohs with HapticHead [19]. They suggest to decrease the frequency in which the motors activate, and we believe that would have caused more comfort with our users. We purposefully kept the vibrations constant during interaction to elicit user responses, but in a next iteration we would transition hat vibrations towards more gestural commands.

Although neither of our VibTac devices were "perfect" according to our participants, they were still able to convey commands properly and discretely. We do not anticipate for one VibTac wearable to emerge as an optimal device, and believe that it is more appropriate to provide a range of options for a Streamer to use.

6.2   RQ2: Third-Party More Trusting of Streamer Than of Viewer

Our survey respondents were interestingly more trusting of a Streamer than of a remote Viewer. Although the Streamer will be the individual who is wearing the hardware, respondents see remote Viewers as the potential wrong-doers; they are the ones consuming the video stream and potentially making recordings. This is exemplified with the general discomfort of the idea of being collocated with a Streamer in private. Still, respondents were not particularly thrilled with the idea of being collocated with a Streamer in public. Prior research has found a negative attitude towards live streaming, especially without consent [27]; but in countries where public video recording is protected, e.g. in the United States, there is no real obligation to inform people that they might be in a stream [25, 47]. With technological advances, some researchers have begun asking questions regarding streaming ethics [10]; future research should target human-to-human telepresence to help understand how Streamers and their remote Viewers are perceived in the scope of ethics and legality.

6.3   Imbalance of Streamer/Viewer Payment

While monetary exchange is not necessary for friends and family to use telepresence, it is implied that it would help to bring about more general use. Our survey respondents indicated an imbalance regarding monetary payment and compensation between the viewer and Streamer, in that they would expect a Streamer to receive more money than they would be willing to pay. This is an issue that would prevent a "physical body marketplace", as conceived by Misawa and Rekimoto [33], from becoming reality, at least for interactions that involve 1 Streamer and 1 viewer. If this is to become a mainstream interaction style, it is clear that there needs to be more incentive to participate, in both ends, as suggested by prior work [5,11]. Future research can help to identify avenues which will provide these incentives; as an example, some researchers are focusing on ways to increase immersion through multisensory stimulation, including touch [22,37] and smell [4,34], which could lead to a more enjoyable experience and thus a stronger desire to participate. Additionally, it may be the case where a 1-to-1 interaction might not be suitable for human-to-human telepresence. Instead, by adopting a 1-to-many paradigm, where a single Streamer could give tours to multiple viewers simultaneously, the cost per viewer could decrease. Although there are additional challenges to be met in this type of interaction, it is possible to achieve. For example, the Faroe Islands remote tourism experience gives control to a single viewer at a time [15], but as such, control time is limited. We look forward to future studies and design ideas regarding how to improve upon the Streamer-viewer experience, to make it desirable by all parties.

6.4 RQ3: Expected Interaction Scenarios

Our participants and survey respondents were able to conceptualize a broad range of scenarios in which human-to-human telepresence may prosper, including more personal cases such as physical therapy or playing augmented reality games with a friend as a Streamer. More intimate scenarios such as giving directions and physical therapy can be found in prior research [7,41], and popular social media sites such as FaceBook, YouTube, and Twitch.tv provide platforms for larger audience engagement such as vlogging of travels and activities [1]. Popular live streams (especially those for games, found on Twitch) typically have a specific goal or direction, but some streamers do poll their viewers to provide more personalized content. Viewers watch these streams for multiple reasons [13,44], including to live vicariously through the experiences of another person [2], but with human-to-human telepresence, Viewers have the opportunity to engage in an even more personal experience. We suggest that the creation of a platform specific to one-on-one telepresence would help create more engaging experiences which are currently unavailable.

6.5 VibTac Devices Not Optimal for Primary Communication Mode

The novelty of VibTac-based navigation gave rise to positive feedback regarding our belt and hat. We did hear some suggestions for improving the devices, including a way to make them more inconspicuous (e.g. replacing the wires with a Bluetooth connection); but, our short-term study did reveal some disinterest with solely relying on VibTac as a primary mode of navigation. Participants on both sides of the interaction expressed a desire for audible communication with their interaction partner. Additionally, our users were on the cusp of becoming annoyed with constant vibrations. As such, we would recommend telepresence designers to consider adding VibTac as an auxiliary mode of communication, as well as exploring additional modes not studied here. As wearable VibTac devices have been broadly researched with positive findings [19,28–30,35], there is opportunity to let Streamer users pick their own as an option.

7 Limitations and Future Work

Although our interaction prototype was met with positive feedback, we did also find apprehensions. As such, there is still much work to be done on many fronts. Our results are from a test where the participants and authors met before conducting the experiment. We do not assume our results to generalize to situations where both parties are absolute strangers. As such, field tests in real-world scenarios are needed to further our understanding; but, ethical considerations must be made to ensure the rights of all parties (viewers, streamers, and third-party) are not infringed upon. Regarding Streamer control, it remains to be seen how users react to extended lengths of interaction exposure. Longitudinal studies should also be conducted to help identify problems which arise over time. Further, our study did not utilize pre-validated instruments, and instead offer insight through custom measures. In our future work, we will identify proper instruments to measure perception towards VibTac devices.

Our prototype was relatively bulky, and iterative ergonomic enhancements can be made to ensure Streamer comfort. Additionally, although we chose to study two of the most prevalent haptic devices found in previous literature, there are others which need to be thoroughly studied. Lastly, legal and ethical considerations must be investigated. In spirit, our study assumed that the interaction would be performed as intended. However, it is possible for a Streamer to be directed to questionable locations, or perform questionable actions (such as commit a crime). Though we do not want to instigate such a scenario, the telepresence community must ask what the proper response would be. We hope that our paper contributes to the discussion for this type of interaction which is rapidly approaching the mainstream.

8   Conclusion

We have presented our prototype in which a person can direct another through vibro-tactile commands. Our results indicate that there is a real opportunity to provide novel and desirable interaction, but more work is needed to make that a widespread reality. We envision this type of system becoming a prominent avenue in social media, allowing Viewers to have a more direct form of experience through the use of a Streamer. We look forward to seeing how this type of technology will engage users of all backgrounds, in order to explore the world around them.

Acknowledgments. Special thanks to Ravikiran Kattoju for assistance with running the user study.

References

1. Alohali, A., Kunze, K., Earle, R.: Run with me: designing storytelling tools for runners. In: Proceedings of the 2016 ACM International Joint Conference on Pervasive and Ubiquitous Computing: Adjunct, pp. 5–8. ACM (2016)
2. Anderson, K.E.: Getting acquainted with social networks and apps: streaming video games on twitch. tv. Library Hi Tech News **35**(9), 7–10 (2018)
3. Baishya, U., Neustaedter, C.: In your eyes: anytime, anywhere video and audio streaming for couples. In: Proceedings of the 2017 ACM Conference on Computer Supported Cooperative Work and Social Computing, pp. 84–97. ACM (2017)
4. Baus, O., Bouchard, S.: Exposure to an unpleasant odour increases the sense of presence in virtual reality. Virtual Reality **21**(2), 59–74 (2017)

5. Bellotti, V., Ambard, A., Turner, D., Gossmann, C., Demkova, K., Carroll, J.M.: A muddle of models of motivation for using peer-to-peer economy systems. In: Proceedings of the 33rd Annual ACM Conference on Human Factors in Computing Systems, pp. 1085–1094. ACM (2015)

6. Cassinelli, A., Reynolds, C., Ishikawa, M.: Augmenting spatial awareness with haptic radar. In: 2006 10th IEEE International Symposium on Wearable Computers, pp. 61–64. IEEE (2006)

7. Chaudary, B., Paajala, I., Keino, E., Pulli, P.: Tele-guidance based navigation system for the visually impaired and blind persons. In: Giokas, K., Bokor, L., Hopfgartner, F. (eds.) eHealth 360°. LNICST, vol. 181, pp. 9–16. Springer, Cham (2017). https://doi.org/10.1007/978-3-319-49655-9_2

8. Cosgun, A., Sisbot, E.A., Christensen, H.I.: Guidance for human navigation using a vibro-tactile belt interface and robot-like motion planning. In: 2014 IEEE International Conference on Robotics and Automation (ICRA), pp. 6350–6355. IEEE (2014)

9. Ellison, L.M., Nguyen, M., Fabrizio, M.D., Soh, A., Permpongkosol, S., Kavoussi, L.R.: Postoperative robotic telerounding: a multicenter randomized assessment of patient outcomes and satisfaction. Arch. Surg. **142**(12), 1177–1181 (2007). https://doi.org/10.1001/archsurg.142.12.1177

10. Faklaris, C., Cafaro, F., Hook, S.A., Blevins, A., O'Haver, M., Singhal, N.: Legal and ethical implications of mobile live-streaming video apps. In: Proceedings of the 18th International Conference on Human-Computer Interaction with Mobile Devices and Services Adjunct, pp. 722–729. ACM (2016)

11. Glöss, M., McGregor, M., Brown, B.: Designing for labour: uber and the on-demand mobile workforce. In: Proceedings of the 2016 CHI Conference on Human Factors in Computing Systems, pp. 1632–1643. ACM (2016)

12. Heshmat, Y., et al.: Geocaching with a beam: shared outdoor activities through a telepresence robot with 360 degree viewing. In: Proceedings of the 2018 CHI Conference on Human Factors in Computing Systems, p. 359. ACM (2018)

13. Hilvert-Bruce, Z., Neill, J.T., Sjöblom, M., Hamari, J.: Social motivations of live-streaming viewer engagement on twitch. Comput. Hum. Behav. **84**, 58–67 (2018)

14. Ishak, C., Neustaedter, C., Hawkins, D., Procyk, J., Massimi, M.: Human proxies for remote university classroom attendance. In: Proceedings of the 2016 CHI Conference on Human Factors in Computing Systems, pp. 931–943. ACM (2016)

15. Islands, V.F.: Remote tourism - visit faroe islands (2020). https://visitfaroeislands.com/remote-tourism/

16. Kasahara, S., Nagai, S., Rekimoto, J.: Jackin head: immersive visual telepresence system with omnidirectional wearable camera. IEEE Trans. Visual Comput. Graphics **23**(3), 1222–1234 (2017)

17. Kasahara, S., Rekimoto, J.: Jackin: integrating first-person view with out-of-body vision generation for human-human augmentation. In: Proceedings of the 5th Augmented Human International Conference, p. 46. ACM (2014)

18. Kasahara, S., Rekimoto, J.: Jackin head: immersive visual telepresence system with omnidirectional wearable camera for remote collaboration. In: Proceedings of the 21st ACM Symposium on Virtual Reality Software and Technology, pp. 217–225. ACM (2015)

19. Kaul, O.B., Rohs, M.: Haptichead: a spherical vibrotactile grid around the head for 3D guidance in virtual and augmented reality. In: Proceedings of the 2017 CHI Conference on Human Factors in Computing Systems, pp. 3729–3740. ACM (2017)

20. Kim, S., Junuzovic, S., Inkpen, K.: The nomad and the couch potato: enriching mobile shared experiences with contextual information. In: Proceedings of the 18th International Conference on Supporting Group Work - GROUP 2014, Sanibel Island, Florida, USA, pp. 167–177. ACM Press (2014). http://dl.acm.org/citation. cfm?doid=2660398.2660409. https://doi.org/10.1145/2660398.2660409

21. Kimber, D., et al.: Polly: telepresence from a guide's shoulder. In: Agapito, L., Bronstein, M.M., Rother, C. (eds.) ECCV 2014. LNCS, vol. 8927, pp. 509–523. Springer, Cham (2015). https://doi.org/10.1007/978-3-319-16199-0_36

22. Kontaris, D., Harrison, D., Patsoule, E.E., Zhuang, S., Slade, A.: Feelybean: communicating touch over distance. In: CHI 2012 Extended Abstracts on Human Factors in Computing Systems, pp. 1273–1278. ACM (2012)

23. Kratz, S., Avrahami, D., Kimber, D., Vaughan, J., Proppe, P., Severns, D.: Polly wanna show you: examining viewpoint-conveyance techniques for a shoulder-worn telepresence system. In: Proceedings of the 17th International Conference on Human-Computer Interaction with Mobile Devices and Services Adjunct, pp. 567–575. ACM (2015)

24. Kratz, S., Kimber, D., Su, W., Gordon, G., Severns, D.: Polly: being there through the parrot and a guide. In: Proceedings of the 16th International Conference on Human-Computer Interaction with Mobile Devices & Services, pp. 625–630. ACM (2014)

25. Kreimer, S.F.: Pervasive image capture and the first amendment: memory, discourse, and the right to record. U. Pa. L. Rev. **159**, 335 (2010)

26. Kristoffersson, A., Coradeschi, S., Loutfi, A.: A review of mobile robotic telepresence. In: Advances in Human-Computer Interaction 2013, p. 3 (2013)

27. Li, Y., Kou, Y., Lee, J.S., Kobsa, A.: Tell me before you stream me: managing information disclosure in video game live streaming. In: Proceedings of the ACM on Human-Computer Interaction 2(CSCW), no. 107 (2018)

28. McDaniel, T., Krishna, S., Balasubramanian, V., Colbry, D., Panchanathan, S.: Using a haptic belt to convey non-verbal communication cues during social interactions to individuals who are blind. In: IEEE International Workshop on Haptic Audio visual Environments and Games, HAVE 2008, pp. 13–18. IEEE (2008)

29. McGrath, B., Estrada, A., Braithwaite, M., Raj, A., Rupert, A.: Tactile situation awareness system flight demonstration. Technical report, Army Aeromedical Research Lab Fort Rucker AL (2004)

30. Meier, A., Matthies, D.J., Urban, B., Wettach, R.: Exploring vibrotactile feedback on the body and foot for the purpose of pedestrian navigation. In: Proceedings of the 2nd International Workshop on Sensor-Based Activity Recognition and Interaction, p. 11. ACM (2015)

31. Minsky, M.: Telepresence (1980)

32. Misawa, K., Rekimoto, J.: Chameleonmask: embodied physical and social telepresence using human surrogates. In: Proceedings of the 33rd Annual ACM Conference Extended Abstracts on Human Factors in Computing Systems, pp. 401–411. ACM (2015)

33. Misawa, K., Rekimoto, J.: Wearing another's personality: a human-surrogate system with a telepresence face. In: Proceedings of the 2015 ACM International Symposium on Wearable Computers, pp. 125–132. ACM (2015)

34. Munyan, B.G., Neer, S.M., Beidel, D.C., Jentsch, F.: Olfactory stimuli increase presence during simulated exposure. In: Lackey, S., Shumaker, R. (eds.) VAMR 2016. LNCS, vol. 9740, pp. 164–172. Springer, Cham (2016). https://doi.org/10. 1007/978-3-319-39907-2_16

35. Myles, K., Kalb, J.T.: Guidelines for head tactile communication. Technical report, Army Research Lab Aberdeen Proving Ground Md Human Research and Engineering Directorate (2010)
36. Neustaedter, C., Venolia, G., Procyk, J., Hawkins, D.: To beam or not to beam: a study of remote telepresence attendance at an academic conference. In: Proceedings of the 19th ACM Conference on Computer-Supported Cooperative Work & Social Computing, pp. 418–431. ACM (2016)
37. Pallarino, T., Free, A., Mutuc, K., Yarosh, S.: Feeling distance: an investigation of mediated social touch prototypes. In: Proceedings of the 19th ACM Conference on Computer Supported Cooperative Work and Social Computing Companion, pp. 361–364. ACM (2016)
38. Pfeil, K., Chatlani, N., Wisniewski, P.: Bridging the socio-technical gaps in body-worn interpersonal live-streaming telepresence through a critical review of the literature. Proc. ACM Hum.-Comput. Interact. (2021, to appear)
39. Pfeil, K., Wisniewski, P., LaViola Jr., J.J.: An analysis of user perception regarding body-worn 360° camera placements and heights for telepresence. In: ACM Symposium on Applied Perception 2019. SAP 2019. Association for Computing Machinery, New York (2019). https://doi.org/10.1145/3343036.3343120
40. Pfeil, K., Wisniewski, P.J., Laviola Jr., J.J.: The effects of gender and the presence of third-party humans on telepresence camera height preferences. In: ACM Symposium on Applied Perception 2020. SAP 2020. Association for Computing Machinery, New York (2020). https://doi.org/10.1145/3385955.3407924
41. Pulli, P., et al.: Mobile augmented teleguidance-based safety navigation concept for senior citizens. In: 2nd International Conference on Applied and Theoretical Information Systems Research (2nd. ATISR2012), pp. 1–9 (2012)
42. Rae, I., Venolia, G., Tang, J.C., Molnar, D.: A framework for understanding and designing telepresence. In: Proceedings of the 18th ACM Conference on Computer Supported Cooperative Work & Social Computing - CSCW 2015, Vancouver, BC, Canada, pp. 1552–1566. ACM Press (2015). http://dl.acm.org/citation.cfm?doid=2675133.2675141. https://doi.org/10.1145/2675133.2675141
43. Scheggi, S., Talarico, A., Prattichizzo, D.: A remote guidance system for blind and visually impaired people via vibrotactile haptic feedback. In: 22nd Mediterranean Conference on Control and Automation, pp. 20–23. IEEE (2014)
44. Sjöblom, M., Hamari, J.: Why do people watch others play video games? An empirical study on the motivations of twitch users. Comput. Hum. Behav. **75**, 985–996 (2017)
45. Slater, M., Linakis, V., Usoh, M., Kooper, R.: Immersion, presence and performance in virtual environments: an experiment with tri-dimensional chess. In: Proceedings of the ACM Symposium on Virtual Reality Software and Technology, VRST 1996, pp. 163–172. Association for Computing Machinery, New York (1996). https://doi.org/10.1145/3304181.3304216
46. Steltenpohl, H., Bouwer, A.: Vibrobelt: tactile navigation support for cyclists. In: Proceedings of the 2013 International Conference on Intelligent User Interfaces, pp. 417–426. ACM (2013)
47. Stewart, D.R., Littau, J.: Up, periscope: mobile streaming video technologies, privacy in public, and the right to record. Journal. Mass Commun. Q. **93**(2), 312–331 (2016)
48. Tang, A., Fakourfar, O., Neustaedter, C., Bateman, S.: Collaboration in 360 videochat: challenges and opportunities. Technical report, University of Calgary (2017)

49. Tsukada, K., Yasumura, M.: ActiveBelt: belt-type wearable tactile display for directional navigation. In: Davies, N., Mynatt, E.D., Siio, I. (eds.) UbiComp 2004. LNCS, vol. 3205, pp. 384–399. Springer, Heidelberg (2004). https://doi.org/10. 1007/978-3-540-30119-6_23

50. Van Erp, J.B., Van Veen, H.A., Jansen, C., Dobbins, T.: Waypoint navigation with a vibrotactile waist belt. ACM Trans. Appl. Percept. (TAP) **2**(2), 106–117 (2005)

51. Wang, H.C., Katzschmann, R.K., Teng, S., Araki, B., Giarré, L., Rus, D.: Enabling independent navigation for visually impaired people through a wearable vision-based feedback system. In: 2017 IEEE International Conference on Robotics and Automation (ICRA), pp. 6533–6540. IEEE (2017)

52. Witmer, B.G., Singer, M.J.: Measuring presence in virtual environments: a presence questionnaire. Presence **7**(3), 225–240 (1998)

Pseudo-haptic Perception in Smartphones Graphical Interfaces: A Case Study

Edmilson Domaredzki Verona$^{(\boxtimes)}$ [ID], Beatriz Regina Brum [ID],
Claiton de Oliveira [ID], Silvio Ricardo Rodrigues Sanches [ID],
and Cléber Gimenez Corrêa [ID]

Universidade Tecnológica Federal do Paraná (UTFPR), Cornélio Procópio, Brazil
edmilsonverona@alunos.utfpr.edu.br,
{claitonoliveira,silviosanches,clebergimenez}@utfpr.edu.br

Abstract. Human-computer interaction is a characteristic that strongly influences the user experience in computer systems, especially Virtual Reality and Augmented Reality. The ability to perform tasks using various human sensory channels (e.g., vision, hearing and touch) can increase the efficiency of these systems. The term pseudo-haptic is used to describe haptic effects (for example, stiffness and viscosity) perceived in touch interaction without actuators. Such effects are generated by visual changes that can improve the user experience. Pseudo-haptic interaction can be created on devices, such as smartphones, with graphical interfaces and touch screens. This paper presents an experiment that uses six types of materials (real and virtual) to check the perception and measure the level of perception of users in relation to the pseudo-haptic effect of stiffness, when the task of pressing the material is performed. A comparison of the perception of each participant in relation to virtual materials was also performed when the effect is applied alone and when it is combined with the device's vibration motor. The results showed that the pseudo-haptic effects are perceived by the participants and in most materials the level of stiffness is similar to that of real materials. The use of the vibration feature combined with the pseudo-haptic approach can mitigate the differences in perception between real and virtual materials.

Keywords: Human-computer interaction · User perception · Pseudo-haptic feedback

1 Introduction

Haptics is the science that studies biological sensations related to touch. This sensation can be generated from a kinesthetic (force) or cutaneous (tactile) feedback [15]. The haptic sensation can be perceived when a person manipulates a real object or when a user interacts with a virtual object in a computer simulation with haptic feedback [13].

© Springer Nature Switzerland AG 2021
J. Y. C. Chen and G. Fragomeni (Eds.): HCII 2021, LNCS 12770, pp. 203–222, 2021.
https://doi.org/10.1007/978-3-030-77599-5_16

In this way, such a sensation can be created from the use of haptic devices such as a haptic pen [34]; devices attached to users' fingers that respond to actions and can simulate heat, force, friction, weight and roughness [2, 23, 24]; and even less conventional devices, like a kind of armor attached to parts of the body [1]. These coupled devices can also be used in Virtual Reality (VR) systems, combined with stereoscopic glasses to insert the user into a virtual environment, for interacting with virtual objects [4, 26, 36, 38, 47, 51] and in Augmented Reality (AR) environments, combining virtual and real elements [22].

Haptic sensations can also be created without the use of any physical haptic device or actuator, through only visual changes or distortions. This type of interaction is called pseudo-haptic [32]. When the shape, speed and trajectory of a given virtual object are changed during human-computer interaction, it is possible to generate feelings of friction, mass, stiffness and characteristics of the curvature of the surface. It is possible to change the user's perception of the shapes of a physical object when the user views changes to a virtual object [5–8], like the spatial properties of a cursor during the interaction [28, 30, 31].

With the popularization of touchscreen devices, improvements can be studied in user interaction, providing some kind of tactile feedback when performing actions without the use of another physical device. Chubb *et al.* (2010) [11] called "haptic surface" touchscreens with haptic feedback. The occurrence of haptic sensations on touchscreens can provide a better experience in human-computer interaction, because it is possible to combine the interaction with some feature of the device and, thus, expand the sensations [20]. This type of tactile feedback can be used by modifying the graphical interface, without the need for additional hardware.

Thus, this paper describes a study on the perception of users for pseudo-haptic effect of stiffness in certain materials, rendered graphically on smartphone interfaces, with graphical elements distortions activated through touch, and compared with the same real materials. The goals are to: prove the pseudo-haptic perception generated from purely visual changes; measure the level of perception for different materials; and check the use of the smartphone vibration feature.

The paper is organized as follows: Sect. 2 describes the main concepts for understanding the paper; Sect. 3 presents the related work; Sect. 4 deals with the case study; and Sects. 5, 6 and 7 address the results, discussions and conclusions, respectively.

2   Background

In this section, the concepts of haptic interaction, haptic surfaces and pseudo-haptic interaction that can be used in VR and AR environments to improve the user experience are presented.

2.1   Haptic Interaction

The human being has several sensors spread throughout the body, which allow to perceive the surrounding environment. Through touch it is possible to perceive textures, measure temperature, evaluate a material and identify edges. According to Montague (1986) [39], touch is the first sense to develop. Touch is usually combined with vision and hearing, and it is this coordinated information, coming from different sensors, that allows to expand the sensations and have a better knowledge or perception of the environment.

Haptic is a term derived from the Greek verb *"Haptesthai"*, meaning "touch", and refers to the science of feeling and manipulating through touch. At the beginning of the 20th century, this word was introduced by researchers in the field of experimental psychology, referring to the active touch of real objects by human beings. In the 1980s, there was a redefinition of the term to broaden its scope and include all aspects of touch, involving human-computer interaction. Today the term is multidisciplinary, covering areas such as Medicine, Psychology, Computer Science and Engineering, which study the human touch and interactions with computer systems [15].

The haptic sense is very important in people's daily lives and the exploration of the haptic sensation is often still marginalized in interactions with computer system interfaces, which focus on visual presentation (graphic effects) and audio (sound effects). The most common way to reproduce haptic effects in these systems, which involve VR and AR applications, is through some haptic device, designed to provide effects, such as stiffness, using force or resistance.

2.2 Haptic Surface

The use of haptic content on touchscreens is known as "haptic surface" [11]. This term refers to surfaces that can generate haptic effects on a physical display to stimulate the biological receptors present in the hands. With the increased use of touchscreens for human-computer interaction, solutions that provide the tactile sensation are sought. In this sense, these solutions can combine these screens with certain features, which can be from the most common and known, as a vibration on a smartphone, to something more complex, such as dynamic surfaces.

Chubb *et al.* (2010) [11] separated the haptic surfaces into three categories as follows: vibrotactile displays; variable friction devices; and shape changing surfaces. Vibrotactile displays are those that use one or more vibration motors that respond to the user's touch action, such as when tactile contact with a smartphone screen occurs when clicking on a button on a graphical interface [43].

The variable friction category is based on the use of lateral forces that can be used to create the illusion of material features and textures on the display. To achieve these effects, electrostatic concepts [59] and acoustic waves at the fingertips [50] can be used.

Finally, there are the shape changing surfaces, such as a dynamic Braille display from a pin-array type tactile display [60] or the use of piezoelectric contactors to create compression and traction stresses [42].

2.3 Pseudo-Haptic Interaction

The pseudo-haptic interaction consists of simulating some haptic effects, called pseudo-haptic effects, without using a haptic device or actuator, that is, only using graphic changes or visual tricks to provide the effects when tactile interaction occurs [28]. By not using any physical haptic device or actuator, which often cannot be applied, due to the shape or relatively high cost, it is possible to increase the haptic sensation through devices present in people's daily lives, such as smartphones and tablets, providing a better experience during human-computer interaction.

Pseudo-haptic is haptic information simulated from a sensory conflict when the tactile information differs slightly from the visual information [21]. Sensory conflicts have been studied for decades. An example is the work of Rock and Victor (1964) [46], in which the authors performed an experiment in which they asked participants to touch a cube, looking through a lens that distorted its shape. In this experiment, visual dominance over tactile was evidenced, because the participants when asked about the shape of the cube touched, answered the visualized shape. Ernst and Banks (2002) [16] proposed a model to explain the predominance between human sensory channels. According to the model created, when sensory conflict is related to spatial perception, the human central nervous system prioritizes vision over touch, as it has greater precision. On the other hand, when sensory conflict concerns textures, touch is selected, as it has more precision in estimating the properties of a material than vision. Spatial "relocation" promotes visual dominance instead of visual-haptic integration, considerably increasing the weight of the dominant sense in the perception [12]. The illusions generated because of these sensory conflicts are errors made by the human brain and not by the senses [49]. Goldstein (1999) [19] found that vision can trick a subject during a task of discriminating conformity between two sources that uses touch, showing that vision can be used to generate haptic illusions [49]. Berthoz (1997) [10] suggested that the sensory illusion cannot be considered as a wrong solution or an error, but as the "best possible hypothesis" identified at that moment by the human brain. Hatwell *et al.* (2003) [21] affirm that the illusions generated from the vision and touch are based on the same rules and representations of real-world properties, that is, the same characteristics identified in previous experiences with real objects are used to identify illusions.

The pseudo-haptic feedback combines visual information in a synchronized way with the user's movement or motor action during the simulation [28]. In this way, a coherent environment or an environment that becomes coherent can be created for the subject during the interaction, allowing the simulation of effects such as weight, stiffness, relief, texture, friction and viscosity. Lécuyer (2009) [28] makes four main statements about the pseudo-haptic feedback, which are: it implies one or more sensory conflicts between visual and haptic information; it is based on the sensory domain of vision on touch in the perception of spatial properties; it can correspond to a new and coherent representation of the environment resulting from a combination of haptic and visual information; it can create haptic illusions, that is, the perception of a haptic property (characteristic perceived by touching the material) different from that present in reality.

Some limitations can be found in the use of pseudo-haptic feedback, including the use of touchscreens. According to Ujitoko *et al.* (2015) [55], the problem of occlusion, which is when the finger that touches the screen hides the visual feature presented, is a limitation, as well as decoupling, which consists of changing the speed ranges of the graphic cursors during interaction to identify their locations and the visual illusion.

A relevant effect on haptic sensations is the stiffness of a material. The stiffness is the level of flexion or deformation of a material under pressure or force during a period (time). And in the case of the pseudo-haptic interaction, the level of graphic deformation or distortion of the virtual object touched during a period.

3   Related Work

Several studies have been carried out in the area over the years using the pseudo-haptic interaction to prove perception of effects or measure the level. Most studies used the mouse or some other external device, which can be expensive or unconventional, combined with the pseudo-haptic effects. Besides, most studies did not have a large number of participants [9,14,40,44,58] which respectively had the participation of 12, 14, 7, 13 and 12 people.

There are works that used physical objects, which can be used in AR systems; or which used motion sensors to assist in interaction. Subsection 3.1 describes works in this category.

There are also studies that are restricted to only making visual changes, known as pure pseudo-haptic (Subsect. 3.2). Few studies used touchscreens and only one used the vibration motor present in devices, such as smartphones.

3.1   Combined Pseudo-haptic

In the literature, there is research to verify if changes in perception occur or improve the user experience when combined with some other device, mostly, that offers physical feedback.

Studies have been carried out that combine pseudo-haptic effects and haptic devices or actuators to provide physical feedback on tactile interaction. There are also works that use a passive haptic device attached to the fingers, combined with visual changes, to generate pseudo-haptic feedback simulating stiffness [2,23]. Other studies have combined the pseudo-haptic effects with pressure actuators [25,58] or with a force feedback device [29].

The pseudo-haptic approach was also used in AR environments to simulate mass effects on virtual objects projected on markers [22], as well as in VR environments [4,26,36,48].

Studies were carried out to measure the participants' perception using the vibration feature. Ridzuan *et al.* (2012) [45] conducted a study using a vibration feature from a touchscreen device and measured the stiffness effect using this feature and graphical changes to the interface. Hachisu *et al.* (2011) [20] used a mouse device with vibrotactile feedback in their research. Studies combining pseudo-haptic approaches with a pen can also be cited, with, among other things, the vibration feature [35,54]. The use of vibration feature is particularly interesting as it can be used in most current smartphones that have an embedded vibration motor.

Studies that modify the reality in the participants' interaction, hiding their hands or fingers were also conducted, demonstrating that the participants can perceive the illusion created using a pseudo-haptic approach as their reality at that moment in relation to the angle, position, curvature, force and size [5–8,27,44].

Microsoft's Kinect device, which recognizes body movements to increase interactivity in virtual games, was also combined with a pseudo-haptic approach in one study [18].

3.2   Pseudo-haptic Interaction

The studies classified in the category of pseudo-haptic interaction did not use any device with physical feedback, being composed purely of visual changes. Most of them were conducted using only a computer and interaction using the mouse device. Some studies have used other passive devices that do not provide haptic feedback in experiments [30,31,33,37,57].

An approach to perform this simulation on devices that do not have a pressure sensor was proposed by Argelaguet *et al.* (2013) [3]. The authors suggested using time and visual changes regarding the size of graphic objects that represent materials to simulate stiffness. The size changes occurred at the moment of touch, the size of the cursor decreasing to a limit while the finger remained in contact with the screen, and when the release occurred, the cursor returned to its normal size.

Lécuyer *et al.* (2000) [32] and Lécuyer *et al.* (2001) [33] worked with the hypothesis that the stiffness effect could be simulated by the visual deformation of an object. For this, they used a Spaceball, an isometric input device with six degrees of freedom, and a virtual object represented on the screen, which had the pressure ratio changed, that is, the more rigid an object was, the less deformation it suffered and the less rigid he was, the more deformation it suffered. Even though Spaceball is not a haptic device, because it is static, passive and does not have pressure reaction feedback, the participants had the perception of different levels of stiffness when interacting with different virtual objects that suffered varied deformations.

Two other pseudo-haptic studies conducted experiments using springs to measure the participants' perception of different levels of stiffness. In the first study, participants interacted using the Spaceball device and visualized the deformation of the virtual object that represented the spring. In this study, participants answered about similarities in stiffness of a virtual spring in relation to a real spring [32]. In the second study, real torsion springs were used, as well as virtual torsion springs simulated using pseudo-haptic feedback. In this study, participants pushed the springs and had a similar perception of stiffness when comparing real and virtual springs [41].

Works focused on touchscreens were conducted by changing objects in the graphical interfaces for pseudo-haptic interaction. These works verified the perception of the participants in relation to the simulated effects in this type of screen during the interaction [9,14,40,55].

4   Case Study

The main purpose of the case study was to verify and measure the level of perception of the haptic sensation of stiffness when interacting with real and virtual materials, the latter being through pseudo-haptic effects on a smartphone's touchscreen; as well as checking the pseudo-haptic effect with and without vibration. For this, an experiment was carried out with participants, collecting data on perception through questionnaires. According to Lécuyer et al. (2000) [32] some haptic sensations can be perceived by participants with similar levels when interacting with real objects. It should be noted that the haptic sensation must be caused by visual or graphical changes, deforming the calibrated virtual materials to represent the studied effect of the corresponding real materials, without using any actuator external to the smartphone. Each virtual material was made with the appearance similar to the corresponding real material in a superior view of the material. Real materials were made available to participants to allow comparisons of perceived sensations, according to the literature [32,41,58]. The hypothesis is that there were not great differences for the same materials among three scenarios.

Fig. 1. Real materials used in the experiment (from left to right): rubber, sponge, fabric, plastic, cardboard and wood.

4.1   Experiment Materials

The experiment had real objects at the disposal of the participants, which consisted of six materials with different levels of stiffness. As can be seen in Fig. 1, following the order from least to most stiff, the materials used were: rubber, sponge, fabric, plastic, cardboard and wood. To represent the rubber a balloon was used. The sponge was represented by the softer side of a common cleaning sponge and the fabric by a common cotton cloth. The plastic was represented by a lid of a common pot, while for the cardboard was used a part from a thick and hard cardboard shipping box. Finally, a piece of solid wood was used, being the only material totally rigid.

The order was defined manually, pressing each real material, since there may be variations of a certain material. For example, there are different plastics, which can have different levels of stiffness. All materials were fixed on individual supports measuring in centimeters (cm), 11 cm × 8.5 cm × 5 cm, for length, width and height. The materials occupied the same area, had the same shape and were visible only from the top face to the participant.

The experiment also included a smartphone with a native vibration feature to perform interaction with virtual materials through its touchscreen. The smartphone used to carry out the experiment was a Motorola G5 Plus with a 5.5-in. screen, with no pressure measurement sensor on the screen or an external feature. For the creation of the Android application containing the virtual materials, Framework7 v5.4.2 [56] and Cordova v9.0.0 [52] technology were used. To simulate realism, the textures of the virtual materials were obtained from high-resolution images of each corresponding real material. The presentation of the face of the virtual materials was represented by a 4.5 cm^2.

The JavaScript Rebound v0.0.7 library [17] was used to provide the pseudo-haptic effect, allowing the resizing and distortion of an image through tension and friction adjustments. This software library allowed to generate a visual effect of sinking the material (displacement of parts of the texture of the image in direction to the center in a period (time), creating an elastic deformation) when the user touches the virtual material, similar when the user touches the real materials, without changing the borders. The calibration was done manually by the researchers, comparing the visual distortion generated between real and virtual materials, modulating the deformation coefficient for the softness/stiffness of each material setting the friction and tension values.

For the performance of the experiment, a computer lab room with sound insulation, closed door and windows without external view was made available. Inside the room, there was a table measuring 400 cm × 150 cm × 75 cm in length, width and height, respectively; and a chair measuring 55 cm × 57 cm in length and width, with a seat 42 cm high in relation to the floor.

The camera of an LG K10 smartphone was used to record participant interactions in each task. The camera was focused on the material or smartphone and on the participant's dominant hand, recording the moment of the interaction. The participants did not have their faces or bodies recorded to avoid their identification. The camera was freely manipulated by the researcher who was conducting the experiment, starting and stopping recording for each task performed. The visualizations of the recordings were used later in the analysis of the results of the experiment, allowing to verify behaviors and also identify if any participant did not perform the task correctly or discrepancies between responses and actions of the participants were found, invalidating the participation.

For statistical analysis, seeking to verify significant differences between the same materials in the scenarios, the R programming language [53] was used. Finally, ballpoint pens and printed questionnaires identified by unique numbers were made available, so that the participants could inform their perceptions during the data collection phase. The numbers would be used to remove data from the survey in case of withdrawal, since the confidentiality of personal information must be respected.

Each questionnaire was divided into three parts, one for each scenario, composed of six questions (one for each material). Only the scenario was described in the questionnaires, without informing the order or descriptions of the materials. At the end of each task in each material in a scenario, the participant was asked to answer the following question: On a scale of 1 to 5, being: 1 - Very soft; 2 - Little soft; 3 - Soft; 4 - Hard; 5 - Very hard, what is your perception of the level of stiffness/hardness when pressing the center of the material? It can be seen that ties were possible, since the scale has five values for the notes of perception and there are six materials.

4.2   Participants and Tasks

The experiment had the participation of nine male students, volunteers, without any remuneration or bonus, from the fifth semester of the undergraduate course in Information Systems, in the age range of 21 to 25 years. As they are from the computing area and from a generation accustomed to using smartphones in their daily lives, no barriers were encountered that could occur with any participant unfamiliar with the device used. Due to the profile explained and the simplicity of the task required to be performed, there was no need for prior training to perform the experiment. The participants only used the real materials and the smartphone of the experiment to perform the task, not being allowed to access or use any other resources during the experiment.

The main task consisted of pressing the center of the material (real or virtual) with the index finger of the dominant hand, so that the participant perceives the level of distortion, as can be seen in Fig. 2. The participants were free to press as many times as they wished, with no time set for execution, in order to have the perception of the stiffness of the material, as long as they always pressed in the center. The material was made available on the table, in front of the participant, who should press it from top to bottom against the table to avoid displacement. In this way, the visual distortion of sinking generated during the experiment, whether in real or virtual material, would be visualized in the same way. No further manipulation with the materials and the smartphone was permitted.

After performing the task with the material, the participant should answer the question of the printed questionnaire, informing their level of perception about the stiffness of the material. During the task, the objective was to collect the perception in relation to each material and avoid comparisons. Therefore, to

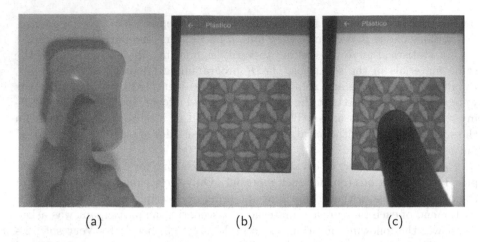

(a)   (b)   (c)

Fig. 2. Participant performing task on materials: (a) real, (b) virtual - before interaction, (c) virtual - during interaction.

prevent the participant from trying to adjust their responses, creating a scale of material levels, the participant could not change a previous answer informed in the questionnaire or perform a task on a previous material again.

4.3 Scenarios

The experiment consisted of three scenarios for each participant, as follows: *(i)* interaction with real materials; *(ii)* interaction with virtual materials; and *(iii)* interaction with virtual materials and with the vibration feature. In both the second and third virtual scenarios, visual distortion occurs, generating a sinking effect when the participant touches the screen of the smartphone. The level of this sinking is based on the stiffness coefficient configured for the material, making the materials behave differently when they are touched. The difference between the second and third scenarios was the use of the smartphone's native vibration motor, starting when the participant's finger touched the screen and ending when it moved away from it. The vibration was continuous, with standard amplitude and frequency of the smartphone's native vibration motor during touch for all materials.

As the experiment aimed at the individual measurement of sensation by each participant, the exchange of messages between participants could influence perception and data collection. For this reason, the participants did not have contact with each other while they were participating in the experiment.

4.4 Experiment Design

Each participant entered the room individually and received an identification number, which was used in the experiment questionnaires answered by him for future analysis. Any question could be asked by the participant before starting the experiment, so that they would feel comfortable and be confident in the experiment. The experiment did not represent any particular type of risk to the participants' health or required personal or confidential information. It is important to mention that the final objective of the experiment was not informed to the participant, that is, that their responses would be used to measure perception and make comparisons of perception levels. This information was omitted so that the participant was not encouraged to try to place the same level among the same materials in different scenarios.

The participant performed the experiment individually sitting on a chair with the table in front of them. The real materials and the smartphone with the virtual materials were made available individually at different times to the participant, according to the predefined order of the scenarios and materials for carrying out the experimental tasks. The participant only interacted with the next material after indicating the perceived level of stiffness of the material in the scenario questionnaire and only advanced to the next scenario after interacting with all the materials in the scenario.

The experiment had a researcher instructor in the room to monitor the progress. He informed the participant of the names of the materials used in the experiment. In the smartphone screen was presented the name of the material at each moment of the experiment. The instructor's role consisted only of: (i) conducting the sequence of the experiment observing the predefined sequence; (ii) providing basic instructions and ethical information without interfering with the participant's perception; (iii) delivering and collecting the real materials, the smartphone with the application and the questionnaires that were used in each task; and (iv) filming the participant's hand performing the proposed task for further verification.

The order of the scenarios varied by participant, using the possible combinations between the three scenarios. Thus, one participant started the experiment by manipulating real materials while another participant manipulated virtual materials without vibration, and a third one manipulated virtual materials with vibration. Likewise, the possible combinations related to the real and virtual materials available in each scenario were used. Thus, one participant started with **Wood** material, while another with **Sponge** and a third with **Rubber** in the same scenario. Using the combinations between the scenarios and between the materials, each participant performed the tasks following a different order in the experiment.

The participant was not allowed to: (i) return to a previous scenario; (ii) have access to the materials previously, except at the time of the task; and (iii) have access to the order of availability of materials. The researcher instructor was the one who individually delivered and collected the material at the time of the task, following the predefined sequence without informing the subsequent material or scenario.

5   Results

All participants performed the three scenarios individually, interacting with all the materials available for each scenario. In total, 162 responses were collected on the participants' level of perception. The average levels by material and scenario, as well as their distribution, can be seen in Table 1 and through Fig. 3a. The following subsections detail the results considering the goals of this paper, to: *(i)* prove the pseudo-haptic effect perception in smartphones for certain materials (Subsect. 5.1); *(ii)* measure the levels of perception (Subsect. 5.1); and *(iii)* check the sensations with and without the use of vibration (Subsect. 5.2).

Table 1. Overall average of the participants' perception level according to the scale: 1 - Very soft; 2 - Little soft; 3 - Soft; 4 - Hard; 5 - Very hard.

Material	Real	Virtual	Virtual/Vibration
Rubber	1.4	1.4	1.6
Sponge	1.7	2.5	2.1
Fabric	1.8	2.3	2.1
Plastic	3.5	3.5	3.3
Cardboard	3.7	4.2	4.2
Wood	4.8	5	4.5

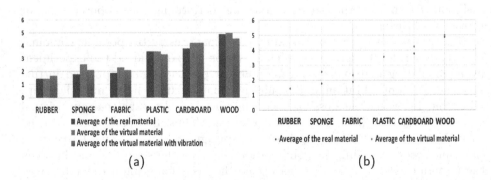

(a)   (b)

Fig. 3. (a) Perception levels of stiffness (Y axis) among materials (X axis) (b) Perception levels of stiffness (Y axis) among real and virtual materials (X axis).

5.1   Perceived Level of Stiffness

Analyzing the averages, it can be identified that the participants perceived the pseudo-haptic effect of stiffness in virtual materials, with and without the use of vibration, as there is a gradual perception of the stiffness level in virtual materials according to real materials (Fig. 3a). It is important to highlight that some similar responses would be possible, especially between pairs of materials, since there were six materials and five levels on the scale of responses. Thus, the perception of the pseudo-haptic effect of stiffness by the participants was proven. Additionally, the level of stiffness was measured, following the proposed scale, although it was expected that for the materials of the extremes (totally soft and totally rigid) the responses would not present discrepancies.

However, when comparing the averages of the participants' responses for virtual materials without vibration with the real materials, it can be seen that in most comparisons between materials, the virtual material was perceived to be a little stiffer than the corresponding real material. The results are shown in the scatter plot of Fig. 3b.

The Friedman nonparametric test was applied to identify statistically significant differences between the three scenarios for each material, checking the hypothesis. The reason for using this statistical test is related to the data and analysis characteristics, such as: *(i)* the residuals of the data does not have normal distribution; *(ii)* there are more than two sample groups for comparing; and *(iii)* the same individual provides more than one response of perception, participating in different scenarios.

After applying Friedman test, **no significant differences** were found (hypothesis corroborated), since a $p - value \leq 0.05$ (confidence level at 95%) was expected, and the $p - values$ were higher than 0.05 for all materials. For the **Rubber** material, it was obtained a Chi-Squared or $X^2 = 0.4$ and a $p - value = 0.8187$; the **Sponge** material reached a $X^2 = 2.7692$ and a $p - value = 0.2504$; for the **Fabric** material the test presented a $X^2 = 2.1739$ and a $p - value = 0.3372$; and for the **Plastic** material the result was a $X^2 = 0.63636$ and a $p - value = 0.7275$. For the **Cardboard** and **Wood** materials the X^2 were 1.3333 and 2.0; and $p - values$ were 0.5134 and 0.3679, respectively.

In the end of some sessions of the experiment, three participants made comments about the study. Two of them said that they needed to add force during interaction with virtual materials that had higher stiffness levels; and one of them commented that it was not necessary to add force to press the materials because the screen of the smartphone is not flexible.

5.2   Combination with Vibration Feature

When the analysis is related to the averages of virtual materials, comparing the use or not of the vibration feature of the smartphone, the result was that the participants, in most materials, perceived a lower level of stiffness with the feature than without it, as shown in Fig. 4a. Except for **Rubber** and **Cardboard**, all other materials had a reduction in the perceived average level. In the case of the **Cardboard** material the average was equal with and without using the vibration feature.

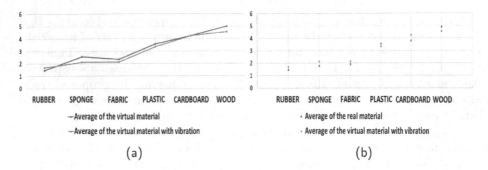

Fig. 4. (a) Perception levels of stiffness (Y axis) among virtual materials with and without vibration feature (X axis) (b) Perception levels of stiffness (Y axis) considering each pair of real and virtual materials with vibration (X axis).

6   Discussions

From the results it is possible to evidence that the simulation of the stiffness effect using a pseudo-haptic approach was perceived by the participants, and that in most materials the level of perception was close to the level of the real material. These results were obtained without previous training with the participants, restricting the participants' access to the materials only at the moment of the task. The names of the materials were not identified in the questionnaires, it was not allowed to change responses attributed and different combinations were used for presenting to the participants the three scenarios and the six materials. Thus, each participant carried out the experiment following a different order, which did not respect the scale of stiffness of the materials and which could start with a scenario containing virtual or real objects.

Discrepancies on the extreme materials (totally soft and totally rigid) were not expected. Additionally, the tie between the materials on the scale was expected, especially between two approximate materials at the stiffness level, since there were six materials and five levels on the scale.

The **Sponge** material had the higher difference in relation to the scenarios according to the statistical test, although the difference is not significant. This occurred possibly due to the visual presentation, which although based on the image of a real sponge, the predominantly yellow color did not contribute to the representation of this virtual material, making it difficult to visualize when the participant performed the task, because the stiffness effect is caused by a visual distortion which causes the image to sink when touching according to a predetermined setup.

On the other hand, **Rubber** and **Plastic**, that had an appearance considered rich, obtained the values closer to each other for the three scenarios. This can be seen in Table 2, which shows the standard deviation between the scenarios.

Variations in the level perceived by participants was expected in this study, even with the hypothesis corroborated, because the stiffness perception could

Table 2. Standard deviation between three scenarios for each material.

Rubber	Sponge	Fabric	Plastic	Cardboard	Wood
0.10475656	0.31860464	0.181443685	0.10475656	0.20951312	0.188852575

vary according to previous individual experiences with the materials. The case of the **Wood** material can be used to exemplify this perception difference, since it was the only material in all scenarios in which there was no distortion or deformation in the touch, and four responses from participants (two after handling real materials and two after handling virtual materials with vibration) were not the level 5, the maximum scale stiffness (fully stiff material). The use of other resources, such as sound effects, can help, reducing the doubts in the perception.

Analyzing the responses from participants, it can be seen that most of the responses varied little with respect to the calculated average level of the participants for each material, except for two cases in the scenario of virtual materials with vibration, which did not follow the presented pattern and can be seen in Figs. 5a and 5b. The participant 8 identified the **Rubber** as a stiff material, defining the level 5 (highest level of stiffness), and the participant 5 identified the **Wood** as a soft material (level 2). If these responses were disregarded, the average in the virtual scenario with vibration for the material **Wood** would be 4.7, compared to the averages 4.8 and 5.0 in the other scenarios for the same material; and the **Rubber** material would have an average lower than 1.4, similar to this material in other scenarios, with a value of 1.2, also reducing the perceived level when using the vibration feature as in most other virtual materials. It is important to highlight that these conflicting values were not the responses to the first task performed by the participants in the experiment, and in the other scenarios these participants answered according to the average for the material. It is also important to note that the recorded videos of the tasks of all participants were evaluated and problems were not identified, such as doubts and unexpected movements during interaction.

Also when analyzing the videos of the recordings made at the time of handling the virtual materials, it was found that most participants seemed to apply a certain amount of force with their finger to press depending on the material, trying to identify the level of stiffness. This analysis shows that even the participants being from the computing area, with knowledge about the device used in the experiment, that is, knowing that the screen was not flexible and did not have any type of pressure sensor, they needed to apply a certain force to try to complete the task of pressing the materials.

The information provided about names and textures of the materials could have influenced the responses. The participants could think about levels of stiffness according to previous experiences with these materials. However, each material has variations, e.g., a plastic can be hard or soft, depending on its composition. This could cause problems in the perception because of previous experiences with these materials. We observed that the participants strove to identify the stiffness of each material based on visual distortions provided in that moment.

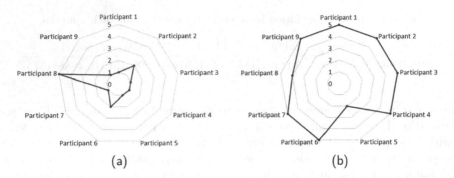

Fig. 5. Responses for the scenario of virtual materials with vibration (a) **Rubber** and (b) **Wood**.

The use of the vibration feature of the smartphone in virtual materials, provided the participants the perception that most materials were less stiff, and in some cases even less than some real materials, such as **Plastic** and **Wood**, which can be seen in Fig. 4b. The results showed that the vibration can mitigate the differences perceived, since the screen of the smartphone is not a flexible surface, such as a real material that is not stiff, and the deformation does not happen during the interaction. Except for **Plastic** and **Wood**, the responses to other real materials presented average values of perception less than the mean values for the same virtual materials when the vibration feature was employed. This observation evidenced that the addition of the vibration must be rigorously studied, because it can influence the pseudo-haptic effect perception.

Finally, the number of participants of the experiment is similar to the numbers found in the main related work. However, we believe that it is important to carry out the experiment with a higher number of participants, including different profiles, to compare with the results obtained in this study.

7   Conclusion

The current study aimed at proving and measuring the stiffness effect perception using a pseudo-haptic approach for certain materials, as well as checking the use of the vibration feature, through a smartphone with touch screen. The haptic feedback can improve the users' experience during the interaction with systems.

According to the results of the experiment, the participants perceived the effect, and the stiffness levels perceived were similar for each pair of real and virtual materials (considering the same material type). When comparing the perceived level between real and virtual materials, a small increase, without statistically significant difference between the scenarios, in the level of stiffness in the perception of the participants was observed for most virtual materials compared to the real ones. A comparison was also made between the virtual material scenarios without the vibration feature with those that had this feature.

The results showed that the participants perceived a lower level of stiffness when the pseudo-haptic effect is combined with the vibration feature for most materials than when this effect is not combined with the same feature.

The contribution was to evidence that is possible to develop computational systems, especially systems based on VR and AR, with pseudo-haptic interaction using graphical interfaces of devices with touchscreens and vibration motor, at least for the profile of the participants of the experiment. These interfaces, during the human-computer interaction, can stimulate two sensory channels (vision and touch), improving the immersion and the experience of the user to perform tasks.

For future work, other materials can be used to measure the perception of the pseudo-haptic effect by participants. Materials with different appearances, formats and sizes could be used. Other tasks can be planned, such as: moving or grabbing the materials. Experiments in which the participants do not receive information, such as the name and the texture of the materials, could be made. As the human brain uses several sensory channels scattered throughout the body to identify properties of real materials, the addition of a sound effect in the interaction would activate another channel and, with vision and touch, could assist in the perception of stiffness.

References

1. Achibet, M., Girard, A., Talvas, A., Marchal, M., Lécuyer, A.: Elastic-arm: human-scale passive haptic feedback for augmenting interaction and perception in virtual environments. In: 2015 IEEE Virtual Reality (VR), pp. 63–68. IEEE (2015)
2. Achibet, M., et al.: Flexifingers: multi-finger interaction in VR combining passive haptics and pseudo-haptics. In: 2017 IEEE Symposium on 3D User Interfaces (3DUI), pp. 103–106. IEEE (2017)
3. Argelaguet, F., Jáuregui, D.A.G., Marchal, M., Lécuyer, A.: Elastic images: perceiving local elasticity of images through a novel pseudo-haptic deformation effect. ACM Trans. Appl. Percept. (TAP) 10(3), 1–14 (2013)
4. Azmandian, M., Hancock, M., Benko, H., Ofek, E., Wilson, A.D.: Haptic retargeting: dynamic repurposing of passive haptics for enhanced virtual reality experiences. In: Proceedings of the 2016 CHI Conference on Human Factors in Computing Systems, pp. 1968–1979 (2016)
5. Ban, Y., Kajinami, T., Narumi, T., Tanikawa, T., Hirose, M.: Modifying an identified angle of edged shapes using pseudo-haptic effects. In: Isokoski, P., Springare, J. (eds.) EuroHaptics 2012. LNCS, vol. 7282, pp. 25–36. Springer, Heidelberg (2012). https://doi.org/10.1007/978-3-642-31401-8_3
6. Ban, Y., Kajinami, T., Narumi, T., Tanikawa, T., Hirose, M.: Modifying an identified curved surface shape using pseudo-haptic effect. In: 2012 IEEE Haptics Symposium (HAPTICS), pp. 211–216. IEEE (2012)
7. Ban, Y., Narumi, T., Tanikawa, T., Hirose, M.: Modifying an identified position of edged shapes using pseudo-haptic effects. In: Proceedings of the 18th ACM Symposium on Virtual Reality Software and Technology, pp. 93–96 (2012)
8. Ban, Y., Narumi, T., Tanikawa, T., Hirose, M.: Modifying an identified size of objects handled with two fingers using pseudo-haptic effects. In: ICAT/EGVE/EuroVR, pp. 1–8 (2012)

9. Ban, Y., Ujitoko, Y.: Enhancing the pseudo-haptic effect on the touch panel using the virtual string. In: IEEE Haptics Symposium 2018 (HAPTICS), pp. 278–283. IEEE (2018)
10. Berthoz, A.: Le sens du mouvement. Odile Jacob (1997)
11. Chubb, E.C., Colgate, J.E., Peshkin, M.A.: Shiverpad: a glass haptic surface that produces shear force on a bare finger. IEEE Trans. Haptics 3(3), 189–198 (2010)
12. Congedo, M., Lécuyer, A., Gentaz, E.: The influence of spatial delocation on perceptual integration of vision and touch. Presence Teleoperators Virtual Environ. 15(3), 353–357 (2006)
13. Corrêa, C.G., Nunes, F.L., Ranzini, E., Nakamura, R., Tori, R.: Haptic interaction for needle insertion training in medical applications: the state-of-the-art. Med. Eng. Phys. 63, 6–25 (2019)
14. Costes, A., Argelaguet, F., Danieau, F., Guillotel, P., Lécuyer, A.: Touchy: a visual approach for simulating haptic effects on touchscreens. Front. ICT 6, 1 (2019)
15. Eid, M., Orozco, M., Saddik, A.E.: A guided tour in haptic audio visual environments and applications. Int. J. Adv. Media Commun. 1(3), 265–297 (2007)
16. Ernst, M.O., Banks, M.S.: Humans integrate visual and haptic information in a statistically optimal fashion. Nature 415(6870), 429–433 (2002)
17. Facebook Inc: Rebound (2020). https://facebook.github.io/rebound-js/. Accessed 25 June 2020
18. Gaucher, P., Argelaguet, F., Royan, J., Lécuyer, A.: A novel 3D carousel based on pseudo-haptic feedback and gestural interaction for virtual showcasing. In: 2013 IEEE Symposium on 3D User Interfaces (3DUI), pp. 55–58. IEEE (2013)
19. Goldstein, E.B.: Sensation and Perception. Brooks/Cole, Kentucky (1999)
20. Hachisu, T., Cirio, G., Marchal, M., Lécuyer, A., Kajimoto, H.: Pseudo-haptic feedback augmented with visual and tactile vibrations. In: 2011 IEEE International Symposium on VR Innovation, pp. 327–328. IEEE (2011)
21. Hatwell, Y., Streri, A., Gentaz, E.: Touching for Knowing: Cognitive Psychology of Haptic Manual Perception, vol. 53. John Benjamins Publishing, Amsterdam (2003)
22. Issartel, P., Guéniat, F., Coquillart, S., Ammi, M.: Perceiving mass in mixed reality through pseudo-haptic rendering of newton's third law. In: 2015 IEEE Virtual Reality (VR), pp. 41–46. IEEE (2015)
23. Jang, I., Lee, D.: On utilizing pseudo-haptics for cutaneous fingertip haptic device. In: 2014 IEEE Haptics Symposium (HAPTICS), pp. 635–639. IEEE (2014)
24. Kim, H., Kim, M., Lee, W.: Hapthimble: a wearable haptic device towards usable virtual touch screen. In: Proceedings of the 2016 CHI Conference on Human Factors in Computing Systems, pp. 3694–3705 (2016)
25. Kimura, T., Nojima, T.: Pseudo-haptic feedback on softness induced by grasping motion. In: Isokoski, P., Springare, J. (eds.) EuroHaptics 2012. LNCS, vol. 7283, pp. 202–205. Springer, Heidelberg (2012). https://doi.org/10.1007/978-3-642-31404-9_36
26. Kohli, L.: Exploiting perceptual illusions to enhance passive haptics. In: IEEE VR Workshop on Perceptual Illusions in Virtual Environments, pp. 22–24 (2009)
27. Kokubun, A., Ban, Y., Narumi, T., Tanikawa, T., Hirose, M.: Representing normal and shearing forces on the mobile device with visuo-haptic interaction and a rear touch interface. In: IEEE Haptics Symposium 2014 (HAPTICS), pp. 415–420. IEEE (2014)
28. Lécuyer, A.: Simulating haptic feedback using vision: a survey of research and applications of pseudo-haptic feedback. Presence Teleoperators Virtual Environ. 18(1), 39–53 (2009)

29. Lécuyer, A., Burkhardt, J.M., Coquillart, S., Coiffet, P.: "Boundary of illusion": an experiment of sensory integration with a pseudo-haptic system. In: Proceedings IEEE Virtual Reality 2001, pp. 115–122. IEEE (2001)

30. Lécuyer, A., Burkhardt, J.M., Etienne, L.: Feeling bumps and holes without a haptic interface: the perception of pseudo-haptic textures. In: Proceedings of the SIGCHI Conference on Human Factors in Computing Systems, pp. 239–246 (2004)

31. Lécuyer, A., Burkhardt, J.M., Tan, C.H.: A study of the modification of the speed and size of the cursor for simulating pseudo-haptic bumps and holes. ACM Trans. Appl. Percept. (TAP) 5(3), 1–21 (2008)

32. Lecuyer, A., Coquillart, S., Kheddar, A., Richard, P., Coiffet, P.: Pseudo-haptic feedback: can isometric input devices simulate force feedback? In: Proceedings IEEE Virtual Reality 2000 (Cat. No. 00CB37048), pp. 83–90. IEEE (2000)

33. Lécuyer, A., Cuquillart, S., Coiffet, P.: Simulating haptic information with haptic illusions in virtual environments. Technical report, Anatole Lécuyer Suresnes (France) Aerospatiale Matra CCR (2001)

34. Lee, J.C., Dietz, P.H., Leigh, D., Yerazunis, W.S., Hudson, S.E.: Haptic pen: a tactile feedback stylus for touch screens. In: Proceedings of the 17th Annual ACM Symposium on User Interface Software and Technology, pp. 291–294 (2004)

35. Li, M., Ridzuan, M.B., Sareh, S., Seneviratne, L.D., Dasgupta, P., Althoefer, K.: Pseudo-haptics for rigid tool/soft surface interaction feedback in virtual environments. Mechatronics 24(8), 1092–1100 (2014)

36. Maereg, A.T., Nagar, A., Reid, D., Secco, E.L.: Wearable vibrotactile haptic device for stiffness discrimination during virtual interactions. Front. Robot. AI 4, 42 (2017)

37. Mandryk, R.L., Rodgers, M.E., Inkpen, K.M.: Sticky widgets: pseudo-haptic widget enhancements for multi-monitor displays. In: CHI 2005 Extended Abstracts on Human Factors in Computing Systems, pp. 1621–1624 (2005)

38. Matsumoto, K., Ban, Y., Narumi, T., Yanase, Y., Tanikawa, T., Hirose, M.: Unlimited corridor: redirected walking techniques using visuo haptic interaction. In: ACM SIGGRAPH 2016 Emerging Technologies, pp. 1–2. Association for Computing Machinery, New York (2016)

39. Montague, A.: Touching: The Human Significance of the Skin. Harper & Row (1986)

40. Murata, K.A., et al.: A touch panel for presenting softness with visuo-haptic interaction. In: International Conference on Artificial Reality and Telexistence & Eurographics Symposium on Virtual Environments 2018 (ICAT-EGVE), pp. 123–130 (2018)

41. Paljic, A., Burkhardtt, J.M., Coquillart, S.: Evaluation of pseudo-haptic feedback for simulating torque: a comparison between isometric and elastic input devices. In: 12th International Symposium on Haptic Interfaces for Virtual Environment and Teleoperator Systems 2004 (HAPTICS 2004), pp. 216–223. IEEE (2004)

42. Pasquero, J., Hayward, V.: STReSS: a practical tactile display system with one millimeter spatial resolution and 700 HZ refresh rate. In: Proceedings of Eurohaptics 2003, pp. 94–110 (2003)

43. Poupyrev, I., Maruyama, S.: Tactile interfaces for small touch screens. In: Proceedings of the 16th Annual ACM Symposium on User Interface Software and Technology, pp. 217–220 (2003)

44. Pusch, A., Martin, O., Coquillart, S.: Hemp-hand-displacement-based pseudo-haptics: a study of a force field application. In: 2008 IEEE Symposium on 3D User Interfaces, pp. 59–66. IEEE (2008)

45. Ridzuan, M.B., Makino, Y., Takemura, K.: Direct touch haptic display using immersive illusion with interactive virtual finger. In: Isokoski, P., Springare, J. (eds.) EuroHaptics 2012. LNCS, vol. 7282, pp. 432–444. Springer, Heidelberg (2012). https://doi.org/10.1007/978-3-642-31401-8_39

46. Rock, I., Victor, J.: Vision and touch: an experimentally created conflict between the two senses. Science **143**(3606), 594–596 (1964)

47. Sagardia, M., et al.: VR-OOS: the DLR's virtual reality simulator for telerobotic on-orbit servicing with haptic feedback. In: 2015 IEEE Aerospace Conference, pp. 1–17. IEEE (2015)

48. Samad, M., Gatti, E., Hermes, A., Benko, H., Parise, C.: Pseudo-haptic weight: changing the perceived weight of virtual objects by manipulating control-display ratio. In: Proceedings of the 2019 CHI Conference on Human Factors in Computing Systems, pp. 1–13 (2019)

49. Srinivassan, M.A.: The impact of visual information on the haptic perception of stiffness in virtual environments. Proc. ASME Dynamic Syst. Control Div. **58**, 555–559 (1996)

50. Takasaki, M., Kotani, H., Mizuno, T., Nara, T.: Transparent surface acoustic wave tactile display. In: 2005 IEEE/RSJ International Conference on Intelligent Robots and Systems, pp. 3354–3359. IEEE (2005)

51. Tatsumi, H., Murai, Y., Sekita, I., Tokumasu, S., Miyakawa, M.: Cane walk in the virtual reality space using virtual haptic sensing: toward developing haptic VR technologies for the visually impaired. In: 2015 IEEE International Conference on Systems, Man, and Cybernetics, pp. 2360–2365. IEEE (2015)

52. The Apache Software Foundation: Apache cordova (2020). https://cordova.apache.org/. Accessed 25 June 2020

53. The R Foundation: The R project for statistical computing (2020). https://www.r-project.org/. Accessed 09 July 2020

54. Ujitoko, Y., Ban, Y., Hirota, K.: Modulating fine roughness perception of vibrotactile textured surface using pseudo-haptic effect. IEEE Trans. Visual Comput. Graphics **25**(5), 1981–1990 (2019)

55. Ujitoko, Y., Ban, Y., Narumi, T., Tanikawa, T., Hirota, K., Hirose, M.: Yubi-Toko: finger walking in snowy scene using pseudo-haptic technique on touchpad. In: SIGGRAPH Asia 2015 Emerging Technologies, pp. 1–3. Association for Computing Machinery, New York (2015)

56. Vladimir Kharlampidi: Framework7 (2020). https://framework7.io/. Accessed 25 June 2020

57. Watanabe, J.: Pseudo-haptic sensation elicited by background visual motion. ITE Trans. Media Technol. Appl. **1**(2), 199–202 (2013)

58. Yabe, S.I., Kishino, H., Kimura, T., Nojima, T.: Pseudo-haptic feedback on softness induced by squeezing action. In: 2017 IEEE World Haptics Conference (WHC), pp. 557–562. IEEE (2017)

59. Yamamoto, A., Ishii, T., Higuchi, T.: Electrostatic tactile display for presenting surface roughness sensation. In: IEEE International Conference on Industrial Technology, vol. 2, pp. 680–684. IEEE (2003)

60. Yang, G.H., Kyung, K.U., Srinivasan, M.A., Kwon, D.S.: Quantitative tactile display device with pin-array type tactile feedback and thermal feedback. In: Proceedings 2006 IEEE International Conference on Robotics and Automation, ICRA 2006, pp. 3917–3922. IEEE (2006)

A Research on Sensing Localization and Orientation of Objects in VR with Facial Vibrotactile Display

Ke Wang[2]([⊠]), Yi-Hsuan Li[2], Chun-Chen Hsu[2]([⊠]), Jiabei Jiang[1], Yan Liu[1], Zirui Zhao[1], Wei Yue[3], and Lu Yao[4]

[1] Nanjing University of Arts, Nanjing, China
[2] National Yang Ming Chiao Tung University, Hsinchu, Taiwan
chuncheng@nctu.edu.tw
[3] Anhui University, Hefei, China
[4] Nanjing Audit University Jinshen College, Nanjing, China
wondermm930@sina.com

Abstract. Tactile display technology has been widely proved to be effective to human-computer interaction. In multiple quantitative research methods to evaluate VR user experience (such as presence, immersion, and usability), multi-sensory factors are significant proportion. Therefore, the integration of VR-HMD and tactile display is a possible application and innovation trend of VR. The BIP (Break in Presence) phenomenon affects the user's spatial awareness when entering or leaving VR environments. We extracted orientation and localization tasks to discuss the influence of facial vibrotactile display on these tasks. Correlational researches are mainly focused on the parts of human body such as torso, limb, and head regions. We chose face region and to carry out the experiment, a VR-based wearable prototype "VibroMask" was built to implement facial vibrotactile perception. Firstly, the behavioral data of subjects' discrimination of vibrotactile information were tested to obtain the appropriate display paradigm. It was found that the discrimination accuracy of low-frequency vibration was higher with loose wearing status, and the delay offset of one-point vibration could better adapt to the orientation task. Secondly, the effect of facial vibrotactile display on objects' localization and orientation discriminating task in VR was discussed. Finally, subjects' feedback was collected by using open-ended questionnaire, it is found that users have a higher subjective evaluation of VR experience with facial vibrotactile display.

Keywords: Sense of facial haptic · VR experience · Motion perception

1 Introduction

Since the late1990s, the development of VE (Virtual Environment) technology led to researches on sense of presence and immersion of VE. Slater M. et al. [1] published evaluate questionnaire of presence "SUS" from an objective perspective. Scholars such as Witmer et al. [2] and Lesslter [3] have also released some commonly used subjective

J. Y. C. Chen and G. Fragomeni (Eds.): HCII 2021, LNCS 12770, pp. 223–241, 2021.
https://doi.org/10.1007/978-3-030-77599-5_17

questionnaire, which are Presence Questionnaire (PQ), Immersive Tendencies Questionnaire (ITQ) and ITC-SOPI. Among the most of evaluate questionnaires, Sense factor, Control factor and Distraction factors are occupying a significant proportion. According to the summary of performance metrics proposed by Nash [4], Display rendering and Field of view are important factors in the field of VE performance which is also an important breakthrough in VE user experience iteration in recent years. In Nash's performance matrix, researches on spatial localization, haptic & touch, and motor & kinematic perception in VE is also listed, which is summarized in haptic feedback devices and navigation and knowledge acquisition, emphasizing the important influence of the two on the experience of sense of presence.

Since tactile also belongs to the category discussed in perception factors, it is easier to simulate compared with olfaction and gustation, so tactile display has been frequently mentioned in recent studies. Servotte [5] proposed the Servotte-Ghuysen Framework for depicting the relevance between factors identified and sense of presence in VR based on the prior studies. It puts forward that the multi-sensory experience is the congruent cues of sense of presence. Spatial localization is also a factor mentioned in VR experience evaluation models. It is closely related to not only distraction factors, but also involved in the discussion of motor perception and involvement. Therefore, in this study, we focus on the two important topics of tactile display and VR spatial information to explore the effectiveness of tactile display in VR and whether it can positively influence the evaluation of VR experience from the perspective of spatial information acquisition and perceptual consistency.

Researches on tactile technology mainly focuses on vibration, pressure, and thermal display. In recent years, a variety of tactile display realization methods have emerged rapidly, most of which are based on more precise electromechanical components. Users to avoid negative emotions and discomfort in the process of experiment, this study considered the sensitivity of the facial skin and user's concern about security and experience of new electromechanical components, so we chose a more stable vibration display method for dynamic tactile display. Prior studies mainly focus on the diversity of tactile perception among different sexes and ages [6], and the application of tactile perception among blind people [7]. This study hopes to expand the scope of the application population, exploring the possibility of vibrotactile display intervention and future development opportunities in VR environment.

This study is mainly composed of two parts. The first part is the study of vibrotactile discrimination accuracy and time consumption. Before the experiments, we made a prototype called "VibroMask", it was used to verify the user's task performance in discriminating the orientation and intensity of vibrotactile display information, discussing whether vibrotactile display has a positive effect on information and motion interaction. We used task performance evaluation method, Scheduling model answers of user's perspective are set according to the VR environment, synchronously measuring subjects' time consumption and accuracy for objects motive information in the environment before and after the intervention of tactile display. The effect of tactile intervention was summarized according to the trend of correct or false results. The second part is the study of presence and immersion in VR with vibrotactile display. While using VR-HMD, subjects was wearing "Vibromask" prototype, sensing the display stimuli of visual and vibrotactile consistency. We collected subjects' discrimination results of objects' motive information, and discussed the appropriate expression forms and behavioral interaction scenarios of tactile display involvement in VR experience. By using open-ended questionnaire, the diversity performance of user feedback in different scenes was collected and compared to explore the impact of tactile display in VR.

2 Related Work

The development of VR technology follows the relevant research results of researches on VE performance evaluation and subjective experience evaluation, but there are certain differences in the use experience between VR and traditional VE environment. Schwind [8] summarized the measures of sense of presence and immersion in VR environment in recent years, which are mainly divided into: behavioral Measures, physiological Measures, and subjective rating Scales. There is a discussion of multi-sensory in all the above evaluation methods and some research results have further verified the effect of haptic display on VE performance. The representation of tactile and spatial orientation in each test questionnaire will be detailed in the following paragraphs.

2.1 Tactile in VR Presence and Immersion

Tactile is a significant component of the multi-sensory experience, some researches have focused on implementation, influencing factors, and evaluation models of improving VR experience. It is expounded that tactile perception can improve subjects' immersion and behavioral task performance under specific task conditions. Chi Wang et al. [9] published "Masque", Nimesha Ranasinghe et al. [10] published "Ambiotherm", and Roshan Lalintha Peiris [11] published "ThermoVR". These three studies all included design practices concentrated on VR experience. By using VR Sense of presence and immersion scale, the effects of tactile perception technology application on VR were measured.

Among the measures used in the studies mentioned, there was a high degree of consistency in the representation of tactile. In PQ & ITQ [2], Witmer proposed "Factors Hypothesized to Contribute to a Sense of Presence". There are Sensory Factors composition of sensory modality, Environmental richness, and Multimodal presentation, which are related to tactile display. In IPQ [12], Schubert T. et al. summarized the abbreviated as "felt present in the VE", sense of being in the virtual space, and sense of acting in predictor defined as Spatial presence of items related to haptic. In SUS [1], Slater states that the Reasons given for transitions to the real in virtual environments, one of the causes is "External touch or force", which summarizes two significant models of tactile display. In MPS [13], intuitive sense and sense of bodily extension are defined under the category of self-presence. Makransky [13] subdivided presence into physical presence, social presence, and self-presence, integrating the cognitive differences between Slater and Witmer on the concept of presence. However, the author believes that the localization of tactile perception should not only be limited to self-perception, but also should be considered in the physical presence.

Nash [4] has completed a review of the prior studies and stated that haptic feedback with input devices is a type of input device types that affecting "Task Performance In Virtual Environments". Several scholars also proposed the study of tactile signal capture, Kouta Minamizawa [14] uses microphone and speakers to create tactile contents for the consistence of auditory sensation source and tactile sensation source. Yusuke Ujitoko et al. [15] uses conditional generative adversarial networks to achieve generation of vibration during moving a pen on the surface. Combined with the input devices described above, the two can build a more complete VE tactile I/O model.

2.2 Facial Vibrotactile in Haptic Display

Vibration in Tactile. Tactile interaction is subdivided into vibration display, temperature display, kinesthetic display, and pressure display. Paula J. Durlach et al. [16] measured motion performance based on hand motion fidelity through speed and accuracy in VE. Paula used the questionnaire survey through phenomenological experience, and obtained the tactile feedback that tactile display could increase the sense of presence and reduce disorientation. Tsetserukou [17] published a tactile prototype based on hugging behavior, he also realized the simulation of a characteristic behavior of tactile display in VE. Al-Sada [18] combined the tactile display principle of vibration and pressure to complete a prototype of haptic display with gesture interaction simulation called "HapticSerpent". Based on summarization of user experience feedback of the former, Al-Sada further developed a new tactile interaction device called "Hapticsnakes" [19]. The device can simulate four different tactile experiences in VR environment: Brush, Grab, Blow, and Touch, combining the VR interactive games to harvest a good subjective preference evaluation. Chongsan Kwon [20] integrated temperature perception and air blowing into virtual reality, and found that VR with skin sensation has enhanced vividness and presence. The deficiencies of the existing tactile display methods are also described in the above studies. The display methods based on electrical stimulation are easy to cause discomfort to users, the display methods based on motor drive are cumbersome and unwearable due to the limitation of mechanical structure. On the contrary, the device based on vibrotactile is simple to construct and can efficiently express the texture information of the objects' surface. The vibrotactile display can accurately realize user information interaction, it is also easier to carry out experiments on the influence of the movement performance of subjects. Tsukada [21] proposed the wearable interface prototype "Activebelt", which used the vibrotactile display to convey direction information to users, and confirmed the possibility of practical use. The upper limb skin was used as the experimental region to test vibration and thermal stimulation based on 31.5 Hz–125 Hz frequencies. The results showed that age had no significant effect on the vibrotactile threshold, and the performance was the best in the frequency range of 100–115 Hz. Preeti Vyas [22] overcame inter-toe discrimination ambiguity by constructing a vibrotactile spatial map of digital information on the user's toes, and improved the accuracy of information transmission, responsive time and cognitive load. Scott D. Novich [23] tried to measure the interaction information of tactile receptors in the back skin, stated that the best form of tactile information interaction is spatial and temporal encoding. But adjacent vibration motors need to be at least 6cm distance to allow for two independent tactile modes (>80% correct).

Facial Vibrotactile. Although trunk and limbs are the main regions of vibrotactile perception in studies, the vibration display of the head region has become the focus of vibrotactile perception research recently. Some studies on the correlation between vibration frequency, amplitude and perceived efficiency provide a reference for further researches. Hollins [24] firstly measured the appropriate amplitude and frequency of facial vibrotactile display from the perspective of perception and psychophysics, and obtained the corresponding vibrotactile threshold evaluation. Lalit Venkatesan [6] estimated the vibrotactile detection thresholds (VDTs) of face and hands, which were tested in multiple facial and hand skin regions using different mechanical stimulation frequencies (5–300 Hz), stated the impact of ages and genders on the target test value. The perceptual differences may be brought about by tissue conformation and thickness, mechanoreceptor densities, skin hydration, or temperature characteristics. Dobrzynski [25] identified the minimum and comfort strength of vibrotactile stimulation, and measured the precision in perceiving the accurate number of active motors as well as the precision in localizing the stimuli on the head. This study strongly suggests to avoid multi-point stimulation.

2.3 Vibrotactile and Spatial Localization

Spatial localization and orientation in VR have significant impact on user experience performance. There are certain differences in spatial perception and localization methods between the real world and the virtual environment. There are also different interpretations of the differences between the two performances from the perspectives of Cybersickness, usability and learning effect. Schwind [8] states that the "BIP (break-in-presence)" problem of subjective measurement in VR, which means the questionnaire test must be conducted after the completion of the experience, and leaving or re-entering the VE may cause disorientation and seriously affect user experience performance. This negative effect can be overcome by using tactile simulation to reduce the time and attention consumption of relocalization and orientation in both real and virtual environments.

Darken [26] discussed the methods of maintaining position and direction in virtual environments, emphasizing the key role of body perception in spatial localization in virtual environments, also stats that mapping relationship between coordinate feedback and the global position indicator in the real environment. Erik Borg [27] published a study on orientation discrimination of vibrotactile perception in 2001. Since then, several studies have shown that head vibrotactile perception can help with orientation and localization tasks. David Swapp [28] introduced the research on spatial localization task performance of audio-visual feedback sensory synergy in VR environment, and stated that when audio-visual feedback are combined with tactile feedback, stats that user task performance can be greatly improved. Tomi Nukarinen [29] conducted an experiment comparing directional tactile cues and visual cues in a vehicle navigation task. The results showed that the response time of tactile cues was significantly faster than that of visual text cues, but tactile cues were also evaluated as worse than visual cues. In both subjective and objective evaluation, tactile glasses performed slightly better than tactile seats. Oliveira [30] designed and evaluated tactile guidance techniques for 3D environments. He firstly explored the modulation of vibration frequency to indicate the position of the object in the horizontal elevation plane, then evaluated to plot the position of an object in 3D space around the object by varying the stimulation site and vibration frequency, the results showed that the frequency modulated by the quadratic growth function can provide more accurate, precise and faster target localization in the active head-pointing task. Kaul [31] measured the task performance of tactile feedback compared with visual and auditory for spatial object localization by constructing a head-mounted device with multiple tactile actuators, and stated the experimental conclusion that tactile feedback was superior to spatial audio. Oliveira [32] evaluated the sensitivity of the head skin to the perception of tactile stimulation, and stated the advantages of region around the forehead in the vibration recognition sensation and spatial discrimination.

2.4 Hypotheses

In this study, we applied the results of above-mentioned researches to concentrate on the spatial perception of vibrotactile sensation in VR, including the adaptive research on facial vibrotactile display, the research on performance of spatial localization task and the evaluation of qualitative user experience. The hypotheses in the adaptive study of facial tactile display include:

H1. Variation of wearing pressure affects discrimination accuracy and time consumption.

H2. Variation of vibration frequency affects discrimination accuracy and time consumption.

H3. Variation of sensing regions affect discrimination accuracy and time consumption.

H4. The time consumption of correct discrimination and wrong discrimination of single-point vibration have differences.

H5. Comparing with simultaneous multi-point vibration, one-point delay offset vibration has a different discrimination accuracy.

H6. Variation of interval time affects discrimination accuracy in multi-point vibration.

H7. In multi-point vibration, the discrimination accuracy of vibration with curvilinear frequency variation is different from vibration with consistent frequency.

H8. Comparing with visual display, vibrotactile and visual display has a better performance in discrimination accuracy and time consumption of object localization in VR.

H9. Comparing with visual display, vibrotactile and visual display has a better performance in discrimination accuracy and time consumption of object information in VR.

H10. Comparing with visual display, vibrotactile and visual display has a better performance in discrimination accuracy and time consumption of object orientation in VR.

3 Experiment

In the research topic related to spatial localization and orientation in VR, accuracy and time interval are two significant quantitative factors [16, 30]. In some of the studies, accuracy is also understood as sensitivity, which is interpreted as the correct perception rate of vibrotactile display. Subjects use the interval time between two independent simulations to complete the perception of tactile display information and the integration perception of environmental information. The length of the interval time and the user's familiarity with the vibrotactile display affect the discrimination accuracy of vibrotactile at the same time. Oliveira [30] proposed a VR-HMD that integrated the vibrotactile display function, using static objects in VR to achieve the assistance of visual simulation, and revealed the appropriate perception method of spatial perception of facial vibrotactile. The mode of existence of objects in VR space is transformed from static to dynamic including the direction of motion. On the basis of orientation and frequency, the direction of vibrotactile display is realized by combining with the array of vibration generator. The core condition of the experiment is vibrotactile display and visual display, aiming to illustrate an effective visual and vibrotactile integration method to enhance the capture of object motive orientation and localization in VR. The key independent variables in the experiment are the frequency of vibration, the time interval of vibration, the sequence of vibration and the corresponding position of the vibration trigger. The subjects in this study were all college or graduate students with art and design background, with good perceptual function and aged between 19 and 23 years old.

3.1 Experiment 1 Single-Point Vibrotactile Sensing

This study mainly discusses the discrimination accuracy of vibrotactile display, which is divided into two experiments: single-point (Experient1) and multi-point (Experient2). The hypotheses of single-point vibration discrimination test include H1, H2, H3 and H4. The hypotheses of multi-point vibration discrimination test include H5, H6 and H7.

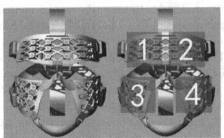
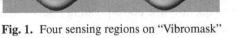

Fig. 1. Four sensing regions on "Vibromask"   **Fig. 2.** Wearing status of "Vibromask".

Vibration Prototype Construction. We chose the embedded 1027 flat vibration motor module with strong reliability and stability to complete the prototype construction, to ensure the consistency of vibration intensity in the experiment and to accurately control the intensity and frequency of vibration according to the change of input voltage. VIVE-HMD was selected to be applied in this experiment. As it occupied a certain facial space in the status of wearing, the prototype of the face device needed to reserve the facial region covered by VR-HMD, forming a combination of four sensing regions composed of forehead and cheek (Fig. 1).

Directional display requires linear displacement arrangement of vibration motors. We hope that the spacing of vibration motors can realize multiple independent perception at the same time, rather than the vibration of one region. Dobrzynski [25] suggested the problem of spacing setting of vibration generators. However, the vibration thresholds (VDTS) of face have individual differences, and lack corresponding facial research data. Novich [23] stats the independent vibration perception rate of the back skin, 6cm (recognition rate >80%) or 4 cm (recognition rate 50 > %). But it is not feasible to apply then to the facial region, because the values of head circumference are relatively small. So, we chose the minimum number of areas and linear arrangement (2 areas × 3 vibration motors) to set the vibration matrix of the mask prototype. In each sensing region, an array of 3 × 3 vibration motors array is set to ensure that the linear operation of 3 vibration units can be realized in each direction.

Since "Vibromask" prototype have 36 vibration motors, we used four Arduino Mega plates to perform the control work to ensure enough analog output pins, and the response time slot of each vibration unit was set to 100 ms. All vibration motors on the vibration mask prototype can independently compile the vibration execution scheme according to the actual requirements in VR.

We found amount of actual wearing problems before the experiment. The size of different subjects' head and facial dimension data have great difference. Because of the status of prototype wearing preference, different sensing regions could also lead to the difference of wearing pressure. The vibration frequency of subjective sensing has larger divergence, causing disturbance variable. Therefore, we used silica gel material with lower hardness instead of the 65-label flexible 3D printing material, and combined with the use of elastic woven ribbon (Fig. 2.). The pressure difference of prototype wearing was well controlled and the pressure balance of each sensing regions were basically realized.

Software and Integration Design of Prototype. In the pre-research, subjects reflected the influence of different wearing pressures on discrimination tasks, so we invited 8 subjects to perform pressure tests on the descriptions of loose and tight wearing. Since the value of pressure perception is not the key issue of this study, only a small number of subjects were invited to complete this test. The preliminary results show that the average value of feeling in the loose wearing is 296.79 Pa (SD = 22.815), and the average value of feeling in the tight wearing is 890.37 Pa (SD = 26.011). Therefore, the values of the pressure tap in the experiment are set to loose (296.79 Pa), standard (593.58 Pa), and tight (890.37 Pa). In the study of Al-Sada [19], percussion actions with different strength in different regions of the trunk were set to quantify the corresponding discrimination accuracy. Similar research methods were used in this experiment.

This study needs to test the appropriate frequency paradigm of facial tactile display and study the influence of display parameters of pressure and frequency on discrimination accuracy and time consumption. According to the research of Hollins [34] and Venkatesan [8], the effective frequency range of facial vibrotactile perception is 5–200 Hz, but the perception thresholds of different vibration frequencies are different. Five gears are uniformly set in this frequency range, which are 40 Hz, 80 Hz,120 Hz, 160 Hz and 200 Hz. We used "Firmataboard" node in VVVV to achieve independent frequency and time control for each individual vibration motor on the Arduino Mega control board.

Experimental Procedure. 8 College students from design and art background were invited to serve as subjects (Age = 22.01 SD = 1.548, 5 Females). In order to collect the data of accuracy and time consumption value of vibrotactile discrimination, 20 vibration frequency trials sequences were randomly prefabricated, and 5 different ratings occurred 4 trials each. The cheeks and forehead were tested respectively. The subjects performed this exercise a total of 60 trials under three different wearing pressures, to avoid the learning effect.

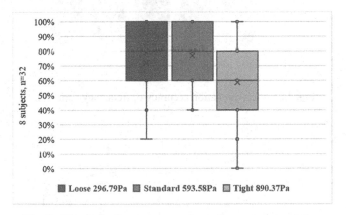

Fig. 3. Discrimination accuracy of wearing pressure variation.

Results. *Factor of Wearing Pressure (H1):* In the forehead regions, the subjects in loose and standard wearing status obtained higher discrimination accuracy, while the discrimination accuracy evaluation in tight wearing status was reduced. In all tests, the discrimination of 40 Hz vibration frequency trials were correct, so we eliminated this part of data in statistical analysis. Since the accuracy data under different pressures are non-normal distribution, we chose Wilcoxon Signed Rank Test to Test the difference of the arrays. As shown in (Fig. 3), there was a difference (p = 0.013) between the discrimination accuracy of loose wearing status (M = 0.719, SD = 0.232, n = 32) and the discrimination accuracy of tight wearing status (M = 0.769, SD = 0.216, n = 32), and there was a statistically significant difference between the identification accuracy of loose wearing status and tight wearing status (M = 0.587, SD = 0.300, n = 32) (p = 0.003). However, there was no statistical difference between the status of loose wearing and standard wearing (p = 0.269). In the cheek regions, the discrimination accuracy of the subjects under two wearing pressures was similar (M_1 = 0.642, SD_1 = 0.286, M_2 = 0.658, SD_2 = 0.317, n = 32), and there was no statistical difference between them. We also discuss possible interactions between the data, which will be detailed in subsequent sections.

Factor of Frequency Variation (H2): As shown in (Fig. 4a), the subjects obtained high discrimination at frequency of 40 Hz, 80 Hz and 120 Hz, while discrimination at frequencies of 160 Hz and 200 Hz were low. This conclusion was basically consistent with the experimental conclusion of Dobrzynski [35]. There was a certain amount of confusion

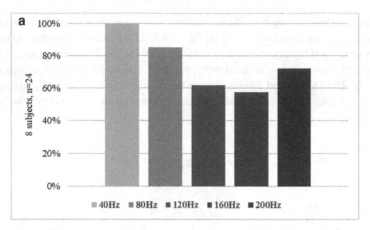

Fig. 4a a. Discrimination accuracy of frequency variation.

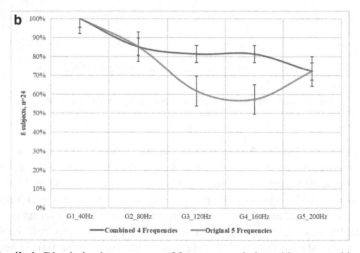

Fig. 4b b. Discrimination accuracy of frequency variation with gear combined.

between the wrong answers at 120 Hz and 160 Hz. We tried to count the number of confused answers of these two gears, and found that when the confused answers of these two subjects were regarded as correct trials, the discrimination rate of the combined vibration range could rise to a higher level (Fig. 4b). Therefore, we believe that when setting the vibration frequency of a mid-high frequency in 5–200 Hz, appropriately increasing the coverage width of the frequency is conducive to increasing the discrimination accuracy of the vibration frequency in this range.

Factor of Cheek and Forehead Regions (H3): Factor of cheek and forehead regions (H3). As shown in (Fig. 5), the average value M = 0.744 (SD = 0.224, n = 96) of forehead discrimination accuracy of the subjects was higher than that of cheeks M = 0.642 (SD = 0.294, n = 96), which was also consistent with the study of Oliveira [30].

Wilcoxon Signed Rank Test results showed that there was a statistical difference in the discrimination rate between forehead and cheek (p = 0.024).

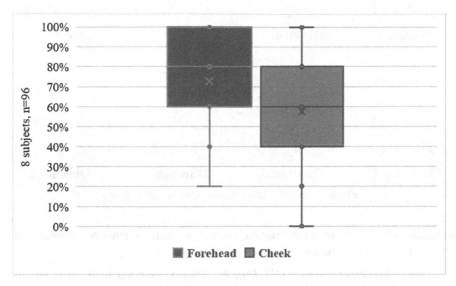

Fig. 5. Discrimination accuracy values of cheek and forehead regions.

Impact of Validity on Sensing Time Consumption (H4): To test the relationship between validity of discrimination and time consumption, we collected time consumption of correct and error trials to distinguish between the statistics, the means (M_C = 1.649, SD_C = 0.553 n_C = 303, M_E = 1.631 SD_E = 0.563 n_E = 123) are close. There was no statistical difference between them (p = 0.058).

Simple Effect Analysis: We also investigated the interaction effects brought by multivariate. We used SPSS tool to complete the inter-subject effect test, and the results showed that the interaction effects of "gender * pressure (p = 0.761)", "gender * frequency (p = 0.585)" and "pressure * frequency (p = 0.923)" were not significant.

3.2 Experiment 2 Multi-point Vibrotactile Perception

Based on the results of single-point vibrotactile experiment (Experiment1), we discuss the subject's performance in multi-point vibrotactile orientation task. As shown in (Fig. 6), in each vibrotactile display region, there are 8 vibration display directions. In the random sequence test, each direction appears 5 times, a total of 40 times. The subjects were consistent with experiment 1.

Results. *Simultaneous Multi-point Vibration (H5):* It is defined as simultaneous vibration of 3 vibration motors in any direction. According to the feedback of the 12 tested subjects (Age = 21.375 SD = 1.690, 6 Females), the vibration of any frequency and time can only produce the feeling of regional vibration, and it is almost impossible to identify the

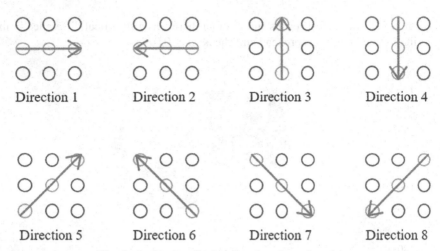

Fig. 6. 8 vibration display directions in each region.

localization and orientation of the vibration motor, so the test cannot be completed. It is consistent with the conclusions of Dobrzynski [25].

One-point Delay Offset Vibration (H5, H6): We defined one-point delay offset vibration as cycles in sequence for 3 vibration in one direction, and only one vibrator is working at the same time. The vibration cycles are repeated in the section of 3s, and the time interval of each vibration cycle is 0.5 s. In the first stage of experiment2, the duration of each time was set to 0.5 s, the average discrimination accuracy value was M = 0.483 (SD = 0.862, n = 96), the feedback from subjects stated a lack of continuity vibration. Later, we modified the duration to 0.3 s, the average value of discrimination accuracy was reduced to M = 0.423 (SD = 0.060, n = 96), the subjects responded that the duration was too short, resulting in difficulty in discrimination. When duration was set to 0.4 s, subjects didn't give any common negative feedback and achieved a higher mean of discrimination accuracy M = 0.579 (SD = 0.149, n = 96).

According to paired-samples T test results, there was a statistically significant difference between the two groups discrimination accuracy when the duration was set to 0.3 s and 0.4 s (p = 0.004). There was no statistically significant difference between the two groups discrimination accuracy when the duration was set to 0.3 s and 0.5 s (p = 0.075). There was a statistically difference between the two groups discrimination accuracy when the duration was set to 0.4 s and 0.5 s (p = 0.047).

One-Point Delay Offset Vibration with Varying Frequency (H7): It is defined as cycles in sequence for 3 vibration with frequency variation in one direction. According to the results of Oliveira [32], the discrimination performance of numerical variation of quadratic curve was the best. However, since there were only three duration in a vibration cycle, quadratic curve couldn't be continuously represented, so the step frequency variation (40 Hz, 80 Hz, 200 Hz) was selected for the test, and the average discrimination value obtained was M = 0.577 (SD = 0.121, n = 96). (Fig. 7) compared the different duration setting and change frequency discrimination accuracy contrast, we found that under the status of standard vibration frequency, and the duration is set to

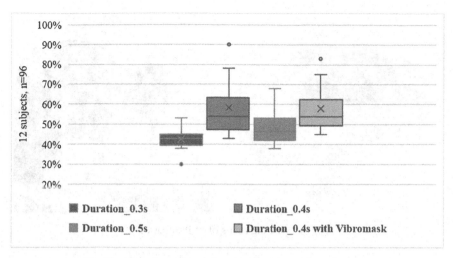

Fig. 7. Accuracy values of one-point delay offset vibration.

0.4 s, orientation discrimination accuracy performance has a highest value. The discrimination accuracy of vibration with varying frequency was close to 0.4 s, and there was no statistical difference (p = 0.892).

3.3 Experiment 3 Comparison of VR and VR with Facial Vibrotactile Display

As mentioned above, spatial awareness in VR has a direct impact on user experience. According to Oliveira [30], spatial awareness is deconstructed into localization and orientation problems in this experiment. We set the VR environment and the vibrotactile display signal of the object in VR to discuss the influence of facial vibrotactile display on the localization and orientation of the object in VR.

Prototype Optimizing for "Vibromask 2". In this experiment, wearing pressure parameters are no longer discussed, and prototype need to be using together with VR-HMD. Therefore, we optimized the original prototype "Vibromask". The elastic band was removed, Velcro was used to combine the silicone module directly with VR-HMD, and the freedom of wearing was realized by adjusting the position of the silicone module. The frequencies and duration that performed better in Experiment 1 were set on the experimental prototype "Vibromask 2" (Fig. 8).

VR Environment Construction and Data Communication Design. In order to enhance the interesting of visual display and avoid the visual perception difference caused by study effect, we chose the scene of underwater theme as the visual environment, we used Unity3D as the VR developing platform.

In the process of determining the scope of object spatial information capture, the width of view of VIVE-HMD is a significant parameter, with a value of about 115°. Considering the dynamic error of the head capture, we set 120° as the maximum effective perceptual breadth. Oliveira [32] stated that the frontal region on the forehead (0° ± 4.5 cm) had higher vibration sensitivity. After conversion, we set ±5° as the boundary

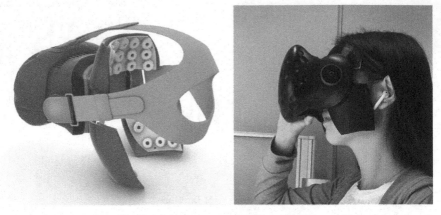

Fig. 8. Wearing status of "Vibromask 2".

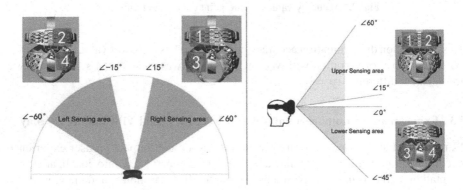

Fig. 9. Scope of object spatial information capture.

of the effective vibration trigger areas of the left and right VR objects, that is, the effective area on the left is $-60°$ to $-15°$ from the center of the viewing Angle, and the effective area on the right is $15°–60°$ from the center of the viewing Angle, as shown in (Fig. 9). In the setting of the vertical effective area of VR object, we adopted a similar method. The height of the upper effective area is $15°$ to $-60°$ in the horizontal direction, and the height of the lower effective area is $0°$ to $-45°$, as shown in (Fig. 9).

Experimental Procedure. In the design stage of the visual and tactile display sequence, we counted possible vibration displays in four regions and eight directions, and each situation was repeated three times for 96 times in total. Each vibration signal lasted for 3 s, and the interval was set as 1s. Fish models with the same movement direction and perception region were placed in VR environment (Fig. 10). Different fish models mapped the diversity of frequency to set the vibrotactile display signal.

According to the two experimental conditions of vibrotactile display and VR visual display, we completed two groups of experiments. The first group of experiments only had VR visual display, the second group of experiments had both facial vibration display

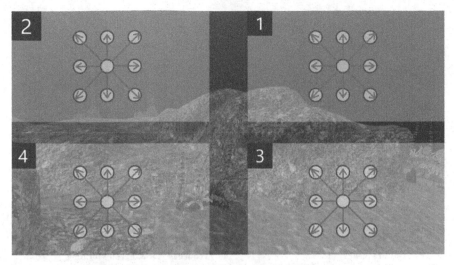

Fig. 10. Fusion of vibrotactile display and VR environment.

and VR visual display. In both experiments, users' discrimination accuracy and time consumption of spatial objects' type information, relative orientation and direction of movement were captured.

Results. *Objects' Localization Discrimination Task (H8):* We completed two random vibration trials in 8 directions and 4 regions respectively, a total of 64 times. The answers in two different experiences were all correct. In the time consumption statistical analysis of data, the average value of the VR experience environment with facial vibrotactile display ($M = 0.809$, $SD = 0.170$, $n = 768$) was lower than that without facial vibrotactile display ($M = 0.933$, $SD = 0.210$, $n = 768$). (Fig. 11). Paired-samples T test results showed significant differences between them.

Specie Model Information Discrimination Task (H9): We set 4 different fish models in 4 different regions corresponding to diversity of vibration frequencies (40 Hz, 80 Hz, 120 Hz, 200 Hz), and each frequency was repeated 4 times, a total of 64 times. All the answers in the two different experiences were correct, but the average time consumption of the VR experience with facial vibrotactile display ($M = 0.987$, $SD = 0.206$, $n = 768$) was lower than that without facial vibrotactile display ($M = 1.097$, $SD = 0.270$, $n = 768$). Paired-sample T test results showed significant differences between them (Fig. 11).

Object Motive Orientation Task (H10): We set 8 different directions of fish movement in 4 different regions, each direction repeated 3 times, a total of 96 times. The time consumption of the VR experience was longer ($M = 1.52$, $SD = 0.466$, $n = 768$) than that with facial vibrotactile display ($M = 1.406$, $SD = 0.386$, $n = 768$). Paired-sample T test results showed significant differences between them (Fig. 11).

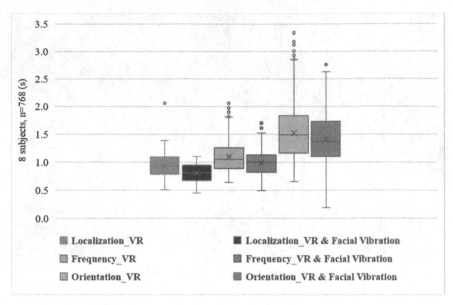

Fig. 11. Performance of object's discrimination task.

4   Subjective Feedback Evaluation

During the experiment, 38 subjects' feedback on the facial vibrotactile prototype were collected (Table 1).

Negative Feedback Related to Prototype Wearing Includes.

A The pressure distribution of "Vibromask" is inhomogeneous when wearing.

B The perceived intensity of each vibration range in "Vibromask 2" is not consistent.

C The wearing status of loose and standard are more comfortable.

Feedback on Vibration Discrimination that are Consistent with the Experimental Results.

D Low frequency vibration is easier to be recognized than high frequency vibration.

E Simultaneous multiple-points vibration in the same area is difficult to discriminate.

F Facial Vibrotactile display could reduce the difficulty of the discrimination task.

Feedback that Cannot be Measured by Experimental Data.

G Adding vibrotactile display can increase vividness and fun, and hope to experience again.

H The learning effect is significant.

I Single-point delay offset vibration can show direction well.

J Among which 6 subjects believe that frequency change is more helpful for directional discrimination, and 2 subjects believe that directional discrimination can be achieved easily with constant frequency.

Table 1. Summary of Subjects' feedback (n = 38)

Tab	Classification	Object	Content	Quantity
A	Manner of wearing	Vibromask 1	Inhomogeneous pressure of wearing	11
B		Vibromask 2	Consistency difference of vibration intensity sensing	17
C		Vibromask 1&2	Loose wearing is more comfortable	36
D	Vibration discrimination	Frequency	Low frequency vibration is easier to discriminate than high frequency vibration	33
E		Multi-point	Simultaneous multi-point vibration is indiscernible	37
F		Task difficulty	Vibrotactile display could reduce degree of discrimination difficulty	21
G	Qualitative evaluation	Experience	Vibrotactile creates vividness & enjoyment	22
H		Task difficulty	Learning effect is remarkable	26
I		Task difficulty	One-point delay offset vibration fits expressing orientation	17
J1		Task difficulty	Vibration with frequency variation helps with orientation discrimination	6
J2		Task difficulty	Vibration of consistent frequency helps with orientation discrimination	2

5 Conclusion and Discussion

The main significance of this study is to discuss a combination of facial vibrotactile sensing and VR visual experience. We quantified the effectiveness of vibrotactile sensing in VR, as well as statistical analysis of subjects' feedback. We found that the large variance of all the experimental results was related to the insufficient number of subjects, and the learning effect and individual physiological characteristics as well. The experimental results can better complete the hypothetical test in this paper. The differences of wearing pressure, vibration frequency and feeling parts affect the vibrotactile discrimination accuracy performance, but have no effect on the time consumption. The discrimination accuracy of multi-point simultaneous vibration is lower than that of single-point delay offset vibration mode, and the change of vibration frequency does not significantly affect the discrimination accuracy. Facial vibrotactile display does not change the discrimination accuracy of localization and orientation in VR environment, but it can change the time consumption. VR environments with facial vibrotactile displays received better evaluation for subject's feedback.

This study can not only provide an application method for VR vibrotactile sensing enhancement for subsequent research, but also provide an appropriate vibration display paradigm for the subsequent design of facial vibrotactile display prototype. From the perspective of behavioral measurement, facial vibrotactile display does not completely solve the specific problems caused by the spatial awareness of VR experience. However, from the perspective of experience evaluation, most subjects gave positive comments, which confirmed the development feasibility of VR experience with facial vibrotactile display.

References

1. Slater, M., Usoh, M.: Presence in immersive virtual environments. In: IEEE Annual Virtual Reality International Symposium, pp. 90–96 (1993)
2. Witmer, B., Singer, M.: Measuring presence in virtual environments: a presence questionnaire. Presence: Teleoper. Virtual Environ. **7**(3), 225–240 (1998). https://doi.org/10.1162/105474 698565686
3. Lessiter, J., Freeman, J., Keogh, E., Davidoff, J.: A cross-media presence questionnaire: the ITC-sense of presence inventory. Presence **10**(3), 282–297 (2014)
4. Nash, E.B., Edwards, G.W., Thompson, J.A., Barfield, W.: A review of presence and performance in virtual environments. Int. J. Hum.-Comput. Interact. **12**(1), 1–41 (2000)
5. Servotte, J., et al.: Virtual reality experience: immersion, sense of presence, and cybersickness. Clin. Simul. Nurs. **38**, 35–43 (2020). https://doi.org/10.1016/j.ecns.2019.09.006
6. Venkatesan, L., Barlow, S., Kieweg, D.: Age- and sex-related changes in vibrotactile sensitivity of hand and face in neurotypical adults. Somatosens. Motor Res. **32** (2014)
7. Mcdaniel, T., Krishna, S., Balasubramanian, V., Colbry, D., Panchanathan, S.: Using a haptic belt to convey non-verbal communication cues during social interactions to individuals who are blind. IEEE International Workshop on Haptic Audio-visual Environments and Games, pp. 13–18(2008)
8. Schwind, V., Knierim, P., Haas, N., Henze, N.: Using Presence Questionnaires in Virtual Reality (2019)
9. Wang, C., Huang, D.-Y., Hsu, S.-W., et al.: Masque: Exploring lateral skin stretch feedback on the face with head-mounted displays. In: Proceedings of the 32nd Annual ACM Symposium on User Interface Software and Technology (UIST '19). Association for Computing Machinery, pp. 439–451 (2019)
10. Ranasinghe, N., Jain, P., Karwita, S., Tolley, D., Do, E.: Ambiotherm: Enhancing Sense of Presence in Virtual Reality by Simulating Real-World Environmental Conditions, pp. 1731–1742 (2017)
11. Peiris, R.L., Peng, W., Chen, Z., Chan, L., Minamizawa, K.: ThermoVR: Exploring Integrated Thermal Haptic Feedback with Head Mounted Displays (2017)
12. Schubert, T., Friedmann, F., Regenbrecht, H.: The experience of presence: factor analytic insights. Presence **10**(3), 266–281 (2001)
13. Makransky, G., Lilleholt, L., Aaby, A.: Development and validation of the multimodal presence scale for virtual reality environments: a confirmatory factor analysis and item response theory approach. Comput. Hum. Behav. **72**, 276–285 (2017)

14. Minamizawa, K., Kakehi, Y., Nakatani, M., Mihara, S., Tachi, S.: TECHTILE toolkit: a prototyping tool for designing haptic media (2012)
15. Ujitoko, Y., Ban, Y.: Vibrotactile signal generation from texture images or attributes using generative adversarial network (2019)
16. Durlach, P.J., Fowlkes, J., Metevier, C.J.: Effect of variations in sensory feedback on performance in a virtual reaching task. Presence **14**(4), 450–462 (2005)
17. Tsetserukou, D.: HaptiHug: a novel haptic display for communication of hug over a distance. In: International Conference on Human Haptic Sensing and Touch Enabled Computer Applications, pp. 340–347 (2010)
18. Al-Sada, M.,, Jiang, K., Ranade, S., Piao, X., Höglund, T., Nakajima, T.: HapticSerpent: A Wearable Haptic Feedback Robot for VR. In: Extended Abstracts of the 2018 CHI Conference on Human Factors in Computing Systems (CHI EA '18), Association for Computing Machinery, Paper LBW624, pp. 1–6 (2018)
19. Al-, M., Jiang, K., Ranade, S., Kalkattawi, M., Nakajima, T.: HapticSnakes: multi-haptic feedback wearable robots for immersive virtual reality. Virtual Reality **24**(2), 191–209 (2019). https://doi.org/10.1007/s10055-019-00404-x
20. Kwon, C.: A study on the verification of the effect of sensory extension through cutaneous sensation on experiential learning using VR. Virtual Reality **25**(1), 19–30 (2020). https://doi.org/10.1007/s10055-020-00435-9
21. Tsukada, K., Yasumura, M.: Activebelt: Belt-type wearable tactile display for directional navigation. In: International Conference on Ubiquitous Computing. Springer, Berlin, Heidelberg (2004)
22. Vyas, P., Taha, F.A., Blum, J.R., Cooperstock, J.R.: HapToes: Vibrotactile Numeric Information Delivery via Tactile Toe Display. Haptics Symposium 2020 (2020).
23. Novich, S.D., Eagleman, D.M.: Using space and time to encode vibrotactile information: toward an estimate of the skin's achievable throughput. Exp. Brain Res. **233**(10), 2777–2788 (2015)
24. Hollins, M., Goble, A.K.: Vibrotactile adaptation on the face. **49**(1), 21–30 (1991)
25. Dobrzynski, M.K.: Quantifying information transfer through a head-attached vibrotactile display: principles for design and control. IEEE Trans. Biomed. Eng. **59**(7), 2011–2018 (2012)
26. Darken, R.P., Sibert, J.L.: A toolset for navigation in virtual environments. In: Proceedings of the 6th Annual ACM Symposium on User Interface Software and Technology. ACM (1993)
27. Borg, E., Rönnberg, J., Neovius, L.: Vibratory-coded directional analysis: evaluation of a three-microphone/four-vibrator DSP system. J. Rehabil. Res. Dev. **38** 257–63 (2001)
28. Swapp, D., Pawar, V., Loscos, C.: Interaction with co-located haptic feedback in virtual reality. Virtual Reality **10**, 24–30(2006)
29. Nukarinen, T., Rantala, J., Farooq, A., Raisamo, R.: Delivering Directional Haptic Cues through Eyeglasses and a Seat (2015)
30. Oliveira, V.A., Brayda, L., Nedel, L., Maciel, A.: Designing a Vibrotactile Head-Mounted Display for Spatial Awareness in 3D Spaces. IEEE Trans. Vis. Comput. Graph. 1 (2017)
31. Kaul, O.B., Rohs, M.: HapticHead: 3D Guidance and Target Acquisition through a Vibrotactile Grid. Chi Conference Extended Abstracts. ACM (2016)
32. Oliveira, V.A.D.J., Nedel, L., Maciel, A., Brayda, L.: Spatial discrimination of vibrotactile stimuli around the head. IEEE Haptics Symposium. IEEE (2016)

HaptMR: Smart Haptic Feedback for Mixed Reality Based on Computer Vision Semantic

Yueze Zhang[1]([🖂]) [iD], Ruoxin Liang[2] [iD], Zhanglei Sun[2] [iD], and Maximilian Koch[1] [iD]

[1] Technical University of Munich, Arcisstraße 21, 80333 Munich, Germany
yueze.zhang@tum.de, max_koch@gmx.net
[2] Technical University of Darmstadt, Karolinenplatz 5, 64289 Darmstadt, Germany
{ruoxin.liang,zhanglei.sun}@stud.tu-darmstadt.de

Abstract. This paper focuses on tactile feedback based on semantic analysis using deep learning algorithms on the mobile Mixed Reality (MR) device, called HaptMR. This way, we improve MR's immersive experience and reach a better interaction between the user and real/virtual objects. Based on the Mixed Reality device HoloLens 2. generation (HL2), we achieve a haptic feedback system that utilizes the hand tracking system on HL2 and fine haptic modules on hands. Furthermore, we adapt the deep learning model – Inception V3 to recognize the rigidity of objects. According to the scenes' semantic analysis, when users make gestures or actions, their hands can receive force feedback similar to the real haptic sense. We conduct a within-subject user study to test the feasibility and usability of HaptMR. In user study, we design two tasks, including hand tracking and spatial awareness, and then, evaluate the objective interaction experience (Interaction Accuracy, Algorithm Accuracy, Temporal Efficiency) and the subjective MR experience (Intuitiveness, Engagement, Satisfaction). After visualizing results and analyzing the user study, we conclude that the HaptMR system improves the immersive experience in MR. With HaptMR, we could fill users' sense of inauthenticity produced by MR. HaptMR could build applications on industrial usage, spatial anchor, virtual barrier, 3D semantic interpretation, and as a foundation of other implementations.

Keywords: Mixed reality · Interacted force feedback · Deep learning for computer vision

1 Introduction

Mixed Reality (MR) is a hybrid system to describe the blending of virtual and physical environments, which is currently explored in many fields, e.g., entertainment, education, and medical treatment [1–4]. The interface of MR allows displaying the virtual scenes to human senses while users explore the real world [5]. Therefore, MR is different not only from virtual reality (VR) that makes users immerse entirely in a pure virtual environment, but also from augmented reality (AR) that modifies the users' physical surroundings by overlaying virtual elements [6, 7]. In other words, MR highlights the integration of virtual objects and the real world, while AR emphasizes the overlying.

© Springer Nature Switzerland AG 2021
J. Y. C. Chen and G. Fragomeni (Eds.): HCII 2021, LNCS 12770, pp. 242–258, 2021.
https://doi.org/10.1007/978-3-030-77599-5_18

An excellent immersive experience with multisensory input is a crucial factor for MR applications. Haptic sense can help to seamlessly blend the real world and virtual objects to create a more believable environment comprising fantastic and actual [8]. MR systems should support the haptic sense in order to convey physical feedback in the virtuality continuum [9]. The haptic output is mostly achieved in AR and VR by multiple techniques, including string-based haptic feedback systems [10, 11], air-jet driven force feedback devices [12–14], and laser-based systems [15]. However, haptic feedback is not widely applied in scenes based on MR. Unfortunately, there are also not many applications of haptic feedback with semantic analysis in the MR environment.

In this paper, we proposed the achievement of a fine haptic system, which is based on the MR environment on HL2 (see Fig. 1). Moreover, we adapted a deep learning model of computer vision towards the force feedback, which is regarded as a semantic analysis of the scene in real-time to improve the immersive experience. When users make some actions with a virtual object, e.g., putting a book on the desk, they can know when the virtual book touched the desktop through the haptic feedback. Due to the different rigidities of materials, the haptic sense touching the desk is certainly not similar to touching the sofa, thanks to the scenes' semantic analysis. Therefore, the haptic feedback combined with the scenes' semantic analysis is a good supplement to the multimodal interaction model under MR, which significantly improves the immersive experience.

Fig. 1. Overview of the HoloLens (2. generation) device with HaptMR system

2 Related Work

Our study builds upon notions of the MR-based modeling system by HL 2, the tactile perception system on hands, and the auxiliary deep learning model.

2.1 Human-Computer Interaction Under MR

MR is a blending of physical and digital worlds, unlocking the links between human, computer, and environment interaction [16]. Compared with the traditional human-computer interaction, mixed reality possesses the ability to perceive the environment, which as the input is also a part of the interactive closed loop. HL2 provides excellent performance for hand tracking. Moreover, it has two lidars, one is utilized for the spatial scanning and the spatial mapping, and the other is dedicated to the tracking of hand details. The hand-tracking model in HL2 has predefined 26 joints in the Mixed Reality Tool Kit (MRTK)'s hand tracking system [17]. Additionally, this hand-tracking model has high robustness, which can be still accurate in the case of glove covered hands, wire interference, and partial occlusion. As introduced in the HL2 interaction design, the instinctual interaction concept is conveyed by three multimodal interaction models, hands and motion controllers, hands- free, gaze and commit [18]. Instinctual interactions are intuitive and easy for users due to low physical and cognitive effort and high learnability. Especially for achieving hand gestures, users don't have to memorize symbolic gestures to interact with the holograms, where instinctual gestures and direct manipulation by hands are introduced by HL2.

2.2 Tactile Perception Module

The tactile perception module plays an important role in interactions. Several strategies can explore this concept by transferring constraints in the real world to 3D modeling [19]. For instance, ModelCraft carries the pen annotation and edits forms on the surface of the physical 3D objects [20]. CopyCAD utilizes the scanned 2.5D directly to remix physical things with copy and paste from the real world [21].

Another method to offer interactive feedback is to utilize the haptic motor controller, eccentric rotating mass and linear resonance actuator on hands (see Fig. 2). Firstly, we introduce the details of the controller. Adafruit DRV2605L Haptic Motor Controller, which encapsulates the DRV2605 Haptic Driver from Texas Instruments, owns multiple haptic models to achieve different force feedbacks. The DRV2605L controller with a small volume possesses a powerful development package, which simplifies coding complexity [22]. Furthermore, it's flexible for controlling motors by the shared I2C-compatible bus efficiently. The versatility and compactness make the DRV2605 driver and DRV2605L controller ideal for touch-enabled actuators. Besides, the eccentric rotating mass can be pasted on fingertips to offer a haptic vibration due to its small volume. The linear resonance actuator generates a wide range of haptic feedback along the Y-axis, which is more suitable for simulating the real haptic sense on the palm.

2.3 Deep Learning Model for Computer Vision

Many deep learning models with convolutional networks are applied at the core of most state-of-the-art computer vision tasks, e.g., GoogLeNet [23], Inception V2 [24], and Inception V3 [25–28] to meet requirements in semantic tasks. In this paper, the Inception V3 model is applied in scene recognition with semantic functions.

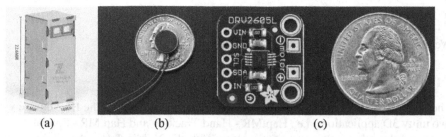

(a)   (b)   (c)

Fig. 2. (a) Linear actuator – product model: HQXZ091022V60–160/320, (b) linear resonance actuator, and (c) DRV2605L Haptic Controller (right) [22]

The Inception V3 model comprises 42 layers, including 11 inception modules with different structures, pooling layers, simple convolution layers, and fully connected layers with dropout and activity function Soft-max (see Fig. 3). The most apparent improvement in the Inception V3 model, compared with other mentioned models, is the convolution kernels' factorization [29]. For instance, a large convolution kernel with the shape 7×7 is decomposed into two one-dimensional kernels with a smaller shape 1×7 and 7×1, respectively. On the one hand, it is advantageous because this method saves many parameters, speeds up the calculation, and reduces the risk of overfitting. On the other hand, this asymmetric factorization improves the model's expression ability compared to the convolution kernel, which is symmetrically decomposed into several smaller kernels of the same size. The lower computational cost of the Inception V3 model is mainly due to the decomposition.

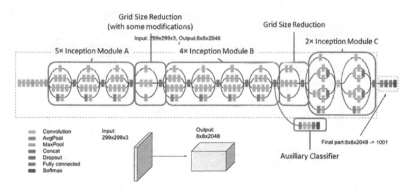

Fig. 3. Structure of Inception V3 model [30]

3   System Design

We now explain the details of our system design.

3.1   System Overview

The HaptMR system consists mainly of two independent devices, the HL2 device with two unity 3D applications, i.e., HaptMR - Hand Tracking and HaptMR - Spatial Awareness, and the other is the fine haptic glove with the Nvidia Jetson-Nano. These two devices communicate via 5GHz Wi-Fi. The HL2-side applications are responsible for tracking hand movements and capturing scenes in front of the user with the HL2 RGB camera (in HaptMR - Spatial Awareness only). And then, HL2 sends captured images to the Jetson-Nano device as server side. The server-side program parses this instruction, and then, communicates with the control chip driving the motor via I2C based on the real-time hand tracking data. If the message contains a RGB image from HL2, this image will be transmitted to the deep learning model, and the inferred result will decide the motor drive command dynamically. Figure 4 presents an overview of the system design.

The HaptMR system achieves the haptic feedback, based on original MR interaction modules. Therefore, compared with the original MR experience on HL2, HaptMR offers a more refined tactile experience for gesture operations. Additionally, utilizing the RGB camera data from HL2, HaptMR could adjust the pattern and intensity of tactile feedback when a collision happens between the virtual object and real objects. In summary, the whole system proposes a mapping from object recognition and semantic to haptic feedback under mixed reality.

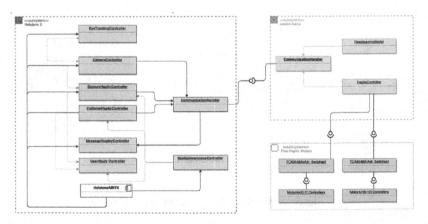

Fig. 4. Overview of HaptMR system design and sub-system decomposition diagram

3.2   Haptic Module in HaptMR

In the HaptMR system, the design of the haptic module adheres to the concept of the intuitive interaction, where the goal is to provide a natural feel and improve intuitiveness to the user. We implemented haptic feedback to multiple gesture interaction models based on HL2. We pasted the eccentric rotating mass motor at each fingertip and each knuckle location, and a linear resonant actuator (LRA) motor on the palm. Furthermore, we also installed ten solvers to five fingertips and five knuckles, in order to make each of them trackable in position and orientation according to the HL2 pre-defined algorithm. Additionally, HaptMR could adjust the haptic behavior for each joint dynamically, including calculating the collision's relative speed with the hand joints (see Fig. 5) and the virtual object. Thus, we could give different intensities to the haptic reaction. We also know which joints are with the virtual object's surface inside, outside, or collided.

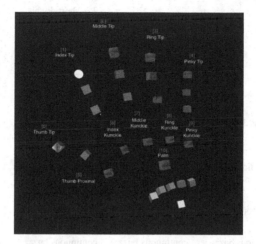

Fig. 5. Hand joints and fine haptic motors with highlight

Moreover, we introduce designed modes corresponding to different operations as following.

Collideable Fingertip. In HaptMR's hand tracking mode, we mapped the tactile feedback to each fingertip, utilizing both eye-tracking and an approach that determines the target object currently being manipulated. Our designed mode could solve some unexpected and unpredictable collisions with holograms caused by multiple collideable fingertips at the same time. **Pressable Button.** We achieved different strengths of double-clicking feedback to the pressable button. **Bounds Control.** When rotating things, pulsing feedback is generated for every 45° of rotation on the Y-axis. For the scaling operation, triple-click feedback is sent for every 10% increase of the object. **Slider.** The strong-clicking feedback is generated every 0.1 tick. **Touching.** When the user performs the touching operation, the force feedback is generated up to 1000 ms. **Object Manipulator.** When the user holds the object for manipulation, buzzing feedback continues until this manipulation stops. During the manipulation, when a virtual object collides with a virtual or physical object, it generates clicking feedback of varying intensity attached to the continuous buzzing. The designed working modes are presented in Table 1.

Table 1. Designed modes in different working modes, the percentage presents the vibration levels, e.g., 100% presents a very strong vibration. DL – Deep Learning.

Working Modes [A/B]	Mode A: no RGB Camera, closed Spatial Awareness, no DL		Mode B: RGB Camera, Spatial Awareness, DL	
Intensity	1 = high	0 = low	1 = high	0 = low
0 = collision between a virtual object to virtual object and virtual to real object when on Hold	buzz, 40%	buzz, 20%	predicted rigidity by DL model 1 = short double clicks, 60% 2 = short double clicks, 80% 3 = short double clicks, 100% 4 = double clicks, 100% 5 = buzz, 100%	predicted rigidity by DL model 1 = short double clicks, 40% 2 = short double clicks, 60% 3 = short double clicks, 80% 4 = short double clicks, 100% 5 = double clicks, 100%
1 = rotation per 45 degrees along Y-axis	pulsing, 100%	–	pulsing, 100%	–
2 = scale per 10% on volume	triple clicks, 100%	–	triple clicks, 100%	–
3 = slider bar per 0.1 scale	click, 100%	–	click, 100%	–
4 = manipulation starts	continuous buzz, 100%,	continuous buzz, 60%	continuous buzz, 100%	continuous buzz, 100%
5 = manipulation ends	stop	stop	stop	stop
6 = press button	double clicks, 100%	–	double clicks, 100%	–
7 = touch	1000-ms alert, 100%	750-ms alert, 100%	1000-ms alert, 100%	750-ms alert, 100%

4 System Implementation

4.1 Software Implementation

For software implementation, we developed two applications on HL2, including Hand Tracking and Spatial Awareness, and the deep learning model on Jetson-Nano. And the communication between Jetson-Nano and HL2.

HaptMR - Hand Tracking. In this scenario, we activated the spatial awareness on HL2, where the real-world environmental awareness was enabled. We utilized two virtual baseball bat prefabs and gave them different masses while turning on the gravity (see

(See Fig. 6 left). In this scenario, users can experience multiple interactions, e.g., pressing, touching, grabbing, scaling, rotating, sliding, direct manipulating with the object, and colliding within virtual objects (see Fig. 7). We set up four identical pieces of cheese to record and analyze interactions with them during the user study.

(a)   (b)

Fig. 6. HaptMR – (a) Hand tracking scene and (b) Spatial awareness scene

Fig. 7. A type of manipulation viewed on HL2: grabbing a virtual coffee cup

HaptMR - Spatial Awareness. In this scenario, we activated the spatial awareness on HL2, where the real-world environmental awareness was enabled. We utilized two virtual baseball bat prefabs and gave them different masses while turning on the gravity (see Fig. 6 right). Since we added solvers at hand joints, the awareness module sends commands to the motor controllers corresponding to different triggered solvers when the user picks up the baseball bat. In practice, we found that holograms on HL2 might disappear momentarily by taking photos. Thus, an image is taken by the RGB camera of HL2 every one second and sent to the server while the baseball bat is being operated, in order to achieve a better user experience. The Deep Learning model on the server side continuously classifies interface-types on the received pictures and the results are saved in a buffer of length 3. When HL2 detects a collision between the virtual object and the real object's mesh, it will send the collision event and the information of the joints of the hand inside the surface of the virtual object to the server. The server must not wait for the transmission of a new image or model inference at this time. Still, it will immediately select the haptic intensity by majority vote in the buffer. In case of inconsistency between all model inferences in the last 3 s, the latest result will be used.

We have set up a general menu and buttons for the recording of user study data. When the user presses the "Launch Haptic Engine" button, the application on HL2 sends a launch request to the server (Jetson-Nano). Users can also press the "Export User Study Data" button to manually export data(.csv) to the HL2 side. The exported data includes the duration of each user's action and the initial/end states of the operated object. All messages, including users' interaction data and tactile control commands for each joint, are saved by the server. Furthermore, when the user pushes the "Stop User Study" button manually, the server receives the request, and the user experiment ends.

We have set up a general menu and buttons for the recording of user study data. When the user presses the "Launch Haptic Engine" button, the application on HL2 sends a launch request to the server (Jetson-Nano). Users can also press the "Export User Study Data" button to manually export data(.csv) to the HL2 side. The exported data includes the duration of each user's action and the initial/end states of the operated object. All messages, including users' interaction data and tactile control commands for each joint, are saved by the server. Furthermore, when the user pushes the "Stop User Study" button manually, the server receives the request, and the user experiment ends.

Communication Between HL2 and Jetson-Nano. The Connection-Oriented TCP Protocol is Utilized to Send and Receive the Information with Stability and High Speed Between the HL 2 Device and the Jetson-Nano. In Our Case, the HL2 Device is the Sender, and Jetson-Nano is the Recipient, Where the Format of the Data Being Passed is Either the String Data or the RGB Image.

The communication module on HL2 binds a fixed IP address with the Jetson-Nano. The size of contents is firstly sent, which can prevent sticky packets. And then, the commands in string form or images in array form are sent to the receiver. The message receiving mode is activated with the confirmed link. Cooperating with HL2, the contents' size is first obtained on Jetson-Nano, which must correspond to the length at the sending side. Otherwise, the transmission of the information cannot be authorized. When everything is ready, haptic commands and figures are transmitted and recorded in order.

To reduce the amount of data sent and to improve robustness, we pre-stored the hand haptic model from the previous section into the parsing module on the Jetson-Nano side. Only the global operating mode, intensity, interaction mode, and the switch status of each joint in 12 bits are included in the sent data items (see Fig. 8). As shown in the example below, every four bits are encoded in hexadecimal as a string and sent. The parsing module then attaches the pre-stored haptic method to transmit to the haptic controller according to the different working and interaction modes.

Deep Learning Model. Inception V3 deep learning model completes the semantic analysis to identify objects' different rigidity levels. The parameters in pre-trained convolutional networks are frozen, including the number of convolutional layers, the size of

1010   0110   0001   0100 0000 0000 = A61400
| Working mode | interaction | Intensity | Joints 0-10 switch |

Fig. 8. Example of a haptic command of Button Pressed gesture.

convolutional kernels, and pooling layers. Only the parameters in the fully connected neural network are updated after training in our training dataset. The training dataset includes 5,000 figures captured with multiple scenes. When the user study is conducted, the Inception V3 model with trained weights predicts the rigidity level of objects

4.2 Hardware Implementation

As shown in Fig. 9, we utilized two TCA9548A modules (1-of-8 bidirectional translating switches) connected to the Jetson-Nano and 11 DRV2605L haptic controllers. Each of them controls one LRA on gloves.

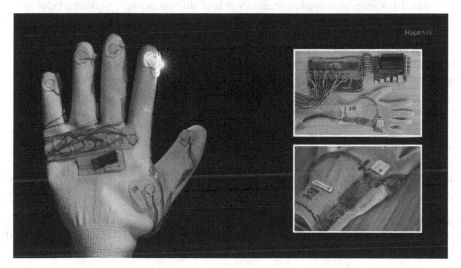

Fig. 9. Hardware implementation of HaptMR

To not interfere with the HL2's hand tracking performance, we lined up the cabling on the side of the finger. We added operating status indicator LEDs for each motor for a better visual experience, which can be synchronized with the motor's operating status or turned off completely (see Fig. 10).

5 User Study and Result Analysis

A within-subjects user study was conducted to test and verify whether our designed HaptMR system on HL2 could enhance the immersive experience. The objective variables in the user study were analyzed, including the manipulation accuracy and required time

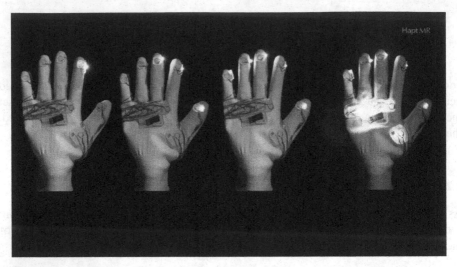

Fig. 10. Gloves with fine haptic motors in four different example working modes

without/with haptic feedback in tasks, and the semantic recognition accuracy by the deep learning model. Furthermore, the subjective MR experience was also presented according to participants' comments, including intuitiveness, engagement, satisfaction. We hypothesized that MR combined with our designed HaptMR system would significantly improve the enjoyment and immersive experience.

5.1   User Study

Participants performed two designed tasks in condition MR equipped without/with HaptMR.

Apparatus. Participants wore the HL2 device and the glove with haptic motors described in previous sections. Participants completed the required actions without/with haptic feedback.

Participants. Our user study was performed by 18 participants, 14 males and 4 females (mean age: 26 years old). All participants were informed of all operations before experiments. Two of them were very familiar with the operations in HL2 previously. The participants' comments were transcribed after achieving tasks.

Tasks. *(1) Hand Tracking.* There are four objects (cheese model) with the same initial state. Participants performed the designed rotation operations with some angles, including 45°, 90°, 135°, 180° (5 times for each rotation/each participant), and then the scaling with determining percentages, including 100%. 120%, 150%, and 180% (5 times for each scaling/each participant). *(2) Spatial Awareness.* Participants grabbed a virtual baseball bat to hit real objects with five different rigidity levels, including 1-very soft, 2-soft, 3-neutral, 4-hard, and 5-very hard. Each participant hit different objects five times in total. These objects were assigned to each participant randomly. However, the amounts of different rigidity levels are the same, which means, there are 18 same/different objects for every rigidity. That means, participants might hit objects with all five rigidity levels, they might also meet only three rigidity levels in total five times.

Procedure. In order to be familiar with the HL2 device, we let each participant be familiar with basic gestures on HL2, automatically adjust the display and vertical offset (VO) according to each participant's interpupillary distance (IPD). Firstly, without haptic feedback, each participant performed the first task, where participants rotated objects with the above-mentioned angles relative to the initial state, and then, they scaled the cheese continuously also relative to its initial state. In addition, participants repeat the above-mentioned procedure in condition with haptic feedback. The real rotating angles and scaling percentages without/with haptic feedback were recorded. Furthermore, participants performed the second task in semantic analysis conditions. When participants hit the object, each haptic feedback predicted by the semantic algorithm was recorded.

5.2 Result Analysis

When we conducted the user study, the HL2 application could be roughly stable at 60 fps. In most cases, the response latency of fine haptics is very low, especially when pressing a button with almost no perceptible latency. Figure 11 shows the data parsed at the receiving end, visualizing the signal for each motor separately.

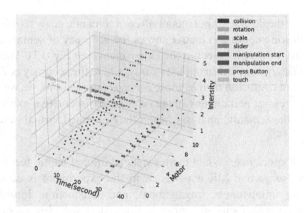

Fig. 11. Data parsed at the receiver (Jetson-Nano) with time

Objective Interaction Experience. For the first task, the data in two conditions (MR applied without/with HaptMR) are analyzed. Figure 12(Left) shows the absolute difference between the real rotated angles and the ground truth when participants rotated objects without/with haptic feedback. If the participant rotated precisely to the ground truth, the difference is almost equal to zero. Similar to the rotating operation, the absolute difference of the real scaling percentage and the ground truth in condition without/with haptic feedback (HF) is presented in Fig. 12(Right). For not only the rotation operation but also the scaling manipulation, the median and standard deviation of differences in condition with haptic feedback are obviously smaller than without haptic feedback. Therefore, the manipulation accuracy increases obviously in condition with haptic feedback. Besides, participants don't have to cautiously focus on their manipulations due to the haptic reminder.

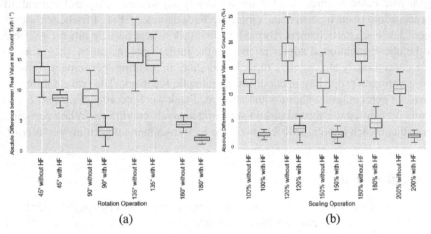

(a)   (b)

Fig. 12. (a) Absolute difference between the real angle values in experiments and the true values, and (b) absolute difference between the real scaling percentage in experiments and the true values

In second task, the deep learning model offers a semantic analysis when users hit the objects. The following confusion matrix shows the accuracy of semantic analysis, that means, the rigidity of the hit object in the experiment (see Fig. 13). There were totally 120 times semantic adjustments in our user study, where the accuracy is 77.5%. Besides, we could observe in confusion matrix, those incorrect predictions are very similar to the ground truth. Therefore, participants obtained a richer interactive experience due to a high accuracy of the semantic analysis, when they operated virtual objects in the real physical world.

Subjective MR Experience. When there exists additional haptic feedback in the MR environment, the subjective MR experience in the experiment is described in three aspects, including intuitiveness, engagement, and satisfaction. Intuitiveness means whether participants must focus on their operations cautiously, Engagement means how helpful the haptic feedback is for participants to complete the designed manipulations, and Satisfaction presents an overall evaluation for the whole process with HaptMR. The result is shown in Fig. 14. 38% of the users strongly agree, and 28% agree that the haptic feedback improves the intuitiveness. For the improved engagement, 67% of users strongly agree, and 8% agree. Moreover, 67% (57% strong agreement and 10% agreement) of users judged higher satisfaction for the whole experiment, when objects were manipulated with haptic feedback. Therefore, the haptic feedback improves the users' immersive MR experience according to the subjective senses.

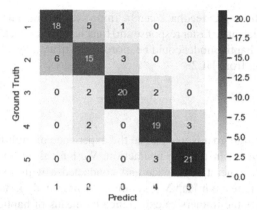

Fig. 13. Confusion matrix of the semantic analysis for identifying the objects' rigidity

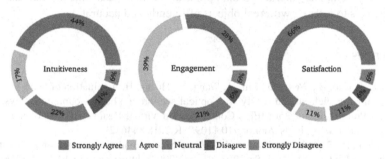

Fig. 14. Review results in three aspects: intuitiveness (left), engagement (middle), satisfaction (right)

5.3 Discussion of Our Findings

The user study supports our previous hypothesis, i.e., the haptic feedback makes the interactive operations more accurate and saves time for the interaction, when participants wear the HL2 device with our HaptMR. Furthermore, the semantic analysis combined with the haptic feedback indeed increases the immersive experience, when participants manipulate the virtual object in the real world. Overall, the participants satisfy the HaptMR system.

Besides, according to the comments, the direct haptic feedback from hands will make the interaction more intuitive than through other interactive channels (such as sound and vision). It makes users feel touched objects more realistically. The haptic feedback can also save the interaction time of fine-grained operations. It's not necessary that users manipulate objects slowly and carefully. In addition, according to some responses, haptic feedback allows participants to ignore to a certain extent the fatigue caused by waving their hands in the air. However, there exists a few delayed or erroneous feedback due to slight delays or inaccuracies of the hand tracking. Moreover, the delayed communication between devices might cause accumulated messages.

In future work, the haptic feedback can be improved. For instance, the use of piezo-electric actuators which have faster response and finer haptic feedback promises even better results. Also, our haptic model could be more sophisticated by additionally utilizing the depth information from HL2.

6 Conclusion

In this article, our design goal is to enhance the experience of multimodal interactions, following the concept of instinctual interaction. We built the HaptMR system based on the HoloLens (2. generation) device and conducted a within-subjects user study with 18 participants to test our HaptMR system. The user study indicates that HaptMR significantly improves the immersive experience by means of haptic feedback and the deep learning model for computer vision. The main benefit of our approach is that users can not only complete interactive manipulations with virtual objects, but also utilize virtual objects to interact with real objects efficiently and accurately.

References

1. Zhang, Z., Cao, B., Weng, D., Liu, Y., Wang, Y., Huang, H.: Evaluation of hand-based interaction for near-field mixed reality with optical see-through head-mounted displays. In: VR 2018 - Proceedings of 25th IEEE Conference on Virtual Reality and 3D User Interfaces, pp. 739–740 (2018). https://doi.org/10.1109/VR.2018.8446129
2. Knoerlein, B., Székely, G., Harders, M.: Visuo-haptic collaborative augmented reality ping-pong. ACM Int. Conf. Proc. Ser. 203, 91–94 (2007). https://doi.org/10.1145/1255047.125 5065
3. Hughes, C.E., Stapleton, C.B., Hughes, D.E., Smith, E.M.: Mixed reality in education, entertainment, and training. IEEE Comput. Graph. Appl. 25(6), 24–30 (2005). https://doi.org/10. 1109/MCG.2005.139
4. Maman, K., et al.: Comparative efficacy and safety of medical treatments for the management of overactive bladder: a systematic literature review and mixed treatment comparison. Eur. Urol. 65(4), 755–765 (2014). https://doi.org/10.1016/j.eururo.2013.11.010
5. Feiner, S.K.: Augmented reality: a new way of seeing. Sci. Am. 286(4), 48 (2002). https://doi.org/10.1038/scientificamerican0402-48
6. Flavián, C., Ibáñez-Sánchez, S., Orús, C.: The impact of virtual, augmented and mixed reality technologies on the customer experience. J. Bus. Res. 100(January 2018), 547–560 (2019). https://doi.org/10.1016/j.jbusres.2018.10.050
7. Ping, J., Liu, Y., Weng, D.: Comparison in depth perception between virtual reality and augmented reality systems. In: VR 2019 - Proceedings of 26th IEEE Conference on Virtual Reality and 3D User Interfaces, pp. 1124–1125 (2019). https://doi.org/10.1109/VR.2019.879 8174
8. Hettiarachchi, A., Wigdor, D.: Annexing reality: enabling opportunistic use of everyday objects as tangible proxies in augmented reality. In: Conference on Human Factors in Computing Systems - Proceedings, pp. 1957–1967 (2016). https://doi.org/10.1145/2858036.285 8134
9. Yokokohji, Y., Hollis, R.L., Kanade, T.: What you can see is what you can feel - development of a visual/haptic interface to visual environment. In: Proceedings - Virtual Reality Annual International Symposium, pp. 46–53 (1996). https://doi.org/10.1109/vrais.1996.490509

10. Di Diodato, L.M., Mraz, R., Baker, S.N., Graham, S.J.: A haptic force feedback device for virtual reality-fMRI experiments. IEEE Trans. Neural Syst. Rehabil. Eng. **15**(4), 570–576 (2007). https://doi.org/10.1109/TNSRE.2007.906962
11. Laboratoty, I.: SPIDAR and Virtual Reality, pp. 17–24 (n.d.)
12. Gupta, S., Morris, D., Patel, S.N., Tan, D.: AirWave: non-contact haptic feedback using air vortex rings. In: UbiComp 2013 - Proceedings of the 2013 ACM International Joint Conference on Pervasive and Ubiquitous Computing, pp. 419–428 (2013). https://doi.org/10.1145/2493432.2493463
13. Sodhi, R., Poupyrev, I., Glisson, M., Israr, A.: AIREAL: interactive tactile experiences in free air. ACM Trans. Graph. 32(4) (2013). https://doi.org/10.1145/2461912.2462007
14. Suzuki, Y., Kobayashi, M.: Air jet driven force feedback in virtual reality. IEEE Comput. Graph. Appl. **25**(1), 44–47 (2005). https://doi.org/10.1109/MCG.2005.1
15. Ochiai, Y., Kumagai, K., Hoshi, T., Rekimoto, J., Hasegawa, S., Hayasaki, Y.: Fairy lights in femtoseconds: aerial and volumetric graphics rendered by focused femtosecond laser combined with computational holographic fields. ACM Trans. Graph. **35**(2), 680309 (2016). https://doi.org/10.1145/2850414
16. Microsoft Mixed Reality Homepage. https://docs.microsoft.com/zh-cn/windows/mixed-reality/discover/mixed-reality
17. Microsoft Mixed Reality Toolkit Homepage. https://microsoft.github.io/MixedRealityToolkit-Unity/Documentation/Input/HandTracking.html
18. Microsoft Homepage. https://docs.microsoft.com/zh-cn/windows/mixed-reality/design/interaction-fundamentals
19. Peng, H., et al.: Roma: interactive fabrication with augmented reality and a robotic 3D printer. In: Conference on Human Factors in Computing Systems - Proceedings (Vol. 2018-April) (2018). https://doi.org/10.1145/3173574.3174153
20. Song, H., Guimbretière, F., Hu, C., Lipson, H.: ModelCraft: capturing freehand annotations and edits on physical 3D models. In: UIST 2006: Proceedings of the 19th Annual ACM Symposium on User Interface Software and Technology, pp. 13–22 (2008)s. https://doi.org/10.1145/1166253.1166258
21. Follmer, S., Carr, D., Lovell, E., Ishii, H.: CopyCAD: remixing physical objects with copy and paste from the real world. In: UIST 2010 - 23rd ACM Symposium on User Interface Software and Technology, Adjunct Proceedings, pp. 381–382 (2010). https://doi.org/10.1145/1866218.1866230
22. Adafruit. Adafruit DRV2605 Haptic Controller Breakout (2014)
23. Szegedy, C., et al.: Going deeper with convolutions. In: Proceedings of the IEEE Computer Society Conference on Computer Vision and Pattern Recognition, 07–12-June-2015, pp. 1–9 (2015). https://doi.org/10.1109/CVPR.2015.7298594
24. Joseph, S.: Australian literary journalism and "missing voices": how Helen garner finally resolves this recurring ethical tension. J. Pract. **10**(6), 730–743 (2016). https://doi.org/10.1080/17512786.2015.1058180
25. Qian, Y., et al.: Fresh tea leaves classification using inception-V3. In: 2019 2nd IEEE International Conference on Information Communication and Signal Processing, ICICSP 2019, pp. 415–419 (2019). https://doi.org/10.1109/ICICSP48821.2019.8958529
26. Wang, C., et al.: Pulmonary image classification based on inception-V3 transfer learning model. IEEE Access **7**, 146533–146541 (2019). https://doi.org/10.1109/ACCESS.2019.2946000
27. Kin, N.G.: Tuned Inception V3 for Recognizing States of Cooking Ingredients (2019). ArXiv. https://doi.org/10.32555/2019.dl.009
28. Demir, A., Yilmaz, F., Kose, O.: Early detection of skin cancer using deep learning architectures: Resnet-101 and inception-v3. In: TIPTEKNO 2019 - Tip Teknolojileri Kongresi, 3–6 January 2019 (2019). https://doi.org/10.1109/TIPTEKNO47231.2019.8972045

29. Szegedy, C., Vanhoucke, V., Ioffe, S., Shlens, J., Wojna, Z.: Rethinking the inception architecture for computer vision. In: Proceedings of the IEEE Computer Society Conference on Computer Vision and Pattern Recognition, 2016-December, pp. 2818–2826 (2016). https://doi.org/10.1109/CVPR.2016.308
30. Xiao, X.: The evolutionary history of the Inception model: from GoogLeNet to Inception-ResNet. In: ZHIHU Zhuanlan Forum. https://zhuanlan.zhihu.com/p/50754671

Position Estimation of Occluded Fingertip Based on Image of Dorsal Hand from RGB Camera

Zheng Zhao[✉], Takeshi Umezawa, and Noritaka Osawa

Chiba University, Chiba, Japan

Abstract. Development of Virtual Reality (VR) and popularization of motion capture enables a user's hands and fingers to directly interact with virtual objects in a VR environment without holding any equipment. However, an optical motion capture device cannot track the user's fingers where the fingers are occluded from the device by the hand. Self-occlusion hinders correct estimation of the fingertips, resulting in failure to achieve natural interaction. This paper proposes a method for estimating 3D position of occluded fingertips using an image of the dorsal hand which a head-mounted camera can capture. The method employs deep neural networks to estimate 3D coordinates of the fingertips based on an image of the dorsal hand. This paper describes a processing pipeline used to build training datasets for the deep neural networks. Hand segmentation is used to preprocess the image, and coordinate alignment is applied to transform coordinates in two camera coordinate systems. The collected dataset includes data with different hand types of subjects, different interaction methods, and different lighting conditions. Then, this paper evaluates the effectiveness of the proposed method based on the collected dataset. The model based on ResNet-18 had a smallest average 3D error of 7.19 mm among three models used to compare. The same model structure is used to build a model to estimate 3D coordinates from an image of a palm as a baseline. An evaluation on the models shows that the difference between errors of the models for palm and dorsal hands is smaller than 1.5 mm. The results show that can effectively predict a fingertip position with a low error from an image of dorsal hand even if the fingertip is occluded from a camera.

Keywords: Self-occlusion · Deep learning · Fingertip position estimation

1 Introduction

In a VR environment, a user can interact with virtual objects by manipulating the controller and other devices. A more natural user interface can be achieved by eliminating the need to hold and wear any equipment on the hand [1]. An optical hand motion tracker such as Leap Motion in front of Head Mounted Display (HMD; for example, HTC VIVE) enables a user's fingers to interact with virtual objects.

However, a hand sometimes occludes its fingertips from the optical motion tracker. The hand motion tracker cannot accurately recognize the position of the occluded fingertips. Although self-occlusion often happens, the motion tracker can capture an image of the user's dorsal hand. The silhouette and skin texture like fine wrinkles of the dorsal

© Springer Nature Switzerland AG 2021
J. Y. C. Chen and G. Fragomeni (Eds.): HCII 2021, LNCS 12770, pp. 259–271, 2021.
https://doi.org/10.1007/978-3-030-77599-5_19

hand are influenced by finger postures. This implies that the silhouette and texture of the skin on the dorsal hand is strongly related to the position of the fingertips [2]. If the fingertip position can be estimated from an image of the dorsal hand, robust position estimation can be achieved even if self-occlusion occurs.

In this work, we propose a method to predict 3D positions of fingertips by analyzing the silhouette and texture of a dorsal hand on an RGB image, even if the fingertips are occluded. We apply hand segmentation for image pre-processing to separate the hand area from the background. In order to train a deep neural network model for estimation of 3D positions, a large-scale dorsal hand dataset containing ground truth is needed. Due to the lack of such a dataset, we created a dataset of images of hands in basic operations for interaction of users with virtual objects.

This paper is organized as follows: In the following section, we give an overview of hand pose estimation and related work. Then, we describe the proposed method and the pipeline of dataset labeling. After that, we evaluate the effectiveness of our proposed method. Finally, we summarize our study and discuss future work for future development.

2 Related Work

Capturing the 3D motion of human hands through a camera is still a long-standing problem in computer vision. Recently, the emergence of consumer-level motion captures, such as Leap Motion and Kinect, provides people with interactive methods that do not require a user to wear devices like a sensor glove. The image-based hand pose estimation methods are mainly classified into Depth-based, RGB-based, and RGBD-based methods.

2.1 Depth-Based Methods

The appearance of depth sensors enabled a lot of studies to focus on hand posture prediction based on a depth image. Oberweger et al. [3] adapted a ResNet architecture to estimate the 3D coordinates of all the finger joints from a depth image. Wetzler et al. [4] generated a hand pose dataset called HandNet and compared the fingertip estimation of the Random Forest (RF) and Convolutional Neural Networks (CNN) models. Guo et al. [5] uses both a depth image and an edge image generated by inputting depth image to RF to improve the accuracy of the model. These studies use CNN-based models to achieve hand pose estimation with high precision.

Training of deep learning models requires a large amount of labeled data. There are three large-scale public datasets in this field: NYU [6], ICVL [7], and MSRA [8]. These datasets are often used as benchmarks to compare and evaluate the results of studies based on the same datasets. Malik et al. [9] also created a large-scale dataset that consists of million-scale synthetic data generated from these three datasets.

The depth information of keypoints in a depth image is useful to predict 3D hand posture. However, use of infrared radiation from the depth sensor degrades the accuracy of the depth information in strong specular reflection, direct sunlight, incandescent light, and outdoor environments. These factors reduce the effectiveness of the depth-based methods.

2.2 RGB-Based Methods

RGB images contain more textural information than depth images. It is possible to use a deep learning model to extract hand features from a complex RGB image and return to finger joint coordinates.

In the AR field, using a deep learning model and images from a camera in devices such as google glass can realize interaction by user gestures. Huang et al. [10] and Jain et al. [11] realized real-time interaction by estimating the 2D position of the user's index fingertip. These studies mainly used lightweight networks such as MoblieNet [12] for real-time processing. In the VR field, an accurate finger 3D position is required. Many studies have used deep learning models to produce 2D "heatmaps" to predict the key points [13, 14, 15] and implement 2D-3D lifting tasks through Inverse Kinematics (IK). Zimmermann et al. [16] also used the learning model to predict the camera's viewpoint and convert the 2D coordinates to 3D. Our study will directly predict the 3D coordinates of all fingertips from an RGB image. The image includes fine skin wrinkles on the back of the hand, which reflect postures of the fingers. Shimizume et al. [2] used a monocular RGB image of the dorsal hand which occludes its fingertips, to estimate the distance between the fingertips of a thumb and an index finger by analyzing skin textures and the silhouette of the dorsal hand. The study showed that a distance between the fingertips could be estimated from an image of the dorsal hand which has occluded fingertips. We extend the estimation method of the distance between occluded fingertips to the estimation of 3D positions of occluded fingertips.

In order to process RGB images with higher dimensionality than depth images, more labeled data is also needed to train models with deeper layers. Simon et al. [17] provided a method to generate a labeled dataset automatically. This method uses a multi-view camera system to generate highly reliable coordinate prediction iteratively through a hand skeleton detector. There is also a large-scale dataset, Stereo Hand Pose Tracking Benchmark (STB) [18], which contains 18,000 hand images under 6 different backgrounds and lighting conditions, as well as the Rendered Hand Pose Dataset (RHD) [16], which is a synthetic dataset containing 42,000 labeled RGB images. In the VR environment where a camera is installed in front of the HMD to detect the user's hand, the hand often occludes its fingertips. However, as far as we know, there are no dorsal hand datasets from a first-person view. Therefore, a dorsal hand dataset labelled with correct 3D coordinates is necessary. This paper will describe an automatic pipeline to generate a dorsal hand dataset in Sect. 4.

2.3 RGBD-Based Methods

Nguyen et al. [19] proposed a multi-task SegNet to segment the finger part in an RGB image and predict the 2D position of the fingertip. They utilize the depth thresholding method to preprocess the image and segment the hand part. The study completes the hand segmentation task with a deep learning model without a depth sensor. Garcia-Hernando et al. [20] provided a large-scale RGB-D dataset of hand-object interaction under the first-person perspective.

3   Proposed Method

The proposed method uses an RGB camera to capture an image of a dorsal hand, as shown in case A of Fig. 1. A deep learning model is employed to accurately estimate 3D positions from the fine textures of the skin and slight differences in the silhouette of the hand. In order to evaluate our model, we need to collect a large number of pairs of data with the 3D coordinate of the fingertips and RGB dorsal hand image.

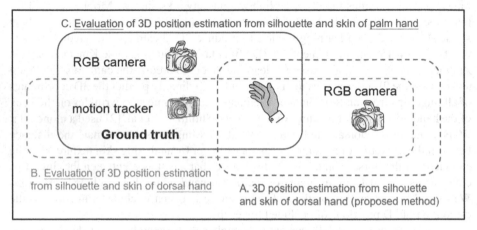

Fig. 1. Evaluation of the proposed method

However, it is not easy to label fingertip data from the back of the hand when self-occlusion occurs. Therefore, we use a motion tracker placed in the front of the hand to measure 3D coordinates of the fingertips as ground truth, as shown in case B of Fig. 1.

Then, another RGB camera is placed in the front of the hand to capture an image of the palm, as shown in case C of Fig. 1. The camera is used to evaluate a model that estimates 3D coordinates of the fingertips from an image of the palm of the hand as a baseline of our study. The proposed method aims to train a high-precision model for predicting fingertip coordinates. The accuracy of the model for the RGB camera in case B should be close to that in case C.

4   Data Acquisition and Annotation

Figure 2 shows a pipeline for fingertip 3D position estimation (upper part) and an evaluation method using fingertip position measurements from a motion tracker as ground truth. It applies to both case B and case C in Fig. 1. First, we need registration of the RGB camera and the motion tracker. We obtain the matrix representing the positional relationship between them through camera registration. The matrix is used to convert the ground truth coordinates in the motion tracker coordinate system to coordinates in the RGB camera coordinate system. Then, hand images collected by the RGB camera are processed by the hand segmentation model whose output is the input of the fingertip coordinate prediction model.

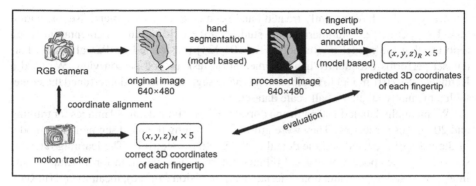

Fig. 2. Estimation pipeline for fingertip position estimation and its evaluation

We describe Coordinate alignment, Hand Segmentation, and Fingertip coordinate annotation in the following subsections.

4.1 Coordinate Alignment

When using a multi-view camera system, camera registration and calibration is frequently used to calculate the positional relationship between the cameras at different positions and angles.

In order to align the coordinates measured in the motion tracker coordinate system to those in the RGB camera coordinate system, we use a chessboard for registration and calibration according to the method of Zhang [21]. The two cameras capture an image of the chessboard synchronously. Then, the intrinsic parameter matrix of RGB camera I_R, intrinsic parameter matrix of motion tracker I_M, and the extrinsic parameter matrix relative to the world coordinate system (chessboard) E_R and E_M are calculated with a matching algorithm of 2D coordinates of the corners in the image and the predefined real 3D coordinates of the corners.

An error of the alignment was evaluated by Root Mean Square (RMS) of the reprojection error, and the error was 0.274 pixel in our experiment.

4.2 Hand Segmentation

In hand pose estimation, hand segmentation is frequently used for image pre-processing. Segmentation can help the fingertip detection model better to capture the features of the hand in the image.

Grabcut [22] is commonly used in hand segmentation, but it is not easy to achieve real-time processing due to complex calculations. Another method is color-based skin detection algorithms. However, the algorithm sometimes fails to perform hand segmentation properly due to changes in lighting conditions and appearance of skin-like texture in the background. It is possible to use the depth thresholding method similar to [19]. But the method is not suitable for our present study due to coarse-grained measurement by the depth sensor and the need to conduct experiments in a specific environment.

Many studies have recently treated hand segmentation as a semantic segmentation task. Urooj et al. [23] summarized the studies in the field of hand segmentation. They reported that the model of RefineNet-Res101 [24] pre-trained on Pascal Person-Part dataset performs excellently hand segmentation task in first-person view. We used a RefineNet-Res101 model to implement our hand segmentation and fine-tuned the model with a manually labeled small-scale dataset.

We manually labeled 100 palm and dorsal images, divided into 80 images for training and 20 images for testing. They were utilized for training the hand segmentation model of the palm of the hand and the dorsal of the hand, respectively. The learning rate was set to 10^{-5}, the epoch was 30, and bilinear interpolation was used for upsampling the image. We used three evaluation criteria: mean Precision (mPrec), mean Recall (mRec), and mean Intersection over Union (mIOU). The evaluation results are shown in Table 1, which implies that the fine-tuned model sufficiently separates the hand and background area for our dataset.

Table 1. Hand segmentation evaluation

Data	mPrec	mRec	mIOU
Palm of hand image	0.966	0.962	0.930
Dorsal of hand image	0.988	0.971	0.960

4.3 Fingertip Coordinate Annotation

This subsection describes cameras used in the experiment, a specific collection pipeline of fingertip coordinates, and the structure of the collected dataset below.

Camera
Our evaluation scenario described in Sect. 3 requires cameras for short-range usage. Therefore, we use two intel RealSense D435i RGBD cameras. One of them is placed in the back of the hand to capture RGB images of the dorsal hand. The other is placed in the front of the hand to capture RGB images of the palm hand for the baseline model. The camera is also used to measure the 2D coordinates of the fingertips as a hand motion tracker.

Annotation Pipeline
MediaPipe Hands [25] is a state-of-the-art hand tracking solution that can estimate a 2.5D hand skeleton of a human from a single RGB image. We use MediaPipe Hands to label the 2D coordinates of fingertips on an inputted image of the palm hand. On the basis of the RGB camera intrinsic parameter matrix I_R obtained in Subsect. 4.1, and the distance $d_i = D(x_i, y_i)$ from the depth sensor of D435i, 3D coordinate p_i of fingertips in the RGB camera coordinate system is calculated by algorithm T deprojecting a pixel to a point, which is expressed by $p_i = T(I_R, d_i, (x_i, y_i))$. Finally, the correctly labeled 3D coordinate l_i is obtained by inputting the extrinsic parameter matrix of the RGB

camera and motion tracker into the coordinate transform function L, which is expressed by $l_i = L(E_R, E_M, p_i)$.

Collected Dataset

We need to pay more attention to various shapes and sizes of hands, hand postures, and lighting conditions to train a more robust model.

We collected images of a hand in 6 types of common VR interaction:

(1) Moving virtual objects pinched by a thumb and an index finger.
(2) Rotating virtual objects pinched by a thumb and an index finger.
(3) Pick objects with a thumb and an index finger and drop them
(4) Moving virtual objects grasped by all fingers.
(5) Rotating virtual objects grasped by all fingers.
(6) Pick objects by all fingers and drop them.

The number of subjects was 6 men in their twenties. The dataset was collected under two lighting conditions, daytime and night, as shown in Table 2.

Table 2. Dataset summary. The last row and the last column respectively indicate the amount of data for each interaction and the amount of data for each subject. The block in the lower right corner represents the total amount of dataset. The unit is frame

	(1)	(2)	(3)	(4)	(5)	(6)	Total
Subject 1 (night)	294	267	370	245	270	291	1737
Subject 1 (daytime)	369	460	274	237	336	255	1931
Subject 2 (night)	277	127	133	210	240	345	1332
Subject 2 (daytime)	165	90	68	167	179	143	812
Subject 3 (night)	281	352	269	266	289	290	1747
Subject 3 (daytime)	325	366	413	101	189	244	1638
Subject 4 (night)	206	250	124	144	229	200	1153
Subject 5 (daytime)	366	228	110	148	118	238	1208
Total	2283	2140	1761	1518	1850	2006	11,558

We divided the collected data of each interaction into an 80-percent training dataset and a 20-percent test dataset. Therefore, a total of 11,558 data were divided into 9246 data for training and 2312 data for evaluation. The image size is 640×480 pixel.

5   Model to Estimate Fingertips

5.1   Model Structures and Parameters

We compared and evaluated some recently proposed deep learning convolutional architectures, ResNet18 [26], ResNet50 [26], and VGG16 [27] using our dataset. To adapt
to the regression task for position estimation, we modified the output dimension of the
last fully connected layer to 15. All models were trained on a computer with an Intel i7
with 4.2 GHz and 32 GB of RAM, and an NVIDIA GTX 1080 graphics card.

We employed Adam as an optimizer with default parameters in PyTorch [28] to train
our model. The appropriate learning rate was 10^{-5}, and the epoch was 50.

5.2   Evaluation

Predicted 3D Coordinates
. We evaluated comparatively estimation accuracies of models trained on the palm of
hand image (baseline) and the dorsal of hand image in our proposed method. The evaluation criterion was average 3D error, which means an average of the Euclidean distance
between the correct 3D coordinate and the predicted 3D coordinate.

The results are shown in Table 3. ResNet-18 has the smallest error of 7.19 mm on
the dorsal of the hand, and ResNet-50 has the smallest error of 6.17 mm on the palm of
the hand. Moreover, the ResNet using Residual Block performs better than VGG.

Table 3.   Average 3D error of each architecture in two cases

Model structure	Average 3D error from palm (baseline)	Average 3D error from dorsal
ResNet-18	6.44 mm	**7.19** mm
ResNet-50	**6.17** mm	7.48 mm
VGG16	9.07 mm	8.06 mm

Then, we plotted the cumulative fraction of images where all fingertips are within a
distance from the ground truth, as shown in Fig. 3. There is no obvious difference in the
predictions of the three models in (b), and the accuracy of VGG16 is slightly reduced in
(a).

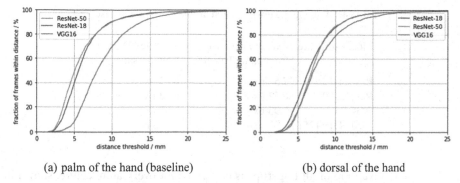

(a) palm of the hand (baseline)   (b) dorsal of the hand

Fig. 3. Cumulative ratio of correct keypoints of the three architectures in 3D

We also evaluated the average 3D error of each fingertip in Case A in Fig. 1, which is shown in Fig. 4. The result shows that there is no significant difference in the prediction error among fingers.

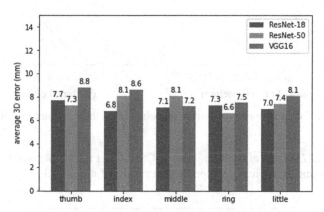

Fig. 4. The average 3D error of fingertip

Verification in 2D Coordinates

We visualize the prediction results of the model in 2D by using the intrinsic parameter matrix of the motion tracker I_M obtained in Subsect. 4.1. Then, we evaluated the average 2D error of all architectures.

In Case A, we also evaluated the accuracy of the MediaPipe, which is summarized in Table 4. The accuracy of our three trained models performs well than MediaPipe, and the accuracy of ResNet-50 is the highest on both palm and dorsal of the hand. Since we used MediaPipe to label the palm image, there is no average 2D error from palm of the hand.

Table 4. Average 2D error of each architecture in two cases

Model structure	Average 2D error from palm (baseline)	Average 2D error from dorsal
ResNet-18	7.51 px	6.32 px
ResNet-50	**6.52** px	**5.83** px
VGG16	9.93 px	8.07 px
MediaPipe [25]	–	17.76 px

The cumulative ratio of all fingertips is computed for every architecture, shown in Fig. 5. The results show that ResNet-50 outperformed in all architectures.

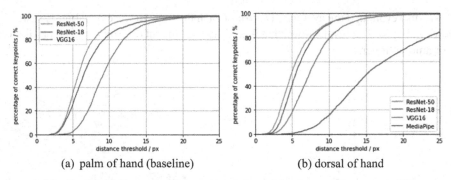

(a) palm of hand (baseline)   (b) dorsal of hand

Fig. 5. Cumulative ratio of correct keypoints of the three architectures in 2D

The average 2D error of each fingertip in Case A in Fig. 1 is shown in Fig. 6. Then, Fig. 7 shows some examples of the prediction results of the model.

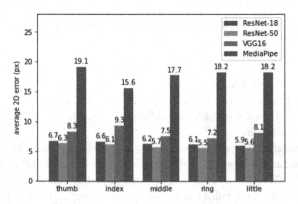

Fig. 6. The average 2D error of fingertip

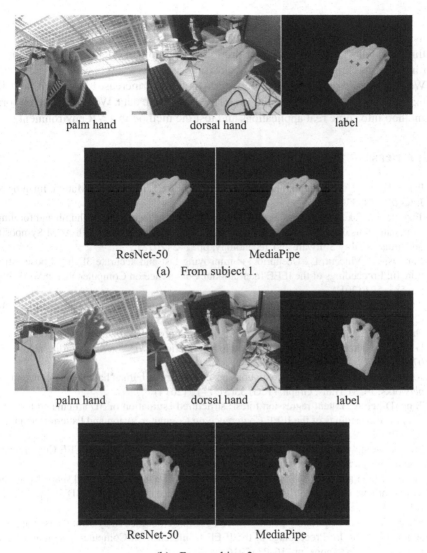

palm hand   dorsal hand   label

ResNet-50   MediaPipe
(a)   From subject 1.

palm hand   dorsal hand   label

ResNet-50   MediaPipe
(b)   From subject 2.

Fig. 7. Examples of prediction results of each model. The image contains two groups, each of which represents, the image of the palm hand, the image of the dorsal hand, the correctly labeled image, the prediction of our ResNet-50 (the best performance of all models when predicting 2D coordinates), and the prediction of MediaPipe

6   Conclusion and Future Work

This paper proposed a method to estimate the 3D positions of occluded fingertips from an RGB image of the dorsal hand. Hand segmentation is used to separate the user's hand from background areas. The 3D coordinates of fingertips measured by MediaPipe are transformed into the correct labeled coordinates through coordinate alignment. Then, three deep learning models were trained on our dataset. Experimental results show that the average 3D error of ResNet-18 is 7.19 mm, which is the highest accuracy among the three models. This shows that our proposed method can effectively predict the 3D coordinate of the fingertip where self-occlusion occurs.

We will investigate efficient data collection methods to increase training data and data augmentation method to improve the model by using more data. We will also incorporate our method into some real applications and test the method in a VR environment.

References

1. Park, G., et al.: Virtual figure model crafting with VR HMD and Leap Motion. Imaging Sci. J. **65**(6), 358–370 (2017)
2. Takuma, S., Takeshi, U., Noritaka, O.: Estimation of distance between thumb and forefinger from hand dorsal image using deep learning. In: Proceedings of the 24th ACM Symposium on Virtual Reality Software and Technology, pp. 1–2 (2018)
3. Markus, O., Vincent, L.: Deepprior++: improving fast and accurate 3D hand pose estimation. In: Proceedings of the IEEE International Conference on Computer Vision Workshops, pp. 585–594 (2017)
4. Aaron, W., Ron, S., Ron, K.: Rule of thumb: deep derotation for improved fingertip detection (2015). arXiv preprint: arXiv:1507.05726
5. Guo, H., Wang, G., Chen, X.: Two-stream convolutional neural network for accurate RGB-D fingertip detection using depth and edge information (2016). arXiv preprint: arXiv:1612.07978
6. Jonathan, T., et al.: Real-time continuous pose recovery of human hands using convolutional networks. ACM Trans. Graph. (ToG) **33**(5), 1–10 (2014)
7. Tang, D., et al.: Latent regression forest: structured estimation of 3D articulated hand posture. In: Proceedings of the IEEE Conference on Computer Vision and Pattern Recognition, pp. 3786–3793 (2014)
8. Sun, X., et al.: Cascaded hand pose regression. In: Proceedings of the IEEE Conference on Computer Vision and Pattern Recognition, pp. 824–832 (2015)
9. Jameel, M., et al.: DeepHPS: end-to-end estimation of 3D hand pose and shape by learning from synthetic depth. In: 2018 International Conference on 3D Vision (3DV), pp. 110–119. IEEE (2018)
10. Huang, Y., et al.: A pointing gesture based egocentric interaction system: dataset, approach and application. In: Proceedings of the IEEE Conference on Computer Vision and Pattern Recognition Workshops, pp. 16–23 (2016)
11. Varun, J., Ramya, H.: AirPen: a touchless fingertip based gestural interface for smartphones and head-mounted devices (2019). arXiv preprint: arXiv:1904.06122
12. Mark, S., et al.: Mobilenetv2: inverted residuals and linear bottlenecks. In: Proceedings of the IEEE Conference on Computer Vision and Pattern Recognition, pp. 4510–4520 (2018)
13. Wei, S.-E., et al.: Convolutional pose machines. In: Proceedings of the IEEE Conference on Computer Vision and Pattern Recognition, pp. 4724–4732 (2016)
14. Zhe, C., et al.: OpenPose: realtime multi-person 2D pose estimation using part affinity fields. IEEE Trans. Pattern Anal. Mach. Intell. **43**(1), 172–186 (2019)
15. Adrian, S., et al.: Cross-modal deep variational hand pose estimation. In: Proceedings of the IEEE Conference on Computer Vision and Pattern Recognition, pp. 89–98 (2018)
16. Christian, Z., Thomas, B.: Learning to estimate 3D hand pose from single RGB images. In: Proceedings of the IEEE International Conference on Computer Vision, pp. 4903–4911 (2017)

17. Tomas, S., et al.: Hand keypoint detection in single images using multi-view bootstrapping. In: Proceedings of the IEEE Conference on Computer Vision and Pattern Recognition, pp. 1145–1153 (2017)
18. Zhang, J., et al.: 3D hand pose tracking and estimation using stereo matching (2016). arXiv preprint: arXiv:1610.07214
19. Hai, N.D., et al.: Hand Segmentation and Fingertip Tracking from Depth Camera Images Using Deep Convolutional Neural Network and Multi-task SegNet (2019). arXiv preprint: arXiv:1901.03465
20. Guillermo, G.-H., et al.: First-person hand action benchmark with RGB-D videos and 3D hand pose annotations. In: Proceedings of the IEEE Conference on Computer Vision and Pattern Recognition, pp. 409–419 (2018)
21. Zhang, Z.: Flexible camera calibration by viewing a plane from unknown orientations. In: Proceedings of the Seventh IEEE International Conference on Computer Vision, Vol. 1, pp. 666–673 (1999)
22. Carsten, R., Vladimir, K., Andrew, B.: GrabCut" interactive foreground extraction using iterated graph cuts. ACM Trans. Graph. (TOG) **23**(3), 309–314 (2004)
23. Aisha, U., Ali, B.: Analysis of hand segmentation in the wild. In: Proceedings of the IEEE Conference on Computer Vision and Pattern Recognition, pp. 4710–4719 (2018)
24. Lin, G., et al.: Refinenet: multi-path refinement networks for high-resolution semantic segmentation. In: Proceedings of the IEEE Conference on Computer Vision and Pattern Recognition, pp. 1925–1934 (2017)
25. Zhang, F., et al.: MediaPipe Hands: On-device Real-time Hand Tracking (2020). arXiv preprint: arXiv:2006.10214
26. Kaiming, H., et al.: Deep residual learning for image recognition. In: Proceedings of the IEEE Conference on Computer Vision and Pattern Recognition, pp. 770–778 (2016)
27. Karen, S., Andrew, Z.: Very deep convolutional networks for large-scale image recognition (2014). arXiv preprint: arXiv:1409.1556
28. Paszke, A., et al.: Pytorch: an imperative style, high-performance deep learning library (2019). arXiv preprint: arXiv:1912.01703

Head-Mounted Displays and VR Glasses

Usability and User Experience of Interactions on VR-PC, HoloLens 2, VR Cardboard and AR Smartphone in a Biomedical Application

Manisha Suresh Balani[ID] and Johannes Tümler[✉][ID]

Anhalt University of Applied Sciences, Köthen, Germany
johannes.tuemler@hs-anhalt.de

Abstract. The Augmented (AR), Mixed (MR) and Virtual Reality (VR) technologies, here subsumed as "xR", have matured in the last years. The research focus of this paper is to study interaction on four different xR platforms to improve medical applications in the future. Often medical applications could be created either as VR or AR scenario. It may depend on multiple factors which xR platform should be used in a specific use case. Therefore, it is interesting to know if there are any differences in usability or user experience between those.

There are various manipulation possibilities that can be done with a virtual object in xR. These major interaction possibilities are explored here: addressing, grasping, moving and releasing of objects. We use a specific virtual scenario to assess user experience and usability of the aforementioned interactions on the four xR platforms. We compare differences and commonalities of the way the interactions are achieved on all platforms.

A study with twenty-one participants gives insight on three main aspects: First, even though the used four platforms have very different interaction capabilities, they can be suitable for biomedical training tasks. Second, all four platforms result in high usability and user experience scores. Third, the HoloLens 2 was the most attractive device but usability and user experience stayed lower in some aspects than even the very simple VR Cardboard.

Keywords: Augmented reality · Virtual reality · Interactions · Biomedical application

1 Motivation

Healthcare systems in every country are tangled with numerous challenges that result from a combination of factors like socio-cultural, economic, and political. Planning and implementation of local health policies and programs often is challenging. Especially on the ground level the situation often seems to be in a permanent state of demand greatly exceeding the supply. There are purely

© Springer Nature Switzerland AG 2021
J. Y. C. Chen and G. Fragomeni (Eds.): HCII 2021, LNCS 12770, pp. 275–287, 2021.
https://doi.org/10.1007/978-3-030-77599-5_20

logistical issues for example when the patient is located in a difficult-to-access place. Next to that, sometimes equipment is outdated or not as effective as it should be or access to it is limited. In addition, there can be problems with lack of available personnel in local institutions. The reality of the situation is that many local hospitals are struggling to handle intense work flow, especially during emergencies [5]. In these situations training the personnel is very important but can become difficult.

Biomedical engineers develop equipment and processes to improve medical applications. Healthcare is an industry where stakes are really - high as it is human life itself. The effectiveness of the health care system highly depends on use of suitable and advanced solutions considering the public interest and involvement as well as funding. Healthcare is open to new technologies [5] like Virtual technologies. A taxonomy for these virtual technologies was proposed by Milgram et al. [7] and is widely accepted in literature. Here, we subsume AR, VR, MR into "xR", where the x can be seen as a placeholder for A/V/M.

Some of the challenges for healthcare can be addressed with the implementation of xR technology [9]. Medical applications of virtual and augmented reality have been extensively developed during the last decade. In the current era of data fusion, virtual technologies provide an ideal approach for educational and training purposes as well as intra-operative guidance. If the xR systems are prepared well they allow for standardized training even in difficult environments. Virtual technologies may be employed to shorten the learning curve related to surgical procedures and increase overall education efficiency, thereby providing patient safety [15]. Future work of biomedical engineers will deal more with digital processes and technologies like xR.

The tools must fit well to the task and be as precise as possible. This is a considerable challenge for developers of xR applications and requires more work and research in terms of precision and usability of xR technologies in biomedical applications.

2   xR Interaction and Research Goals

A defining feature of xR is the ability to manipulate virtual objects interactively, rather than to simply view a passive environment. Manipulating a virtual object is a fundamental and essential interaction task for users experiencing xR. To achieve this, the selection, moving, rotating, and scaling of virtual objects are basic tasks [8]. Instead of issuing an abstract command or specifying coordinates and rotation angles, users may reach out a hand, grasp an object (using a button or a gesture), and move it around the virtual environment using natural, physical motions [3]. There are multiple possibilities to represent the interaction device (e.g. controller, hands) with different effects on efficiency [16].

An interaction starts with user's intention to manipulate an object. To define the interaction object, this intention needs to be populated to the xR system - the object must be addressed. Grasping an object is necessary when an object has to be picked. The user must at least specify which object to grasp and may also denote the center of rotation for the following manipulation phase [4]. For many interactions in xR, grasping the object is the foremost user interaction which is done. For e.g. translation movement, when users move a physical object, they usually grasp it with their fingers or controllers, move it mid air and place it at the desired target position. Once the user is satisfied with the new position of the virtual object, the releasing of the object finishes the interaction with the virtual object [8]. For scaling, user can grasp a virtual object at an angle and move away or close the hands or controllers to each other, the grasped object is scaled up or down respectively [2,4].

Depending on the xR platform type users may be confronted with different devices like head mounted displays, controllers or touch screens. All of these have different interactive possibilities and platform-specific limitations. For many biomedical use cases it is important to understand differences between the platforms. Therefore, we here aim at comparing usability of interactions on different relevant xR platforms in a typical biomedical use case. The two main objectives are: (1) To find commonalities of interactions on common xR platforms and (2) to compare user ratings for usability and user experience on all four platforms in the sample use case.

3   Use Case and Implementation

Anatomy is an essential component of medical education as it is critical for the accurate diagnosis in the human system. Detailed animations and interactive 3D models of human body such as the Visible Human 3D Anatomical Structure Viewer have been developed to facilitate learning of anatomy, radiology and surgical procedures [12]. In circumstances where dissections are limited, students often heavily depend on written and verbal explanations, as well as 2D representations. Computer aided learning and 3D computer models are developed with the aim of decreasing the cognitive load. 3D computer models can be useful for illustrating anatomy, where dissection is considered an ineffective teaching tool due to inaccessibility, inherent complexity and/or size of structure [11].

One main purpose of xR in biomedical tasks is training medical personnel with interactive 3D data visualizations. Therefore we implemented a medical training use case. An anatomic 3D model of human hand served as a puzzle to make it a game like training experience for the participants (Fig. 1). Eight bones were spread 360° around the participant's space. Participants had to physically move their own body in space to find and interact with one bone at a time (address it, grasp it) then fit it into the final hand model position (move it, release it). Possibly correct positions were visualized by a transparent bone object within the hand model. Each single task was fulfilled correctly if a minimum distance between the selected bone and its correct position was reached. Then, the selected bone would snap into its final position to be released by the user. The application was closed after a short pause if all bones were positioned correctly.

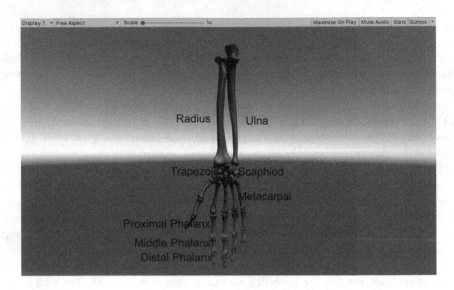

Fig. 1. 3D-model of human hand in Unity

The puzzle use case allows to have more than one interaction of same type during the whole procedure. At the end of each procedure this also helps us to understand which interactions were easier to use.

Four platforms were used for the study, which are:

- **PC-VR**, using HP Reverb (G1) with two controllers, on a machine equipped with Intel Core i7-8700, nVidia RTX 2080 and 16 GB of Ram, Windows 10
- AR using Microsoft **HoloLens 2** with Windows Holographic, version 2004
- **VR Cardboard** with an Android 9.0 based Samsung SM-G950F smartphone
- **AR smartphone** with the same SM-G950F device

These platforms have very different interaction possibilities, e.g. controllers, hand gestures, gaze or touch screen. For the study we aimed at a realistic comparison between typical platform scenarios, so we let our each platform use its standard interaction capabilities. The interactions of all device platforms were implemented using Unity engine (2019.2.17f1). The following SDKs were used:

- MRTK 2.1.0 for PC-VR and HoloLens 2
- GVR SDK v1.200.1 for cardboard VR
- ARCore SDK v1.6.0 for smartphone based AR

The implemented scene geometry and materials were exactly same on all platforms. The size of the hand model was approximately 3 m. It consisted of roughly 100k triangles. Users were positioned 4 m away from it. The spread eight bones also had a distance of 4 m from the user. The interactions made use of the named platform specific SDKs.

For **PC-VR** addressing was achieved by aiming a controller at the object. The controller was visualized using its Windows Mixed Reality standard 3D model. A ray was cast along the forward vector of the controller geometry. As long as an object was hit by the ray, it was addressed. While addressed, the object would be shown in red color. This method of representing an addressed object was the same for all four platforms. The VR controller was used to grasp, move and release the object. The trigger button of the VR controller grasped or released an object. An object could be moved by keeping the trigger button pressed on an selected object and then physically changing the controller pose.

For **HoloLens 2** the object was addressed either by a ray starting at users hands or by walking towards the object until in reach of hands. The object was grasped by pinch gesture, then moved and released by opening the fingers. The virtual hand model was not visualized, so that users would not get distracted from differences between the virtual and real hands.

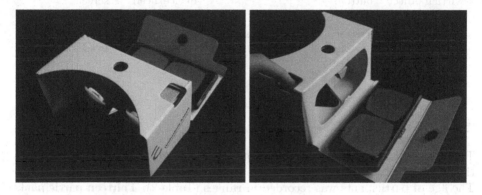

Fig. 2. Photographs of the VR Cardboard with cardboard button. A button press results in a "tap" on the phone screen. (Sample smartphone)

The **VR Cardboard** (Fig. 2) we used included a simple physical button for interaction that generated a touch input on the phone. The device was set up with the Google Cardboard Android app[1] and a device-dependent QR-code. Addressing the object was done by a simple gaze interaction, because the cardboard SDK only allows for 3 degrees-of-freedom rotational tracking. A combination with positional tracking like from ARCore would be possible, but this is not the typical use for VR Cardboards. To address an object, users had to rotate their head and bring the gaze pointer on top of the final object. The object was selected by pushing the aforementioned cardboard button. The users would rotate their view and release the object by pushing the button.

The **AR smartphone** did not have controllers or free hand interaction within the virtual scene. Instead, objects were addressed by finger tap on the

---

[1] https://play.google.com/store/apps/details?id=com.google.samples.apps.cardboard demo.

displayed object and then moved by a swipe gesture. This could lead to the situation, that the view on the 3D model was partially covered by user's hands or fingers. A final tap released the object.

Table 1 summarizes the interactions on the four different device platforms.

Table 1. Comparison matrix for common interactions on the chosen four platforms

Common interaction	PC-VR HP Reverb	Microsoft HoloLens 2	VR Cardboard	AR Smartphone
Address the virtual object	Gaze and controller	Gaze and hand gesture	Gaze	One finger tap
Grasp the virtual object	Trigger button	Hand gesture	Button click	One finger tap
Move the virtual object	Trigger button: pressed	Hand gesture	Rotate the device/head	Move finger on screen
Release the object	Trigger button: released	Release hand gesture	Button click	Release finger from screen

4   Procedure

Twenty-one participants (N = 21) took part in the study without any compensation (within-subject design). They were students and staff of Anhalt University. The age of participants was recorded in ranges (Table 2). Thirteen participants had previous experience with virtual technologies, ranging from minimum one month to 15 months. None of them use it on a daily basis. Eight participants had no experience with virtual technologies at all. None of the participants suffered from any vision of stereoscopic disorder, according to the pre-test questionnaires.

Table 2. Age of participants

Age range	15–20	21–25	26–30	31–35
Number of participants	1	8	9	3

The participants were greeted when they arrived and filled out a pre-test-questionnaire, e.g. about demographics. They were given the chance to familiarize with each platform interaction in a demo scenario, through interaction with simple 3D cubes. They could take as much time as they wanted for this. After familiarization they had to fulfill the interaction task on all four platforms. The order of the device platforms was randomized equally among the participants.

When all device platforms were finished, feedback was recorded by filling out two questionnaires in English language: System Usability Scale (SUS) and User Experience Questionnaire (UEQ). Besides that they had the chance to report their own thoughts and give feedback in oral form. The study took about 45 to 60 min for each participant. Figure 3 shows use of each platform.

Fig. 3. Use of four xR platforms. Top left: AR-smartphone. Top right: VR Cardboard. Bottom left: Microsoft HoloLens 2. Bottom right: VR-PC with HP Reverb (G1) and VR controllers

The SUS score between 0 and 100 gives an insight on usability performance in the aspects of effectiveness, efficiency and overall ease of use [13]. It consists of 10 item questionnaire with 5 response options from strongly agree to strongly disagree[2]. An average value of 68 and would mean a "medium" usability, higher

---

[2] https://www.usability.gov/how-to-and-tools/resources/templates/system-usability-scale-sus.html.

is better. An adjective is used to building on the idea of using words instead of numbers to describe an experience. For example, scores above 85 are associated with "Excellent". "Good" is just above 71 and "Ok" for scores from 51. Another variation on using words to describe the SUS is to think in terms of what's "acceptable" or "not acceptable". Acceptable corresponds to roughly above 70. Unacceptable to below 50 (closely corresponds to our designation of scores lower than 51.6 with grade of F. Three classes of recommenders can be derived based on their responses to the likelihood to recommend question. Promoters score 9 and 10, passive 7 and 8, detractors 6 and below. While promoters are more likely to recommend the product/website/application to a friend, detractors are more likely to discourage rather than recommend [10]. Following is the interpretation of SUS Score [18]:

- Grade A: SUS Score >80.3. The adjective rating is "Excellent".
- Grade B: SUS Score between 68–80.3. The adjective is rating "Good".
- Grade C: SUS Score 68. The adjective rating is "Okay".
- Grade D: SUS Score between 51–68. The adjective rating is "Poor".
- Grade F: SUS Score <51. The adjective rating is "Awful".

The UEQ covers a comprehensive impression of user experience. Both classical usability aspects (efficiency, perspicuity and dependability) and user experience aspects (originality and simulation) are measured [6]. The participants had to fill out a survey of 26 constraint adjective pairs. Those randomly ordered word groups represent six scales which are crucial for good User Experience (UX). The scales of UEQ can be grouped into attractiveness, pragmatic quality (perspicuity, efficiency, dependability) and hedonic quality (stimulation, originality) [17]. Pragmatic quality describes task related quality aspects, hedonic quality the non task related quality aspects. We used the online version of the UEQ [1] and the full version of Schrepps "UEQ Data Analysis Tool"[3] to analyze the data. The tool provides a benchmark with adjectives reaching from "excellent" to "bad" to compare user experience in relation to existing values from a benchmark data set. In addition, Matlab was used for statistical analysis.

Both hardware (display, controllers, etc.) and software (our developed application, motion tracking, etc.) of the xR systems have an influence on user ratings for the SUS and the UEQ.

5 Results

All platforms reached values above medium usability according to SUS results (Fig. 4). Recorded data was not normally distributed, thus for statistical analysis we used a Wilcoxon signed rank test (alpha level 5%). It shows a significant difference between HoloLens 2 and Smartphone AR ($Z = 2.02$, $p = 0.043$). Table 3 gives more insight and shows that the score for PC-VR was denoting excellent performance and likely to be promoted by the participants. AR Smartphone

---

[3] https://ueqtryitout.ueq-research.org/.

follows closely at a score of 79.52. VR Cardboard was ranked third with score
of 75.83 and HoloLens 2 at score of 73.69. The grade ranges from A to with C,
while only the PC-VR and AR smartphone reach the best grade.

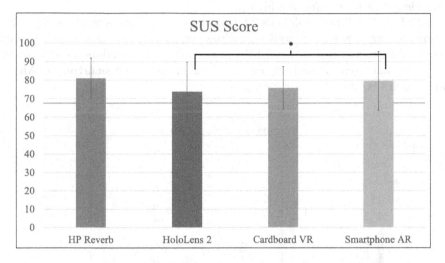

Fig. 4. SUS average score per platform. (The blue line indicates a "medium" usability
at a score of 68, higher is better. * indicates a significant difference.) (Color figure
online)

Figure 5 and Table 4 present the UEQ results for the four platforms. To
analyze for statistical differences we used a Wilcoxon signed rank test at an
alpha level of 5%. We found statistically significant differences in novelty aspects
between PC-VR and Cardboard ($Z = -2.276$, $p = 0.023$), HoloLens 2 and Cardboard ($Z = -2.544$, $p = 0.011$) and AR smartphone and Cardboard ($Z = 2.491$,

Table 3. SUS score

Features	PC-VR HP Reverb	Microsoft HoloLens 2	VR Cardboard	AR Smartphone
SUS Average Score	80.95	73.69	75.83	79.82
SUS SD	10.90	16.02	11.61	15.94
Grade (A-F)	A	C	B	A
Adjective	Excellent	Good	Good	Good
Acceptable parameter	Completely acceptable	Marginally acceptable	Completely acceptable	Completely acceptable
Net Promoter Score (NPS)	Likely to be Promoted	Passive	Passive	Likely to be Promoted

p = 0.013). For perspicuity (Z = 2.045, p = 0.041) and dependability (Z = 2.282, p = 0.023) there is a significant difference between HoloLens 2 and AR Smartphone. For efficiency there is a significant difference between PC-VR and Cardboard (Z = −1.975, p = 0.048). The effect strength for all statistically significant results is between medium and high.

Both for PC-VR and HoloLens 2 the values of attractiveness, efficiency, stimulation and novelty reach "excellent", while perspicuity and dependability reach "good" user experience. Cardboard VR perspicuity and stimulation reach "excellent", the other scales reach "good" user experience. For smartphone AR all scales reach "excellent" user experience.

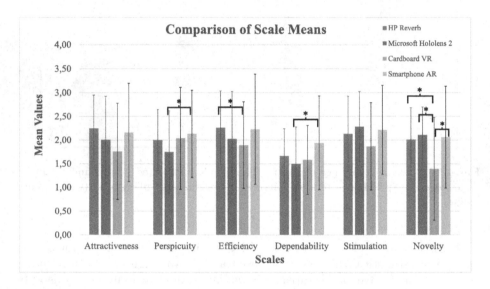

Fig. 5. UEQ scores for the different scales. (* indicates a significant difference)

Table 4. Mean and SD values for UEQ scales

	PC-VR HP Reverb	Microsoft HoloLens 2	VR Cardboard	AR Smartphone
Attractiveness	2.25 ± 0.70	2.01 ± 0.92	1.76 ± 1.01	2.16 ± 1.03
Perspicuity	2.00 ± 0.64	1.75 ± 0.87	2.04 ± 1.07	2.13 ± 0.92
Efficiency	2.26 ± 0.77	2.02 ± 1.00	1.89 ± 0.91	2.23 ± 1.16
Dependability	1.67 ± 0.57	1.50 ± 0.78	1.58 ± 0.73	1.94 ± 0.99
Stimulation	2.13 ± 0.79	2.29 ± 0.74	1.87 ± 0.92	2.21 ± 0.94
Novelty	2.01 ± 0.67	2.11 ± 0.59	1.39 ± 1.08	2.06 ± 1.07

In accordance to the UEQ and SUS results we noticed, that users had problems to work with the HoloLens 2 hand interaction. The hand interaction code was strictly taken from MRTK, it performed as planned from developer's perspective. Nevertheless, compared to the three other platforms users had problems to hit virtual objects with the hand rays. Selecting and grasping the virtual objects were very difficult and cumbersome using the hand ray interaction. This lead to partial frustration. Similar problems were not noticed with the other platforms. Moving and placing objects by hand gesture seemed easy for the users, though.

6 Discussion

By analysis of the SUS questionnaire we conclude that PC-VR is the most popular choice for our use case. The participants rated it as grade A with supreme performance and they were more likely to promote it to other people. In general, all four platforms reached a usability rating at least of "good". HoloLens 2 reached a lower SUS score than VR Cardboard, which was surprising to us.

The analysis of answers to the UEQ allows us to conclude the AR smartphone is a popular choice for participants in terms of attractiveness, practicality, leading edge, value and motivation. It is closely followed by PC-VR which is attractive, efficient, interesting for the participants. The least favorite among the participants is the VR Cardboard as it is ranked conservative, dull and conventional but still is more practical to be used than HoloLens 2.

The differences for perspicuity and dependability between AR smartphone and HoloLens 2 are interesting, especially because both devices belong to the AR device category. From Schrepp's UEQ handbook [14] we can read:

- *Perspicuity*: Is it easy to get familiar with the product? Is it easy to learn how to use the product?
- *Dependability*: Does the user feel in control of the interaction?

We can assume that most participants were used to today's screen-based smartphone interaction. But the free hand AR interaction was a challenge for participants, compared to the known touch screen based AR interaction. We noticed, that the users were overwhelmed by HoloLens 2 hand tracking interaction because it was not easy to use. This might be a reason for the worse values of perspicuity and dependability of the HoloLens 2.

Both SUS and UEQ show the simple VR Cardboard can rank better than HoloLens 2 in certain aspects and scenarios similar to ours. To us this has three implications:

1. First, it is necessary to adjust the user interface to the device properties. It is not possible to just copy a scenario from one platform to another. Instead, maybe a combination of best practices of one platform (i.e. gaze selection) and additional possibilities of the other platform (i.e. hand interaction or physical controllers) can be beneficial. It should be verified if natural hand interaction is necessary or if physical manipulation devices (controllers, touch pads) are a better choice.

2. A second implication is that users of modern xR hardware must be trained to these devices. Many of our participants were xR novices, a training might have helped for better usability and user experience ratings.
3. As a third implication it is obvious to say that the most modern device is not necessarily the best solution to all problems. It always helps to follow the KISS-principle[4].

A limitation of our study is the small sample set of surveyed subjects. A larger number of participants could give a wider range of perspective and results - especially, if these were trained to device specific characteristics. Besides that, the number of possible interactions or capabilities of each platform could be increased. For example it would be possible to use hand tracking in PC-VR or gaze timer interaction in VR Cardboard or add a translational tracking to VR Cardboard. This would help to understand dis/advantages of such enhancements. Another limitation is the simple application task. Medical training of course are not limited to moving objects from A to B. More complex visualizations and interactive tasks could sharpen the view on results achieved here.

Each of the four platforms has very different interaction capabilities, device performance and immersion quality. So it must be questioned if these systems can be compared at all. Our intention was to think of a realistic stakeholder decision: Which device should we use to implement our application? We implemented the applications with the same visualizations, same virtual object behaviour and same user tasks. The intention of the used questionnaires SUS and UEQ is to compare different systems. Therefore we think, our approach is valuable.

7   Conclusion and Outlook

We were able to create interactive xR scenarios on the four xR platforms PC-VR, HoloLens 2, VR Cardboard and AR smartphone. All presented the same biomedical educational scenario. Participants were able to fulfill the required tasks on all four platforms to solve a puzzle of bones within a 3D model of human hand. The scene content the participants saw was same on each platform. The technique the participants used to achieve the interactions were different, depending on the device capabilities. By analysis of SUS and UEQ we were able to find differences in usability and user experience ratings between the platforms in various aspects.

In conclusion, different xR platforms can be compared to each other through same virtual object manipulation tasks. Depending on the use case even a simple xR device can be seen as more practical than a novel xR device like HoloLens 2.

Building on these results, we create a common framework for multi-user multi-platform xR experiences. This allows future users to decide for themselves which device to use in what use case and will allow seamless cross-platform collaboration. The far goal is to enable xR technology in a broad range of biomedical applications - with individual free choice of the xR platform per user.

---

[4] Keep It Simple, (and) Stupid!.

References

1. Alberola, C., Walter, G., Brau, H.: Creation of a short version of the user experience questionnaire UEQ. i-com **17**(1), 57–64 (2018)
2. Aliprantis, J., Konstantakis, M., Nikopoulou, R., Mylonas, P., Caridakis, G.: Natural interaction in augmented reality context. In: VIPERC@ IRCDL, pp. 50–61 (2019)
3. Bowman, D.A., Hodges, L.F.: An evaluation of techniques for grabbing and manipulating remote objects in immersive virtual environments. In: Proceedings of the 1997 Symposium on Interactive 3D Graphics, p. 35ff (1997)
4. Hürst, W., Van Wezel, C.: Gesture-based interaction via finger tracking for mobile augmented reality. Multimedia Tools Appl. **62**(1), 233–258 (2013)
5. Khor, W.S., Baker, B., Amin, K., Chan, A., Patel, K., Wong, J.: Augmented and virtual reality in surgery–the digital surgical environment: applications, limitations and legal pitfalls. Ann. Transl. Med. **4**(23) (2016)
6. Laugwitz, B., Held, T., Schrepp, M.: Construction and evaluation of a user experience questionnaire. In: Holzinger, A. (ed.) USAB 2008. LNCS, vol. 5298, pp. 63–76. Springer, Heidelberg (2008). https://doi.org/10.1007/978-3-540-89350-9_6
7. Milgram, P., Takemura, H., Utsumi, A., Kishino, F.: Augmented reality: a class of displays on the reality-virtuality continuum. In: Telemanipulator and Telepresence Technologies, vol. 2351, pp. 282–292. International Society for Optics and Photonics (1995)
8. Oh, J.Y., Park, J.H., Park, J.M.: Virtual object manipulation by combining touch and head interactions for mobile augmented reality. Appl. Sci. **9**(14), 2933 (2019)
9. Pantelidis, P., et al.: Virtual and augmented reality in medical education. In: Medical and Surgical Education-Past, Present and Future, pp. 77–97 (2018)
10. Pradini, R.S., Kriswibowo, R., Ramdani, F.: Usability evaluation on the sipr website uses the system usability scale and net promoter score. In: 2019 International Conference on Sustainable Information Engineering and Technology (SIET), pp. 280–284. IEEE (2019)
11. Preece, D., Williams, S.B., Lam, R., Weller, R.: "Let's get physical": advantages of a physical model over 3D computer models and textbooks in learning imaging anatomy. Anat. Sci. Educ. **6**(4), 216–224 (2013)
12. Pujol, S., Baldwin, M., Nassiri, J., Kikinis, R., Shaffer, K.: Using 3D modeling techniques to enhance teaching of difficult anatomical concepts. Acad. Radiol. **23**(4), 507–516 (2016)
13. Sauro, J.: Measuring usability with the system usability scale (SUS) (2011). https://measuringu.com/sus/
14. Schrepp, M.: User Experience Questionnaire Handbook (2019). https://www.ueq-online.org/Material/Handbook.pdf
15. Sutherland, J., et al.: Applying modern virtual and augmented reality technologies to medical images and models. J. Digit. Imaging **32**(1), 38–53 (2019)
16. Veldhuizen, M., Yang, X.: The effect of semi-transparent and interpenetrable hands on object manipulation in virtual reality. IEEE Access **9**, 17572–17583 (2021)
17. Weschke, D.: UEQ-user experience questionnaire: the UX testing tool that was here all this time-for free (2019)
18. Will, T.: Measuring and interpreting system usability scale (SUS) (2017). https://uiuxtrend.com/measuring-system-usability-scale-sus/

Simulation of the Field of View in AR and VR Headsets

Sarah Brauns[1] and Johannes Tümler[2]([envelope]) [iD]

[1] Volkswagen AG, Wolfsburg, Germany
sarah.brauns@volkswagen.de
[2] Anhalt University of Applied Sciences, Köthen, Germany
johannes.tuemler@hs-anhalt.de

Abstract. Technical parameters of today's Optical See-Through Head Mounted Displays (OST-HMDs) do not fully match the industrial requirements yet: Especially the small field of view (FoV) of current OST-HMDs is a hindrance for industrial use. The FoV is a technical parameter the user is always confronted with while the immersive experience of Augmented Reality takes place: It defines the extent of the observable augmented world where virtual objects can be perceived. This experience is limited by the augmented objects being cut off at the screen boundaries. This paper describes a scientific approach to simulate the FoV of OST-HMDs with the help of AR and VR devices. It aims at enabling tests and validation of necessary FoV-specifications of HMDs. Therefore, a study to simulate different FoVs and evaluate the necessary FoV size for manual two-handed automotive assembly tasks is presented. Results show significant differences in ratings between AR and VR but nearly no differences between the participant groups "AR/VR experts" and "assembly line workers".

Keywords: Augmented Reality · Virtual Reality · User Interfaces · Field of view · Manual assembly · Automotive industry · Head Mounted Display

1 Introduction

Industrial applications are longing for Optical See-Through Head-Mounted Displays (OST-HMDs) for many years already [4]. Advantages of such devices like working hands free and displaying the information directly where needed using Augmented Reality (AR) promise to simplify complex tasks, e.g. in manual assembly or training. Current hardware is still restrictive and limited, which conflicts with the straightforward use in industrial tasks [16]. In addition, the number of research studies in this area increases which is caused by a high interest in evaluation of the technology [7].

The aim of production industry, e.g. automotive, is not to develop HMDs themselves. They rather depend on HMDs developed by third party suppliers. But on the other hand this industry has a strong stakeholder's perspective on

© Springer Nature Switzerland AG 2021
J. Y. C. Chen and G. Fragomeni (Eds.): HCII 2021, LNCS 12770, pp. 288–300, 2021.
https://doi.org/10.1007/978-3-030-77599-5_21

configuration of useful HMDs. For suppliers of industrial HMDs it is inevitable to know these parameters and configurations to create suitable products. To assess parameters and configurations for suitable HMDs it is necessary to develop adequate tools in cooperation with future users. These must be able to estimate the potential of a HMD for specific usecases before it comes to market. In this paper, we present an approach to verify specifications relevant for industrial use before the technology is ready.

2   Related Work

2.1   Evaluations of Head Mounted Displays in Industrial Applications

De Souza Cardoso et al. [3] give a comprehensive overview on industrial use of AR and HMDs. They conclude *"that they [HMDs] still need some technological improvements (...). Ergonomics and legal aspects of their usage is still unknown, so they represent a significant risk to companies employing the device"*. Thus, a general large implementation of HMDs in industrial or automotive processes did not happen until now. Further investigations on all related topics (application, user, technology) are required.

One key element that is necessary to enable high quality interactive AR is tracking. Besides academic research on that topic there even is industry-focused research of automotive industry itself [26]. Another important aspect of current HMD research is the user interface, which was addressed for example by Blattgerste et al. [2] and Renner et al. [21]. Theis et al. [25] and Grubert et al. [8] carried out studies on effects of the technology on user's strain and describe shortcomings in ergonomic aspects. Henderson and Feiner [11] as well as Khuong et al. [14] present examples on HMD applications for manual assembly.

Besides public articles like those, industry has developed own best practices for use of AR and HMDs. Often large industrial 10,000+ employee companies have multiple distinct development teams that create solutions or demonstrators for internal use. Usually that knowledge is not discussed in public but could be extrapolated from patent applications (e.g. [5,17]). The authors of this paper belong to that group and have a 15+ years history working on AR applications for industrial corporations and therefore developed own best practices for industrial use of HMDs.

Our view on the current state of "HMDs for industrial use" is the following:

- HMD-based applications must be developed together with potential future users from beginning to end of the project.
- AR-support is not implemented "for fun". Not all applications need AR-support or HMDs. Sometimes the technology seduces project engineers or decision makers.
- HMD suppliers tend to create devices where "one device fits all needs". From our experience, there are big differences between all sorts of applications. Thus, specific or customizable HMDs are required.

- Success in an application does not come from advanced technical parameters of AR or a HMD. It rather is a mix of addressing user's needs, workflow integration and respect of company regulations.
- In general it is not clear which parameters of a device are most relevant for different manual assembly tasks.

Especially that last item is important to know for developers of industrial HMD applications and has no satisfactory answer yet. Further research is necessary.

2.2   Simulation of Augmented Reality

HMD parameters could be examined in AR and VR or combined scenarios. Combining AR and Virtual Reality (VR) is not new. Wafaa et al. [27] were one of the first to develop an architecture for an AR simulation in VR. They evaluated the effects of the simulation on a systemic level using simple test scenarios. Ware et al. [28] evaluated different FoVs of Video See-Through (VST) AR systems. They could show that a limited FoV reduces task performance. Based on this work, Steindecker et al. [24] put a focus on the design of optics of an AR system. In a similar scenario, Alce et al. [1] stated that usability problems in VR can have negative impact on the evaluation of the simulated AR system.

One limitation of VR simulations is that haptic feedback is usually missing or limited to, e.g. to rumble feedback [19]. Still, there are reports about experiments including haptic feedback which were conducted in large screen installation and video-based streaming of simulated AR content to mobile devices. These experiments, however, require expensive hardware and may suffer from high latencies [20,22].

In addition, the human perception differs between AR and VR: Looking at virtual objects causes more fatigue to user's eyes than real objects would do [6]. This must be considered when dealing with augmenting industrial tasks and simulating AR in VR. The FoV itself can be directly linked to the estimation of distance [12]. A small FoV supports an underestimation of object distances in virtual environments.

The validity of the Mixed Reality Simulation approach for AR system design has been addressed by several studies [11]. Using a CAVE-based AR simulation system, Gupta et al. [9] could replicate a prior AR experiment on the effects between latency and performance and found that a potential latency of the VR simulation (not a latency between movement and AR registration) had little to no effect on task performance. Lee et al. [15] found that differences in visual realism regarding three levels of geometry, texture and lighting, all in the same style, did not have an effect on task performance in VR. However, visual realism could affect validation: In their examples high and low contrast lighting areas were difficult in the physical conditions, challenges that were not simulated in their Mixed Reality (MR) condition.

3   Method and Study Design

In our work, we build upon reported experiences. Section 2.1 described that for each type of industrial application different needs must be addressed. One main application we focus on is manual two-handed assembly because high potential for production is known [18]. For this application we used a questionnaire to evaluate, which parameter of a current AR-HMD limits manufacturing tasks most. We asked 20 AR-experts from different industrial areas and companies (e.g. automotive, marine, aeronautics; company names may not be printed) to rate characteristics of an OST-HMD for a manual assembly use case. They were given 15 parameters of OST-HMDs and had to rank them regarding their relevance for the use case from one (lowest relevance) to 15 (highest relevance).

Table 1. Relevance (least: 1 to most: 15) of visualization parameters for an industrial assembly usecase. Mean represents averaged relevance, minimum represents minimal rated relevance, maximum represents maximal rated relevance over all participants.

HMD-parameter	Ranking	Mean	Min	Max	SD
Stable tracking	15	12.79	1	15	2.82
FoV	14	11.00	2	15	3.46
Latency	13	10.66	2	15	3.68
Focal plane	12	10.59	2	15	3.60
Resolution	11	9.17	1	15	3.90
Stereo-display	10	9.03	2	15	3.99
Frame rate	09	8.79	2	14	3.33
Adjustment of IPD	08	7.34	1	15	3.62
Brightness	07	6.86	2	14	2.87
Form of visualization	06	6.69	1	15	4.01
Size of eyebox	05	6.28	1	15	3.77
Transmission	04	6.41	2	13	3.68
Contrast	03	6.38	1	14	2.43
Black level	02	4.24	1	14	3.50
Color space	01	3.97	1	15	3.95

Table 1 presents results of the questionnaire. The most relevant parameter that limits the use of OST-HMDs in assembly tasks is stable tracking, according to the experts. Tracking is subject to research for many scientific and industry groups, e.g. [26]. Therefore, we focused our research on the second most important parameter, the limited FoV.

The study intended to find the minimum necessary FoV that helps to fulfill a typical manual two-handed assembly task. So we limited the field of view of one AR device used to simulate other smaller-FoV HMDs. At the same time we wanted to know if simulating AR in VR (see Sect. 2.2) would produce the same results compared to AR-only. This is interesting for industry because often the physical assembly stations are expensive, in daily use and exist only in limited numbers per factory. If an AR simulation in VR would create the same results then future "AR simulations" could be carried out without influence on current ongoing production.

Within industry, there are many parameters such as noise and lighting conditions or danger by moving objects that all have an effect on the participants and their way of interaction with the HMD and displayed information. It is not possible to keep those conditions stable during a scientific experiment without monetary consequences for the ongoing real production. For that reason the study was carried out in stable industrial laboratory conditions (noise, light, temperature, time, work tasks). Every user was shown the same scene with the same environmental conditions.

There is a high variability of part structures and sizes at the assembly line. As a typical two-handed automotive assembly process we chose the vehicle door assembly. This had two big advantages in contrast to other possible assembly parts: The portability and availability of the parts for laboratory use and the different parts in size and geometry which had to be assembled. Besides that, this task was discussed internally as a potential candidate for future support by AR glasses.

We used a within-subject design to get an assessment of all simulated FoVs for each person. Thus, participants could directly compare the same FoV in AR to the VR visualization. One of our experiences from previous experiments is that the UX and usability rating differs between AR/VR experts and assembly line workers. For that reason half of our subjects came from assembly line, the other half were company-internal AR/VR experts from different departments. Moreover, different experience levels could be compared when repeating the assembly several times. This enabled participants to rate the different FoVs according to the specific use case in comparison to the combinations that were already tested.

4   Implementation

There are numerous OST-HMDs on the market. Not many of them are suitable for industrial tasks, e.g. regarding robustness or computing performance. Three HMDs have typical FoV values that could be used in industry: The Epson BT-300 with 23° FoV, the Microsoft Hololens (1) with 35° FoV and the ODG R7 with 50° FoV (all diagonal FoVs).

Table 2 describes all seven possible setups the participants had to use in randomized order: Two in "real AR" and five "VR-simulated AR". At the time of the study we were not able to use the HoloLens 2. The FoVs of 23° (see Epson BT-300) and 35° (see HoloLens 1) were visualized with the help of the Microsoft HoloLens in AR and the HTC Vive for VR. Moreover, we also visualized the FoV of 50° (see Dreamglass), 90° (see Oculus Rift) and 110° (see HTC Vive) using the HTC Vive in VR to evaluate forseeable future FoVs of AR headsets.

Table 2. Different combinations of diagonal FoVs in AR and VR used in the study for supporting the assembly scenario (yes: FoV was evaluated with the device, no: FoV could not be evaluated with the device due to its spec limitations)

HMD	23° FoV (Reference: Epson BT-300)	35° FoV (Reference: MS HoloLens)	50° FoV (Reference: Dreamglass)	90° FoV (Reference: Oculus Rift)	110° FoV (Reference: HTC Vive)
Microsoft HoloLens	Yes	Yes	No	No	No
HTC Vive	Yes	Yes	Yes	Yes	Yes

The simulation used Unity3D (2017.4) to present virtual information in AR and VR. The scene was modeled in Unity with 3D-models of the real parts and a roughly reproduced surrounding. To simulate the limited FoV a self-implemented clipping shader was used on assembly-relevant virtual objects. Participants were shown where and in which way the parts had to be positioned and fixed. This was visualized by virtual installation animations that showed the virtual parts move correctly into their final position. These animations were derived from the real instruction manual.

– For the AR condition the Microsoft HoloLens (1) was used at 60 fps. Virtual objects were registered to the physical door by using 3D to 3D correspondences [10,13] on the native HoloLens tracking. The real vehicle door and the real parts that had to be assembled by hands of the user as well as the real tools to fulfill the assembly task were provided. The next step could be activated by voice command (Fig. 1, top).
– For the VR condition the HTC Vive was used on a PC with a nVidia P6000 videocard at 90 fps. Only the "AR objects" were clipped by the shader whereas the virtual environment was still completely visible on the complete FoV of the HTC Vive. The participants used the Vive controllers which gave haptic feedback while fixing screws and at collision with virtual objects. The next step was activated automatically when the part was assembled (Fig. 1, bottom).

A 3D path implemented according to experiences of Schwerdtfeger et al. [23] supported by textual instructions was used to show where the real part had to be placed. We made sure that for each FoV it was possible to see enough of the AR-instructions to fulfill the work task by asking production experts during the study design. The task outcome (duration, errors) were not measured in accordance with internal work council guidelines.

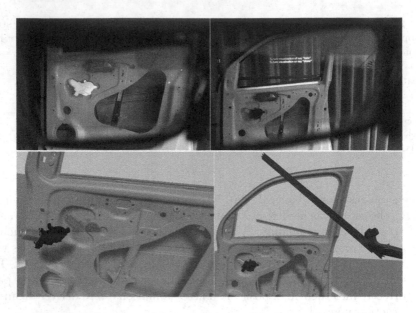

Fig. 1. Assembly guidance in AR in the Microsoft HoloLens (top) and in VR in the HTC Vive (bottom, clipped "AR" object in blue) (Color figure online)

5   Procedure

The study followed a within-subject design and incorporated 26 male and female volunteers that got no compensation for their participation. All were internal employees. 13 of them were AR-experts either for development or use of AR and VR in automotive processes. 13 were workers from internal automotive production lines which had little to no experience with the technology but knew the specific assembly process very well.

Before using any of the AR/VR devices statistical data and previous experience with AR/VR was recorded through a questionnaire. Afterward, the used AR/VR technologies as well as the necessary tasks were explained. Users got some minutes for familiarization in a non-related AR/VR scenario and had time to ask questions. When the participant felt ready the assembly tasks started. Every participant was working on the task with all seven conditions (two different AR-FoVs and five different "VR-simulated AR"-FoVs) in a random order.

The assembly had two main parts. For a complete assembly, participants had to place the window lift motor at the right position and fix it with three screws to the door body using two hands. Then, they had to clip the window shaft seal. This had to be done seven times in total, each time with a different FoV-size on either the AR- (with two different FoV-sizes) or the VR-HMD (with five different FoV-sizes). The order of devices and FoVs was randomized equally for the group.

After each complete assembly in AR or VR, a questionnaire in German language was filled out by the participants. Participants had to rate the following questions on a Likert scale from 1 to 5. For this paper we translated the questions to English:

- Q1: How do you rate the execution of the given task with the HMD? (very easy (1) to very difficult (5))
- Q2: How was the effect of the displayed FoV for supporting the given task? (very helpful (1) to very cumbersome (5))
- Q3: How restrictive felt the displayed FoV for the given task? (very restrictive (1) to not restrictive at all (5))
- Q4: How much did you change your behavior and movements due to the HMD? (very much (1) to not at all (5))
- Q5: How supportive was the HMD with the displayed FoV for the given task? (very supportive (1) to not supportive at all (5))

6 Hypotheses

The study intended to identify the minimum FoV that is necessary to support the automotive assembly task in a useful manner.

Due to differences in AR systems compared to VR systems we expected a difference in ratings for AR and VR. This resulted in the following hypotheses that we examined by analysis of the questionnaires of the two participant groups:

H1   Rating of our specific work task is different for "real AR" compared to "VR-simulated AR" for at least one of our questions Q1–Q5.

For HoloLens (1) we experienced in previous internal evaluations that a 35° FoV is not suitable for most two-handed assembly tasks. In our Q2 a rating of 2 ("helpful") or lower should be achieved. Hence:

H2   The FoV 35° will be rated as insufficient (Q2 larger than 2.0) both in "real AR" and "VR-simulated AR".

We also expected that for the two different groups of participants with diverse experiences either regarding the assembly task or the interaction with AR and VR their evaluation would differ as well:

H3   Regardless of personal experience, workers and AR/VR experts rate visualization characteristics and their limits in the same way.

7 Results

Overall, the results between AR and VR were divergent. The same assembly task was rated significantly different for AR and VR (see Table 3). The statistical analysis of the results in the form of a t-test of dependent samples shows that participants rated the FoV of 35° very different for the Microsoft HoloLens compared to the HTC Vive. For the FoV of 23° condition, the results were also

Table 3. t-test of dependent samples for the comparison of AR and VR question pairs (group dependency given (all participants rated the seven combinations), variables interval scalabe (rating scale the same over all five questions), difference of paired values normally distributed (difference in between AR and VR))

Pairs	Mean difference	SD	Significance*
AR Q1 vs. VR Q1	0.75	0.95	**p = 0.001**
AR Q2 vs. VR Q2	0.69	1.2	**p = 0.007**
AR Q3 vs. VR Q3	0.69	1.06	**p = 0.003**
AR Q4 vs. VR Q4	0.35	0.87	p = 0.053
AR Q5 vs. VR Q5	0.71	1.12	**p = 0.003**

* (significance level 5%)

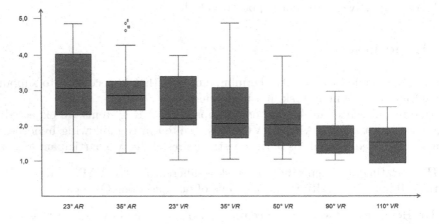

Fig. 2. Box plot for the question: How supportive do you rate the given FoV for the assembly task? (not supportive at all (5) to very supportive (1))

divergent. Only for one of five questions, the participants did not rate a significant difference between AR and VR.

Thus, the evaluation shows that for visualizing the FoV of an AR OST-HMD with the help of VR there is a high probability that AR in VR will be rated differently compared to "real AR". Hypotheses **H1** cannot be rejected. The conclusion is that in general characteristics of an AR-HMD should not be tested in a VR-environment or at least results of such evaluations should be handled with care. Moreover, the ergonomics of HMDs need to be developed further so that users can behave normally while using these devices.

Figure 2 corresponds with **H1**. AR-FoVs were rated worse than similar "VR-simulated AR"-FoVs. All in all, the rating got better (closer to 1.0) the bigger the displayed FoV was. Both for AR and VR the 23° and 35° the rating if Q2 did not reach a value smaller than 2.0 and **H2** should not be rejected. In addition, the result of Q2 shows that the FoV of 50° and upwards, the support of the given task was rated more helpful (at least 2.0) than with the smaller FoVs.

There was a significant difference in ratings for the support (Q5) and the limitation of the FoV (Q3) between the participant experience groups. Table 4 presents a statistical analysis for Q3 and Q5 between the AR/VR expert group and the assembly experts. As an example the values for 50° FoV give a significant difference between the two user groups. For future studies it is important to always consider the target group for the task to be supported (in this case the production experts). A rating by technological experts is not representative and can be misleading. **H3** must be rejected.

Table 4. Man-Whitney-U-test of independent samples for group affiliation, question and FoV

Null hypothesis	Question	Significance**
The distribution of 50° FoV and Q5 is the same over the categories E/P*	How supportive was the HMD with the displayed FoV for the given task?	**p = 0.044**
The distribution of 50° FoV and Q3 is the same over the categories E/P*	How restrictive felt the displayed FoV for the given task?	**p = 0.019**

*E: expert, P: production employee; **(significance level 5%)

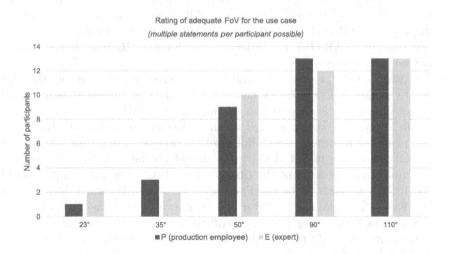

Fig. 3. Rating of adequate FoV for the use case (one statement per participant)

Figure 3 shows the rating of the different FoVs regarding their fit for the given task and answers the fifth question Q5. More than 50% of the participants assessed the FoV of 50° as being adequate for the given vehicle door assembly task. All larger FoVs were rated as supportive. Smaller FoVs were mostly perceived as a hindrance. The results need to be validated with an OST-HMD and a FoV of 50° in the future.

8   Discussion and Conclusion

This study addressed three topics:

1. Compare user evaluations in "VR-simulated AR" and "real AR"
2. Compare AR/VR evaluations of two user groups "AR/VR experts" and "assembly line workers"
3. Find clues on which FoV is required for manual assembly tasks

(1) This paper shows the parameter 'FoV' can be tested with an AR and a VR-simulated AR scenario, but will be rated differently between those. Reasons might lay a limited view on reality through the opaque AR display frame, poor resolution per degree of the VR display compared to the HoloLens, self-glowing of only the virtual information (AR) or the full visualization (VR) and interaction devices (VR controller vs. real hands and tools in AR). Participants could easily distinguish between the two worlds in AR and the limited FoV was standing out more. Especially the clipped FoV was difficult to evaluate in VR as there was no offset or time lag in between the VR-simulated AR objects and the virtual static objects. With the HoloLens "real AR" there always was a small but noticable time lag (latency) of the AR visualization while moving around the real physical object. Therefore it seems not plausible that a static transfer function exists that would convert results of a VR-simulation into an AR-compatible result. If the target display is an AR OST-HMD then technical parameters should be evaluated using an actual AR OST-HMD device - results of a VR-simulated AR might not be transferable.

(2) The two experts groups rated the FoVs differently which means that for future studies it is absolutely necessary to consider the assessment of the target group that is supposed to be supported by AR.

(3) In our study a 50° FoV was rated as "large enough" by technical AR experts and production employees to fulfill a vehicle door assembly task, when using an AR simulation in VR. This result should not be transferred to general assembly tasks because of the discussed limitations of the comparison of AR in VR. It needs to be validated with an AR-HMD which has at least 50° FoV, e.g. HoloLens 2. Nevertheless, it proves that the FoV of 35° of the Microsoft HoloLens (1) is not sufficient enough for the chosen typical automotive assembly task because the augmented sight is too limited for that kind of use case.

The transferability of the results must be validated in further studies, industries and scenarios. Moreover, our recommendation is to continue this study within future research with different tasks and a bigger assembly-expert user group to avoid repetition effects when executing the same task several times.

References

1. Alce, G., Hermodsson, K., Wallergård, M., Thern, L., Hadzovic, T.: A prototyping method to simulate wearable augmented reality interaction in a virtual environment - a pilot study. Int. J. Virtual World Hum. Comput. Interact. **3**, 18–28 (2015). https://doi.org/10.11159/vwhci.2015.003
2. Blattgerste, J., Strenge, B., Renner, P., Pfeiffer, T., Essig, K.: Comparing conventional and augmented reality instructions for manual assembly tasks. In: Proceedings of the 10th International Conference on Pervasive Technologies Related to Assistive Environments (PETRA 2017), pp. 75–82 (2017). https://doi.org/10.1145/3056540.3056547
3. De Souza Cardoso, L.F., Mariano, F., Zorzal, E.: A survey of industrial augmented reality. Comput. Ind. Eng. **139**, 106159 (2019). https://doi.org/10.1016/j.cie.2019.106159
4. Friedrich, W.: ARVIKA - augmented reality for development, production and service. In: Proceedings of the International Symposium on Mixed and Augmented Reality (ISMAR 2002), pp. 3–4 (2002)
5. Fuchs, V., Kamradt, M., Peters, A.: Device and method for the visual support of a user in a working environment (patent application DE102017219067A1) (2019)
6. Gao, Y., Liu, Y., Normand, J.M., Moreau, G., Gao, X., Wang, Y.: A study on differences in human perception between a real and an AR scene viewed in an OST-HMD. J. Soc. Inf. Disp. **27**(3), 155–171 (2019). https://doi.org/10.1002/jsid.752
7. Gialos, A., Zeimpekis, V.: Defining and testing system parameters for enhancing vision picking technology in warehouse operations. Int. J. Logist. Syst. Manag. **11**(1), 19–30 (2020)
8. Grubert, J., et al.: Extended investigations of user-related issues in mobile industrial AR. In: 2010 IEEE International Symposium on Mixed and Augmented Reality, pp. 229 230 (2010). https://doi.org/10.1109/ISMAR.2010.5643581
9. Gupta, A., Fox, D., Curless, B., Cohen, M.: DuploTrack: a real-time system for authoring and guiding duplo block assembly. In: UIST 2012 - Proceedings of the 25th Annual ACM Symposium on User Interface Software and Technology, pp. 389–402 (2012). https://doi.org/10.1145/2380116.2380167
10. Hartley, R., Zisserman, A.: Multiple View Geometry in Computer Vision. Cambridge University Press, Cambridge (2004)
11. Henderson, S., Feiner, S.: Exploring the benefits of augmented reality documentation for maintenance and repair. IEEE Trans. Visual Comput. Graphics **17**, 1355–1368 (2011). https://doi.org/10.1109/TVCG.2010.245
12. Jones, J., Ii, J., Bolas, M.: Peripheral stimulation and its effect on perceived spatial scale in virtual environments. IEEE Trans. Visual Comput. Graphics **19**, 701–10 (2013). https://doi.org/10.1109/TVCG.2013.37
13. Kellner, F., Bolte, B., Bruder, G., Rautenberg, U., Steinicke, F., Lappe, M., Koch, R.: Geometric calibration of head-mounted displays and its effects on distance estimation. IEEE Trans. Visual Comput. Graphics **18**(4), 589–596 (2012)
14. Khuong, B., Kiyokawa, K., Miller, A., Viola, J., Mashita, T., Takemura, H.: The effectiveness of an AR-based context-aware assembly support system in object assembly. In: Proceedings of the IEEE Virtual Reality Conference 2014, pp. 57–62 (2014). https://doi.org/10.1109/VR.2014.6802051
15. Lee, C., Rincon, G.A., Meyer, G., Höllerer, T., Bowman, D.A.: The effects of visual realism on search tasks in mixed reality simulation. IEEE Trans. Visual Comput. Graphics **19**(4), 547–556 (2013)

16. Miller, J.: Overcoming the limitations of commodity augmented reality head mounted displays for use in product assembly. Master's thesis, Iowa State University (2019)
17. Peacock, J.L., Watsonand, J.J., Wilcox, S.M.: Augmented reality assembly assistance and monitoring (patent application US10366521) (2019)
18. Radkowski, R., Herrema, J., Oliver, J.: Augmented reality-based manual assembly support with visual features for different degrees of difficulty. Int. J. Hum.-Comput. Interact. **31**, 337–349 (2015). https://doi.org/10.1080/10447318.2014.994194
19. Ragan, E., Wilkes, C., Bowman, D., Höllerer, T.: Simulation of augmented reality systems in purely virtual environments. In: IEEE Virtual Reality Conference, pp. 287–288 (2009). https://doi.org/10.1109/VR.2009.4811058
20. Ren, D., Goldschwendt, T., Chang, Y., Höllerer, T.: Evaluating wide-field-of-view augmented reality with mixed reality simulation. In: Proceedings of the IEEE Virtual Reality Conference 2016, pp. 93–102 (2016). https://doi.org/10.1109/VR.2016.7504692
21. Renner, P., Pfeiffer, T.: Evaluation of attention guiding techniques for augmented reality-based assistance in picking and assembly tasks. In: Proceedings of the 22nd International Conference on Intelligent User Interfaces Companion, pp. 89–92 (2017). https://doi.org/10.1145/3030024.3040987
22. Rodriguez, L., Quint, F., Gorecky, D., Romero, D., Siller, H.: Developing a mixed reality assistance system based on projection mapping technology for manual operations at assembly workstations. Procedia Comput. Sci. **75**, 327–333 (2015). https://doi.org/10.1016/j.procs.2015.12.254
23. Schwerdtfeger, B., et al.: Pick-by-vision: a first stress test. In: 2009 8th IEEE International Symposium on Mixed and Augmented Reality, pp. 115–124. IEEE (2009)
24. Steindecker, E., Stelzer, R., Saske, B.: Requirements for virtualization of AR displays within VR environments. In: Shumaker, R., Lackey, S. (eds.) VAMR 2014. LNCS, vol. 8525, pp. 105–116. Springer, Cham (2014). https://doi.org/10.1007/978-3-319-07458-0_11
25. Theis, S., Mertens, A., Wille, M., Rasche, P., Alexander, T., Schlick, C.: Effects of data glasses on human workload and performance during assembly and disassembly tasks. In: Proceedings 19th Triennial Congress of the IEA, vol. 9, pp. 14–21 (2015)
26. Thiel, K., Jundt, E., Klinker, G.: [POSTER] automated evaluation and configuration of object tracking for augmented reality. In: 2017 IEEE International Symposium on Mixed and Augmented Reality Adjunct Proceedings, pp. 132–134 (2017). https://doi.org/10.1109/ISMAR-Adjunct.2017.48
27. Wafaa, A., de Bonnefoy, N., Dubois, E., Torguet, P., Jessel, J.P.: Virtual reality simulation for prototyping augmented reality. In: International Symposium on Ubiquitous Virtual Reality (ISUVR 2008), pp. 55–58 (2008). https://doi.org/10.1109/ISUVR.2008.9
28. Ware, C.: Information Visualization: Perception for Design, 3rd edn. Morgan Kaufmann Publishers Inc., San Francisco (2012)

Exploring Perspective Switching in Immersive VR for Learning First Aid in Lower Secondary Education

Tone Lise Dahl[1]([✉]) [ID], Olve Storlykken[2], and Bård H. Røssehaug[2]

[1] SINTEF Digital, S.P. Andersens veg 5, 7034 Trondheim, Norway
`tone.lise.dahl@sintef.no`
[2] Making View, Grønnegata 83, 2317 Hamar, Norway
`{os,br}@makingview.com`

Abstract. There is an increased interest in how immersive learning can be used to support educational practices. Immersive virtual reality (IVR) with head-mounted displays (HMDs) is a technology that provides for immersive and smart learning environments where learners can interact and participate in an entirely virtual world. Based on literature and lessons learned from an ongoing research project, we identify potential benefits and challenges by incorporating perspective switching in an immersive VR application with. The VR application will be used to teach and stimulate learning within first aid in lower secondary education. The overall goal is to develop a user-centered VR application through Participatory Design (PD). The main contribution of this paper is a conceptual framework and guidelines for the process of developing IVR where users can switch between a first-person perspective and a third-person perspective.

Keywords: Immersive VR · Perspective switching · 360-degree video

1 Introduction

Virtual Reality (VR) is a technology that can immerse people into a computer-generated reality, where they can view and engage in 360-degree videos or 3D animations. There is an increased interest in using immersive learning for educational practices, e.g. by using simulations, educational games, and serious games [1, 2]. The potential for VR to revolutionize education has been discussed for decades. However, publicly available and affordable IVR with HMDs is a relatively recent phenomenon [3]. It was not until affordable versions of HMDs were introduced that the technology reached a required level to be applied in education at large [4].

With immersive virtual reality (IVR) with head-mounted displays (HMDs), immersive and smart learning environments can be created. The users can experience a range from passive to more interactive experiences, e.g., by only looking around in the virtual world or by navigating and manipulating virtual objects [3]. Because of the feeling of presence, motivation, enjoyment, and immediacy of control, students seem to prefer IVR compared to desktop VR [5]. By using game engines and gamification elements to

© Springer Nature Switzerland AG 2021
J. Y. C. Chen and G. Fragomeni (Eds.): HCII 2021, LNCS 12770, pp. 301–316, 2021.
https://doi.org/10.1007/978-3-030-77599-5_22

create user interactivity, high learning rates can be achieved [1]. Learners can explore environments freely, and exploration is one of the key strengths of game-based learning [2].

As part of an ongoing research project, we are exploring the use of perspective switching in an IVR application for learning first aid for pupils in lower secondary education. Hence, the research question for this paper is: *"What benefits and challenges can be identified when incorporating perspective switching in an immersive virtual reality (IVR) application with 360-degree video?"*. Based on literature and lessons learned from the R&D- project, we propose a conceptual framework and guidelines for incorporating perspective switching in IVR applications.

2 Research Context

The research context for this paper is an R&D project where a municipality wants to explore the use of immersive VR as a learning technology. A VR application is being developed to teach and stimulate learning within first aid. The overall goal is to develop a user-centered VR application through Participatory Design (PD). Therefore, project partners and pupils are involved in the design process. This is in alignment with the core tenet of the PD by giving those who are destined to use the product a critical role in its design. PD is characterized as a process of reciprocal learning, co-realization, and the sharing of decision-making power among relevant stakeholders in the design process [6]. The final VR application will be used within the interdisciplinary topic "health and life skills" for pupils aged 13–16 years old at lower secondary education. The VR application is expected to improve the pupils' ability to make good risk assessments and subsequent decisions in critical real-life situations by enabling them to recognize and act appropriately in emergency situations. By using virtual reality, students can learn first aid by being exposed to real-life scenarios in a virtual environment where they feel a sense of presence, that otherwise would not have been possible due to resources, risks, and ethical reasons [7]. The project partners consist of a municipality (school owner), two schools, a production company, the National Association for Heart and Lung Diseases, and an independent research institute.

We wanted to explore incorporating perspective switching in the virtual environment based on several reasons. We wanted the pupils to play a character through a first-person view and to be able to interact in the virtual environment so they can feel a high sense of presence, embodiment, and immersion. By enabling the pupils to make choices on behalf of a character we could reduce the number of choices and create choices that seem realistic for the character. Our hypothesis was that this might reduce frustration for not having access to all different kinds of options the different pupils might feel would represent themself the most. We also had an assumption that having the ability to experience the character from another perspective can create a different experience and enable reflection and in-depth learning. Also, sharing reflections about their own experiences in front of peers in a classroom might feel private considering that identity formation, negotiating social status, and acceptance are pertinent processes for many adolescents [8]. Enabling pupils to talk about the subject based on a character instead of their own choices might help to reduce this potential challenge.

3   Theoretical Background

Immersive Virtual Reality as a Learning Technology
There are many learning benefits and affordances with using immersive VR with HMDs in education, as well as challenges related to embedding it into classrooms. Based on the SMADICT framework, successful use of VR as a learning technology in education requires a combination of technological knowledge, content knowledge, pedagogical knowledge, didactical considerations, and external factors like technical support, personal learning network, and support from school management [7].

The rationale of using VR for learning and training is often based on learning theories like constructivism and situated learning, e.g., for training first aid and reanimation [9]. The use of VR can support an experiential learning process where pupils can recognize virtual experiences as direct experiences [10, 11]. Interest, motivation, self-efficacy, embodiment, cognitive load, and self-regulation are six affective and cognitive factors that can lead to IVR-based learning outcomes [12]. Presence and agency have been identified as the general psychological affordances of learning in IVR. A sense of agency is described as the feeling of generating and controlling actions, while presence can be described as a feeling of being there in the virtual environment. The three technological factors immersion, control factors, and representational fidelity are important factors for a sense of presence in virtual environments. Also, control factors, e.g., being able to control the body representation and modify the environment and its objects are regarded as the most important predictor of agency [12].

To be able to reap the benefits of this technology, one should aim to minimize the feeling of symptoms of discomfort produced by VR exposure (cybersickness) and maximize the experience of presence [13]. Immersive storytelling and cinematic virtual reality (CVR) are two potential methods to achieve that.

Cinematic Virtual Reality and Immersive Storytelling with 360° Videos
Storytelling is a method of presenting information through a coherent story and might present itself in many forms. With VR, you can create unique experiences, but it is a complex process since established rules for filmmaking do not apply to VR and 360-degree films[14]. To shoot a 360-degree video, equipment like a spherical camera with a 360-degree lens, drones, and 360 microphones can be used. For post-production, there might be a need for an editing software to bring all the footage in one piece and ensure high quality of visuals. 360-degree video does not have a defined frame, but the viewer still has a personal frame, or field of view (FoV). In 360-degree videos, users are often limited to viewing. There is however a range of complexity and interactivity, from simple 360-degree live action where the viewers can make limited choices concerning their field of view, to more complex stories with choice points for branching narratives that are selected by the viewer [15].

For 360-degree videos, immersion is based on spatial aspects. It includes an interplay of temporal, spatio-temporal, and emotional immersion [16]. Spatial immersion is mostly a visual aspect. The aspect shows the place and time of the story by using narrative elements like characters' dialogues or actions. Temporal immersion centers on the story, the plot's structure, and set expectations. Spatio-temporal immersion builds on the story world. It is partly determined by characters and their actions. It includes the integration of the viewer in multiple forms: as a character in the first-person Point of View (POV), or as a viewer as a second-person Point of View (POV). A switch between POVs serves a narrative purpose. It can increase plausibility or give more information. Emotional immersion is linked to temporal immersion. This type of immersion is driven by conflicts between characters or consequences of the character's actions [16].

Cinematic Virtual Reality (CVR) has become a more common method in storytelling where stories are told in a 360° sphere. Instead of creating a computer-generated, game-engine-based world, CVR aims to create immersive experiences of real-world scenes [17]. The viewer can compose their own story by choosing the FOV. This enables new creative methods for storytelling. However, people can be afraid of missing out on essential aspects of the story, so it might be necessary to guide the viewer to increase the enjoyment of CVR [17]. By using sound, lighted objects, and movement, the attention of the viewer can be directed [18].

There are few scientific studies about the differences between classical filmmaking and filmmaking in 360 and VR. However, Gödde et al. [14] describe six major challenges for cinematic narration in VR. The challenges are related to guiding the user's attention, choosing the role of the viewer and the right place for cameras and story elements, balancing story density, and rethinking both framing and editing [14]. Dooley [15] highlights the need to place the viewer at the center of the VR narrative. With VR one must consider the viewer's free will, and at the same time aim to guide them down a predetermined path. Since the VR viewer can be an active agent or a more passive witness, the creator might face several challenges and opportunities when considering viewer immersion and interaction in the 360-degree environment. The role of the viewer is a major challenge, and it is recommended to define the role of the viewer very clearly as only an observer with no connection to the scene or the viewer as part of the scene [14].

The Role of the Viewer
There are advantages in using different perspectives, e.g., first-person perspective (1PP) and third-person perspective (3PP). Evaluating the effect of 1PP and 3PP in gameplay experiences via the new generation of HMD systems is an unexplored topic [19]. It seems like 3PP is preferred in action games with a protagonist roaming in a virtual world. The design of HMDs spontaneously inspires a 1PP and seems like a perfect option for VR to immerse people into the story. However, a 3PP is more suitable when there is a need for more macroscopic information of the environment [20]. Both perspectives enable a high spatial presence feeling, but the best condition to induce a sense of embodiment toward a virtual body seems to be through 1PP [21]. By using 1PP one can enable maximal user inclusion within the virtual environment and provide for more suitable conditions for the accuracy of interactions. By using 3PP one can improve spatial awareness and perception of the virtual environment [21]. Monteiro et al. [19] found that 3PP-VR is less likely to make people have simulator sickness when compared with 1PP-VR. However, the former is not perceived as immersive, but this might not be a problem because presence

is not mandatory for enjoyment. Their findings suggest that there is no clear preference between 1PP-VR and 3PP-VR for gameplay.

Perspective Taking

Understanding other people's thoughts, feelings, and intentions is considered critical in social life. Perspective taking is described as the ability to look beyond your point of view. This enables you to consider other´s thoughts and feelings. Batson [22] describes perspective taking as an imaginative act of perceiving another person from a point of view that differs from your original point of view [22]. An important difference in the way people understand story characters is whether they take an actor's or an observer's perspective. When taking an observer's perspective, people observe the character's behaviors and maintain a separate self-identify from the character. When taking an actor´s perspective, people actively participate in the behavior [23].

There has been some previous research that has examined perspective taking and perspective switching in VR in recent years. Aitamurto et al. [17] examined the sense of presence, attitude change, perspective-taking, and usability of a split-sphere, first-person perspective 360-degree video for Cinematic Virtual Reality (CVR). A first person 360-degree video with good enough usability with access to two perspectives can be effective for perspective taking. Switching between the two perspectives may enhance the impact of perspective taking, particularly when the film is shot from a first-person perspective and filmed from the main characters' point of view. However, usability issues, such as difficulty following the narrative, a fear of missing out and concern about missing the full story (FOMO), can challenge the user experience [17].

Cmentowski et al. [24] explored giving players the ability to switch from a first-person to a third-person god-mode perspective in games. Players could use first-person point-of-view to experience the world like they are used to, and the third-person mode to watch and command their avatar from a bird's eye perspective. This allowed the players to cover larger distances easily. Cmentowski et al. [24] claim that this technique increased the perceived presence and did not lead to cybersickness compared to established techniques. The proposed dynamic switching was intuitive and increased spatial orientation and allowed players to maintain a high degree of presence throughout the game.

4   Lessons Learned

Participatory Design (PD) is the methodology of this project, and several co-design sessions have been conducted with project partners to create an immersive VR application. A manuscript group with representatives from all the project partners worked together to create a storyline and manuscript for approximately 8 months. Around 40 pupils participated at a "VR inspiration day" where they could test and try out different VR applications and suggest first-aid scenarios without any limitations. Also, two- co-design sessions with twelve 13–14-year-old pupils were conducted. Lessons learned from the conducted co-design involve group selection and group dynamics, methods and artifacts, and dissemination and adaptation to VR [8]. It is important to take into consideration how to organize and put together groups and promote effective and balanced collaboration. Also, a thoughtful choice of methods and artifacts can help to create a safe space and pleasant atmosphere for knowledge sharing. Also, one should disseminate insights as soon as possible and implement them in the development of the VR application [8].

As a result of all these PD activities, a manuscript has been written and a software program has simultaneously been developed to create an interactive 360-degree video by incorporating choice buttons and perspective switching between a 1PP and a 3PP.

The Production Process

The theme for the storyline for VR- application is risk management and self-evaluation in critical situations. The selected scope is a party scenario. We incorporate perspective switching by letting the pupils experience the story in a 1PP as the main character where they see through the main character's eyes. Also, the players can choose to be the character from a 3PP where they can see and be the character from a distance and observe the impact and consequences of their choices. The aim was to create a gamified story where the sequence of events within the narrative is defined through the choices made by the main character. See Fig. 1.

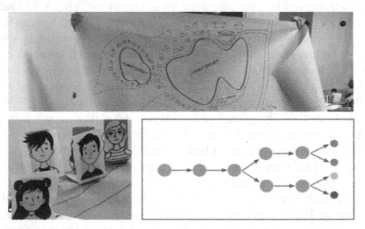

Fig. 1. Pupils made storylines with artefacts in co-design workshops as input to the manuscript

To enable reflection and learning, we did not incorporate functionalities that give the users the possibility to regret their choices or rewind since we want them to experience the consequences of their actions. We wanted the outcome of the story to change based on the choices made along the way and create branching scenarios as routes through the learning content. This might lead to a too long and complex manuscript and a difficult production process regarding recording and editing. We, therefore, used a decision tree template and designed a branching narrative that spreads out and gathers again adjusted to certain scenes and choices to ensure an effective production process. The ending has different outcomes to allow the users to experience the story differently based on their choices. See Fig. 2.

Incorporating perspective switching has affected the production process in several ways. For instance, every scene needs to be filmed twice to have two different perspectives that can flow seamlessly into each other. This requires that the actors can repeat

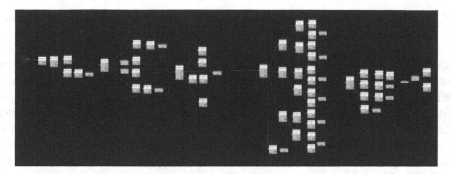

Fig. 2. An illustration of a decision tree template and branching narrative

exactly what they have done and said when the same scene will be filmed twice, and the two takes should ultimately be as precise as possible. In some of the scenes, the main character has a dialogue with the other characters to prevent the main character from behaving as a spectator in the story. Rehearsal with actors was therefore essential since there is not much room for improvisation. The actors need to know the timing of the dialogue well enough to know what the main character is supposed to say at what time.

A 360 microphone will be used to record audio from all angles. We can place the sound in 3D-space after recording so that no matter where the player turns in the 360-degree video, the sound will be based on the player's position and rotation. All added audio needs to be placed in the virtual environment aligned with the correct position in the room. The audio tracks must be placed correctly in the editing afterward by adding the audio file on the video filmed in 1 POV/FOV. For the user to understand that the sound comes from the main character they are playing, we will add sound-effects.

The video producer and the software/XR engineer needed to collaborate closely to make sure that the manuscript and storyline would consider the limitations of the software system that was being developed as part of the project, as well as give input to further development of the system.

Story Architect
The software system Story Architect was developed to create a software program that would be perceived as easy to use to enable pupils to make choices that affect the sequence of events in VR applications. Some existing products had linear timelines where one could place buttons and videos, but they would be difficult to work with when designing stories with many videos and button choices. Besides, when a player switches between perspectives, the new video must continue where the last video ended for the user to experience the story as seamlessly as possible. Interactive 360-degree videos can be made in Unity by adding buttons to play and pause the experience, graphics, animations, interactive choices, menus, and more. However, Unity requires code development skills and familiarity with the interface. This might be a barrier to use the technology since most teachers and pupils do not have the required skills for using Unity [25].

Story Architect was developed in Unity 3D and consists of two software programs: Story Reader and Story Writer. With Story Reader, you can experience interactive stories of branching VR narratives, and with Story Writer, you can create stories of branching

VR narratives. By having Story Reader installed, the pupils and teachers can download, and access content made in Story Writer with their HMDs.

With Story Architect, the use of "saves" and reuse of custom values can create different directions and outcomes of the story. Choices the players make in the beginning can therefore affect which alternatives and videos they see later. The data types supported are INTEGER (WholeNumber), STRING (Text), and BOOLEAN (True/False). With this system, it is possible to save choices that have been made, e.g. a choice of collecting a key early in the story can be saved and when the user later enters a locked door, the system knows that the user has a key, and the user can open the door. This functionality was incorporated so we would not have to build two parallel stories from start to be finished.

At the beginning of the project, a playtest of another IVR- application within first aid using Story Architect was conducted. Three representatives from the production company tested the application with 15 pupils at an upper secondary school. The pupils were divided into small groups where they could play a story. When they were finished, they answered a questionnaire with a mix of questions with a five-point Likert scale, open-ended questions, and ratings from 1 to 5 points. The results showed that 11 of the 15 pupils liked the story well or liked it a lot, and 80% of the pupils experienced the application as intuitive and easy to use. They did however not like that they were told to go back and try again when they answered "incorrectly" in the application. These results were used and impacted the further development of the system. This version of the system did not include perspective switching.

Story Writer
With Story Writer, you can create and edit the different narrative branches and place choice buttons in the 360-degree video (Fig. 3). You can create custom variables and fill them with data, as well as specify where in the scene the choice buttons should be placed for each perspective with the possibility to switch between the perspectives. You can also change the text and position of the buttons as well as when in the video they will be visible for the viewer.

Fig. 3. How a VR- scene with multiple buttons is shown in Story Writer

You can drag and drop from one scene to another to create different choice options and branches. In Fig. 4 you can see the structure of a story and how the different nodes and buttons are leading a story in different directions. Every box is a node that has different functionalities. Most of them are wide nodes containing one or more videos, buttons (outcome), and specific settings for videos.

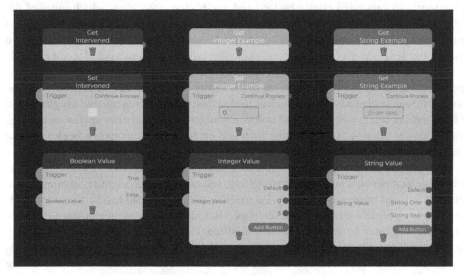

Fig. 4. Nodes showing different data and how to edit the different data types

Story Reader
Story Reader interprets the stories created in Story Writer and makes it a playable story for pupils. Story Reader identifies and prepares stories and disables stories that are no longer available. The flow chart of nodes is converted to actual videos that play, and the content of the nodes and scenes is visualized and processed in Story Reader. The choices the player makes are saved along the way, so that "custom variables" can be used to block or open directions later in the story. Story Reader accesses a server to see what stories are available to the player and downloads them (and the videos they contain) to make them available for offline playback. We have chosen to do it this way because Norwegian school networks are not good enough to handle more than 20 video streams of the 4K 360-degree videos.

5   Conceptual Framework

In this section, we will describe our conceptual framework *PERspeCtivE Switching in ImmersiVE VR* (PERCEIVE). The PERCEIVE framework illustrates what to consider when incorporating perspective switching in an immersive VR application that will be used in an educational context based on literature and lessons learned from the ongoing research project. The framework is meant to visually explain and give a comprehensive understanding of key concepts and the relationship between them when incorporating perspective switching in IVR applications with 360-degree videos.

PERCEIVE consists of seven steps of the process of developing the IVR application. Participatory- design is the method and process that led to specifications for the VR- application and a manuscript for immersive storytelling. The specification and manuscript incorporated choice buttons and perspective switching, which initiated the filmmaking to create a 360-degree-video, and the development of a software system to easily edit and create interactive 360-degree videos with choice buttons and perspective switching. This is not a linear process; sometimes different steps take place in parallel.

The users can switch perspectives between first-person perspective (1PP) and third-person perspective (3 PP) while being in the virtual environment and experiencing the story. 1PP can lead to advantages such as user inclusion, embodiment, and a higher sense of immersion, while a 3PP can lead to less simulator sickness, better spatial awareness, and macroscopic view. Incorporating both and enabling users to switch between these two perspectives is less common.

Perspective switching in IVR can lead to several potential benefits and challenges. Five potential benefits are perspective-taking, interactivity, experiential learning, sense of presence, and the sense of agency. Perspective-taking can lead to a better understanding of other people's thoughts, and feelings. User interactivity is an element to achieve high learning rates by using gamification strategies and enable game-based learning where pupils learn through exploration, and experiential learning by allowing the pupils to recognize virtual experiences as direct experiences. Presence is the subjective feeling of being in the virtual environment instigated by immersion, control factors, and representational fidelity. By giving the user a feeling of generating and controlling body representation and modify the environment, another affordance of perspective switching might be creating a sense of agency.

Potential challenges are complicated production processes, especially related to shooting and editing a 360-degree video where the user can experience the same situations and scenes from two different points of view (POVs) in a branching narrative with choice buttons. Having access to a software system that is easy to use and does not require coding skills, can reduce the challenge of editing an interactive story. However, shooting the scenes is complicated and requires a good amount of planning and rehearsal. For the viewer, perspective switching can affect the user experience in a bad way. It might make it difficult to follow the narration and create a fear of missing out (FOMO), which can compromise the sense of presence. See the conceptual framework in Fig. 5.

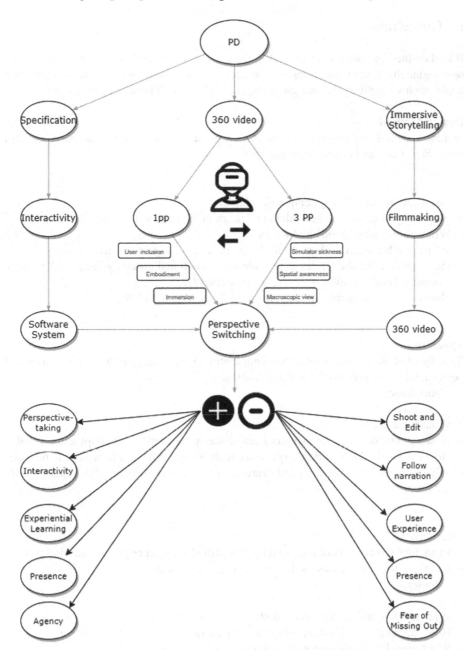

Fig. 5. The Conceptual Framework PERCEIVE

6   Guidelines

Based on the key concepts described in the conceptual framework, we have developed seven guidelines with questions to consider for those who want to develop an IVR application where the users are given the chance to switch between perspectives:

Design Method
Involve stakeholders and users in the design process to make sure that the result will meet their needs and ensure high usability.
Questions:

– For whom is the IVR application developed?
– How can you involve stakeholders and users in the design process?
– What are the users' needs and wants?
– Which methods and artifacts could be useful in co-design sessions?
– How can you distribute roles to provide for a functional group dynamic and promote a balanced collaboration in co-design processes?
– How to disseminate insights effectively and adapt them to VR?

Specification
Specify what the product should be, what it should look like, and what function it will perform based on insights from PD-activities.
Questions:

– What is the goal of the VR application?
– How can you disseminate insights from co-design activities and adapt them to VR?
– How can you build the virtual experience technically? What platform should be used?
– What features should be included to create an immersive and engaging experience for the users?

Interactivity
Find an appropriate level of interactivity that provides for an engaging learning process without it getting in the way of the story and learning goals.
Questions:

– What level of interactivity is needed?
– How can interactivity enhance the virtual experience?
– What gamification elements can enhance the learning process?

Software System
VR should not only look real but feel real. VR software systems and programs can be used to build immersive virtual environments.
Questions:

- What game engines can be used to create interactivity and enhance the learning process?
- Is there a need for additional software programs to edit 360-degree videos?
- How to distribute the VR product and make it easily accessible for the users?

Immersive Storytelling

Immersive storytelling aims to immerse the users in the story. For 360-degree videos, immersion includes an interplay of temporal, spatio-temporal, and emotional immersion.
  Questions:

- Which narrative elements can show the place and time of the story to enhance spatial immersion?
- Which type of characters and actions can increase spatio- temporal immersion and the sense of being placed within the scenes?
- Can a switch between POVs increase plausibility or give more information?
- How can you direct the attention of the viewer and guide her/him through the story?
- How can conflicts between characters or consequences of the character's actions increase emotional immersion?
- What should be the role of the viewer?

Film Making

Established rules for filmmaking do not apply to VR and 360-degree films.
  Questions:

- What equipment is needed for shooting the scenes?
- How should you place the 360 camera and microphone in scenes?
- How much rehearsal is needed?

360-degree Video

The videos must be stitched together and viewed in 360° on VR headsets. Audio and interactive elements may be added.
  Questions:

- Should you add sound in 3D-space after shooting?
- How can you integrate action limited choice options for the field of view?
- How to integrate choice points for branching narratives?

7 Concluding Remarks

Participatory Design (PD) is the methodology of the ongoing research project where several co-design activities have been conducted to create an immersive and user-centered VR application that will be used in the classrooms to teach and stimulate learning within first aid. The virtual experience and story will be presented through a 360-degree video delivered via HMDs. We wanted to explore the use of perspective switching to create a more engaging and interactive learning process. Several potential affordances and challenges with letting users choose between a first-person perspective and a third-person perspective have been identified.

The main contribution of this paper is a conceptual framework- PERCEIVE. The framework presents key concepts to consider when developing IVR where the user can switch between perspectives throughout a fictional story in a 360-degree video between a 1PP and a 3PP. Based on the literature and lessons learned from an ongoing research project, seven steps describing the process of developing a user-centered application have been identified. Five potential affordances with perspective switching are perspective-taking, interactivity, experiential learning, presence, and agency. Potential challenges are shooting and editing 360-degree videos. It may damage the user experience and make it difficult for users to follow the narration and create a fear of missing out. There is also a risk that it may reduce the sense of presence instead of increasing it. Based on these elements, we have provided some guidelines to help others who want to explore perspective switching in IVR.

Due to COVID-19 restrictions and lock-down, the shooting of the 360-degree video with pupils was canceled. It is currently postponed until recording is considered safe and aligned with the infection control restrictions in the municipality. In the future, we will conduct more systematic evaluations of the final VR application based on the identified factors outlined in the PERCEIVE framework to get a more comprehensive understanding of the effect of perspective switching in IVR.

Acknowledgements. The ongoing research project and this work is funded by the Regional Research Fund Viken (#296188).

References

1. Checa, D., Bustillo, A.: A review of immersive virtual reality serious games to enhance learning and training. Multimed. Tools Appl. **79**(9), 5501–5527 (2020). https://doi.org/10.1007/s11042-019-08348-9
2. Freitas, S., Liarokapis, F.: Serious Games: A New Paradigm for Education? pp. 9–23 (2011)
3. Southgate, E.: Immersive virtual reality, children and school education: A literature review for teachers. DICE Report Series Number 6. Newcastle: DICE Research (2018). Retrieved from http://dice.newcastle.edu.au/DRS_6_2018.pdf
4. Jensen, L., Konradsen, F.: A review of the use of virtual reality head-mounted displays in education and training. Educ. Inf. Technol. **23**, 1–15 (2018). https://doi.org/10.1007/s10639-017-9676-0
5. Makransky, G., Lilleholt, L.: A structural equation modeling investigation of the emotional value of immersive virtual reality in education. Educ. Technol. Res. Develop. **66**, 1141–1164 (2018). https://doi.org/10.1007/s11423-018-9581-2
6. Van Mechelen, M.: Designing technologies for and with children: theoretical reflections and a practical inquiry towards a co-design toolkit (2016)

7. Dahl, T.L., Fjørtoft, S.O., Landmark, A.D.: Developing a conceptual framework for smart teaching: using VR to teach kids how to save lives. In: Uskov, V., Howlett, R., Jain, L. (eds) Smart Education and e-Learning 2020. Smart Innovation, Systems and Technologies, vol. 188, pp. 161-170. Springer, Singapore (2020). https://doi.org/10.1007/978-981-15-5584-8_14

8. Dahl, T.L., Høiseth, M.: Co-designing immersive VR with and for adolescents in elementary school. In: Proceedings of the 2020 ACM Interaction Design and Children Conference: Extended Abstracts, London, United Kingdom (2020).https://doi.org/10.1145/3397617.339 7848

9. Bucher, K., Blome, T., Rudolph, S., von Mammen, S.: VReanimate II: training first aid and reanimation in virtual reality. J. Comput. Educ. 6(1), 53–78 (2019). https://doi.org/10.1007/s40692-018-0121-1

10. Jantjies, M., Moodley, T., Maart, R.: Experiential learning through Virtual and Augmented Reality in Higher Education (2018)

11. Kwon, C.: Verification of the possibility and effectiveness of experiential learning using HMD-based immersive VR technologies. Virtual Reality 23(1), 101–118 (2019). https://doi.org/10.1007/s10055-018-0364-1

12. Makransky, G., Petersen, G.: The cognitive affective model of immersive learning (CAMIL): a theoretical research-based model of learning in immersive virtual reality Educ. Psychol. Rev. (2021). https://doi.org/10.1007/s10648-020-09586-2

13. Weech, S., Kenny, S., Barnett-Cowan, M.: Presence and cybersickness in virtual reality are negatively related: a review. Front. Psychol. 10(158), 1–19 (2019). https://doi.org/10.3389/fpsyg.2019.00158

14. Gödde, M., Gabler, F., Siegmund, D., Braun, A.: Cinematic narration in VR – rethinking film conventions for 360°. In: Chen, J.Y.C., Fragomeni, G. (eds.) Virtual, Augmented and Mixed Reality: Applications in Health, Cultural Heritage, and Industry, pp. 184–201. Springer International Publishing, Cham (2018). https://doi.org/10.1007/978-3-319-91584-5_15

15. Dooley, K.: Storytelling with virtual reality in 360-degrees: a new screen grammar. Stud. Australas. Cinema 11, 1–11 (2017). https://doi.org/10.1080/17503175.2017.1387357

16. Elmezeny, A., Edenhofer, N., Wimmer, J.: Immersive storytelling in 360-degree videos: an analysis of interplay between narrative and technical immersion. J. Virtual Worlds Res. 11, 1–15 (2018). https://doi.org/10.4101/jvwr.v11i1.7298

17. Aitamurto, T., Zhou, S., Sakshuwong, S., Saldivar, J., Sadeghi, Y., Tran, A.: Sense of Presence, attitude change, perspective-taking and usability in first-person split-sphere 360° video. In: Proceedings of the 2018 CHI Conference on Human Factors in Computing Systems, p. 545. Association for Computing Machinery (2018)

18. Rothe, S., Hussmann, H., Allary, M.: Diegetic cues for guiding the viewer in cinematic virtual reality (2017)

19. Monteiro, D., Liang, H., Xu, W., Brucker, M., Nanjappan, V., Yue, Y.: Evaluating enjoyment, presence, and emulator sickness in VR games based on first and thir person viewing perspectives. Comput. Anim. Virtual Worlds 29, e1830 (2018)

20. Yang, Z., Zhang, M., Zhang, T., Linhao, F., Nakajima, T.: Real world third-person with multiple point-of-views for immersive mixed reality. In: Pereira, P., Ribeiro, R., Oliveira, I., Novais, P. (eds.) Society with Future: Smart and Liveable Cities: First EAI International Conference, SC4Life 2019, Braga, Portugal, December 4-6, 2019, Proceedings, pp. 97–108. Springer International Publishing, Cham (2020). https://doi.org/10.1007/978-3-030-45293-3_8

21. Gorisse, G., Christmann, O., Amato, E.A., Richir, S.: First- and third-person perspectives in immersive virtual environments: presence and performance analysis of embodied users. Front. Robot. AI 4(33), 1–12 (2017). https://doi.org/10.3389/frobt.2017.00033

22. Batson, C. D.: Two forms of perspective taking: Imagining how another feels and imagining how you would feel. Handbook of imagination and mental simulation, pp. 267–279. Psychology Press New York, NY, US (2009)

23. Zhou, S.: Actor's and Observer's Perspective in Narrative Processing. Cornell University (2017)
24. Cmentowski, S., Krekhov, A., Krueger, J.: Outstanding: a perspective-switching technique for covering large distances in VR games. In: Extended Abstracts of the 2019 CHI Conference on Human Factors in Computing Systems, Glasgow, Scotland Uk. (2019). https://doi.org/10.1145/3290607.3312783
25. Unity Technologies, https://unity.com/

Beyond Visible Light: User and Societal Impacts of Egocentric Multispectral Vision

Austin Erickson[✉], Kangsoo Kim, Gerd Bruder, and Gregory F. Welch

University of Central Florida, Orlando, FL 32816, USA
ericksona@knights.ucf.edu

Abstract. Multi-spectral imagery is becoming popular for a wide range of application fields from agriculture to healthcare, mainly stemming from advances in consumer sensor and display technologies.Modern augmented reality (AR) head-mounted displays already combine a multitude of sensors and are well-suited for integration with additional sensors, such as cameras capturing information from different parts of the electromagnetic spectrum. In this paper, we describe a novel multi-spectral vision prototype based on the Microsoft HoloLens 1, which we extended with two thermal infrared (IR) cameras and two ultraviolet (UV) cameras. We performed an exploratory experiment, in which participants wore the prototype for an extended period of time and assessed its potential to augment our daily activities. Our report covers a discussion of qualitative insights on personal and societal uses of such novel multi-spectral vision systems, including their applicability for use during the COVID-19 pandemic.

Keywords: Multi-spectral vision · Augmented reality · Optical see-through head-mounted displays · Extended perception · Thermal vision · Ultraviolet vision · User study

1 Introduction

With new developments in low-cost imaging sensors that can be tuned to different wavelengths of the electromagnetic spectrum, sensors are becoming more affordable and attractive for potential users and practitioners in different application fields. At the same time, we are also seeing advances in novel display technologies. Consumer augmented reality (AR) displays, in particular optical see-through head-mounted displays (OST-HMDs) such as the HoloLens 1 and 2 or the Magic Leap One, have been released over the last few years that integrate a variety of visual and auditory sensors, displays, and processing hardware. While these solutions already combine a multitude of sensors, including infrared (IR) and RGB cameras, these display platforms are capable of easily integrating additional sensors that cover more or different parts of the electromagnetic spectrum.

© Springer Nature Switzerland AG 2021
J. Y. C. Chen and G. Fragomeni (Eds.): HCII 2021, LNCS 12770, pp. 317–335, 2021.
https://doi.org/10.1007/978-3-030-77599-5_23

Several different systems and research prototypes have been developed over the last several years that incorporate additional sensors onto an AR HMD in an effort to augment the user's visual capabilities by feeding data from multi-spectral imaging sensors into user's view of their environment. Most prominent are thermal displays, such as a FLIR thermal camera integrated into the DAQRI Smart Helmet or the U.S. Army's IVAS version of the HoloLens 2. Another example is a research prototype by Erickson et al., who integrated a HoloLens with two FLIR thermal cameras that could be overlaid stereoscopically over the user's view of the real world [16]. Orlosky et al. also developed a framework called VisMerge that supports developers in spatially and temporally calibrating HMDs with infrared cameras [37].

While these multi-spectral imaging sensors are relatively new in combination with AR displays, they are already widely used in different professional application fields. A prominent example is in healthcare, where we have seen thermal infrared sensors used in many contactless thermometers during the current COVID-19 pandemic. Near-infrared wavelength sensors are also used to determine the amount of blood in a given area of tissue and the amount of blood that is oxygenated [10,49]. Another example is in agriculture, where IR or ultraviolet (UV) multi-spectral imaging sensors, sometimes mounted on airborne sensor platforms [40], are widely used to determine variations in the texture of soils to identify different soil zones and locating variability in crop emergence and biomass [23,28,44]. Beyond these domains, multi-spectral sensors tuned to the human body temperature among the thermal wavelength IR band have also been widely used for many defense or disaster management applications [5,43].

Because of the diverse range of domains that utilize these sensors and the ease of their integration into AR HMDs, it is possible that consumer grade AR HMDs will incorporate such sensors into their designs in the near future. This means that users of the AR HMD have access to these sensors for use in not only professional domain-specific applications, but also for daily use under otherwise normal circumstances. This raises interesting research questions about how having access to multi-spectral vision can affect the daily lives of users:

1. What are the possible use cases that regular consumers can benefit from this multi-spectral vision?
2. How does having access to this multi-spectral vision affect the behavior of users?
3. What are the social implications of widespread usage of this technology?

In this paper, we present our methods of implementing a prototype multi-spectral vision AR HMD that incorporates consumer off the shelf (COTS) thermal infrared and ultraviolet sensors onto the Microsoft HoloLens 1. We also present an exploratory user study where users were tasked with wearing the prototype system for an extended period of time, and we discuss the results in terms of the above research questions.

This paper is structured as follows. Section 2 presents an overview of related work. Section 3 describes the our multi-spectral vision prototype and study design. Our findings are presented in Sect. 4 and are discussed in Sect. 5. Section 6 concludes the paper.

2   Related Work

In this section, we discuss related work on the uses of IR and UV imaging sensors in the scope of our multi-spectral AR research. As discussed earlier, most of the previous work in this domain has focused on professional applications with hand-held or drone-mounted imaging sensors, with limited work investigating AR displays and daily activities.

2.1   Thermal Infrared Spectrum

With the advent of low-cost commercial off-the-shelf (COTS) thermal IR cameras over the last years, e.g., from FLIR, thermal IR images have been utilized extensively for applications spanning across a wide range of domains, including medical applications [24], defense [2,3,8], surveillance [47,56], and firefighting [45]. While the resolution of these cameras is still far behind the state of the art in RGB camera technologies, it has greatly improved over the last years, as has their form factor and developer support [11,14,26].

In medical diagnostics, the use of thermobiological information traces back to the writings of Hippocrates around 480 BC [24], and IR-based thermography has been used for decades due to the ability to monitor the temperature distribution on human skin. Jones pointed out the usefulness of such IR imaging to detect abnormalities in physiology while summarizing the methodology and applications for body temperature detection and analysis [25]. Non-invasive near-infrared spectroscopy (NIRS) methods have been introduced to monitor muscle oxygenation and blood flow and detect tissue vasculature problems, such as vascular sarcomas [10,49].

In the context of disaster control or first responder activities, thermal IR cameras have been used by firefighters for a long time [7]. Recently, Sosnowski et al. developed a prototype firefighter helmet that integrates both an OLED display and thermal IR cameras [45]. Such a design enables firefighters to see through the blinding thick smoke that often fills the environments that they work in. Enhanced perception with such devices can protect the firefighter from stepping into unseen danger and allow them to be more efficient in rescuing people trapped in danger. Rudol and Doherty integrated the thermal imaging system in unmanned aerial vehicles (UAVs) and found that the thermal images could improve the human (victim) detection rate in rescue missions from a distance [43].

Such thermal IR-based human body detection are further used in defense and surveillance applications, where the narrow band of normal human body temperature of 36.5–37.5 $°C$ can be identified [2,3,8]. Beyond body detection, thermal images can also be used for emotion detection in social contexts. Pavlidis et al. suggested an IR-based anxiety detection method to identify suspects engaged in illegal or harmful activities in military or civilian installations [39]. Military systems have also been utilizing IR sensors to detect and track non-human targets for space and missile defense [5].

Thermal images have also been used in many other application domains. In building diagnostics, thermal cameras have a long history of being used to detect structural defects and design flaws [4,27,46]. In agriculture, IR images have been utilized to monitor plants and detect diseases [13,23,36,44]. Urban heat distribution, such as urban head island effects, can be analyzed by the integration of IR images in geographic information systems (GIS) [29]. The automotive industry uses thermal images to detect humans or animals based on their body heat in the dark [18,55].

Despite the large volume of professional IR use cases, not much research has focused on daily activities or its effects on human perception.

2.2   Ultraviolet Spectrum

Compared to IR, the UV spectrum is largely unexplored with respect to the field of AR. This mainly stems from UV light being near-absent in the indoor spaces where AR was used traditionally.

However, UV light has several interesting properties that have been examined in the past. UV rays primarily come from the sun and are categorized in UV-A, B, and C, each corresponding to a specific wavelength. UV-A and B are responsible for causing sunburns, but can also induce eye conditions, such as cataracts and macular degeneration [42], and skin conditions like melanoma [35].

Fulton described how UV-filtered photos show the effects of UV exposure, which are now commonly used in dermatology clinics to educate patients on the dangers of UV exposure [17]. Zhang et al. developed a prototype AR HMD that detects the presence and amount of UV in the user's environment through UV sensors and alerts them to the dangers of UV exposure by changing the user's skin color through the AR display to appear as though it had burned from UV exposure [54]. Their users, in general, agreed that the system was helpful in alerting them to the presence of UV, and they felt that they were better protected from UV by this system.

UV rays are not always harmful and have benefits for human health such as vitamin D synthesis when exposure is moderated [30,53], and in medicine such as in ultraviolet germicidal irradiation (UVGI), which has been historically used as a means of decontamination [41], and dental inspection [21,38]. UV fluorescence imaging is further used to detect flaws in insulators of transmission lines [1] and in photovoltaic plants [32], the latter showing superior performance compared to the common inspection techniques using thermography [33].

Wilkes et al. pointed out that the high cost of such systems is affecting their widespread use and to remedy this issue they developed a low-cost UV imaging system marketed for cellphone cameras [50]. With volcanology as one of the main areas utilizing UV imaging [9,31], Wilkes et al. deployed a modified version of their previous low cost system to measure the sulphur dioxide gas emissions of volcanoes, finding that their system's performance was comparable to more expensive scientific cameras [51].

There is a lot of potential for the use of the UV spectrum for educational, art, and interactive purposes. Munnerley et al. discussed the benefits of augmenting students' senses with multi-spectral imagery to challenge them about the limitations of their vision and how it affects their perception and understanding [34]. Eck et al. used multi-spectral sensors (UV, x-ray and IR) to perform art inspections (e.g., underdrawings in paintings [6]) in an interactive museum experience, where visitors were able to switch between these multi-spectral images and reveal the effects of each image captures on the digital replicas of the paintings by using a spray can interface with an IR light which was tracked by a Wiimote [48]. They pointed out that even with some technical limitations such as tracking issues, visitors exhibited a lot of enthusiasm.

3   Experiment

In this section we describe our implementation of a prototype multi-spectral vision AR HMD and present an exploratory experiment that was conducted to better understand the potential benefits and drawbacks of AR multi-spectral vision for daily activities.

3.1   Multi-spectral Vision OST-HMD Prototype

For the purposes of this experiment, we developed a prototype multi-spectral AR OST-HMD that consists of a Microsoft HoloLens 1, augmented with two pairs of spectral imaging sensors:

- **Thermal Infrared Cameras:** Two FLIR Lepton 3.5 Radiometric thermal IR cameras (housed in PureThermal 2 I/O modules) and
- **Ultraviolet Cameras:** Two XNiteUSB2S-MUV 2 Megapixel UV cameras.

The prototype display is shown in Fig. 2. Effectively, we turned a COTS AR display into a multi-spectral display using COTS IR and UV cameras. The thermal cameras have a resolution of 160×120 pixels and a field of view of $56°$ horizontally and $44°$ vertically, which is slightly larger than the HoloLens ($30°$ horizontally and $17°$ vertically). These IR cameras sense a range of 8–14 μm in the infrared spectrum known as thermal vision. The Lepton 2 breakout boards were attached to the top of the headset, 0.08 m above the participant's eyes and at a separation of 0.17 m apart. The UV cameras sense the range of light between 365–380 nm, with a resolution of 1920×1080 pixels and a field of view of $163°$ horizontal and $92°$, vertical. They were mounted on a bracket alongside the thermal cameras 0.08 m above the participant's eyes, at a slightly greater separation of 0.245 m.

Due to the lack of USB ports on the HoloLens itself, the cameras were tethered to a backpack computer (MSI, Intel Core i7-7820HK 2.9 GHz CPU, 16 GB

RAM, Nvidia GTX 1070 graphics card, Windows 10 Pro) which utilized a cellular mobile hot-spot to stream imagery to the HoloLens via Unity version 2018.2.11f1 in holographic remoting mode. We used the FLIR Lepton user app to connect and configure the infrared cameras, and the UV cameras were used as plug-and-play web-cams with default settings, then the camera streams were accessed through Unity. In our Unity implementation, the sensors were treated as USB webcams, which allowed imagery to be streamed in real time over the network where it was presented on built-in Unity UI canvas and rawimage game objects.

We aimed to test the prototype both indoors and outdoors, however the imagery presented by the HoloLens 1 is difficult to observe outdoors due to the limited luminance capabilities of the display [15]. For this reason, we created a visor that could be attached to the HoloLens when outside. This visor consists of two stacked sheets of neutral density filters, one with an optical density of 0.6 and another with a density of 0.9. This combination blocks 37.5% of all incoming light and greatly improves the contrast between the virtual imagery and user's physical environment.

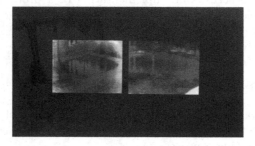

Fig. 1. The combined display mode features side by side views of the UV imagery (left) and thermal imagery (right).

Multi-spectral Vision Modes. Three different display modes were implemented, which could be toggled by pressing a button on a wireless mouse that users carried with them while using the prototype system. These views included stereoscopic views of the thermal infrared or ultraviolet sensors separately, and also included a combined view where a single camera stream from one thermal infrared sensor was shown on the right portion of the display and the stream from one ultraviolet sensor was shown on the left (see Fig. 1.) A stereoscopic view of both sensor pairs simultaneously was tested, but ultimately was not used due to running into network limitations when attempting to stream imagery from all four sensors simultaneously.

We further implemented a scaling feature that allowed us to use the scroll wheel on the wireless input device to scale the size of the image regions depicting the camera feeds in the field of view. We included this feature to allow us to get a closer view and inspect features in the camera feeds or reduce them in the

Fig. 2. Annotated photo showing the multi-spectral HoloLens prototype we used in the experiment, including the backpack computer and attached thermal IR and UV cameras.

visual field. Screenshots of these display modes, taken via the HoloLens' mixed reality capture, can be seen in Figs. 1 and 6.

The thermal IR camera feed was presented to the participants using a shader that mapped the temperature of the scene to particular colors. The camera also made use of an automatic gain control feature that would find the hottest and coldest areas of the scene, and automatically calibrate the shader so that the coldest object appeared black and the hottest appeared white, which thus maximizes the discernible range of temperatures within each view. The shader uses a linear mapping of temperatures to colors from coldest to warmest, where black is used to depict the coldest temperatures, followed by red, orange, yellow, and then white.

The UV camera feed was presented to the participants in standard grayscale, offering a distinct contrast in imagery between the footage from the UV and thermal IR cameras.

3.2 Participants

Five male and two female (ages between 19 and 37, $M = 28.6$, $SD = 7.0$) participated in our exploratory study. All had normal or corrected-to-normal vision. Four participants wore glasses during the experiment. None of the participants reported known visual or vestibular disorders, such as color or night blindness, dyschromatopsia, or a displacement of balance. All participants were students, researchers, or professionals in AR/VR sensor and display technologies.

3.3 Methods

We asked our participants to explore the usefulness of the multi-spectral vision prototype for daily activities and societal uses for at least 45 min with the option to continue on for up to two hours. We instructed participants to take notes and/or take screenshots on the HoloLens when they observed an interesting use of the IR/UV views. We also used retrospective probing, in which an experimenter asked questions during short breaks and after completion of the experiment. At the end of the experiment, everyone filled out a demographics and experience questionnaire with open questions.

Following the completion of the study by all participants, we had a debriefing session where all of the participants discussed their experience and observations.

4   Results

Based on the observations of the participants, we see two main advantages of multi-spectral vision for our daily activities and society at large (not focusing on professional applications):

1. **A1** Simplifying tasks that would have otherwise required more time or effort.
2. **A2** Providing novel signals that have the potential to be useful as cues for interpersonal communication, in daily activities, or personal health.

In the following section, tags (such as **A1** or **A2**) will be placed at the end of sentences that support these advantages of multi-spectral vision.

Identifying Medical Conditions. Due to the narrow band of 36.5–37.5 °C of normal human body temperature, most peoples' skin temperature looked roughly the same in thermal vision, however if their temperature was changed to be out this range it was a very apparent change on the display. During the experiment, we came across a specific situation that indicated a person's skin temperature appeared much lower than that of other people. We first attributed this to other effects, e.g., environmental or activity-related, but we investigated it further in different environments and found an explanation in the person's known medical condition of low blood pressure. Figure 3 shows a side-by-side comparison of a person's normal temperature on the right and the person's decreased temperature on the left. These differences remained consistent and apparent over different environments and on other days following the study; they were most apparent on the face and the hands. Furthermore, that person had a history of subjectively feeling colder than other people in the lab, which is a known by-product associated with low blood pressure, just as high blood pressure is associated with subjective feelings of warmth or heat. While low blood pressure is usually no reason for concern, according to the CDC, 32% of Americans have high blood pressure, which is a primary or contributing cause of death for more than 1,100 deaths/day in 2014 [12]. Only 54% of people with high blood pressure have their condition under control, e.g., by taking medication.

Beyond this example, we could see thermal skin temperature measures being used to identify symptoms for other medical conditions, and even prevent the spread of diseases such as COVID-19 [**A2**]. While this was not encountered

Fig. 3. Identifying medical conditions: Example thermal IR view with the person on the left having low blood pressure compared to normal blood pressure on the right.

during our study, the multi-spectral vision prototype should be able to easily detect people running fevers, which could alert the user to avoid contact with them. Several participants noted that they "could see a reflection of [their] body while looking at see-through glass, but the reflection was a heat image of [their] body." It became apparent that the thermal feed could also be examined via reflections off specular surfaces similar to traditional RGB wavelengths. If such a property is exploited, it could potentially alert a user if they themselves are running a fever when checking their reflection in the bathroom mirror in the morning, or future AR mirrors might include thermal IR imagery to facilitate this health feature without the need to wear an AR HMD (e.g., see Microsoft's Holoflector [52]) [**A1,A2**]. The ability to see one's own temperature with AR displays, e.g., when checking one's thermal reflection in a mirror in the morning, could provide a quick and useful measure in maintaining a healthy life [**A1,A2**].

Measuring Temperatures at a Glance. A practical aspect of seeing thermal IR was that it allowed users to make objective measurements of temperature without physically being in contact, or even near, the object of interest [**A1**].

In several situations, in particular occurring at home during the study, participants were alerted of hot toasters and stoves in thermal IR vision that appeared to be normal room temperature when viewed in the visible light spectrum. By being able to know the temperature prior to coming into contact with the appliance or object, accidental burns could be prevented. Practically, just by looking around with thermal vision, one could not help but be situationally aware of potential threats due to visual areas that are noticeably too hot (bright yellow; could burn oneself if touched) or too cold (black; could freeze oneself if touched) [**A2**]. Participants indicated that for the goal to *prevent accidents*, a simplified color scheme would be sufficient or even better suited, e.g., glowing blue for "too cold" and glowing red for "too hot." Using such a color scheme, normal room temperature objects could be ignored and left un-annotated in terms of AR effects.

One participant completed their entire trial around their home, and was surprised by the wealth of information that could be gathered by using the multi-spectral vision device. They stated that they were "able to notice wet spots on the carpet" with the thermal vision that were unseen to the naked eye (a scenario many pet owners are likely familiar with) [**A1**]. With the device, the user was able to locate the exact position of the mess as well as see that it had been cleaned up properly, all by examining the differences in temperature between the affected portion of carpet and the unaffected area around it. The same participant also noticed that they could "identify which houseplants were watered recently" by their spouse and which had not. The recently watered plants had cool dark-colored soil when observed with thermal IR vision, whereas the soil surrounding the plants in need appeared to be at room temperature [A1].

When examining doorways and windows under thermal vision, several participants had interesting observations. One participant noted that they "could tell exactly where the doors leading outside were because of the intense heat on the door". Another participant noted that it was possible to "see which doors were letting heat in from outside" [A1]. Upon close inspection of the latter it was noted that the weather strip was not making an airtight seal between the door and the frame. Such a feature may be useful to people who are interested in keeping air conditioning and heating costs down, by helping them find the specific places that could be better sealed or insulated. Similarly, when opening a door or window, it became possible to see how the room temperature changed, e.g., seeing a progression of colors in the room that were in line with being drained of warmth or heating up depending on the temperature outside, before it "leveled out" and remained at a constant temperature level.

One of the participants spent their trial during lunch time, and wore the multi-spectral vision device while walking across the street to a local smoothie restaurant. One of their observations was that they could "tell how much smoothie [they] had left in [their] opaque cup without needing to touch it or take the lid off," which is related to a difference in surface temperature on the cup as shown in Fig. 4 [A1]. This same participant also ordered a hot lunch, and noted that they were able to see how hot the food was upon receiving it from the server, as well as see it cool down over time as it was left on the tray. Spending their time in an office environment, other participants reported as useful that they could see if their coffee was already cold in their mug without having to taste it [A1].

Fig. 4. Opaque mugs and cups and their thermal representation. In particular, the right image shows how much of the smoothie is left inside the cup.

Residual Heat Affects Behavior. When walking around their work environment, participants noted that they could tell which furniture was recently used by observing the residual heat left over on the cushion [A1,A2]. This information might further affect one's behavior by avoiding a chair when entering a meeting room that is clearly warmer than the others due to a feeling of "someone else is/was sitting there," which is shown in Fig. 5. In that sense, the residual heat could be associated with a *residual presence* of that person [19]. Residual heat could even be seen on the floor if someone had stood in the same place for an extended period of time.

Fig. 5. *Which chair would you sit in?* RGB and thermal IR views showing office chairs of which one has been occupied recently.

Heightened Sensitivity to Security Concerns. During the study, several participants performed routine tasks while seeing the thermal IR imagery that increased their sensitivity to security related issues, e.g., led them to be more careful when interacting with keycode or password protected doors or computers. For instance, one participant observed that they transferred heat between themselves and keypads/keyboards. This transfer of heat was clearly visible in the thermal IR spectrum, and can give the user an idea of what buttons were pressed recently, e.g., within the last minute (usually between 25 and 50 s) [**A1**]. Further, we noticed that the transfer of heat can go in either direction, such as leaving a hot fingerprint behind as seen in Fig. 6, or by touching the keyboard of a hot laptop computer, in which case a colder dark fingerprint is left instead of the former. After noticing how easy it was to pick out the characters or numbers in a password, participants became more conscious of this and one even noted that they adopted behaviors to compensate for this, e.g., by typing faster or wiping the panel.

Fig. 6. Sensitization to security concerns: Residual heat from button presses on a keypad.

Enhanced Visibility of Humans and Other Entities. As mentioned previously, due to their comparatively high body temperature, humans are easy to spot when looking at them through the thermal IR display mode in the multispectral vision device. This phenomena is not limited to people, and also occurs for certain animals and other dynamic entities. Two participants in the study noted that they were able to clearly make out the warm bodies of a flock of birds that were meandering about outside [**A1**]. The birds were clearly visible against the even coloration of the grass they were walking over. Another participant noticed that they were even able to pick out an airplane flying overhead in the same manner, where the plane appeared hot against the even background of the sky [**A1**]. Contrary to most participants' expectations, most smaller animals could not be made out in the thermal IR mode. In particular, reptiles, amphibians, and insects were not directly visible in the thermal IR view since their body temperature depends largely on the environment. Similarly, not many smaller animals maintain a high body temperature as humans and thus were less easy to make out in the environment.

Understanding Sunscreen and UV Light. We conducted the experiment during the summer and several participants applied sunscreen during their trial, and observed the effects with the UV vision mode. The left picture in Fig. 7 shows an (anonymized) UV image that illustrates the effects of sunscreen (sun protection factor SPF 60) applied to half of the person's face. The sunscreen-protected areas appear darker and a clear line is visible on the person's nose, forehead, and chin that shows the difference between the presence of sunscreen and the absence of it. The right picture shows one of the participants applying a small stripe of sunscreen to their outstretched arm. The sunscreen appears darker in UV light, so it is possible to see exactly where it has been applied. While usually transparent in normal human vision, it became possible to see if one missed a spot when applying sunscreen on one's body before one went out into the sun, which has the potential to avoid sunburns and improve personal health [**A1,A2**].

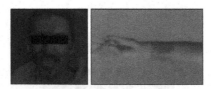

Fig. 7. Effects of sunscreen on the appearance of one's skin in UV vision. Skin areas protected by sunscreen appear darker in UV vision.

Reducing UV Light Pollution. During the course of their trial, several participants noticed that many different lights emit small amounts of UV radiation.

This was noticed in both overhead fluorescent lights, and traditional bulbs, but was not observed on any computer monitors or phone displays. Additionally, they found that certain equipment around the environment such as in tracking systems emitted small amounts of UV light. Similarly, several smart phones were observed, and while the phones themselves appeared pitch black in indoor environments, there was often a flashing LED on the front of the phone that emitted UV light but was invisible to the naked eye. Indoor sources of UV light were easy to make out in the UV vision mode, and replacing light bulbs with ones that emit no UV light could potentially improve personal health [A1,A2]. An indoor UV sterilization lamp was observed by one of the participants of the study, who thought that it may be possible to observe its area of effect through use of the UV sensor. They found that while the lamp itself was clearly visible on the display, it was not possible to see its area of effect via illumination of any of the surrounding surfaces.

A similar observation was made by one of our participants in that the UV cameras did not pick up any ambient UV from within indoor environments, even when positioned near large windows. Participants could see the ambient UV from the sun through the window, however the UV light was not apparent at all on any indoor surfaces.

5   Discussion

In this section, we discuss the main lessons-learned in terms of potential benefits and drawbacks for our society.

5.1   Societal Benefits

Most of the observations we made during the study were positive and suggested that multi-spectral vision could **make tasks easier** to accomplish in our daily life and save time. A primary example is the ability to directly see information, e.g., temperature, without having to find the information using some other means such as a smartphone app to check the weather or a thermostat to check the temperature in one's office. For instance, we often used it to answer the recurring question in our air-conditioned office spaces, "Is it cold in here or is it just me?" Before using thermal vision in our study, we had no proof that temperature actually varied a lot between a thermostat's location and the rest of the room.

A related benefit is that multi-spectral vision can **prevent accidents**, e.g., when we directly see the temperature of a hotplate or the interior of our car that was standing in the sun, which we otherwise would have to touch to know if the surfaces could burn us. Similarly, being able to see people and animals while driving at night or in other low-visibility conditions in the natural human spectral bands can prevent collisions that otherwise would be difficult to avoid. In the same sense, being able to see and avoid potentially dangerous animals that are well-camouflaged and unseen in the visible range of light could save one's life.

Further, multi-spectral vision can **improve situational awareness**. Having direct access to visual information from other spectral bands allowed us to see people and animals in low-visibility conditions, see if animals are hiding among the vegetation around us, see if other people in social situations are feeling hot or cold, see if IR-based tracking equipment in the laboratory is powered and active, or see how much potentially unwanted UV light is being emitted from equipment and lights within the laboratory.

We believe that having access to multi-spectral vision also has the potential to **improve personal health**. As mentioned previously, participants of the study were able to use thermal IR vision to identify abnormal temperature readings on themselves through the use of reflections and on others in the environment. They were able to notice signs of low blood pressure through decreased body temperature and might be able to pick out people who have unusually high temperatures which could be associated with a fever. By having easy access to this information, users could make more informed decisions on their own state of health, as well as point out abnormalities to others in their environment that they may have missed or ignored.

On the UV spectrum, participants were able to observe which areas were receiving the most UV exposure, and either avoid such areas or protect themselves from it by visualizing the places on their body that were not covered in sun screen. Participants were also able to note sources of UV emission in their home or working environments such as fluorescent and overhead lighting, and could use this information to reduce this amount of UV exposure they were experiencing indoors and better protect their eyes and skin from harm. As certain skin and eye conditions are linked to long term exposure to UV light, having access to this UV information may help prevent or slow the onset of some of these conditions, such as macular degeneration and cataracts [42], and skin conditions like melanoma [35].

While not being essential for our society, we believe that such benefits could increase public demand and become a driving force behind commercial products with multi-spectral vision integrated in future ubiquitous AR displays, ranging from personal AR goggles to in-car AR head-up displays.

5.2 Societal Drawbacks

Since our human sense of vision is limited to the red, green, and blue spectral bands, it is not possible to add other spectral information without changing or replacing other sensory information. In this study, participants toggled between different spectral bands or looked at insets in their visual field, but it will be an important challenge for the scientific visualization research community to identify methods to avoid **sensory or cognitive deprivation or overload** that stems from toggling through different bands or trying to compress information from the entire electromagnetic spectrum into the limited human spectral channels. If not solved, it is possible that we will see negative societal examples, such as **more accidents**, where people are distracted by the multi-spectral vision imagery and are not fully aware of their surroundings. This could be exaggerated by displays that are not lined up one-to-one with the user's environment or do not convey appropriate depth information to the user. Such issues may be addressed in future work by compressing relevant multi-spectral information into a single vision mode and by hiding non-relevant information, such as room temperature objects in thermal vision or areas with no UV light. However, such techniques are largely dependant on the user's task at hand and preferences could vary from user to user.

Some participants noted a feeling of **distraction or detachment** from conversations and social interaction while wearing our multi-spectral vision prototype. The HMD and different vision modes made it hard to make eye contact with another person and see the traditional (RGB vision) social cues as they occur during the interaction. The effect likely goes both directions, as the person that the participant is interacting with is likely feeling like they are not completely connecting with the participant due to the barrier of the HMD being between them. However, the participant who went out to lunch during their trial interacted with the cashier at the restaurant and reported that "the cashier didn't even mention the HMD or backpack computer. It was like they didn't even notice." While we found this example to be particularly humorous, it is likely the case that the cashier was simply being polite. As AR technology becomes smaller and more ubiquitous, the barrier between the user of the AR technology and the person they are interacting with will likely diminish, however as we make our way to that point it is important to consider these effects and barriers when designing user interfaces for these type of interactions.

We further have to point out that it is not universally positive that multi-spectral vision allows us to see more information that people in our society traditionally do not have access to, since some of this could be considered **private information**. An example are medical conditions that have discernible symptoms in different spectral bands such as low or high blood pressure, skin conditions, or strong cases of fever. By having access to this information, the user may inadvertently or purposely change their behavior towards that person, which may help prevent the spread of disease if the person actually had a fever, but may also damage interpersonal relationships if the cause of the temperature change was something benign (such as being caused by the environment or as a side effect of a medication).

In the UV spectrum, certain skin features such as freckles and moles are more prevalent than they are in the visible spectrum [17]. Some people do not like the appearance of these features even in visible light, and take measures to cover or obscure them from the people they interact with. These people will likely feel uncomfortable being around users of multi-spectral vision devices, as they will feel self-conscious about the appearance of these features in the UV spectrum. As multi-spectral vision becomes more common, we are likely to see people such as the ones described above, who want to keep certain personal or medical information to themselves, and therefore shy away from multi-spectral vision users due to privacy considerations. Due to issues such as the ones described above, we see a potentially transformative aspect of ubiquitous AR goggles with multi-spectral vision for our society in that it could **change societal norms and behaviors**.

5.3 Limitations

Observations in this study were limited to what the participants could visually perceive with the thermal IR and UV visualization techniques. Human vision is excellent in detecting differences and patterns in three wavelengths and with respect to luminance, but in this study it was capped by the temporal and spatial resolution of the available consumer thermal IR and UV cameras. Future versions of these cameras will likely provide more discernible features and lead to more information gained from these vision modes.

We would also like to note that human vision falls short in identifying certain features with respect to thermal IR and UV that machine learning approached are more suitable for. For instance, He et al. developed a system capable of classifying facial expressions from thermal imagery using a machine learning approach [20]. Additionally, Hu et al. developed a multi-camera system that combined IR and thermal sensors and is capable of monitoring both human heart rate and breathing rate simultaneously [22].

As multi-spectral vision technology and AR displays become more ubiquitous, such machine learning methods could be utilized along with the sensors and displays in order to make full use of the multi-spectral information.

6 Conclusion and Future Work

In this paper, we presented a qualitative report on lessons learned about potential societal uses and implications of AR-based multi-spectral vision enhancements focusing on the thermal IR and UV spectral bands during daily activities. We described a multi-spectral AR prototype based on a Microsoft HoloLens 1 with attached thermal IR and UV cameras. We presented a human-subject study, in which participants performed daily activities while wearing the HMD prototype. We discussed the potential of such AR multispectral vision enhancements with respect to different use cases, e.g., personal health, preventing accidents, and improving situational awareness.

For future work, we believe that more exploratory research is necessary to identify uses and drawbacks of such technologies to understand their societal implications, in particular with respect to vision augmentations that stem from different multispectral visualization methods for the camera streams or AR visual information created based on the output of machine learning approaches.

Acknowledgments. This material includes work supported in part by the Office of Naval Research under Award Number N00014-17-1-2927 (Dr. Peter Squire, Code 34) and the Advent Health Endowed Chair in Healthcare Simulation (Prof. Welch).

References

1. Ai, J., Jin, L., Zhang, Y., Tian, Z., Peng, C., Duan, W.: Detecting partial discharge of polluted insulators based on ultraviolet imaging. In: IEEE 11th International Conference on the Properties and Applications of Dielectric Materials (ICPADM), pp. 456–459. IEEE (2015)
2. Akula, A., Ghosh, R., Sardana, H.K.: Thermal imaging and its application in defence systems. Optics: Phenomena, Materials, Devices, and Characterization, pp. 333–335 (2011)
3. Bae, W., Kim, Y., Ahn, S.: IR-band conversion of target and background using surface temperature estimation and error compensation for military IR sensor simulation. Sensors **19**(11), 2455 (2019)
4. Balaras, C.A., Argiriou, A.A.: Infrared thermography for building diagnostics. Energy Build. **34**(2), 171–183 (2002)
5. Becker, L.: Influence of IR sensor technology on the military and civil defense. In: Quantum Sensing and Nanophotonic Devices III, vol. 6127, p. 61270S (2006)
6. Bendada, A., Sfarra, S., Ibarra, C., Akhloufi, M., Pradere, C., Maldague, X.: Subsurface imaging for panel paintings inspection: a comparative study of the ultraviolet, the visible, the infrared and the terahertz spectra. Opto-Electron. Rev. **23**(1), 90–101 (2015)
7. Bennett, M.V., Matthews, I.: Life-saving uncooled IR camera for use in firefighting applications, vol. 2744 (1996)
8. Bento, N.A.F., Silva, J.S., Dias, J.B.: Detection of camouflaged people. International Journal of Sensor Networks and Data Communications, vol. 5, no. 3 (2016)
9. Bluth, G.J.S., Shannon, J.M., Watson, I.M., Prata, A.J., Realmuto, V.J.: Development of an ultra-violet digital camera for volcanic so2 imaging. J. Volcanol. Geoth. Res. **161**(1–2), 47–56 (2007)
10. Boushel, R., Piantadosi, C.A.: Near-infrared spectroscopy for monitoring muscle oxygenation. Acta Physiol. Scand. **168**(4), 615–622 (2000)
11. Cardone, D., Merla, A.: New frontiers for applications of thermal infrared imaging devices: computational psychopshysiology in the neurosciences. Sensors **17**(5), 1042 (2017)
12. Centers for Disease Control and Prvention (CDC): High blood pressure fact sheet, June 2016. https://www.cdc.gov/dhdsp/data_statistics/fact_sheets/fs_bloodpressure.htm
13. Chen, Y.R., Chao, K., Kim, M.S.: Machine vision technology for agricultural applications. Comput. Electron. Agric. **36**(2–3), 173–191 (2002)
14. Cho, Y.: Mobile Thermography-based Physiological Computing for Automatic Recognition of a Person's Mental Stress. Ph.D. thesis, UCL Interaction Centre (2019)
15. Erickson, A., Kim, K., Bruder, G., Welch, G.: Exploring the limitations of environment lighting on optical see-through head-mounted displays. In: Proceedings of ACM Conference on Spatial User Interfaces (SUI), pp. 1–8 (2020)
16. Erickson, A., Schubert, R., Kim, K., Bruder, G., Welch, G.: Is it cold in here or is it just me? analysis of augmented reality temperature visualization for computer-mediated thermoception. In: Proceedings of the International Symposium on Mixed and Augmented Reality (ISMAR) (2019)
17. Fulton, J.E., Jr.: Utilizing the ultraviolet (uv detect) camera to enhance the appearance of photodamage and other skin conditions. Dermatol. Surg. **23**(3), 163–169 (1997)

18. Gade, R., Moeslund, T.B.: Thermal cameras and applications: a survey. Mach. Vis. Appl. **25**(1), 245–262 (2014)
19. Glushakow, J.M.: Social facilitation: salience and mediated, anticipatory, and residual presence. Ph.D. thesis, Rutgers University-Graduate School-New Brunswick (2011)
20. He, S., Wang, S., Lan, W., Fu, H., Ji, Q.: Facial expression recognition using deep boltzmann machine from thermal infrared images. In: 2013 Humaine Association Conference on Affective Computing and Intelligent Interaction, pp. 239–244 (2013)
21. Hermanson, A.S., Bush, M.A., Miller, R.G., Bush, P.J.: Ultraviolet illumination as an adjunctive aid in dental inspection. J. Forensic Sci. **53**(2), 408–411 (2008)
22. Hu, M., et al.: Combination of near-infrared and thermal imaging techniques for the remote and simultaneous measurements of breathing and heart rates under sleep situation. Plos One **13**(1), 1–14 (2018)
23. Ishimwe, R., Abutaleb, K., Ahmed, F.: Applications of thermal imaging in agriculture - a review. Adv. Remote Sens. **03**(03), 128–140 (2014)
24. Jiang, L.J., et al.: A perspective on medical infrared imaging. J. Med. Eng. Technol. **29**(6), 257–267 (2005)
25. Jones, B.F.: A reappraisal of the use of infrared thermal image analysis in medicine. IEEE Trans. Med. Imaging **17**(6), 1019–1027 (1998)
26. Kruse, P.W.: Uncooled Thermal Imaging Arrays, Systems, and Applications. SPIE Press, Bellingham (2001)
27. Lagüela, S., Armesto, J., Arias, P., Herráez, J.: Automation of thermographic 3D modelling through image fusion and image matching techniques. Autom. Constr. **27**, 24–31 (2012)
28. Lamb, D.W.: The use of qualitative airborne multispectral imaging for managing agricultural crops - a case study in south-eastern Australia. Aust. J. Exp. Agric. **40**(5), 725 (2000)
29. Lo, C.P., Quattrochi, D.A., Luvall, J.C.: Application of high-resolution thermal infrared remote sensing and GIS to assess the urban heat island effect. Int. J. Remote Sens. **18**(2), 287–304 (1997)
30. Mason, R.S., Sequeira, V.B., Gordon-Thomson, C.: Vitamin D: the light side of sunshine. Eur. J. Clin. Nutr. **65**(9), 986 (2011)
31. McGonigle, A.J.S., et al.: Ultraviolet imaging of volcanic plumes: a new paradigm in volcanology. Geosciences **7**(3), 68 (2017)
32. Morlier, A., Siebert, M., Kunze, I., Mathiak, G., Köntges, M.: Detecting photovoltaic module failures in the field during daytime with ultraviolet fluorescence module inspection. IEEE J. Photovoltaics **7**(6), 1710–1716 (2017)
33. Muehleisen, W., et al.: Outdoor detection and visualization of hailstorm damages of photovoltaic plants. Renew. Energy **118**, 138–145 (2018)
34. Munnerley, D., Bacon, M., Wilson, A., Steele, J., Hedberg, J., Fitzgerald, R.: Confronting an augmented reality (2012)
35. Narayanan, D.L., Saladi, R.N., Fox, J.L.: Review: ultraviolet radiation and skin cancer. Int. J. Dermatol. **49**(9), 978–986 (2010)
36. Ochoa, D., et al.: Hyperspectral imaging system for disease scanning on banana plants. In: Sensing for Agriculture and Food Quality and Safety VIII, vol. 9864, p. 98640M. International Society for Optics and Photonics (2016)
37. Orlosky, J., et al.: Vismerge: light adaptive vision augmentation via spectral and temporal fusion of non-visible light. In: Proceedings of the IEEE International Symposium on Mixed and Augmented Reality (ISMAR), pp. 22–31 (2017)
38. Panov, V., Borisova-Papancheva, T.: Application of ultraviolet light (uv) in dental medicine. Med. Inform. **2**, 194–200 (2015)

39. Pavlidis, I., Levine, J., Baukol, P.: Thermal image analysis for anxiety detection. In: International Conference on Image Processing, vol. 2, pp. 315–318. IEEE (2001)

40. Puri, V., Nayyar, A., Raja, L.: Agriculture drones: a modern breakthrough in precision agriculture. J. Stat. Manag. Syst. **20**(4), 507–518 (2017)

41. Reed, N.G.: The history of ultraviolet germicidal irradiation for air disinfection. Publ. Health Rep. **125**(1), 15–27 (2010)

42. Roberts, J.E.: Ultraviolet radiation as a risk factor for cataract and macular degeneration. Eye Contact Lens **37**(4), 246–9 (2011)

43. Rudol, P., Doherty, P.: Human body detection and geolocalization for UAV search and rescue missions using color and thermal imagery. In: IEEE Aerospace Conference, pp. 1–8. IEEE (2008)

44. Sankaran, S., Mishra, A., Ehsani, R., Davis, C.: A review of advanced techniques for detecting plant diseases. Comput. Electron. Agric. **72**(1), 1–13 (2010)

45. Sosnowski, T., Madura, H., Bieszczad, G., Kastek, M.: Thermal camera system integrated into firefighter helmet. Measurement Automation Monitoring, vol. 63 (2017)

46. Stockton, G.R.: The use of thermal imaging technology. Technical report, Stockton Infrared Thermographic Services, Inc. (2015)

47. Torresan, H., Turgeon, B., Ibarra-Castanedo, C., Hebert, P., Maldague, X.P.: Advanced surveillance systems: combining video and thermal imagery for pedestrian detection. In: Thermosense XXVI, vol. 5405, p. 506 (2004)

48. Van Eck, W., Kolstee, Y.: The augmented painting: playful interaction with multispectral images. In: 2012 IEEE International Symposium on Mixed and Augmented Reality-arts, Media, and Humanities (ISMAR-AMH), pp. 65–69. IEEE (2012)

49. Vogel, A., et al.: Using noninvasive multispectral imaging to quantitatively assess tissue vasculature. J. Biomed. Opt. **12**(5), 051604 (2007)

50. Wilkes, T., et al.: Ultraviolet imaging with low cost smartphone sensors: development and application of a raspberry Pi-based UV camera. Sensors **16**(10), 1649 (2016)

51. Wilkes, T., Pering, T., McGonigle, A., Tamburello, G., Willmott, J.: A low-cost smartphone sensor-based UV camera for volcanic so2 emission measurements. Remote Sens. **9**(1), 27 (2017)

52. Wilson, A.D., Zhang, Z., Chou, P.A., Fishman, N.S., Gillett, D.M., LLC, H.B.M.T.L.: Providing a tele-immersive experience using a mirror metaphor. US patent no. us9641805b2 (2017)

53. Wright, F., Weller, R.B.: Risks and benefits of UV radiation in older people: more of a friend than a foe? Maturitas **81**(4), 425–431 (2015)

54. Zhang, X., Xu, W., Huang, M.C., Amini, N., Ren, F.: See UV on your skin: an ultraviolet sensing and visualization system. In: Proceedings of the 8th International Conference on Body Area Networks, pp. 22–28. BodyNets 2013, ICST (Institute for Computer Sciences, Social-Informatics and Telecommunications Engineering), ICST, Brussels, Belgium (2013)

55. Zhou, D., Dillon, M., Kwon, E.: Tracking-based deer vehicle collision detection using thermal imaging. In: IEEE International Conference on Robotics and Biomimetics, pp. 688–693. IEEE (2009)

56. Zhu, Z., Li, W., Wolberg, G.: Integrating LDV audio and IR video for remote multimodal surveillance. In: Proceedings of the IEEE Computer Society Conference on Computer Vision and Pattern Recognition (CVPR) Workshops, p. 10 (2005)

No One is Superman: 3-D Safety Margin Profiles When Using Head-Up Display (HUD) for Takeoff in Low Visibility and High Crosswind Conditions

Daniela Kratchounova[1]([✉]), Inchul Choi[2], Theodore Mofle[2], Larry Miller[3], Jeremy Hesselroth[3], Scott Stevenson[3], and Mark Humphreys[2]

[1] Federal Aviation Administration Civil Aerospace Medical Institute, Oklahoma City, OK, USA
Daniela.Kratchounova@faa.gov
[2] Cherokee Nation 3S, Catoosa, OK, USA
{Inchul.CTR.Choi,Theodore.C-CTR.Mofle}@faa.gov
[3] Federal Aviation Administration Flight Technologies and Procedures Division, Oklahoma City, OK, USA
{Larry.C.Miller,Jeremy.J.Hesselroth,scott.stevenson}@faa.gov

Abstract. The role of crosswinds in the relationship between crew workload and size of safety margin during low visibility takeoffs using HUD was examined. 3-dimensional (3-D) safety margin profiles for different low visibility takeoff conditions and guidance types were generated utilizing the raw and standardized scores for the six NASA-TLX subscales, with and without the effect of crosswinds. The results underlined the critical role for aviation safety of a) building an evocative shared mental model within the pilots' community of the multi-faceted nature of safety margin; and b) having a clear understanding of the complex interplay between the many factors that affect its shape and size.

Keywords: Safety margin · Crew workload · Head-up display (HUD) · NASA-TLX · Low visibility operations

1 Introduction

In a previous research effort [7], we identified the differential effects of head-up display (HUD), HUD with localizer guidance symbology, runway visual range (RVR) and runway centerline lighting infrastructure on crew workload as measured by the NASA Task Load Index (NASA-TLX) scores during low visibility takeoff operations. Only the total weighted NASA-TLX scores were used for those analyses and crosswinds were not a factor of primary interest.

Here, we analyzed the role of crosswinds in the relationship between crew workload and safety margin as measured by the raw NASA-TLX subscale scores. The information gained from these analyses enabled the creation of 3-dimensional (3-D) safety margin profiles across different low visibility takeoff conditions and guidance types. Specifically,

This is a U.S. government work and not under copyright protection in the U.S.; foreign copyright protection may apply 2021
J. Y. C. Chen and G. Fragomeni (Eds.): HCII 2021, LNCS 12770, pp. 336–352, 2021.
https://doi.org/10.1007/978-3-030-77599-5_24

the scores for the six NASA-TLX subscales were used to plot each safety margin profile with and without the effect of crosswinds. In addition, we discuss the importance of pilots recognizing that handling crosswinds safely requires awareness not only of the aircraft and their own personal limitations, but all factors that could directly, or indirectly, affect the size of safety margin.

The notion of margin of safety is fundamental to the notion of aviation itself. Safety margins apply to many areas of flight operations including flight environment (e.g., weather), ground infrastructure (e.g., runway lighting), etc. Furthermore, aircraft design involves multiple layers of safety margins intended to improve safety without unnecessarily limiting aircraft and human performance. Numerous factors affect these safety margin layers and may dynamically change the size of each layer in the different phases of flight, and across varying operational and environmental conditions.

Conceptually, the size of a single safety margin layer could be defined as the "distance" between a crew workload profile, and a potential incident or accident boundary in a given flight situation. In this context, the probability of safety margin reduction as a function of some type of hazard, or a combination of hazards, is referred to as risk. Besides, the way people recognize risk is inherently subjective and reflects their: a) previous experience with particular hazard; b) perception of the potential, direct or indirect, negative consequences and how imminent these consequences are; c) sense of control over the situation; and d) individual biases toward competency and control. Therefore, building strong mental models about how the effects of one factor (e.g., crosswinds) interact with the effects of other operational and environmental factors, and new technologies; is critical for the safety of flight.

2 Background

In aviation, as with other high-risk operational environments, there is a constantly fluctuating margin between two distinct boundaries. That is, a lower boundary that could represent a pilot/crew's current workload level resulting from performing normal pilot tasks and responses to hazards presented by actual conditions; and an upper boundary representing a pilot/crew's total capacity to positively respond to hazards and safely manage tasks under those conditions.

Hart [5] echoes the notion that workload is "the human cost (e.g., fatigue, stress, illness, and accidents) of maintaining performance" (p. 904). When that cost is unacceptably high, the capacity of a human operator to perform a given task safely may be depleted. As the distance between the two boundaries decreases, the safety margin decreases, leaving less spare capacity for the pilot to resolve hazards or successfully complete required tasks.

For the purposes of this research, the raw scores on the six NASA-TLX subscales established the lower boundary. The upper boundary was "mapped" to the upper limit of the subscales [6]. The highest score on the NASA-TLX workload scale is 100, signifying the upper limit of pilots' total capacity to manage tasks safely under those conditions [4].

Figure 1 portrays an example of NASA-TLX Mental Demand profiles for the pilot flying (PF) and the pilot monitoring (PM) across two types of takeoff guidance, three levels of RVR, and various crosswind components. Overall, the PF reported experiencing higher workload than the PM for the given set of conditions. Furthermore, the relative differences between the reported workload levels for the PF and PM also varied across conditions. Consequently, the resulting size and shape of safety margin for each crewmember were different. This was not surprising. The PF and PM perform separate duties on the flight deck. Therefore, a crew workload profile could not be depicted as a single entity and contains the workload profiles of both the PF and the PM.

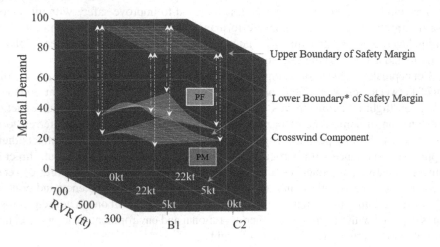

*Lower boundary for each crew member (PF and PM)

Fig. 1. Safety margin's lower boundary for each crewmember on the Mental Demand NASA-TLX subscale.

While the number of actual conditions that could affect safety margin is seemingly unlimited, the impact of crosswinds on takeoff and landing provides a rich example to consider. For high crosswind conditions, the lower boundary could be defined as the workload associated with resolving the aircraft directional control hazard caused by the crosswind component. In this particular case, the upper boundary limit could be determined as the pilot's total capacity to control the aircraft safely under crosswind conditions.

It is important to note that the controllability of the aircraft is not solely based on the all-engines operating case. The crosswind considerations must also include engine failure considerations. Under strong crosswind conditions, the aircraft naturally tends to weathervane into the wind due to side forces exerted on the aircraft fuselage. Additionally, an engine failure in a twin-engine aircraft causes the aircraft to yaw in the direction of the failed engine. The torque generated from the thrust differential makes an upwind engine failure under high crosswind conditions the most critical engine failure case for controllability. If the actual runway crosswind conditions remain below the limits of both the aircraft and the pilot, then the safety margin is preserved. However, if the crosswinds exceed the capabilities of either the pilot or the aircraft, and/or are combined with other risk factors such as inclement weather, then the safety margin may be compromised resulting in an accident.

Nevertheless, safeguards and mitigating factors that positively affect the lower boundary level could preserve or enhance the safety margin. For example, in high cross-wind operations without the use of advanced flight deck technologies such as a HUD, the lower boundary workload level could be optimized by either utilizing a runway direction more closely aligned with the wind, or simply, waiting for the winds to subside. Similarly, factors such as training and experience, crew resource management (CRM), and new technologies may have a profound impact, as well.

2.1 Training and Experience

One potentially large contributor to increasing the safety margin in a crosswind environment would be optimizing the lower boundary limit by increasing pilots' skill level through standardized initial and recurrent training. This includes learning about landing techniques such as de-crabbing[1] the aircraft just prior to touchdown, and building a mental model of the correct sight picture for wings level and on runway centerline, both in the daytime and at night. It also includes rigorous training on what actions are to be taken if the aircraft's performance is outside of specific parameters. For example, an aircraft operator could establish a training standard specifying that if a safe landing cannot be achieved with wings level and within 20 ft of centerline, a missed approach must be executed. The "must" is important as it relates to safety margin because it relieves the pilot of having to quantify the size of the safety margin in a highly dynamic and time-compressed environment.

Correctly determining where the lower boundary actually resides with respect to the upper boundary is a nearly impossible task in real time. However, pilots can easily determine when they are approaching the limits of a specific training standard that is tailored to ensure that as much of the safety margin is preserved as possible. If there were a real or perceived pressure not to execute a missed approach and just land the plane regardless of its position relative to the prescribed one, the safety margin may be reduced.

Through the process of continuous training, a culture of safety is created. More, a well-established safety culture gives pilots the agency and confidence to "do the right thing" every time. Building upon the knowledge and skills gained through training, real-world experience and the practical application of those skills is often the best instructor. This encompasses not only learning directly from personal experiences, but also learning indirectly by observing the experiences of other pilots. For example, a pilot may observe the full effects of crosswind while lined up for takeoff during high crosswind conditions, as the plane ahead rolls off for takeoff. If the preceding aircraft fails to apply sufficient crosswind controls into the wind, the upwind wing would rise and the engines on the downwind wing would come very close to the ground. As a result, the aircraft may experience a wing rock ensuing in a roll angle with the upwind wing low, before returning to a wings-level condition. The pilot(s) in the waiting aircraft would have no way of

---

[1] "Crabbing" is to point the nose of the plane into the wind. The plane flies sideways, similar to how a crab walks. .

knowing all of the factors that contributed to this outcome. However, they could gain valuable insight by observation and in the future, recognize the likely signs of insufficient crosswind controls into the wind followed by a sharp overcorrection in response to the wing rise. Ultimately, retaining and reinforcing knowledge of proper crosswind control techniques improves the safety margin by optimizing the workload profile that defines its lower boundary.

2.2 Crew Resource Management (CRM)

In multi-crew aircraft, CRM has a significant impact on safety margin. Through crew briefings and other activities, CRM affects the lower boundary by creating a shared mental model that serves to quantify, organize, and articulate all of the external factors that the aircrew is managing during a particular phase of flight. This organization of tasks optimizes pilots' cognitive workload, therefore preserving the safety margin. At the same time, by delegating and sharing tasks, pilots are effectively able to redistribute their individual workload level where an optimized crew workload level reflects the pilots working together performing normal pilot tasks and resolving hazards. With regard to crosswind takeoffs and landings, CRM helps both pilots have a shared mental model about how the winds are likely to affect the aircraft, what the acceptable takeoff and landing parameters are, and what actions should be taken if those parameters are exceeded. As a result, the size of the safety margin is maximized, as well.

2.3 New Technologies

New technologies on the flight deck are intended to enhance the safety margin, improve performance, and optimize crew workload. At the same time, such technologies may initially raise the lower boundary and consequently reduce the safety margin due to elevated cognitive workload levels associated with the lack of experience in flying with these technologies. For example, in the case of crosswind takeoffs and landings using a HUD, there are three main tools used: the flight path vector (FPV), the boresight symbol, and the wind readout. The FPV and boresight symbol are very useful, especially at night and in low visibility conditions, because they provide the pilot with a visual cue of the angular difference between the actual flight path and the longitudinal axis of the aircraft when no external visual cues are available. The wind readout is useful during high crosswind landings because the winds are seldom steady throughout the approach and landing.

As the wind velocity and vector continually change, this requires appropriate adjustments in flight control inputs. Without any indication depicting the general trends in wind velocity and direction, the flight control inputs may lag in response to the changing crosswind conditions. The wind readout helps reduce the lag time and, when used in conjunction with the FPV, it helps refine the required flight control inputs. Takeoff operations similarly benefit from the HUD. From immediately after takeoff and throughout the departure climb segments, the FPV compared to the boresight symbol provides a near instantaneous visual depiction of the actual aircraft flight path compared to the aircraft's longitudinal axis. By placing the FPV over the top of the flight director cue, and cross-referencing the wind readout, a pilot is able to reduce the wind drift and tracking error relative to the planned departure track compared to operations without the assistance of the HUD symbology.

The combination of FPV, boresight symbol, and wind readout on the HUD enhances pilot performance and optimizes workload levels because the information is immediately actionable for proper application of control inputs. This eliminates the typical lag associated with waiting for a deviation to occur, for that deviation to be recognized, and then for corrective inputs to be applied to return the aircraft to the planned departure track. Once a pilot overcomes the initial challenge to incorporate this new information into their cognitive process, the use of a HUD positively affects the lower limit by providing the pilot with highly actionable information that reduces pilot response time, thereby enhancing the safety margin.

In summary, and for the purposes of this study, a safety margin is the relative spread between the lower boundary, representing a pilot's current workload level, and the upper boundary limit, representing a pilot's total capacity to handle normal pilot tasks and resolve hazards. The lower boundary limit is profoundly influenced by training and experience, CRM, and the introduction of new technologies on the flight deck. New techniques already exist (e.g., use of a HUD) that are capable of further optimizing the safety margin by limiting the lower boundary to a certain level to ensure it remains well below the upper boundary during all phases of flight, types of operations and environmental conditions.

2.4 Personal Crosswind Limits

On any given day, a pilot's performance is not limited solely by the extent of their training. For decades, the literature has extensively documented factors that potentially negatively affect pilot's performance, including factors such as fatigue, use of over-the-counter medications, alcohol consumption, and other stressors in their personal lives that detract from their ability to focus. It is an established practice that pilots need to assess their individual fitness to perform flight duties before every flight. While that is true for both commercial air carriers and general aviation, the methods of addressing those impacts may differ between the two communities.

Operational limitations for commercial air carriers are very specific, and typically could be found in the Aircraft Flight Manual (AFM), the company's Flight Operations Manual, or the Operations Specifications that govern a carrier. For any set of operational conditions, a pilot is authorized to operate only within the specified limits. Pilots in this community are trained and evaluated for operations according to predefined standards. A pilot is expected to report for duty fully prepared to operate at that level. If any personal factors exist that would prevent them from safely operating up to the standard, it is customary to decline the flight assignment so another pilot is assigned to the flight. This makes the fitness for duty decision a binary choice. For the community of commercial air carrier pilots, this eliminates the need for setting personal minimums based upon other operational or environmental factors.

In contrast, general aviation has less prescribed restrictions imposed on the pilots. This places more responsibility on them to assess not only their personal fitness for flying duties and to determine a set of personal minimums, as well. General aviation pilots may set their personal minimums according to the aircraft limitations in most situations. However, in certain situations the pilot may choose to set a lower personal minimum. In a stark contrast to commercial air carriers, if a limit is not in the AFM then there may be a few situations where a general aviation pilot would set personal minimums based on the Aeronautical Decision-Making (ADM) guidance [2]. Such circumstances might involve weather, runway conditions, location, and in some cases, a known design issue inherent to a certain airframe that pilots learn to pay special attention to, during training.

One situation where a pilot may consider setting a personal crosswind limit lower than the ones set forth by the AFM would be during low visibility takeoff. Under FAR Part 91, which is the sole governing regulation for most general aviation operations, there are no takeoff minimums. Therefore, when the visibility is reduced significantly, pilots may choose not to attempt a takeoff in crosswinds that are close to, or at the limit of the aircraft. For example, a particular aircraft may have a "maximum demonstrated" crosswind of 28 kt for takeoff. This may not be an aircraft limitation per se, but simply the maximum crosswind the test pilots demonstrated during certification [8]. In these situations, pilots often choose to set their personal limit to a value less than the maximum demonstrated crosswind. While 28 kt is a very high crosswind, there are techniques that would help pilots mitigate potential hazards when operating the aircraft close to these demonstrated conditions. For example, one such technique is the use of normal crosswind control inputs then slowly reducing the amount of input as ground/airspeed increases the effectiveness of the control surfaces. A different technique to consider is a slightly higher rotation speed and/or a faster rotation especially if the crosswind is gusting. The intent is to keep the wheels in contact with the ground as long as possible and rotate the aircraft away from the ground as quickly as possible.

In degraded visual conditions, the number of outside visual references are reduced substantially. Therefore, pilots may consider lowering the crosswind they are willing to take off with, and do so relative to the amount of reduced visibility. Following with the example above, if the visibility is low enough; pilots may reduce the crosswind they are willing to accept from 28 kt to 20 kt or even lower, depending on the specific conditions.

Another factor in considering a personal crosswind limit is the runway condition. Contingent on the amount of contamination (e.g., water, ice) on the runway, pilots should consider reducing the amount of crosswind they are willing to accept due to reduced traction of the tires on the pavement. In some AFMs and countries of registry, this is an actual limitation and aircraft registered there would be limited to 28 kt for wet runways with "good" braking reported, 15 kt for "average", 10 kt for "poor" and for a coefficient of friction less than 0.3, the takeoff would be prohibited. Similarly, for "contaminated" runways, the aircraft would be limited to 10 kt crosswind and prohibited with the coefficient of friction less than 0.3. For most countries however, there are no limitations, therefore it becomes the responsibility of the Pilot-In-Command to establish a crosswind limit suitable to the runway conditions. If a limitation is not introduced during training, it is the pilot's responsibility to draw from experience to establish acceptable and safe personal minimums. Flying with more senior pilots may help with establishing such minimums. Essentially, they may be passed down to junior pilots in an informal manner.

In addition, certain aircraft design characteristics might make the pilot more susceptible to error during crosswind takeoffs and landings therefore warranting personal limits that are more conservative. Aircraft with narrowly spaced main gear, a low belly and wings, and highly swept wings may be good examples. Moreover, defined crosswind limitations or "demonstrated" crosswinds may not exist for some aircraft [8]. During initial training, pilots may receive some suggested guidance on acceptable crosswind limits. However, these could vary greatly across flight crews since there are no demonstrated or limiting crosswinds defined by the manufacturer. As a result, crews may report an unexpected and sometimes unnoticed issue of wing "scrape" during high crosswind and excessive pitch takeoffs and landings. A "word-of-mouth" pitch/bank combination could be what crews set when flying such airframes.

Location, unique terrain features, and weather phenomena associated with that location also warrant setting personal crosswind limits lower than what is normal or defined in the AFM. Due to the runway direction and layout of the terrain, when there is a direct crosswind, nearby mountains may create a Venturi effect. These phenomena add up to winds that are significantly stronger at 50–100 ft above the runway than is reported by the automated weather observation service. Consequently, pilots should expect that shortly after rotation while still at low airspeeds, they might encounter moderate to severe turbulence that could potentially affect the controllability of the aircraft. Given these factors, and when winds at the airport are reported to be higher than 10–15 kt of direct crosswind, pilots should plan delaying the departure until winds subside or change direction. Through experience of known weather and terrain phenomena, this is one instance where it may be prudent to set up lower crosswind limits than what would otherwise be considered typical.

2.5 Crosswind Takeoff Considerations

Regardless of whether a pilot is performing flight duties as an air carrier operator or as a general aviation pilot, they likewise require the ability to determine the actual crosswind component of the wind relative to the runway heading. Fortunately, the actual runway crosswind conditions are easy to estimate based on the winds reported from the tower controller. While the Automatic Terminal Information Service (ATIS) broadcasts report the average wind velocity and direction valid at the time of the ATIS recording, for takeoff purposes they are mostly useful only for runway planning and performance data calculations. At tower-controlled airfields, the controller typically provides current runway wind conditions as part of the takeoff clearance to civil aircraft. At those same airfields, it is mandatory for the controller to provide runway wind direction and velocity to military aircraft because crosswinds are specifically factored into aircraft performance data for aircraft that are certified under military specification. Using the tower reported wind direction and velocity; a pilot can calculate the crosswind component of runway wind by analyzing the horizontal component of the wind vector relative to the runway heading. For operations at airports without an operating control tower, an Automated Weather Observation System (AWOS) may be available that broadcasts nearly real-time wind data that can be used for performance calculations.

2.6 Crew Workload Considerations

To achieve optimal system performance, system designers need to take into consideration the overall operator workload at all stages of system design and operation. The NASA-TLX is a human-centered rating scale in which information about the size and sources of six dimensions of workload are combined to develop a sensitive and reliable subjective assessment of workload [6]. It was developed based on the assumption that a combination of six workload related factors (Mental Demand, Physical Demand, Temporal Demand, Performance, Effort, and Frustration) represent the workload experienced by most people performing most tasks. These dimensions were selected after extensive analyses of factors that identify the subjective experience of workload for different people performing activities ranging from simple to complex tasks such as flying an aircraft [4, 6].

According to Hart [5], the majority of studies that used NASA-TLX, addressed a question about the user interface design and 31% of them focused on display design. Furthermore, the author reported that a common variation of the scale is to conduct subscale-rating analyses instead of generating a single overall workload score. Over 40 studies used this approach and demonstrated the potency of the scale and the diagnostic value of the component subscales. The author concluded that the high reliability, sensitivity, and utility of the NASA-TLX component ratings allow for a very narrow identification of sources of a workload or performance problems [5].

Our original research [7] included analyses that used only the total weighted NASA-TLX scores. With this follow-on research, we focused on identifying the size of the safety margin based on the raw scores from each of the NASA-TLX subscales. Specifically, we looked for an insight to whether or not the introduction of the HUD, with either just its basic HUD symbology or with the additional localizer takeoff guidance, contributed to a more optimized crew workload profile and helped preserve the safety margin under low visibility conditions. We hypothesized that any contribution to a more optimized pilot workload profile due to the use of a HUD, and a dedicated set of takeoff guidance symbology, could also allow for a larger takeoff safety margin in higher crosswinds conditions.

During each crew's briefing session, we found that it was easier for the pilot evaluators to look at the six NASA-TLX subscales as two distinct groups. One of the groups included the first three subscales - all pertaining to the task itself. Specifically, we requested that the pilots assess the mental, physical, and temporal demands as sources of workload related to the nature of the task in the specific conditions it was performed. The second group consisted of the last three subscales, all associated with the person performing the task. In this case, the pilots were asked to rate their individual performance on the task, the total level of effort they felt was required to meet the demands of the task and achieve that performance; and the level of frustration they experienced while performing the task in each set of conditions.

Based on the raw NASA-TLX subscale scores, with this follow-on study, we introduced a novel method of visualizing the data in 3-D by generating safety margin profiles across the different guidance types, RVR values, crosswinds, for normal and abnormal flight operations; and with and without the use of a HUD for takeoff. By generating safety margin profiles with the raw and standardized scores for each NASA-TLX sub-scale, the objective was to help the pilot community build an evocative mental model of the effect crosswinds have on the size of safety margins under a variety of operational and environmental conditions; both with and without new flight deck technologies.

3 Method

Twenty-four pilot crews participated in this research: 12 airline crews and 12 business jet crews, who were deemed proficient in using a HUD. For normal operations, five levels of Type of Guidance, three levels of RVR (300 ft, 500 ft, & 700 ft), and two levels of Lighting conditions were examined (see Table 1). Wind speeds ranging between 3 kt (calm) and 22 kt[2] and varying directions were randomly assigned to scenarios. For abnormal operations, winds between 3 kt (calm) and 15 kt were applied. All tailwinds were limited to 10 kt (Boeing 737–800 NG Airplane Flight Manual Limitation).

Crew workload was assessed using the "paper and pen" NASA-TLX [4] The Pilot Flying (PF) and Pilot Monitoring (PM) each completed the NASA-TLX questionnaire immediately following each takeoff scenario. Plotting the PF and PM as separate lower boundary layers is prudent and essential to the understanding of the overall nature of safety margin. More specifically, it affords a deeper insight to the changes of its shape and size as the crew experiences the changes in the operational and environmental conditions.

Our previous research [7] analyzed total weighted NASA-TLX scores, using an ANCOVA method, with two significant main factors: Type of guidance (five levels), RVR (three levels), and one non-significant main factor of lighting conditions (two levels). Crosswind component was considered as a covariate. In this study, the raw NASA-TLX subscale scores were examined separately, and utilized to construct 3-D safety margin profiles. The profiles show the changes that occur to the shape of the safety margin's lower boundaries under the different experimental conditions.

Due to violations of normality and homogeneity of variance, the crosswind coefficient for each subscale was evaluated individually using a Generalized Linear Mixed Model (GLMM). Instead of applying a transformation to the workload data, an identity link function to a normal distribution was applied. The crosswind component values were normalized across all experimental conditions; assessing at ~9 kt for normal operations; and ~4 kt for abnormal operations.

Using mesh graphs, the raw and the standardized NASA-TLX subscale scores for the PF and PM were plotted side-by-side. Crosswind component at ~9 kt for normal operations and ~4 kt for abnormal operations were applied with each crosswind component coefficient. In lieu of a linear interpolation method, the modified Akima (MAKIMA) piecewise cubic Hermite interpolation method [1] in MATLAB® was utilized to generate the 3-D mesh graphs. For the purposes of 3-D visualization, this interpolation method allows for optimal data smoothing while at the same time preserving data validity.

---

[2] AC 120-28D - Criteria for Approval of Category III Weather Minima for Takeoff, Landing, and Rollout .

Table 1. Normal and Abnormal operational conditions

Operation type	Conditions	RVR		
		300	500	700
Normal operations	**Baseline 1:** HUD, No LOC[a] guidance, RCLM[b] only	Day/ Night	Day/ Night	Day/ Night
	Baseline 2: HUD, No LOC guidance, CLL[c,d]	Day/ Night	Day/ Night	Day/ Night
	Baseline 3: No HUD, CLL	Day/ Night	Day/ Night	Day/ Night
	Condition 1: HUD, LOC guidance, RCLM only	Day/ Night	Day/ Night	Day/ Night
	Condition 2: HUD, LOC guidance, No RCLM, No CLL	Day/ Night	Day/ Night	Day/ Night
Abnormal operations	**Failure Condition 1:** Above V_1 continue	Day/ Night	Day/ Night	Day/ Night
	Failure Condition 2: Below V_1 reject	Day/ Night	Day/ Night	Day/ Night
	Failure Condition 3: Below V_{mcg} reject	Day/ Night	Day/ Night	Day/ Night
	Failure Condition 4: LOC Fail	Day/ Night	Day/ Night	Day/ Night
	Failure Condition 5: LOC Bend	Day/ Night	Day/ Night	Day/ Night
	Failure Condition 6: Loss of HUD	Day/ Night	Day/ Night	Day/ Night

[a]LOC = Localizer
[b]RCLM = Runway Centerline Markings
[c]CLL = Center Line Lights
[d]All CLL conditions assume existing RCLM

4 Results

Crosswind component coefficients were determined for each NASA-TLX subscale by conducting GLMM analyses on the scores for normal and abnormal operations. The crosswind coefficients and associated p-values, for each NASA-TLX subscale for normal operations are shown in Table 2. The coefficient of crosswind covariate was positive and significant for each subscale. Table 3 shows the crosswind coefficients and associated p-values, for each NASA-TLX subscale for abnormal operations. The crosswind components coefficients were significant only for Temporal Demand and Frustration.

A set of 3-D crew workload profiles for each NASA-TLX subscale across different Types of Guidance, RVR levels, and crosswinds, during normal operations at night are shown on Fig. 2 and Fig. 3. The workload profiles represent the lower boundary of the

Table 2. Crosswind component coefficient and p-value for each NASA-TLX Subscale (Normal Operations)

NASA-TLX subscale	Crosswind component coefficient	p-Value
Mental demand	0.459	$p < 0.0001$
Physical demand	0.313	$p < 0.0001$
Temporal demand	0.294	$p < 0.0001$
Performance	0.284	$p < 0.0001$
Effort	0.473	$p < 0.0001$
Frustration	0.362	$p < 0.0001$

Table 3. Crosswind component coefficient and p-value for each NASA-TLX Subscale (Abnormal Operations)

NASA-TLX Subscale	Crosswind component coefficient	p-Value
Mental demand	0.279	$p = 0.170$
Physical demand	0.138	$p = 0.476$
Temporal demand	0.454	$p = 0.044$
Performance	0.236	$p = 0.141$
Effort	0.118	$p = 0.601$
Frustration	0.351	$p = 0.060$

safety margin for a given set of flight conditions. The side-by-side profiles are grouped by NASA-TLX subscale, displaying the raw scores before parsing out crosswind effect on the left and the scores with the standardized crosswind effect on the right. Each figure represents a group of three subscales, one for the task demands subscales and one for the subscales related to the subjective experience of the person performing the task.

These profiles reveal the complex interplay between different factors affecting the lower safety margin boundary. The raw NASA–TLX subscale scores for PF and PM identify the sources of crew workload with a high level of granularity. For example, Fig. 2 and Fig. 3 clearly indicate that Mental Demand and Effort were the largest contributors of workload for both PF and PM in normal operations. The relatively higher "peaks" on the virtual "landscape" as shown on Fig. 2 (left) and Fig. 3 (left), portray the effect of crosswind component on the raw NASA-TLX scores in each set of conditions. In contrast, Fig. 2 (right) and Fig. 3 (right) depict the "landscape" when the effect of crosswind was parsed out.

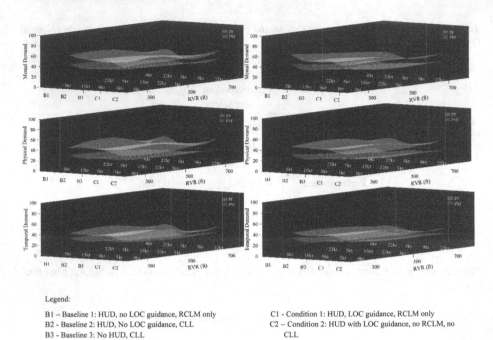

Legend:

B1 – Baseline 1: HUD, no LOC guidance, RCLM only   C1 - Condition 1: HUD, LOC guidance, RCLM only
B2 - Baseline 2: HUD, No LOC guidance, CLL   C2 – Condition 2: HUD with LOC guidance, no RCLM, no
B3 - Baseline 3: No HUD, CLL   CLL

Fig. 2. NASA-TLX Mental Demand, Physical Demand, Temporal Demand (normal operations): raw scores (left) and standardized scores at ~9 kt crosswind component (right)

While the higher "peaks" on the raw score profiles could be interpreted as a decrease in safety margin under these conditions, none of them approached what would be considered unsafe levels of workload (e.g., scores in the upper most quartile on the NASA-TLX scale). We attribute these results to the high levels of information redundancy typical of the design of modern flight decks and the number of safeguards in place for multi-crew operations such as continuous training, practicing good CRM; and new technologies that enhance pilot performance and optimize workload. Nonetheless, having the "landscape" of crew workload visualized in 3-D space provides for a better understanding of the nature of the effect crosswinds (or any other factor of interest) may have on safety margin when interacting with conditions such as inclement weather during a critical phase of flight.

The crosswind conditions included in the failure scenarios did not exceed the maximum authorized 15 kt crosswinds for takeoff operations performed according to FAA Policy Order 8400.13F [3] and OpSpec CO78/079. The operational safeguards specified in these documents are designed to ensure safety margins are preserved and the maximum authorized crosswinds remain below the limits of both the aircraft and the pilot, especially when other risk factors such as inclement weather are present. Not surprisingly, crosswinds did not have a significant contribution to the level of crew workload except for Temporal Demand. One plausible explanation for these results could be that when a failure condition was present, the crew reprioritized crosswind as a factor. Their focus was on quickly resolving the effects of key factors jeopardizing safety of flight (e.g., engine failure) first, and then, on successfully recovering from the failure.

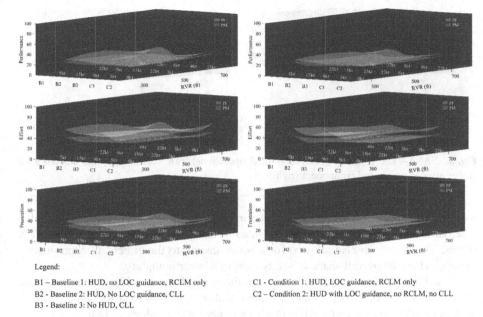

Legend:

B1 – Baseline 1: HUD, no LOC guidance, RCLM only   C1 - Condition 1: HUD, LOC guidance, RCLM only
B2 - Baseline 2: HUD, No LOC guidance, CLL   C2 – Condition 2: HUD with LOC guidance, no RCLM, no CLL
B3 - Baseline 3: No HUD, CLL

Fig. 3. NASA-TLX Performance, Effort, Frustration (normal operations): raw scores (left) and standardized scores at ~9 kt crosswind component (right)

5 Discussion

In the original research effort [7], only the total weighted NASA-TLX scores were used for the analyses, and crosswinds were not a factor of primary interest. The overall crew workload levels reported by the crews across the baseline and experimental conditions were low to moderate for normal operations (Fig. 4). Workload did not exceed moderate levels on the NASA-TLX scale for abnormal operations (Fig. 5).

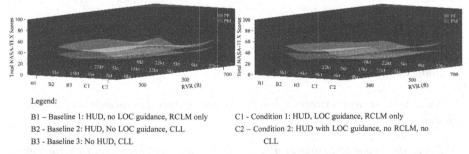

Legend:

B1 – Baseline 1: HUD, no LOC guidance, RCLM only   C1 - Condition 1: HUD, LOC guidance, RCLM only
B2 - Baseline 2: HUD, No LOC guidance, CLL   C2 – Condition 2: HUD with LOC guidance, no RCLM, no
B3 - Baseline 3: No HUD, CLL   CLL

Fig. 4. NASA-TLX Total Weighted (normal operations): raw scores (left) and standardized scores at ~9 kt crosswind component (right)

The novel 3-D visualization proposed here utilized the scores on the six NASA-TLX subscales. The differential contribution of each source of workload to the crew

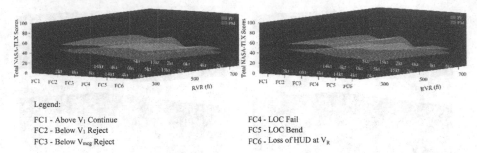

Legend:

FC1 - Above V₁ Continue
FC2 - Below V₁ Reject
FC3 - Below Vmcg Reject

FC4 - LOC Fail
FC5 - LOC Bend
FC6 - Loss of HUD at VR

Fig. 5. NASA-TLX Total Weighted (abnormal operations): raw scores (left) and standardized scores at ~4 kt crosswind component (right)

workload profiles under the different experimental conditions was clearly identifiable when analyzed and plotted separately instead of using the weighted total NASA-TLX scores. This approach also allowed for a better insight to the effects all experimental factors had on the overall shape of safety margin's lower boundary.

In addition, during the data collection for the original research [7], we requested that pilot evaluators give their personal recommendation for the lowest RVR they considered as equally safe for using HUD localizer guidance symbology in lieu of centerline lights (CLL). Their feedback was remarkably consistent with the results and expanded beyond the topic of equivalence of level of safety to cover many other factors that could potentially influence it. Below are excerpts from the pilots' responses directly addressing crosswind as an important safety factor in that context.

"Successful outcomes were demonstrated at crosswinds of 22 kt which is approaching the upper boundaries for a successful low visibility takeoff. I personally would suggest an operational limit of no greater than 15 knots crosswind component if utilizing an RVR value < 1800 for the Boeing 737 aircraft."

"Guidance cue was extremely helpful, mostly during crosswinds and engine failures."

"I found it most useful making initial crosswinds corrections."

"I believe that the cue is a little too sensitive to very small rudder inputs in maintaining centerline in crosswinds."

"Guidance cue was extremely helpful, mostly during crosswinds and engine failures."

"The guidance que and ground roll reference cue appeared to diverge from runway centerline on crosswinds. Guidance cue seemed overly sensitive on initial takeoff roll. Training would be critical component of implementing this on 121 programs."

"Crosswinds affected the symbology on the HUD at rotation and takeoff by slewing rapidly and resulting in momentary confusion. After seeing the flight path vector

slew to the side, the flight guidance cue eventually centered. It was only 1–2 s of uncertainty but because we rarely see very low visibility combined with strong crosswinds, the momentary confusion may cause over-controlling on the part of the PF."

One limitation of our research was the absence of wind gust conditions. Wind gusts are an important factor that could have a significant effect on the margin of safety [8]. However, creating wind gusts with a reasonable level of fidelity in a simulator presents a challenge. The ability to include wind gusts in a study conducted on a simulator may provide even more insightful lower boundary profiles with potentially more dramatic "peaks" and "valleys" representing the effects of wind gusts, in addition to the effects of sustained winds direction and magnitude, on the shape and size of safety margin.

6 Conclusion

A 3-D visualization of safety margin profiles, with and without the effect of crosswinds, has the potential to make the process of pilots setting up their individual crosswind limit more informed and for the following reasons:

- In a given set of operational and environmental conditions, specific sources of workload relevant to a piloting task in such conditions can be readily identified and considered;
- The "peaks" and "valleys" of the workload profiles for each potential source (e.g., Mental Demand, Temporal Demand) provide an insight to the potential changes to these profiles as conditions change;
- The safety margin profiles could provide a foundation for building robust mental models about how the effects of crosswind interact with the effects of other operational and environmental factors, as well as new technologies;
- Safety margin profiles may differ across different phases of flight, therefore understanding such differences, especially for takeoff and landing; could help pilots setting sensible crosswind limits

From a broader perspective, the analyses conducted during this follow-on study, highlighted the notions that a) building an evocative shared mental model of the multi-faceted nature of safety margin, and b) having a clear understanding of the complex interplay between the many factors that affect its shape and size; are essential for the safety of flight.

While limited only to the takeoff phase of flight, these results demonstrated the potency of the NASA-TLX scale and the strong diagnostic value of its component subscales. The high reliability, sensitivity, and utility of these component ratings allowed for a narrow identification of the sources of workload in the specific set of conditions included in the research. However, a similar approach could be applied to other measures of pilot performance (e.g., flight technical error), as well.

Further research is need to expand the building of data-driven 3-D safety margin profiles across different phases of flight, operational and environmental conditions. Such profiles may be just the right tool to include in training materials and utilize in the cultivation of a culture of safety within the pilot community about something that is inherently subjective – perception of risk. Furthermore, as aircraft design involve multiple layers of safety margins intended to improve safety without unnecessarily limiting aircraft and human performance, designers could utilize such data-driven profiles to inform airframe and aircraft systems design, as well.

References

1. Akima, H.: A new method of interpolation and smooth curve fitting based on local procedures. J. ACM (JACM) **17**(4), 589–602 (1970)
2. Federal Aviation Administration, & United States.: Pilot's handbook of Aeronautical knowledge. Aeronautical decision-making, pp. 2-1–2-32) Federal Aviation Administration, United States (2016)
3. Federal Aviation Administration: Order 8400.13F. Department of Transportation, United States (2019)
4. Hart, S.G.: NASA Task load index (TLX) Volume 1.0; Paper and pencil package. NASA Ames Research Center (1986)
5. Hart, S.G.: NASA-task load index (NASA-TLX); 20 years later. In: Proceedings of the Human Factors and Ergonomics Society Annual Meeting, vol. 50, no. 9, pp. 904–908 (2006)
6. Hart, S.G., Staveland, L.E.: Development of NASA-TLX (Task Load Index): results of empirical and theoretical research. Adv. Psychol. **52**, 139–183 (1988)
7. Kratchouova, D., Humpherys, M., Miller, L., Mofle, T., Choi, I., Nesmith, B.L.: Crew workload considerations in using HUD localizer takeoff guidance in lieu of currently required infrastructure. In: International Conference on Human-Computer Interaction, pp. 507–521 (2020)
8. van Es, G.W.H.: Crosswind Certification-How does it affect you?. https://reports.nlr.nl/bitstream/handle/10921/343/TP-2006-324.pdf?sequence=1. Accessed 4 Feb 2021

Robust Camera Motion Estimation for Point-of-View Video Stabilization

Wonwoo Lee$^{(\boxtimes)}$, Byeongwook Yoo, Deokho Kim, Jaewoong Lee,
Sunghoon Yim, Taehyuk Kwon, Gunill Lee, and Jiwon Jeong

Samsung Research, Seoul 06765, South Korea
{wonw.lee,byeongw.yoo,deokho16.kim,jw84.lee,sunghoon.yim,taehyuk.kwon,
gunill.lee,jiwon.jeong}@samsung.com

Abstract. Point-of-View videos recorded by Augmented Reality Glasses contain jitters because they are acquired under users' actions in varying environments. Applying video stabilization on such videos is difficult due to weakness of conventional keypoint-based motion estimation to environmental conditions. They are prone to fail to track in low-textured or dark environments. To overcome this limitation, we propose a neural network-based motion estimation method for video stabilization. Our network predicts frame-to-frame motion in high accuracy by focusing on global camera motion, while ignoring local motion caused by moving objects. Motion prediction takes only up to 10 ms so that we achieve real-time stabilization on modern smartphones hardware. We demonstrate our method outperforms keypoint-based motion estimation and the quality of estimated motion is good enough for video stabilization. Our network is trainable without ground truth and easily scalable to large datasets.

Keywords: Augmented Reality Glasses · Motion estimation · Video stabilization · Neural network

1 Introduction

Taking Point-of-View (PoV) videos in our daily life is considered as one of major applications of Augmented Reality Glasses (AR Glasses), e.g., life logging. PoV videos recorded by head-worn AR Glasses can easily become shaky and jittery because they are acquired under user's actions, such as walking streets and playing sports. Moreover, there exists unintended head motion that causes jitters in the recorded videos even if a user perceives the world as static [14]. These characteristics of PoV videos make video stabilization inevitable.

Video stabilization reduces abrupt changes in frame-to-frame motion, working as a low-pass filter. It requires a robust motion estimation method, especially on AR Glasses, to handle variety of motion and environmental conditions we meet in daily life. Conventionally, keypoint-based motion estimation methods have been used [9], where descriptors on salient patches are matched between consecutive frames in a video [1,8]. However, keypoint matching is prone to

© Springer Nature Switzerland AG 2021
J. Y. C. Chen and G. Fragomeni (Eds.): HCII 2021, LNCS 12770, pp. 353–363, 2021.
https://doi.org/10.1007/978-3-030-77599-5_25

fail because they have fundamental weakness in low-textured environments and changing lighting conditions.

In this paper, we propose a neural network-based motion estimation for video stabilization on PoV videos. We design a fully convolutional network that predicts motion between two video frames. The network learns to find global camera motion from videos by focusing on the static regions and rejecting inconsistent foreground motions. Our network is self-supervised and trainable without groundtruth motion so that it can easily scale up to videos in wild. We demonstrate our method outperforms keypoint-based motion estimation and the quality of estimated motion is good enough for video stabilization.

2   Related Works

Keypoint-based frame-to-frame tracking and motion estimation has been widely used for offline video stabilization. Frame-to-frame motion has been represented as different motion models, e.g., affine and homography [15]. 6DoF motion and dense optical flow have also been adopted in researches [5,6], but they were uncommon in video stabilization because they require relatively large computational power compared to affine and homography models.

Sensor-based approaches have been adopted in modern action cameras and smartphones. They use built-in gyroscope and accelerometer to estimate camera motion and run stabilization online while recording a video [11,12]. Sensors provide exact motion of a device in real-time, but they should be highly precise and accurately synchronized with the camera hardware for video stabilization. Sensor-camera synchronization requires complex and careful engineering but even after that, the algorithm works only a specific sensor-camera combination.

Recently, neural network based motion estimation adopted widely used in 6DoF motion estimation and visual odometry [4,18]. In general, they have been used for reconstruction and scene navigation, rather than for video stabilization. Existing researches retrieve 6 DoF poses in conjunction with depth maps, but it requires more computational resources, which can be a burden on mobile devices. Recurrent structures for temporal consistency increase computational complexity even more [17].

In this work, we choose a neural network-based approach for video stabilization because it has the following advantages. Neural networks are more robust to textures and lighting condition changes than keypoint-based methods. They can learn implicit representation of global motion from training data, while keypoint-based methods depend on sparse local features for tracking. Computational efficiency is another advantage. Motion estimation runs in a constant time on neural network, i.e. inference time, while keypoint-based methods require more time in proportion to the resolution of videos. Thanks to dedicated hardware for running neural network, modern mobile devices can perform network inference in higher efficiency.

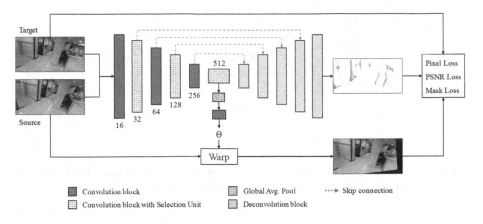

Convolution block   Global Avg. Pool   ····▶ Skip connection

Convolution block with Selection Unit   Deconvolution block

Fig. 1. Network architecture

3   Approach

3.1   Self-supervised Motion Estimation

Figure 1 shows the architecture of our motion estimation network. The network consists of a series of convolution blocks and a global average pooling followed by a 1×1 convolution. The output of the network is Euler angles of camera assuming rotational motion only. We use the mask prediction branch only for training the network and remove in runtime inference.

Figure 2 shows design of convolution and deconvolution blocks. All convolutions use kernel size 3 and stride 2, followed by ReLU activation [10] and batch normalization. We apply Selection Unit [2] in every two convolutional blocks as attention to feature maps. It enhances quality of feature maps passed to the next convolution block. The number of filters are increased twice in each convolutional block. The mask branch consists of a series of deconvolutions with kernel size 3 and stride 2, as show in Fig. 2(c).

Given two consecutive frames, source $\mathcal{I}_s$ and target $\mathcal{I}_t$, our network predicts motion parameters Θ from source to target image. There are several motion models, such as affine, homography and Euler angles. We choose to use Euler angles (role, pitch, and yaw) in the range of $[-\frac{\pi}{2}, \frac{\pi}{2}]$. We convert the predicted Euler angles to homography transformation under planar scene assumption for image warping. We also tried direct homography prediction with 8 parameters, but it didn't show difference in performance compared to Euler angles.

Given motion parameter Θ between the two frames, homography transformation from the source to the target is computed as

$$\mathcal{H} = KRK^{-1}, \tag{1}$$

where K is intrinsic parameter and R is 3×3 rotation matrix computed from Θ.

Then, we apply $\mathcal{H}$ to $\mathcal{I}_s$ to register the source frame to the target frame.

$$\mathcal{I}_s^* = warp(\mathcal{I}_s, \mathcal{H}) \tag{2}$$

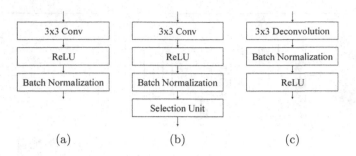

Fig. 2. Convolution and deconvolution blocks: (a) normal convolution block; (b) convolution block with Selection Unit; (c) Deconvolution block

After warping a frame to the other, some of pixels become inconsistent due to camera motion and moving objects. The network needs to learn how to ignore such invalid pixels for motion estimation in high accuracy. To teach the network to focus on static part of scenes, the network predicts a foreground mask $\mathcal{M}_f$ on $\mathcal{I}_t$ in a separate branch. Foreground mask $\mathcal{M}_f$ estimates the probability of pixels belonging to foreground objects so that the predicted motion becomes robust to object motion inconsistent with the motion of a camera. Foreground mask prediction is only for training and it is removed at inference time. This improves the speed of inference time by removing expensive deconvolutions from the network.

We define training losses from $\mathcal{I}_s^*$, $\mathcal{M}_w$, and $\mathcal{M}_f$. Pixel loss is defined as L1 loss weighted by the foreground mask. It is averaged by the number of pixels (H×W×C). PSNR loss is computed by scaling PSNR value exponentially. Mask loss is computed as cross-entropy loss between $\mathcal{M}_w$ and $\mathcal{M}_f$. We use the warping mask as reference to ignore invalid pixels. Total loss is computed as a weighted sum of all three losses.

$$L_i = \frac{1}{HWC} \sum_{h,w,c} \mathcal{M}_f \cdot \|\mathcal{I}_{s^*} - \mathcal{I}_t\| \tag{3}$$

$$L_p = e^{-0.15(psnr(\mathcal{I}_s^*,\mathcal{I}_t)-30)} \tag{4}$$

$$L_f = CrossEntropy\left(\mathcal{M}_w, \mathcal{M}_f\right) \tag{5}$$

$$Total\ Loss = w_i L_i + w_p L_p + w_f L_f \tag{6}$$

3.2   Real-Time On-Device Video Stabilization

We design a streamlined architecture for real-time video stabilization shown in Fig. 3. There are three modules conducting motion estimation, motion stabilization, and image warping. Each module runs in a separate thread so that one does not interfere the other. There is a buffer between two modules to store output of the previous module and each module process the data in the buffers. Incoming

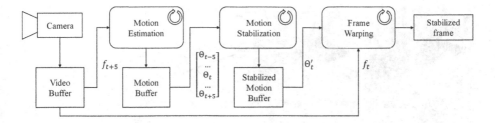

Fig. 3. Architecture of real-time video stabilization on a mobile device

video frames are first fed to motion estimation module. It predicts the motion from the previous frame to current frame and put the results to a motion buffer.

Motion stabilization module generates stabilized motion parameters. We adopt Mesh Flow algorithm [7] for motion smoothing. In [7], a frame is divided by a grid, and the motion of grid points are generated from keypoint tracking. In our approach, there are only motion parameters and no dense motion vectors. Instead, we generate the motion vectors by warping grid points based on $\mathcal{H}$. We set the size of motion smoothing to 11 and use default parameters in [7]. Stabilization module takes a 11 motions in $[t - 5, t + 5]$ and estimates the smoothed motion parameter Θ'_t at time t.

Warping module transform f_t based on Θ'_t, i.e., warping the original frame to the stabilized position. The stabilized frames are cropped to the region of 80% from the raw video resolution. Unlike offline video stabilization, where we can compute the best crop ratio from all stabilized frames, online video stabilization requires a preset crop ratio because the end of sequence is unknown.

Since there is a time window in motion stabilization, outputs of stabilizations are delayed to the half of the window size, i.e., 5 frames in our implementation. The whole stabilization framework runs in 28 ms on Samsung Galaxy S20 Ultra against FHD (1920×1080) videos.

4   Training and Datasets

4.1   Training

Training our network is unsupervised. Given a set of video sequences, two frames are fed to network. We sample the two frames from a video with intervals raining from 1 to 3 frames. Using intervals larger than 1 allows us to mimic fast camera motion, which is often in videos recorded by head-worn AR Glasses. In this way, we can not only increase the variety of input motion, but also easily collect video data without concerns on the speed of motion in videos. Pixel values are normalized to $[0, 1]$. During training, we add distortion to pixel values for data augmentation, i.e., random Gaussian noise, brightness and contrast changes. We also apply random flip in horizontal and vertical, so that we expand coverage of motion even more.

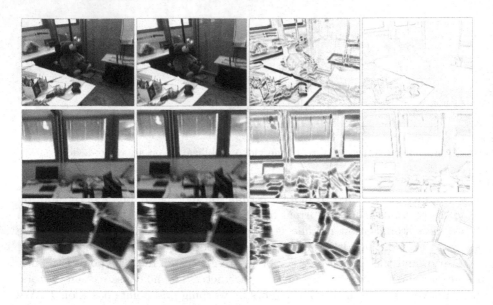

Fig. 4. Frame differences before and after warping to target views on TUM-RGBD dataset; column 1 and 2: source and target frames, column 3 and 4: image difference before and after warping (darker is larger)

We used Adam optimizer with $\beta_1 = 0.9$ and $\beta_2 = 0.999$. Learning rate was set to 2×10^{-4} and decayed by factor of 0.99 at every 2 epochs. Training typically converges after 1,000k iterations with batch size of 16. Weights of each loss was set as $w_i = 1.5$, $w_p = 0.1$, and $w_f = 0.2$.

4.2   Dataset

We use TUM-RGBD dataset [16] providing groundtruth camera poses of video sequences for performance benchmark. To validate our method in real life situation, we also collected video sequences by using a head-mounted camera. We call our dataset *Real-world* dataset.

TUM-RGBD Dataset. We split the dataset to 10 for training and 13 for evaluation out of 23 video sequences. The original video sequences have 640×480 resolution. In training, we resize images to 160×120 to feed them to network. We did not use depth data included in the dataset.

Real-world Dataset. We recorded videos in different indoor and outdoor scenes we meet in our daily life, while making actions, such as walking, running, looking around. We also collected videos at day and night too. Total 100 videos were recorded in FHD (1920×1080) resolution at 30 fps and we split them to 70 for training and 30 for evaluation. Input images are downasmpled to 256×128 for training.

Fig. 5. Frame differences before and after warping to target views on Real-world dataset; column 1 and 2: source and target frames, column 3 and 4: image difference before and after warping (darker is larger)

5   Experimental Results

5.1   Performance Evaluation

We ran SLAM-based pose estimation using keypoint-based tracking [13] on TUM-RGBD dataset, and compared the accuracy of rotational motion. We compute Relative Pose Error (RPE) from a camera rotation vector between two consecutive frames of input videos. We compute frame-to-frame rotational motion from estimated rotation vectors and convert them in 3×3 matrices. Given estimated rotation R and groundtruth R^*, we compute relative rotation between them and convert it to axis-angle notation. RPE is computed as

$$RPE = \frac{1}{N} \sum_i T(R_i^{-1} R_i^*) \tag{7}$$

where N is the number of frames and $T(\cdot)$ is a function converting a rotation matrix to axis-angle notation.

Table 1 shows RPE of the two methods. Our neural network based method outperforms SLAM-based method using keypoint tracking. Thanks to high accuracy of our motion estimation, we achieved lower error than the SLAM-based method. We visualized such an accuracy in Fig. 4. We can see the frame-to-frame difference is greatly reduced after registration using motions estimated by our method.

As shown Fig. 5, difference is large in the regions of moving people and small in background scene. Our network successfully rejected foreground motion and estimation global camera motion in good accuracy. Although errors still exist on edges of 3D objects due to our assumption of planar scene, it is enough for video stabilization (see Fig. 6)

Table 1. Mean relative pose error

	Mean RPE (degrees)
SLAM-based [13]	0.4
Ours	0.34

Fig. 6. 5-frames average on raw and stabilized videos. Our motion estimation is good enough to align frames in video stabilization

To demonstrate our method provides high-accuracy motion estimation enough for videos stabilization, we show video frames averaged in 5-frames from raw and stabilized videos in Fig. 6. As we can see, the unaligned raw videos has large motion blur caused by averaging in time. On the other hand, motions are reduced a lot in stabilized videos and thus, they have less motion blurs. Note that each frame of raw videos already contain some amount of motion blur, apart from the blur generated by 5-frames average. This kind of self-contained blur is not removable by video stabilization and still exists in stabilized videos.

5.2   Robustness in Video Stabilization

One of advantages of our approach is the robustness to changing environmental conditions, such as textures and lightings. In Fig. 7 we show two video sequences stabilized by motions from keypoint-based tracking (top) and our method (bottom). For better understanding, we didn't crop out the warped frames. Instead, we overlaid a red rectangle of the final crop region that is shared by all the video frames to generate the final stabilized frames.

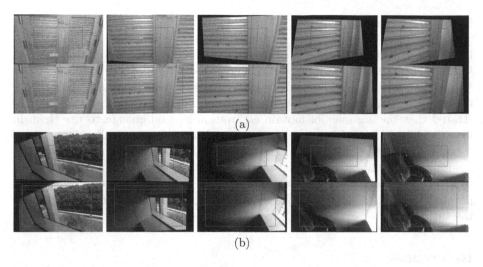

Fig. 7. Robust video stabilization under varying conditions: (a) stabilized videos under low-texture; (b) stabilized videos under bad lighting conditions. Rectangles overlaid in red represent the final crop windows for the production of stabilized videos

In Fig. 7 keypoint-based methods failed to estimate motion in the middle of frames due to lack of textures and lighting condition changes. Due to wrong motion estimations, raw video frames are badly-warped in stabilized video and results in severe crop from the original video consequently. In contrast, our method consistently estimates correct motion under such a varying environments. As a result, the stabilized videos keep a much larger crop window than results from the keypoint-based method.

5.3   Inference Speed

We measured inference speed of our network on Android platform. We used Tensor flow *benchmark_model*[1] to profile inference speed of our network. We ran the tool on Samsung Galaxy S20 Ultra device, the latest smartphone at the time this paper is written.

We ran tests on input size of 256×128, regarding FHD videos. Average inference speed measured on the device is 9.4 ms on GPU. Both timings are fast enough for real-time applications. Note that we achieved this speed without any acceleration techniques, such as weight quantization and DSP hardware that can potentially improve inference speed even faster.

---

[1] https://www.tensorflow.org/lite/performance/measurement.

6 Conclusion

In this paper, we proposed a neural network based motion estimation method for PoV video stabilization. Our neural network-based approach guarantees fast and robust motion estimation from video streams under varying environmental conditions, such as richness of textures and lighting conditions. We demonstrated that the accuracy of motion estimation is good enough to use them in video stabilization and it is applicable to real-time camera applications, where frame-to-frame motion estimation is required. Limitation of our work is in the assumption of calibrated camera, which is closely related to motion estimation from images. Some work has been done to predict both intrinsic and motion parameters simultaneously [3]. We will continue to research in this direction in the future.

References

1. Bay, H., Ess, A., Tuytelaars, T., Gool, L.V.: Speeded-up robust features (surf). Comput. Vis. Image Underst. **110**(3), 346–359 (2008)
2. Choi, J., Kim, M.: A deep convolutional neural network with selection units for super-resolution. In: IEEE Conference on Computer Vision and Pattern Recognition Workshops (CVPRW), pp. 1150–1156 (2017)
3. Gordon, A., Li, H., Jonschkowski, R., Angelova, A.: Depth from videos in the wild: unsupervised monocular depth learning from unknown cameras. In: International Conference on Computer Vision, pp. 8976–8985 (2019)
4. Han, L., Lin, Y., Du, G., Lian, S.: Deepvio: self-supervised deep learning of monocular visual inertial odometry using 3d geometric constraints. In: IEEE/RSJ International Conference on Intelligent Robots and Systems, pp. 6906–6913 (2019)
5. Liu, F., Gleicher, M., Jin, H., Agarwala, A.: Content-preserving warps for 3d video stabilization. ACM Trans. Graph. **28**(3), 1–9 (2009)
6. Liu, S., Yuan, L., Tan, P., Sun, J.: Steadyflow: spatially smooth optical flow for video stabilization. In: IEEE Conference on Computer Vision and Pattern Recognition, pp. 4209–4216 (2014)
7. Liu, S., Tan, P., Yuan, L., Sun, J., Zeng, B.: Meshflow: minimum latency online video stabilization. In: European Conference on Computer Vision, pp. 800–815 (2016)
8. Lowe, D.G.: Distinctive image features from scale-invariant keypoints. Int. J. Comput. Vis. **60**(2), 91–110 (2004)
9. Mur-Artal, R., Montiel, J.M.M., Tardós, J.D.: Orb-slam: a versatile and accurate monocular slam system. IEEE Trans. Robot. **31**(5), 1147–1163 (2015)
10. Nair, V., Hinton, G.E.: Rectified linear units improve restricted boltzmann machines. In: Proceedings of the 27th International Conference on International Conference on Machine Learning, pp. 807–814 (2010)
11. Ovrén, H., Forssén, P.: Gyroscope-based video stabilisation with auto-calibration. In: IEEE International Conference on Robotics and Automation, pp. 2090–2097 (2015)
12. Ringaby, E., Forssén, P.: Efficient video rectification and stabilisation for cellphones. Int. J. Comput. Vis. **96**(3), 335–352 (2012)

13. Runzhi, W., Wan, W., Wang, Y., Di, K.: A new RGB-D slam method with moving object detection for dynamic indoor scenes. Remote Sens. **11**(10), 1143 (2019)
14. Schindler, A., Bartels, A.: Integration of visual and non-visual self-motion cues during voluntary head movements in the human brain. NeuroImage **172**, 597–607 (2018)
15. Shum, H.Y., Szeliski, R.: Construction of panoramic image mosaics with global and local alignment. Int. J. Comput. Vis. **36**(2), 101–130 (2000)
16. Sturm, J., Engelhard, N., Endres, F., Burgard, W., Cremers, D.: A benchmark for the evaluation of RGB-D slam systems. In: IEEE/RSJ International Conference on Intelligent Robots and Systems, pp. 573–580 (2012)
17. Wang, R., Pizer, S.M., Frahm, J.: Recurrent neural network for (un-)supervised learning of monocular video visual odometry and depth. In: IEEE Conference on Computer Vision and Pattern Recognition, pp. 5550–5559 (2019)
18. Zhou, T., Brown, M., Snavely, N., Lowe, D.G.: Unsupervised learning of depth and ego-motion from video. In: IEEE Conference on Computer Vision and Pattern Recognition, pp. 6612–6619 (2017)

Rendering Tree Roots Outdoors: A Comparison Between Optical See Through Glasses and Smartphone Modules for Underground Augmented Reality Visualization

Gergana Lilligreen$^{(\boxtimes)}$ ⓘ, Philipp Marsenger, and Alexander Wiebel ⓘ

University of Applied Sciences Worms, UX -Vis Group, Worms, Germany
`lilligreen@hs-worms.de`

Abstract. In this paper we propose augmented reality (AR) modes for showing virtual tree roots in the nature. The main question that we want to answer is "How is it possible to convincingly represent virtual 3D models of tree roots as being located in the forest soil, underground, while using the AR technology?". We present different rendering and occlusion modes and how they were implemented on two different types of hardware. Two user studies, that we performed to compare the AR visualization for optical see-through glasses (HoloLens head mounted display) and for mobile devices (smartphone), are described. We specifically focus on depth perception and situated visualization (the merging of real and virtual environment and actions). After discussing the experiences collected during outdoor user tests and the results of a questionnaire, we give some directions for the future use of AR in the nature and as a part of an environmental educational setting. The central result of the study is that while supporting depth perception with additional depth cues, specifically occlusion, is very beneficial in the mobile device setting, this support does not change depth perception significantly in the stereo HMD setting.

Keywords: Augmented reality · Visualization and Image rendering · Outdoors · Underground · Environment · Occlusion · Nature · Mobile systems

1 Introduction

Augmenting the real world can be not only fascinating but also valuable. There are many areas, in which augmented reality (AR) is being used and discussed

This work has been performed in project SAARTE (Spatially-Aware Augmented Reality in Teaching and Education). SAARTE is supported by the European Union (EU) in the ERDF program P1-SZ2-7 and by the German federal state Rhineland-Palatinate (Antr.-Nr. 84002945).

J. Y. C. Chen and G. Fragomeni (Eds.): HCII 2021, LNCS 12770, pp. 364–380, 2021.
https://doi.org/10.1007/978-3-030-77599-5_26

(e. g. , maintenance [16], education [10], architecture and marketing [4], edutainment [24]). When it comes to educational goals, enriching the familiar learning environment by adding digital content and interaction, can enable new possibilities for learning. For environmental education school classes or other groups interested in nature often undertake field trips. This is not a typical area for using AR [17], but carries a lot of potential and should be explored more intensively.

Azuma [1] defines three conditions for AR: the real environment must be combined with virtual objects, there must be interaction in real time, and registration in 3D. One of the big advantages of AR is the possibility to make the invisible visible. An example in the nature is showing the hidden parts of a tree – the tree roots. With AR this can happen on-site and in the context of the real environment – the nature. This can be achieved by using a head-mounted AR device (HMD). In our experiments the HMD is a Microsoft HoloLens. Because this kind of hardware is not yet widely distributed and still very expensive, we investigated whether it is also possible to convincingly visualize tree roots using a smartphone, and what kind of differences can be observed. We developed different variants for visualizing 3D tree roots outdoors on the HMD and on a smartphone.

In the following sections we introduce related work, the user interface, and the different modes for visualization of tree roots, which we developed. In Sect. 5 we present the user tests that we conducted, discuss the results in Sect. 6 and conclude in the last section.

2   Related Work

Occlusion plays a major role in AR because it is very important for depth perception [20]. Showing underground infrastructure is a known use case for AR. Schall et al. [19], Zhang et al. [25] and works presented by Behzadan et al. [3] show pipes that are supposed to lie underground using AR. These settings are much more organized than the natural environments we consider and there is no prominent real object occluding parts of the geometry as the tree in our case.

Even older works show different techniques for visualization and interaction with hidden objects. Kolsch et al. [9] present a rendering mode, designed like a tunnel, thus enabling the user to mask out item that occlude otherwise hidden objects. It is divided into regions with different representations: transparent regions, regions where only wireframes are rendered and focus regions with fully rendered objects. The user can move the focus region and thus explore 3D information at any distance like whole complexes of rooms in buildings interactively. For the use in nature such a tool seems too complicated and not necessary. Furthermore, we don't want to visualize that complex data, covering a big part of the user's view – the nature should be still visible.

Regarding outdoor AR for nature settings there has been work for school excursions in the past [8]. In this setting students follow a carbon or oxygen atom through the environment and thus can better understand the carbon cycle in ecosystems. However, this work does not deal with hidden geometry and is not implemented on optical see-through glasses like in our case.

A survey of the use of AR in nature and AR applications dealing with environmental aspects is provided by Rambach et al. [17].

3 User Interface and Model Placement

For the experimental comparison of the techniques presented and discussed in this paper two applications, one for HMDs and one for smartphones, had to be developed. Two user tests with a focus on depth perception and the merging of real and virtual content were performed. The tests took place outdoor next to a tree. More details on the experiments can be found in Sect. 5.

To avoid usability problems that can influence the results of experiments, the design of an easy-to-understand user interface is very important.

3.1 Smartphone User Interface

In the smartphone application, initially a ground plane is detected using the AR framework. When the user looks around a ray is cast in viewing direction. The position where this ray intersects the ground plane is continuously indicated by a marker. When the user taps on the screen of the smartphone the root model is placed directly below the marker position. The place should be chosen near a tree for blending the roots on the real position. All control elements are directly accessible from the main screen, so the main function remains easy to use and there is no need to explain a navigation through menus to the users. A swipe control (swiping left or right) was implemented for switching between the different display modes. For the experiments it is important that users always know the name of the current mode. Therefore, text describing the active mode is displayed at the top of the screen. Additionally, a slider at the bottom of the display (see Fig. 5), shows the progress through the different modes of the experiment. The slider also serves as an alternative control for switching between the modes, in case that the user has problems with swiping.

3.2 HMD User Interface

The HoloLens HMD provides so-called *spatial mapping* [14] which yields a detailed representation of real-world surfaces in its environment. The user's gaze ray intersects with the generated spatial mapping mesh and is used by our application as a base for the positioning of the 3d root model below the intersection point. This way the virtual roots appear as under the ground level. At the beginning the spatial mesh is visualized so the user can see when the environment is scanned. With an AirTap gesture [12] near the real tree stem the virtual root model is positioned. Then, a speech command "toggle mesh" lets the spatial mesh disappear and the roots can be seen better. Switching between the different modes is controlled by speech commands, which we also used as names in the description and the questionnaire (see Table 2 and Table 3). When a speech command is recognized a visual feedback is given to the user – the name of the mode is shown for a short time in the view of the user. We chose to use speech commands because the control with gestures is not familiar for most users and our focus in this paper lies on the depth perception and the situated visualization outdoors in the nature and not on gesture interaction.

4   Rendering and Occlusion Modes

We applied several techniques for the visualization of hidden objects and developed different modes for showing a 3D model of tree roots outdoors, in a natural context. For some of the variants additional features providing additional depth cues are used, these can be found in the detailed description of the modes.

Virtual holes can be used to display hidden elements in the floor more realistically. In some cases, using partly transparent virtual objects can help to control the depth perception [2, 11].

Phantom objects are another helpful technique. A phantom is a virtual representation of a *real object*, which is rendered completely transparent and only the Z-buffer (depth buffer) is manipulated. Thus, the phantom virtual object occludes other virtual contents, but is not visible itself [7]. Usually, transparent objects have no influence on the rendered image, but manipulating the Z-buffer forces the phantom to be considered in the compositing stage of the rendering process. This makes it possible to prevent rendering the parts of virtual objects that are behind the phantom. If the phantom and the real object overlap, an impression, that the *real object* is covering the virtual one, is created.

We developed both applications, for HoloLens HMD and for smartphone, using the Unity engine [23]. We used its stencil shader [22] for the virtual holes. For rendering phantom objects we adapted MRTK's standard shader [13].

A schematic overview of the rendering and occlusion modes described in the following subsections is shown in Fig. 1.

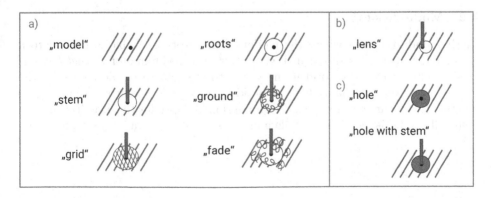

Fig. 1. Rendering and occlusion modes for displaying 3d tree roots. Point = root model, green = real environment, blue = virtual occluders/elements. a) Modes used on HMD and a smartphone, b) Mode used only on HMD, c) Modes used only on a smartphone.

4.1   Mode "model"

In this mode (see Fig. 2), the model of the roots is placed at the selected location under the tree stem without the use of other rendering techniques or other effects. This mode is used as a neutral mode to compare with the other modes, which use different techniques, intended for better depth perception or fusing of the virtual roots into the real environment.

Fig. 2. Mode "model" (picture taken through the HoloLens HMD, the stereoscopic depth experience and colors are not truly displayable as a monoscopic picture)

4.2   Mode "roots"

In this mode the area where the model of the roots is visible is limited to a circular hole (see illustration in Fig. 3). Here the technique of *virtual holes* is used as also in the real world if one wants to see something hidden under the ground one would probably have some kind of hole. The aim is to investigate whether this technique enhances the impression of depth for the user. Technically a stencil shader is used for the hole and the spatial mesh "acts" as a phantom.

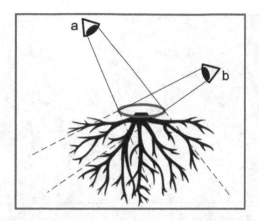

Fig. 3. Seeing different parts of the root depending on view angle.

4.3   Mode "stem"

This mode extends the mode "roots". This is achieved with the help of a *phantom object* tree stem (see Sect. 4). This way the real tree stem hides parts of the roots which are on the backside and the resulting occlusion can be helpful for a correct depth impression.

All of the next modes implement the phantom stem.

4.4   Mode "ground"

In this mode a dense layer of virtual leaves and soil is placed on the edge of the hole. We investigate whether the occlusion of the "sharp" edge could be helpful for a smoother transition between the virtual objects and the real world.

4.5   Mode "grid"

To enhance the impression of depth of the roots below the surface, in this mode the virtual roots and the real soil are hidden by a brown colored grid. The roots only shine through the squares of the grid and this should give the feeling of being able to view the roots through windows in the forest floor. This mode looks different on the different hardware. On the smartphone the grid appears brown, but on the HMD the dark color is not very bright and almost transparent, so it looks more as the user is seeing the root model through a grid of the real soil.

4.6   Mode "fade"

The root model seen in the hole is hidden by semi-transparent leaves (see Fig. 4). The leaves become more transparent towards the border of the hole. With this mode we want to investigate whether the transition between virtual and real world is improved by the additional masking and transparency. Furthermore, we tested if the roots shown under the semi-transparent leaves appear deeper to the observer.

Fig. 4. Mode "fade". Picture taken through the HoloLens HMD. The stereo depth experience and colors are not truly displayable as a picture)

The described modes (4.2. to 4.6.) are all implemented on both devices - HMD and smartphone. The next two modes ("hole" and "hole with stem") are included only on the smartphone. And the last one ("lens") is available only for the HMD.

4.7   Mode "hole"

With this option, an earth-colored, brown background is added to the hole to represent the soil. The background is only visible through the hole and hides the real forest ground that lies under the roots. This should increase the impression of being under the ground. As dark colors appear almost transparent on the HoloLens HMD this feature is not included in the respective application. It is also not required because the visualization on the HMD does not have such bright contrast like the visualization on video see through devices like smartphones and the real soil and root model are supposed to merge better. The depth perception on the HMD is also much better due to the technical features of the device.

4.8   Mode "hole with stem"

Here the mode "hole" is extended with the phantom for the tree stem as described in mode "stem" (Sect. 4.3).

In Fig. 5 the phantom stem is included and the real tree stem "hides" parts of the hole and the roots. In the prototype that we used in the user tests there is only one size of the visualization. For the next iteration a function automatically resizing the model is planned. This way the real tree and the virtual roots can fit better. For the user tests we chose trees which were suitable for the size of our virtual roots.

Fig. 5. Mode "hole with stem" on the smartphone

4.9 Mode "lens"

In this mode the techniques of Magic Lens combined with a virtual x-ray vision are accomplished for the HMD. Billinghurst et al. [5] show a Magic Lens implementation that enables users to view inside virtual datasets, while holding a real handle (a ring mouse). In our visualization we look through the real ground to see the virtual model. Through a virtual "peephole", that follows the user's gaze, parts of the root model can be seen. As a result the users have a smaller but more focused view of the root. The size of the peephole is so small, that it fits in the view area of the HoloLens HMD. That way the cutting of the view is part of the mode itself and is not caused by the device.

5 Evaluation

To investigate if our rendering modes can help to convincingly represent virtual 3d models of tree roots as being located underground, we performed separate user tests for the two devices, HMD and smartphone. For the two tests we chose a location with a tree and enough space to move around it. For the HMD we also paid attention to test in the shadow as virtual models appear nearly invisible if the environment is too bright. Furthermore a quiet location was chosen because we used speech commands for changing the different modes. We focused on depth perception and the quality of merging between real and virtual. In the next subsections we describe details and results of the evaluation.

5.1   Hypotheses

- **H1:** *The modes "hole" and "hole with stem" on the smartphone will have a big impact on the depth perception.*
  We define big impact as follows: the users choose "agree" or "fully agree" for the corresponding statements in the questionnaire (see Sect. 5.4).
  The visualization on the smartphone is very clear and has high contrast as it is a video-see-through device. If the real earth surface next to the tree stem is visible in the rendering of the roots, it does not appear as the roots are in a hole, under the earth. When adding a "fake" soil (brown background) in the virtual hole the visualization of the roots should be more convincing.
- **H2:** *The users will have a good depth perception even in the mode "model" on the HMD.*
  Because the HMD provides stereo rendering our users will choose "agree" or "fully agree" for the depth impression in mode "model" in the questionnaire.
- **H3:** *In mode "lens" on the HMD the virtual hole will be more convincing for the participants than in the other modes.*
  The whole lens region for looking underground fits in the field of view of the HMD and with the real movement and gaze the users can decide by themselves which part of the root they want to see. This should make the experience more convincing as we do not have unexpected clipping without context. Here, limiting the field of view is part of the visualization itself. When clipping is caused by the size of the HMD display, it could be more confusing for users with no or less experience in AR.
- **H4:** *The modes in which the border of the virtual hole is covered ("ground" and "fade") will be helpful for better merging of real and virtual environment.*

5.2   Method

We used mixed methods [6] to evaluate our prototypes and rendering modes and to verify (or disprove) the defined hypotheses. We collected quantitative and qualitative data during user tests, for the two devices – smartphone and HMD. We designed two questionnaires with 5-point Likert-scale[1] to find out what preferences the users have (for the different modes) with regard to (1) depth perception and (2) fusing of real and virtual environment. Both questionnaires were very similar, as most modes were available on both devices. The statements of the HMD-questionnaire are shown in detail in Tables 2 and 3, and supplemented with the additional statements for the smartphone case in the text. We added three open field questions to obtain more qualitative data. The users filled out the questionnaire right after they tested the application. Additionally, a think-aloud-protocol [18] was conducted during the tests to find out what the participants are thinking.

---

[1]   ++ (fully agree), + (agree), = (neutral), − (reject) and −− (totally reject).

5.3   Participant Characteristics

A total of 44 people participated in the tests and filled out the questionnaires. The smartphone test was taken by 22 people, over a period of three days. The average age was approximately 32 years, with the youngest user being 19 years old and the oldest 58. Half of the participants were female and the other half was male. The HMD test was also taken by 22 people (12 male, 10 female). The individual tests were spread over a longer period of time (around two months) due to the outbreak of COVID-19 and the partial contact restrictions. The average age was approximately 41 years, the youngest user being 24 years old and the oldest 62. The age distribution is listed in Table 1.

Table 1. Participants characteristic – age.

Age: years	Smartphone: n (%)	HMD: n (%)
<20	3 (14%)	0 (0%)
20–29	11 (50%)	2 (9%)
30–39	3 (14%)	6 (28%)
40–49	2 (9%)	11 (50%)
50–59	3 (14%)	2 (9%)
>60	0 (0%)	1 (4%)

The users also had to state if they already had experience with AR. 59% of the smartphone and 54% of the HMD users had *no* prior experience with AR.

5.4   Depth Perception

To investigate the preferences of the users for the different modes with regard to the depth perception, the questionnaire contained the statements shown in Table 2. In addition to these statements, it comprised an open field question: *"In which mode did you experience the depth impression best and why?"* This way an explicitly chosen mode was defined and additional qualitative data were collected. We also analyzed the think-aloud-notes, that we made during the test. Information on this can be found in Sect. 5.6.

In the **smartphone** test we also had the modes "hole" and "hole with stem". For these modes, we provided two statements about depth perception in the questionnaire: *"Adding a 'brown soil' in the virtual hole enhances the impression of depth"* and *"The combination of 'brown soil' and real tree trunk enhances the impression of depth"*. Compared to the other modes, for these modes the results show the highest approval among the participants with regard to the experienced depth impression – "hole" with 41% "fully agree" and 50% "agree". The mode "hole with stem" got even 100% acceptance – "fully agree" (68%) and "agree" (32%). These data show, that our first hypothesis (H1) was correct.

Table 2. Statements about depth perception in the HMD-questionnaire

	++	+	=	–	––
1. Mode "model": The tree roots alone give a good impression of depth					
2. Mode "roots": The circular hole underlines the impression that the roots are underground					
3. Mode "stem": The circular hole, combined with the covering of the roots by the real stem, underlines the impression that the roots are underground					
4. Mode "grid": Displaying a brown grid over the root model strengthens the impression that the roots are underground					
5. Mode "lens": Looking at the root through a kind of lens intensifies the impression that the roots are underground					

The mode "model" in the **HMD** version was chosen by more than half of the participants as the best mode for the depth perception in the open field part of the questionnaire (see Fig. 7b). It also has got the highest approval according to statement 1 in Table 2 about the depth perception (see Fig. 7a) – 91% of the users agree or fully agree, that in mode "model" the tree roots alone give a good impression of depth. With these results and with the statements of the participants in the think-aloud-protocol (see Sect. 5.6) it can be stated, that hypothesis H2 in Sect. 5.1 is correct.

Figure 6 presents results from the questionnaire for the different modes on the **HMD**. The vertical axis shows the number of the participants, the horizontal the different statements. The different colors match the Likert-scale options. For a lot of the modes no clear positive or negative trend is to see.

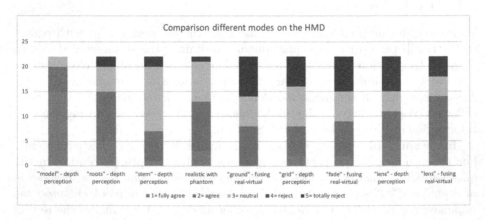

Fig. 6. Results (frequency distribution) for the different modes on the **HMD**

To verify hypothesis H3, that in mode "lens" on the **HMD** the virtual hole will be more convincing for the participants than the other modes, we look at the two statements about mode "lens" (statement 5 in Table 2 and statement 4 in Table 3), as the depth perception and the merging of real and virtual both can be helpful for a better impression of a hole. The last two bars in Fig. 6 show that for about half of the participants the mode "lens" is helpful. Eight people chose the mode as the best for depth perception (5 users) or for fusing of real and virtual elements (3 users).

In the **HMD** case the phantom tree stem was not noticed by many users and they did not see any difference between the modes "roots" and "stem". Therefore they chose the option neutral in the questionnaire. An explanation for this is, that the most users were looking very concentrated to the root model and this way in some positions the phantom stem was not in the HMD's field of view or not in the users focus.

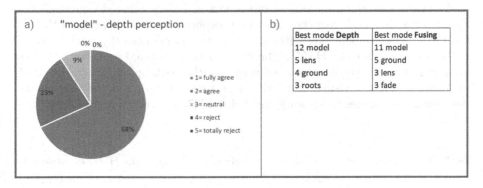

Fig. 7. a) Results (frequency distribution) for mode "model" on the HMD. b) Count of the most mentioned modes (in the open field question for the HMD) as a best mode for depth perception and merging (fusing) of virtual and real. As some participants noted more than one mode, the sum is not equal to the participants' count.

5.5 Merging of Virtual and Real

Similar to the investigation of the users' preferences for depth perception, we also defined statements for the merging (or fusing) of virtual and real (Table 3). We also considered answers to the following open field question in the **HMD** test: *"In which mode did you experience the merging of real and virtual best and why?"* This way, again, an explicitly chosen mode was defined and an additional information was collected.

As mentioned in the last section the mode "lens" was chosen by some participants as best mode for merging of real and virtual. In this case the self determined choice in which part of the roots to look was interesting for the users. More about similar results in the think-aloud-protocol can be read in the last paragraphs of Sect. 5.6.

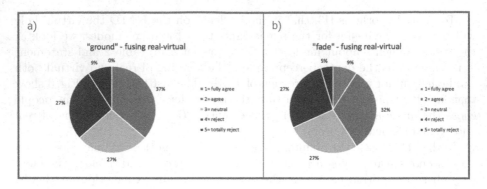

Fig. 8. Results (frequency distribution) for a) mode "ground" and b) mode "fade" on the HMD.

The modes in which the border of the virtual hole is covered ("ground" and "fade") were designed with the idea to be helpful for better merging of the real and virtual environment (H4). But also here the users chose the mode "model" as the best mode for the **HMD**. The merging of the virtual roots with the real environment seems to be more convincing for the participants when the whole 3d model is directly visible. But still more than one third of the participants have found the modes interesting and helpful. This is shown in Fig. 8 and also in Fig. 7b.

Table 3. Statements about the merging of virtual and real in the HMD-questionnaire

	++	+	=	−	−−
1. The positioning of the virtual roots appears more realistic by covering them with the real tree trunk					
2. Mode "ground": Covering the hole's border with earth and leaves makes the transition between virtual objects and the real world more unnatural*					
3. Mode "fade": Covering the hole's border with semi-transparent leaves gives a better, more natural transition between virtual objects and the real world					
4. Mode "lens": Looking at the root through a kind of lens allows a more self-determined exploration of the roots (through self-selected focus)					

In the part of the questionnaire related to merging, we used one inverted statement (marked with * in Table 3). For the results we used the reversed points – if the user chose "reject" we counted "agree" for building a positive total result for the statements.

In the **smartphone** application both modes ("ground" and "fade") were more convincing for the participants than other modes. Around two thirds of the users chose "agree" or "fully agree", that with these rendering modes a better, more natural transition between virtual objects and the real world is given. Mode "ground" was a little bit better.

5.6   Think-Aloud-Method and Participants' Notes

We analyzed the answers of the participants to the free text questions of the questionnaire and the think-aloud protocol of the **HDM** test. Using coding [21] we extracted five categories. The categories are as follows: outdoor conditions, clipping, depth, inaccuracy of spatial mesh/tracking problems, integration in the environment.

Some of the themes were also mentioned in the notes from the smartphone tests. We add a comment on this in the following paragraphs.

Outdoor Conditions. 10 of 22 participants in the **HMD** test commented on colors that they see. It was interesting to hear, that some people perceived the colors differently (e.g., P1 – "slightly bluish color cast/tint", P6 – "more colored, pink"). Several of the differences occurred because on some of the testing days it was sunnier and even in the shadow the sun light caused the different colors on the Optical-See-Through HMD. This shows, that the environment plays a big role for the perception. When an HMD application is used outside the weather and the light conditions have to be considered. Some of the users made remarks related to the real environment or could not see the leaves e.g. in the rendering mode "fade". This can be also an indication why the additional effects were not that strong on the HMD like on the smartphone. On the HMD, the merging of the virtual and real is strengthened by the fact, that in optical-see-through HMDs the contrast is not as big as on the smartphone and this way even the 3d model alone merges with the environment to some degree.

Clipping. Another theme from the think-aloud protocol was the clipping of the roots. Some of the comments (e.g. P4 – "irritating when roots are gone") were based on the hardware-side-caused limitation of the view, as the used HoloLens **HMD** offers only a small field of view for virtual content (called holographic frame on the Hololens). Other remarks referred to the virtual hole, that we implemented in most variations for the displaying of the roots underground (e.g. P5 – "roots: strange that the roots are cut off").

Here also 2/3 of the users of the **smartphone** application commented on smaller or clipped roots. After some directions to move around and look from a different angle, the users mentioned that now they see more and deeper. This shows that an additional guidance for the users can be helpful to discover all the features of a rendering mode and to perceive the depth also underground.

Depth. We observed, that around 1/3 of the participants in the **HMD** test talked about depth in the modes "roots" and "model", but also in all other modes an impression of "roots going deep underground" was mentioned (e.g. P8 – stem: "like a hole, it ends here, almost the feeling of falling in", P15 – model: "now you have to dig out and see if the root is there", P5 – roots: "you can see more when bending/squatting"). This shows that with the HMD a 3d model, which is positioned under the floor level, can already give a good depth perception, which emphasizes the results delivered by the questionnaire. But the virtual hole technique is still a good choice and a different option for a visualisation underground.

Inaccuracy of Spatial Mesh/Tracking Problems. We found out, that about half (HMD) and one third (smartphone) of the participants mentioned some problems or inaccuracy in the positioning of the virtual augmentation (P5 – ground: "now has moved", P4 – fade: "leaves below the ground"). In a newer version of our application we addressed some of the problems employing spatial anchoring [15].

Integration in the Environment. Two thirds of the participants of the **HMD** test talked about the integration of the virtual model in the environment or about real activities associated with the virtual augmentation (e.g. P1 – lens: "I find this mode the most exciting: I follow the roots with the gaze", P5 – grid: "with grid, what function is that supposed to have?"). Also half of the **smartphone** participants commented on the mode "grid", that it does not fit in the context of nature and were irritated.

6   Discussion

We developed different rendering modes for two different devices. In our study we discovered which of these modes works best for each particular device – smartphone or HMD.

From the observations of the **smartphone** tests it can be stated that the underground visualization is best achieved with the use of occlusion. In the best rated mode **"hole with stem"** occlusion is used in 3 different ways: first, the hole that hides the part of the roots; second, the earthy brown background that hides the real forest soil behind the roots; and third, the phantom object that creates the effect as if the real tree trunk is hiding the virtual roots behind it. The depth impression in this mode was the strongest for most participants. On the **HMD**, even when rendering only the 3d root model (when positioned correctly) without additional features (**mode "model"**), the root appears underground for most users and the visualization merges well with the environment. Against the small field view and the unexpected clipping of virtual objects the **mode "lens"** seems to be helpful.

7   Conclusion and Future Work

In this paper we presented different rendering modes for displaying 3d tree roots underground while using AR on an HMD and a smartphone. We used techniques like virtual holes, phantom objects, transparency and stencil shader. We focused on the depth perception and the merging of real and virtual. As expected, adding more depth cues like using additional occlusion and enhancing motion parallax leads to improved depth perception in the smartphone case. Surprisingly, the effect of the additional depth cues provided by the different rendering modes was negligible for the HMD. We assume that the quality of the depth perception using the HMD was already on a very high level due to the availability of stereo rendering.

Regarding future work it is interesting to note that many users mentioned that they do not see the roots very well when they are only visible through the virtual hole. For the questions discussed in this paper, this was not a big problem, because we focused on the depth perception. But for future applications, a mode implemented as a virtual hole might be used as a starting visualization only. After that, the users would be shown the whole model or they would have the ability to perform actions like triggering and displaying root growth or the uptake of nutrients in the tree.

References

1. Azuma, R.T.: A survey of augmented reality. Presence: Teleoper. Virtual Environ. **6**(4), 355–385 (1997). https://doi.org/10.1162/pres.1997.6.4.355
2. Bajura, M., Fuchs, H., Ohbuchi, R.: Merging virtual objects with the real world: seeing ultrasound imagery within the patient. ACM SIGGRAPH Comput. Graph. **26**(2), 203–210 (1992)
3. Behzadan, A.H., Dong, S., Kamat, V.R.: Augmented reality visualization: a review of civil infrastructure system applications. Adv. Eng. Inform. **29**(2), 252–267 (2015). https://doi.org/10.1016/j.aei.2015.03.005
4. Billinghurst, M., Clark, A., Lee, G.: A survey of augmented reality. Found. Trends® Hum.-Comput. Interact. **8**(2–3), 73–272 (2015). https://doi.org/10.1561/1100000049
5. Billinghurst, M., Grasset, R., Looser, J.: Designing augmented reality interfaces. SIGGRAPH Comput. Graph. **39**(1), 17–22 (2005). https://doi.org/10.1145/1057792.1057803
6. Johnson, R.B., Onwuegbuzie, A.J., Turner, L.A.: Toward a definition of mixed methods research. J. Mixed Methods Res. **1**(2), 112–133 (2007). https://doi.org/10.1177/1558689806298224
7. Kalkofen, D., Sandor, C., White, S., Schmalstieg, D.: Visualization techniques for augmented reality. In: Furht, B. (eds.) Handbook of Augmented Reality, pp. 65–98. Springer, New York, NY (2011). https://doi.org/10.1007/978-1-4614-0064-6_3
8. Kamarainen, A., Reilly, J., Metcalf, S., Grotzer, T., Dede, C.: Using mobile location-based augmented reality to support outdoor learning in undergraduate ecology and environmental science courses. Bull. Ecol. Soc. Am. **99**(2), 259–276 (2018). https://doi.org/10.1002/bes2.1396

9. Kolsch, M., Bane, R., Hollerer, T., Turk, M.: Multimodal interaction with a wearable augmented reality system. IEEE Comput. Graph. Appl. **26**(3), 62–71 (2006). https://doi.org/10.1109/MCG.2006.66

10. Lilligreen, G., Keuchel, S., Wiebel, A.: Augmented reality in higher education: an active learning approach for a course in audiovisual production. In: Proceedings of the 16th Annual EuroVR Conference, pp. 23–36 (2019). https://doi.org/10.32040/2242-122X.2019.T357

11. Livingston, M.A., Dey, A., Sandor, C., Thomas, B.H.: Pursuit of "X-Ray Vision" for Augmented Reality, pp. 67–107. Springer, New York, NY (2013). https://doi.org/10.1007/978-1-4614-4205-9_4

12. Microsoft: Microsoft HoloLens 1 gestures. https://docs.microsoft.com/en-us/dynamics365/mixed-reality/guides/authoring-gestures. Accessed 10 Nov 2020

13. Microsoft: Mixed Reality Toolkit Documentation, MRTK Shader. https://microsoft.github.io/MixedRealityToolkit-Unity/Documentation/README_MRTKStandardShader.html. Accessed 11 Jan 2021

14. Microsoft: Microsoft HoloLens 1 spatial mapping. https://docs.microsoft.com/en-us/windows/mixed-reality/design/spatial-mapping. Accessed 20 Jan 2021

15. Microsoft: Microsoft mixed reality documentation. spatial anchors. https://docs.microsoft.com/de-de/windows/mixed-reality/design/spatial-anchors. Accessed 22 Jan 2021

16. Palmarini, R., Erkoyuncu, J.A., Roy, R., Torabmostaedi, H.: A systematic review of augmented reality applications in maintenance. Robot. Comput.-Integr. Manuf. **49**, 215–228 (2018)

17. Rambach, J., Lilligreen, G., Schäfer, A., Bankanal, R., Wiebel, A., Stricker, D.: A survey on applications of augmented, mixedand virtual reality for nature and environment. In: Proceedings of the HCI International Conference 2021. p. in this volume (2021)

18. Rubin, J., Chisnell, D.: Handbook of Usability Testing: How to Plan, Design ad Conduct Effective Tests. John Wiley & Sons, New Jersey (2008)

19. Schall, G., Zollmann, S., Reitmayr, G.: Smart vidente: advances in mobile augmented reality for interactive visualization of underground infrastructure. Pers. Ubiquit. Comput. **17**(7), 1533–1549 (2013). https://doi.org/10.1007/s00779-012-0599-x

20. Schmalstieg, D., Höllerer, T.: Augmented Reality - Principles and Practice. Addison-Wesley Professional, United States (2016)

21. Skjott Linneberg, M., Korsgaard, S.: Coding qualitative data: a synthesis guiding the novice. Qual. Res. J. **19**(3), 59–270 (2019). https://doi.org/10.1108/QRJ-12-2018-0012

22. Unity Technologies: Unity User Manual, stencil. https://docs.unity3d.com/2019.4/Documentation/Manual/SL-Stencil.html. Accessed 10 Nov 2020

23. Unity Technologies: Unity real-time development platform. https://unity.com/. Accessed 27 Jan 2021

24. Von Itzstein, G.S., Billinghurst, M., Smith, R.T., Thomas, B.H.: Augmented reality entertainment: taking gaming out of the box. In: Lee, N. (eds.) Encyclopedia of Computer Graphics and Games, pp. 1–9. Springer, Cham (2017). https://doi.org/10.1007/978-3-319-08234-9_81-1

25. Zhang, X., Han, Y., Hao, D., Lv, Z.: Argis-based outdoor underground pipeline information system. J. Vis. Commun. Image Representation **40**, 779–790 (2016). https://doi.org/10.1016/j.jvcir.2016.07.011

Using Head-Mounted Displays for Virtual Reality: Investigating Subjective Reactions to Eye-Tracking Scenarios

Crystal Maraj[✉], Jonathan Hurter, and Joseph Pruitt

Institute for Simulation and Training, University of Central Florida, Orlando, FL 32826, USA
{cmaraj,jhurter,jpruitt}@ist.ucf.edu

Abstract. Virtual reality head-mounted displays (HMDs) have recently incorporated eye-tracking into hardware design. For the present study, the Varjo VR-1 and HTC Vive Pro Eye HMDs were used for three eye-tracking scenarios; and immersion, simulator sickness, and visual discomfort questionnaires measured subjective reactions. A lack of research exists comparing HMDs equipped with eye-tracking capabilities, in terms of the subjective measures employed. In this study, the HMDs were investigated using between-subjects and within-subjects designs. For the between-subjects design, the independent variable was the HMD (i.e., Varjo VR-1 or HTC Vive Pro Eye) and the dependent variables were the immersion, simulator sickness, and visual discomfort measurements. For the within-subjects design, simulator sickness, and visual discomfort were evaluated across scenarios. Forty participants were asked to detect and confirm the same target stimulus in each of the three eye-tracking scenarios of increasing ecological complexity. For the results, non-parametric statistics were used, given non-normal data. Since between-groups differences were not found for immersion, simulator sickness, and visual discomfort, recommendations are provided for updating the survey measures. Within-groups differences for both simulator sickness and visual discomfort are explained for plausible cause and reduction methods. Correlation results indicate overlap between visual discomfort and simulator sickness; immersion lacked significant correlations with the other measures. Overall, survey updates and individual differences (e.g., ocular aspects) should be considered for future research and development.

Keywords: Eye tracking · Head-mounted displays · Immersion simulator sickness · Target detection · Virtual environments · Virtual reality · Visual discomfort

1 Introduction

1.1 Virtual Reality: Head-Mounted Displays

Head-mounted displays (HMDs) are headsets that attach to a user's head and present visuals to the user's central and peripheral vision; HMDs are commonly associated with virtual reality (VR), as they can be utilized to immerse users in a virtual world for a variety

© Springer Nature Switzerland AG 2021
J. Y. C. Chen and G. Fragomeni (Eds.): HCII 2021, LNCS 12770, pp. 381–394, 2021.
https://doi.org/10.1007/978-3-030-77599-5_27

of purposes (e.g., gaming, military, engineering, and medical purposes, Virtual Reality Society 2017). With recent advancements in VR hardware, technology companies have increasingly begun integrating eye-tracking technologies into HMDs (Clay et al. 2019). Areas of eye-tracking research applications extend to training, education, and cognition, with an emphasis on objective data to determine a system's effectiveness (Curatu et al. 2005). This paper investigates subjective reactions to eye-tracking task scenarios. The Varjo VR-1 (hereinafter, termed VR-1) and HTC Vive Pro Eye (hereinafter, termed Vive Pro Eye) HMDs are used for the tasks, and immersion, simulator sickness, and visual discomfort are used as subjective reactions to the tasks. By examining perceptual differences between HMDs (using a between-groups design for immersion, simulator sickness, and visual discomfort) and across scenarios (using a within-groups design for simulator sickness and visual discomfort), we can parse out VR effects and highlight any concerns for eye-tracking scenarios.

1.2 Head-Mounted Displays: VR-1 and Vive Pro Eye

The VR-1 is an HMD released in 2019, and has a Bionic Display that delivers a resolution of 60 pixels per degree (equivalent to 20/20 vision; Varjo 2020). The VR-1 originally retailed at $5995 (Schulze 2019), and has a larger display (at 1920 pixels × 1080 pixels) and a smaller display (at 1440 pixels × 1600 pixels; Varjo 2020). At the time of writing, the VR-1 had been discontinued. The Vive Pro Eye was released in 2018, includes eye-tracking technology, and offers a combined resolution of 2880 pixels × 1600 pixels (Vive Enterprise, n.d.). The Vive Pro Eye HMD retailed for $999 or $1599 (with the two controllers and base stations included; Vive Enterprise, n.d.). For a visual comparison of the two headsets, see Fig. 1.

Fig. 1. The Varjo VR-1 (left) and HTC Vive Pro Eye (right) head-mounted displays

1.3 Eye Tracking

Eye tracking can be defined as a technique used to measure a user's point of gaze (or fixation) and shifts in movement (or saccades) from one point to another (Poole and

Ball 2006). As a user focuses on objects displayed in a virtual environment, related eye-movement data is logged. Eye-tracking technology permits capture of objective data, such as pupil size, eye position, and detection of movement (Tobii, n.d.). This research effort takes a perceptual approach to examining eye tracking and interaction within VR technologies. Eye-tracking interaction methods have been investigated in the realm of a game for VR; in terms of accuracy and subjective easiness, a purely manual method (using a lightgun and trigger) ranked best, and pure eye-tracking methods (using gaze and blinking) ranked worst (Hülsmann et al. 2011). Although lacking statistical tests, the latter work shows a trend towards challenges in using eye-tracking interfaces. Eye movement information can also be recorded to determine areas of interest in 3D VR (Clay et al. 2019). The automotive industry was one area of exploration for eye-tracking applications in VR and human-computer interactions, whereby a driver's eye movements can help indicate attention and drowsiness (Barbuceanu and Antonya 2009).

1.4 Immersion

For the current investigation, immersion is operationalized as subjective responses to items based on five components: emotional involvement, cognitive involvement, challenge, control, and real-world dissociation (Jennett 2010); immersion relates to an engaging videogame experience (Jennett et al. 2008). We use this meaning for immersion hereinafter. Nevertheless, this definition is in contrast to immersion as based on technological aspects (Slater et al. 1995). We contend immersion can happen in a range of virtual scenarios. Previous research has found some immersion differences, with a first-person point-of-view being more immersive than a third-person point-of-view when gaming (Denisova and Cairns 2015); and an HMD more immersive than a triple flat screen for a driving simulator task (Walch et al. 2017). Immersion was examined in the present work through a between-groups design and through correlations.

1.5 Simulator Sickness

Simulator sickness emerges as adverse physiological issues when experiencing a simulation. Specifically, these issues break down into nausea, disorientation, and oculomotor aspects, which are operationalized as subscales from ranked items in the Simulator Sickness Questionnaire (SSQ; Kennedy et al. 1993). The SSQ has been employed when comparing HMDs, with some SSQ differences between devices found (Guna et al. 2019); and a lack of SSQ differences between devices found (Yildirim 2019; Singla et al. 2017). Still, eye-tracking tasks were not used in these studies. HMDs also induce more intense symptoms of simulator sickness than desktops, at least in a driving simulator (Cao et al. 2020). Simulator sickness was examined in the present work through a between-groups design, a within-groups design, and correlations.

1.6 Visual Discomfort

Observing particular stimuli can produce a set of adverse symptoms known as visual discomfort (O'Hare and Hibbard 2013), including headache, nausea, fatigue (Boyce and Wilkins 2018), eye strain, difficulty focusing, blurred vision, and double vision (Jaiswal et al. 2019). Visual discomfort is distinct from visual fatigue: whereas visual fatigue represents an objectively measured decrease in the human visual system, visual discomfort represents the subjective impact of stimuli on an observer (Lambooij et al. 2009). We operationalize visual discomfort as Headache, Eye Strain, Eye Tiredness, and Visual Clarity items per scenario through a Symptom Questionnaire, as adapted from Hoffman et al. (2008); some overlap with SSQ items in the questionnaire is noted. Disregarding overlap with the SSQ, visual discomfort has not been investigated when comparing HMDs; nor has the role of ecological complexity in inducing visual discomfort between virtual environments. Various factors can influence the severity of visual discomfort. Binocular distortions, the vergence-accommodation conflict, disparity distribution, and motion have all been shown to affect a viewer's level of visual comfort (for a review, see Li et al. 2015). Visual discomfort was examined in the present work through a between-groups design, a within-groups design, and correlations.

1.7 Research Purpose

The purpose of this research was to examine the VR-1 and Vive Pro Eye VR systems through an analysis of perceptual data tied to three scenarios involving eye-tracking tasks. A lack of research exists comparing HMDs equipped with eye-tracking capabilities, in terms of the subjective measures employed. The objective of this research was to evaluate differences in participants' perceptual data, including immersion, simulator sickness, and visual discomfort when using either the VR-1 or Vive Pro Eye. The research questions are as follows:

1. Is there a statistically significant difference between the VR-1 and Vive Pro Eye for immersion, simulator sickness and visual discomfort?
2. Is there a statistically significant difference from pre- to post-test simulator sickness for the VR-1? Vive Pro Eye?
3. Is there a statistically significant difference in visual discomfort across scenarios for the VR-1? Vive Pro Eye?
4. Are there any statistically significant correlations between a) immersion and simulator sickness, b) immersion and visual discomfort, or c) simulator sickness and visual discomfort?

2   Method

2.1 Participants

Forty volunteers from the University of Central Florida (UCF) and its neighboring areas signed-up to participate in the eye-tracking study. There were 20 males and 20 females ($N = 40$), with ages ranging from 18 to 33 years old ($M = 21.88$, $SD = 3.89$). Due to

COVID-19, participants were asked to complete a pre-health screening one day before the study took place, in addition to meeting study sign-up criteria. The inclusion criteria consisted of being at least 18 years old, having normal or corrected-to-normal vision, having a United States citizenship, and having no history of seizures. Participants also were confirmed to have no color-blindness. Each study lasted approximately one hour, and each participant was compensated $10 for time and travel.

2.2 Experimental Design

The eye-tracking study employed a between-subjects design to assess perceptual differences between the VR-1 and Vive Pro Eye HMDs. The independent variable was the type of HMD (i.e., VR-1 or Vive Pro Eye), and the dependent variables were the eye-tracking scenario measurements (i.e., immersion, simulator sickness, and visual discomfort). The study also incorporated a within-subjects design to evaluate simulator sickness and visual discomfort, across scenarios, within the VR-1 and Vive Pro Eye conditions.

2.3 Software

Three eye-tracking scenarios were developed in the Unity game engine software for integration and execution within each HMD. The scenario assets were purchased from the Unity Asset Store and imported into the Unity environment. The scenarios increased in complexity through the addition of models in the environment.

The VR-1 contained a 20/20 Eye Tracker to track eye movement within the HMD. The software was designed, and propriety rights were owned, by the Finnish company. The eye-tracking software works by reflecting an image into the user's eye and calculates information using an algorithm. The eye-tracking software is compatible with Unity to create virtual content for visual display. The Vive Pro Eye has built-in eye-tracking software developed by Tobii (Vive 2020). The software is configured with the Vive Pro Eye to create an immersive user experience. The Tobii eye-tracking software development kit is compatible with the Unity game engine. The user's shift in gaze from one stimuli to another is tracked by the software. Both HMDs included foveal rendering, which provides a sharper image in central vision.

The Qualtrics software is a university-wide site-license for the UCF population. Qualtrics is a web-based software that allows its users to create, distribute, and collect survey data from research participants. Qualtrics was installed on a standard desktop computer to gather perceptual data regarding immersion, simulator sickness, and visual discomfort; and to gather demographic information.

2.4 Scenario Tasks

Upon completion of a tutorial, the user started the experimental scenarios. The participant's objective within each scenario was to detect and confirm the target stimulus: a red car with one wheel missing. The participant could detect multiple objects using their gaze, and confirm detection using buttons with a controller. The participant would be automatically driven to stop-points, wherein the target stimulus would appear for detection. A gazed-upon object would be outlined in red, and after 2 s of dwell time two on-screen buttons allowed the participant to either confirm or reject the object as the target. The participant would be moved to the next stop-point after 15 s in the detection stage, regardless of confirmation or rejection; confirmation was allowed once, but rejection was unlimited. After these 15 s, the user would move to the next stop-point (traveling to stop points happened 15 times per each of the three scenarios). The user could view the surrounding VE via head-tracking from a first-person perspective.

2.5   Scenario Environments

The scenarios in this study were set in a virtual urban environment; the ecological complexity of the three scenarios was increased through the addition of visual elements commonly associated with urban environments. In Scenario 1, the environment consisted of only buildings, road markings, and the target stimuli. Scenario 2 increased in ecological complexity through the addition of streetlights, stop signs, benches, and other objects commonly found in cities. In Scenario 3, assets were added to Scenario 2: cars (other than the target stimuli), pedestrians, and power lines. Figure 2 shows scenario examples.

2.6   Survey Measurements

A demographics questionnaire consisted of a series of general background questions, such as age, gender, education level, and questions targeting technology usage (e.g., proficiency with computers, previous VR use, and time spent playing computer/video games).

The Immersion Measure was adapted from Jennett et al. (2008) to assess the participants' immersion, as operationalized in Sect. 1.4. The survey consisted of eight statements, rated from *strongly disagree* (1) to *strongly agree* (5). The SSQ from Kennedy et al. (1993) was used to assess the severity of a set of symptoms, as operationalized in Sect. 1.5: subscales and a Total SSQ score of all subscales were measured. The questionnaire consisted of 16 symptom items; participants rated the intensity of each symptom from *none* (0) to *severe* (3). There was also a free-response question that allowed for the documentation of any additional symptom unlisted in the questionnaire. The Symptom Questionnaire was adapted from Hoffman et al. (2008) to assess the severity of symptoms associated with visual discomfort, as operationalized in Sect. 1.6. The questionnaire consisted of six questions, rated on a 5-point scale, such as from *less tired than normal* (1) to *more tired than normal* (5). The Cronbach's alphas for the Immersion Measure, SSQ, and Symptom Questionnaire were .80, .86, and .64, respectively.

2.7   Procedure

All participants followed a stepwise procedure, incorporating pre-scenario, scenario, and post-scenario experimental sections. Each participant completed only one condition: either the VR-1 or Vive Pro Eye condition. For the order of tasks per section, see Table 1. The interface training slides provided information regarding the overall experiment, task

Fig. 2. Each column provides examples of the same eye-tracking stop-point location, for Scenarios 1, 2, and 3. From top to bottom are Scenarios 1, 2, and 3, respectively.

procedure, system (i.e., both HMD and controller), eye-tracking calibration, and tutorial. The VR-1 slides also contained information on the HMD's head-positioning guide. For eye-tracking calibration, the VR-1 required calibration before the tutorial and every scenario; the Vive Pro Eye eye-tracking calibration was only required once, before the tutorial.

Table 1. Experiment procedure for both conditions

Section	Task completed
Pre-scenarios	1. Informed consent 2. Color-blindness test 3. Demographics questionnaire 4. Simulator Sickness Questionnaire (pre-test) 5. Interface training slides 6. Tutorial and one-minute break
Scenarios	7. Scenario 1, Symptom Questionnaire, and one-minute break 8. Scenario 2, Symptom Questionnaire, and one-minute break 9. Scenario 3, Symptom Questionnaire, and one-minute break
Post-scenarios	10. Immersion Measure 11. Simulator Sickness Questionnaire (post-test) 12. Receipt for compensation 13. Dismissal

3   Results

Tests for normality, homogeneity of variance, and outliers were conducted. The Kolmogorov–Smirnov test's value was $<.05$, and thus violated assumptions. Homogeneity of variance was also violated. As a result, non-parametric tests were used for analysis.

3.1   Results for Research Question 1: Between-Groups Differences for Immersion, Simulator Sickness, and Visual Discomfort

For Research Question 1 we asked, is there a statistically significant difference between the VR-1 and Vive Pro Eye for immersion, simulator sickness and visual discomfort? Using Mann-Whitney U Tests, no differences for Total Immersion, post-test simulator sickness (for all subscales and Total SSQ scores), and visual discomfort (Symptom Questionnaire) were found, except for the first scenario's scores for Sore Neck and Sore Back. Since these latter items are not indicative of visual discomfort, the significant differences are not shown.

3.2   Results for Research Question 2: Within-Groups Differences for Simulator Sickness

For Research Question 2 we asked, is there a statistically significant difference from pre- to post-test simulator sickness for the VR-1? Vive Pro Eye? Using a Wilcoxon Signed Rank Test, significant differences were found within-groups for both VR-1 and Vive Pro Eye, as shown in Table 2.

Table 2. Simulator sickness questionnaire (SSQ) results for within-groups differences

Symptom	Md		z	p
	Pre-SSQ	Post-SSQ		
Varjo VR-1				
Oculomotor	0.00	7.58	−2.83	.01
Total	0.00	3.74	−2.05	.04
HTC Vive Pro Eye				
Disorientation	0.00	0.00	−2.21	.03
Oculomotor	0.00	7.58	−3.05	.00
Total	0.00	3.74	−3.03	.00

Note: n = 20 for each SSQ, except for post-SSQ in the Varjo VR-1, where n = 19.

3.3 Results for Research Question 3: Within-Groups Differences for Visual Discomfort

For Research Question 3 we asked, is there a statistically significant difference in visual discomfort across scenarios for the VR-1? Vive Pro Eye? For visual discomfort (i.e., Symptom Questionnaire) the results of the Friedman test indicated that there was a statistically significant difference in the Headache item across the three scenarios, $\chi 2$ $(2, n = 20) = 7.6, p = .02$ ($Md = 3$ across scenarios), in the VR-1 condition.

3.4 Results for Research Question 4: Spearman's Correlations for Immersion, Simulator Sickness, and Visual Discomfort

For Research Question 4 we asked, are there any statistically significant correlations between a) immersion and simulator sickness, b) immersion and visual discomfort, or c) simulator sickness and visual discomfort? Spearman's correlations were used to assess relationships between measures. There was no statistically significant relationship between Total Immersion and post-test SSQ subscales (i.e., Nausea, Disorientation, and Oculomotor) or Total SSQ for both the VR-1 and Vive Pro Eye. There was no statistically significant relationship between Total Immersion and Symptom Questionnaire items after Scenario 3 for both the VR-1 and Vive Pro Eye. Table 3 shows significant correlations between SSQ post-test scores and Symptom Questionnaire items for Scenario 3.

Table 3. Simulator sickness questionnaire (SSQ) and symptom questionnaire correlations

Symptom questionnaire	SSQ			
	Nausea	Disorientation	Oculomotor	Total
	Varjo VR-1			
Eye Tiredness	.45*	.61**	.54*	.52*
Eye Strain	–	–	.64**	.56*
Visual Clarity	–	–	.56*	.52*
	HTC Vive Pro Eye			
Eye Tiredness	–	–	.48*	–
Eye Strain	.69**	.49*	.65**	.66**
Headache	.73**	–	–	–

Note: The Varjo VR-1 condition had an $n = 19$. The HTC Vive Pro Eye condition had an $n = 20$. Hyphens represent nonsignificant findings. $^*p < .05$ $^{**}p < .01$

4 Discussion

4.1 Discussion for Research Question 1: Between-Groups Differences for Immersion, Simulator Sickness, and Visual Discomfort

Statistically, differences were not found for immersion, simulator sickness, or visual discomfort, when comparing the VR-1 and Vive Pro Eye systems. Overall, similar outcomes were produced by both systems for between-groups analysis; that is, one system was not better than another. Thus, the following discussion focuses on how scenarios impacted perceptual response. Perhaps surveys should be redesigned or created anew to better scope valuable aspects, such as a distinction between the physical (or hardware) aspects of HMDs and the psychological aspects of scenarios, as a foundation to determine if such valuable aspects are associated or dissociated. The immersion survey was predominately tied to scenario composition, rather than HMD factors. Revising the survey to focus on HMD immersion may add another dimension to findings. Further, immersion measures may be placed after completion of each scenario, to better map immersive effects over time, in terms of both between-groups and within-groups analysis.

Even if the systems were similar in terms of the RQ1 constructs, more specific questionnaires could examine HMD aspects at a more granular analysis. For example, adding open-ended questions to the SSQ, where participants could elaborate on the close-ended ratings of each symptom.

4.2 Discussion for Research Question 2: Within-Groups Differences for Simulator Sickness

Both the VR-1 and Vive Pro Eye had significant pre-to-post increases in the Oculomotor subscale and Total SSQ scores; and the Vive Pro Eye had a significant difference in pre-to-post Disorientation subscale. Example Oculomotor subscale items include Eye Strain, Difficulty Focusing, and Headache (Kennedy et al. 1993). Eye strain may also be caused by environmental issues, as reported by a participant, where scenario visuals would act jittery. The scenarios appear to increase certain simulator sickness aspects, but not all aspects. Based on a user perspective, scenarios for up to 30 min (in 10-min intervals) involving vection (i.e., a false sense of movement), head movements, and eye-tracking can induce significant levels of at least Oculomotor subscale and Total SSQ scores. For such tasks, increasing time between scenarios may help reduce these SSQ issues.

4.3 Discussion for Research Question 3: Within-groups Differences for Visual Discomfort

The only significant finding for Research Question 3 was a significant difference in the Headache item for the VR-1. Perhaps, calibration with the VR-1 was inconsistent, such as due to certain individual differences: glasses, pupil size, color of the iris, and eye dominance have been found to impact eye-tracker data (Nyström et al. 2013). Ultimately, future research should elucidate a map of how individual aspects relate to headache symptoms. Further, the dwell time required for object selection (i.e., 2 s) could negatively impact users. Past research suggests long dwell times can lead to visual discomfort (i.e., subjective visual fatigue); conversely, a focal-fixation method is shown as an alternative to a dwell-time method, as the latter can maintain accuracy and reduce visual discomfort (Velichkovsky et al. 2014). As an overlap, the Headache item is considered an exclusively Oculomotor subscale issue on the SSQ. This difference in the Headache item is complemented by the changes in the Oculomotor subscale in the VR-1 condition.

4.4 Discussion for Research Question 4: Spearman's Correlations for Immersion, Simulator Sickness, and Visual Discomfort

Some visual discomfort items found in the Symptom Questionnaire were associated positively with the Oculomotor subscale of the SSQ. In the Varjo, Eye Tiredness, Eye Strain, and Visual Clarity were associated positively with the Oculomotor subscale; visual discomfort issues rose as the oculomotor issue rose. Eye Tiredness was also positively associated with Nausea and Disorientation subscales. In the Vive Pro Eye, Eye Tiredness and Eye Strain were also associated positively with the Oculomotor subscale. Some dissociation between the visual discomfort and simulator sickness exists. For example, the Headache item reported through the Symptom Questionnaire was not correlated to the Oculomotor subscale, despite the Headache item being exclusive to the Oculomotor subscale. Subjective surveys, and their placement within a procedure, may account for this effect.

One would expect immersion to negatively relate to the negative aspects of visual discomfort and simulator sickness: if one's focus was on their own physiological concerns, then one would not be able to increase engagement with the scenarios. Yet, a lack of significant correlations was found between immersion and such negative aspects.

4.5 Limitations and Next Steps

Based on the current research design, considerations are given to survey updates. To complement the visual discomfort survey, additional physiological optometric measures may be integrated as a pre-screening baseline, as well as for comparison to subjective data. Increasing sample size may reveal statistical differences between the participant's reactions to the HMDs.

In terms of calibration between headsets, we focused on the product's organic (or factory default) method, providing a specific end-user case per each headset. However, our design does not account for controlling calibration in a more consistent fashion, where both HMDs would follow the same calibration procedures. A next step would be to confirm whether this consistency impacts user response(s) differently.

5 Conclusion

Since no between-groups differences were found for immersion, simulator sickness, or visual discomfort, plausible recommendations of survey-design updates were discussed: survey placement and survey elaborations. A pre-to-post increase in the Oculomotor subscale was shown for both HMDs, and a significant pre-to-post difference in the Disorientation subscale was shown only for the Vive Pro Eye. Tasks involving movement around routes and detecting objects of interest via head movements may benefit, such as conducting a patrol route, by understanding simulator sickness concerns: breaks longer than the 1 min used in our work may be researched. The VR-1 had differences across scenarios (whereas the Vive Pro Eye did not) for visual discomfort: specifically, the Headache item differed, perhaps due to individual differences (e.g., pupil size). Overall, some overlap, or association, was found between visual discomfort and simulator sickness (i.e., strongly in the positive direction). The study establishes considerations for surveys; perhaps, the current surveys need updating for eye-tracking tasks. As eye-tracking becomes part of culture, subjective reactions should be customized to better understand eye-tracking tasks.

Acknowledgments. This research was sponsored by Mr. Clayton Burford of the U.S. Army Futures Command, CCDC-SC, Simulation and Training Technologies Center (STTC) under contract W911QX-13-C-0052. However, the views, findings, and conclusions contained in this presentation are solely those of the authors and should not be interpreted as representing the official policies, either expressed or implied, of the U.S. Government.

References

Barbuceanu, F., Antonya, C.: Eye tracking applications. Bull. Transilvania Univ. Brasov, Ser. 1: Eng. Sci. **2**(51), 17–24 (2009)

Boyce, P.R., Wilkins, A.: Visual discomfort indoors. Lighting Res. Technol. **50**(1), 98–114 (2018)

Cao, S., Nandakumar, K., Babu, R., Thompson, B.: Game play in virtual reality driving simulation involving head-mounted display and comparison to desktop display. Vir. Reality, 1–11 (2020)

Clay, V., König, P., König, S.U.: Eye tracking in virtual reality. J. Eye Mov. Res. **12**(1) (2019)

Curatu, C., Hua, H., Rolland, J.: Projection-based head-mounted display with eye-tracking capabilities. In: Novel Optical Systems Design and Optimization VIII, vol. 5875. International Society for Optics and Photonics, August 2005

Denisova, A., Cairns, P.: First person vs. third person perspective in digital games: do player preferences affect immersion? In: Proceedings of the 33rd Annual ACM Conference on Human Factors in Computing Systems, pp. 145–148, April 2015

Guna, J., et al.: Virtual reality sickness and challenges behind different technology and content settings. Mob. Netw. Appl. 1–10 (2019)

Hoffman, D.M., Girshick, A.R., Akeley, K., Banks, M.S.: Vergence–accommodation conflicts hinder visual performance and cause visual fatigue. J. Vis. **8**(3), 1–30 (2008)

Hülsmann, F., Dankert, T., Pfeiffer, T.: Comparing gaze-based and manual interaction in a fast-paced gaming task in virtual reality. In: Proceedings of the Workshop Virtuelle & Erweiterte Realität (2011)

Jaiswal, S., Asper, L., Long, J., Lee, A., Harrison, K., Golebiowski, B.: Ocular and visual discomfort associated with smartphones, tablets and computers: what we do and do not know. Clin. Exper. Optom. **102**(5), 463–477 (2019)

Jennett, C.I.: Is game immersion just another form of selective attention? An empirical investigation of real world dissociation in computer game immersion [Doctoral thesis]. University College London (2010)

Jennett, C., et al.: Measuring and defining the experience of immersion in games. Int. J. Hum.-Comput. Stud. **66**(9), 641–661 (2008)

Kennedy, R., Lane, N., Berbaum, K., Lilienthal, M.: Simulator sickness questionnaire: an enhanced method for quantifying simulator sickness. Int. J. Aviat. Psychol. **3**(3), 203–220 (1993)

Lambooij, M., Fortuin, M., Heynderickx, I., IJsselsteijn, W.: Visual discomfort and visual fatigue of stereoscopic displays: A review. J. Imaging Sci. Technol. **53**(3), 030201–030201-14 (2009)

Li, J., Barkowsky, M., Le Callet, P.: Visual discomfort in 3DTV: Definitions, causes, measurement, and modeling. Novel 3D Media Technologies, pp. 185–209. Springer, New York (2015). https://doi.org/10.1007/978-1-4939-2026-6_10

Nyström, M., Andersson, R., Holmqvist, K., Van De Weijer, J.: The influence of calibration method and eye physiology on eyetracking data quality. Behav. Res. Meth. **45**(1), 272–288 (2013)

O'Hare, L., Hibbard, P.B.: Visual discomfort and blur. J. Vis. **13**(5), 7 (2013)

Poole, A., Ball, L.J.: Eye tracking in HCI and usability research. In: Encyclopedia of Human Computer Interaction, pp. 211–219. IGI Global (2006)

Schulze, E.: A new $6,000 virtual reality headset lets you see with 'human-eye' resolution. CNBC. https://www.cnbc.com/2019/02/19/finnish-start-up-varjo-launches-5995-vr-1-headset.html. Accessed 19 Feb 2019

Singla, A., Fremerey, S., Robitza, W., Raake, A.: Measuring and comparing QoE and simulator sickness of omnidirectional videos in different head mounted displays. In: 2017 Ninth international conference on quality of multimedia experience (QoMEX), pp. 1–6. IEEE, May 2017

Slater, M., Usoh, M., Steed, A.: Taking steps: the influence of a walking technique on presence in virtual reality. ACM Trans. Comput.-Hum. Interact. (TOCHI) **2**(3), 201–219 (1995)

Tobii (n.d): What is eye tracking?. https://tech.tobii.com/technology/what-is-eye-tracking/. Accessed 25 Nov 2020

Varjo (2020): VR-1. https://varjo.com/products/vr-1/

Velichkovsky, B.B., Rumyantsev, M.A., Morozov, M.A.: New solution to the midas touch problem: identification of visual commands via extraction of focal fixations. Procedia Comput. Sci. **39**, 75–82 (2014)

Virtual Reality Society: Head-mounted displays (HMDs). VRS. https://www.vrs.org.uk/virtual-reality-gear/head-mounted-displays/. Accessed 28 June 2017

Vive (2020): VIVE Pro Eye with Tobii Eye. https://vr.tobii.com/products/htc-vive-pro-eye/. Accessed 25 Sept 2020

Vive Enterprise (n.d.): Vive Pro Eye Office. https://enterprise.vive.com/us/product/vive-pro-eye-office/

Walch, M., et al.: Evaluating VR driving simulation from a player experience perspective. In: Proceedings of the 2017 CHI Conference Extended Abstracts on Human Factors in Computing Systems, pp. 2982–2989, May 2017

Yildirim, C.: Don't make me sick: investigating the incidence of cybersickness in commercial virtual reality headsets. Virt. Reality, 1–9 (2019)

Omnidirectional Flick View

Ryota Suzuki$^{(\boxtimes)}$, Tomomi Sato, Kenji Iwata, and Yutaka Satoh

National Institute of Advanced Industrial Science and Technology,
Tsukuba, Ibaraki, Japan
{ryota.suzuki,tomomi.satou,kenji.iwata,yu.satou}@aist.go.jp

Abstract. We propose a novel interface that naturally and dynamically augments practical horizontal field-of-view via Head-Mounted Display (HMD). Instead of showing whole omnidirectional sight, we realize augmentation of dynamic field-of-view (FoV) by composition of two methods: (i) Neck-yaw Boosting: magnification of amount of movement of sight against neckyawing, and (ii) Dynamic FoV Boosting: slight translation between local view and global view. Neck-flicking motion of users expands FoV and extends direction of neck-yawing. Simultaneous usage of these methods extremely reduces burden of turning head while degrading optical flow for suppressing VR sickness.

Keywords: Vision boosting · Head-mounted display · Usability

1 Introduction

Humans have evolved their vision for precise interaction with a limited FoV (field of view). Although humans have high cognitive abilities such as depth and speed in the near-frontal area, the spatial area that can be immediately recognized is narrow. In contrast, many animals have very wide FoV. The pigeons have a FoV of more than 300° and has the vision to constantly observe all directions and respond immediately. Even in humans, such visual ability would be useful in many cases. For example, in sports that require omni-directional interaction, such as football and basketball, spatial perception is important. It has been achieved by active sensing and advanced simulation in the brain, but the load is high and depends on individual talent. In addition, wheelchair users often have accidents with pedestrians around them. The reason for this is that it is difficult to turn the body and neck due to the immobilization of the lower half of the body, and the cognitive ability of the surrounding environment is lower than that of able-bodied person. Also, the accessibility of the elevator is an issue because wheelchair users have poor visibility behind them.

However, it is difficult for human perceive the surroundings immediately because of two problems: (i) Physical problem. In order to recognize a range that cannot be covered by eye movement, it is necessary to turn around the neck, but the cost of swinging the head is large. (ii) Visual problem. It is difficult for humans to visually perceive the entire circumference even if they are presented in the same visual field at once.

© Springer Nature Switzerland AG 2021
J. Y. C. Chen and G. Fragomeni (Eds.): HCII 2021, LNCS 12770, pp. 395–414, 2021.
https://doi.org/10.1007/978-3-030-77599-5_28

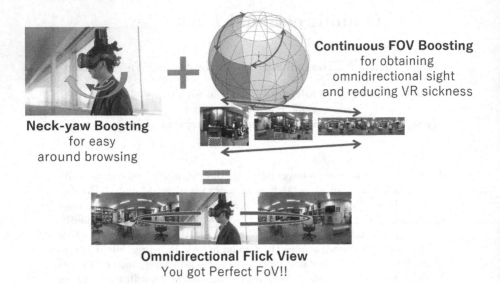

Neck-yaw Boosting
for easy
around browsing

Continuous FOV Boosting
for obtaining
omnidirectional sight
and reducing VR sickness

Omnidirectional Flick View
You got Perfect FoV!!

Fig. 1. Omnidirectional flick view

On the other hand, developments in VR devices, such as high resolution and improved sensors, have made it possible to virtually create novel vision that cannot be obtained by human vision. In this paper, we propose an interface that solves these two problems and effectively extends the FoV. Our proposal consists of two modules: (i) Neck-yaw Boosting: Significantly reducing the amount of neck orientation by expanding the virtual neck orientation. (ii) Dynamic FoV Boosting: Smooth and dynamic transition between wide FoV and narrow FoV. The system for realizing them consists of an omnidirectional multi-camera and a pose trackable HMD (head-mounted display).

These two modules come into their own when they are used simultaneously. Neck-yaw Boosting accelerates the virtual gaze movement, while increasing the optical flow, then inducing VR sickness. Therefore, Dynamic FoV Boosting can be used at the simultaneously to reduce the optical flow due to the zoom-out effect during FoV expansion, thus reducing VR sickness.

The contributions of this study are as follows:

- Development of a system for dynamic FoV expansion and reduction of pivoting loads.
- Development of a package device consisting of a multi-camera array, a tracker, and a HMD to implement this system.
- Designing dynamics to achieve visual boosting without discomfort.

2   Related Work

A lot of research about expanding field of view have been conducted. It could be majorly distinguished into two paradigms. One is an expansion of static field of view. For example, Fisheye vision Orlosky et.al. proposed that implemented a device consists of an HMD and two fisheye cameras pasted on HMD corresponding to left/right eyes of users, and provides 180° FoV while maintaining steleoscopy [4]. It corrected lenz distortion among binocular view areas of cameras and keep distortion of peripheral view areas of each cameras. Yamada et.al. developed a simple device to realize extension of blurred peripheral view without requiring any computational process [6]. Almost of the works were limited to expand FoV until likely 180°.

Researches realizing over 180° FoV expansion also exists. Peñaranda et.al. developed less-distorted FoV expansion until 360° by employing hyperbolic Möbius transform on Riemann sphere [5]. Our work has the same direction toward expansion on a sphere for the static FoV expansion, but we are able to expand FoV more than 360° theoretically.

As the other paradigm, active field of view expansion has also researched. Jeakl et.al. conducted an experiment of virtually boosting neck direction, and the result shows that not only users could accept the virtual boosting of neck direction but they felt boosted movement more natural than normal movement in virtual reality [2]. Jay et.al. conducted an experiment that evaluated quickness of searching particular objects in a VR room under condition of boosting neck direction with virtual avatar of users' hand [3]. They reported that the condition of boosting both neck direction and hand avatar direction quickened the task.

Our strategy is the combination of these paradigm. A research of applying the strategy can also be found. Yano et.al. proposed a FoV expansion system that incorporated static/active FoV expansion with a device of an HMD and two fisheye cameras [7]. However, they were limited for the FoV expansion up to 180°, and they did not consider about slight transition between narrow/wide FoV and connection between static/active FoV expansion.

3   System Overview

3.1   Device

Our devices consists of a pose trackable omnidirectional multiple camera array and a pose trackable HMD. Figure 2 shows appearance of the devices. We use HTC Vive pro for HMD and pose tracking system. The camera array consists of six web cameras[1] and a pose tracker. We configure position and pose of the cameras that they are side-topping and cover whole horizontal 360° direction while intersecting field of view of the cameras (see Fig. 4). All cameras and the pose tracker are fixed on a mount printed by 3D printer so as to fix positional relationship among them. Intrinsic parameters of the cameras, positional relationship between the cameras and the pose tracker are required for adequate construction of virtual space. We calibrated intrinsic parameters of each cameras using OpenCV. Moreover, we calibrated positional relationship between

---

[1] BSW20KM11BK, Buffalo inc. Horizontal FoV: 120° , vertical FoV: 80° (approx.). Resolution: 1920 × 1080 pixels. 30 fps. USB connection.

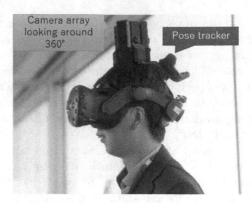

Fig. 2. Pose-trackable multiple camera array on HMD

the cameras and the pose tracker by referring positional relationship between a checkerboard and the cameras. Positional relationship between two cameras can be obtained by observing a same static checkerboard at once. The tracker position relative to a representative camera $P_{C \to T}$ can be solved by applying a non-linear optimization method on the Eq. (1):

$$P_{Ci \to Cj} = P_{C \to T} \cdot P_{Ti \to Tj} \cdot P_{C \to T}^{-1}. \tag{1}$$

Here, $P_{Ti \to Tj}$ is difference of the tracker's pose between two shot timing i, j by the camera.

We use a machine consists of Intel Core i7 CPU ad NVIDIA GeForce RTX 2080Ti GPU for a calculation unit. We use NVIDIA OptiX for ray casting process and OpenGL for the other entire rendering process.

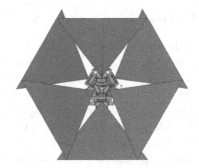

Fig. 3. 3D CAD data of multiple camera array

Fig. 4. Sight of cameras on multiple camera array

3.2 Virtual Space Settings and Boosting Modules

Camera images taken by the camera array are virtually put around a virtual camera. Users are able to look around the virtual space through the HMD. Owing to the calibration processes mentioned in above section, we can put camera images into VR without distortion.

Camera images are put on a distance of 2 m from the virtual camera on referring the calculated camera intrinsic parameter and the relative pose. Thus the camera images forms an octagonal pole around the virtual camera. We define the distance according to heuristics. By referring Sociology, the distance of 2m means middle of Social distance of Interpersonal distance, that a Sociologist Edward T. Hall defined [1], so that it would be comfortable to make social interaction.

By the way, we maintain intersection area of camera images by applying blending by distance from center position of each images. We define the pixel value of a camera image that is to be rendered onto the HMD as $I_i(\bar{u}_i, \bar{v}_i)(i = 0, ..., N-1)$, whereas i means a number of a camera image. We also define $(\bar{u}_i, \bar{v}_i)$ as UV coordinate of the corresponding point on the image that is normalized in range of $[-1, 1]$ and the center position as $(0, 0)$. We calculate the corresponding pixel value on the HMD I_{HMD} as:

$$I_{HMD} = \frac{\sum_i w(\bar{u}_i, \bar{v}_i) I_i(\bar{u}_i, \bar{v}_i)}{\sum_i w(\bar{u}_i, \bar{v}_i)}. \tag{2}$$

where,

$$w(\bar{u}_i, \bar{v}_i) = (1 - |\bar{u}_i|)^2 (1 - |\bar{v}_i|)^2. \tag{3}$$

$w(\bar{u}_i, \bar{v}_i)$ shows relative weight of image i. It is designed so that the weight of the center pixel is the largest and degrading slightly up to 0 toward peripheral area.

By controlling optical system and pose of the virtual camera, the boosting of human vision can be accomplished. The boosting consists of two modules:

Neck-yaw Boosting. Boosting horizontal camera direction against real face direction. With quite short rotation of head let users see every direction over 360°. It is adaptive to neck-flicking speed and users can control the amount of boosting by neck-flicking motion.

Dynamic FoV Boosting. Boosting FoV according to users' motion of neck-flicking. Spherical polar coordinate is employed to realize over 360° FoV.

We design an elaborate dynamics of the adaptive boosting control for providing both high utility and avoidance of VR sickness. We explain the detail of these two boosting modules in the next section.

4 Design of Boosting Modules

4.1 Neck-Yaw Boosting

Neck-yaw Boosting amplifies the virtual view direction by referencing angular distance between a base direction and a real view direction. We assume that the base direction is ordinarily a body direction of user. The base direction would be configurable depending on an application.

The simplest idea of the boosting is to multiply an azimuth angle (i.e. an angle between the base direction and the real view direction) by a constant. However, because it also boosts noises, it is difficult for user to finely adjust a virtual viewpoint. When a user gazes at a specific point, blurring caused by a wiggle of a head is always amplified, and it vitiates the stability of a virtual viewpoint. On the other hand, when we choose a low boosting rate for stability, the range of virtual viewpoint where user can reach only by the neck-yawing is limited. Thus, the dynamical FoV is narrowed in this setting. Therefore we apply adaptive boosting rate control.

As a guideline for the boosting rate control, we introduce the following conditions:

Cond. a. Giving a large boosting rate when a real viewpoint moving quickly to look around. When a user is gazing at a specific point or searching a narrow range, giving a small (close to identity) boosting rate.

Cond. b. When a real viewpoint directs toward the base direction, a virtual viewpoint also directs toward the base direction.

Cond. c. A moving direction of virtual viewpoint is same as the real viewpoint.

Cond. b is important especially in an application where the base direction has a specific meaning, for example, in a case of a user needs to recognize the positional relationship between the user's own pose and a virtual viewpoint.

If Cond. c is not satisfied, change of view conflicts with movement of the neck, which would induce VR sickness.

In order to satisfy Cond. a, the system needs to apprehend a purpose of a user's action. We make the following assumption:

Asm. a. When a user moves viewpoint largely and overlooks, an angular velocity of a real viewpoint takes large. When a user gazes and searches in a narrow area, an angular velocity slightly moves.

Thus, we rephrase Cond. a as:

Cond. a'. Giving a large boosting rate for a large angular velocity, and a small boosting rate for a small angular velocity.

Hence, we design the following boosting rate control function:

$$\dot{\theta}_{BV} = k^+ \dot{\theta}_R, \quad k^+(\dot{\theta}_R) = 1 + k_{\max}(1 - \exp[-|\dot{\theta}_R/\dot{\theta}_0|]). \tag{4}$$

$\theta_{R/BV}$ is the azimuth of real or boosted virtual viewpoint, and $\dot{\theta}_{R/BV}$ is the angular velocity of them. From Eq. (4), we obtain

$$
\begin{aligned}
k^+(\dot{\theta}_R \ll \dot{\theta}_0) &\rightarrow 1 + k_{\max}\dot{\theta}_R/\dot{\theta}_0, \\
k^+(\dot{\theta}_R \rightarrow \infty) &\rightarrow 1 + k_{\max}.
\end{aligned}
\tag{5}
$$

This equation is given in the form of a differential equation of time evaluation. Thus, the actual value of the virtual viewpoint θ_{BV} is given by integrating the equation.

Because the actual value of θ_{BV} depends on the angular velocity of the real viewpoint, Cond. b is not always satisfied as it is. So we device the function to satisfy Cond. b. Firstly, we divide the control function into the cases of outward movement and inward movement:

$$
\theta_{BV} = \begin{cases} \theta_{BV}^+ \left(\dfrac{d}{dt}|\theta_R| > 0 \right) \\[2mm] \theta_{BV}^- \left(\dfrac{d}{dt}|\theta_R| \leq 0 \right) \end{cases}
\tag{6}
$$

For the outward moving control function θ_{BV}^+, we evolves the above differential equation in time. On the other hand, for the inward moving control function θ_{BV}^-, we have to re-design it while satisfying Cond. b. Here we give priority to Cond. b against Cond. a to design θ_{BV}^-, because it is fatal to lose correspondence between a user's pose and a viewpoint.

Although the azimuth of the real viewpoint θ_R and the angular velocity $\dot{\theta}_R$ depends on the user's action, we assume that the viewpoint moves at a constant velocity, and determine the control function at each time. By Cond. b, the following constraint is given to θ_{BV}^- at time t:

$$
\textbf{ia.} \quad \theta_{BV}^- \left(\theta_R \rightarrow 0, \dot{\theta}_R(t) \right) = 0.
\tag{7}
$$

At the base direction ($\theta_{BV} = 0$), the inward control function θ_{BV}^- connects to the outward control function θ_{BV}^-. Here, the following condition is required for smoothly connecting between $\theta_{BV}^+ - \theta_{BV}^-$:

$$
\textbf{ib.} \quad \dot{\theta}_{BV}^- \left(\theta_R \rightarrow 0, \dot{\theta}_R(t) \right) = \dot{\theta}_{BV}^+ \left(\dot{\theta}_R(t) \right).
\tag{8}
$$

The above conditions depend on the azimuth angle θ_R and angular velocity $\dot{\theta}_R$ of real viewpoint, and they are changing over time depending on a user's behavior. We add the following constraints to make the azimuth angle of the virtual viewpoint varying continuously and smoothly:

$$
\textbf{iia.} \quad \theta_{BV}^- \left(\theta_R(t), \dot{\theta}_R(t+dt) \right) = \theta_{BV}(t).
\tag{9}
$$

$$
\textbf{iib.} \quad \dot{\theta}_{BV}^- \left(\theta_R(t), \dot{\theta}_R(t+dt) \right) = \dot{\theta}_{BV}(t).
\tag{10}
$$

The meaning of the above conditions iia, b is easier to understand with time discretization. Here we consider an update process that gives $\theta_{BV}^-, \dot\theta_{BV}^-$ at step $i+1$ (time $t = t_{i+1}$) from that at step i ($t = t_i$). When $\theta_R(t), \dot\theta_R(t), \theta_{BV}(t), \dot\theta_{BV}(t)$ are expressed as the known constant $\theta_{R,i}, \dot\theta_{R,i}, \theta_{BV,i}, \dot\theta_{BV,i}$, the following condition is obtained:

$$\textbf{ia'} \quad \theta_{BV}^-(\theta_R \to 0, \dot\theta_{R,i+1}) = 0.$$
$$\textbf{ia'} \quad \dot\theta_{BV}^-(\theta_R \to 0, \dot\theta_{R,i+1}) = \dot\theta_{BV}^+(\dot\theta_{R,i}).$$
$$\textbf{iia'} \quad \theta_{BV}^-(\theta_{R,i}, \dot\theta_{R,i+1}) = \theta_{BV,i}. \tag{11}$$
$$\textbf{iib'} \quad \dot\theta_{BV}^-(\theta_{R,i}, \dot\theta_{R,i+1}) = \dot\theta_{BV}.$$

The above equations are given as boundary conditions for the unknown functions $\theta_{BV}(t), \dot\theta_{BV}(t)$. Assuming that θ_{BV}^- can be expressed as a function of θ_R without explicit dependence on time t, we get

$$\dot\theta_{BV}^- = \frac{d\theta_{BV}^-}{dt} = \frac{d\theta_R}{dt}\frac{d\theta_{BV}^-}{d\theta_R} = \dot\theta_R \frac{d\theta_{BV}^-}{d\theta_R}. \tag{12}$$

Thus,

$$\textbf{a''-ii} \quad \frac{d\theta_{BV}^-}{d\theta_R}(\theta_R \to 0, \dot\theta_{R,i}) = k_i^+ \equiv k^+(\dot\theta_{R,i}).$$
$$\textbf{b''-ii} \quad \frac{d\theta_{BV}^-}{d\theta_R}(\theta_{R,i}, \dot\theta_{R,i+1}) = \theta_{BV,i}' \equiv \frac{d\theta_{BV}^-}{d\theta_R}(\theta_{R,i}, \dot\theta_{R,i}). \tag{13}$$

The function $\theta_{BV}^-(\theta_R)$ which satisfies these equations is given as following:

$$\theta_{BV,i+1}^- \equiv \theta_{BV}^-(\theta_{R,i+1}, \dot\theta_{R,i+1})$$
$$= k_{i+1}^+ \theta_{R,i+1} + \{-(2k_{i+1}^+ + \theta_{BV,i}')\theta_{R,i} + 3\theta_{BV,i}\}\left(\frac{\theta_{R,i+1}}{\theta_{R,i}}\right)^2 \tag{14}$$
$$+ \{(k_i^+ + \theta_{BV,i}')\theta_{R,i} - 2\theta_{BV,i}\}\left(\frac{\theta_{R,i+1}}{\theta_{R,i}}\right)^3.$$

With sufficiently small time interval,

$$\frac{\theta_{R,i+1}}{\theta_{R,i}} = 1 - \Delta\theta_i \quad (0 \le \Delta\theta_i \ll 1). \tag{15}$$

Thus, we use the following equations in the actual update process:

$$\theta_{BV,i+1}^- = k_{i+1}^+ \theta_{R,i+1} + \{-(2k_{i+1}^+ + \theta_{BV,i}')\theta_{R,i} + 3\theta_{BV,i}\}(1 - \Delta\theta_i)^2$$
$$+ \{(k_{i+1}^+ + \theta_{BV,i}')\theta_{R,i} - 2\theta_{BV,i}\}(1 - \Delta\theta_i)^3$$
$$\approx k_{i+1}^+ \theta_{R,i}(1 - \Delta\theta_i) + \{-(2k_{i+1}^+ + \theta_{BV,i}')\theta_{R,i} + 3\theta_{BV,i}\}(1 - 2\Delta\theta_i) \tag{16}$$
$$+ \{(k_{i+1}^+ + \theta_{BV,i}')\theta_{R,i} - 2\theta_{BV,i}\}(1 - 3\Delta\theta_i)$$
$$= \theta_{BV,i} - \theta_{BV,i}'\theta_{R,i}\Delta\theta_i = \theta_{BV,i} + \theta_{BV,i}'(\theta_{R,i+1} - \theta_{R,i}).$$

$$\theta'_{BV,i+1} \equiv \left.\frac{d\theta^-_{BV,i+1}}{d\theta_R}\right|_{\theta_R=\theta_{R,i+1}}$$

$$= k_i^+ + 2\left(-2k_{i+1}^+ - \theta'_{BV,i} + 3\frac{\theta_{BV,i}}{\theta_{R,i}}\right)\frac{\theta_{R,i+1}}{\theta_{R,i}}$$

$$+ 3\left(k_{i+1}^+ + \theta'_{BV,i} - 2\frac{\theta_{BV,i}}{\theta_{R,i}}\right)\left(\frac{\theta_{R,i+1}}{\theta_{R,i}}\right)^2 \tag{17}$$

$$\approx k_{i+1}^+ + 2\left(-2k_{i+1}^+ - \theta'_{BV,i} + 3\frac{\theta_{BV,i}}{\theta_{R,i}}\right)(1-\Delta\theta)$$

$$+ 3\left(k_{i+1}^+ + \theta'_{BV,i} - 2\frac{\theta_{BV,i}}{\theta_{R,i}}\right)(1-2\Delta\theta)$$

$$= \theta'_{BV,i} - 2\left(k_{i+1}^+ + 2\theta'_{BV,i} - 3\frac{\theta_{BV,i}}{\theta_{R,i}}\right)\Delta\theta.$$

The update equation of θ^-_{BV} (Eq. 16) is expressed as $\dot{\theta}^-_{BV} = \dot{\theta}_R\theta'_{BV}$ in the continuous limit. So we obtain the inward movement boosting rate as

$$k^-(t) = \theta'_{BV}(t) \tag{18}$$

We use the values $\theta_{BV}(t)$, $k^+(t)$ at previous step as the initial value for $\theta_{BV,i}$ and $\theta'_{BV,i}$. In the most cases, the angular velocity is zero at the switching timing between inward/outward movement, hence the initial value of $\theta'_{BV,i}$ will be 1.

Cond. c is always satisfied in outward moving θ^+_{BV}, because the coefficient $k^+ > 0$. In inward moving θ^-_{BV}, it is not guaranteed that the condition are satisfied [2]. However, in our experience that it is very rare or not happen.

We show plot of time sequence of Neck-yaw Boosting for a certain movement of neck-yawing in Fig. 5. From Fig. 5a, it is found that moving speed of a virtual viewpoint is small and less boosted for low speed, and large for high speed by contrast. It is also found that a virtual viewpoint turns to 0 when a real viewpoint turns to 0, that means the virtual viewpoint must turn toward front when users turn their head to front. Although We separate the function into outward and inward, from Fig. 5b, it is found that the outward function and the inward function is connecting smoothly. Note that the shape of the inward function before going to 0 is distorted due to implementing Cond. b.

---

[2] It is not satisfied on $k^+ < 3\theta_{BV}/\theta_R$.

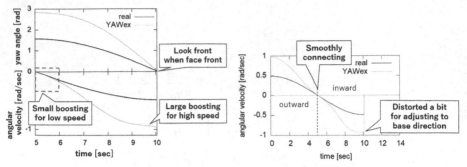

(a) Time sequence for inward movement   (b) Time sequence around interchange from outward to inward

Fig. 5. Example plot of time sequence of Neck-yaw boosting

4.2 Dynamic FoV Boosting

Core Idea. Dynamic FoV Boosting is achieved by controlling FoV of the camera adaptively to neck-yawing motion of a user. If we employ a general perspective projection model as the optical system of the virtual camera, reachable FoV is less than 180°, and it dose not increase linearly. Therefore, we employ the spherical polar coordinate camera model which has a partial spherical projection screen and a spherical square pyramid shape visual volume. Herewith, we are able to achieve hypervisual FoV expansion over 360°, theoretically.

We can control the FoV by scaling the phase components θ, ϕ (azimuth and elevation angle) in the polar coordinate system. We take a virtual viewpoint coordinate in a VR space, and define a vector toward the depth direction as a virtual line-of-sight vector. We define the coordinate system (r, θ, φ) so that the virtual line-of-sight vector is described as $\theta = 0, \varphi = 0$, and a azimuth angle θ varying in $[-\pi, \pi]$. The phase scaling function is described as following:

$$(r, \ \theta, \ \varphi) \to (r, \ \theta', \ \varphi') = (r, \ \theta/c, \ \varphi/c) \quad (c \geq 1). \tag{19}$$

In the case of $c \leq 1$, it expresses phase shrinking. It means zooming-out, and has a effect of suppressing optical flow. Hereafter, we call c as the phase shrinking rate.

An amplified angular velocity of a virtual viewpoint by the Neck-yaw Boosting is also shrunk by the phase scaling as following:

$$\dot{\theta}_{BV} \to \dot{\theta}'_{BV} = \dot{\theta}_{BV}/c. \tag{20}$$

Choosing c for the neck-yaw boosting rate k to be $k/c \lesssim 1$, we suppress the angular velocity to less or equal than the original.

Appearance of the Phase Shrinking. Because a projected image in an HMD is drawn after the phase scaling, virtual FoV is scaled to c times. Taking an x axis to the horizontal direction, a y axis to the vertical direction and a z axis to the depth direction, a point on the screen around the virtual line-of-sight vector ($\theta \ll 1$, $\varphi \ll 1$) is expressed as:

$$(x,\ y,\ z) = r\left(\sin\left(\theta\right),\ \sin\left(\varphi\right), \cos\left(\theta\right)\cos\left(\varphi\right)\right) \approx r\left(\theta,\ \varphi,\ 1\right). \tag{21}$$

The point are translated as $(x,\ y,\ z) \rightarrow (x',\ y', z) \approx (x/c,\ y/c,\ z)$ by the phase scaling. In the center view, the phase shrinking is observed as simple zooming-out. In the peripheral view, although the above approximation is broken, the behavior is similar that each point converges on the center of the field of view. Furthermore, in the outermost, the region outside of original FoV comes into a user's view, thus the user obtains wide view without swinging head anymore.

With sufficiently large c, the effective viewing angle, i.e. the c times redoubled HMD viewing angle, is able to exceed $\pm\pi$. On this occasion, we duplicate and use the region corresponding to azimuth angle $|\theta| > \pi$. Whereas, if we take a similar operation to elevation angle φ, the point corresponding north/south pole $\varphi = \pm\pi/2$ is undefined. Hence, we clamp the region corresponding to $|\varphi| \leq \pi$ not to draw the region. By doing above, we obtain a panorama image with horizontal expansion of the omnidirectional visual information.

The clamp of φ also has a effect of suppressing VR sickness. With the clamp, the top and bottom of the view is always the background. Is will have the same effect as the tunneling technique that has been widely used to suppress VR sickness.

Implementation. The phase scaling is easily implemented by ray tracing technique. The ray vector in ray tracing is the vector that connects from the center coordinates of the camera to the drawing points on the screen. The phase scaling for the coordinate system of a drawing target is equivalent to the phase expansion for the coordinate of a ray vector. We are able to draw the virtual reality world by applying the following:

$$\begin{aligned} v_x &= \sin\left(\theta_v\right) \rightarrow \sin\left(c\theta_v\right), \\ v_y &= \sin\left(\varphi_v\right) \rightarrow \sin\left(c\varphi_v\right), \\ v_z &= \cos\left(\theta_v\right)\cos\left(\varphi_v\right) \rightarrow \cos\left(c\theta_v\right)\cos\left(c\varphi_v\right). \end{aligned} \tag{22}$$

By the way, we do not draw in the region of $|c\varphi_v| \geq \pi/2$ for clamping.

Control of Phase Shrinking Rate. The phase shrinking not only suppresses optical flow amplified by Neck-yaw Boosting, but also extends the user's static field-of-view to entire direction. On the other hand, because the phase shrinking also acts as zooming-out, it interferes with a work if a user focuses on a narrow region. Therefor, we need to control the phase shrinking rate c dynamically. Here, we should be careful about the effect of zooming. A fluctuation of the rate causes virtual accelerative sensation, that is vection, which will cause VR sickness and impair a user's balance.

Guideline. With large angular velocity of the virtual viewpoint $\dot{\theta}_{BV}$, large phase shrinking is required to reduce large optical flow. We can consider that a user do not pay attention to a particular point but search surroundings while the user swings head largely.

Based on experience, we establish the following guidelines for controlling phase shrinking rate:

1. Suppressing subtle fluctuations of phase shrinking rate, and keeping it constant as possible.
2. When decreasing phase shrinking rate, changing it as smooth and calm as possible.
3. When increasing the rate, changing it as smooth and rapid as possible. At this time, allowing some degree of acceleration due to zooming-out.

The guideline 1 is established in the aim of reducing the transition frequency of the FoV Boosting. Because the FoV Boosting performs distortion of the entire view, optical flow is increasing during boosting. Although the amplifying rate of the Neck-yaw Boosting goes up and down depending on action of a user, it is problematic to perfectly synchronize the phase shrinking rate against the neck-yaw boosting rate. Because the phase shrinking rate c should be larger than the neck-yaw boosting rate k to suppress optical flow, we tend to maintain a high phase shrinking rate. Note that we need an upper limit for the phase shrinking rate, because an excessive rate interferes with a user's recognition of the environment.

The guideline 2 is established in the aim of reducing vection of acceleration due to zooming-in caused by the decreasing the phase shrinking rate. When the phase shrinking rate decreases, optical flow is formed from the center view to the peripheral view, and it causes virtual sense of going forward which is inconsistent with the physical sense.

The guideline 3 is for an immediate response against increasing optical flow by Neck-yaw Boosting. We allow an increase of the optical flow due to zooming-out to some extent, and quickly suppress the optical flow due to viewpoint movement. Under the Neck-yaw Boosting without the FoV Boosting, an interesting object of a user permanently moves fast in the view. It is difficult to find the interesting object. When large zooming-out in short time occurs, it temporally difficult to track the interesting object, but the difficulty is just a moment while transition time of FoV Boosting short. Once after FoV expanded, a user can find and track an interesting object while amount of movement of the object is small in the zoomed-out view. Although we have to avoid exceeded high speed of zooming-out that could make a user feeling of unnatural, the guideline 2 will maintain it.

From the guidelines 2 and 3, we introduce an asymmetric relaxation process for increasing and decreasing of the phase shrinking rate. In other words, the phase shrinking rate should be increased relatively quickly, while it should be decreased as slowly as possible. Due to the relaxation, the phase shrinking rate which once raised tends to remain high, and when the speed of the FoV Boosting

$\dot{\theta}_{BV}$ is above a certain level, it remains almost constant. This feature is good with the guideline 1. On the other hand, when $\dot{\theta}_{BV}$ varies in the low region, it has an issue of frequent fluctuations in the phase shrinking rate. Thus we need some effort to avoid the issue.

Based on the above, we reconsider the guidelines for the control of the phase shrinking rate c:

– Using a response function of value range $[1, c_{max}]$, that shows monotonically increasing or close to the behavior with respect to the angular velocity $\dot{\theta}_{BV}$ of the virtual viewpoint, whereas c_{max} is the upper limit of c.
– The response function that rises rapidly with increasing of $\dot{\theta}_{BV}$, and decays slowly with decreasing of $\dot{\theta}_{BV}$. In low and high $\dot{\theta}_{BV}$ regions, it shows low responsiveness.

Control Function. The specific control method we adopt for the time dependent phase shrinking rate $c(t)$ is described as below. First of all, we set the target value c_{dst} for $c(t)$, which depends only on the angular velocity $\dot{\theta}_{BV}$, as follows:

$$c_{dst}(\dot{\theta}_{BV}) = \max\left(1, c_{max}(1 - \exp[-|\dot{\theta}_{BV}|/\dot{\theta}_0])\right) \tag{23}$$

Where, $\dot{\theta}_0$ is the reference value of the angular velocity.

Next, for a gradual transition from the current rate c to the target value c_{dst}, the relaxation factor is introduced as follows:

$$w(t) = \begin{cases} \exp\left[-\dfrac{dt}{T_{stat \to seek}}\right] & (c(t, \dot{\theta}_0) < c_{dst}) \\ \exp\left[-\left(\dfrac{dt}{T_{seek \to stat}}\right)^2\right] & (c(t, \dot{\theta}_0) > c_{dst}) \end{cases} \tag{24}$$

Where, $dt = t - t_0$, and t_0 is the timing of switching the magnitude relation between c and c_{dst}. From the guidelines 2 and 3, we choose the relaxation durations $T_{stat \to seek}$, $T_{seek \to stat}$ to be $T_{stat \to seek} \leq T_{seek \to stat}$.

The actual phase shrinking rate c is time-evolved with c_{dst} and w, according to the following:

$$c\left(t, \dot{\theta}_{BV}\right) = c_0\left(1 - w(t)\right) + c_{dst}\left(\dot{\theta}_{BV}\right) w(t). \tag{25}$$

where, $c_0 = c(t = t_0)$.

We show plot of time sequence of Dynamic FoV Boosting for a certain movement of neck-yawing in Fig. 6. It is found that FoV scale is entirely smooth. By watching around time 0 and 10, where angular velocity suddenly up from 0 or down to 0, it is found that it zooms-in faster while maintaining smoothness. It also found that FoV scale delays against the target value $c_d st$, that is for suppressing noise of users' neck motion. The FoV boosting is adaptive to boosted neck-yawing speed.

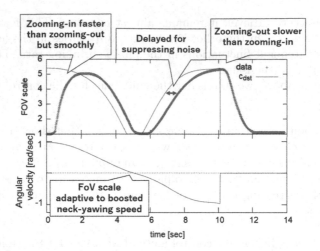

Fig. 6. Example plot of time sequence of dynamic FoV boosting

5   Virtual Accessories for Avoiding VR Sickness

5.1   Avoiding VR Sickness

Avoiding VR sickness is one of the essential task for VR applications. In this work, we employ three accessories of tunneling, base mesh and nose model.

Tunneling is a known technique of VR for suppressing VR sickness that replaces peripheral view to some fixed things relative to real world coordinate. Users can implicitly adjust their sense of body balance by referring the fixed things. We implement it by slightly decaying peripheral view and replacing to base mesh.

Base mesh is grids corresponding to real world coordinate.

Nose model is a virtual model fixed to an HMD screen as a virtual nose of a user's. It also has similar effect as tunneling.

5.2   Cognition of Direction

Omnidirectiona Flick View also have a problem of confusing users' cognition of body pose between virtual and real. The system positively modifies a virtual gaze direction which is different from a real face direction, that breaks intuition of body reference. To deal with the problem, we employ three accessories of abstract avatar, virtual compass and light rays.

Abstract avatar is constructed by 3D primitive objects that shows users' virtual upper body and face. With an additional pose tracker attached on users' body, it shows users' real pose relative to the virtual view direction.

Virtual compass is a directional marker shown in center direction of the view, that indicates virtual face direction from base direction. If users turn right their neck, virtual compass turns clockwise, and if they turn neck to front (same as body direction), it turns to up. Thus users can find which is face direction relative to body direction.

Light rays flow from users back to front in VR. Users can identify their body direction in VR with the rays. Light rays flow with random speed for each to prevent vection.

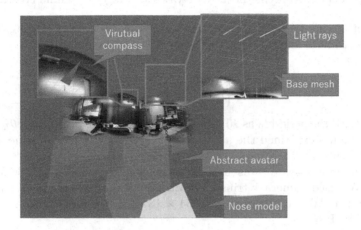

Fig. 7. Virtual accessories

6   Evaluation

6.1   Goal

For the purpose of quantitatively evaluating effect of Neck-yaw Boosting and Dynamic FoV Boosting against users' performance of cognition, we measure optical flow. We executed an experiment under two conditions as below:

Cond. simulation. Calculation of theoretical optical flow for virtual primitive cubic object.

Cond. VR. Measurement of optical flow in two VR of generated mosaic pattern images and practical real photos.

The characteristics would be expected as:

- Without Dynamic FoV Boosting, magnitude of optical flow is in proportion to speed of movement of real viewpoint. That is, it is in proportion to the neck-yaw boosting rate.
- With Dynamic FoV Boosting, magnitude of optical flow is in inverse proportion to Dynamic FoV Boosting rate. Optical flow caused by zooming is not in the rule.

6.2   Settings

For each cases, we conducted measurement by three patterns:

Normal. Not applying both Neck-yaw Boosting / Dynamic FoV Boosting.
YAWex. Applying Neck-yaw Boosting without Dynamic FoV Boosting.
YAWex+FOVex. Applying both Neck-yaw Boosting / Dynamic FoV Boosting.

By considering fairness, we generate motion of users' neck-yawing. We simulated the azimuth angle of real viewpoint θ_R as cyclic motion as:

$$\theta_R(t) = \begin{cases} \frac{\pi}{2}\sin\left(2\pi\frac{t}{t_0}\right) & (t < t_0) \\ 0 & (t \geq t_0) \end{cases}. \tag{26}$$

We defined the period t_0 as 20 s. In the case of Neck-yaw Boosting, θ_R boosted by the dynamics explained the above section. We show a plot of time sequence of θ_R in Fig. 9(a).

Sampling rate was 11 ms and measurement duration was 13.75 s (1250 frames). We used camera intrinsic parameter as the parameter of left eye of HTC Vive Pro. We set resolution as 1234×1370, that is half for each dimension of HTC Vive Pro.

Optical Flow. We define optical flow as below:

For the optical flow F_t at time t in a target movie, corresponding points between consecutive frames I_t, I_{t+1} are given as;

$$I_{t+1}(x,y) = I_t\left(t; x + F_t^x(x, y), \ y + F_t^y(x,y)\right). \tag{27}$$

Where, $F_t(x, y) = (F_t^x(x, y), \ F_t^y(x,y))$. We employed L2 norm $F_t(x, y) \equiv \|F_t(x,y)\|_2$ as magnitude of optical flow.

Simulation Condition. We simulated optical flow by the following method:

1. Translating the point P corresponding to a pixel in an taken image to the point Q on a cylinder which approximate an octagonal pole that is constructed by projected camera images in VR by 3D projection using the camera parameter.
2. Calculating Q' by applying translation of camera motion between frames.
3. Performing inverse projection from Q' to P', that is a corresponding point in the next frame.
4. Calculating $F_t = P' - P$.

Here, we did not evaluate in the area over $\pm 60°$ of elevation angle.

VR Condition. We evaluated optical flow for the situation of practical usage. We put prepared images of taken by the omnidirectional multi-camera and generated ones in VR and then the virtual camera shot them.

We used the following two sets of images:

Mosaic. Six images of random mosaic pattern. Gradation is also applied.
Real. Six images taken by omnidirectional multi-camera in a laboratory room.

Each images had almost 60° vertical field of view. We show example of displayed image in an HMD in Fig. 8.

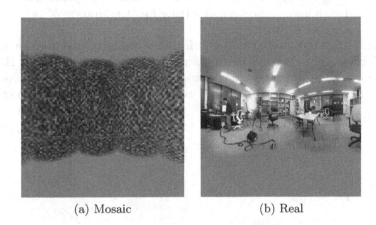

(a) Mosaic   (b) Real

Fig. 8. Example of rendered image of the conditions

We used Gunnar Farneback algorithm of the OpenCV function shown in listing 1.1 for calculating optical flow.

Listing 1.1. Snippet of optical flow calculation

```
1  cv::calcOpticalFlowFarneback(prevImg, nextImg, flow, /*pyrScale =*/ 0.5, /*
      levels =*/ 3, /*winsize =*/ 101, /*iterations =*/ 3, /*polyN =*/ 7, /*
      polySigma =*/ 1.5, /*flag =*/ cv::OPTIFLOW_USE_INITIAL_FLOW | cv::
      OPTIFLOW_FARNEBACK_GAUSSIAN);
```

6.3   Statistics

Calculation of optical flow for practical images does not always perform expected value. It is difficult for textureless area and performs lower value than expected. Using sum of magnitude of optical flow of whole image is not adequate because complexity of texture is different for each images and unfair. Hence, we considered that optical flows of their magnitude were less than a threshold F_{th} were invalid. After disposing the invalid optical flows, we took average magnitude of remained optical flows. We defined $F_{th} = 10^{-5}$ pix/frame on the experiment. Optical flows of peripheral area were also disposed because they are not affected on gazing something. We uses an ellipse cone of horizontal 50° and vertical 35° for vertical angle of the cone as visual volume.

6.4 Result

Figure 9(b), (c), (d) shows time sequence of magnitude of optical flow for each case. In every cases, it is observed that high magnitude of optical flow is measured in YAWex setting, and short term high value and long term low value are measured in YAWex+FOVex setting.

The short term high values in YAWex+FOVex setting is caused by zooming as we expected. Effective term of high magnitude of optical flow is tighten to be very short while zooming-out, and optical flow gradually increases while zooming-in to avoid losing interesting objects. It can be seen that optical flow is largely degraded and even lower than normal setting for the duration of swinging head to search (1–4 s and 7–10 s).

It is found that less magnitude of optical flow was measured in more practical setting. This would be relative to complexity of textures of the images. However, there are not large difference and it would be an evidence that our designed boosting control functions works as we expected even in real environment.

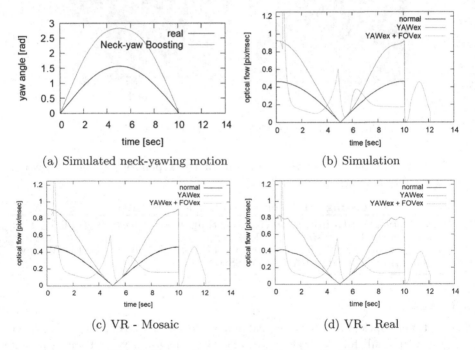

(a) Simulated neck-yawing motion   (b) Simulation

(c) VR - Mosaic   (d) VR - Real

Fig. 9. Comparison of magnitude of optical flow

7   Demonstration

Omnidirectional Flick View enable users to look every direction with quite small amount of neck swinging and choose narrow/wide FoV properly immediately as they wish. So it is applicable to various purpose.

We show an example of picking omnidirectional particular things (see Fig. 10). An operator can correctly seek out and pickup particular things that are given by surrounding people with quite less neck yawing. The operator momently flicks his neck to zoom-out up to potentially over 360°, then he stops his neck to gaze an interesting thing that results slight zooming-in and it enables the operator let precise operation using his body. Neck-yaw boosting also help operators extremely reduce burden of looking every direction.

Fig. 10. Demonstration scene of picking omnidirectional particular things

8   Conclusion

We proposed Omnidirectional Flick View, that realize augmentation of human vision to acquiring over 360° field of view. One of the modules Neck-yaw Boosting lets users look around every direction with quite less neck motion even for wheelchair user to easily look back. The other module Dynamic FoV Boosting lets users control field of view up to over 360° by users' motion of neck-flicking.

Although these two modules have been discussed separately, we showed that simultaneous usage of both modules is effective on the point of maintaining optical flow.

We developed a pose trackable multiple camera array that can observe around 360° to be mounted on an HMD. We also elaborate a special dynamics of adaptive boosting control for providing utility and suppression of optical flow. Moreover, through an evaluation, we showed that our system can provide the function of boosting with suppressing optical flow as we expected even in a practical situation.

References

1. Hall, E.T.: A system for the notation of proxemic behaviour. Am. Anthropologist **65**(5), 1003–1026 (1963). https://doi.org/10.1525/aa.1963.65.5.02a00020
2. Jaekl, P., et al.: Perceptual stability during head movement in virtual reality. In: Proceedings IEEE Virtual Reality, pp. 149–144 (2002)
3. Jay, C., Hubbold, R.: Amplifying head movements with head-mounted displays. Presence **12**(3), 268–276 (2003)
4. Orlosky, J., Wu, Q., Kiyokawa, K., Takemura, H., Nitschke, C.: Fisheye vision: peripheral spatial compression for improved field of view in head mounted displays. In: Proceedings of the 2nd ACM Symposium on Spatial User Interaction, pp. 54–61. SUI 2014, Association for Computing Machinery, New York, NY, USA (2014). https://doi.org/10.1145/2659766.2659771
5. Peñaranda, L., Velho, L., Sacht, L.: Real-time correction of panoramic images using hyperbolic möbius transformations. J. Real-Time Image Process. **15**(4), 725–738 (2018). https://doi.org/10.1007/s11554-015-0502-x
6. Yamada, W., Manabe, H.: Expanding the field-of-view of head-mounted displays with peripheral blurred images. In: Proceedings of the 29th Annual Symposium on User Interface Software and Technology, pp. 141–142. UIST 2016 Adjunct, Association for Computing Machinery, New York, NY, USA (2016). https://doi.org/10.1145/2984751.2985735
7. Yano, Y., Orlosky, J., Kiyokawa, K., Takemura, H.: Dynamic view expansion for improving visual search in video see-through AR. In: Reiners, D., Iwai, D., Steinicke, F. (eds.) ICAT-EGVE 2016 - International Conference on Artificial Reality and Telexistence and Eurographics Symposium on Virtual Environments. The Eurographics Association (2016). https://doi.org/10.2312/egve.20161435

**VAMR Applications in Design,
the Industry and the Military**

Virtual Fieldwork: Designing Augmented Reality Applications Using Virtual Reality Worlds

Kota Gushima[✉] and Tatsuo Nakajima

Waseda University, Okubo 3-4-1, Tokyo, Japan
{gushi,tatsuo}@dcl.cs.waseda.ac.jp

Abstract. AR technology continues to develop and is expected to be used in a much wider range of fields. However, existing head-mounted displays for AR are still inadequate for use in daily life. Therefore, we focused on using VR to develop AR services and explored the possibility of virtual fieldwork. By comparing fieldwork using AR and virtual fieldwork using VR, we revealed the feasibility and limitations of virtual fieldwork. It was shown that virtual fieldwork is effective in an indoor environment where no other people are present. By using virtual fieldwork, researchers can obtain qualitative results more easily than with traditional fieldwork. On the other hand, it was suggested that it is difficult to realize virtual fieldwork in a large environment such as outdoors and in the presence of others. In particular, participants do not perceive the virtual fieldwork as fieldwork in the real world because the experience of walking in a large space is difficult to experience in conventional VR.

Keywords: Virtual fieldwork · Augmented reality · Virtual reality

1 Introduction

In this paper, we aim to examine Augmented Reality (AR) services in the Virtual Reality (VR) space. We expect that AR services will play a role in various contexts when see-through Head-Mounted Displays (HMDs) such as HoloLens become more advanced. This will require service designers to consider what issues will arise when services are used in different contexts and what changes should be made depending on the context. However, existing see-through HMDs are not sufficiently powerful to be utilized in a variety of contexts. For example, a narrow Field of View (FoV) causes AR content to be only partially visible in the FoV, resulting in a 3D model in which the service being displayed is only partially visible. This leads to poor user experience for the AR service. Because existing see-through HMDs have various problems, when we prototype the AR service and conduct user evaluations to identify the issues and feasibility of the service, we cannot evaluate it correctly because of the noise of the see-through HMD problems.

© Springer Nature Switzerland AG 2021
J. Y. C. Chen and G. Fragomeni (Eds.): HCII 2021, LNCS 12770, pp. 417–430, 2021.
https://doi.org/10.1007/978-3-030-77599-5_29

In addition, fieldwork in various contexts is often limited by time and location. In particular, fieldwork in public spaces such as stations and towns is costly in terms of permissions for the experiment. Therefore, fieldwork is often conducted at the final stage when designing a service before releasing the service. In recent years, there have been many methods of improving services by iterating through the development process, such as agile development. However, user evaluations in public spaces are difficult to iterate owing to the high cost of each iteration.

These two problems make AR fieldwork challenging to use in a variety of contexts. Therefore, this paper discusses whether virtual fieldwork can be utilized by using VR technology to evaluate AR services. Current VR devices have a wider FoV than see-through HMDs, and once a VR world is built, it can be utilized as often as possible. Therefore, we believe they are better suited for evaluating the use of services in various contexts. In this paper, we identify from two experiments, whether it is possible to evaluate AR services in VR. In the first experiment, we show whether the evaluation of a prototype using VR can deliver the same qualitative results as evaluating a prototype using AR in a virtual environment that simulates the same situation as the prototype using AR. In the second experiment, we used VR to simulate outdoor experiments that would be difficult to achieve in real-world fieldwork. Finally, we discuss whether these results make the virtual fieldwork equivalent to real-world fieldwork.

2   HoloMoL: Memorization AR Application

HoloMoL is an application that uses AR technology to display what you want to remember in the real world and aims to improve memory by linking real-world locations and information [1]. We previously evaluated this application. This experiment was conducted in the laboratory using HoloLens (Fig. 1). We found that individuals may have different patterns of placing the information to remember.

- Pattern 1: Mapping the recalled meanings from a nation's description to some objects located in the real space.
- Pattern 2: Creating a patrol route to the room and arranging the information.
- Pattern 3: Using the marker's texture to memorize the nation's description.

3   Two Research Questions

In this paper, we investigate the feasibility of virtual fieldwork with VR technology. We focus on two research questions:

- RQ1: Can a qualitative user evaluation of AR services be conducted in the VR environment?
- RQ2: Can services be considered within VR for situations that are difficult to implement in the real world?

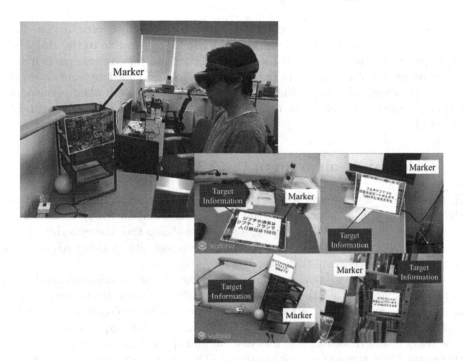

Fig. 1. Overview of HoloMoL

The study of RQ1 focuses on how services are used by users. This is because the role of VR in virtual fieldwork is to develop ideas for new services and products and to observe how these ideas are used. Therefore, we use VR to replicate the qualitative experiments of HoloMoL conducted in Sect. 2. If the results are identical to those presented in Sect. 2, we can indicate that AR and VR can perform similar qualitative experiments.

Regarding RQ2, since AR services are expected to be used in a variety of contexts in the future, it is necessary to examine how the services will be used in various contexts when considering future AR services. AR services with the implementation of the virtual fieldwork concept can be considered within the VR world. Therefore, we discuss whether the use of HoloMoL in outdoor city settings can be considered in VR. However, unlike in RQ1, we cannot directly compare it with AR experiments because there are various barriers to conducting AR experiments outdoors. In addition, even if a VR environment is used, users cannot walk around in a massive space like a city. Therefore, walking in the room is realized by using a controller. Thus, we will also discuss to what extent we can substitute one real-world element for another. In the virtual world, like the dots in a 2D game, abstract expressions can be used to achieve persuasive presentations, but people do not perceive the dots as similar to the real world in the VR world. Through this discussion, we will examine what makes the difference between virtual worlds that can be treated as equivalent to the real world and those that are not.

We will conduct three experiments to answer these two questions. The first experiment is conducted in VR, which is as similar as possible to the HoloMoL experiment conducted in the real world. In the second experiment, participants will experience a VR experiment that simulates HoloMoL outdoors and an experiment. They are asked to use the AR prototype as if they were walking outdoors indoors in the real world. In the following sections, we describe these experiments in detail.

4 HoloMoL Evaluation in the VR World

In this section, we examine whether the fieldwork of HoloMoL, a case study of the AR service, can be conducted in VR. As mentioned earlier, because it is challenging to conduct AR fieldwork, if it can be shown that the experiment can be conducted in VR, then we can evaluate the possibility of using AR services in more different contexts than ever before.

Therefore, in this section, we compare the features of experiments conducted in the AR environment with those conducted in the VR environment by performing the same experiments in the VR environment as those conducted in Sect. 2 and comparing the results obtained from them. This VR experiment revealed how users of the HoloMoL link information and space. The results showed that there were three types of memory patterns. The experiment conducted in Sect. 2 focused on how users use the service. Since the goal of this section is not to evaluate services in detail but to examine their potential and explore their pitfalls in the virtual environment, the VR evaluation, like the evaluation in Sect. 2, is appropriate for this goal.

4.1 Experimental Environment

We designed a virtual space to evaluate HoloMoL using VR. The previous HoloMoL experiment was conducted in our lab. We built 3D models of the room to conduct the experiment, focusing on how the user places information in the virtual room. The experimental system was developed by Unity, and the 3D model of the room was referenced to a free asset[1] . Participants enter this room through a VR device, the VIVE PRO[2]. In this room, there are cards with ten pieces of information to be memorized, nd users can grab these cards by using the VIVE controller, as shown in Fig. 2. The grabbed cards can be placed anywhere in the virtual space.

---

[1] https://assetstore.unity.com/packages/3d/environments/urban/furnished-cabin-71426?locale=ja-JP.

[2] https://www.vive.com/jp/product/vive-pro-full-kit/.

Fig. 2. Overview of HoloMoL indoors in VR

4.2   Experimental Procedure

The experimental procedure was designed similarly to the one conducted in Sect. 2.

1. Briefing and Tutorial Phase: after a short briefing about our study, participants wear VIVE PRO and use the HoloMoL demo to familiarize themselves with the controls.
2. Construction Phase: They place all the cards in the virtual room in 3 min. The cards contain the name of an African country and information about that country. We anticipate that subjects will place temporarily in this part because they will see the information to be remembered for the first time in this section.
3. Reconstruction Phase: They have 3 min to scrutinize and reposition the cards. In this phase, they can place the information in the places where they can remember more easily because they are looking at all of the information.
4. Training Phase: They have 3 min to memorize the information they place. This phase does not allow the participants to move the cards.
5. Quiz Phase: The participants answer with the country's name and the location where they place the information.
6. Interview Phase: Subjects responded to a semistructured interview about their memory methods. In this interview, they were asked about 1) how they placed the information and 2) how they remembered the information.

There were eight Japanese participants (six males and two females, average age 24.1 years).

4.3   Experiment Results

We observed patterns in the participants' memories in this experiment.

1. Pattern 1. Information and place, or information and object combination: One participant linked images associated with the country's name to objects in the room. This participant remembered information about the country by assigning the pronunciation of the country name to an object. For example, as a result of associating the "Republic of Mali" with the video game "Mario," Mali's information was placed in front of the television.
2. Pattern 2. Setting a patrol route and placing information on that route: The three participants placed their cards on objects in the room. They then decided on a starting point and learned the information sequentially from the point. One participant partially utilized Pattern 1. This participant placed "Republic of Chad" on a brown couch. In the interview, he said that he was able to link it to the object because the pronunciation of Chad was similar to the Japanese pronunciation of brown (Cha). Another participant said in the interview that if he had an African map, he would have remembered to assign the geographical arrangement to the virtual space. Therefore, the participants that used pattern two also partially used pattern 1 to place information within a reasonable range.
3. Pattern 3. Arrange all of the information insight: Unlike Patterns 1 and 2, four participants did not place the cards on the objects in this pattern but arranged them in the air where they could be easily seen. One participant arranged the cards in random order and another who placed them in a Hiragana order.

5   HoloMoL Evaluation in Outdoors in VR World

In this paper, we evaluate whether our AR application, HoloMoL, can be used outdoors. Because this application uses HoloLens, this device should not be used outdoors. Therefore, in this paper, we test whether VR enables us to evaluate the possibility of HoloMoL outdoors. We aim to clarify the advantages and disadvantages of VR prototypes by scenario-based experiments that compared AR with VR.

5.1   Introduction of Virtual Fieldwork Outdoors

In this section, we discuss findings from a preliminary experiment on the use of HoloMoL outdoors. When proposing a new application for use in public spaces, it is necessary to fully consider the potential danger to the user before conducting large-scale fieldwork because fieldwork is costly. Therefore, before conducting large-scale experiments, a small-scale evaluation should be conducted to identify the application's possibilities and drawbacks. In particular, AR technology overlays information into the field of view. Therefore, an AR application should be considered when designed for use in public space, where the user faces a risk

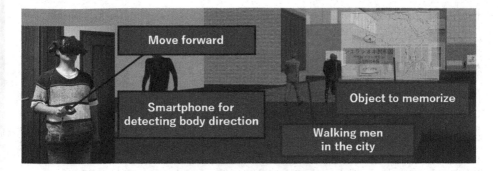

Fig. 3. Overview of HoloMoL in virtual reality

of colliding with people or objects. In addition, when using an AR device out-doors, brightness becomes an issue. HoloLens can function indoors [4]; however, its brightness is not sufficient for its use outdoors, especially on a sunny day.

Therefore, as a preliminary evaluation, we evaluated the AR prototype using virtual reality (VR). The HoloLens brightness issue can be solved by VR outdoor simulation. Study [2] attempted to use VR to evaluate AR, and the difference between that study and ours is the purpose of our research. This study focused on completely controlled AR studies. Ours focuses on the difficulty of fieldwork. In this paper, we aim to clarify the advantages and drawbacks of using VR for evaluation by comparing the VR simulation with a traditional evaluation using an AR prototype conducted indoors.

5.2 Implementation

We developed a system to simulate outdoor fieldwork in VR Fig. 3. We used Unity as the development environment and HTC VIVE PRO as the VR device. We used a free 3D model of the city provided by Zenrin and a free male 3D model provided by Unity to simulate the outdoor environment. The male model was programmed to walk along a street in the city in combination with animation. The turning points were established at the intersections in the city, and the men turned there randomly and walked along the streets. This aimed to represent the crowds in a city.

We developed a simple walking system for VR. Recently, researchers have attempted to create natural walking in VR [3]. In our case, the walking system was designed to move toward the front of the body. Because the body direction was not detected when using the VIVE only, this system uses a combination of VIVE and a smartphone. Zigsim [1] allows developers to use sensor data detected by a smartphone. Participants can move in the VR space toward the front direction of their body by pulling the VIVE controller's trigger. This method allows participants to walk straight while looking around the city.

We developed the AR prototype using HoloLens, which places objects to be remembered in the real space to compare the AR with the VR simulation. In the AR experiment, we placed the information to be remembered statically in the real space because the experiment was based on a scenario.

5.3   Experimental Procedure

This experiment was based on user enactment. Participants role-play a scenario [7,8] because this prototype was designed to help people use the prototype with a clear image of its use in a real city. Participants read a scenario and then experienced the prototype based on the scenario. The scenario used in our procedure was that an officer memorizes African countries' names while walking on a street. We conducted the experiment with eight male participants in their 20 s (average age, 23.4 years) with experience in creating AR or VR content. The participants were divided into Group A and Group B. Group A experienced the AR prototype first, completed a questionnaire, encountered the VR experience, and filled out the questionnaire again. Group B experienced VR with the questionnaire first, followed by AR with the questionnaire. The questionnaire consisted of 5-scale Likert questions (5 = agree, 1 = disagree). Finally, the participants completed a questionnaire, and a semistructured interview was conducted with them.

5.4   Results and Discussion

The questionnaire results suggest that evaluating the AR application with VR is not a substitute for AR experiments Fig. 4. Three participants said that *"walking with the controller was not suitable for simulating the real world, "* and two participants said that *"3d model is too unreal to believe that I am in the real world. "*

On the other hand, in the interviews, some participants said that the VR prototype was needed for the preliminary experiment. Two participants commented that "it in the AR prototype, I could understand how the system displays the information in the real world and how the object looks when I move my body. In the VR prototype, I could imagine the situation using the system in the city. Each prototype has unique characteristics." Another participant said, "it Completing AR fieldwork is too costly, and it also costs a lot to develop and a VR device that maximizes reality. As in this case, it may be possible to perform the essential evaluation of an application relatively easily by combining AR, which performs simple fieldwork, and VR, which allows participants to experience complicated situations." These comments suggest that a combination of AR and VR could be useful in the early stages of application design. This can help participants imagine a more concrete use case for the application.

Another participant said, "it By experiencing the ideal situation of the service in VR first and then experiencing a realistic prototype. It became easier to recognize the problem that the application should overcome. Therefore, it is worth experiencing the AR prototype after VR." In other words, VR prototypes could take on the role played by scenarios and concept movies. In particular, in the case of content that changes according to movement, such as in AR, participants can imagine the use case more realistically than when they see it in a movie. This may allow for the evaluation of the application concept in the early stages of application development. Typically, VR has been used to evaluate dangerous situations [9]. However, the results of this experiment show that VR is useful not only for conditions that cannot be implemented in the real world but also for evaluating the concept of daily AR application in public spaces.

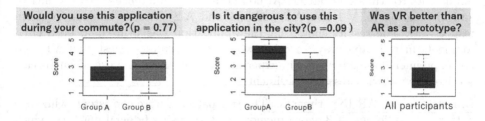

Fig. 4. Questionnaire results

5.5   Limitations and Future Work

On the other hand, some participants commented that using only AR was sufficient. They felt that the VR and AR prototypes were utterly different experiments. They thought that the virtual world could not be treated as an alternative to the real world. Thus, it should be considered whether VR evaluation as a method of providing scenarios is useful for everyone in the future.

In addition, there is the cost of developing VR. Two participants felt that the 3D models of the men were not realistic. To meet their demands, more realistic virtual worlds are needed. However, distinct virtual worlds require high development costs. Researchers developing AR prototypes may not have the resources to create a high-quality VR prototype to evaluate the application. In other words, we need to create a VR system of moderate quality. In this experiment, we could not clarify how high the quality of the VR prototypes should be. In the future, it needs to be clarified what level of VR quality is necessary to make the experience more beneficial than just reading a scenario to imagine use cases.

6   Discussion

6.1   Answer to RQ1

This section compares the patterns obtained from the AR experiments conducted in Sect. 2 with this VR experiment. The patterns obtained in the AR experiment were of three types:

1. a pattern that links the names of countries to objects in the real world, and
2. a pattern that places information on a route that is easily patrolled, and

3. a pattern that links objects to the meaning of the texture of the fiducial marker.

The patterns obtained in the AR experiment are called Pattern A-1, Pattern A-2, and Pattern A-3, and the patterns obtained in the VR experiment are called Patterns V-1, Pattern V-2, and Pattern V-3.

Similarities to AR Experiments: Although there are differences between the real and virtual spaces, V-1 and A-2 and V-1 and A-2 showed the same pattern, respectively. The results show that the application was utilized in both environments in the same way. In other words, the results suggest that VR and AR experiments are equivalent in experiments that reveal the use of small-scale services such as the present experiment.

Differences from AR Experiments: The two patterns were consistent, while one pattern was different. A-3 was a memory method using fiducial markers, which was a memory method that we did not anticipate. This pattern will not be used in the final product because the fiducial markers will not be included in the final product. V-3, on the other hand, is a method of card placement that does not depend on the laws of physics. Therefore, this pattern could not be used in the AR prototype. This is because it was not possible to place fiducial markers in the air.

Discussion About RQ1. The results of the experiments in Sect. 4.3 showed that the results obtained from real-world fieldwork using the AR prototype and the results obtained from fieldwork in the virtual world using the VR prototype were almost the same, although there were a few differences between them. These results suggest that the use of VR environments can be useful in observing how services are used in the real world. In addition, the implementation of AR content requires the use of spatial recognition, which makes the development of prototypes more difficult, while VR prototypes are relatively easy to implement because developers have a complete grasp of the 3D space before implementing them. Therefore, VR allows service developers to achieve almost the same qualitative results as real-world fieldwork in an environment where they can develop prototypes more easily. We expect this to create both the benefit of lowering the cost of developing AR services and the benefit of quickly testing different ideas.

6.2   Answer to RQ2

From Fig. 4, we found that VR simulations of outdoor fieldwork are not equivalent to AR simulations.

Discussion About RQ2. While the first indoor VR experiment showed similar results to previous experiments conducted in AR environments, several participants in the second experiment, which was conducted outdoors in VR, noted problems with respect to immersion. A major factor in the loss of user immersion was the unnaturalness of the walking and human models and movements.

The difference between the first experiment and the second was the number of variables in the virtual world. The first experiment was identical to the AR experiment, except that it used the virtual room and controller. The second experiment was conducted in addition to them, with the addition of converting the walking method. We believe that these additional factors contributed to the participants feeling unrealistic.

The Problem of Walking: Walking is an inherently unconscious activity that a person can perform. People can talk or listen to music while walking. Because walking in the second experiment was a controller-based movement different from the walking users had done unconsciously in real space, we speculate that participants felt that this experiment was not equivalent to reality.

When conducting a study of real-world services in a virtual world, it is necessary to consider the extent to which real-world elements can be converted. It was shown in the first experiment that switching the background world was not a problem. It has been shown that the background world is the background of people's consciousness and that it was possible to represent that world with virtual objects. On the other hand, the conversion of walking, which is also a background of consciousness, was not successful. This issue is often discussed in the field of VR, with the walk-in place and redirecting walking being the most common methods, and methods of walking through the large VR world still under consideration [3,6].

The Problem of 3D Models: The experiment in Sect. 5.4 aimed to display crowds walking through the city and observe how the system was used in crowds. However, some participants did not feel like they were using the system in a crowded environment because the others were unnatural. While using more realistic 3D models or making the animations more realistic could solve this problem, we discuss this problem from another aspect. Since our first experiment suggests that we were able to conduct good experiments even though we were experimenting with a cheap 3D world, we believe that in the virtual fieldwork, there are cases where 3D models are sufficient and cases where more accurate 3D models are required.

These two issues reveal the characteristics of VR when it is not equivalent to AR in evaluating AR services. In virtual fieldwork, we assumed that the difference between the real world and the virtual world is the background world. Essentially, that understanding is correct, but this experiment reveals that the reality required to reproduce the background world in the VR world differs depending on the object type. That is, the required reality is different when copying or transforming reality into the virtual world. For example, as shown in the experiment in Sect. 4, reality is not needed when representing furniture and a house in the virtual world. Simultaneously, objects that can be perceived in the foreground of a person's consciousness, such as other people, require a higher level of reality, as shown in the experiments in Sect. 5. In particular, creatures, including humans, have a large variety of information. For example, humans regularly produce various types of information: the movement of the body, facial expressions, and fashion. If this information is not represented, users may not recognize people in the virtual world as equivalent to people in the real world. It is currently possible to implement 3D models and animations that can represent this complex information with significant development costs. However, realistic models cannot yet be treated as commodities, and therefore evaluating VR to include people may be difficult. It is expected that this issue will be solved in the future when developers can easily use high-quality 3D models.

7   General Discussion

To summarize what has been revealed by RQ1 and RQ2, when the background world is being converted from the physical world to the virtual world, considering services in the virtual world is equivalent to considering them in the real world. However, when simulating a larger environment, we found that the virtual world is no longer equivalent to the real world because existing techniques require the use of controllers to convert the movement. Furthermore, when simulating crowds, a more realistic 3D model must be used, or the virtual world will not be equivalent to the real world.

In other words, it has been shown that the virtual world is equivalent to the real world only in limited cases with current technology. To study how to utilize services used in a wide range of situations and services that involve multiple people, the above problems must be solved. On the other hand, if the above conditions can be avoided, it is suggested that the real world and the virtual world are equivalent. Therefore, it may be possible for room-scale and one-person services to implement various considerations using the virtual world. For example, it is possible to examine VR designs when designing an AR application to support the work of a single person in a factory.

Examining services within a virtual world has been done in the past [5]. In this study, Mäkelä et al. proposed three conditions under which the evaluation of public displays should be conducted in a VR environment.

1. that a variety of conditions should be tested.
2. that the same settings can be used over and over again.
3. the real target environment cannot be used.
4. it must be conducted in room-scale VR.
5. no other humans are to be included.

Therefore, we infer that these findings were not obtained because the evaluations could have been fully implemented on the room scale. In public display experiments, research on crowds has also been pointed out as a future issue. Since our study showed that representing crowds in a VR world is difficult, we suggest that their future challenges will also be validated depending on VR technology advances.

Their paper also mentions a scenario-based evaluation method. The researchers argue that scenario-based evaluation methods are not suitable for ecological data collection owing to accuracy issues. Since our use of the VR environment is focused on using it for consideration rather than the detailed evaluation of services, we infer that this accuracy issue does not affect the consideration of the AR service. Our experiments also suggest that combining scenario-based experiments in real space and scenario-based experiments in the virtual space will allow users to examine the service more precisely. Combining scenarios in two worlds is a new idea from our experiments. Currently, although both AR and VR technologies still have shortcomings, each technology can compensate for their deficiencies.

8   Conclusion

We explored the possibilities of virtual fieldwork. By comparing fieldwork using AR and virtual fieldwork using VR, we identified the feasibility and limitations of virtual fieldwork. It was shown that virtual fieldwork works well in an indoor environment where no other people are present. By using virtual fieldwork, researchers can obtain qualitative results more quickly than traditional fieldwork.

On the other hand, the results suggest that it is challenging to realize virtual fieldwork in a large environment such as outdoors and others' presence. In particular, participants do not perceive the virtual fieldwork as fieldwork in the real world because the experience of walking in a large space is difficult to experience in conventional VR. The lack of realism of the human being in the VR world was also an inferior aspect of virtual fieldwork. Since these problems rely on traditional VR technology limitations, we believe that advances in VR technology will lead to making virtual fieldwork more versatile.

References

1. 1-10drive (2020) Zig-project. https://zig-project.com/. Accessed 18 July 2020
2. Lee, C., Bonebrake, S., Hollerer, T., Bowman, D.A.: A replication study testing the validity of ar simulation in vr for controlled experiments. In: 2009 8th IEEE International Symposium on Mixed and Augmented Reality, pp. 203–204 (2009)
3. Lee, J., Kim, M., Kim, J.: A study on immersion and vr sickness in walking interaction for immersive virtual reality applications. Symmetry 9(5), 78 (2017). https://doi.org/10.3390/sym9050078, https://www.mdpi.com/2073-8994/9/5/78
4. Liu, Y., Dong, H., Zhang, L., Saddik, A.E.: Technical evaluation of hololens for multimedia: A first look. IEEE MultiMedia 25(4), 8–18 (2018)
5. Mäkelä, V., et al.: Virtual field studies: conducting studies on public displays in virtual reality. In: Proceedings of the 2020 CHI Conference on Human Factors in Computing Systems, pp. 1–15. Association for Computing Machinery, New York, NY, USA, CHI 2020 (2020). https://doi.org/10.1145/3313831.3376796
6. Nilsson, N.C., et al.: 15 years of research on redirected walking in immersive virtual environments. IEEE Comput. Graph. Appl. 38(2), 44–56 (2018). https://doi.org/10.1109/MCG.2018.111125628
7. Odom, W., Zimmerman, J., Davidoff, S., Forlizzi, J., Dey, A.K., Lee, M.K.: A fieldwork of the future with user enactments. In: Proceedings of the Designing Interactive Systems Conference, pp. 338–347. Association for Computing Machinery, New York, NY, USA, DIS 2012 (2012). https://doi.org/10.1145/2317956.2318008

8. Odom, W., Zimmerman, J., Forlizzi, J., Choi, H., Meier, S., Park, A.: Unpacking the thinking and making behind a user enactments project. In: Proceedings of the 2014 Conference on Designing Interactive Systems, pp. 513–522. Association for Computing Machinery, New York, NY, USA, DIS 2014 (2014). https://doi.org/10.1145/2598510.2602960

9. Williams-Bell, F.M., Kapralos, B., Hogue, A., Murphy, B.M., Weckman, E.J.: Using serious games and virtual simulation for training in the fire service: a review. Fire Technol. **51**(3), 553–584 (2015). https://doi.org/10.1007/s10694-014-0398-1

Contextually Adaptive Multimodal Mixed Reality Interfaces for Dismounted Operator Teaming with Unmanned System Swarms

Michael Jenkins[1]([⊠]), Richard Stone[1], Brodey Lajoie[1], David Alfonso[1],
Andrew Rosenblatt[1], Caroline Kingsley[2], Les Bird[2], David Cipoletta[1],
and Sean Kelly[1]

[1] Pison Technology, Boston, MA 02111, USA
mjenkins@pison.com
[2] Charles River Analytics, Cambridge, MA 02138, USA

Abstract. US dismounted Special Operations Forces operating in near-threat environments must maintain their Situation Awareness, survivability, and lethality to maximize their effectiveness on mission. As small unmanned aerial systems and unmanned ground vehicles become more readily available as organic assets at the individual Operator and team level, these Operators must make the decision to divert attention and resources to the control of these assets using touchscreens or controllers to benefit from their support capabilities. This paper provides an end-to-end overview of a solution development process that started with a broad and future-looking capabilities exploration to address this issue of unmanned system control at the dismounted Operator level, and narrowed to a fieldable solution offering immediate value to Special Operation Forces. An overview of this user-centric design process is presented along with lessons learned for others developing complex human-machine interface solutions for dynamic and high-risk environments.

Keywords: Human factors · Human-Robot Interaction (HRI) · Multimodal interfaces · Situational awareness · Teleoperation · Autonomy · Mixed reality · Augmented reality · Human-Computer Interaction (HCI) · Human-Robot teaming · Unmanned vehicles · Swarms · UAS · SUAS · UGV · UXS

1 Introduction

1.1 Problem/Opportunity

US dismounted Special Operations Forces (SOF) operating in near-threat environments must maintain their Situation Awareness (SA), survivability, and lethality to maximize their effectiveness on mission. As small unmanned aerial systems (SUAS) and unmanned ground vehicles (UGV) become more readily available as organic assets at the individual Operator and team level, these Operators must make the decision to divert attention and resources to the control of these assets using touchscreens or controllers to benefit

© Springer Nature Switzerland AG 2021
J. Y. C. Chen and G. Fragomeni (Eds.): HCII 2021, LNCS 12770, pp. 431–451, 2021.
https://doi.org/10.1007/978-3-030-77599-5_30

from their support capabilities. These control modalities both require combat users to disengage from their weapon and other hand-operated equipment and may fail under certain contexts of use. For example, touchscreens cannot be manipulated without an Operator taking time to remove their gloves (and then redon them after the control task is completed) and can fail in environments with significant moisture (e.g., rain, snow, sea spray). Additionally, smartphone touchscreens mounted on an Operator's chest cannot be accessed when an Operator is prone, and when the device is engaged (i.e., flipped down) it may prevent ease of access to extra magazines or other abdomen mounted equipment. Physical controllers typically require both hands to operate and must be carried and stored securely until needed. They can also be cumbersome to operate while wearing gloves and/or in a prone position. SOF Operators require a solution to efficiently control and benefit from unmanned system (UXS) capabilities in near-threat environments that will not compromise their SA, survivability, or lethality.

1.2 Background

In July of 2019, Pison Technology and Charles River Analytics (CRA) participated in a SOFWERX-sponsored hackathon event focused on explorations into fielding UXS swarms to support dismounted SOF in near-threat environments as part of the Special Operations Command (SOCOM) vision of applying artificial intelligence for small unit maneuvers (AISUM). At this event, our team's focus was on exploration of novel and future-looking Operator-Swarm interfaces (OSIs) that will allow dismounted SOF Operators to effectively team with large autonomous UXS swarms (50+ UXS nodes) to bolster their own survivability and/or lethality.

During this week-long event, our team worked with SOF subject-matter experts to understand the constraints and affordances of interacting with UXS technology while maneuvering through a threat environment and engaging confirmed threats. Based on this understanding, our team designed and developed a proof-of-concept multimodal information display, mixing augmented reality (AR) visual, audio, and haptic feedback, to enable dismounted Operators to maintain SA of: (1) a battlefield swarm's status, goals, and progress towards those goals; and (2) available battlefield swarm autonomous capabilities (termed 'tactics') that the Operator can engage or employ on demand. This multimodal information display solution was then paired with a contextually adaptive AR multimodal interaction suite that combines gesture as the primary input modality, with gaze and speech interfaces to enable Operators to effectively configure, select, and direct swarm assets and tactics while preserving their own survivability and lethality (i.e., remaining heads up, eyes out, and weapon ready). The combined mixed reality (MR) multimodal information display and interaction suite formed the basis for an OSI for SOF, which was envisioned for future (5 to 10 years in the future) SOF missions. The initial proof-of-concept prototype was rapidly developed during the week-long event to function with the consumer Magic Leap One AR headset and a micro-swarm of three DJI Tello unmanned aerial systems (UAS). This system was demonstrated for and by SOF personnel and SOCOM Science and Technology (S&T) leadership to inform requirements and a roadmap for future SOCOM capability funding.

After this initial rapid prototyping event (RPE), Pison sought to continuously advance and evolve the initial concepts to produce a fieldable solution offering for heads-up and eyes-out UXS control for dismounted Operators. This paper provides an overview of the iterative user-centric design, development, and test approach that Pison adopted following the initial RPE. The following sections discuss how the technology offering evolved over the course of 18 months as more end users were able to test the capabilities and provide their feedback on a path to shipping a fieldable offering. Additionally, the outcomes from the RPE informed initial design and development of user interfaces for rapid operational teaming with autonomous swarms, led by CRA. Section 2.3 discusses how learnings from the RPE impacted the initial multimodal AR interface design process, and ultimately how that work informed subsequent future design iterations.

2 Approach

2.1 SOFWERX RPE Foundations

The SOFWERX RPE served to establish an initial vision and high-level objective for delivering UXS capabilities at the dismounted Operator squad level and to define an initial set of considerations, constraints, and requirements in pursuit of that objective. The overarching objective that our team took away from the RPE was to:

> *Design a command and control (C2) solution for dismounted Operators to effectively use and benefit from UXS drones and/or swarms of drones by providing intelligence, surveillance, and reconnaissance (ISR) and other capabilities, while preserving Operator survivability and lethality.*

In addition to establishing this high-level objective, the RPE served to provide a useful vignette for how current and near-future SOF want to leverage UXS capabilities at the squad level. The vignette is provided here for reference (e.g., for other UXS solutions developers). Note that this is a fictional mission scenario generated in collaboration with the SOF Operators at the RPE to help RPE participants contextualize the design of a UXS capabilities roadmap for a 5- to 10-year horizon.

> **Mission:** *Conduct a Special Reconnaissance (SR) of a target area to confirm or deny the presence of a biological weapons facility.*
>
> *If you do confirm the presence, complete and transmit in real time the following tasks:*

- Localize material within the facility.
- Determine program maturity.
- Determine manufacturing team size and facial information.
- Determine security apparatus by type and size.

> *While executing this mission, the following should be prioritized:*

1. Avoid Detection.
2. Identify and Localize Weapons Compound and HIS Platforms.

3. Determine Signals of Interest within Target Area
4. Find, Explore, and 3D Map Weapons Compound
5. Implement Persistent Monitoring of Target Environment
6. Identify and Monitor Potential LW Support Network
7. Collect as Many Key Identifiers as Possible
8. Determine Time and Scale of Attack

In addition to these priorities, the following considerations and constraints on mission execution must be adhered to:

1. No personnel are currently located within 10 km of Area of Interest (AOI).
2. No SUAS movement allowed above 100FT above ground level (AGL).
3. No satellite communications permitted inside 10 km radius of AOI.
4. No commercial telephone or Wi-Fi allowed inside 10 km radius of AOI.
5. Inhabitants of AOI cannot be trusted.

These vignette details helped frame knowledge elicitation discussions with the SOF Operator subject matter experts (SMEs) during the RPE, while also generating several requirements and future concepts for exploration and evaluation. For example, one key design outcome from the RPE was establishing different "mission operating modes" that are defined by the time an Operator must interface with the system, the tasks the Operator hopes to achieve at that time, and the interaction modalities that are likely preferred by the user based on feedback from the SOF Operator SMEs. Table 1 summarizes these operating modes. These modes further emphasized the importance of enabling Operators to remain heads-up, eyes-out, and weapon-ready when maneuvering in environments with potential for proximal threats, which is where our team tailored our subsequent design efforts (i.e., the third and fourth operating modes presented in Table 1). Based on outcomes like these from the RPE (and the characterization of SOF Operators executing missions in complex, dynamic, and high-risk environments), our initial focus was on the design and prototyping of human-machine interfaces (HMIs) that promoted heads-up, eyes-out, and weapon ready UXS C2. This prioritization narrowed the team's initial focus to augmented reality (AR) visual and haptic interfaces (see Fig. 1) as each is well suited to enable Operators to maintain SA and readiness during close combat operations and were cited as preferred battlefield modalities by SOF Operators at the RPE. These modalities are in comparison to traditional control inputs for UXS platforms such as physical controllers and touchscreen controllers.

Fig. 1. Concept image generated to help elicit feedback during the SOFWERX RPE showing a notional battlefield HMI combining gesture and AR visuals to enable Operator control of UXS.

Table 1. SOF elicited UXS mission operating modes as characterized by the time Operators anticipate having to issue commands/consume UXS sensor information, the tasks Operators seek to accomplish with respect to interacting with the UXS, and Operators' preferred interaction modalities (assuming fieldable technology exists in a battlefield proven form).

Operating mode	Description	Time to interface	Tasks to achieve	Preferred modalities
Pre-mission configuration	Operator knows the mission plan and anticipated context when UXS will be employed; Operator is in a secure location with very low chance of a proximal threat	Unrestricted	Configure UXS and UXS HMI for anticipated mission needs	Smartphone Touchscreen Keyboard and Mouse
On-mission infiltration safe UI	Operator is on the mission en route to the objective, e.g., helicopter infiltration, but threat is low	Minutes	Reconfigure UXS and UXS HMI based on shifting mission goals/priorities and mission progress	Smartphone touchscreen
On-mission safe UI	Operator is on the mission within the vicinity of the objective in the field, but located in a secure location where the proximal threat is low	Minutes	Reconfigure UXS and UXS HMI based on shifting mission goals/priorities and mission progress	Smartphone touchscreen
On-mission tactical UI	Operator is actively maneuvering on the battlefield or in the objective area in a location where proximal threats are unknown or high	Seconds	Quickly direct UXS to new position or engage specific UXS autonomy	Gesture and AR
On-mission situational awareness (SA) UI	Operator is actively maneuvering on the battlefield or objective area in a location where proximal threats are unknown or high	Seconds	Consume UXS ISR/sensor information from the UXS to enhance SA	Haptics and AR
On-mission exfiltration Safe UI	Operator is on the mission en route to their base low to high proximal threat	Minutes	Reconfigure UXS and UXS HMI based on shifting mission goals/priorities and mission progress focused on clearing exfiltration route	Smartphone touchscreen

2.2 User-Centric Iterative Solution-Narrowing Approach

Post-RPE, our design approach followed a user-centric method of iteration through information gathering, capability prototyping, and live demonstrations for, and testing with, representative end users to rapidly increase system fidelity and feasibility of the solution for fielded use. To this end, Table 1 provides a summary of the various end-user testing events that were executed. Across all these events, the end users were typically comprised of a mix of dismounted SOF Operators and SOCOM or Army Special Forces Command (USASOC) leadership, with the Combat Capabilities Development Command (CCDC) demonstrations being the notable exceptions where the demonstrations were provided for senior Army Command representatives and their staff.

Table 2. An iterative user-centric design approach, using rapid prototyping and evaluations with end users, was enabled by our team's ability to access end users. Across these events different AR headsets (ML = Magic Leap One; HL = HoloLens), UAS (Tello = DJI Tello; S2 = Skydio S2; A = Parrot Anafi), and UGV (Spot = Boston Dynamics Spot UGV; Ghost = Ghost Robotics Vision 60 UGV) were utilized for a range of SOF Operator groups (RPE = Rapid Prototyping Event; NSW = Naval Special Warfare; SOCOM = Special Operations Command; USASOC = United States Army Special Operations Command; CCDC = Combat Capabilities Development Command; AISUM = Artificial Intelligence for Small Unit Maneuvers).

Event	Site	Date	Days	Users	AR	Haptic	UAS	UGV	Iteration
SOFWERX RPE	Tampa, FL	7/19	5	10+	ML	Y	Tello	–	1
NSW Demo	Camp Morena	9/19	3	10+	HL	Y	S2	–	2
SOCOM Demo	Louisville, KY	9/19	2	20+	–	Y	A	–	3
USASOC Demo	Southern Pines, NC	12/19	2	10+	–	Y	S2/Anafi	–	4
USASOC Demo	Hunter Airfield	2/20	2	30+	–	Y	S2/Anafi	–	4
NSW Demo	Camp Roberts	2/20	3	10+	–	Y	–	Ghost	5
SOCOM AISUM Demo	Tampa, FL	7/20	5	10+	–	Y	Anafi	Spot	6
USASOC AISUM Demo	Southern Pines, NC	7/20	2	30+	–	Y	Anafi	Spot	6
USASOC Demo	Southern Pines, NC	10/20	2	20+	–	Y	Anafi	–	7
USASOC Delivery	Southern Pines, NC	1/21	2	5+	–	Y	Anafi	–	7

2.3   Multimodal AR Interface Design

The following section describes the initial multimodal AR interfaces designed by CRA, building on the results from the RPE. Figures 2 through Fig. 5 show a subset of the candidate designs, with a focus on comparing and contrasting persistent versus on-demand interfaces, as well as location of display elements within the Operator's field of view (FOV).

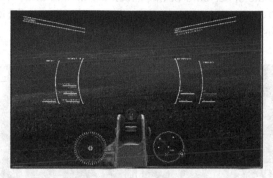

Fig. 2. Persistent rifle-tethered AR visual interface design.

Figure 2 is the resulting AR interface design from the RPE. This design uses arcs on the left and right to depict plays and the tactics within. This concept is text-heavy rather than icon-based. While text can pose issues in terms of readability and rapid understanding, it serves as a great cue for voice-based interfaces. This design concept is persistent, appearing on either side of an Operator's FOV, tethered to the rifle location.

Fig. 3. Persistent FOV-tethered AR visual interface design.

Figure 3 is also a persistent interface yet it is positioned out of the Operator's natural FOV, tethered to the left edge of the AR head-mounted display (HMD) FOV. To select a tactic, the user would turn their head and/or shift their eyes away and to the left from the rifle. Rather than a text-based interface like Fig. 2, this design is icon based, which likely provides a quicker visual indication to the user but lacks a verbal cue.

The first two designs concepts show information that is persistent and always accessible. The following designs involve a two-step process, where higher level indicators and menus are persistent, and a user must select and/or open a menu to access more in-depth information and interface controls (i.e., tactic selection).

Figure 4 utilizes the upper left and right corners of the AR FOV. In the passive viewing mode (image on the left) the upper left corner displays progress/confidence bars for all tactics currently running and the upper right displays a closed menu. The design elements in the upper third of the screen are up and away from the Operator's natural FOV. When a user opens the menu, the status indicators on the left screen become more salient and the menu on the right opens.

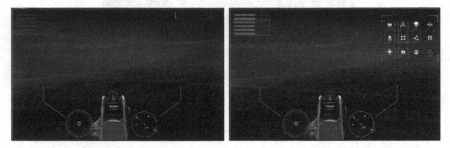

Fig. 4. Accessible FOV-tethered corner AR visual interface design.

Figure 5 is another rifle tethered accessible design, however using the left and right sides of the display for menu expansion rather than the upper corners. This is designed to be outside of the Operator's natural FOV.

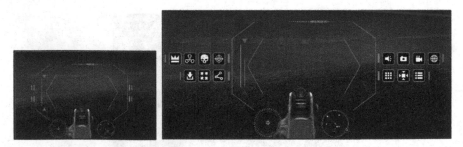

Fig. 5. Accessible FOV-tethered left/right AR visual interface design.

Finally, Fig. 6 shows another two-step accessible design, however tethered to the rifle rather than the AR HMD FOV in Figs. 4 and 5. In the passive viewing mode (image on the left), there are two closed menu icons to the left and right of the rifle. In the upper right-hand corner of the display, out of the Operator's FOV, is an overall tactic progress indicator for all tactics. If a user opens the menu icons, a partial radial menu spawns in an upwards arc to the left and right of the rifle.

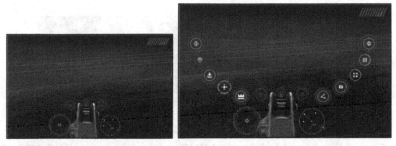

Fig. 6. Accessible rifle-tethered AR visual interface design. This design shows the menus coming arcing from bottom to top. The menu could also arc downwards from the rifle to occlude less of the Operator's FOV however generally it is much easier for humans to move their eyes up and away rather than down and away.

CRA rapidly prototyped these AR interface design concepts in Unity and internally tested the displays in a VR environment designed to represent the AR display and rifle tether (i.e., using a VR controller to represent the rifle). This allowed rapid evaluation not only of different visual interfaces but also different interaction modalities and how the different design elements (e.g., text vs. icon, persistent vs. accessible, location within display) fared across different interaction modalities: gaze only, gaze with voice command, and voice only.

Through internal testing and rapid prototyping and iteration, CRA refined and down-selected two leading interface designs with information equivalency and isolated variables to enable formal evaluation and comparison of visual interfaces across interaction modalities. CRA designed an IRB-approved experimental study protocol to evaluate this and ran an internal pilot. However, execution of the formal study was put on hold due to the low probability of AR HMDs being fielded in the next 1–2 years to Soldiers for operational (vs. training) use. As a result, the overall effort moved forward with a focus on bringing a fieldable solution to the battlefield.

2.4 Technology Overview

The initial SOFWERX RPE event was designed as a rapid exploratory event with little thought to the near-term fieldability of the technology conceived. As such, one of the key requirements from SOCOM leadership exiting that event was that any near-term solution would require hardware that was currently in use or approved for use by SOF. As a result, the DJI platform was abandoned as the primary SUAS as DJI platforms were not approved for Defense use at the time. Likewise, the Magic Leap One AR HMD was not, to our team's knowledge, being actively considered for future fielding for Defense use. For the AR HMD, our team selected the Microsoft HoloLens for AR HMI exploration, based on Microsoft winning the US Army's prime contract for the Integrated Visual Augmentation System (IVAS). While not guaranteed, we believed Microsoft's prime role on this contract created the most significant pathway for a binocular AR HMD to be fielded in the next 2–3 years (see Fig. 7), initially for training and later for operational use.

Fig. 7. Microsoft Generation 1 HoloLens AR HMD (*left*) and the Army's IVAS AR implementation led by Microsoft as of November 2020 (*right*).

With respect to selection of UXS, SOF users noted there were several disadvantages to current commercially available-off-the-shelf (COTS) SUAS offerings, most notable of which were: (1) limited battery life/flight times; (2) lack of portability/ease of fitting it in a pouch or pack to enable Operators to carry them into the field; (3) lack of autonomous crash avoidance capabilities; (4) inability to operate at night; and (5) inability to carry custom payloads on the battlefield (e.g., chemical, biological, radiological, and nuclear (CBRN) threat sensors). Based on this initial feedback, Pison conducted a rapid trade study of the best candidate UXS to address SOF needs. No single UXS platform was identified with potential to address all these challenges. For example, there were no portable COTS SUAS with an operational flight time greater than approximately 25 min. As a result, our team selected four candidate UXS platforms for capability exploration. Shown in Table 3, this included two UGVs and two SUAS. The UGV platforms were selected based on their extended runtimes (compared to SUAS), ability to carry custom payloads, and potential to extend the range of SUAS by carrying them as a payload into battle. The SUAS were also selected based on their participation in the Defense Innovation Unit's (DIU's) Blue SUAS program, indicating current or near-future feasibility for Defense acquisition. For both UGV and SUAS, selections were made to enable exploration of different end-user priorities, specifically comparing the ability to support night operations (e.g., the Parrot Anafi and Vision 60 can be outfitted with thermal cameras) versus autonomous collision avoidance capabilities, which were both mentioned by at least 5 SOF Operators at the SOFWERX RPE as high priority.

Table 3. Ghost Robotics' Vision 60 quadruped UGV (*upper left*); Parrot's Anafi SUAS (*upper right*); Boston Dynamics' Spot quadruped UGV (*lower left*); and Skydio's Skydio 2 SUAS (*lower right*).

Autonomy	Night Ops	UGV	SUAS
None	Yes	Ghost Robotics' Vision 60	Parrot Anafi
Collision Avoidance	No	Boston Dynamics' Spot	Skydio 2

2.5 Design Iteration 2 – Autonomous SUAS Integration

Following the RPE prototyping effort, our second design iteration was focused on standing up a demonstratable SUAS capability to showcase both direct (i.e., manual maneuvering of the SUAS via pitch, yaw, roll, and thrust inputs) and indirect (i.e., designation of a geospatial or drone-referenced waypoint for the SUAS to navigate to autonomously) flight control combined with HMI support for AR and gesture modalities. This design was intended to provide a set of capabilities to facilitate feedback from Operators to help with the initial narrowing of capabilities and interfaces for a fieldable solution. As shown in Fig. 8, this system iteration utilized the Skydio S2 platform, the Microsoft HoloLens AR HMD, and Pison's gesture control wearable (Fig. 9), which also provides integrated haptic feedback. With this design, Operators could: (1) directly fly the SUAS using gesture with wrist roll mapped to SUAS roll, arm pitch at the elbow mapped to SUAS pitch (i.e., tilting forward to achieve increased thrust), and arm yaw at the elbow mapped to SUAS yaw; or (2) indirectly fly the SUAS by using gesture to point and designate a point in 3D space as a waypoint for the SUAS to autonomously navigate. Using this control scheme, the Operator is presented with AR visuals to indicate the designated control mode (direct vs. indirect), the relative position of the SUAS to their own position, and the heading the SUAS is traveling if in motion. Haptic feedback in the wrist wearable was also used to provide confirmation when a gesture-input was successfully transmitted to the SUAS. The Skydio S2's crash avoidance autonomy was always enabled to both prevent accidental collisions and to assist with indirect waypoint-guided control (i.e., the Skydio S2 was programmed to attempt to fly in a straight path to its waypoint and if an obstacle is encountered it will automatically adjust course until the path is clear to continue). This avoidance technology also allowed us to explore the perceived benefits of this capability with Operators.

The second iteration of the solution was demonstrated to ~10 SOF Operators at Camp Morena who observed Pison employees using the system and then tried it firsthand. Majority feedback on the system included: (1) the AR concepts were potentially beneficial, but not enough to sacrifice natural FOV or risk virtual display clutter in a

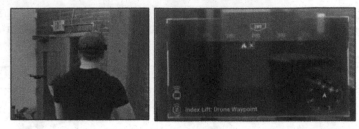

Fig. 8. Second iteration prototype showing a Pison employee piloting a Skydio S2 (*left*; S2 SUAS hovering by the door in the image) with an AR visual HUD overlay that shows the relative location of the SUAS and its current bearing/orientation to enable selection and flight command inputs (*right*; presented on a HoloLens AR HMD).

Fig. 9. Pison's Gesture Activated Machine Biological Interface Tether (GAMBIT) is a wristwatch-sized wearable that uses patented electroneurography (ENG) sensing technology to acquire biopotential and motion signals created by the neuromuscular system. Machine learning (ML) algorithms interpret this data in real-time to infer human intent and state, and Pison builds custom solutions that apply that intent and state information to offer elegant and robust human-machine interfaces (HMIs), primarily via by gesture-based control solutions.

close combat situation (i.e., Operators would not use it); (2) lack of confidence that AR will work effectively with night-vision goggles (NVGs); (3) preference for video feed on their chest-mounted end-user device (EUD) so with a single glance they can check the video and their ATAK map; (4) direct flight mode is a must so they can precisely control position and orientation of the SUAS; (5) indirect mode is useful as a less-refined adjustment capability for very quickly repositioning the SUAS; and (6) the haptic feedback incorporated into the gesture wearable was beneficial to confirm inputs were being transmitted without needing AR or heads-down visual confirmation.

2.6   Design Iteration 3 – Non-autonomous SUAS Integration

This system design used the same direct control methods as the prior iteration but abandoned indirect control and the AR HMD while transitioning to the Parrot Anafi. The visual feedback and video feed were built into a smartphone application that could be worn on the Operator's chest (simulating an ATAK EUD). Transitioning to the Anafi meant a thermal camera could be used for nighttime operations, but also eliminated crash avoidance autonomy. This was intentional to allow us to test direct control performance with both gesture and a touchscreen interface when the Operator had to be more precise and intentional with their inputs to avoid SUAS collisions. This iteration was demonstrated to 20+ SOF Operators within a domestic subterranean facility located in Louisville, KY. As shown in Fig. 10, this facility was fully underground and was GPS-denied, which restricted the use of indirect flight that relies on GPS-based waypoints (therefore it was not included as a feature in this iteration).

The overall Operator consensus was that manual control was valuable for precisely controlling the SUAS in confined quarters. They described a subterranean scenario where they would slowly advance through a tunnel system while manually keeping the SUAS 100 feet in front of them to serve as a forward scout. They expressed interest in understanding how the collision avoidance capability would perform in confined environments, but stressed: (1) the need for operating in dark/nighttime environments; and (2) ability to override automated collision avoidance capabilities as needed (e.g., if the collision avoidance buffer is too tight to enable flight through a narrow space). With respect to the touchscreen interface, Operators were clearly aligned on when they would prefer it over gesture. If Operators are in a secure position taking cover with no immediate threat of enemy fire, using the touchscreen to remotely pilot the SUAS into a forward position would be preferred to using gesture, which they felt is more conducive to on-the-move piloting of the SUAS.

Fig. 10. The third iteration of the system being demonstrated by a Pison employee with the chest-mounted smartphone application (*left*) and gesture-controlled flight (*right*).

2.7 Design Iteration 4 – SUAS Comparison

The fourth iteration of the system enabled toggleable control of the Skydio S2 and Parrot Anafi. Both drones could be flown with gesture or touchscreen controls for direct or indirect flight commands. This iteration was tested at two events with over 40 current and former SOF Operators. Operators were trained on the system and then able to test both platforms, comparing performance aspects of both the S2 and Anafi SUAS.

Despite the large number of Operators and the ability for them to directly compare both SUAS against one another, there was relatively little new information. Instead, Operators confirmed top-level priorities were support for: (1) night operations; (2) direct flight; (3) both gesture and touchscreen control; and (4) use of a smartphone EUD for viewing the SUAS video feed. It was also confirmed that some SOF units were already using the Parrot Anafi on missions, which only served to further confirm that, based on these top-level priorities, the Anafi was the better SUAS to support.

2.8   Design Iteration 5 – UGV Integration

With the preferred SUAS selected, our team shifted to add support for the non-autonomous UGV (i.e., the Ghost Robotics Vision 60). Using the same framework as the SUAS, this enabled direct and indirect control of the Vision UGV via gesture and touchscreen inputs. The primary difference is that all inputs were flattened to ground level (i.e., elevation inputs relevant to adjust SUAS were zeroed out for the UGV). This prototype iteration was presented to approximately 10 Operators at Camp Roberts in California. Operators were able to navigate the UGV outdoors (on both asphalt paved areas and desert terrain) and indoors (within large hangers and through doorways).

Majority of Operators appreciated the potential for the UGV to operate for prolonged periods of time and its potential to carry more significant payloads forward onto the battlefield (compared to UAVs). They also felt it would be superior for forward scouting in very confined environments where elevation changes are restricted, specifically environments where a vehicle could transport the UGV to secure an entry point (e.g., inside a building, in a subterranean environment). The maximum speed of the UGV was a critical factor for preference of control input modality. The preferred control input was indirect control since Operators could physically move faster than the UGV, so they did not want to have to constantly stop and advance the system manually. However, they noted that without collision avoidance they would be unlikely to trust indirect control for fear of the platform driving itself into an obstacle and crashing.

2.9   Design Iteration 6 – Autonomous UGV and SUAS

The sixth iteration of the system was meant to serve as a capstone capability exploration to inform the selection of the set that would be supported in the final fieldable solution. It incorporated the Parrot Anafi (the preferred SUAS) and the Boston Dynamics Spot UGV (given its autonomous collision avoidance to facilitate the preferred indirect control mode). This iteration was purpose built for a USSOCOM S&T AISUM Technology Demonstration event. The event allowed the prototype solution to be integrated into a simulated breach and target exfiltration mission being conducted by Operators at a controlled installation that replicated a small-scale multi-building environment (see Fig. 11).Our team constructed a payload mount that included a network router, edge compute device, and SUAS launching system that allowed Spot to carry up to four Anafi SUAS and launch them individually or as a swarm of four. Two of these UGV and SUAS swarm setups were constructed to be deployed with a squad of four Operators, one of which was tasked with controlling the full swarm of unmanned assets to support the mission. Based on this, the squad planned tactics for the mission and decision points where they would leverage the swarm. Figure 12 shows an illustration of one tactic whereby the Operators wished to leverage the swarm to provide forward scouting ISR as they approach a potential threat, and then to monitor the perimeter of a building for potential threats that attempted to run away and escape (termed "squirters").

All Operators had access to the ISR video feeds from any of the UGV or SAUS on their EUD smartphones. Operators could also see the positions of the UGV and SUAS on their EUD map. The Operator with the ability to control the UGV and SUAS, referred to as the "Handler," was positioned in the rear of the squad stack and tasked with

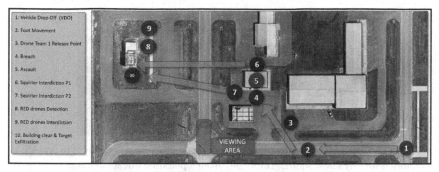

Fig. 11. USSOCOM S&T AISUM Technology Demonstration event breach and exfiltration mission plan overview. The viewing area designated in the image was for civilian and Government observers who were not actively taking part in the exercise.

Fig. 12. Concept sketch illustrating the use of the prototype swarm capability to scout a building and position to monitor for squirters exiting the building during breach and exfil tactics.

maneuvering the various UGV and SUAS elements around the environment to support the mission. Figure 13 and Fig. 14 illustrate some of the control tactics for the UGV and SUAS that were used throughout the mission.

Fig. 13. AISUM team moving forward with UGVs in forward close formation as a SUAS launches off the UGV pictured to the left.

Unlike the prior iterations where the Operators only need to control a single UGV or SUAS platform, this iteration allowed them to control any combination of the available 2 UGV and 8 SUAS assets. This was accomplished using a robust but intuitive gesture HMI

Fig. 14. AISUM team advancing forward and relying on UGV in rear position to provide video for monitoring for any latent squirters emerging from a potential threat building.

that allowed the Operator to quickly select which specific UXS they wanted to control, and then gesture with the control input for that selection. The following page shows the decision tree and conditions for this selection HMI to illustrate how logic can be designed into the HMI, based on tasks users need to accomplish, to enable even a simple user input to accomplish a complex technical task (Fig. 15). Similar decisions trees were created for each control state after an Operator selected: (1) a single SUAS; (2) multiple SUAS; (3) a single UGV; (4) both UGV; or (5) a mix of UGV and SUAS. For a single SUAS, Operators could use either direct or indirect flight. This was the only scenario where direct control was enabled as Operators never highlighted a scenario where they would want to directly control more than one UXS at a time, and our prior testing indicated that they always preferred indirect control for UGVs so long as they had collision avoidance (which the Spot had). For control of multiple SUAS, preset formation tactics were established prior to the mission with feedback from the Operators on how they envision future swarm autonomy supporting them. These hardcoded tactics replicated basic autonomy (e.g., a selection of four SUAS could be directed to form a square around a given area to provide full 360-degree inward looking video ISR coverage). Additionally, the Operator could use indirect control to move all selected SUAS in their current formation by some geospatial offset (e.g., move them all 20 m East), which also worked if the selection included a mixture of UGV and SUAS assets.

During the event, the Operator team walked through the mission scenario several times to enable them to familiarize and test both our team's system and several unrelated technologies from other companies contributing to the AISUM Tech Demo event. These dry runs were run over the course of several days in preparation for the "full-speed" primary event on the final day of the event. Feedback was collected after each dry run to fine tune the capabilities for the final full-speed run through. Most of the feedback received prior to the full-speed run was based on tweaking the simulated autonomy (e.g., changing the positioning of how a default formation was setup), with limited feedback on the actual HMI components as Operators had sufficient time to practice with them and get comfortable with what interactions were possible and how to control those interactions.

Most of the feedback from Operators and SOCOM leadership that were in attendance focused on how to take this iteration and adapt it for very near-term (i.e., within 3–6 months) fielding. Nearly all parties agreed that the UGV in its current form was not well suited to operations in open environments where a vehicle could easily carry the UGV forward to the point of need. The slow speed of the UGV and the inability for it to be a man-portable (i.e., Operator-carried) asset were too much of a burden. There was potential benefit in clearing confined environments (e.g., multistory building, subterranean environment) where the UGV could be brought safely to the entrance and then used to scout the building for threats, but this potential would require additional autonomy and considerations for payloads that would enhance its sensing capabilities. With respect to the UGV's ability to carry and launch SUAS, users agreed it was not necessary and an excessive capability at this time as the Anafi could easily fold its propeller arms in and be stored in a pouch or pack on the Operator.

With respect to the Anafi, Operators were happy with the gesture-based HMI method to enable command of more than one SUAS that was airborne in the environment. However, the general feeling was that a single Operator would be unlikely to put up more than one SUAS at a time without performant autonomy to support: (1) collision avoidance; (2) strategic positioning and camera orientation; and (3) video feed event/object detection and alerting. This was due to a concern with managing coordinated movements of multiple SUAS when they were not in a secure position, and the need to effectively monitor multiple camera feeds for threats or other salient pieces of information (which puts them in a head-down state). The direct and indirect gesture controls were confirmed

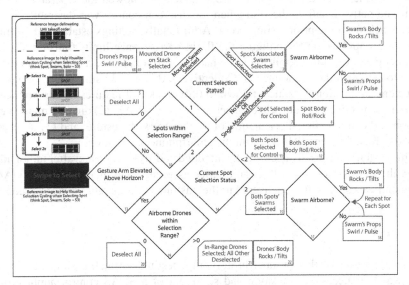

Fig. 15. Example illustrating part of the mixed UGV and SUAS swarm control gesture HMI map. This diagram illustrates the system process and HMI for how an Operator selects one or more UGV and/or SUAS to which they wish to issue a command. In this image the gesture to select a UGV and/or SUAS is to simply swipe your arm in an arc that covers the physical position of the platform(s) you wish to select. The rest of this figure then delineates the logic for how the swarm responds to that selection to appropriately add the right UGV and/or SUAS to your selection. Finally, the same setup was tested a second time at a location in Southern Pines, NC in a less formal setting. Active and former Operators were able to try out the system in an uncontrolled manner outside and within a small warehouse setting. While no novel insights resulted from these demonstrations, the feedback results in further confirmation on many of the settings.

as beneficial, with the same feedback that direct control was more valuable. One novel piece of feedback uncovered during the full-speed scenario run was that the touchscreen controls designed for our application were considered less beneficial than the native Parrot Anafi application. Operators commented that Parrot's touchscreen flight application offered more features and refined limiters on the platform (e.g., capping maximum speed, altitude, bank angle, turn radius) so they could more comfortably use gesture to directly control the aircraft within the context of a mission environment (e.g., using faster maximum speeds in more open environments and lower maximums when the SUAS is in position and only needs minor adjustments). Operators requested to add equivalent features (e.g., fully configurable flight performance parameters, preconfigured adjustments of those parameters for differing operating modes) within the custom solution application or to eliminate it completely and simply allow them to use the native Anafi app when touchscreen control was required.

2.10   Design Iteration 7 – Final SUAS Iteration and Delivery

The final iteration of the system was designed for delivery and deployment. The baseline capability was direct gesture-based control of the Parrot Anafi SUAS. The application did not include touchscreen flight controls, instead it allowed the Operator to switch over to the native Anafi application when touchscreen control was desirable based on the feedback from the prior testing event. Additionally, settings established within the native Anafi application to configure the flight performance limits transferred over to the direct gesture-control application to enable Operators to use a single configuration source to establish those parameters. Collectively, this greatly simplified the nature of the custom application to reduce it down to only the set of features needed to meet the end-users' objectives: (1) quickly connect to an Anafi SUAS; (2) directly maneuver the position and camera gimbal orientation of the SUAS with gesture; and (3) observe the ISR video feed from the SUAS within the smartphone application.

This system was tested once with the intended end-user group and after minor adjustments, the final system went through quality assurance and quality control (QA/QC) testing and was successfully delivered to the customer for operational use as seen fit.

3   Results

The overall result of this product prototyping, testing, evaluation, and development effort was the successful transition and shipment of a SUAS control application for dismounted SOF Operators. Following a user-centric and iterative design methodology, that was heavily anchored in frequent end-user demonstrations, testing, and feedback events, allowed our team to rapidly iterate and narrow capability focus to the subset that provided the utility necessary to address a gap in the end-users' mission need. Throughout this process there were several critical insights that were gained with respect to the design of both mixed reality and unmanned system interfaces that can be carried beyond the scope of the specific solution our team narrowed in on.

With respect to the general HMI for both the different AR HMD and UXS systems, we confirmed with over 50 SOF Operators their preference for battlefield HMIs. Their primary motivation is maintaining their survivability and lethality above all else. Said differently, they will always prioritize surviving a fight and/or eliminating a threat in a situation where that is an option, as one SOF TACP stated "I am going to neutralize any immediate threat to myself or my team, I become a liability if I cannot keep up". As a result, if an HMI to leverage a technology reduces their SA, survivability, or lethality, the likelihood they will rely on that technology in critical situations is also reduced. For this reason, HMIs that allow Operators to remain heads-up, eyes-out, and weapon ready are always their preference in high-threat/unknown threat environments. Based on this information, Pison crafted a Primary, Alternative, Contingency, and Emergency (PACE) plan for dismounted SOF Operator control that is meant to create the same levels of HMI redundancy that similar PACE communications plans benefit from on the battlefield. The logic here is that much like communications plans allow Operators to interact with teammates and support elements, HMIs allow Operators to communicate and interact with battlefield technology.

As shows, within this PACE plan gesture serves as the primary HMI modality. This is because gestures can be performed: (1) quickly (inclusive of the action itself as well as any precursor to input such as unlocking a phone, doffing a glove, taking out a piece of hardware, etc.); (2) without requiring any shift in visual or auditory attention; (3) in almost any posture; and (4) without creating an easily detectable signature by enemy forces that could compromise survivability (Fig. 16).

Fig. 16. PACE plan for battlefield HMIs used by close combat dismounted SOF Operators.

Voice and gaze-based inputs serve as an alternative and/or redundant HMI modality, potentially pairing well with gesture to be complementary (e.g., using gesture to activate a push-to-talk radio or toggling on eye-tracking or serving as an activation input on an AR HMD). Gaze-based HMIs fail to serve as a primary input due to the requirement that Operators fixate their gaze on some interactable object. This means both that: (1) AR or other HMD hardware is required to provide a visually selectable digital overlay (i.e., technology that is not yet in widespread use by the military and which has potential to obscure FOV and compromise SA); and (2) visual attention, and specifically foveal vision, is required to be diverted for some period of time to the interaction target/region which inherently means they are shifting visual attention off some other element of interest (e.g., a threat).

Speech-based interfaces have significant potential as a battlefield HMI, but a lack of performant technology (e.g., speech libraries that perform effectively in noisy environments, on existing hardware, and across a range of user accents, pitches, amplitudes, and tones), and the potential to interfere with existing human-to-human battlefield communications standards (i.e., radio chatter and inter-squad callouts) and discreet operations limits their ability to serve as a primary input. This point is made salient even when considering the current battlefield standard for voice communications whereby a physical HMI (i.e., a radio's pushbutton) is required as a precursor to issuing any voice communications, and specific tactics, techniques, and procedures (TTPs) have been established on how to effectively use voice communications on the battlefield (e.g., to prevent critical information from being "stepped on" by someone keying their radio at an inopportune time). As a result, speech-based HMIs for battlefield technology is likely to be severely limited to a short subset of key command words or phrases that are sparsely used and only accessible after some other keying HMI is used to tell the system a speech command is about to be issued.

Contingency interfaces in the PACE HMI plan are physical/direct control HMIs (e.g., physical controllers, keypads, etc.). The benefit of these is their reliability, which comes with a significant tradeoff of requiring an Operator to lower their weapon, unpack/access the physical controller, spend time interacting with it until the desired command inputs are issued, and then repack the controller to continue with the mission. Additionally, physical controllers are not always accessible or usable depending on the context of a given situation (e.g., laying prone a chest-mounted controller may be difficult to access and use effectively). An Army Ranger Team Leader for the 75th Ranger Regiment stated, "I have another Ranger cover me whenever I use my controller, its highly inefficient in a small maneuver teams".

Finally, touchscreen interfaces (primarily mediated through a smartphone) are seen as an emergency HMI and ultimately a last resort for interaction. This is because they require the Operator to: (1) go fully heads-down to interact with them (losing all visual awareness of their surrounding); (2) remove gloves or other PPE before interacting with them (and then redon them after use); (3) can interfere with access to other equipment when being employed (e.g., a chest-mounted smartphone in the open position can inhibit access to magazines stored in an abdomen pouch which is common placement for both); and (4) typically offer less precision than physical controllers dedicated to a specific endpoint HMI solution. A SOF JTAC stated "touch screens are a liability at night with more night vision devices becoming readily available, I have to kneel and cover my phone to avoid highlighting myself and my team". It is critical to note that touchscreen requires the Operator to put their weapon down in a non-ready position. This drastically increases the time for an Operator to either put their weapon in a ready position to scan for a threat or transition to a firing position for an observed threat.

Across all four of the PACE plan tiers, the other considerations that were uncovered related to how the spectrum of PACE tiers largely align with: (1) time available for interaction; (2) security/safety of Operator position at time of interaction; and (3) precision of interaction required. All of these factors are inversely related to the left-to-right PACE

HMI alignment. For example, gesture HMIs lend themselves to very rapid inputs that can be executed very quickly even while maneuvering in high-threat situations, but typically compromising the precision of that input (i.e., gestures will typically be successful when mapped to binary or gross control inputs). On the other end of the spectrum, Operators confirmed that use of a touchscreen interface would rarely be employed unless Operators were in a secure position with the time required to access and interact with the HMI safely, while also noting that controllers and touchscreens typically offer more precision in the inputs vs. gesture, speech, and gaze HMI modalities.

4 Conclusions

This paper presented an end-to-end overview of an iterative user-centric process to discover, explore, prototype, test, and ultimately field a useful unmanned vehicle capability for dismounted SOF Operators. The approach taken was enabled by frequent access to demonstrate and allow hands-on testing of technology with end users. This allowed for rapid iteration of functional prototypes as features initially expanded and then rapidly narrowed to converge on the final capabilities set that was deployed to the end users and customer as the delivered product offering. Lessons learned from this approach included identification of standard measures or spectrums on which HMI and technology solutions for dismounted SOF Operators should be characterized to inform design and feature decisions.

Virtual Solutions for Gathering Consumer Feedback on Food: A Literature Review and Analysis

Summer D. Jung[✉][iD], Sahej Claire, Julie Fukunaga, Joaquin Garcia, and Soh Kim

Stanford University, Stanford, CA 94305, USA
{summerjung,saclaire,juliefa,joaqg3,sohyeong}@stanford.edu

Abstract. Addressing consumer needs is key to success in new product development. Due to COVID-19, however, gathering feedback on food products has become challenging. Our preliminary research on the food industry revealed that the socially distanced lifestyle has deprived food practitioners of in-person testing platforms, inspiring our research questions. Although a myriad of virtual methods for food testing have been reported in the past two decades, the literature does not provide systematic assessment of their applicability. Therefore, in this review of 108 papers, we delineate the landscape of virtual technologies for food testing and present their practical implications. From our analysis, VR emerged as a promising tool, yet it was not being used by practitioners. Other technologies (e.g. flavor simulators) were too preliminary to be adopted in industry. Furthermore, the types of technologies were fragmented, leaving much room for cross-tech integration. Future research goals to address the gaps are discussed.

Keywords: Human food interaction · Sensory technology · Virtual testing

1 Introduction

1.1 The Need for Virtual Technologies During the Pandemic

Understanding the needs of consumers is a must for food companies to design successful products [56]. Use of consumer insight techniques not only helps companies to identify new market opportunities but also to test the validity of the prototypes before launching [36]. By doing so, food companies can address the ever-changing needs of consumers [35]. As a result, a myriad of methodologies for applying consumer needs have been reported in the literature. Traditional examples of such methodologies range from initial ideation tools, such as observation and self-reporting, to testing tools, such as descriptive sensory analysis [49,67].

© Springer Nature Switzerland AG 2021
J. Y. C. Chen and G. Fragomeni (Eds.): HCII 2021, LNCS 12770, pp. 452–471, 2021.
https://doi.org/10.1007/978-3-030-77599-5_31

However, the landscape of new food design is changing quickly as new technologies are introduced. For instance, the emergence of the Internet has allowed consumers to access, apply, and share relevant knowledge that can help companies' new product design processes [82]. Among many tools on the Internet, social media can serve as a crowdsourcing platform for new ideas [80]. Hardware technologies, such as 2D and 3D food printing, can aid the prototyping of new food products [33,83], and virtual realities allow us to understand food-related consumer behaviors and test products in absence of a physical testbed [116,127]. In their timely review on the potential applications for Virtual and Augmented Reality (VR/AR), Crofton et al. identified the technologies hold significant potential in five key areas in sensory science: introducing different consumption contexts, gathering biometric data, visualizing food structure and texture, providing tools for sensory marketing, and augmenting sensory perception [20]. Such technologies altogether constitute the new, emerging field of Human-Food Interaction (HFI), which broadens our understanding of how technology can and should be applied to our everyday food experiences [3].

In addition to the current tech-oriented trends, we project that the new technologies will be increasingly applied to the new food design process in the current COVID era. COVID-19 takes a double toll on food companies; it is not only pushing them to create new products for the fast-changing consumer lifestyle but has also deprived them of the venues traditionally used to market products and gauge consumer reactions, such as restaurants and cafes [75]. Food shows, expos, and festivals, which require mass gatherings, have been cancelled or postponed indefinitely. In this troubling time, leveraging technology can help fill the gap between companies and their consumers. For instance, the healthcare and education industries have already adopted virtual patient care and virtual learning in lieu of traditional in-person practices [2,131].

Despite the strong need for the food industry to adopt virtual alternatives, the existing literature does not provide structured information on what knowledge is readily available, nor on applications of that knowledge to the food industry. Individual studies on virtual alternatives for new food development provide only scattered and partial insights. A recent review by Hartmann and Siegrist offers a thorough overview of Virtual Reality's potential for contextual food testing [116], but it does not tap into other technologies, such as a digital taste simulator [96]. On the other hand, the current HFI framework developed by Bertran et al. covers a much too broad range of interactions, from food sourcing to food consumption. Its broad approach provides limited insight into how to practically apply the knowledge to new food design [3]. The present study contributes to the literature by shedding light on the currently available virtual alternatives and their implications for food practitioners in the specific context of new food design. Furthermore, it brings attention to the gaps in the current space, guiding future research.

1.2 Preliminary Data to Scope the Research

To ground our research, we conducted a series of interviews with practitioners in the food industry. Twenty-two Consumer-Packaged Goods food startups across California were interviewed on COVID-19's impact on their new food design process. All interviews, which lasted approximately an hour, were semi-structured and guided by a set of pre-generated questions. Later on, the recorded interviews were thematically coded by the research team to single out mentions of COVID's impact. All of the procedures described above were pre-approved by an Institutional Review Board.

The interviews allowed us to effectively narrow down the scope of our research. Different models of product development processes exist in the literature, often based on Cooper's stage-gate model [19]. Kukko-liedes et al.'s four-stage model, which is adapted to suit the development process of food startups, consists of ideation, concept development, product development, and delivery [53]. Our interviews revealed that the product development stage presented the biggest challenge because the food startups could not gather in-person sensory feedback. One startup founder remarked, "Pre-COVID, when we were doing sampling in retail stores, we learned a lot from customers that way as well. But obviously with COVID, you can't." Another reported, "a common way to market products... is to do events, to do grocery store demonstrations, where you're inside the grocery stores, sampling products, farmers markets...so all of that stuff is out the window." Before COVID-19, giving a product demo at a grocery store or sampling at a farmer's market was a natural way to test prototypes, gather feedback, and get new product ideas. The literature also attests that in-person food tasting plays a critical role in food purchasing, along with the haptic information that consumers get when holding and feeling products [81,84]. Because of COVID-19, such experiences have been significantly reduced. From this specific need, we set the scope of our research to food product testing, among the many stages of new food design. Thus, our research questions are as follows:

- What are currently available technologies that can virtualize food product testing?
- What practical implications do those technologies offer?
- How is the current human food interaction research addressing the gap between concept creation and testing?

2 Methodology

2.1 Building the Dataset

To answer our research questions, we first conducted an exhaustive search of existing studies on Google Scholar based on the set of keywords we generated, such as "virtual food" or "human food interaction." The full list of the search keywords is attached in the appendix. To ensure we covered all bases, we further looked at the studies cited by the searched articles. Then, all the papers' titles and abstracts were evaluated on the following inclusion and exclusion criteria:

Inclusion Criteria

- Written in English
- Including at least one user study that assesses a virtual alternative to the physical food experience OR at least one user study with findings related to virtual food product testing
- Presented in a full paper or an extended abstract, in contrast to an abstract submission or a demo

Exclusion Criteria

- Published before the year of 2000
- Addressing solely theoretical matters of virtual alternatives (e.g. literature reviews)
- Testing the technology in a non-food-related context
- Using the technologies to study medical implications (e.g. eating disorders)
- Same paper introduced at different venues (When multiple versions of the same technology were found, we included only the latest version.)

2.2 Dataset

At the end of our manual filtering process, we ended up with 108 studies on virtual tools that can aid or partially replace the in-person feedback gathering process for food companies. The majority of the studies were published in the following three academic communities: Human-Computer Interaction, Technology, and Food. Technology included engineering-focused venues like IEEE (Institute of Electrical and Electronics Engineers) as well as computing-related or VR/AR-related venues. In total, 20 articles from HCI, 20 from Technology, and 46 from Food-related conferences or journals were included in the dataset. The venues of the rest of the articles (22) varied from psychology to marketing.

2.3 Data Analysis

Each study was then qualitatively analyzed using a set of themes inspired by Bertran et al. [3] and two additional themes, types of technology and practical implications. In their HFI framework, Bertran et al. introduce three lenses through which to analyze HFI studies: Domain, Focus, and Agency. In their suggested framework, Domain concerns the stage of food interaction, such as sourcing ingredients or eating food. Focus maps the papers on a spectrum of functionality and experience, depending on whether the technology demonstrates a function or enhances an experience (e.g. social bonding). Agency assesses whether the agency of humans or technology is supported. In our analysis, we used Domain as a lens, but different subcategories emerged as the scope of our research was narrower. Similarly, we adopted a new set of subcategories for the Focus lens because the majority of the studies were function-oriented and Bertran et al.'s binary classification yielded limited insights. Similarly, the Agency lens was removed because the vast majority of the studies present low-agency technologies. Along with Domain and Focus, we summarized the type of technology used and the practical implications of each study to guide industry professionals.

3 Results

3.1 Domain

From our review of 108 papers that encompasses sensory technology, VR/AR, and online survey tools, we identify three domain subcategories: (1) purchasing and selecting food, (2) tasting food, and (3) perceiving food (Table 1).

Table 1. Domain

Domain	Count
Purchasing and selecting	34 (31.5%)
Tasting food	49 (45.4%)
Perceiving food	23 (21.3%)
Miscellaneous	2 (1.9%)
Total	108

Purchasing and Selecting Food. Concerning consumer selection and purchasing, we primarily present studies using VR as a testbed to better understand and probe consumer purchasing and selection habits. Many create a virtual replica of an immersive environment as the backdrop for user studies. For instance, two studies recreate virtual bars to understand their impact on wine selection or liking [37,105]. A number of virtual supermarkets are used to understand the influence of different factors, such as price, on purchasing choices [122,123]. Other virtual environments include a food court [78], buffet [17], and outdoor setting [110].

Tasting Food. Our review generates a large number of user studies involving sensory technologies related to sight, smell, taste, touch, and/or sound, mainly in the form of pseudo-gustatory interfaces. Another set of studies uses VR testing settings to simulate the food tasting process and assess the impact of VR on the eating experience [18,110]. It is in this category that hardware devices shine, simulating and stimulating the various senses in the food-tasting process. However, despite the large number of the studies, many flavor simulation prototypes are limited to generating elementary sensations.

Certain patterns emerge regarding the different senses. Studies utilizing sensory technology (of which a subset use AR) are overwhelmingly multisensory, using a combination of techniques such as projections of color or other visuals [92] as well as electric stimulation of the tongue and jaw muscles, to influence taste and/or consumption amount [68]. Given the multisensory nature of taste and flavor, we find that 33 of these studies overlap across two or more senses, with the vast majority focusing on a combination of sight, smell, and taste, neglecting sound and haptics. Sixteen studies focus on establishing proof of concept for a single sense.

Perceiving Food. Regarding online tools, we see virtual pathways for sourcing consumer feedback on different food products. Through projective techniques, such as free word association, researchers try to understand consumer perceptions of a variety of food items such as cheese [48], fermented milk [87], amaranth [100], and ready-to-eat salads [121]. Others use surveys to characterize consumer perceptions of and motivations to buy products [1,28,120], or use findings gathered from online communities to help promote food companies' engagement with consumers [24].

These three categories in Domain are frequently siloed in the type of technology used, leaving much room for cross-tech integration. Purchasing and selecting food primarily consists of VR user studies, while the perceiving food category mainly comprises online survey tools. Overall, intersections between technology types are rare, existing mainly in the realms of consumer psychology and sensory technologies augmented by hardware and immersive technology (AR/VR), such as those combining eye tracking technology with projective techniques in both immersive and non-immersive environments [11,63].

3.2   Focus

We next mapped our findings across a new set of categories inspired by Bertran et al.'s Focus lens in order to gain insight into each paper's overall goal [3]. Seven distinct subcategories were identified within this lens.

Table 2. Focus

Focus	Count	References
1. To validate VR as a testbed	23 (21.3%)	[4–6,14,17,34,37,40,57,65,78, 89,90,104,106,107,116,117,122– 124,127,134]
2. To test different factors in a virtual retail environment	7 (6.5%)	[26,41,62,125,126,128,135]
3. To test a tool's influence on food consumption	23 (21.3%)	[9,18,25,27,39,42,43,51,54,71,73, 77,79,85,86,102,105,108,110,112, 114,119,133]
4. To offer a virtual tool to understand consumers	21 (19.4%)	[1,7,8,10,11,28,30,31,48,63,64,66, 74,87,88,100,109,113,120,121,132]
5. To virtualize eating	22 (20.4%)	[21,38,44,46,50,60,68–70,76,92– 99,101,103,111,115]
6. To examine virtual communities	7 (6.5%)	[12,22–24,45,47,130]
7. To enhance eating experience	5 (4.6%)	[13,29,61,72,129]
Total	108	

To Validate VR as a Testbed. In looking at VR's comparability to real life environments, 19 of 23 studies (Table 2) compare specified locations such as supermarkets [14,40,57,65,89,90,104,106,117,122–124,127], buffets [17,116], a food court [78], a wine bar [37], a pub [107], and a cafe [134] in both virtual and physical environments to test for any visible deviations in consumer experience and choice. Additionally, one study compares how virtual and physical cookies are perceived differently [34], while another uses chocolate to see whether a virtual environment can effectively generate disgust as in a real environment [4]. Although many studies find that there are no significant differences between a virtual and physical environment [4,116,127], fewer studies find that consumer behavior in fact differs [40,57,117], a point to be further discussed in Discussion.

To Test Different Factors in a Virtual Retail Environment. Taking this concept of VR as a testbed into consideration, seven studies investigate consumer behavior through VR with the assumption that a virtual environment is a comparable test method. All use a virtual supermarket as their setting to explore factors influencing purchasing behavior such as labels [26], pricing [126,128], packaging [41], and discounts [125].

To Test a Tool's Influence on Food Consumption. In our first category that did not rely solely on VR as a testbed, we explored 23 studies investigating different tools' influence on food consumption. Eleven of the 23 use VR in conjunction with AR or physical environments to test the environments' effect on perceptions of freshness [108], flavor [18,25,39,51,77,79,110], aroma [114], satiety [71], and cravings [54]. Studies show that modification or augmentation of the food in question in one virtual, augmented, or immersive environment compared to another can lead to a magnification of sensory experience such as perceived sweetness of beverage [18], aroma of wine [114], emotional association with dark chocolate [51], and more [77,108,110]. Other non-VR or non-AR technologies included automatically generated chewing sounds, for which impacts on the food consumption quantity [27] and perceived freshness [133] are investigated.

To Offer a Virtual Tool to Understand Consumers. This subcategory includes a total of 21 studies. Six of the 21, in further application of VR, combine virtual environments with other measures such as eye tracking [63,88], wearable cameras [74], and analysis of path tortuosity [132] to investigate consumer behaviors in a shopping environment. Conversely, this subcategory also included 15 studies using solely online assessment methods, such as free word association [7,8,28,48,64,87,88,100,121], questionnaires [28,113], and Haire's shopping list [87,121], to gauge consumer perception of different food products.

To Virtualize Eating. Eleven of the 22 of the studies in this category aim to achieve the same result: stimulating or simulating flavor through the application of electronics, both hardware and software. The other 11 studies focus instead on physical sensations such as chewing, drinking, and texture. Consensus seems to be in either the application of electrical signals to simulate the physical sensation of chewing and drinking through devices such as chopsticks [68,99] and straws [38,68,94], or in the use of electrical or thermal signals to stimulate or emulate flavor profiles such as sweet and sour [21]. The technologies further enhance the perceived flavors through visual cues such as color and texture [46,68,92,94,97].

To Examine Virtual Communities. This category, encompassing seven studies, explores virtual food communities with the potential for new methods of delivering user feedback. Four studies emphasize methods of enhancing engagement from community members and go on to discuss the implications of these virtual communities for food companies, particularly from marketing and branding perspectives [22,24,45,47]. The other three explore virtual food networks as alternatives to physical spaces such as farmer's markets, demonstrating that such networks can supplement but not substitute for physical spaces [12], tend to attract a more educated and price-conscious demographic [130], and can drive sustainable purchasing and consumption [23].

To Enhance Eating Experience. Our final category, focused on enhancing the current physical eating experience rather than virtualizing it, encompasses five studies. Two, an augmented eating system [61] and CoDine, a dining table embedded with interactive subsystems [129], create experiential changes to augment and test different eating experiences, in contrast to eating sensations. The other three focus on enhancing sensation to impact flavor in a more focused application of a tool: generation of chewing sounds to enhance perceived flavors [29], mobile telesmell to prime emotional responses to food [13], and an edible marker system to change food's appearance and scent [72].

Table 3. Types of technologies

Type	Count
VR	49
Sensory tech	32
Online	22
AR	10
Miscellaneous	3

Overall, we found there to be a heavy focus on VR/AR solutions in the first four Focus categories. Table 3 also summarizes the count of each type of technology in the dataset. The total count exceeds 108 because some studies implement more than one type of technology. As Table 3 indicates, VR is the most frequently used tool in our dataset, followed by sensory technology, such as an electric taste simulator.

4 Discussion

4.1 Practical Implications and Challenges of Technology Adoption

So far, we presented the landscape of the currently available technologies. The 108 reviewed studies collectively provide six major insights for future designers of Human Food Interaction, including practitioners in the food industry, on how virtual technologies can be applied to food testing, as Table 4 illustrates.

Table 4. Practical Implications

Practical Implication	Example	References
1. A VR/AR environment can change the perceived flavor or liking of a product	Consumers are more likely to perceive a product as sweet when consumed in a sweet-congruent VR environment [18]	[6,9,18,25,39,43,51,77,79, 85,108,110,114]
2. VR is a comparable testbed to recreate food shopping experiences	Selection of cereals does not differ significantly in a VR aisle vs. a physical store [106]	[4,5,11,17,26,31,34,37, 41,63,65,74,78,89,90, 106,107,116,119,122– 128,132,134,135]
3. Consumer behavior differs in a VR environment	Participants spend more money and buy more products in a VR store than in a physical store [40]	[14,40,54,57,62,86,104, 105,117]
4. Multiple technologies (e.g., haptic interfaces and simulators) can recreate basic flavors and eating sensations	Flavors can be simulated through devices that emit scent and send electric signals to the tongue [98]	[13,21,29,38,44,46,50,68– 70,72,73,76,92– 99,101,103,111,115]
5. Non-VR online tools can provide valuable consumer insights	Free word association is used to gauge consumer perception of a novel ingredient, amaranth [100]	[1,7,8,10,28,48,64,66,87, 88,100,113,120,121]
6. Social media can be an effective platform for gathering feedback	A case study of craft beer brewers' use of social media to engage consumers [30]	[22,24,30,45]

Overall, our findings draw a promising picture, but a few challenges stand in the way of the technologies' wider adoption in the food industry. First, more research is needed to understand the specifics of how VR environments influence consumer behavior. We found some controversy within the literature on how comparable a VR environment is to a real food environment; many studies suggest that there are no discernible differences between real life and VR in terms of how they impact food choice [5,116,127]. Others, however, report that purchasing behaviors differ in a VR environment [14,57,117]. One research team finds that consumers spend more money, buy more national brands, and respond more strongly to price promotions in a virtual supermarket than in a physical store [40]. Thus, VR is an effective tool for studying consumers, but its influence may not be negligible depending on the study's dependent variable. More research is needed, and when adopting a VR environment for consumer testing, practitioners should be keenly aware of the technology's implications.

Second, hardware-based flavor simulators should achieve a higher level of multimodality. Although many of the flavor simulators incorporate more than one sense, tactile and auditory senses are mostly neglected. Eating is fundamentally a multisensory experience [91], and our perception of flavors is constructed from an amalgamation of gustatory, olfactory, and tactile sensations rather than any individual sensation [91]. Even the sound of food, such as the crunchiness of potato chips, has a significant influence on the perceived flavor [133]. Therefore, flavor simulators should incorporate more senses in order to improve their functionality and more fully simulate the flavors of existing products.

Third, different types of technologies can be integrated to increase the reality of eating experiences. Overall, intersections between technology types are fragmented. Many studies have already established that VR is an effective tool to enhance perceived flavors. Those studies examine how environmental, particularly immersive 3D and/or VR, cues affect consumer preference and perception of different foods [4,18,108]. Such studies can combine their VR testing environments with hardware-based electric flavor simulators in order to create fuller eating experiences.

4.2   Gap Between Academia and Industry

In their preliminary review on multisensory technologies for flavor augmentation, Velasco et al. critically evaluate that a vast gap exists between HCI research and the industry [118]. Such technologies as those discussed are rarely introduced to the industry for commercial purposes, and the majority of the studies are one-off demonstrations of the technologies, lacking any prolonged development or considerations for long-term usage. Overall, our findings are aligned with this criticism.

Many of the studies present demonstrative technologies that are not readily applicable to the industry. Some technologies are, in fact, readily applicable, but they are not being utilized by practitioners. For instance, VR is a tool with the potential to overcome even the limitation of conventional sensory testing. Past research shows that sensory testing in either a conventional lab environment [52] or an unusual consumption environment [15] is a poor predictor of actual consumer satisfaction. VR can effectively address the issue by creating "naturalistic" contexts. Unfortunately, none of the practitioners in our interviews were considering using VR as a testbed, and to the best of our knowledge, the literature does not provide any case study of a food company actively adopting the reviewed technologies for consumer testing. One explanation for this is that the food industry has traditionally been a low-tech sector of incremental innovation rather than disruptive innovation [16,59]. Currently, all of the techniques in use identified in the interviews took the conventional form of sending samples and collecting sensory feedback remotely. Although there are a few emerging high-tech services that integrate machine learning, such as Flavorwiki (https://flavorwiki.com/), or matching algorithms, such as Sussio (https://www.sussio.com/), most of the services used by food companies are conventional tools such as social media or email lists. In fact, the only type of technology that shows convergence between our interview data and literature review is social media. Social media can certainly be useful, but the food industry can further benefit from adding the other virtual technologies reported in the review to their toolkit and combining them with existing tools.

5   Conclusion

The present study contributes to the literature by describing the current landscape of virtual food testing tools, summarizing the practical implications for future design of HFI, and highlighting the gaps, which serve as the future research agenda. We observed that current technologies are heavily focused on VR/AR solutions and flavor-simulating hardwares. However, the technologies are frequently siloed, leaving much room for cross-tech integration. The practical implications for practitioners reveal that the reviewed tools are certainly promising yet must overcome major hurdles prior to the food industry's adoption. Our literature review, in combination with the interview data, collectively points us to a gap between the industry and academia that must be bridged as we enter the new normal lifestyle shaped by the pandemic.

The present research, however, has some limitations. The dataset can be further validated by external researchers in the relevant academic communities. We plan to continue the research by informing ourselves of new studies in the field and correspondingly updating the dataset. Furthermore, the scope of the food industry that we look at can be broadened; most of the food companies recruited are small in size, and Small-to-Medium Enterprises (SMEs) tend to lack resources and expertise [32,55]. Big food corporations might be using virtual technologies more actively or even developing them internally. If so, more case studies on such companies are needed, and their findings should be analyzed for managerial implications for smaller companies.

A crisis like the pandemic is detrimental, but it can also be an impetus for major growth in the food industry [58]. Due to COVID-19, food companies now must seek virtual alternatives, such as a remote feedback gathering service or a new Direct-to-Consumer website. Though this change was certainly unexpected, those virtual options can open up new opportunities for practitioners. Furthermore, researchers can gain valuable insights into what virtual tools can and cannot do by observing practitioners in the field during this unprecedented pandemic. They can not only gather rich naturalistic data but also test a hypothesis of a new virtual tool. As more researchers address the future research agenda suggested in the present review, practitioners will be equipped with more effective tools for food testing, and researchers will be able to apply valuable user insights to their virtual solutions, thus establishing a symbiotic relationship between academia and industry.

Appendix

Complete list of search keywords: Consumer choice virtual, Consumer choice virtual food, Consumer psychology food feedback, Consumer testing technology, Customer feedback, Digital food sensory, HCI food, Human food interaction, Online food, Marketing, Social media, Technology food virtual, Virtual alternative, Virtual food, Virtual human food interaction, Virtual reality sensory, Virtual reality food, Virtual sensory food, Virtual food community, Virtual food future, Virtual flavor, Virtual food emotional responses, and Virtual food communication marketing.

References

1. Albert, A., Varela, P., Salvador, A., Hough, G., Fiszman, S.: Overcoming the issues in the sensory description of hot served food with a complex texture. application of qda® flash profiling and projective mapping using panels with different degrees of training. Food Qual. Prefer. **22**(5), 463–473 (2011)
2. Almarzooq, Z., Lopes, M., Kochar, A.: Virtual learning during the COVID-19 pandemic: a disruptive technology in graduate medical education (2020)
3. Altarriba Bertran, F., Jhaveri, S., Lutz, R., Isbister, K., Wilde, D.: Visualising the landscape of human-food interaction research. In: Proceedings of the 2018 ACM Conference Companion Publication on Designing Interactive Systems, pp. 243–248 (2018)
4. Ammann, J., Hartmann, C., Peterhans, V., Ropelato, S., Siegrist, M.: The relationship between disgust sensitivity and behaviour: a virtual reality study on food disgust. Food Quality Prefer. **80** (2020)
5. Ammann, J., Stucki, M., Siegrist, M.: True colours: Advantages and challenges of virtual reality in a sensory science experiment on the influence of colour on flavour identification. Food Quality Prefer. **86** (2020)
6. Andersen, I.N.S.K., Kraus, A.A., Ritz, C., Bredie, W.L.: Desires for beverages and liking of skin care product odors in imaginative and immersive virtual reality beach contexts. Food Res. Int. **117**, 10–18 (2019)
7. de Andrade, J.C., de Aguiar Sobral, L., Ares, G., Deliza, R.: Understanding consumers' perception of lamb meat using free word association. Meat Sci. **117**, 68–74 (2016)
8. Ares, G., Deliza, R.: Identifying important package features of milk desserts using free listing and word association. Food Qual. Prefer. **21**(6), 621–628 (2010)
9. Bangcuyo, R.G., Smith, K.J., Zumach, J.L., Pierce, A.M., Guttman, G.A., Simons, C.T.: The use of immersive technologies to improve consumer testing: The role of ecological validity, context and engagement in evaluating coffee. Food Qual. Prefer. **41**, 84–95 (2015)
10. Bernabéu, R., Tendero, A.: Preference structure for lamb meat consumers. A Spanish case study. Meat Sci. **71**(3), 464–470 (2005)

11. Bigne, E., Llinares, C., Torrecilla, C.: Elapsed time on first buying triggers brand choices within a category: a virtual reality-based study. J. Bus. Res. **69**(4), 1423–1427 (2016)
12. Bos, E., Owen, L.: Virtual reconnection: The online spaces of alternative food networks in england. J. Rural. Stud. **45**, 1–14 (2016)
13. Braun, M.H., et al.: Emotional priming of digital images through mobile telesmell and virtual food. Int. J. Food Des. **1**(1), 29–45 (2016)
14. Bressoud, E.: Testing FMCG innovations: experimental real store versus virtual. J. Prod. Brand Manage. (2013)
15. Cardello, A.V., Schutz, H., Snow, C., Lesher, L.: Predictors of food acceptance, consumption and satisfaction in specific eating situations. Food Qual. Prefer. **11**(3), 201–216 (2000)
16. Carlucci, D., Lerro, A., Muscio, A., Nardone, G., Dottore, A.: Understanding demand for innovation in the food industry. Measur. Bus. Excell (2010)
17. Cheah, C.S., et al.: Validation of a virtual reality buffet environment to assess food selection processes among emerging adults. Appetite 104741 (2020)
18. Chen, Y., Huang, A.X., Faber, I., Makransky, G., Perez-Cueto, F.J.: Assessing the influence of visual-taste congruency on perceived sweetness and product liking in immersive VR. Foods **9**(4), 465 (2020)
19. Cooper, R.G.: The new product process: an empirically-based classification scheme. R&D Manage. **13**(1), 1–13 (1983)
20. Crofton, E.C., Botinestean, C., Fenelon, M., Gallagher, E.: Potential applications for virtual and augmented reality technologies in sensory science. Innov. Food Sci. Emerg. Technol. **56** (2019)
21. Cruz, A., Green, B.G.: Thermal stimulation of taste. Nature **403**(6772), 889–892 (2000)
22. Cui, Y.: Examining farmers markets' usage of social media: an investigation of a farmers market facebook page. J. Agricult. Food Syst. Commun. Dev. **5**(1), 87–103 (2014)
23. De Bernardi, P., Bertello, A., Venuti, F.: Online and on-site interactions within alternative food networks: sustainability impact of knowledge-sharing practices. Sustainability **11**(5), 1457 (2019)
24. De Valck, K., Van Bruggen, G.H., Wierenga, B.: Virtual communities: a marketing perspective. Decis. Support Syst. **47**(3), 185–203 (2009)
25. Delarue, J., Brasset, A.C., Jarrot, F., Abiven, F.: Taking control of product testing context thanks to a multi-sensory immersive room. A case study on alcohol-free beer. Food Qual. Prefer. **75**, 78–86 (2019)
26. Ducrot, P., et al.: Impact of different front-of-pack nutrition labels on consumer purchasing intentions: a randomized controlled trial. Am. J. Prev. Med. **50**(5), 627–636 (2016)
27. Elder, R.S., Mohr, G.S.: The crunch effect: food sound salience as a consumption monitoring cue. Food Qual. Prefer. **51**, 39–46 (2016)
28. Eldesouky, A., Pulido, A., Mesias, F.: The role of packaging and presentation format in consumers' preferences for food: an application of projective techniques. J. Sens. Stud. **30**(5), 360–369 (2015)
29. Endo, H., Ino, S., Fujisaki, W.: The effect of a crunchy pseudo-chewing sound on perceived texture of softened foods. Physiol. Behav. **167**, 324–331 (2016)
30. Foster, D., Kirman, B., Linehan, C., Lawson, S.: The role of social media in artisanal production: a case of craft beer. In: Proceedings of the 21st International Academic Mindtrek Conference, pp. 184–193 (2017)

31. Gayler, T., Sas, C., Kalnikaite, V.: Taste your emotions: an exploration of the relationship between taste and emotional experience for HCI. In: Proceedings of the 2019 on Designing Interactive Systems Conference, pp. 1279–1291 (2019)
32. Gilmore, A., Carson, D., Grant, K.: SME marketing in practice. Mark. Intell. Plan. (2001)
33. Godoi, F.C., Prakash, S., Bhandari, B.R.: 3d printing technologies applied for food design: Status and prospects. J. Food Eng. **179**, 44–54 (2016)
34. Gouton, M.A., Dacremont, C., Trystram, G., Blumenthal, D.: Validation of food visual attribute perception in virtual reality. Food Qual. Prefer. 104016 (2020)
35. Grunert, K.G., van Trijp, H.C.: Consumer-oriented new product development. Encyclopedia Agricult. Food Syst. **2**, 375–386 (2014)
36. Grunert, K.G., Verbeke, W., Kügler, J.O., Saeed, F., Scholderer, J.: Use of consumer insight in the new product development process in the meat sector. Meat Sci. **89**(3), 251–258 (2011)
37. Hannum, M., Forzley, S., Popper, R., Simons, C.T.: Does environment matter? assessments of wine in traditional booths compared to an immersive and actual wine bar. Food Qual. Prefer. **76**, 100–108 (2019)
38. Hashimoto, Y., Inami, M., Kajimoto, H.: Straw-like user interface (II): a new method of presenting auditory sensations for a more natural experience. In: Ferre, M. (ed.) EuroHaptics 2008. LNCS, vol. 5024, pp. 484–493. Springer, Heidelberg (2008). https://doi.org/10.1007/978-3-540-69057-3_62
39. Hathaway, D., Simons, C.T.: The impact of multiple immersion levels on data quality and panelist engagement for the evaluation of cookies under a preparation-based scenario. Food Qual. Prefer. **57**, 114–125 (2017)
40. van Herpen, E., van den Broek, E., van Trijp, H.C., Yu, T.: Can a virtual supermarket bring realism into the lab? comparing shopping behavior using virtual and pictorial store representations to behavior in a physical store. Appetite **107**, 196–207 (2016)
41. van Herpen, E., Immink, V., van den Puttelaar, J.: Organics unpacked: the influence of packaging on the choice for organic fruits and vegetables. Food Qual. Prefer. **53**, 90–96 (2016)
42. Hirose, M., Iwazaki, K., Nojiri, K., Takeda, M., Sugiura, Y., Inami, M.: Gravitamine spice: a system that changes the perception of eating through virtual weight sensation. In: Proceedings of the 6th Augmented Human International Conference, pp. 33–40 (2015)
43. Huisman, G., Bruijnes, M., Heylen, D.K.: A moving feast: effects of color, shape and animation on taste associations and taste perceptions. In: Proceedings of the 13th International Conference on Advances in Computer Entertainment Technology, pp. 1–12 (2016)
44. Ikeno, S., Watanabe, R., Okazaki, R., Hachisu, T., Sato, M., Kajimoto, H.: Change in the amount poured as a result of vibration when pouring a liquid. In: Kajimoto, H., Ando, H., Kyung, K.-U. (eds.) Haptic Interaction. LNEE, vol. 277, pp. 7–11. Springer, Tokyo (2015). https://doi.org/10.1007/978-4-431-55690-9_2
45. Irwansyah, I., Triputra, P.: Indonesia gastronomy brand: netnography on virtual culinary community. Soc. Sci. **11**(19), 4585–4588 (2016)
46. Iwata, H., Yano, H., Uemura, T., Moriya, T.: Food simulator: a haptic interface for biting. In: IEEE Virtual Reality 2004, pp. 51–57. IEEE (2004)
47. Jacobsen, L.F., Tudoran, A.A., Lähteenmäki, L.: Consumers' motivation to interact in virtual food communities-the importance of self-presentation and learning. Food Qual. Prefer. **62**, 8–16 (2017)

48. Judacewski, P., Los, P.R., Lima, L.S., Alberti, A., Zielinski, A.A.F., Nogueira, A.: Perceptions of Brazilian consumers regarding white mould surface-ripened cheese using free word association. Int. J. Dairy Technol. **72**(4), 585–590 (2019)

49. Kendall, P.A., et al.: Observation versus self-report: validation of a consumer food behavior questionnaire. J. Food Prot. **67**(11), 2578–2586 (2004)

50. Koizumi, N., Tanaka, H., Uema, Y., Inami, M.: Chewing jockey: augmented food texture by using sound based on the cross-modal effect. In: Proceedings of the 8th International Conference on Advances in Computer Entertainment Technology, pp. 1–4 (2011)

51. Kong, Y., et al.: Virtual reality and immersive environments on sensory perception of chocolate products: a preliminary study. Foods **9**(4), 515 (2020)

52. Kozlowska, K., Jeruszka, M., Matuszewska, I., Roszkowski, W., Barylko-Pikielna, N., Brzozowska, A.: Hedonic tests in different locations as predictors of apple juice consumption at home in elderly and young subjects. Food Qual. Prefer. **14**(8), 653–661 (2003)

53. Kukko-Liedes, V., Mikkonen, M., Björklund, T.: Experimentation throughout the product development process-lessons from food and beverage ventures. In: Proceedings of the Design Society: International Conference on Engineering Design, vol. 1, pp. 1145–1154. Cambridge University Press (2019)

54. Ledoux, T., Nguyen, A.S., Bakos-Block, C., Bordnick, P.: Using virtual reality to study food cravings. Appetite **71**, 396–402 (2013)

55. Lee, K.S., Lim, G.H., Tan, S.J.: Dealing with resource disadvantage: generic strategies for SMES. Small Bus. Econ. **12**(4), 299–311 (1999)

56. Linnemann, A.R., Benner, M., Verkerk, R., van Boekel, M.A.: Consumer-driven food product development. Trends Food Sci. Technol. **17**(4), 184–190 (2006)

57. Lombart, C., Millan, E., Normand, J.M., Verhulst, A., Labbé-Pinlon, B., Moreau, G.: Effects of physical, non-immersive virtual, and immersive virtual store environments on consumers' perceptions and purchase behavior. Comput. Hum. Behav. 106374 (2020)

58. Macpherson, A., Herbane, B., Jones, O.: Developing dynamic capabilities through resource accretion: expanding the entrepreneurial solution space. Entrepreneur. Reg. Dev. **27**(5–6), 259–291 (2015)

59. Martinez, M.G., Briz, J.: Innovation in the Spanish food & drink industry. Int. Food Agribus. Manage. Rev. **3**(2), 155–176 (2000)

60. Maynes-Aminzade, D.: Edible bits: Seamless interfaces between people, data and food. In: Conference on Human Factors in Computing Systems (CHI 2005)-Extended Abstracts, pp. 2207–2210. Citeseer (2005)

61. Mehta, Y.D., Khot, R.A., Patibanda, R., Mueller, F.: Arm-a-dine: towards understanding the design of playful embodied eating experiences. In: Proceedings of the 2018 Annual Symposium on Computer-Human Interaction in Play, pp. 299–313 (2018)

62. Meißner, M., Pfeiffer, J., Peukert, C., Dietrich, H., Pfeiffer, T.: How virtual reality affects consumer choice. J. Bus. Res. **117**, 219–231 (2020)

63. Meißner, M., Pfeiffer, J., Pfeiffer, T., Oppewal, H.: Combining virtual reality and mobile eye tracking to provide a naturalistic experimental environment for shopper research. J. Bus. Res. **100**, 445–458 (2019)

64. Mitterer-Daltoé, M., Carrillo, E., Queiroz, M., Fiszman, S., Varela, P.: Structural equation modelling and word association as tools for a better understanding of low fish consumption. Food Res. Int. **52**(1), 56–63 (2013)

65. Mizdrak, A., Waterlander, W.E., Rayner, M., Scarborough, P.: Using a UK virtual supermarket to examine purchasing behavior across different income groups in the United Kingdom: development and feasibility study. J. Med. Internet Res. **19**(10) (2017)
66. de Morais, E.C., Lima, G.C., de Morais, A.R., Bolini, H.M.A.: Prebiotic and diet/light chocolate dairy dessert: chemical composition, sensory profiling and relationship with consumer expectation. LWT-Food Sci. Technol. **62**(1), 424–430 (2015)
67. Murray, J., Delahunty, C., Baxter, I.: Descriptive sensory analysis: past, present and future. Food Res. Int. **34**(6), 461–471 (2001)
68. Nakamura, H., Miyashita, H.: Augmented gustation using electricity. In: Proceedings of the 2nd Augmented Human International Conference, pp. 1–2 (2011)
69. Nakamura, H., Miyashita, H.: Development and evaluation of interactive system for synchronizing electric taste and visual content. In: Proceedings of the SIGCHI Conference on Human Factors in Computing Systems, pp. 517–520 (2012)
70. Nambu, A., Narumi, T., Nishimura, K., Tanikawa, T., Hirose, M.: Visual-olfactory display using olfactory sensory map. In: 2010 IEEE Virtual Reality Conference (VR), pp. 39–42. IEEE (2010)
71. Narumi, T.: Multi-sensorial virtual reality and augmented human food interaction. In: Proceedings of the 1st Workshop on Multi-sensorial Approaches to Human-Food Interaction, pp. 1–6 (2016)
72. Narumi, T., Nishizaka, S., Kajinami, T., Tanikawa, T., Hirose, M.: Augmented reality flavors: gustatory display based on edible marker and cross-modal interaction. In: Proceedings of the SIGCHI Conference on Human Factors in Computing Systems, pp. 93–102 (2011)
73. Narumi, T., Sato, M., Tanikawa, T., Hirose, M.: Evaluating cross-sensory perception of superimposing virtual color onto real drink: toward realization of pseudo-gustatory displays. In: Proceedings of the 1st Augmented Human International Conference, pp. 1–6 (2010)
74. Ng, K.H., Shipp, V., Mortier, R., Benford, S., Flintham, M., Rodden, T.: Understanding food consumption lifecycles using wearable cameras. Pers. Ubiquit. Comput. **19**(7), 1183–1195 (2015)
75. Nicola, M., et al.: The socio-economic implications of the coronavirus pandemic (covid-19): a review. Int. J. Surg. (London, England) **78**, 185 (2020)
76. Niijima, A., Ogawa, T.: Virtual food texture by electrical muscle stimulation. In: Proceedings of the 2016 ACM International Symposium on Wearable Computers, pp. 48–49 (2016)
77. Nishizawa, M., Jiang, W., Okajima, K.: Projective-AR system for customizing the appearance and taste of food. In: Proceedings of the 2016 workshop on Multimodal Virtual and Augmented Reality, pp. 1–6 (2016)
78. Nordbo, K., Milne, D., Calvo, R.A., Allman-Farinelli, M.: Virtual food court: a VR environment to assess people's food choices. In: Proceedings of the Annual Meeting of the Australian Special Interest Group for Computer Human Interaction, pp. 69–72 (2015)
79. Okajima, K., Spence, C.: Effects of visual food texture on taste perception. I-Perception **2**(8), 966–966 (2011)
80. Olsen, N.V., Christensen, K.: Social media, new digital technologies and their potential application in sensory and consumer research. Curr. Opin. Food Sci. **3**, 23–26 (2015)
81. Oomen, R.: The role of tasting in the purchasing process. In: BIO Web of Conferences, vol. 5, p. 03010. EDP Sciences (2015)

82. O'Hern, M.S., Rindfleisch, A.: Customer co-creation: a typology and research agenda. Rev. Mark. Res. **6**(1), 84–106 (2010)
83. Pallottino, F., et al.: Printing on food or food printing: a review. Food Bioprocess Technol. **9**(5), 725–733 (2016)
84. Peck, J., Childers, T.L.: To have and to hold: the influence of haptic information on product judgments. J. Mark. **67**(2), 35–48 (2003)
85. Pennanen, K., Närväinen, J., Vanhatalo, S., Raisamo, R., Sozer, N.: Effect of virtual eating environment on consumers' evaluations of healthy and unhealthy snacks. Food Qual. Prefer. **82** (2020)
86. Picket, B., Dando, R.: Environmental immersion's influence on hedonics, perceived appropriateness, and willingness to pay in alcoholic beverages. Foods **8**(2), 42 (2019)
87. Pinto, L.D.P.F., et al.: Understanding perceptions and beliefs about different types of fermented milks through the application of projective techniques: a case study using Haire's shopping list and free word association. J. Sens. Stud. **33**(3), e12326 (2018)
88. Piqueras-Fiszman, B., Velasco, C., Salgado-Montejo, A., Spence, C.: Using combined eye tracking and word association in order to assess novel packaging solutions: A case study involving jam jars. Food Qual. Prefer. **28**(1), 328–338 (2013)
89. Pizzi, G., Scarpi, D., Pichierri, M., Vannucci, V.: Virtual reality, real reactions?: Comparing consumers' perceptions and shopping orientation across physical and virtual-reality retail stores. Comput. Hum. Behav. **96**, 1–12 (2019)
90. Ploydanai, K., van den Puttelaar, J., van Herpen, E., van Trijp, H.: Using a virtual store as a research tool to investigate consumer in-store behavior. JoVE (J. Visual. Exper.) (125), e55719 (2017)
91. Prescott, J.: Multisensory processes in flavour perception and their influence on food choice. Curr. Opin. Food Sci. **3**, 47–52 (2015)
92. Ranasinghe, N., Jain, P., Karwita, S., Do, E.Y.L.: Virtual lemonade: Let's teleport your lemonade! In: Proceedings of the Eleventh International Conference on Tangible, Embedded, and Embodied Interaction, pp. 183–190 (2017)
93. Ranasinghe, N., Karunanayaka, K., Cheok, A.D., Fernando, O.N.N., Nii, H., Gopalakrishnakone, P.: Digital taste and smell communication. In: Proceedings of the 6th International Conference on Body Area Networks, pp. 78–84 (2011)
94. Ranasinghe, N., Lee, K.Y., Do, E.Y.L.: Funrasa: an interactive drinking platform. In: Proceedings of the 8th International Conference on Tangible, Embedded and Embodied Interaction, pp. 133–136 (2014)
95. Ranasinghe, N., Lee, K.Y., Suthokumar, G., Do, E.Y.L.: Virtual ingredients for food and beverages to create immersive taste experiences. Multimedia Tools Appl. **75**(20), 12291–12309 (2016)
96. Ranasinghe, N., Nakatsu, R., Nii, H., Gopalakrishnakone, P.: Tongue mounted interface for digitally actuating the sense of taste. In: 2012 16th International Symposium on Wearable Computers, pp. 80–87. IEEE (2012)
97. Ranasinghe, N., Nguyen, T.N.T., Liangkun, Y., Lin, L.Y., Tolley, D., Do, E.Y.L.: Vocktail: a virtual cocktail for pairing digital taste, smell, and color sensations. In: Proceedings of the 25th ACM International Conference on Multimedia, pp. 1139–1147 (2017)
98. Ranasinghe, N., Suthokumar, G., Lee, K.Y., Do, E.Y.L.: Digital flavor: towards digitally simulating virtual flavors. In: Proceedings of the 2015 ACM on International Conference on Multimodal Interaction, pp. 139–146 (2015)

99. Ranasinghe, N., Tolley, D., Nguyen, T.N.T., Yan, L., Chew, B., Do, E.Y.L.: Augmented flavours: Modulation of flavour experiences through electric taste augmentation. Food Res. Int. **117**, 60–68 (2019)
100. Rojas-Rivas, E., Espinoza-Ortega, A., Thomé-Ortiz, H., Moctezuma-Pérez, S.: Consumers' perception of amaranth in mexico. British Food J. (2019)
101. Sakurai, S., et al.: Mechanism of inhibitory effect of Cathodal current tongue stimulation on five basic tastes. In: 2016 IEEE Virtual Reality (VR), pp. 279–280. IEEE (2016)
102. Sakurai, S., Narumi, T., Ban, Y., Tanikawa, T., Hirose, M.: Calibratable: tabletop system for influencing eating behavior. In: SIGGRAPH Asia 2015 Emerging Technologies, pp. 1–3 (2015)
103. Samshir, N.A., Johari, N., Karunanayaka, K., David Cheok, A.: Thermal sweet taste machine for multisensory internet. In: Proceedings of the Fourth International Conference on Human Agent Interaction, pp. 325–328 (2016)
104. Schnack, A., Wright, M.J., Holdershaw, J.L.: Immersive virtual reality technology in a three-dimensional virtual simulated store: investigating telepresence and usability. Food Res. Int. **117**, 40–49 (2019)
105. Sester, C., et al.: "having a drink in a bar": an immersive approach to explore the effects of context on drink choice. Food Qual. Prefer. **28**(1), 23–31 (2013)
106. Siegrist, M.: Consumers' food selection behaviors in three-dimensional (3d) virtual reality. Food Res. Int. **117**, 50–59 (2019)
107. Sinesio, F.: Do immersive techniques help to capture consumer reality? Food Qual. Prefer. **77**, 123–134 (2019)
108. Sinesio, F., Saba, A., Peparaio, M., Civitelli, E.S., Paoletti, F., Moneta, E.: Capturing consumer perception of vegetable freshness in a simulated real-life taste situation. Food Res. Int. **105**, 764–771 (2018)
109. Speicher, M., Cucerca, S., Krüger, A.: Vrshop: a mobile interactive virtual reality shopping environment combining the benefits of on-and offline shopping. In: Proceedings of the ACM on Interactive, Mobile, Wearable and Ubiquitous Technologies, vol. 1, no. 3, 1–31 (2017)
110. Stelick, A., Penano, A.G., Riak, A.C., Dando, R.: Dynamic context sensory testing-a proof of concept study bringing virtual reality to the sensory booth. J. Food Sci. **83**(8), 2047–2051 (2018)
111. Suzuki, C., Narumi, T., Tanikawa, T., Hirose, M.: Affecting tumbler: affecting our flavor perception with thermal feedback. In: Proceedings of the 11th Conference on Advances in Computer Entertainment Technology, pp. 1–10 (2014)
112. Suzuki, E., Narumi, T., Sakurai, S., Tanikawa, T., Hirose, M.: Illusion cup: interactive controlling of beverage consumption based on an illusion of volume perception. In: Proceedings of the 5th Augmented Human International Conference, pp. 1–8 (2014)
113. Torres, F.R., Silva, H.L.A.D., Cutrim, C.S., Cortez, M.A.S.: Consumer perception of petit-suisse cheese: identifying market opportunities for the Brazilian dairy industry. Food Sci. Technol. (AHEAD) (2020)
114. Torrico, D.D., Han, Y., Sharma, C., Fuentes, S., Gonzalez Viejo, C., Dunshea, F.R.: Effects of context and virtual reality environments on the wine tasting experience, acceptability, and emotional responses of consumers. Foods **9**(2), 191 (2020)
115. Tsutsui, Y., Hirota, K., Nojima, T., Ikei, Y.: High-resolution tactile display for lips. In: Yamamoto, S. (ed.) HIMI 2016. LNCS, vol. 9735, pp. 357–366. Springer, Cham (2016). https://doi.org/10.1007/978-3-319-40397-7_34

116. Ung, C.Y., Menozzi, M., Hartmann, C., Siegrist, M.: Innovations in consumer research: the virtual food buffet. Food Qual. Prefer. **63**, 12–17 (2018)
117. Van Herpen, E., Yu, T., Van den Broek, E., Van Trijp, H.: Using a virtual grocery store to simulate shopping behaviour. In: Proceedings of the Measuring Behavior (2014)
118. Velasco, C., Obrist, M., Petit, O., Spence, C.: Multisensory technology for flavor augmentation: a mini review. Front. Psychol. **9**, 26 (2018)
119. Verhulst, A., Normand, J.M., Lombart, C., Moreau, G.: A study on the use of an immersive virtual reality store to investigate consumer perceptions and purchase behavior toward non-standard fruits and vegetables. In: 2017 IEEE Virtual Reality (VR), pp. 55–63. IEEE (2017)
120. Viana, M.M., Silva, V.L., Deliza, R., Trindade, M.A.: The use of an online completion test to reveal important attributes in consumer choice: An empirical study on frozen burgers. Food Qual. Prefer. **52**, 255–261 (2016)
121. Vidal, L., Ares, G., Giménez, A.: Projective techniques to uncover consumer perception: application of three methodologies to ready-to-eat salads. Food Qual. Prefer. **28**(1), 1–7 (2013)
122. Violante, M.G., Vezzetti, E., Piazzolla, P.: How to design a virtual reality experience that impacts the consumer engagement: the case of the virtual supermarket. Int. J. Interactive Des. Manuf. (IJIDeM) **13**(1), 243–262 (2019)
123. Waterlander, W., Ni Mhurchu, C., Steenhuis, I., Tang Rijeka, X.: The use of virtual reality in studying complex interventions in our every-day food environment. Virtual Real. Hum. Comput. Interact. **229**, 260 (2012)
124. Waterlander, W.E., Scarpa, M., Lentz, D., Steenhuis, I.H.: The virtual supermarket: an innovative research tool to study consumer food purchasing behaviour. BMC Public Health **11**(1), 589 (2011)
125. Waterlander, W.E., Steenhuis, I.H., de Boer, M.R., Schuit, A.J., Seidell, J.C.: The effects of a 25% discount on fruits and vegetables: results of a randomized trial in a three-dimensional web-based supermarket. Int. J. Behav. Nutr. Phys. Act. **9**(1), 11 (2012)
126. Waterlander, W.E., Steenhuis, I.H., de Boer, M.R., Schuit, A.J., Seidell, J.C.: Introducing taxes, subsidies or both: the effects of various food pricing strategies in a web-based supermarket randomized trial. Prev. Med. **54**(5), 323–330 (2012)
127. Waterlander, W.E., Jiang, Y., Steenhuis, I.H.M., Mhurchu, C.N.: Using a 3d virtual supermarket to measure food purchase behavior: a validation study. J. Med. Internet Res. **17**(4) (2015)
128. Waterlander, W.E., Mhurchu, C.N., Steenhuis, I.H.: Effects of a price increase on purchases of sugar sweetened beverages. results from a randomized controlled trial. Appetite **78**, 32–39 (2014)
129. Wei, J., Wang, X., et al.: Codine: an interactive multi-sensory system for remote dining. In: Proceedings of the 13th International Conference on Ubiquitous Computing, pp. 21–30 (2011)
130. Wills, B., Arundel, A.: Internet-enabled access to alternative food networks: a comparison of online and offline food shoppers and their differing interpretations of quality. Agric. Hum. Values **34**(3), 701–712 (2017)
131. Wosik, J., et al.: Telehealth transformation: COVID-19 and the rise of virtual care. J. Am. Med. Inform. Assoc. **27**(6), 957–962 (2020)
132. Yaremych, H.E., Kistler, W.D., Trivedi, N., Persky, S.: Path tortuosity in virtual reality: a novel approach for quantifying behavioral process in a food choice context. Cyberpsychol. Behav. Soc. Netw. **22**(7), 486–493 (2019)

133. Zampini, M., Spence, C.: The role of auditory cues in modulating the perceived crispness and staleness of potato chips. J. Sens. Stud. **19**(5), 347–363 (2004)
134. Zandstra, E., Kaneko, D., Dijksterhuis, G., Vennik, E., De Wijk, R.: Implementing immersive technologies in consumer testing: Liking and just-about-right ratings in a laboratory, immersive simulated café and real café. Food Quality and Preference, p. 103934 (2020)
135. Zhao, H., Huang, F., Spence, C., Wan, X.: Visual search for wines with a triangle on the label in a virtual store. Front. Psychol. **8**, 2173 (2017)

Modernizing Aircraft Inspection: Conceptual Design of an Augmented Reality Inspection Support Tool

Clay D. Killingsworth, Charis K. Horner, Stacey A. Sanchez,
and Victoria L. Claypoole^(✉) ⓘ

Design Interactive Inc., Orlando, FL 32817, USA
{Clay.Killingsworth,Charis.Horner,Stacey.Sanchez,
Victoria.Claypoole}@designinteractive.net

Abstract. Aircraft maintenance is critical to the Navy's fleet readiness, however, ongoing delays in completing maintenance tasks and increases in maintenance-related mishaps, highlight a need for improvement in the fleet's maintenance processes. Central to correcting the current maintenance shortfall is improving the training and support of maintenance personnel, as many transitioning experts are currently being replaced by junior, inexperienced maintainers. Augmented, virtual, and mixed reality (AR/VR/MR) – known collectively as extended reality (XR) – present a promising avenue by which to fill these skill and knowledge gaps. The present paper details the conceptual design of an AR-based operational support tool targeting point-of-need support during nondestructive inspection of aircraft, referred to as Augmented Reality Technician Inspection for Surface Anomalies and Noncompliance (ARTISAN). ARTISAN is an AR tool that provides step-wise information for inspection procedures and overlays augmented AI predictions regarding location of anomalies to enhance operational support. It also allows for the real-time, continuous capture of identified anomalies; using an AR head-worn device (HWD), maintainers are able to take first-person point of view media and geo-spatially tag surface anomalies, reducing ambiguity associated with anomaly detection and ultimately increasing readiness. The current article describes how ARTISAN was conceptualized, from initial solution to placement of augmented content to finalized system architecture. Finally, the article concludes with a discussion on how ARTISAN was optimized for the end-user through iterative user testing via remote platforms with Naval stakeholders, SMEs, and relevant end users.

Keywords: Job performance aid · Augmented Reality · Aircraft inspection

1 Introduction

Aircraft readiness is paramount to Naval Aviation, as apparent by a press release by Vice Adm. DeWolfe H. Miller, III, Commander, Naval Air Forces (CNAF): "…readiness is not where it needs to be for today's combat environment. Improving readiness remains

J. Y. C. Chen and G. Fragomeni (Eds.): HCII 2021, LNCS 12770, pp. 472–485, 2021.
https://doi.org/10.1007/978-3-030-77599-5_32

our main focus across the entire NAE-from leaders, to Sailors and Marines, to our civilian engineers and artisans, to our industry partners" (Naval Aviation News Public Affairs 2019). One significant area within aircraft maintenance is the inspection and repair of special coatings requiring precision and accuracy. Corrosion alone is responsible for more than 20% of the U.S. Navy's maintenance costs, accruing more than $8.5 billion annually (LMI 2018). A need exists to improve aircraft readiness and maintenance is a critical avenue for exploration. Recently, Naval aviation maintenance activities have been linked to increasing numbers of Class C mishaps. In fact, the number of Class C mishaps doubled between 2012 and 2018, and two thirds of Class C mishaps can be tied directly to maintenance (Eckstein 2018). Further, much of this can be traced back to less experienced maintainers conducting critical tasks. Another factor exacerbating the need for more experienced maintainers is the so-called 'Silver Tsunami' – where Baby Boomers are retiring at a rate faster than their expertise can be replenished (Claypoole et al. 2020). As the current workforce heads towards retirement, the silver tsunami has led to an increased number of junior technicians in need of support. This phenomenon is even more apparent in military maintenance due the high transition rates of maintainers. The result is clear; there is a need to improve the quality of maintenance activities through the support of maintenance personnel – especially in the domain of aircraft inspection.

1.1   Aircraft Inspection Use Case: Non-destructive Inspection

When discussing the quality of Naval Aviation maintenance activities, a key area of interest is Nondestructive Inspection (NDI). A specialty of the aircraft structural mechanics rate, NDI is a complex and ever improving area where sophisticated methods are used to verify component suitability while leaving them operable (Naval Air Force Atlantic Public Affairs 2016). NDI is the "most economical way of performing inspection and the only way of discovering defects [not visible to the naked eye]" (Stancu et al. 2011, p. 820). NDI has been consistently used since the 1950s and over the last seventy years has seen significant changes and enhancements to methodologies. In fact, NDI is considered to be "one of the fastest growing technologies from the standpoint of uniqueness and innovation" (Hellier 2013, p 1.1). This growth should be considered in light of NDI's expansiveness; in regard specifically to Naval Aircraft maintenance, NDI is done on 70%–80% of the aircraft.

Beyond visual inspection, five NDI methods are in use by the US Navy, including liquid penetrant, magnetic particle inspection, eddy current inspection, ultrasonic inspection, and radiographic inspection (Naval Air Force Atlantic Public Affairs 2016). Liquid Penetrant is a physical and chemical nondestructive procedure created to detect and expose surface connected discontinuities in nonporous engineering materials. A liquid is applied to components to expand the contrast between a discontinuity and its background (Stancu et al. 2011). The Magnetic Particle relies on "the principle that magnetic flux in a magnetized object is locally distorted by the presence of discontinuity. The distortion causes some of the magnetic field to exit and re-enter the object at the discontinuity" (Stancu et al. 2011, pp. 820–821). An electromagnet yoke is used to inspect irregular shaped parts for surface defects (Stancu et al. 2011). Eddy Current is used for "inspecting electrically conductive materials at very high speeds that [do] not require any contact between the test piece and the sensor" (García-Martín et al. 2011,

p. 2525). Ultrasonic NDI is used during in-service testing of aircraft structures when inspecting "for planar discontinuities lying parallel to the test surface" (Stancu et al. 2011, p. 821). Finally, Radiography applies x-rays and gamma-rays to a material, and in areas where thickness, density variations, or defects are present the rays are not homogeneously absorbed, an image is imprinted showing the defects (Lopez et al. 2018). Each of these methods involve the complex use of tools, experiential knowledge, and components and require experienced technicians to complete.

These methods in use by the US Navy, however, are not the only ones gaining popularity in modern times. Additional inspection innovation had led to advancements in the process and additional methods like Thermal Infrared Testing and Acoustic Emission Testing (Hellier 2013). As the process of NDI consistently advances, the equipment, procedures, methodologies, and knowledge necessary to conduct NDI gains complexity. This is emphasized by the importance of certification; NDI technicians not only need to be certified in NDI as a whole within the aircraft structural mechanics job area, but they also must be certified individually in each NDI method. This reinforces the complexity of the tasks at hand. Beyond this, it has been posited that the success and reliability of NDI is greatly dependent on the expertise and thoroughness of the technician conducting the inspection (Ahmad and Bond 2018). As the value of NDI is so intrinsically tied to technician expertise and thoroughness, it follows that technicians should be supported to the utmost while conducting these inspections to supplement their existing codified knowledge with tangible job support.

Despite this need and the continued investment and advancement of NDI methods, support for NDI practitioners remains surprisingly analog. Technicians chiefly rely on paper-based documents like Component Maintenance Manuals (CMM) issued by manufacturers (Kamsu Foguem 2012). Technicians may need multiple manuals, like the CMM, the manual explaining how to conduct the specific type of NDI, and the manual for the NDI equipment used. This means technicians must flip back and forth between multiple paper-based manuals while conducting NDI. This process can be cumbersome, as NDI methods themselves often involve physical interaction with components and equipment. Due to this, technicians often come to rely on existing knowledge through their training rather than reliance on official manual documentation. While technicians with years of experience often have this encoded knowledge to fall back on, not all technicians share this hard-earned tacit knowledge. This phenomenon is becoming increasingly pervasive with the rise of expert workers leaving the force – either through transition or retirement (Claypoole et al. 2020). With the inherent reliance on experiential knowledge within the conduct of NDI, this becomes a significant area in need of support. A need thus exists to modernize operational support for NDI technicians. Recent research has called for the use of innovative technologies, like Augmented Reality (AR), to fill this knowledge gap and provide next-generation operational support (Claypoole et al. 2020).

1.2 Augmented Reality (AR)

Augmented Reality (AR) is an experience in which the real environment is enhanced with computer-generated content, which can take the form of two- and three-dimensional objects, multimodal cues, and other digital entities seamlessly overlaid on the real world.

Typically, digitized AR content is tied to specific geo-spatial locations to provide spatially relevant information and contextualized content, allowing users to expand their perception and interaction capabilities in the real world (Izkara et al., 2007). Recently, AR has been used in military and commercial domains to support training and aid job performance (Claypoole et al. 2020). For maintenance contexts, AR has the capability to present step-by-step instructions overlaid onto relevant parts, components, and equipment. The benefits of AR are immense; reported maintenance benefits include reduced errors, execution time, downtime, and cost, as well as, increased productivity, efficiency, compliance, and readiness (Potter 2019). AR is a powerful emerging technology that can be used to support the reliability and maintainability of aviation assets that will directly reduce life cycle costs by augmenting manual operations. Based on these capabilities, it was postulated that AR could modernize and provide additional support to aircraft maintenance and inspection.

2   Modernizing Aircraft Inspection

Leveraging the innovating and empowering capabilities of AR, Augmented Reality Technician Inspection for Surface Anomalies and Noncompliance (ARTISAN) was conceptualized to modernize aircraft inspection. At its core, ARTISAN is an AR tool that provides stepwise information for inspection procedures and overlays augmented Artificial Intelligence (AI) predictions regarding location of anomalies to enhance operational support. ARTISAN allows for the real-time, continuous capture of identified anomalies. Using an AR head-worn device, maintainers are able to take first-person point of view media and geo-spatially tag surface anomalies. This AR captured material is then stored within a repository for expert NDI review, verification, and logging. Over time, this process leads to an organized catalog of historical data that can be used as input data needed for advanced predictive modeling and analyses, such as anomaly forecasting, as well as refresher training and job performance aids (JPAs). The following sections describe the ARTISAN capabilities as well as the conceptual design process taken to develop the solution.

2.1   ARTISAN

To use ARTISAN, technicians first open their AR device and search the content library for the appropriate inspection guide and JPA. The JPA presents AR-based step-wise information and assistance as technicians complete the NDI process. Technicians are presented step-by-step procedural guidance that includes pictures, videos, audio notes, holograms, and virtual models to assist the technicians as they complete the inspection. The AR overlays show contextually relevant information, such as where a step occurs and what tools are needed, that fully support the technician as they work. The AR capabilities display augmented content in the technicians' world view so that they can receive support spatially, in view, as opposed to flipping through one or more technical manuals – ultimately modernizing and simplifying their operational support.

To provide additional assistance, during the inspection, ARTISAN prompts the technicians to capture any additional AR content (e.g., pictures, videos, voice notes, etc.)

relevant to the anomaly they are inspecting. This capability allows for real-time enhancement during inspections, wherein technicians can digitally capture faults effectively during their inspection process. The real-time insight into identified anomalies through continuous capture and review can increase inspection efficiency by an estimated 30%. Moreover, by allowing maintainers across the enterprise to provide additional augmented media during their inspections, a database of historical data for inspection records is created, ultimately leading to improved aircraft readiness through records of aircraft state over time.

Once the maintainer has completed the inspection, the additional media captured during the session will be logged, reviewed, and approved by leadership or management. From there, it can be integrated into the aircraft's record and redistributed to the enterprise, where appropriate. By capturing and storing all relevant data associated with aircraft inspection, a catalog of historical data will be developed. This data is then used in predictive models to provide forecasting information on anomalies during future inspections. Therefore, ARTISAN provides not only augmented procedural support, it also supplies predictive AI analyses on where anomalies are likely to be detected – ultimately modernizing operational support for aircraft maintenance and inspection.

2.2 Conceptual Design

Product design encompasses all processes related to the conception, visualization, development, and refinement of a solution (French et al. 1985). The early, and most critical, stage of product design is conceptual design – where the major decisions on the product/solution are still being made (French et al. 1985). The conceptual design process discussed here takes a human factors engineering and cognitive approach to the conceptual design framework, which critically analyses usability, safety operability, and reliability of the system (Sun et al. 2018). Particularly, a heavy focus is applied to the interaction between the system and the end user to ensure an empowering end-result. The conceptual design process described herein discusses how the AR form factor for ARTISAN was selected, what front-end analyses were conducted, and how user-centered design principles were leveraged to optimize the solution.

Determining the AR Form Factor. Once the initial solution idea for ARTISAN was determined, the appropriate AR form factor had to be selected prior to the execution of user interface and user experience (UI/UX) explorations and other front-end analyses. Two approaches for AR displays exist: optical see-through and camera see-through. Optical see-through displays project virtual elements onto a display medium such as glass or plastic, allowing for interaction with both real and virtual objects, while camera see-through displays overlay virtual elements onto real-time video of the environment. While the latter may be more accessible, the greater potential of optical AR has led to more investment and development.

Camera See-Through Displays. As an emerging technology, AR would seem to be a universally expensive endeavor. However, many applications can be downloaded onto a tablet or smartphone and used right away. Smartphone or tablet applications are accessible ways to utilize AR. Users are likely to be familiar with the technology – 81% of

Americans currently own a smartphone (Pew Research Center 2020) – and may have already used AR apps from the consumer world. The learning curve, therefore, is likely to be shallower for smartphone-based AR than for head worn devices. Anecdotal evidence from the authors' initial studies of usability of AR devices, however, has suggested this learning curve may not be significantly lower in camera-see through than optical see-through devices, and may in fact, be higher. The prevalence of personal smartphones also facilitates rapid implementation of AR solutions throughout a company or industry, reducing the need for expensive and specialized hardware.

The potential utility of camera AR, however, is limited. The primary strength of AR lies in the user retaining the ability to see and interact with the physical environment; camera AR removes the user from reality by one degree and introduces potential sources of inefficiency. Streaming video may, even when not passed over a network, lag behind inputs by a perceptible amount. Such latency can lead to sim-sickness (Pausch et al. 1992) and is a more serious detractor from user experience in AR than all other factors combined (Brooks 1999; Holloway 1997). Minimizing the amount of sensory input that is vulnerable to latency issues is desirable, so perceiving the physical environment directly (i.e., optical AR) is preferable for applications requiring users to interact with the environment. Because the requirements of aircraft inspection include moving around an airframe and manipulation of inspection tools, AR aids will need to be low latency and primarily hands-free in operation, making camera AR solutions such as smartphones or tablets suboptimal.

Optical See-Through Displays. Optical see-through AR devices take many forms, but the central design of head-worn devices (HWD's) resembles goggles or glasses with computing hardware around the circumference of the head. HWD's may be self contained computers, as with the Microsoft HoloLens, or may be tethered to a computer as with many virtual reality (VR) devices. Due to the inherent mobility, hands free nature, and increased contextualization and perception of the physical environment, optical see-through AR is the preferred modality for ARTISAN. When introducing an AR headset to aircraft inspection technicians, however, careful attention must be taken to understand ergonomic considerations.

Numerous recommendations for the design and implementation of helmet-mounted devices (HMD's, e.g., night-vision goggles) have been identified. HWDs such as AR headsets require largely, though not wholly, the same considerations for their application. Of primary importance is the physical effect of wearing the hardware on the head and any discomfort or risk of injury it presents. Neck strain and injury is among the most prevalent occupational hazards for rotary-wing pilots, in part due to the weight of equipment worn on the head (van den Oord et al. 2010). Helmet-mounted night vision goggles have been shown to increase workload on muscles in the neck and upper back by shifting the head's center of mass (CM) up and forward relative to the biomechanical pivot point (the occipital condyles; Tai et al. 2010). This CM shift increases muscle demands on the neck erectors for the duration of wear, and this effect is exaggerated in postures which move the CM further forward, as when looking down, leaning, or lying prone. Increases of as little as 50 g in the weight of night-vision HMD's produce significantly greater muscle activation. Reducing this demand is desirable, and counterweights located at the back of the head have shown to effectively mitigate the increased muscular stress associated with head-mounted night vision goggles in pilots (Harrison et al. 2007). The Department of Defense's Design Criteria for Human Engineering, MIL-STD-1472G (Department of Defense 2019) indicates that equipment should be designed such that the weight of the load is distributed through as many muscle groups as possible. Melzer et al. (2009) similarly emphasize the importance of keeping the center of mass for the equipped head and the head alone as closely aligned as possible, as counterweighting measures are intended to do. However, postures which require tilting the head forward (e.g., inspecting objects below the visual horizon) may not show benefits of counterweighting (Harrison et al. 2016). The nature of aircraft NDI requires a variety of head postures, not limited to downward-looking orientations, and thus any HWD implemented in this context is likely to benefit from evenly distributing weight to minimize the demand placed on any one muscle group, such as found in the design of the Microsoft HoloLens 2.

In addition to the weight distribution of the HWD, the secureness of the headset fit and risk of transmitting outside forces to the user must be considered. MIL-STD-1472G (Department of Defense 2019) indicates that any helmet-mounted cables should not provide avenues to transmit unsafe loads to the head or neck of the wearer (e.g., Meta2 and MagicLeap). Standalone headsets – those which place all necessary hardware on the wearer's head – are thus preferable to tethered designs or those that spatially separate display and computing hardware and connect the two components via cable. Similarly, the headset itself should be adjustable to ensure proper fit for a variety of head sizes. Models which rely on elastic tension for fit adjustment, such as the BANC3 ThirdEye X2, present a risk of exerting undue pressure on sensitive areas of the head such as the temples, which is against MIL-STD-1472G recommendations (Department of Defense 2019).

Based on these considerations, the Microsoft Hololens 2 was selected as the AR form factor of choice for ARTISAN. The 2nd generation Microsoft HoloLens updates its predecessor from 2016 with a faster processor, more RAM, and higher-resolution options for still picture and video capture. It also adds an additional microphone to the original array of 4 in a bid to improve the device's environment monitoring and voice command functionality. Display characteristics are also substantially changed. The new generation utilizes a display aspect ratio of 3:2, considerably closer to square than the original 16:9 ratio. While 2D displays like TV's and computer monitors have progressively expanded in the horizontal plane, a more equal distribution between vertical and horizontal axes is better suited for AR applications because of their unique use cases. Expanding 2D displays horizontally produces less repetitive strain than expanding vertically, AR does not assume a stationary user in the way a desktop computer does. Software upgrades are likely the most notable changes for user experience. The HoloLens 2 has considerably more capable gesture tracking moving from the whole-hand tracking of the 1st generation to tracking of individual fingers. This not only improves responsiveness but affords a greater number and variety of gestures, moving toward more naturalistic interaction schemes.

Front-End Analyses. The front-end analysis for this conceptual design effort included a gap analysis, a task analysis, and developing personas for the intended end users. First, a gap analysis was conducted on existing aircraft and NDI inspection processes. The purpose of this gap analysis was to determine what gap exist for the current end users, where enhanced capabilities would be best leveraged, and how to best modernize operational support. From this analysis, it was determined that three main gaps exist within current aircraft inspection operational support. First, inspection procedure support aids need to be modernized past the current paper-based form factors. Digital and/or augmented content must be provided to technicians in order to enable hands-free usage of the support tool. Second, technicians need additional support during the actual anomaly capture process. Current job aids only provide procedural guidance, they do not offer any assistance in actually capturing, tagging, or locating faults and anomalies. Finally, technicians would be better supported if AI optimization provided guidance on the likelihood of an anomaly is present on the zones of the aircraft. Currently, technicians collect significant data that is filed away on a computer system. To truly modernize operational support, this collected data should be used to provide AI predictions on the likelihood of anomaly detection. This capability would aid the aircraft technicians as they executed the inspection. These three capabilities were identified as the major themes for ARTISAN. With respect to the conceptual design, themes are higher-level components that the solution must have to afford an innovative design that truly empowers the end user.

Once the major gaps to be solved by ARTISAN were identified, a task analysis was conducted to determine how technicians currently execute an inspection and what pain points and frustrations currently exist within these processes. Task analyses provide detailed descriptions of both physical and cognitive activities associated with task completion. They can reveal the complexity, requirements (e.g., physical requirements, environmental conditions, technological limitations, etc.), and unique constraints of the task. By conducting a task analysis, conceptual designers can better understand their users, the task requirements, and limitations to be overcome. The task analysis for aircraft inspection determined where, how, and to what extent the aforementioned themes could be implemented within an AR solution for aircraft inspection. Specifically, it was determined that capabilities, such as extensive voice commands, would need to be implemented in order to make the system more usable. As aircraft technicians typically use several pieces of equipment during an inspection, they need to be hands-free when using the AR device as to not constrain their tool usage.

To complete the front-end analysis, a user persona was created. The basic tenant of user centered design is to start with the user and build everything around their needs. However, a wide range of people with different, and sometimes competing, goals will interact with any given system. To capture and simplify the variety of end-users, user experience designers create an abstraction of these users called user personas. Through the process of user interviews, clear roles and user segments can be identified. Those end users that share similar objectives can be grouped together into a representative and fictional persona. The structure of a user persona is often as varied as the people they represent, but the core aspects of a persona are their name, demographics, technical skill level, end goals, and current impediments that prevent them from reaching those goals. With respect to the conceptual design process, these fictional personas will serve as a proxy for user experience designers to humanize and empathize – ultimately leading to a user-centric design and system image (Fig. 1).

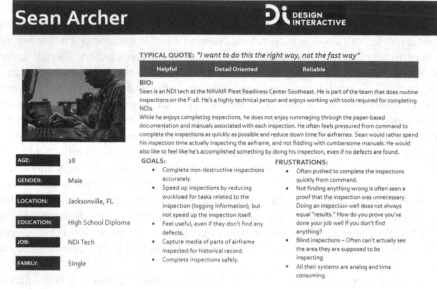

Fig. 1. Example User Persona for ARTISAN.

Based on the outcomes of the AR hardware analysis and the front-end analyses, the initial conceptual design of ARTISAN was created. The initial conceptual design included low- and high-fidelity wireframes and other system image documentations.

User Centered Principles. To enhance the initial conceptual design, User Centered Design (UCD) Principles and the Anthropomorphic and Cognitive Approaches to Human-Computer Interaction (HCI) Design were further examined and incorporated into the system image. For example, cognitive load (e.g., the amount of information able to be held in working memory, Sweller 2011) is minimized by requiring recognition rather than recall wherever possible. For example, system status, the current point in the procedure, and the tail number of the aircraft being serviced/inspected are perceptible at all times. Cognitive load is further minimized by non-textual indication of historical vs. new media when comparing in AR (hue/intensity of image shadow is used to distinguish old from new media). The universal option to "go back" allows users to (1) undo the last action or (2) reverse their previous navigation without requiring that they remember how they got there. Prompting is used to ensure that media is captured where appropriate (or predicted to be needed) (Fig. 2).

Two main approaches from HCI design were incorporated: Anthropomorphic and Cognitive. The anthropomorphic approach seeks to attribute human characteristics to nonhuman objects (Cuevas 2004). In particular, it is concerned with ensuring that the communication from the system to the user is a naturalistic as possible; it uses human to human communication patterns as the predominate model for human to system inter-action. The cognitive approach refers to ensuring that the user's cognitive resources are

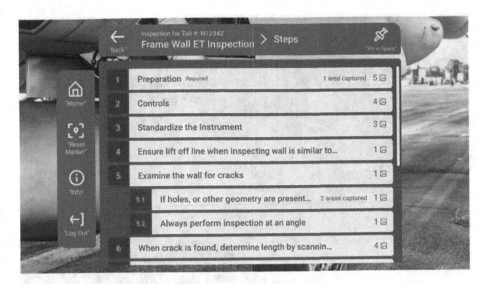

Fig. 2. Example of cognitive load reduction techniques within ARTISAN.

not overtaxed by using the system (Cuevas 2004). Principles and theories of perceptual processing, memory, and attention are leveraged to increase the efficiency associated with interacting with the system. The most common techniques associated with the cognitive approach include centering the interaction based on existing mental models and integrating metaphors and analogies into the solution to facilitate learnability and reduce abstraction.

Based on these approaches, it was determined that the system image should present affordances and constraints liberally throughout the process. This reduces the users' long-term memory and cognitive load, as the visual indications always let them know what they can and cannot do within the system. Additionally, metaphors and analogies are used throughout the system to more closely match the user's mental model and to reduce working memory. The metaphors and analogies used throughout the system allows users to match their mental representations with the system's image. For example, with respect to the conceptualized Continuous Capture capability, aircraft technicians currently use "Aircraft Approved Marking Devices", or Markers/Sharpies, to physically draw on the Aircraft to indicate an anomaly. To modernize this process and match the user's mental models, ARTISAN conceptualized an AR-based telestration process that used relevant icons and voice commands (i.e., Marker) that were analogous to the user's real-world actions (Fig. 3).

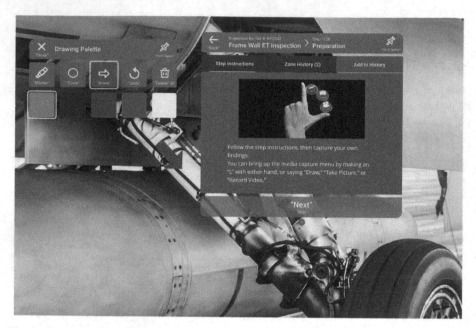

Fig. 3. Example of the "Aircraft Approved Marking Devices" mental model incorporated within ARTISAN.

3   Optimizing for the End User

User needs are a critical component of ensuring that the final solution and system are optimized for the end user. In the evaluation of user needs, the examined users were subject matter experts (SMEs) and the end users (aircraft inspection technicians). The user needs analysis was executed by conducting one-on-one semi structured interviews. When speaking with the SMEs, their needs centered on finding ways to allow maintainers to have proper inspection procedure knowledge. To allow maintainers to have the correct inspection procedure knowledge, the SMEs believes the system must be tailored to the specific inspection process. Some inspection processes can be difficult to complete, even for experienced maintainers, so giving maintainers assistance in conducting these procedures would improve aircraft turnaround. Feedback was also identified as an area of importance, as the system should allow for inspection managers to provide performance information to technicians so that technicians could understand if they correctly detected anomalies. The system should accommodate for engineers in the loop, so the information from the systems should go back to the engineers to review inspections and give feedback to the maintainers. Based on this feedback, these core capabilities were developed within the final system.

The aircraft inspection end users primarily wanted a system focused on reducing errors, validating mental models, and connecting the new systems with current tools and processes – all of which were already incorporated within the initial conceptual design. To reduce errors, ARTISAN uses a lightweight and hands-free AR system to use in tandem with their inspection tools. By keeping the technology hands-free and light, it allows technicians to keep situational awareness and not have difficulty conducting inspections on aircraft. Moreover, technicians often must crawl into tight spots while conducting inspections, and therefore the technology must be portable and not handheld. To validate mental models, ARTISAN has the ability to map the standards to the actual aircraft by overlaying inspection zones. By creating an overlay, it allows for technicians to be able to better see the areas of the aircraft they need to focus on for inspection. These identified user needs were incorporated in the final conceptual design and system image.

Once finalized, both the conceptual design and resulting system image was reviewed with representative end users and informal usability testing was conducted. Qualitative one-on-one semi structured interview questions were administered to representative end users after the completion of the prototype demonstration. Feedback was solicited and incorporated into the final design of ARTISAN. Overall, representative end user and SME feedback was collected early and often throughout the conceptual design process to ensure that ARTISAN provided true benefit to aircraft inspection and empowered the end users. The resulting ARTISAN system was a modernized operational support tool that utilized AR capabilities to present procedural information in a spatialized content and present AI predictions on anomaly locations.

4 Conclusions

NDI is a critical maintenance activity to enable aircraft readiness, but the existing processes to support technicians are due for modernization. A need exists to provide a sophisticated JPA to aircraft inspection technicians to enable efficient inspection procedures. Additionally, organizations need a way to harness the critical information found during NDI inspections to introduce efficiencies and optimize NDI processes through AI predictive analytics. Designed for Nondestructive Inspection (NDI) maintainers who require high levels of precision and accuracy, ARTISAN is an AR JPA providing stepwise information for inspections. ARTISAN reduces ambiguity associated with anomaly detection and is expected to result in a 30% increase in efficiency during NDI inspections. A software solution grounded in Sailor-centric design, ARTISAN provides: 1) Continuous inspection record capture, 2) An up-to-date repository of historical data, and 3) AI insights and optimization. The conceptual design process described here provides a baseline framework for how to integrate human factors and cognitive science principles into the design and development of operational support tools. The outcome of this process was an innovative and modernized solution that is aimed at empowering the end users.

References

Ahmad, A., Bond, L.: J Reliability of Flaw Detection by Nondestructive Inspection (2018). https://dl.asminternational.org/handbooks/book/55/chapter-abstract/650537/Reliability-of-Flaw-Detection-by-Nondestructive?redirectedFrom=fulltext

Boff, K.R., Lincoln, J.E. (eds.): User's Guide Engineering Data Compendium: Human Perception and Performance. Armstrong Aerospace Medical Research Laboratory (1988)

Brooks, F.P.: What's real about virtual reality? IEEE Comput. Graph. Appl. 12 (1999)

Claypoole, V.L., Stanney, K.M., Padron, C.K., Perez, R.: Enhancing Naval Enterprise Readiness through Augmented Reality Knowledge Extraction. In: Proceedings of the Interservice/Industry Training, Simulation, and Education Conference (I/ITSEC) Annual Meeting, Orlando, FL (2020)

Cuevas, H.M.: An illustrative example of four HCI design approaches for evaluating an automated system interface. In: Proceedings of the Human Factors and Ergonomics Society Annual Meeting, vol. 48, no. 5, pp. 892–896. SAGE Publications, Los Angeles (2004)

Department of Defense. Design Criteria Standard for Human Engineering [MIL-STD-1472G_CHG-1] (2019). http://everyspec.com/MIL-STD/MIL-STD-1400-1499/MIL-STD-1472G_CHG-1_56051/

Eckstein, M.: Less Experienced Maintainers Contribute to Rise in Naval Aviation Mishaps (2018). https://news.usni.org/2018/06/22/less-experienced-maintainers-contribute-rise-naval-aviation-mishaps

French, M.J., Gravdahl, J.T., French, M.J.: Conceptual Design for Engineers. Design Council, London (1985)

García-Martín, J., Gómez-Gil, J., Vázquez-Sánchez, E.: Non-destructive techniques based on eddy current testing. Sensors (Basel, Switzerland), 11(3), 2525–2565 (2011). https://doi.org/10.3390/s110302525

Harrison, M.F., Forde, K.A., Albert, W.J., Croll, J.C., Neary, J.P.: Posture and helmet load influences on neck muscle activation. Aerospace Med. Hum. Perform. 87(1), 48–53 (2016). https://doi.org/10.3357/AMHP.4301.2016

Harrison, M.F., Neary, J.P., Albert, W.J., Veillette, D.W., McKenzie, N.P., Croll, J.C.: Physiological effects of night vision goggle counterweights on neck musculature of military helicopter pilots. Mil. Med. 172(8), 864–870 (2007). https://doi.org/10.7205/MILMED.172.8.864

Hellier, C.J.: Handbook of Nondestructive Evaluation (2013). https://www.accessengineeringlibrary.com/binary/mheaeworks/bfbbb83568319de5/7834db859fc583ea6210e585c3ce400f74ce eee5a08ee6852d8b8ecea1db0507/book-summary.pdf

Holloway, R.L.: Registration error analysis for augmented reality. Presence: Teleoper. Virt. Enviro. 6(4), 413–432 (1997). https://doi.org/10.1162/pres.1997.6.4.413

Huang, T.-L., Liao, S.: A model of acceptance of augmented-reality interactive technology: the moderating role of cognitive innovativeness. Electron. Comm. Res. 15(2), 269–295 (2014). https://doi.org/10.1007/s10660-014-9163-2

Izkara, J. L., Pérez, J., Basogain, X., & Borro, D. Mobile augmented reality, an advanced tool for the construction sector. (2007).

Kamsu Foguem, B.: Knowledge-based support in Non-Destructive Testing for health monitoring of aircraft structures. Adv. Eng. Inform. 26, 859–869 (2012)

Lopez, A., Bacelar, R., Pires, I., Santos, T.G., Sousa, J.P., Quintino, L.: Non-destructive testing application of radiography and ultrasound for wire and arc additive manufacturing. Addit. Manuf. 21, 298–306 (2018)

Melzer, J.E., Brozoski, F.T., Letowski, T.R., Harding, T.H., Rash, C.E.: Guidelines for HMD design: (614362011–018). Am. Psychol. Assoc. (2009). https://doi.org/10.1037/e614362011-018

Naval Air Force Atlantic Public Affairs: Checking for Integrity: Non-destructive Inspection Technicians (2016). https://navalaviationnews.navylive.dodlive.mil/2016/04/04/checking-for-integrity-non-destructive-inspection-technicians/

Naval Aviation News Public Affairs. Air Boss on Readiness Reform (2019). https://www.navy.mil/submit/display.asp?story_id=109434

Nilsson, N.C.: Perceptual illusions and distortions in virtual reality. Encyclopedia Comput. Graphics Games (2018). https://doi.org/10.1007/978-3-319-08234-9_245-1

Pausch, R., Crea, T., Conway, M.: A literature survey for virtual environments: Military flight simulator visual systems and simulator sickness. Presence: Teleoper. Virt. Environ. **1**(3), 344–363 (1992)

Pew Research Center: Demographics of Mobile Device Ownership and Adoption in the United States | Pew Research Center. (n.d.). https://www.pewresearch.org/internet/fact-sheet/mobile/. Accessed 4 Sept 2020

Potter, K.: Augmented Reality becoming a focus in maintenance technology. Geopspacial World, Jan 2019. https://www.geospatialworld.net/blogs/augmented-reality-becoming-a-focus-in-maintenance-technology/

Stancu, C., Grigore, E., Stoian, D., Dumitru, A.: Integration of nondestructive testing in aircrafts maintenance. International Conference of Scientific Paper (2011)

Sun, H., Ma, P., Liu, X., Tian, W., Qiu, S., Su, G.: Conceptual design and analysis of a multipurpose micro nuclear reactor power source. Ann. Nucl. Energy, **121**, 118–127 (2018)

Sweller, J.: Cognitive load theory. In: Psychology of learning and motivation, vol. 55, pp. 37–76. Academic Press (2011)

Tai, H.-S., Lee, Y.-H., Kuo, C.-L., Liu, B.-S.: Effects of postures and wearing night vision goggle on EMG activities in Upper Neck and Trapezius. In: Proceedings of the 6th World Congress of Biomechanics (WCB 2010), vol. 31, pp. 71–74. (2010). https://doi.org/10.1007/978-3-642-14515-5_19

van den Oord, M.H.A.H., De Loose, V., Meeuwsen, T., Sluiter, J.K., Frings-Dresen, M.H.W.: Neck pain in military helicopter pilots: prevalence and associated factors. Mil. Med. **175**(1), 55–60 (2010). https://doi.org/10.7205/MILMED-D-09-00038

Yung, R., Khoo-Lattimore, C.: New realities: a systematic literature review on virtual reality and augmented reality in tourism research. Curr. Issues Tourism **22**(17), 2056–2081 (2019). https://doi.org/10.1080/13683500.2017.1417359

LMI Estimated Impact of Corrosion on Cost and Availability of DoD Weapon Systems FY18 Update Report SAL62T1 (2018). https://www.corrdefense.org/static/media/content/11393.000.00T1-March2018-Ecopy.pdf

The Potential of Augmented Reality for Remote Support

Stefan Kohn$^{(\boxtimes)}$ (iD) and Moritz Schaub (iD)

FOM Hochschule Für Oekonomie and Management Gemeinnützige Gesellschaft mbH,
Leimkugelstraße 6, 45141 Essen, Germany
stefan.kohn@fom-net.de

Abstract. This paper addresses the question whether an AR enabled remote service based on standard hardware offers benefits for remote support or not. To answer this question a lab experiment has been conducted with 66 participants to examine the current potential of AR for field service tasks. The authors compare the productivity of a pure video-based remote support system with the productivity of an AR enabled remote support system. The AR system offers real-time video sharing and additionally virtual objects that can be used by the remote experts as "cues" to guide the field engineer. Thirdly a system consisting of a head mounted display with cues has been tested. The results of the lab experiment show that the guided engineers could clearly benefit from AR based remote support. Nevertheless, the influence of both the engineer's prior skillset as well as the remote experts' ability to instruct is bigger than of the deployed tool.

Keywords: Augmented Reality · Lab experiment · Remote support

1 Introduction

1.1 Background

Having expertise knowledge readily available independent of the location of the experts offers benefits for field service tasks like maintenance, repair, or installation jobs. Experts do not need to travel which safes travel costs and time.

This idea of remote support is not new. While remote phone support is nowadays the norm, remote video support is growing. Augmented Reality (AR) might improve the quality as well as the potential areas of applicability even further [11]. AR is defined in this paper based on Azuma's [1] definition as systems that fulfill the following three criteria:

- Combination of real and virtual objects
- real-time interaction and
- real and virtual objects are related which each other.

J. Y. C. Chen and G. Fragomeni (Eds.): HCII 2021, LNCS 12770, pp. 486–498, 2021.
https://doi.org/10.1007/978-3-030-77599-5_33

While Azuma points out that AR systems can address all human senses, we focus in this paper on visual augmentation only.

The concept of remote support enabled by AR technology has already been around since several years. An early prototype had been realized in 1993 [4]. There are several studies on the deployment of AR in industries: as approach for the remote support in the automotive industry [10], the maintenance of aircrafts [2] as well as support for shipbuilder operators [5]. Nevertheless, almost 30 years after the initial research of Feiner [4] there is no broad application of AR in the field of industrial support, yet.

Gartner even predicts that AR technology needs another 5 to 10 years to reach its plateau of productivity [6]. On the other hand, we see widespread availability of AR-capable hardware in the market. Almost all new smartphones include the necessary sensors and processing power.

1.2 Results and Analysis of Recent Studies

The current state of AR remote support has been analyzed by Masood & Egger in an experiment for guided assembly using the Microsoft HoloLens and an AR guided construction task. This research compared the task-completion-time and the task-load of the candidates [3, 9].

As the employed high-end AR-glass utilized for the experiment, might not be suitable for harsh industrial environments and will not comply with work safety regulations [7,8] the authors wanted to examine the potential of AR support utilizing hardware that is readily available for field service tasks.

1.3 Research Gap and Research Question

Based on the past research of Masood & Egger [9] the question arises whether an AR enabled remote service based on standard hardware offers benefits for remote support or not.

To answer this question the productivity of a pure video-based remote support system needs to be compared with the productivity of an AR enabled remote support system. The AR system offers real-time video sharing, and additionally virtual objects that can be used by the remote experts as "cues" to guide the field engineer. These cues will be called "virtual cues" in the following. Ideally those cues are persistent in space, i.e., do not change their position relative to the physical objects. In this case we call them "persistent virtual cues".

Additionally, existing literature does not quantify or rank the potential impact of AR compared to other influence factors like existing knowledge of the field engineer or the remote expert.

Besides the general applicability of AR for remote support applications the authors wanted to identify existing challenges and success factor for real-world deployment.

2 Methodology

2.1 Research Design

The goal of this research is to evaluate the benefit of real-life deployments of AR-based remote support in comparison with standard video-based remote support. Additionally, the impact of prior knowledge of the field engineer as well as the remote expert should be examined.

For the research design the following elements had to be considered and defined:

- Task: What is the challenge to be solved remotely?
- Remote expert: Who are the experts, who support from the distance with advanced knowledge?
- Field engineer: Who requires additional support for the completion of a task in the field?
- Communication tool: What is the technology employed for guiding the field engineer by the remote expert?
- Goal measurement: What is the success measurement to judge the impact of the different variables?

The highest external validity could be achieved through a field study, but initial tests showed, that the reproducibility of the remote support sessions would be quiet challenging. Especially the uncontrollable variety of tasks would hinder the comparability. Therefore, the research has been designed as a lab experiment with the following elements ensuring a controlled environment and thus a high internal validity.

Task: The construction of a Lego model seemed suitable, as the manual could be used by the remote expert, whereas the construction parts were at the participant's side.

Remote Experts: Three instructors with expert knowledge had been chosen for the guidance of the task. The remote experts had prior experience with Lego and had been qualified as they built the model on their own. Furthermore, they instructed at least two candidates through the building sequence before the start of the measured experiments.

Field Engineers: The field engineers are represented by the participants of the research; each participant was given an unknown assembly task to be fulfilled, with the guidance of a remote expert.

Communication Tool: The communication in-between candidates and remote experts has been conducted with different tools, providing a voice call with video functionality. The utilized hardware and the usage of visual cues distinguishes the groups:

1. **Research group A: Video call on iPad.** Skype has been chosen as a reference tool for video communication tools. Video call technology also represents the current baseline, as it has reached an ubiquitarian level, being supported by various messenger such as FaceTime, WhatsApp Messenger, and others. As a hardware an iPad had been chosen. Figure 1 shows the set-up with one field engineer. The video stream of the iPad's camera was transmitted to the instructor while they initiated a voice call. As shown in Fig. 1 the iPad had been standing elevated in-between candidate and assembly parts ensuring high visibility for the remote experts. Candidates also had the possibility to freely move the iPad if necessary – for example to search for a specific part in the pile.

Fig. 1. Setup of research group A: basic video call with an instructor

2. **Research group B: Video call on iPad with persistent visual cues.** Candidates of the second research group were using a similar experimental setup as research group A. But instead of Skype the application TeamViewer Pilot was used, allowing the instructors to place visual annotations in the video view of the candidates. Those annotations stay persistently at their location, also when the device is being moved by the candidates. These persistent visual cues therefore stand for the visual AR support. An example of the annotations used is shown in Fig. 2. The instructor highlighted required parts with numbered arrows and drew their placement on to the model. Those visual cues were individually placed by the remote expert to facilitate sequences, afterwards they were manually deleted by the remote expert.

Fig. 2. Setup of research group B: Visual annotations highlight the construction procedure

Fig. 3. Setup of research group C: The RealWear provides a head worn display and camera. Additionally, a screenshot of the display is shown in the center.

3. **Research group C: Video call on RealWear glasses with visual cues.** In the third research group instead of an iPad a head mounted display (HMD) with camera had

been used with Oculavis Share software. Figure 3 shows two candidates wearing the RealWear glasses. The display is positioned in front of one eye of the participants. The live camera view is displayed, enriched with highlights positioned by the instructor. These visual cues therefore stand for the visual AR support. Unlike the persistent annotations utilized in research group B, the markings did not stick to the physical objects and vanished seconds after being placed. In combination with the head's movement, this limits the clear mapping of the markings.

As head mounted devices are not as common as tablets the field engineers needed to be prepared before the tests. On the one hand side the RealWear required time to set up the device for each individual candidate. On the other hand, the candidates had additional time to familiarize with the head worn display before the start of the experiment.

Goal Measurement: The goal for each participant of the research groups was to complete the Lego model within 30 min as far as possible. Previous test with the instructors indicated that the full construction would not be feasible within this time frame; most of the pretest-candidates could only finish half of the task.

The experimental setup also mimicked the real nature of remote support, as the remote experts were at home guiding the candidates in a different physical location.

2.2 Data Collection

Besides the control variables (age, professional background), the prior Lego experience of the field engineer as well as the assigned remote expert had been recorded. The construction progress was evaluated with a dedicated score which represented the number of parts assembled within the 30 min time frame. The candidates documented their progress on a questionnaire as well as the additional information that characterized the participants.

After the experiment, participants evaluated their experience based on the raw *NASA-Taskloadindex (NASA-TLX)* and gave a qualitative feedback with a questionnaire as well.

2.3 Sample and Sample Size

The experiment has been executed with a total of 66 candidates[1]. The sample characteristics are shown in Table 1. From the 66 participants 30 had a professional background as field engineers, 36 had different, non-technical professions. The group represented various ages as well as different level of experiences with Lego and/or similar construction activities.

The candidates were randomly and equally divided between the three experimental groups and remote experts as shown in Table 2.

---

[1] Two additional experiments had been excluded, as they could not be completed to the set standards.

Table 1. Overview on the participants and their characteristics

	Field Engineer	Other profession	Total
Participants	30	36	66
Age			
Under 26	7	16	23
26–40	10	11	21
41–55	7	7	14
Over 55	6	2	8
Prior experience of candidates			
Beginner	4	8	12
Average	23	17	39
Advanced	3	17	15

Table 2. Distribution of research groups and instructors

	Research Group A: Video	Research Group B: Video with persistent cues	Research Group C: Video with cues on HMD	Total
Remote expert 1	8	7	7	22
Remote expert 2	7	8	7	22
Remote expert 3	7	7	8	22
Total	22	22	22	66

3   Results and Analysis

3.1   Raw Data

After the execution of the experiments, a dataset of 66 valid experiments had been collected. The dependent variable *progress* is the key metric of this research, additionally the *NASA-TLX* has been collected. Table 3 shows an overview of the dependent factors.

Table 3. Overview of key metrics and statistics

	Min	Mean	Max	Std Dev
Progress	65,00	135,07	206,50	34,60
NASA-TLX cumulative	42,09	44,50	75,00	16,73

Initially the *progress* was planned to be measured on a scale from 0 to 177 points. Candidates reaching 177 would fully complete the construction of the Lego model. As it turned out there were 9 candidates which completed the construction progress in less than 30 min. Therefore, the scale for *progress* has been extended through extrapolation: For each minute which was left after completion of the build, additional 177: 30 = 5,9 points have been added to the overall *progress*.

A closer examination of the 9 candidates that completed the task shows, that all of them were either guided by the same remote expert and/or had advanced prior knowledge.

3.2 General Findings: Influencing Factors

Based on the collected data the influence of the independent variables has been analyzed using a multilinear regression. The overall quality of the model is high, the p-values of the variables proof the significance of the model (Table 4).

Table 4. Linear regression for the task progress

Variable	Coefficient	Standard error	t-value	$P > |t|$
Research group	12,6799	3,5972	3,5249	0,0008 **
Remote expert	20,4297	3,976	5,1382	2,90E−6 **
Participants prior experience	32,8758	4.0602	8.0971	2,41E−11 **
Multiple R-Squared: 0.9582 Adjusted R-Squared: 0.9562	** P < 0,001			

Based on these results it becomes visible that both the prior experience of the field engineer and the guidance of the instructors have a higher impact, then the utilized communication tool. These factors will be analyzed in detail in the following.

3.3 Prior Knowledge of Participants

Previous experience refers to the candidate's judgement regarding their skills with Lego and similar assembly tasks. As seen in the analysis of the independent factors in Table 4, previous experience of our participants had the highest impact on the task progress. To further analyze this factor Fig. 4 shows a comparison of the task progress for the different skill levels: candidates with prior *advanced* knowledge performed better. Candidates which rated themselves as *average* and *beginner* showed no significant difference in progress. Therefore, these datasets will be merged and jointly analyzed as *non-advanced* and compared to the *advanced* candidates.

Our statistical analysis (p-value < 0,001) shows that *advanced* prior experience of our participants has a significant influence on the progress. Contrary to the initial assumption, actually 9 out of the 15 candidates with *advanced* prior knowledge finished the model in 30 min or faster. In fact, *advanced* prior knowledge of the participants has such a high positive influence on the result of the experiment, that the other factors do not show significant influence any more for the advanced participants. However, as the sample size of those candidates is small (15 candidates), further analysis will focus on candidates with *non-advanced* prior experience only.

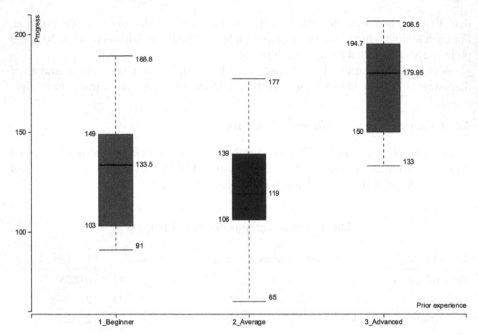

Fig. 4. Comparison of the task progress based on the participants prior experience.

3.4 Guidance of the Remote Experts

Although the remote experts had been carefully chosen and qualified in both the guidance of the specific task as well as the efficient usage of the tools, the remote experts impacted the results of the experiment.

Analysis of the data reveals a significant effect on the task progress: on the one hand based on the individual learning curve of the instructors, on the other hand based on the different skill level of the instructors.

Learning Effect Over the Course of the Experiments. During the course of the experiment, every remote instructor explained the same construction sequence repeatedly more than 22 times. When analyzing the data, a clear learning effect becomes visible as the task progress grows higher over time. The graph in Fig. 5 shows the progress of the conducted experiments over time. The values of candidates with *advanced* prior experience have been excluded. The regression line highlights the trend of the progress increase over time.

The graph indicates an improvement of the instructor's ability to guide the construction. Their remote directions seem to become more efficient, which allowed the candidates to accomplish the task quicker. Therefore, a learning effect can be assumed.

Different Levels of Guidance. Figure 6 compares the progress based on the three remote experts. When comparing the boxplot of the instructors, the progress of remote expert 3 is much higher. A test was performed (see Table 5), which validated that the difference is significant. Therefore, it can be stated, that the skillset of the remote expert impacts the candidate's progress.

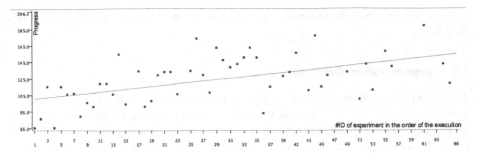

Fig. 5. Task progress on a timeline (without candidates with *advanced* prior experience).

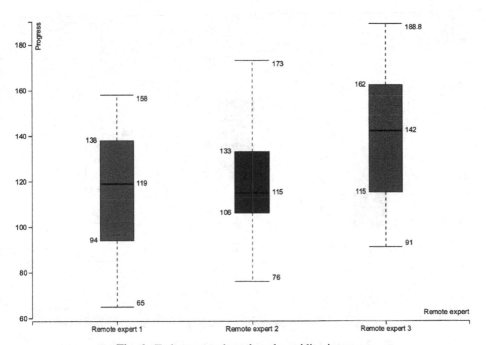

Fig. 6. Task progress based on the guiding instructor

Table 5. T-test results of the guiding remote experts

Progress	Expert 1 Expert 3	Expert 3 Expert 2	Expert 2 Expert 1
T-Test	0,0148 p *	0,0333 p *	0,5709 p
* p < alpha 0,05			

Furthermore, the frustration level – measured by the *NASA-TLX* – of the candidates guided by this remote expert was significant lower (p < 0,1). This indicates that the individual guidance of the instructors impacts both the task progress and the candidate's well-being.

3.5 Communication Technology

As shown in Fig. 7 the average task progress was the lowest in research group A using the standard video call only and the highest for research group B using the video transmission with persistent visual cues. The comparison reveals a significant gain in productivity of research group B (see Table 6). Although the average task progress in research group C is higher than in group A, the difference was not significant.

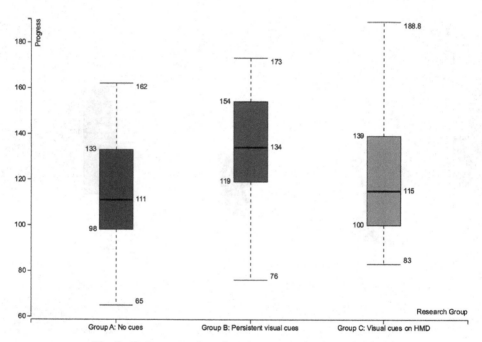

Fig. 7. Task progress based on the communication technology

When comparing the NASA-TLX there were no significant results in-between the research groups.

The findings indicate that persistent visual cues have the potential to improve the productivity of remote support tasks. Nevertheless, the overall progress of candidates using the RealWear is not significant higher.

Based on the candidate's feedback of research group C, the RealWear was not well perceived, furthermore the visual cues were hardly helpful. Especially the monocular display which was positioned in front of one eye was difficult to see. It required time for the candidates to habituate to look through the small display while working on the task. As the visual cues of this research group did not support persistent positioning, the markings moved with the candidate's head movement and did not stick to real objects.

Table 6. T-test results of the research groups

	Group A: No cues Group B: Persistent cues	Group A: No cues Group C: Cues on HMD	Group B: Persistent cues Group C: Cues on HMD
Progress			
T-Test	0,0449 p *	0,4677 p	0,2209 p
Nasa-TLX			
T-Test	0,4135 p	0,6441 p	0,7620 p
* p < 0,05			

4 Conclusion

4.1 Contribution

Our experiment-based research shows that AR enabled remote support can offer productivity benefits compared to standard video-based remote support using existing and readily available technology already today.

Besides our research shows that besides the hard- and software also other factors, especially the level of expert knowledge as well as the existing prior knowledge have a huge and even greater influence of the remote support productivity.

- **Prior knowledge of participants:** The most important factor according to our date is prior knowledge with similar task of the participants. This has a positive impact on the task completion time.
- **Expert knowledge:** The second most important factor is the skill level of the remote expert. Analysis of the data reveals that the expert knowledge has also an impact on task completion time as the data shows a significant effect of their individual learning curve.
- **Communication technology**: And the third most important factor is the tool in form of persistent visual cues. While AR enabled remote support seems to be superior compared to video-based remote support our research shows that certain parameters should be considered. While HMD seem to have advantages as the user can operate hands-free, the insufficient display of the RealWear glasses resulted in a low performance as many candidates were having issues seeing the displayed instructions.

4.2 Implications for Academia

Our research expands the research on AR-based remote collaboration. Our lab experiment with 66 participants mimics real-world conditions quite well and proofs the potential of AR-based remote support that is existing already today.

While sensors and software are already quite advanced and seem to fulfill the requirements of the users, hardware is still a limitation. As our research design allowed the participants to conveniently place the iPad and operate hands-free this is not always the case in real-world situations. The HMD that would be suitable for such cases showed the shortcomings of this hardware category. Further research should focus on solutions to overcome this challenge.

Additionally, our research reveals the huge influence of human skill set. While technology can improve the performance of humans, the prior skill level is essential for overall performance. This interdependence between human basic capabilities and the leveraging factor of technology should be the subject of further research.

4.3 Implications for Practice

Companies who strive to increase the productivity of their field service organization, can benefit from the results. Based on existing standard hardware AR can add productivity gains. But the true potential of remote support will be exploited when a strong expert is guiding the process and the person who is being instructed has at least a decent prior knowledge.

As there are various solutions available on the market and technology advances rapidly, further research should analyze additional AR tools and hardware.

References

1. Azuma, R., et al.: Recent advances in augmented reality. IEEE Comput. Graphics Appl. 21(6), 34–47 (2001)
2. Ceruti, A., Marzocca, P., Liverani, A., Bil, C.: Maintenance in aeronautics in an industry 4.0 context: the role of augmented reality and additive manufacturing. J. Comput. Des. Eng. 6(2019), 516–526 (2019)
3. Egger, J., Masood, T.: Augmented reality in support of intelligent manufacturing – a systematic literature review. Comput. Ind. Eng. 140, 1–32 (2020)
4. Feiner, S., Macintyre, B., Seligmann, D.: Knowledge-based augmented reality. Commun. ACM 36(7), 53–62 (1993)
5. Fernández-Caramés, T., Fraga-Lamas, P., Suárez-Albela, M., Vilar-Montesinos, M.: A fog computing and cloudlet based augmented reality system for the industry 4.0 shipyard. Sensors 18(6), 1–18 (2018)
6. Gartner.   https://www.gartner.com/smarterwithgartner/5-trends-emerge-in-gartner-hype-cycle-for-emerging-technologies-2018/. Accessed 22 Feb 2021
7. Lorenz, M., Knopp, S., Klimant, P.: Industrial augmented reality: requirements for an augmented reality maintenance worker support system. In: 2018 IEEE International Symposium on Mixed and Augmented Reality Adjunct, Munich, Germany, pp. 151–153. IEEE (2018)
8. Masoni, R., Ferrise, F., Bordegoni, M., et al.: Supporting remote maintenance in industry 4.0 through augmented reality. Procedia Manuf. 11(2017), 1296–1302 (2017)
9. Masood, T., Egger, J.: Adopting augmented reality in the age of industrial digitalisation. Comput. Ind. 115, 1–14 (2020)
10. Mourtzis, D., Zogopoulos, V., Xanthi, F.: Augmented reality application to support the assembly of highly customized products and to adapt to production re-scheduling. Int. J. Adv. Manuf. Technol. 105(9), 3899–3910 (2019). https://doi.org/10.1007/s00170-019-03941-6
11. Obermair, F., Althaler, J., Seiler, U., et al.: Maintenance with augmented reality remote support in comparison to paper-based instructions: experiment and analysis. In 2020 IEEE 7th International Conference on Industrial Engineering and Applications (ICIEA), Bangkok, Thailand, pp. 942–947. IEEE (2020)

A Review of Distributed VR Co-design Systems

Jean-François Lapointe(✉)[iD], Norman G. Vinson[iD], Keiko Katsuragawa[iD], and Bruno Emond[iD]

National Research Council Canada, Ottawa, Canada
{jean-francois.lapointe,norman.vinson,keiko.katsuragawa,
bruno.emond}@nrc-cnrc.gc.ca
https://nrc-cnrc.canada.ca

Abstract. This paper presents a systematic literature review to identify the challenges and best practices of distributed VR co-design systems, in order to guide the design of such systems. It was found that VR, due to its intuitive format is useful at co-design review meetings since it allows everyone, not just experts, to provide their inputs, thus resulting in additional practical insights from project stakeholders. It also allows the identification of design deficiencies that were not observable using traditional methods and that were overlooked by the traditional panel of expert reviewers. Our review also indicates that VR should complement, not replace, traditional 2D CAD drawings. Our review, however, shows there is little conclusive evidence about the features and functions that should be included in the design of such systems and that more quantitative studies are needed to support the findings from qualitative studies.

Keywords: Co-design · Codesign · VR · Virtual reality · Collaborative design review

1 Introduction

Because of progress in the availability and performance of information and communication technologies combined with economic and safety reasons (including the current pandemic context), work is increasingly distributed across space and time. As such, more and more virtual teams are assembled remotely by audio or videoconferencing to design and assess objects or scenes. Distributed systems reduce costs and increase productivity compared to the traditional way where experts typically travel physically to be co-located to accomplish these tasks [5]. In parallel, the potential of distributed virtual reality (VR) systems is still mostly untapped for collaborative design (aka co-design) tasks.

This paper consists of a literature review identifying the challenges and best practices of distributed VR co-design systems, and highlighting particular aspects of distributed co-design systems. These VR systems are about systems that allow the real-time interactive use of virtual and graphical 3D models.

© National Research Council of Canada 2021
J. Y. C. Chen and G. Fragomeni (Eds.): HCII 2021, LNCS 12770, pp. 499–510, 2021.
https://doi.org/10.1007/978-3-030-77599-5_34

One aspect of co-design that is the focus of many articles is the *design review*. A design review is an activity undertaken by a group of people to examine a design and its relationship to various requirements and constraints, and to make suggestions about how the design can be improved, if needed [1, 26, 32]. Design reviews are typically used in industries involving the design of physical objects [1], such as the automotive sector [29], but they can also be used in the development of non-physical entities, such as software [32]. Of course, VR is mainly relevant to design reviews of physical product design.

Two major objectives of design reviews are cost reduction [29] and quality control [1]. If a design is pushed into development and later found to be inadequate, much of the post-design work must be redone, thus increasing costs and delays. Non-technical stakeholders, such as managers or end-users, sometimes participate in design reviews in various domains [11, 23]. The presence of non-technical participants is an important issue for VR. Non-technical participants are more likely to benefit from a VR-enabled review since they will have trouble imagining what blueprint-based designs will look like in 3D. Of course, physical mock-ups can be used instead of VR, but mock-ups can take longer to make [29], and may not necessarily meet review objectives as well as VR (as discussed below). With non-technical reviewers, VR can also support important communication and persuasion functions [23].

2   Background

This section reviews some categories of distributed systems in use today. This will provide a baseline for comparison.

2.1   Traditional Distributed (Audio/Video Conferencing) Co-design Systems

With these systems, users minimally need an audio channel for conversation, a shared visual space, and ideally the possibility to use gestures for additional communication [14]. They do that by using audio and/or video conferencing systems.

Audio conferencing systems support communication through an audio channel. Any visual material has to be shared before the meeting and meeting overhead is expended coordinating the references to the visual material. Video conferencing adds a video channel, which typically allows visual material to be shared. Some systems even accommodate communication via gestures [14].

2.2   Distributed Desktop VR Co-design Systems

These non-immersive systems use 3D renderings of objects or scenes but display them on flat 2D screens. They are often referred to as desktop VR systems [25]. Distributed desktop VR systems can be used as multi-channel systems by combining audio/video conferencing systems. However, the users cannot see the collaborator's gestures or expressions with respect to the 3D rendered objects.

2.3   Distributed Immersive VR Co-design Systems

The use of immersive display technologies and in particular Head-Mounted Displays (HMDs) and associated hand controllers allow new possibilities that have the potential to further improve the productivity of distributed co-design systems. This is because the use of virtual 3D models has proven to be effective [24].

To provide natural means of communication the use of audio/visual/gestural communication channels are needed [14] although the gestural channel can quickly become overloaded if, for example, hand controllers are used to both interact with the virtual environment and communicate via gesture.

Several attempts have been made to develop distributed immersive co-design systems, some using HMDs [5], others with projection-based environments such as the Cave Automatic Virtual Environment (CAVE) [6,18] for display.

A virtual environment supports rich communication channels and helps overcome the limitation of the traditional distributed co-design environment. In Sect. 4, we report the recommendations made in papers studying distributed collaborative VR for design reviews. However, before we present the recommendations, we discuss our methodology.

3   Literature Review Method

We conducted a systematic literature review based on methods developed by Guyatt and his colleagues for the medical domain [19,20] and Torres-Carrion et al. [35] for engineering and education.

Since our objective is to provide design guidelines to develop a distributed VR co-design system, we aimed to identify user interface (UI) features for such systems that enjoy empirical support. We would then include those features in our system. Our systematic review research question is therefore:

Q: What is the empirical support for various UI features of VR co-design review systems?

Answering this question required us to both find those UI features, and to evaluate the empirical evidence supporting them. Below we discuss the method for finding the features as well as the method for evaluating their empirical support. A summary of the steps sequence is presented in Fig. 1.

3.1   Searches

Databases. We searched two databases, each with broad coverage: Scopus and Google Scholar.

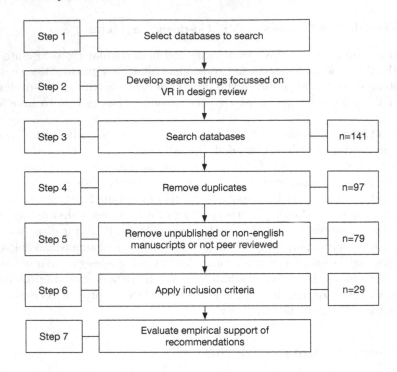

Fig. 1. Summary of the systematic review selection process.

Search Strings. We employed several different search strings to retrieve only relevant articles. The search strings are listed below.

- (S1) (virtual AND reality AND "design review") all in title.
- (S2) "Immersive co-design" OR "Immersive codesign".
- (S3) "physical task collaborative environment".
- (S4) (VR AND "design review") all in title.
- (S5) [(VR OR "virtual reality") AND ("codesign" OR "co-design")] all in title.
- (S6) [(VR OR "virtual reality") AND ("remote collaboration") AND design] all in title.
- (S7) (Immersive AND "design review") all in title
- (S8) (Immersive AND "remote collaboration" AND design) all in title.

The search results were current as of January 6, 2021.

Inclusion and Exclusion Criteria. From our search results, we excluded documents that were:

- Citations or patents (from Google Scholar);
- Unpublished manuscripts, including theses and dissertations;

- Documents in languages other than English;
- Articles in magazines (as opposed to journals), and articles that were not peer reviewed;
- Conference workshops.

We further reduced the number of articles by requiring that the articles and systems meet the following inclusion criteria:

- The article must include one or more empirical evaluations of user interface functionality;
- The system must support multi-user collaborative design or design review;
- The system must involve virtual reality.

We did not explicitly search for, nor excluded articles describing Augmented Reality (AR) systems, which allow users to see real as well as virtual objects.

Each author of this article reviewed several articles to determine whether each met the inclusion/exclusion criteria. None of these judgments were verified by the other authors.

Evaluation. To generate evidence-based recommendations for UI features, we evaluated findings on the basis of the criteria listed in Table 1.

Table 1. UI feature assessment criteria

Evidence type	Impact	Methodological issues
RCT with quantitative performance data	Statistically significant performance increase	No obvious issues
Usability test	Quantitative data showing a performance increase (but no statistical test)	Minor issues
Iterative design	Preferred by users	Serious issues
Summative user preference questionnaire		

RCT = Randomized Controlled Trial. Row items are sorted from best to worst. Note that a single article can have any combination of the values across columns, and could present several types of evidence, each with its own impact and methodological issues. For example, one article could report a user preference questionnaire (col. 1, row 4), showing the system is preferred by users (col. 2, row 3), and with no obvious methodological issues (col. 3, row 1).

Combining the assessment criteria from Table 1 provides the strength of evidence. A *Strong* evidence required a properly conducted randomized control experiment with a statistically significant increase in effectiveness. *Moderate* evidence required an iterative design process, a usability test, or a controlled experiment that was not statistically significant. Flawed controlled experiments with significant results could also be considered to provide moderate evidence. A *Weak* evidence was provided by summative user preference questionnaires. Interview and other qualitative studies provided a *very weak* evidence. This is not to say that such studies are not valuable, as they provide rich data, but they do not provide conclusive evidence.

4   Results

Our initial search and exclusion screening left 79 articles. Applying the inclusion criteria reduced that set to 29. Table 2 shows the UI features described in the articles, their associated empirical support, and various recommendations found in the papers.

Table 2. Recommendations found in the papers

Recommendation	Evidence
Immersion is an important factor in creating a sense of presence during design evaluation, but does not seem to provide better design comprehension [3]	Weak
Immersive VR (CAVE) supports design review better than using traditional stand-up briefing PowerPoint slides but cost constraints may hinder the ability to use CAVE as a tool [2]	Weak
VR improves the user's ability to understand Computer-Aided Design (CAD) geometry [13]. The paper suggests that the ability to hide components, use exploded views, and parametrically update a model in real time provide better user performance than simply being able to pan, rotate, and scale a model	Strong
HMD-based VR boosts users' confidence and rapidity in design understanding. It also helps users to better understand the consequences of a proposed design change [12]	Strong
Dynamic viewpoint interactions with 3D models on a flat screen are more effective than static viewpoints of the same 3D models for design reviews due to the greater amount of visual and spatial information available to the user [4]	Strong
The use of HMDs is recommended over CAVEs, domes, or theatres for co-design review [12, 17]	Very weak
Analyzing the effect of visualization technologies during design reviews should include variables related to design reviewers' expertise and focus on the process variables rather than the outcomes [22]	Moderate
Desktop VR is superior to immersive VR for design review of mechanical subassemblies [27]. Note that the main author of [27] is also co-author of [22] so the expertise of design reviewers should be taken into account	Strong
This article contains visual illustrations of various collaborative car or architectural design reviews featuring tablets, HMDs, and large displays scenarios [33]. Authors are optimistic that mobile mixed reality applications will find their way into real life applications soon	Very weak
Provides ranking of functions in high demand by design reviewers such as selection of components, individual pointer, and set up of a model view [34]	Very weak
A virtual mock-up model (CAVE) helps reviewers quickly reach consensus on some design decisions. Compared to a physical mock-up model, it offers a better medium of communication for participants from a diverse set of organizations and disciplines [28]	Moderate
VR demonstrated two incremental benefits over traditional design reviews, specifically identification of design deficiencies that: - Were not observable using traditional design review methods; - Were overlooked by the traditional panel of expert reviewers. The intuitive format of VR is also accessible to the various stakeholders of a project thus resulting in additional practical insights from people who would otherwise have been excluded from the design review process [15]	Moderate

(continued)

Table 2. (*continued*)

Recommendation	Evidence
An HMD-based VR system increased the accuracy of the users' understanding of elements and aspects of the virtual environment. Although the immersive simulation itself seems to leverage the overall spatial perception of users as opposed to traditional media, the immersive VR system as a whole is still incapable of providing a certain level of detail, and interactivity and collaborative features that would allow for a truly effective design review [31]	Moderate
The session protocol proposed in this study represents a comprehensive basis and reference framework for quantitative research aiming at measuring the added value of VR systems, in terms of communication and analysis capability, in each phase of a digitally enabled usability-focused design review meeting. The VR system was a semi-immersive VR environment featuring a stereoscopic projector and a single portable rear-projected wall with a user-tracking system, while a 3D mouse, a fly-stick and a keyboard were used as VR controllers [37]	Very weak
In the Architecture, Engineering, Construction and Facility Management industry, VR for design review is intended primarily to support analysis and communication [36]	Very weak
Recommendations: (a) Be bilaterally hybrid (analog/digital) to support mutual communication between different skills and realms (b) Support multiple kinds of representations, from graphical images and physical models to animations (c) Implement multiple scales including full immersion (d) Support active and intuitive co-design [7,8]	Weak
Use the combination of social VR (a VR system where users can communicate with each other because they don't use an occlusive headset) and physical models to support non-designers' involvement [10]	Very weak
A multi-touch tablet used as an interface device for VR. Supported tasks were moving a 3D cursor, navigating, sketching, selecting and editing. Multi-touch proved more precise than position tracking for 3D cursor placement [9]	Moderate
To support a large number of 3D CAD data in the multi-user VR setting, use a client/server protocol [16]	Very weak
In the building design review process, VR-supported design review has an advantage in the design phase and augmented reality (AR) supported design review is suitable in the construction phase. In the VR and AR supported design review setup, it is suggested to filter information based on the project's type, complexity, and users [21]	Very weak
In an engineering design review process, use VR as an addition to the traditional CAD displays. The users can find a few more faults in a 3D model with VR-supported design review than a CAD model on a PC screen. It also reduces the risk of exclusion of certain professional groups from the design review process and allows users faster entry into the design review [38]	Moderate
Immersion (walk through) and interactivity were important to discover hazards and less than optimal spatial arrangements of furniture and equipment [11]	Very weak
Users liked AR for interior design [30]	Moderate
Users found VR helpful to assess ergonomics, styling, and product fit in design reviews. Authors claim stereoscopy is important for perceiving the fit of the pieces [29]	Weak
1:1 scale is a useful aspect of VR not available in 2D representations [39]	Weak
VR alone is no better than traditional 2D design review media. The best performance results from a combination of VR and traditional media (drawings, maps, digital models) [26]	Moderate
VR's advantages over 2D are: greater fidelity (as opposed to the use of symbols and designs distributed over several documents); better recall of similar/related experiences; simulation of workflow; support of sight-line inspection through immersion; more accurate user perception of size, scale, volume, and depth. VR's disadvantages: disorientation, loss of context; inappropriate representation for some tasks (analysis of plumbing system for example); cybersickness. VR should be used when the object is difficult to visualize in 3D, when spatial relationships are important, or when the object is complex [26]	Very weak
There are usability issues with VR in general [1]	Very weak

5 Discussion

If we focus on studies showing strong or moderate evidence, we find that various forms of 3D displays (desktop, CAVE, HMD) do support the design process [4,12, 13,15,28,30,31,38]. VR for example boosts users understanding and confidence of their judgment of a design geometry [12,13,31]. VR also seems helpful in detecting *additional* design flaws [15,38]. VR can also help involve additional stakeholders who may be marginalized in a traditional design review [15,28,38]. It can also increase the efficiency of the design review [26,28].

However, comparisons between the various forms of VR (immersive (including HMD and CAVE), desktop (including 3D CAD)) provide inconsistent results [12,13,17,22,27,38]. Horvat et al. (2020) [22] suggest that the reviewers' experience with the display technologies, 3D CAD or VR, can have an impact on the effectiveness of the type of 3D display. This is not surprising of course. Moreover, other authors have noted usability issues with VR, such as motion sickness and navigation difficulties [26,31,39]. VR is still an emerging technology, whereas CAD is a well-established technology that we expect to better meet the needs of experienced users. Expertise and usability issues may therefore explain the inconsistent results comparing desktop VR to immersive VR for design reviews.

Nonetheless, there do seem to be advantages of immersive VR (CAVE, HMD) over desktop VR (or 3D CAD), but the evidence is generally weak. Immersive VR does appear to be superior to desktop VR (3D CAD) for non-experts [28] (moderate strength of evidence), which is not surprising given Horvat et al.'s (2020) findings on desktop VR (3D CAD) expertise [22]. The life-size scale of immersive VR *may* also provide some advantages [7,39], particularly in terms of ergonomics (space for human movement for example) [11,26,29]. The results from Wolfartsberger [38] indicate that an immersive VR-supported design review allows users to see slightly more faults in a 3D model than in a desktop VR (3D CAD) software-based approach on a PC screen. Goh et al. (2019) [17] suggest that HMD-based immersive VR is better than their CAVE-based and dome-based immersive VR because it is more affordable, requires less space and allows users to view virtual objects that are close to them, but the evidence is very weak.

It is important to keep in mind that co-design, even design review, involves many sub-tasks and topics. VR will be more helpful for some than others. For example, we can expect VR to be most helpful when reviewing 3D objects, and not so much when reviewing software (see Parnas and Weiss (1987) [32]). Similarly, VR would be less useful in planning or preparing the design review (see Adwernat et al. (2020) [1]) or reviewing how regulations relate to requirements (see Kim [23]). On the other hand, there is some evidence that VR may be particularly useful in communication during design review meetings [31,39]. This is not unexpected, especially when the design review includes stakeholders who are unfamiliar with technical 2D documents [38].

Because VR is not suited for all aspects of design review, some authors [7, 8,26,38] recommend that VR be used in addition to the usual 2D documents, rather than in their stead.

To provide design guidelines for a VR design review system, we were interested in determining which specific features would be helpful. Unfortunately, there is no strong evidence supporting particular individual features. Nonetheless, based on an experimentation with 32 participants, Freeman et al. [12,13] do suggest that the ability to hide components, use exploded views, and parametrically update a model in real time provide better user performance than simply being able to pan, rotate, and scale a model.

Without much to guide us from an empirical perspective, we performed a task analysis to generate requirements for features that could be particularly helpful. Adwernat et al. (2020) [1] performed a similar exercise. A few of the less obvious features we thought were important were supporting and capturing annotations on the models themselves [1], the use of avatars (so reviewers could see each other's positions), recording the review sessions' audio [1] and video, and providing the users with a means to point to objects. Because our review did not provide empirical evidence for these features, we will conduct reviews and empirical on each type of feature (avatars, annotations).

One reason empirical evidence was so limited is that many articles report real-world case studies with post-experience user satisfaction questionnaires or interviews, in which users typically state that VR is helpful (for example, see [11,39]). Moreover, most of these studies only have a few participants so summary statistics of user questionnaires are not particularly informative. We appreciate the importance of testing VR in real-world settings. Unfortunately, this makes it very difficult to compare systems empirically to determine the specific benefits of VR.

6 Conclusion

In this paper, we presented a systematic literature review of distributed co-design systems in a VR environment. Based on each article's methodology and results, we assessed the strength of the evidence for the reported findings, which we presented in the results section. We then synthesized those results in the discussion section.

There are about half a dozen studies that provide strong evidence that VR displays, whether desktop or immersive (e.g. HMD-based or CAVE-based), support design review. However, our review shows there is little conclusive evidence on the differences between these visual displays, which aspects of the design review they support better, and what specific UI features or functions are important for design reviews.

Having established that VR supports design reviews in general, it is now important to investigate *quantitatively and empirically* which types of VR and which UI features are most helpful, and for which design review tasks. At this point, there is a surfeit of qualitative case studies with few subjects. While real world case studies are of critical importance to validate lab results, we should not neglect quantitative lab studies. The research community should probably now emphasize lab studies involving more users in an attempt to generate quantitative evidence that converges with existing qualitative evidence.

References

1. Adwernat, S., Wolf, M., Gerhard, D.: Optimizing the design review process for cyber-physical systems using virtual reality. Procedia CIRP **91** (2020)
2. Banerjee, P., Basu-Mallick, D.: Measuring the effectiveness of presence and immersive tendencies on the conceptual design review process. J. Comput. Inf. Sci. Eng. **3**(2) (2003). https://doi.org/10.1115/1.1578500
3. Banerjee, P., Bochenek, G., Ragusa, J.: Analyzing the relationship of presence and immersive tendencies on the conceptual design review process. J. Comput. Inf. Sci. Eng. **2**(1), 59–64 (2002). https://doi.org/10.1115/1.1486218
4. de Casenave, L., Lugo, J.E.: Effects of immersion on virtual reality prototype design reviews of mechanical assemblies. In: 30th International Conference on Design Theory and Methodology, vol. 7, pp. 1–11 (2018). https://doi.org/10.1115/DETC2018-85542
5. Conner, B., et al.: An immersive tool for wide-area collaborative design. In: TeamCAD, the First Graphics Visualization, and Usability (GVU) Workshop on Collaborative design Atlanta, GA: TeamCAD, pp. 139–143 (1997)
6. Cruz-Neira, C., Sandin, D.J., DeFanti, T.A., Kenyon, R.V., Hart, J.C.: The CAVE: audio visual experience automatic virtual environment. Commun. ACM **35**(6), 64–72 (1992). https://doi.org/10.1145/129888.129892
7. Dorta, T., Kinayoglu, G.: Towards a new representational ecosystem for the design studio. In: 19th International Conference on Computer-Aided Architectural Design Research in Asia (CAADRIA), pp. 699–708 (2014)
8. Dorta, T., Kinayoglu, G., Boudhraâ, S.: A new representational ecosystem for design teaching in the studio. Des. Stud. **47** (2016)
9. Dorta, T., Kinayoglu, G., Hoffmann, M.: Hyve-3D and the 3D cursor: Architectural co-design with freedom in virtual reality. Int. J. Archit. Comput. **14**(2), 87–102 (2016)
10. Dorta, T., Safin, S., Boudhraâ, S., Marchand, E.B.: Co-designing in social VR. process awareness and suitable representations to empower user participation. In: Intelligent & Informed 24th Annual Conference of the Association for Computer-Aided Architectural Design Research in Asia (CAADRIA), vol. 2, pp. 141–150 (2019)
11. Dunston, P.S., Arns, L.L., Mcglothlin, J.D., Lasker, G.C., Kushner, A.G.: An immersive virtual reality mock-up for design review of hospital patient rooms. In: Wang, X., Tsai, J.J.H. (eds.) Collaborative Design in Virtual Environments, pp. 167–176. Springer, Dordrecht (2011). https://doi.org/10.1007/978-94-007-0605-7_15
12. Freeman, I., Salmon, J., Coburn, J.: A bi-directional interface for improved interaction with engineering models in virtual reality design reviews. Int. J. Interact. Des. Manuf. (IJIDeM) **12**(2) (2018)
13. Freeman, I.J., Salmon, J.L., Coburn, J.Q.: CAD integration in virtual reality design reviews for improved engineering model interaction. In: Proceedings of the ASME International Mechanical Engineering Congress and Exposition. vol. 11, pp. 1–10. American Society of Mechanical Engineers (2016). https://doi.org/10.1115/imece2016-66948
14. Fussell, S.R., Setlock, L.D., Yang, J., Ou, J., Mauer, E., Kramer, A.D.I.: Gestures over video streams to support remote collaboration on physical tasks. Hum.-Comput. Interact. **19**(3) (2004)

15. Ghadban, W., Kozina, V., Kelly, B.: Improving project delivery using virtual reality in design reviews - a case study. In: Abu Dhabi International Petroleum Exhibition & Conference, pp. 1–8. Society of Petroleum Engineers (2019). https://doi.org/10.2118/197745-ms

16. Girbacia, F., Butnaru, T., Beraru, A., Butila, E., Mogan, G.: A framework for tele-immersive design review of 3D CAD models. Recent Res. Manuf. Eng. 199–202 (2011)

17. Goh, K.K.: Ship design review and collaboration with virtual reality tools. Marine Eng. **54**(5) (2019). https://doi.org/10.5988/jime.54.735

18. Gross, M., et al.: Blue-c: A spatially immersive display and 3D video portal for telepresence. ACM Trans. Graph. **22**(3) (2003). https://doi.org/10.1145/882262.882350

19. Guyatt, G.H., Oxman, A.D., Kunz, R., Vist, G.E., Falck-Ytter, Y., Schünemann, H.J.: What is "quality of evidence"and why is it important to clinicians? BMJ **336**(7651) (2008). https://doi.org/10.1136/bmj.39490.551019.BE

20. Guyatt, G.H., et al.: GRADE: an emerging consensus on rating quality of evidence and strength of recommendations. BMJ **336**(7650) (2008). https://doi.org/10.1136/bmj.39489.470347.AD

21. Haahr, M.T., Svidt, K., Jensen, R.L.: How can virtual reality and augmented reality support the design review of building services. In: Proceedings of the 19th International Conference on Construction Applications of Virtual Reality, pp. 84–93 (2019)

22. Horvat, N., Škec, S., Martinec, T., Lukačević, F., Perišić, M.: Identifying the effect of reviewers' expertise on design review using virtual reality and desktop interface. In: Proceedings of the Design Society: DESIGN Conference, vol. 1, pp. 187–196. Cambridge University Press (2020)

23. Kim, J.: Survey Results. In: What Do Design Reviewers Really Do? Understanding Roles Played by Design Reviewers in Daily Practice, pp. 95–121. Springer, Cham (2019). https://doi.org/10.1007/978-3-030-05642-1_8

24. Kulkarni, A., Kapoor, A., Iyer, M., Kosse, V.: Virtual prototyping used as validation tool in automotive design. In: Proceedings of the 19th International Congress on Modelling and Simulation, pp. 419–425 (2011)

25. LaViola, J.J., Kruijff, E., McMahan, R., Bowman, D.A., Poupyrev, I.: 3D User Interfaces: Theory and Practice, 2nd edn. Addison Wesley Professional, USA (2017)

26. Liu, Y., Castronovo, F., Messner, J., Leicht, R.: Evaluating the impact of virtual reality on design review meetings. J. Comput. Civ. Eng. **34**(1), 1–13 (2020)

27. Lukačević, F., Škec, S., Törlind, P., Štorga, M.: Identifying subassemblies and understanding their functions during a design review in immersive and non-immersive virtual environments. Front. Eng. Manage. (2020)

28. Majumdar, T., Fischer, M.A., Schwegler, B.R.: Conceptual design review with a virtual reality mock-up model. In: Joint International Conference on Computing and Decision Making in Civil and Building Engineering, pp. 2902–2911 (2006)

29. Moreau, G., Fuchs, P.: Stereoscopic displays for virtual reality in the car manufacturing industry: application to design review and ergonomic studies. In: Stereoscopic Displays and Virtual Reality Systems IX. vol. 4660, pp. 504–513. International Society for Optics and Photonics (2002)

30. Oksman, V., Siltanen, S., Ainasoja, M.: User participation in co-creative services: developing virtual and augmented reality tools for do-it-yourself home design. In: Proceedings of the 16th International Academic MindTrek Conference, pp. 229–230 (2012)

31. Paes, D., Irizarry, J.: A usability study of an immersive virtual reality platform for building design review: Considerations on human factors and user interface. In: Construction Research Congress, pp. 419–428 (2018)
32. Parnas, D.L., Weiss, D.M.: Active design reviews: Principles and practices. J. Syst. Software **7**(4) (1987). https://doi.org/10.1016/0164-1212(87)90025-2
33. Santos, P., Gierlinger, T., Stork, A., McIntyre, D.: Display and rendering technologies for virtual and mixed reality design review. In: 7th International Conference on Construction Applications of Virtual Reality, pp. 165–175 (2007)
34. Steger, W., Kim, T.S., Gebert, M., Stelzer, R.: Improved user experience in a VR based design review. In: International Design Engineering Technical Conferences and Computers and Information in Engineering Conference, vol. 1B. American Society of Mechanical Engineers (2016). https://doi.org/10.1115/DETC2016-59840
35. Torres-Carrión, P.V., González-González, C.S., Aciar, S., Rodríguez-Morales, G.: Methodology for systematic literature review applied to engineering and education. In: 2018 IEEE Global Engineering Education Conference (EDUCON), pp. 1364–1373. IEEE (2018)
36. Ventura, M.S., Castronovo, F., Nikolić, D., Ciribini, A.L.: A framework of procedural considerations for implementing virtual reality in design reviews. In: Proceedings of the 2019 European Conference on Computing in Construction, pp. 442–451 (2019). https://doi.org/10.35490/EC3.2019.160
37. Ventura, S.M., Castronovo, F., Ciribini, A.L.: A design review session protocol for the implementation of immersive virtual reality in usability-focused analysis. J. Inform. Technol. Construction (ITcon) **25**(14) (2020)
38. Wolfartsberger, J.: Analyzing the potential of virtual reality for engineering design review. Autom. Constr. **104**, 27–37 (2019)
39. Zaker, R., Coloma, E.: Virtual reality-integrated workflow in BIM-enabled projects collaboration and design review: a case study. Visual. Eng. **6**(1), 1–15 (2018). https://doi.org/10.1186/s40327-018-0065-6

The Mobile Office: A Mobile AR Systems for Productivity Applications in Industrial Environments

Daniel Antonio Linares Garcia[1,2](✉), Poorvesh Dongre[2],
Nazila Roofigari-Esfahan[1], and Doug A. Bowman[2,3]

[1] Department of Building Construction, Virginia Tech, Blacksburg, VA 24060, USA
{dlinares,nazila,dbowman}@vt.edu
[2] Department of Computer Science, Virginia Tech, Blacksburg, VA 24060, USA
poorvesh@vt.edu
[3] Center for Human-Computer Interaction, Virginia Tech,
Blacksburg, VA 24060, USA

Abstract. This article proposes the Mobile Office, an AR-Based System for productivity applications in industrial environments. It focuses on addressing workers' needs while mobilizing in complex environments and when workers want to do productive work similar to a workstation setting. For this purpose, the Mobile Office relies on a bi-modal approach (mobile and static modes) to addresses both scenarios while considering critical aspects such as UI, ergonomics, interaction, safety, and cognitive user abilities. Its development relies first on a systematic literature review for establishing guidelines and system aspects. Then AR-UI mockups are presented to incorporate literature and authors' expertise in this area. Three hardware configurations are also presented for the implementation of the Mobile Office. Validation of the Mobile Office was made through a survey to potential users that provided their feedback about their perceptions of proposed system. The survey results revealed concordance of critical aspects of particular importance for effective productivity support on the Mobile Office's focus scenarios. We incorporated these critical aspects and suggested future research direction for the Mobile Office's further development and significance.

Keywords: Adaptive and personalized interfaces · Context-dependent system · HCI in industry and business · HCI theories and methods · Heuristics and guidelines for design · Augmented reality (AR)

1 Introduction

Multiple factors challenge workers performing their work in industrial environments. These include their physical context, receiving and processing information, their cognitive abilities, ergonomics, and safety [17]. At the center of all, information understanding while mobile or stationary is essential to enable workers to translate their skills to the products and services within their industry

© Springer Nature Switzerland AG 2021
J. Y. C. Chen and G. Fragomeni (Eds.): HCII 2021, LNCS 12770, pp. 511–532, 2021.
https://doi.org/10.1007/978-3-030-77599-5_35

capabilities and be productive. Devices such as smartphones, laptops, and tablets have been used to complement worker activities. However, these impose limitations on the worker, such as lack of context awareness and the inability to be used and be productive in all the working conditions [9]. Augmented reality (AR) systems have the potential to be a more integrated solution to address the needs of industrial workers. AR systems can potentially be used to replace smartphones, tablets, and laptops if the system dynamics where AR performs is better understood [2]. In this regard, AR systems can improve workers' productivity by providing support to workers during their mobile and stationary operations. This study aims to propose an AR system based on guidelines, interface, and hardware solutions to improve AR's effect during mobile and stationary workers' operations in industrial environments to improve their productivity. Literature from Human-centered [19], Virtual environment approaches [28], and AR System Control [19] was considered for the system development. System aspects include UI, ergonomics, interaction, safety, and cognitive user abilities. Based on literature findings, we propose system guidelines, AR-UI mockups and hardware solutions that inform how the system might work in the given scenarios. We named our recommended system, the "Mobile Office". The Mobile Office has AR-User Interface (AR-UI), hardware features, and multi-modal interaction methods to increase industrial workers' mobile productivity while maintaining safety and ergonomics.

2   Related Works

Early research efforts in productivity applications of AR has been focused on office-like environments. The oldest research item identified that use AR-like approaches in a productivity setting was made by Raskaret al. [23]. The virtual workstation enabled in this research was made by projecting images on walls to mimic the interaction of the user with the virtual content to facilitating collaboration. Later developments focused on presenting interactivity in workstation spaces such as works made by Regenbrecht et al. [24]. They used barcodes to enable the projection of virtual objects in the user's Field of View (FOV), so an object was projected over a bar code, and the manipulation of the bar code location let the user also manipulate the virtual object location. Citibank [4] has a video prototype for a hybrid AR solution for a static workstation where a user sits on a desk-like space with monitors on the sites, but additional visualizations are projected through a Hololens in the center. The previous setting enables a banker to interact with 3D visualizations that helps him on taking decisions. These research developments and applications were exploratory and serve to stimulate the use of AR as an enhancer for workstations in office-like spaces. More dynamic versions of workspaces have been explored. For example, Janssen et al. [12] developed productivity spaces within the automobile cabin so a user, such as a passenger or a driver, can have a collaboration-like environment within the confinement of the car. Their approach assumes that the AR technology will reach maturity, so self-driving and motion sickness will be diminished or eliminated in these settings. Workspaces have also been explored in dynamic environments such as the construction industry. Li et al. [18] analyzed AR/VR technology and how it is impacting safety in these environments; however, they do not address the interface and interactions aspects but proposed potential uses and applications. The previous research highlights how AR has the potentials to address human support in both static and dynamic environments. However, a hybrid approach that addresses both scenarios is unclear. Considering the paradigm that workstation settings are exclusive to static locations, developing a system that brings those scenarios to new frontiers might enable new research directions previously under-explored. The dynamics of a system that does static and mobile scenarios impose additional challenges considering transitions and the minimum threshold that the system provides at least an equivalent user experience for the independent scenarios.

3 Research Methods

The main objective of this article is to develop and evaluate an AR-UI for productive applications in industrial environments. The methodological process to include: first, guidelines for System Design were developed based on the relevant literature concerning the topics related to the Mobile Office; then, a recommended system is proposed based on interface mockups and case scenarios that illustrate key aspects of the proposed Mobile Office system; a survey was conducted to evaluate and get feedback from potential users of the system; finally, the proposed system design was updated, and future work suggested.

4 Guidelines for System Design

Guidelines from System Design were reviewed from the literature and summarized in this section in this section. Specifically, guidelines for AR user-interface (AR-UI) design and AR system control are further discussed.

4.1 AR User-Interface (AR-UI) Design Guidelines

In Graphical User Interfaces (GUIs), virtual objects are restricted to a 2D screen, and in VR, the virtual objects are restricted to the 3D environment. In contrast, AR 3D virtual objects are combined with real objects. Because of this, interactions in AR differ from those in GUIs and VR. There are some similarities between the interactions in AR and VR; however, the real world's presence in AR makes it a unique case. Our study found that substantial research has been done around AR hardware and software development, but less has been done for AR-UI development. Existing research on AR-UI development are application-specific and work related to AR-based mobile systems is also lacking. Therefore, we utilized the general guidelines proposed by researchers to design an AR-UI and categorized such research based on the approach they followed to propose the guidelines. These categories are (1) the Human-centered approach, (2) the VE approach, and (3) the Application-based approach.

Human-Centered Approach. The most important research for designing a system for emerging technologies like AR was a used-based method given by Gabbard and Swan. [7]. They proposed an iterative method to design UIs for AR that can also lead to the development of AR-UI design guidelines. Their iterative method comprises UI design, user-based studies, and expert evaluation. Gabbard and Swan (2008) also recommend using MS Powerpoint to create the initial concept design and consult with the users and experts to confirm the validity of the design before moving on to the actual UI design development.

Livingston [19] proposed a human-factor method in designing AR-UI. He discusses the interface-feature conundrum and concludes that a well-designed interface with fewer features is always better than a poorly designed interface with more features. Livingston [19] suggested creating multiple designs by assessing the perceptual needs of humans and choose the best design to test for cognitive needs. Dünser, Grasset, Seichter, & Billinghurst [5] used the design principles of Human-Computer Interaction (HCI) to propose a human-centered approach for designing AR UIs. These principles are affordance, cognitive load, low physical effort, learnability, flexibility.

Virtual Environment (VE) Approach. The VE approach takes inspiration from the well-defined guidelines to design VE UIs to design AR-UIs. The most important work in this approach is LaViola et al. [16]. In their book, the authors detail "designing for human" and "investing 3D UIs" strategies to design UIs for VE. The "designing for human" strategy matches the design of interaction techniques and applications that are human-centered. The "investing 3D UIs" strategy is based on common sense approaches, creative exploration, and rules of thumb. Stanney et al. [25] followed a multi-structural approach based on usability characteristics to develop an automated system for evaluating VEs. The multi-structural approach categorizes the usability characteristics into "system interface" that focuses on interaction and system output and "user interface" that focuses on engagement and side effects in VEs.

Application-Based Approach. Apart from the guidelines mentioned above, researchers also proposed some application specific guidelines to design AR-UIs. Ganapathy [8] focused on addressing the factors that influence the design of mobile augmented reality (MAR) applications based on usage scenarios, interaction modalities, and device form factor. These guidelines are about having clear textual information, contrast, grouping, placement, alert/attention sensitivity, interaction methods, distinct icons, visibility, and distance. Wetzel et al. [29] gave a set of design guidelines which are drawn from comparing three mixed reality games based on used AR technique, hardware, tracking, playing area, interaction devices, and interaction techniques.

4.2   AR System Control

In this section, various techniques to establish an efficient system control for the Mobile Office AR-UI is discussed. Tangible User Interfaces (TUIs) and Natural

User Interfaces (NUIs) are further discussed and then considered in the context of the Mobile Office.

Tangible User Interfaces (TUIs). TUIs are physical objects that seamlessly integrate with the virtual objects to facilitate interaction in AR experiences. The use of familiar physical objects can also increase affordances in the design. Henderson and Feiner [11] developed opportunistic TUIs by using affordances offered by commonly existing surfaces that otherwise are unused in the domain environment. Billinghurst et al. [3] developed TUIs using real objects to design the layout of virtual furniture in a room. These objects offer easily perceivable affordance to efficiently interacts with an AR application.

Natural User Interfaces (NUIs). NUIs are intuitive control mechanisms that use natural human interaction such as sound, touch, and gestures to interact with the AR system. Bartie and Mackaness [1] developed a speech-based interface for an AR system to support cityspace exploration. Other NUIs were explored by Yeh et al. [13] which developed a system control for projection-based AR system for on-site building information retrieval that can understand user commands using touch screens and accelerometers. Mistry and Maes [20] developed a wearable gestural interface comprised of a pocket projector, a mirror, and a camera. Although NUIs seems like a handy technique for system control in AR, it is limited by its modalities. For instance, the speech-based interface by [1] was limited by background noises, and in the touch-based interface by [13], users were facing difficulties in operating the touch screen and focusing on the AR display at the same time. Moreover, Norman [21] argues that gestures are cultural-specific; thus, not every user may naturally recognize a gestural command.

5   The Mobile Office System Proposal

To proceed with the Mobile Office design, the iterative user-based approach proposed by Gabbard and Swan [7] was used. The first iteration of the Mobile Office integrated literature findings, authors' experiences in AR-UIs, and authors' experiences in industrial environment to propose a version that seeks to attend to the needs of workers and increase their productivity. The human-factors approach by Livingston [19] was followed to create multiple mockup designs based on these aspects. The guidelines given by Dünser et al. [5] were explored to reduce cognitive load, and increasing learnability and explored the use of multimodal NUIs for improving the flexibility of system control. Guidelines from the application-based approach such as having clear textual information, contrast, grouping, placement, and alert/attention sensitivity were also used to design a user-friendly AR-UI for the Mobile Office.

5.1   System Modes

Productivity in industrial environments is considered within the boundaries of workers mobilizing and doing productivity work in the factory floor. Because of this, our design for the Mobile Office considers two main specific modes, namely the mobile mode and the static mode.

Mobile Mode. The mobile mode refers when the user navigates the industrial environment to mobilize among spaces or to explore this environment as part of his productivity work. While a user is using the Mobile Office in mobile mode, the user has specific needs such as (1) locate places, other users, or objects, (2) receive contextual information about the environment that is relevant to his current work activity or navigation support, (3) receive notifications from data sources and communication proactively, and (4) make the user feel safe and promote his healthy occupation. Constrains in the Mobile Mode include (1) user's FOV has limitations and zones with a varied degree of value, (2) the AR hardware limits the user's perceptions of his surroundings so the user needs to be supported concerning external hazards and information to be provided, (3) cognitive abilities of the user while in the mobile mode limits the user to complete more analytical or complex productivity work (e.g., checking excel data, or reviewing 3D models).

Static Mode. The static mode refers to the uses that the Mobile Office receive when more demanding cognitive and visual work is undertaken. This mode is similar to working in a desktop-like setting where the user has the following needs (1) user demands more efficient real state in productivity applications in his FOV, without concerning of contextual information from the environment, (2) user still needs to receive notifications from data sources and communication proactively, (3) system control and interaction should more streamlined so productivity work such as typing can be efficiently done. Constrains in the static mode include (1) this mode is focused on multitasking, with the ability to pull up multiple fully opaque windows. To enable interaction with these applications, physical input methods such as mice and keyboards should work with the system, presenting a cursor on the screen for rapid selection tasks if needed. In addition to having the capacities of a laptop computer in this mode, the system would still retain its capacity to enable natural input methods such as gestures for window manipulation or voice inputs for dictation where appropriate, (2) user's safety, ergonomics, and health status needs to be monitored and enforced at all times. However, hazards from the environment should be controlled based on the enabling of the static mode.

5.2   Mobile Office: AR-UI

Supporting Human Cognition. The cognitive capability of a person is limited. Besides, a person actively engages with all the different modalities perceived at any moment, and in an AR application, the cognitive ability of a person can be saturated. This is especially the case for the visual modality, given that the additional information superimposed in the user's FOV is an unnatural phenomenon. In this context, the user's attention should be prioritized based on the user's cognitive load, environmental conditions and hazards, and how the system interface interacts with these.

Fig. 1. Mobile Office's basic AR-UI

Figure 1 is a mockup of a user's point of view with the first iteration of the AR-UI for the Mobile Office. This takes place in a standard in-the-field mobile mode, wherein no navigation or focus intensive productivity tasks are occurring. This is based on the recommendations given by [22] for attention. A warehouse is used for these and all future mockup images to showcase the design in a consistent setting.

Managing FOV and Information. In normal conditions, a person's attention continually seeks to recognize the implicit information from the environment. In an AR system, the environment is saturated with additional information being added to the user's visual cue, which can cause distraction and provoke loss of attention. Therefore, the way to present information in AR should be precise and located in the user's center FOV to relieve the user of finding the information they needed. Also, the way the user receives information in this setting should be direct, such as graphics instead of text, given that text needs the user to interpret the information received [22]. According to [22], if the information is projected on the periphery of the vision, this information is informative or a warning if the appropriate color scheme and symbols are used.

Because this is a work-centric UI, and the physical nature of the area is important for the work being performed, it is most appropriate that only objects

Fig. 2. Field of view ranges for UI elements

in the immediate environment and highlights pertaining to tasks at hand should
have virtual elements in the center and mid-peripheral ranges of the user's vision,
see Fig. 2. This is to prevent visual clutter and allow the user to retain awareness
of their environment, following a general paradigm that elements should never
obscure the real world, only highlight aspects of it [27]. Sometimes, however,
information cannot be displayed in such a passive way, and for these cases there
are sidebars present at the edges of the user's vision, which present domain-
dependent modules relevant to the user's work scenario. A handful of modules
that generalize well are pictured in Fig. 1 (a task list, notifications feed, map,
and system clock); however, as prior research indicated, the way information is
shown can matter just as much as the information itself [22], so to facilitate this,
the sidebars are simply generic containers for customized modules, which can be
made to be efficient for conveying specific information.

The faded after-image displayed on the furthest edges of the screen are
intended to demonstrate that these sidebars should have both an active and
docked position, with the active position being readily readable, but the docked
position placed within the user's far peripheral vision. This not only frees up
the center of the user's vision from dense visual clutter, but also leverages the
peripheral vision's motion detection capabilities to alert the user to new content, such as items being added to their task list or notifications [15]. To change
position from docked to activate, eye tracking can be used to detect when the
user is looking towards their peripheral vision for an extended period of time
and move the sidebar in response to this. By utilizing gaze instead of gestures
or physical controllers, user fatigue can be reduced at no cost to convenience.

Managing User's Attention. The users' attention or the detrimental distraction cues while immersed in AR can also be caused by improper management
of content given to the user. This is also exacerbated when the information projected in AR does not match the real-world conditions; in other words, projected
information does not recognize physical objects, and their interactions are unnatural and, in some cases deceiving. Because of that, integration is relevant, and

context needs to be considered from the perspective of the cognitive load to the user. To address the issue of multiple content sources that are not integrated with the sensed environment, a content fusion approach has been suggested by Zhang et al. [30]. This approach suggests integrating multiple data sources with the sensed real-world environment giving the user a consistent visualization of information within the contextual visual perception observed, see contextual cues in Fig. 1. Still, this approach relies dramatically on the intelligent interpretation of the context where the user is located and how this information is coupled with the other different data sources. Contextual AR was also explored by Walczak et al. [28]; one interesting development they present is that concordance of virtual and physical objects can even be considered in the context of interaction, so the user is capable of interacting with the virtual objects in addition to the real-world objects as correctly recognized by the system.

Managing Visual Clutter. After considering data fusion or situational awareness of the AR system, the AR interface should also address visual clutter. This is especially important because a contextually aware system might recognize multiple environment pieces of information and saturate the user with feedback information. Researchers have identified this issue, and the mechanism has been developed to present mostly useful feedback to the user without saturating their FOV while avoiding visual clutter. One of these research efforts includes the adaptive information density method by Tatzgern et al. [27]. They exemplify the case of a library where the user can be bombarded with feedback from too many sources; therefore, a system cluster information to declutter the user's visual. The challenges remain in this area as the meaningful mechanisms to cluster information should be done case by case to reach a meaningful understanding. Besides itemizing an item, a multistage selection process should be undertaken by the user, which in some cases, might be impractical.

Fig. 3. AR-UI for the Mobile Office Static Mode

The Mobile Office Static Mode. Many of the AR-UI aspects in the Mobile Office relates more to the mobile mode. However, some aspects are more specific to the static mode. In this mode, applications work in a way similar to a personal computer, with window switching being available in an infinitely scrolling carousel around the user, maneuvered with swiping gestures, see Fig. 3. In the absence of a physical input method, various virtual input methods could be projected, the exact natures of which are task-dependent and outside the scope of this article, see Fig. 4.

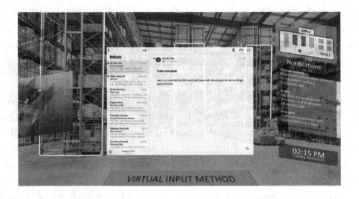

Fig. 4. Static mode AR-UI with alert and input methods

5.3   Mobile Office: Physical Considerations

Safety. We hypothesize that the mobile productivity applications considered in this article will find use cases in uncontrolled environments such as outdoors or very dynamic environment such as factory floors. Researchers have explored the use of AR in outdoor environments, and safety concerns have been highlighted such as visual clutter, then the display becomes a distraction from hazards from the real world, and increasing the cognitive load of the user while controlling the interface which might also cause distraction from external risks [15]. Other problems observed while using AR devices are the interface elements occluding relevant environmental aspects and the warning of environmental hazards outside the FOV of the user. For example, see Fig. 5. Addressing this issue has been of interest to researchers, and methodologies have been developed to reduce the hazards present because of the user's limitations in FOV [14] in AR-UI.

To indicate where a hazard is coming from and its urgency, a color wave at the edges of the user's FOV is used to warn the user in the current Mobile Office design, see Fig. 6. This wave moves in from the edge of the user's FOV depending on the severity of the hazard detected, and is accompanied by haptics and sound cues which increase in intensity as the wave encroaches further into the center of the user's vision. By using a graphical design, a great deal of information about the hazard can be conveyed immediately, without the use of symbols or text.

(a) AR-UI occluding environmental haz- (b) Hazard in the environment without AR-
ards   UI component

Fig. 5. AR-UI occlusion example

Fig. 6. Hazard warning on in the Mobile Office's AR-UI

Our design includes the safety considerations in this section by adding the following features in our design: (1) the Mobile Office, actively monitor the environment to identify hazards inside and outside the user's FOV, (2) the system interface, proactively identify visual locations that are of utmost importance to the user, so the interface does not occlude this spots, (3) warning hazards are highlighted at the edge of the user's FOV and are shown in the position where the hazards are discovered.

System Transitions. When the user is not performing tasks that demand their full environmental awareness, the Mobile Office switches to the static mode. The switching to the static mode in the Mobile Office can be done in two main methods. An **automatic** switching method depends on sensors and algorithms that detect the user in doing productivity work appropriate for the static mode and also verifies the safety and ergonomic constraints to enable this mode. An **on-demand** method enabled manually by the user. However, sensors are still a need to enable the static mode in this approach, given that the system should guarantee the user's safety and ergonomic. An intermediate solution when ergonomic and safety is not assured can allow the user to activate the static mode and actively monitor the user's safety and ergonomics. In this regard, the system can detect the user idling in an active workzone for too long and suggest moving to a safer or more ergonomic location.

Ergonomics. The Mobile Office is expected to perform in working environments as varied as industrial and office stations. Thus, Occupational Health and Safety (OHS) is relevant in these scenarios. OHS considerations are related to the physical conditions of the worker provided in the work environment. How these conditions are maintained is critical so issues that negatively affect a worker in the long and short term while performing his job are averted. When considering work environments within VR/AR, OHS is still relevant because the user is within the boundaries of the physical working environment that can cause harm, or OHS aspects need to be considered for the welfare of the user. Research works suggest that the evaluation of ergonomics on VEs is essential; however, ways to evaluate these aspects qualitatively are not completely established. Sun et al. [26] explored metrics for ergonomics in VEs and developed a method to evaluate workspace ergonomics in the context of OHS for a ship manufacturing application. In this sense, the Mobile Office can do an OHS check-up so it can give recommendations to the user about the ergonomic and environmental issues that need to be addressed to work safely and without ergonomic repercussions.

Ergonomics factors for user interaction and the VE is also a need to consider. In this regard, Figueiredo et al. [6] evaluated hand and controller user input within VEs, and their finding suggests that control with the hand only is possible but issues might arise. However, when compared to interaction with a controller, the interaction becomes superior and more natural for system control. Given that our envisioned mobile productivity system might not include a controller, the current hand only control of the system needs to be improved, or new methodologies to control the interface might be required. Ergonomics also depends on the length of exposure in the VE. In particular long-term exposure to virtual environments present challenges that impact the physiological and psychological effects on the user. Guo et al. [10] evaluated exactly this effect and used the Maslow's Hierarchy of Needs to support the first four levels in the hierarchy, which correspond that the basic needs of a person.

Our recommended design addresses the issue of ergonomics by taking the following considerations: (1) the AR system actively monitors the user while in a static mode where ergonomics need to be assured, (2) the ergonomics considerations also include the tracking of OHS aspects based on the standards, (3) the characteristics for the length and comfort of the user is addressed through the inclusion of modes in the system that provide different levels of comforts to the user based on the duration of exposure to the AR system of the user, the users focus on the task, and the physical setup provided.

5.4   Proposed Hardware Configurations

Three main hardware configurations are presented for a possible implementation of the Mobile Office. These configurations are a kiok, a vehicle, and a personal device, see Fig. 7. These configurations are constrained based on the system capabilities previously mentioned including Head-Mounted Display, Environmental Sensors, User Sensors, and Multiple Modalities for interaction. Each hardware configuration considers a different status of the AR technology maturity. More details about these configurations are provided in this section.

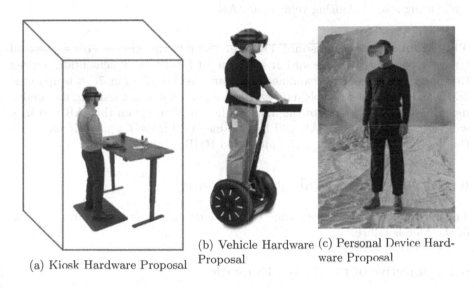

(a) Kiosk Hardware Proposal   (b) Vehicle Hardware Proposal   (c) Personal Device Hardware Proposal

Fig. 7. Static mode mockups for the Mobile Office AR-UI

The Mobile Office Kiosk. The Mobile Office Kiosk is the most feasible solution in response to the current status of the AR technology capabilities. The hardware configuration provided in Fig. 7a, present a solution where the Head Mounted Device (HMD) is wore by the user while mobilizing around the industrial environment. However, the static mode is only enabled when the user is found present in the kiosks located around the environment. By fixing the location of the kiosk, the system guarantees that physical constraints such as safety and ergonomics are guaranteed at all times. Besides, the kiosk eliminates the need for the sensors embedded in the Mobile Office hardware which nowadays might prove challenging to implement in a real prototype. Finally, the kiosk configuration, resolves the issue of guaranteeing a productivity parameters such as typing and an ergonomic surface. The biggest drawback of this implementation is that the mobile implementation is lost given that the static mode is only available where the kiosks are located. In addition, the investment in building kiosks might also a complication for implementing in a industrial environment.

The Mobile Office Vehicle. The Mobile Office vehicle is an intermediate but exciting proposal for a hardware solution. The hardware configuration provided in Fig. 7b, presents a personal self-balancing vehicle that provides a self-contained hardware solution. The hardware solution presented do not limit mobility and potentially increase user mobility. This hardware configuration also support the embedding of sensors for environment and user perception within the vehicle. In addition, a surface at the hands height might also incorporate input hardware and ergonomic support to the user. The drawback of this implementation is the unclear effect on the user's perception and physiological capabilities while using a self balancing vehicle and AR.

The Mobile Office Personal Device. Finally, the Mobile Office personal device is considered by the author as the most futuristic implementation given the limitations of such a streamlined hardware. As shown in Fig. 7c, it is up to the HMD and potential wearable hardware to include all display, sensing, and multi-modality implementation for the mobile office. It is uncertain that AR maturity will reach the point were AR will be capable of all these features. However, in the last years, advances such as untethered HMDs make it promising.

6 Mobile Office Evaluation: Surveys

This section presents the evaluation by conducting a survey for the first iteration of the Mobile Office.

6.1 Objective of the Survey Evaluation

The survey evaluation seeks to obtain feedback from professionals with experiences working in industrial environments. Their feedback seeks to indicate how the Mobile Office is truly addressing the needs and challenges of the workers in this scenarios and how feasible is the implementation of the Mobile Office.

6.2 Questionnaire Development

The survey questionnaire included seven sections where participants were asked about their industry experiences and how the Mobile Office might support their productive work in these environments. These sections are:

- The **introduction** describe the Mobile Office and its objectives in industrial environments.
- **Demographic** information was asked to the participants to understand their characteristics.
- **Technology and Industry Experiences** was included to accommodate the varying collection of industry experiences and engagement with AR technology. In regards to industry experience, participants were asked about (1) their employment status, including students with previous experiences in

manufacturing firms, (2) Industry sector experiences, and (3) Years of industry experience In regards to AR experience, participants were asked about (1) experience using AR, (2) familiarity with AR technologies, and (3) work Experiences with AR.

- **Guidelines and Recommendations** asked participants their perception about their needs and requirements while implementing a system such as the Mobile Office in their work. Participants were asked about their perception about (1) potential uses of AR in productivity work, (2) assessment of physical aspects, (3) interface aspects, and (4) concerns or drawbacks in using the Mobile Office in the participants' work.
- In the **Design Critique** section, participants were presented with demos for the interface for key scenarios for the Mobile Office. Participants were asked about the Mobile Office Modes' user interface. For the mobile mode, participants were asked how the interface presented to address obstruction from the environment, fulfill user needs, relevant information and functions the interface provides, and manage information overload. For the productivity mode, participants were asked their assessment about the interface presented regarding the supporting of productivity workflow, typing, and multi-display support.
- The **transition** section asked participants to critique how enabling the static mode address user's safety and ergonomics, whether the switching of modes happen automatically, or activated based on the user's desire, how the interface adapts to the new mode, and if the user awareness of the switching of modes is important.
- Finally, the **feasibility** section asked the participants if, based on their industry experiences, how likely is the Mobile Office to be implemented. The questionnaire asked the participants their opinion about whether hardware and software technology is capable of implementing the Mobile Office in their industry and if the industry, users, and companies they work might support the implementation of the mobile office.

The questionnaire covers these aspects to elucidate system interaction with the users and the users' opinions about such a system in the industry they work. The survey for this study was reviewed and approved by the Industry Review Board (IRB) at Virginia Tech under protocol number IRB-20-954.

6.3   Target Respondents

The target participants for the survey are professionals who have had industry experiences in the past. Two main participants groups were targeted. First, industry professionals were targeted by contacting the alumni at the Industrial and Systems Engineering (ISE) department at Virginia Tech. Secondly, students with previous experiences in industry.

6.4 Results

The survey gathered responses from 22 participants. However, incomplete responses were removed and an analysis of the results were made with 7 valid responses.

Demographics. Demographics denotes that most of our respondents are graduate students at Virginia Tech given that the highest percentage for employment status is student with previous experience in industry and industry experience between 0 to 1 years. Participants experiences with AR denotes no substantial use, familiarity or experiences with AR.

Guidelines. Figure 8 presents the survey response for the guidelines aspects of the Mobile Office. The first question asks about potential uses of AR in productivity work. Respondents agreed that the most important uses are: get visual or instructional support while doing activities, navigate your surroundings, and review databases. Activity support (e.g., proactive support to a labor worker when doing activities such as welding or assembly) was the use case with the respondents' higher ponderation, but the Mobile Office does not thoroughly consider this aspect but it is a consideration for future versions of the Mobile Office. Navigation and review databases align with the Mobile Office's design aspects that focus on bi-modal approaches such as the mobile mode for navigation and the static mode that can be optimized for information review such as databases. Communicating with co-workers or management is also important based on participants' responses and can be enabled in the mobile office's current iteration despite not thoroughly explained.

The second question asked about the assessment of physical aspects. In this regard, the most concerning aspect is the hazards from the environment. Consequently, when the third question asked about interface aspects, respondents agreed that warning about these hazards was also critical. Therefore, the safety design aspects presented in the Mobile Office design significantly seeks to address environmental hazards, information management, and AR-UI interaction aspects, see Fig. 5 and 6. Furthermore, hardware configurations are also based on the hardware capabilities to enable sensing and monitoring of the environmental hazards and user's ergonomics, see Fig. 7. Also, showing visual and audio information was also considered very important. Finally, the last question asked about concerns and drawbacks about AR in these environments. In this sense, the biggest concern among the respondents are information might overwhelm the user and also it might cause distractions.

Design Critique. Figure 9 presents the survey results for the Design Critique presented to the participants during the survey. In general, positive feedback was received about information presented to the user in the Mobile Office's modes. Concerning the mobile mode, respondents perceive that the interface seems to address information overload and addressing the user's needs in the

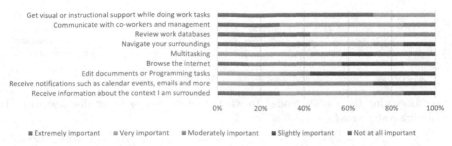

(a) What is your assessment of the following potential uses while using AR in productivity work?

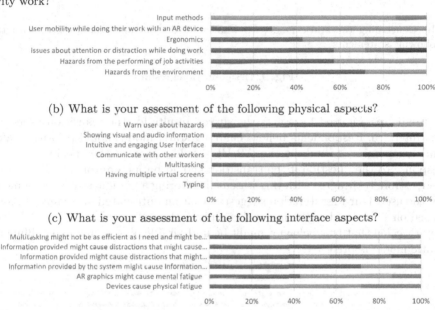

(b) What is your assessment of the following physical aspects?

(c) What is your assessment of the following interface aspects?

(d) What are your concerns or drawbacks about implementing this technology in productivity tasks based on your experiences?

Fig. 8. Guidelines results

environment. However, some respondents believe that the interface might hinder the user's perception of the environment. Our design addresses the last issue by considering gaze-based highlight for AR-UI elements; however, the mockups' static nature did not convey this idea as captured in the survey responses. Concerning the static mode, respondents perceived that the interface might allow multi-display support and copying information from multiple programs. However, some respondents were concern about typing effectiveness in the interface mockup presented.

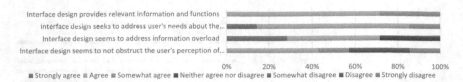

(a) Concerning the mobile mode, To what level do you agree or disagree with the following statements?

(b) Concerning the static mode, To what level do you agree or disagree with the following statements?

Fig. 9. Design critique results

Transition. Figure 10 presents the survey results for the transition aspects of the interface. Respondents believe enabling static mode should prioritize safety and ergonomics, as well as the AR-UI should adapt to the specific mode. In response to the question if the transition should happen automatically, respondents strongly disagree with this statement favoring a manual switching of modes by the user. Our first iteration suggested that an automated switching of modes based on safety and ergonomic will comply with user's needs. However, the survey revealed that this behavior might be undesirable, and manually enabling the static model is preferred.

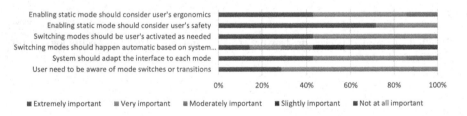

Fig. 10. Transition results. Question: Concerning mode transition, What is your assessment of the following transition aspects?

Feasibility. Figure 11 presents the survey results for the feasibility questions. Our design suggest that the current available hardware might not be capable of supporting the development of all the capabilities envisioned for the Mobile Office. However, users believe this is not the case, and they perceived it as feasible. Interestingly, respondents believe that software technology is currently capable to implement the Mobile Office with the hardware technology have a

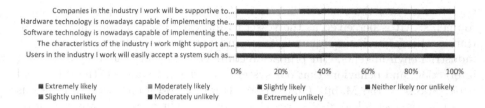

Fig. 11. Feasibility results. Question: What is your assessment of the feasibility of implementing a system such as the Mobile Office in your work experiences?

slightly less positive feedback. Also, users believe that the industry they work might support a system such as the mobile office; however, in response to the users' acceptance of such a system, respondents consider that is not as likely.

7 Discussion

The Mobile Office is an integrative approach to provide worker support in industrial environments. Previous research efforts have sought to tackle independent worker support aspects, but to our knowledge, any previous research has integrated the multiple approaches as proposed in the Mobile Office. Thus, the detailed aspects of such a system are not clearly defined; therefore, this study seeks to develop the intricacies of this multi-modal system. We based our system development on previous works' theories, authors' experiences in AR-UIs, and authors' experiences in industrial environments. The surveys then serve as an evaluation methodology and get feedback from potential Mobile Office users.

Overall, the Mobile Office proposed design aligns with the participants' expectations and needs in the survey. Aspects such as the bi-modal approach, environmental hazards, attention, and distraction align with AR-UI and physical considerations for the Mobile Office. This alignment was expected given that our design was based on the established methods and theories from the literature and authors' experiences. The survey also provided new perspectives that might need to be further explored in our Mobile Office design, such as the activity support and transition preference.

Given the limitations of the currently available hardware, multiple hardware configurations were proposed as presented in Fig. 7. The most significant hardware challenge is incorporating all the sensing and processing capabilities in a hardware device that is small enough to fit in the hardware configuration to implement. Considering this, the Mobile Office kiosk and vehicle hardware configurations in Fig. 7 might be considered feasible as of now; however, the personal device configuration still seems unattainable as of now.

8 Conclusions and Future Work

This article presents a novel approach to design a hybrid system based on AR to improve workers' productivity in industrial environments. Our proposed system goes further into the research direction of human support in productive environments. AR is perceived as the vessel to integrate context-awareness, visualization of information, communication, and perception within the challenging industrial environments. Our primary recommendations are the design features, interaction, and behaviors that our system implement to address the needs and expectations of the Mobile Office users. However, we found some limitations based on the technology limitations; however, it might open the gate to a novel and relevant AR applications if enabled based on future AR technology developments.

Despite the survey limitations in the sample obtained, it still provided evidence that confirms the Mobile Office design decisions. However, conducting a survey with a larger sample or a different inquiry method such as interviews is potentially a future work direction. We also recommend that an interactive prototype of this design be made for VR or current cutting-edge augmented reality device. Furthermore, though the guidelines would indicate the recommended design should work in theory, a usability study with both consumer and expert populations would greatly aid in determining the actual effectiveness of the design, as well as informing where alterations are appropriate. Quantitative approaches such as productivity measurements in the Mobile Office application might also be compared with other solutions used to increase productivity in industrial environments. Lastly, expanding the scope of this research beyond solely industrial use cases into other fields, such as mobile work for business or visualization for academia, would also provide valuable insight into whether there are effective universal elements for AR user interfaces or if they must be carefully tailored to individual uses.

Author contributions. Daniel Linares contributed to developing the theoretical framework including review literature, and the Mobile Office Design. He also helped develop, conduct, and interpret survey results. He also contributed to writing the article. Dr. Bowman led the project and provided expert guidelines and recommendations for the Mobile Office. He also helped to edit the article. Poorvesh Dongre helped to develop the theoretical framework, including the review of the literature. He also helped during the IRB review and also helped writing and to review the article. Dr. Roofigari helped in reaching out to participants for the survey and helped in reviewing the article.

References

1. Bartie, P., Mackaness, W.: Development of a speech-based augmented reality system to support exploration of cityscape. Trans. GIS **10**, 63–86 (2006). https://doi.org/10.1111/j.1467-9671.2006.00244.x
2. Berg, L.P., Vance, J.M.: Industry use of virtual reality in product design and manufacturing: a survey. Virtual Reality **21**(1), 1–17 (2016). https://doi.org/10.1007/s10055-016-0293-9
3. Billinghurst, M., Grasset, R., Looser, J.: Designing augmented reality interfaces. SIGGRAPH Comput. Graph. **39**(1), 17–22 (2005). https://doi.org/10.1145/1057792.1057803

4. Citi: Citi HoloLens holographic workstation. https://youtu.be/0NogltmewmQ
5. Duenser, A., Grasset, R., Seichter, H., Billinghurst, M.: Applying HCI principles to AR systems design (2007)
6. Figueiredo, L., Rodrigues, E., Teixeira, J., Teichrieb, V.: A comparative evaluation of direct hand and wand interactions on consumer devices. Comput. Graph. **77**, 108–121 (2018). https://doi.org/10.1016/j.cag.2018.10.006
7. Gabbard, J.L., Swan II, S.E.: Usability engineering for augmented reality: employing user-based studies to inform design. IEEE Trans. Vis. Comput. Graph. **14**(3), 513–525 (2008)
8. Ganapathy, S.: Design guidelines for mobile augmented reality: user experience. In: Huang, W., Alem, L., Livingston, M. (eds.) Human Factors in Augmented Reality Environments, pp. 165–180. Springer, New York (2013). https://doi.org/10.1007/978-1-4614-4205-9_7—
9. Grubert, J., Langlotz, T., Zollmann, S., Regenbrecht, H.: Towards pervasive augmented reality: context-awareness in augmented reality. IEEE Trans. Vis. Comput. Graph. **23**, 1706–1724 (2016). https://doi.org/10.1109/TVCG.2016.2543720
10. Guo, J., et al.: Mixed reality office system based on Maslow's hierarchy of needs: towards the long-term immersion in virtual environments. In: 2019 IEEE International Symposium on Mixed and Augmented Reality (ISMAR), pp. 224–235 (2019). https://doi.org/10.1109/ISMAR.2019.00019
11. Henderson, S., Feiner, S.: Opportunistic tangible user interfaces for augmented reality. IEEE Trans. Vis. Comput. Graph. **16**(1), 4–16 (2010). https://doi.org/10.1109/TVCG.2009.91
12. Janssen, C., Kun, A., Brewster, S., Boyle, L., Brumby, D., Chuang, L.: Exploring the concept of the (future) mobile office (2019). https://doi.org/10.1145/3349263.3349600
13. Kang, S.C., Yeh, K., Tsai, M.H.: On-site building information retrieval by using projection-based augmented reality. J. Comput. Civil Eng. **26**, 342–355 (2012). https://doi.org/10.1061/(ASCE)CP.1943-5487.0000156
14. Kasapakis, V., Gavalas, D., Galatis, P.: An efficient geometric approach for occlusion handling in outdoors augmented reality applications. In: De Paolis, L.T., Mongelli, A. (eds.) AVR 2016. LNCS, vol. 9768, pp. 418–434. Springer, Cham (2016). https://doi.org/10.1007/978-3-319-40621-3_30
15. Kerr, S.J., et al.: Wearable mobile augmented reality: evaluating outdoor user experience. In: Proceedings of the 10th International Conference on Virtual Reality Continuum and Its Applications in Industry (VRCAI 2011), pp. 209–216. Association for Computing Machinery, New York (2011). https://doi.org/10.1145/2087756.2087786
16. LaViola, J.J.: 3D User Interfaces: Theory and Practice. Addison-Wesley, Boston (2017)
17. Leyer, M., Richter, A., Steinhüser, M.: "Power to the workers": empowering shop floor workers with worker-centric digital designs. Int. J. Oper. Prod. Manage. **39**(1), 24–42 (2019). https://doi.org/10.1108/IJOPM-05-2017-0294
18. Li, X., Yi, W., Chi, H.L., Wang, X., Chan, A.P.C.: A critical review of virtual and augmented reality (VR/AR) applications in construction safety. Autom. Constr. **86**, 150–162 (2018). https://doi.org/10.1016/j.autcon.2017.11.003
19. Livingston, M.A.: Evaluating human factors in augmented reality systems. IEEE Comput. Graph. Appl. **25**(6), 6–9 (2005). https://doi.org/10.1109/MCG.2005.130

20. Mistry, P., Maes, P.: Sixthsense: a wearable gestural interface. In: ACM SIG-GRAPH ASIA 2009 Art Gallery & Emerging Technologies: Adaptation (SIG-GRAPH ASIA 2009), p. 85. Association for Computing Machinery, New York (2009). https://doi.org/10.1145/1665137.1665204

21. Norman, D.A.: Natural user interfaces are not natural. Interactions **17**(3), 6–10 (2010). https://doi.org/10.1145/1744161.1744163

22. Nwakacha, V., Crabtree, A., Burnett, G.: Evaluating distraction and disengagement of attention from the road. In: Shumaker, R. (ed.) VAMR 2013. LNCS, vol. 8022, pp. 261–270. Springer, Heidelberg (2013). https://doi.org/10.1007/978-3-642-39420-1_28

23. Raskar, R., Welch, G., Cutts, M., Lake, A., Stesin, L., Fuchs, H.: The office of the future: a unified approach to image-based modeling and spatially immersive displays. In: Proceedings of the 25th Annual Conference on Computer Graphics and Interactive Techniques (SIGGRAPH 1998), pp. 179–188. Association for Computing Machinery, New York (1998). https://doi.org/10.1145/280814.280861

24. Regenbrecht, H., Baratoff, G., Wagner, M.: A tangible AR desktop environment. Comput. Graph. **25**(5), 755–763 (2001). https://doi.org/10.1016/S0097-8493(01)00118-2

25. Stanney, K.M., Mollaghasemi, M., Reeves, L., Breaux, R., Graeber, D.A.: Usability engineering of virtual environments (VEs): identifying multiple criteria that drive effective VE system design. Int. J. Hum. Comput. Stud. **58**(4), 447–481 (2003). https://doi.org/10.1016/S1071-5819(03)00015-6

26. Sun, T.-L., Feng, W.-Y., Chao, C.-J.: Dynamic generation of human-populated VR models for workspace ergonomic evaluation. In: Duffy, V.G. (ed.) ICDHM 2007. LNCS, vol. 4561, pp. 979–987. Springer, Heidelberg (2007). https://doi.org/10.1007/978-3-540-73321-8_110

27. Tatzgern, M., Orso, V., Kalkofen, D., Jacucci, G., Gamberini, L., Schmalstieg, D.: Adaptive information density for augmented reality displays. In: 2016 IEEE Virtual Reality (VR), pp. 83–92. https://doi.org/10.1109/VR.2016.7504691

28. Walczak, K., Rumiński, D., Flotyński, J.: Building contextual augmented reality environments with semantics. In: 2014 International Conference on Virtual Systems & Multimedia (VSMM), pp. 353–361. https://doi.org/10.1109/VSMM.2014.7136656

29. Wetzel, R., McCall, R., Braun, A.K., Broll, W.: Guidelines for designing augmented reality games. In: Proceedings of the 2008 Conference on Future Play: Research, Play, Share (Future Play 2008), pp. 173–180. Association for Computing Machinery, New York (2008). https://doi.org/10.1145/1496984.1497013

30. Zhang, Z., Hui, P., Kulkarni, S., Peylo, C.: Enabling an augmented reality ecosystem: a content-oriented survey. In: Proceedings of the 2014 Workshop on Mobile Augmented Reality and Robotic Technology-Based Systems (MARS 2014), pp. 41–46. Association for Computing Machinery, New York (2014). https://doi.org/10.1145/2609829.2609835

Virtual Reality Compensatory Aid for Improved Weapon Splash-Zone Awareness

Richi Rodriguez[1], Domenick Mifsud[1], Chris Wickens[1],
Adam S. Williams[1(✉)] ⓘ, Kathrine Tarre[3], Peter Crane[2],
and Francisco R. Ortega[1] ⓘ

[1] Colorado State University, Fort Collins, CO, USA
{richi.rodriguez,dmifsud,chris.wickens,adamwil,
f.ortega}@colostate.edu.com
[2] Virtual Reality Rehab, Orlando, FL, USA
pcrane@virtualrealityrehab.com
[3] Florida International University, Miami, FL, USA
ktarr007@fiu.edu

Abstract. Military personnel often have very little time to make battle-field decisions. These decisions can include the identification of weapon splash-zones and of the objects in and near that zone. With the advances made in commercially available virtual reality technologies, it is possible to develop a compensatory aid to help with this decision-making process. This paper presents a virtual reality system that was designed to be such an aid. This system was tested in a user study where participants had to identify whether objects were in a splash-zone, where those objects were relative to that splash-zone, and to identify what the objects were. This user study found that the system was well-received by participants as measured by high system usability survey responses. Most participants were able to identify objects with high accuracy and speed. Additionally, throughout the user study participant performance improved to near-perfect accuracy, indicating that the system was quickly learned by participants. These positive results imply that this system may be able to serve as a viable, and easy to learn aid for splash-zone related decision making.

Keywords: Virtual reality · Human-computer interaction · Visualizations · Compensatory aid

1 Introduction

Military personnel often have seconds to decide whether to fire or not [7]. These personal can have improved firearm safety through cognitive aids and training [7].

Distribution A - Approved for Public Release (Unlimited Distribution). Document Control Number (DCN #): 43-7564-21.

J. Y. C. Chen and G. Fragomeni (Eds.): HCII 2021, LNCS 12770, pp. 533–544, 2021.
https://doi.org/10.1007/978-3-030-77599-5_36

As the military adopts new display technologies [3], there is an opportunity to develop compensatory aids that can reduce casualties. These aids may also serve as a way to reduce the amount of gear needed to be carried or switched between in the field. As an example, a map and a notepad can both be shown on a head-up display, reducing the homing time needed for users to move their attention from either device to the other.

This paper outlines a user study evaluating one such compensatory aid. That aid utilized a virtual reality (VR) system that concentrated on the usability of splash-zone representations, which could indicate the impact area of a weapon. This aid was developed with military use in mind, as such, the tasks given in the study are set to emulate a portion of the workflow completed by joint terminal attack controllers (JTACs). JTAC's are tasked with integrating information about targets, personnel movements, aircraft coordination, and attack coordination [11]. Currently these tasks are supported by a variety of digital (i.e., tablet, phone, radio, digital map), and analog (i.e., paper pad, binoculars) technologies [9]. This system uses a VR head-mounted display (HMD) to render synthetic battlefield information in participant's field of view. This can be considered to take the place of a digital map and a communication device. That said, the system can be extended to have the functionalities of other tools needed in this workflow (i.e., annotation of the map, notepad).

The portion of the JTAC workflow most closely implemented in and tested with this system were the tasks of identifying a target area, identifying the locations of objects, and identifying those objects positions relative to the target area. Often the identification of target zones, and the associated objects near that zone, is relayed to aircraft pilots whose view of the world may be different from the JTAC's. The terms "left" and "right" are too ambiguous to be used in this scenario, especially given the intense time pressures that JTAC operators function under. Due to that, this system is designed using a north up bird's eye view (Fig. 1).

As technologies continue to advance, the military's adaptation of augmented reality (AR) and VR displays is becoming more prevalent [3]. By leveraging this emerging technology to facilitate a JTAC style workflow, this system can reduce the need for military personal to carry additional devices (i.e., digital map, rangefinder) through incorporating them into a single system. While optical see-though solutions such as augmented reality HMDs can provide more contextual awareness, their limited field of view and difficulties rendering objects in bright areas makes them sub-optimal for testing this system. Due to that, this system has been developed on an VR-HMD. This choice allows for a wider field of view and more exact control of the rendered objects visibility. Most importantly, this system offers a salient and accessible means of showing target zones. This style of compensatory aid can be of much benefit to end-users in the field.

This studies objectives were:

- To find how effectively participants could use the visualization shown to assess whether entities or objects (e.g., vehicles, troops) were inside the target zone (Fig. 1)

- To assess the extent to which the visualization features might inhibit other judgments of importance such as recognition of the entity and its relative bearing from the center of the zone
- To examine the learning of these judgments across the experimental session

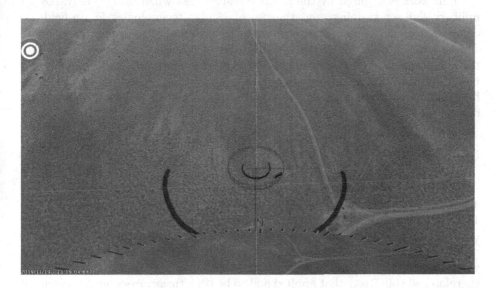

Fig. 1. Example of experimental stimulus.

2   Related Work

The military has pursued using VR-HMDs as a training aid for technical job requirements. In support of that, the 2018 "Joint Fire Support Executive Steering Committee" report specifies that some portion of JTAC live training can be replaced by the use of virtual simulations [4]. VR-HMD training for military applications has seen some success. Sui et al. (2016) found that the use of VR training can effectively retrain military medical professional on operational skill-sets that have been degraded by infrequent use [10].

Within the context of JTAC workflows, prior work has shown that a combination of human factors design and AR-HMDs can be successfully used in JTAC workflow related tasks [11]. However, that work primarily focused on testing the feasibility of various information displays as measured by human-factors based evaluations. Where that work focused on the feasibility of information displays, this work focuses on the usability of those displays.

The study of VR-HMD compensatory aid design has been somewhat limited. Work on battlefield aids usually focuses on the use of AR-HMDs, and mobile AR (i.e., a cell phone display with video-pass-through technology) [1,5]. One such aid using mobile AR on commercially available phones was shown to be both usable for in field sensor fusion information display, and as a military viable option [5]. Other work has shown that the use of AR-HMDs can be beneficial as navigation aids [1], as well as for the identification of building obscured troops locations [6,8].

This work is inspired by the positive results seen when using VR-HMDs for military skill-set training, and the use of similar technologies for in-field use compensatory aids. This paper represents a push forward in evaluating the real-time use of a virtual battlefield aid. In order to do that, this paper establishes the acceptance and effectivity of this aid's use in a controlled environment. This paper differentiates itself from prior work by examining learning rates and visual information assessment, as opposed to examining the feasibility of information display on these technologies.

3   Methods

A user study was conducted with 24 unpaid volunteers. All 24 volunteers were active students (age 18 or older) at Colorado State University and out of those 18 were enrolled in the United States Army Reserve Officers' Training Corps (ROTC). Of the 24 volunteers, 5 were females and 19 were males. The average age of the volunteers was 19.96 with a standard deviation of 2.99. At the time when the experiment was conducted, the experiment was under export control, therefore, all volunteers that applied had to be US citizens. A second requirement was that the volunteers had a 20/20 vision or corrected to close to 20/20 via glasses/contacts/surgery.

All volunteers that fulfilled the requirements were asked to sign an informed consent, an attestation that they were citizens, and that they had an acceptable vision to continue as participants in the experiment. After filling out those forms, each participant was briefed on the tasks that would be presented to them. The briefing was done via instructions, which each participant had to read. After reading the instructions, a dialogue would take place with the participant, where questions were asked to confirm that the instructions had been understood. The next couple of minutes was optional if the participant had other questions.

Next, the head-mounted display was shown, along with the function of each knob/button and how to how to properly wear it. They were given as long as necessary to adjust it so that their viewing was not impaired due to calibration. A set of menus/images were shown to verify that the participant's vision was focused, and when that was not the case, an additional amount of time was reserved for that purpose.

For each trial participants viewed a virtual environment, which contained a splash-zone and an object. Participants were asked to respond to three questions regarding that scene:

- Is the object inside or outside the splash-zone? (In/out).
- What is the Azimuth position of the object? (Clock position of the object).
- Please describe the object. (Object description).

Participants were trained to respond to these scenes as quickly as possible. When shown the scene in Fig. 1, participants were expected to respond to question 1 ("in"), question 2 ("4 o'clock"), and question 3 ("bus"). There were 6 possible objects (Fig. 2). There were 12 possible clock positions (1–12), and 2 possible splash-zone locations (In/Out). During the experimental trials, these three variables were combined orthogonally in a $2 \times 12 \times 6$ experimental design. Trials lasted approximately 5–10 s; this time is determined by how long it took a participant to make each judgment.

A block consisted of six scenes. Participants were first given a chance to train on the system with two blocks (Blocks 1–2). The next four blocks (Blocks 3–6) were the experimental blocks considered for the analysis. Therefore, each question was presented a total of 24 times (excluding the training blocks) to each of the 24 participants.

It was hypothesized that some of the participants would not have experienced a virtual reality system before, which could have caused some eye strain. Therefore, an optional short break was highly encouraged between blocks.

At the end of each experiment, a system usability score (SUS) questionnaire was presented to each participant so that each participant can rate the system's usability [2].

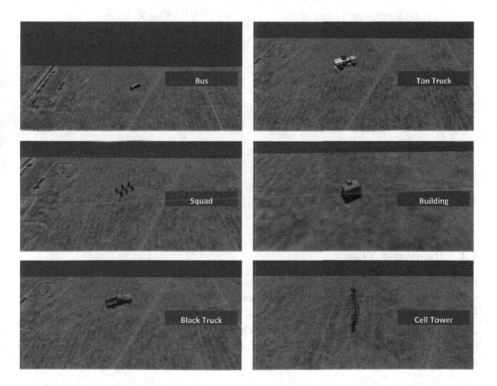

Fig. 2. The six objects and their names.

3.1 Apparatus

The computer used to perform the experiment consisted of an Alienware Aurora
R8 with 1TB SSD, 2TB SATA HDD, an NVIDIA GeForce RTX 2070 with 8GB
GDDR6 RAM, an Intel i7 9700K CPU, and 64GB RAM. The head-mounted
display used was the HTC Vive Pro Eye. Two generic tripod stands were used
to setup the Vive's base stations. A Yeti USB Microphone was used to record
each participant's responses. An external 2TB hard drive was used to keep a
backup of the data under lock and key.

4 Results

There was a significant impact of block on response time which manifested as
a decrease in response time over blocks or "practice" (Fig. 3). This was supported by an analysis of variance (ANOVA) ($F(3,1717) = 6.68, p < .001$).
Total response time was then subdivided into the time used to make each of the
three consecutive judgments.

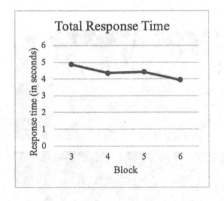

Fig. 3. The list of recommended hotels

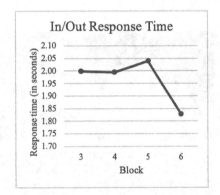

Fig. 4. In/Out response time (in seconds).

4.1 Response Time

Figure 4 shows the effect of block on judgment time (in/out). Although Fig. 4
suggests faster time during the last session, an ANOVA showed that this was
not statistically significant ($F(3,567) = 0.82, p = .48$). There was a continuous
decrease in azimuth judgment time with practice ($F(3,567) = 6.37, p < .001$)
(Fig. 5). There was also a significant effect of blocks on object recognition time
with $F(3,567) = 3.43, p = 0.017$ (Fig. 6).

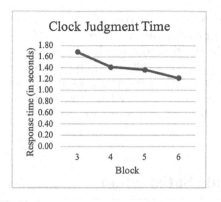

Fig. 5. Azimuth position/clock judgment time.

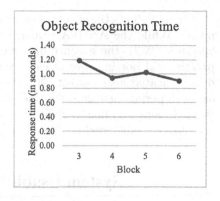

Fig. 6. Object recognition time (in seconds).

4.2   Accuracy

The accuracy of the first judgment, in/out of the splash-zone was nearly at ceiling performance from the start (97%) and, as such, was not affected by practice. The accuracy of the azimuth judgment as a function of block is shown in Fig. 7. Clock position accuracy was high overall (approximately 88%). Block did not have a significant impact on this judgment ($F(3, 92) = 0.42, p = 0.74$). A closer inspection of the data revealed that participants made near perfect judgments of clock position when the azimuth lay along the line of sight (12:00 or 6:00) and orthogonal (9:00 or 3:00), but had more difficulty judging the off-angle azimuths of 1, 2, 4, 5, 7, 8, 10, and 11 o'clock, where there was only an 80% accuracy rate.

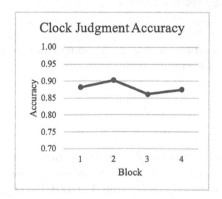

Fig. 7. Clock judgment accuracy.

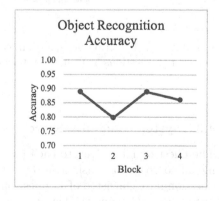

Fig. 8. Object recognition accuracy.

Figure 8 shows the effects of block on the accuracy of participant object recognition. While the ANOVA revealed a marginally significant effect ($F(3, 92) = 2.67, p = .052$), the absence of a monotonic trend across blocks suggests that practice did not improve object recognition accuracy. Closer analysis of these data indicated near perfect (99%) accuracy when the object was located at an azimuth perpendicular to the line of sight; reduced accuracy (93%) when it was located along the line of sight, and still further reduced accuracy (81%) when the object was located on the off-angle azimuths.

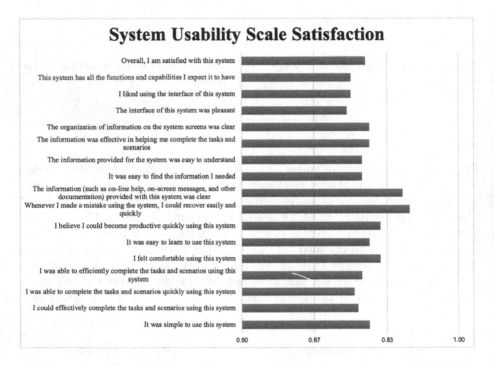

Fig. 9. SUS satisfaction per question, showing a ratio representing the sum of all user ratings per questions against the total number of maximum points.

4.3 System Usability Score

The questionnaire given to each participant at the end of each experiment was meant to give us an insight into what worked and what needed to improve. The questionnaire consisted of 17 questions, where each question could be rated from one to seven (1 being the lowest satisfaction and 7 being the highest satisfaction rating). Figure 10 contains a list of the questions, the mean of all participants per questions on the left, as well as each participant's individual response to each question on the right side of the question. A total of 10 questions were not answered by participants, which were replaced by a rating of 4, as it is

Mean	Question	Participant																							
		1	2	3	4	5	6	7	8	9	10	11	12	13	14	15	16	17	18	19	20	21	22	23	24
3.92	It was simple to use this system	2	1	5	1	7	1	1	1	7	1	1	1	1	1	1	7	7	1	7	7	6	7	7	7
3.79	I could effectively complete the tasks and scenarios using this system	1	1	6	1	6	1	1	7	1	1	1	1	2	1	6	7	1	7	6	6	7	7	6	7
3.75	I was able to complete the tasks and scenarios quickly using this system	2	1	4	1	6	1	1	7	1	1	1	1	1	1	7	6	1	7	7	6	7	7	6	7
3.83	I was able to efficiently complete the tasks and scenarios using this system	2	1	5	1	6	1	1	7	1	1	1	1	1	1	7	7	1	7	7	6	7	7	6	7
4.04	I felt comfortable using this system	3	1	4	1	7	1	3	7	1	1	1	2	1	1	7	7	1	7	7	7	7	7	6	7
3.92	It was easy to learn to use this system	1	1	5	1	7	1	1	7	1	1	1	1	1	1	7	7	1	7	7	7	7	7	7	7
4.04	I believe I could become productive quickly using this system	2	1	5	1	7	1	1	7	1	1	1	1	4	1	7	6	1	7	7	7	7	7	7	7
4.38	Whenever I made a mistake using the system, I could recover easily and quickly	1	2	3	4	7	4	4	6	4	4	4	1	4	1	6	5	1	7	5	5	7	7	6	7
4.29	The information (such as on-line help, on-screen messages, and other documentation) provided with this system was clear	1	2	5	4	5	1	4	7	1	4	4	1	1	1	7	7	1	7	6	6	7	7	7	7
3.83	It was easy to find the information I needed	2	1	3	1	6	1	1	7	4	1	1	1	1	1	7	7	1	7	6	7	7	6	6	7
3.83	The information provided for the system was easy to understand	2	1	4	1	7	1	1	7	1	1	1	1	1	1	7	7	1	7	7	7	7	6	6	7
3.92	The information was effective in helping me complete the tasks and scenarios	2	1	6	1	6	1	1	7	1	1	1	2	1	1	7	7	1	7	7	6	7	7	6	7
3.92	The organization of information on the system screens was clear	2	1	5	1	7	1	3	7	1	1	1	1	1	1	7	7	1	7	7	6	7	5	7	7
3.67	The interface of this system was pleasant	2	1	5	1	5	1	3	7	1	1	1	1	1	1	6	5	1	7	7	6	7	5	6	7
3.71	I liked using the interface of this system	2	1	4	1	5	1	2	7	1	1	1	1	1	1	7	6	1	7	7	6	7	6	6	7
3.71	This system has all the functions and capabilities I expect it to have	2	1	6	1	6	1	2	7	1	1	1	2	1	1	7	6	1	7	7	7	3	5	6	7
3.88	Overall, I am satisfied with this system	2	1	5	1	6	1	2	7	1	1	1	2	1	1	7	6	1	7	7	7	6	7	6	7

Fig. 10. The **Question** column list the questions that were presented in the SUS with the mean on its right and the individual responses per participant on the right side.

the average between the ratings (1 and 7) and can act as a neutral number. Although the instructions for the ratings (1 being the lowest and 7 the highest) were provided at the beginning of the SUS and they were reminded at intervals, some participants confessed, after finishing, that they were confused and thought that a rating of 1 was better. The maximum number of points for all questions were 119 ($7 \times 17 = 119$, 7 corresponding to the highest satisfaction and 17 to the number of questions). Figure 9 illustrates the ratio of the sum for each question over the total maximum points. This shows that the overall satisfaction rate for all questions were well above 75%.

5 Discussion

The primary objective of the experiment was to assess if the entities were inside or outside of the splash zone. As the overall correct response rate of participants were over 99%, one could see that participants did not have any problems affirming the object's location. Another objective was to assess if the visualization features might inhibit some of the judgment calls. The object recognition accuracy fluctuated between 80%–90%. Some of the concerns that participants expressed after the experiment were that the color of the object and the texture of the background closely resembled each other, which at times made it difficult to recognize the type of object being presented. Object identification was also occasionally inhibited by the display. When objects were located perpendicular to the line of sight they were never interposed, and their identity was judged with near perfect accuracy. When objects were along the line of sight, or at off angles, roughly half of the time they would have been partially obscured by the fence, which degraded performance.

The final objective was to assess the learning effect of the presented judgments across the experiment sessions. The clock judgment accuracy (Fig. 7) revealed that the mean stayed between 85%–90%. Likewise, the object recognition accuracy (Fig. 8) mean was always between 80%–90%. Making these judgments from a long distance and in the case of most participants, doing this for the first time, the resulting accuracy was to be expected. However, when the response times of the clock judgment (Fig. 5) and the object recognition time (Fig. 6) are reviewed, the graphs indicate that the required time to respond was decreasing. The decreasing time graphs (Figs. 5 and 6), along with the over 80% accuracy graphs (Figs. 7 and 8) indicate that a learning effect was taking place.

The learning effect indicates that the system is easy to learn in a short amount of time as seen by the users improved performance over each block. This learning rate also indicates that this system can improve splash-zone awareness for minimally trained participants, whose first exposure to the system was the same day as the experiment (6 out of 24 participants had experience with VR). It is possible that these trends may hold true in augmented reality HMD systems as well. If that is found to be true, this system may be able to aid military personal as a field use compensatory aid. The low training overhead, and quick target identification times could both the success of this aid.

The SUS is important as it will help the team to reshape the future of this project. While a 75% overall satisfaction ratio is high, there are some areas that need improvement, such as "The interface of this system was pleasant" and "I was able to complete the tasks and scenarios quickly using this system", both of which had ratings in the low 70 s. Since some of the lower ratings were due to the participant mistaking the high ratings for the low ratings, it would be beneficial to mention the SUS scales to the participant verbally at intervals and to place a reminder of these ratings at the beginning of every other question using a larger font. Overall, the SUS results show that this system is usable and well received by minimally trained participants. We believe this is a positive indication that this system would similarly be usable by military personal, which have some overlapping military training with the participant pool used in this study due to the participants ROTC training.

6 Future Work

Some of the deficiencies previously mentioned is that the foreground object would need to be distinct from the background texture. One approach would be to change the shape of the object, as the light rendered on it will make it look different. Consequently, choosing a different color for the object or the background is another way to separate one from the other, making the interface easy to follow. This experiment showed that a learning effect takes place while the participant is performing the experiment. A prospective experiment could be one that shows a participant's accuracy when a participant needs to identify an object given several objects scattered in the splash zone. An awareness of this type given in a specific situation would need to be instantaneous. JTACs are required to make instant judgment calls on any terrain at any cardinal location and understanding their reaction time and requirements will help them achieve their goal.

7 Conclusion

Participants could determine if the objects were in or out of the splash-zones with near perfect accuracy. The judgments of object identity appeared to have been slightly inhibited. When the objects were located perpendicular to the line of sight they were recognized with near perfect accuracy, whether inside or outside the fence (Fig. 1). Occasionally misidentification of targets was due to the fence obscuring the object itself, or due to the similarity of the texture of the object shown and the texture of the background. Mistakes caused by the fence obscuring objects were most common in trials where the objects were along or at off angle to the line of sight. Participants became quicker with practice, shortening their overall response time by nearly 1 second. It was the only the in/out judgments that did not improve with practice, but these were so simple that response time would be difficult to shorten. These results demonstrate that this system can improve splash-zone understanding.

Acknowledgments. This effort is based on research supported by the Office of Naval Research under SBIR topic N171-091 "Synthetic Vision System for Ground Forces via Fused Augmented Realities (FAR-UI)", SV4GF contract # N00014-19-C-2026. We would like to thank Albert Armonda and the ARMY ROTC cadets at Colorado State University.

References

1. Aaltonen, I., Laarni, J.: Field evaluation of a wearable multimodal soldier navigation system. Appl. Ergon. **63**, 79–90 (2017)
2. Brooke, J.: Sus: a "quick and dirty' usability". In: Usability Evaluation in Industry, p. 189 (1996)
3. Brustein, J.: Microsoft wins $480 million army battlefield contract, November 2018. https://www.bloomberg.com/news/articles/2018-11-28/microsoft-wins-480-million-army-battlefield-contract
4. Chairman of the Joint Chiefs of Staff Instruction, M.: Joint fire support executive steering committee governance and management. Report CJCSI 5127.01A DISTRIBUTION: A, B, C, S (2018). www.jcs.mil/Portals/36/Documents/Library/Instructions/CJCSI%205127.01A.pdf

5. Chmielewski, M., Kukiełka, M., Fraszczak, D., Bugajewski, D.: Military and crisis management decision support tools for situation awareness development using sensor data fusion. In: Światek, J., Borzemski, L., Wilimowska, Z. (eds.) ISAT 2017. AISC, vol. 656, pp. 189–199. Springer, Cham (2018). https://doi.org/10.1007/978-3-319-67229-8_17

6. Gans, E., et al.: Augmented reality technology for day/night situational awareness for the dismounted soldier. In: Display Technologies and Applications for Defense, Security, and Avionics IX; and Head-and Helmet-Mounted Displays XX, vol. 9470, p. 947004. International Society for Optics and Photonics (2015)

7. Hamilton, J.A., Lambert, G., Suss, J., Biggs, A.T.: Can cognitive training improve shoot/don't-shoot performance? Evidence from live fire exercises. Am. J. Psychol. **132**(2), 179–194 (2019). https://doi.org/10.5406/amerjpsyc.132.2.0179

8. Livingston, M.A., Ai, Z., Decker, J.W.: Human factors for military applications of head-worn augmented reality displays. In: Cassenti, D.N. (ed.) AHFE 2018. AISC, vol. 780, pp. 56–65. Springer, Cham (2019). https://doi.org/10.1007/978-3-319-94223-0_6

9. Office of the Naval Inspector General, Navy: Alleged vulnerabilities of the kinetic integrated low-cost software integrated tactical combat handheld (KILSWITCH)/android precision assault strike suite (APASS) application. Report of Investigation, NIGHTS, OSC DI-17-3391 NAVINSGEN 201702142 132 (2018). www.cyber-peace.org/wp-content/uploads/2018/12/us_navy.pdf

10. Siu, K.C., Best, B.J., Kim, J.W., Oleynikov, D., Ritter, F.E.: Adaptive virtual reality training to optimize military medical skills acquisition and retention. Mil. Med. **181**(suppl 5), 214–220 (2016). https://doi.org/10.7205/MILMEDD1500164

11. Wickens, C., Dempsey, G., Pringle, A., Kazansky, L., Hutka, S.: Developing and evaluating an augmented reality interface to assist the joint tactical air controller by applying human performance models. In: Proceedings of the Human Factors and Ergonomics Society Annual Meeting, vol. 62, no. 1, pp. 686–690 (2018). https://doi.org/10.1177/1541931218621155

Mixed Reality Visualization of Friendly vs Hostile Decision Dynamics

Simon Su[1]([⊠]) [iD], Sue Kase[1] [iD], Chou Hung[1] [iD], J. Zach Hare[1] [iD],
B. Christopher Rinderspacher[1] [iD], and Charles Amburn[2]

[1] DEVCOM Army Research Laboratory, Adelphi, MD 20783, USA
simon.m.su.civ@mail.mil
[2] DEVCOM Soldier Center, Orlando, FL 32826, USA

Abstract. We present an investigation using mixed reality technology to visualize decision-making dynamics for a Friendly vs Hostile wargame in a Multi-Domain Operation environment. The requirement of penetrate and dis-integrate phases under Multi-Domain Operations aligns well with the advantages of Artificial Intelligence/Machine Learning because of 1) very short planning timeframe for decision-making, 2) simultaneous planning requirement for multiple operations, and 3) interdependence of operations. In our decision dynamics research, we propose to advance the art/science for wargaming by leveraging brain science to extend the use of Artificial Intelligence/Machine Learning algorithms and the use of mixed reality technology to visualize complex battlespace scenarios requiring a better understand of the dynamics in a complex decision making process.

Keywords: Immersive visualization · Multi-domain operation · Multi-modal visualization

1 Introduction

To bridge the gap between computer games and Multi-Domain Operations (MDO) wargaming, a concerted programmatic effort is needed to develop artificial intelligence and machine learning (AI/ML) research, grounded in brain and decision science principles, and embedded in an immersive advanced visualization environment. The AI/ML research will discover the foundational theories needed to develop universal tools for conceptual understanding that can recombine and interpret different sources of information to aid complex MDO decision-making. Modeling and visualizing these decision-making strategies at all levels of operations requires new algorithms applied to dynamic environments characterized by changing rules, cognitive states, uncertainty, individual biases and heuristics [1]. The capability to rapidly respond to and mitigate unexpected hostile capabilities as well as exploit new opportunities and friendly technological capabilities is critical for decision-making overmatch in a MDO environment.

For complex MDO situations with imperfect knowledge and uncertainty, an AI that provides a landscape of near-optimal solutions may be more helpful than one that provides a single 'optimal' solution [2]. How the AIs can convey these solution alternatives

This is a U.S. government work and not under copyright protection in the U.S.; foreign copyright protection may apply 2021
J. Y. C. Chen and G. Fragomeni (Eds.): HCII 2021, LNCS 12770, pp. 545–555, 2021.
https://doi.org/10.1007/978-3-030-77599-5_37

in a transparent manner to command and operational staff is a research gap that needs to be addressed [3]. Experimentation of conditions such as near-optimality and uncertainty [2], with new warfighter machine interfaces (WMIs) and advanced visualization technologies can lead to new AI/ML algorithm development and universal tools and principles that better synergize the human + AI exploration of complex decision-making [4]. In this paper, we begin to explore the ties between AI/ML-generated solutions, WMIs, and advanced visualization technology by utilizing the Augmented REality Sandtable (ARES) [5] battlespace visualization platform.

The ARES platform provides mixed reality visualization capabilities for our investigation of Friendly vs Hostile Decision Dynamics for complex MDO decision-making. ARES is a battlespace visualization research and development testbed using commercial off-the-shelf products to create a low-cost method of geospatial terrain visualization with a tangible user interface. Currently, ARES is primarily used for simulation and training with the goal of offering battlespace visualization capabilities and a user-defined common operating picture of the battlespace environment. The ARES platform supports multimodal visualization capabilities such as a traditionally used military sand filled table enhanced with commercial off the shelf components and projection technology used in combination with a depth sensor; browser-based 2D and 3D interfaces; head mounted and hand-held devices; and mixed reality integration. Figure 1 shows ARES running in a multi-user visualization view.

In the next section, we overview two research projects related to our Friendly vs Hostile Decision Dynamics research conducted on the ARES visualization platform. Section 3 describes Phase 1 implementation details of visualizing the Friendly vs Hostile Decision Dynamics research on the ARES platform. Section 4 discusses the challenges of algorithm development and Phase 1 testing the wargame using a text-based visualization

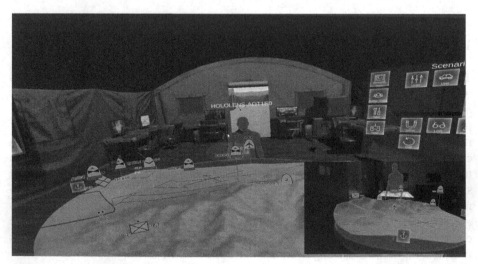

Fig. 1. Augmented REality Sandtable (ARES) running on Mixed Reality and Head Mounted Display with the larger viewport showing the complete immersive view from a Head Mounted Display and the smaller viewport showing the mixed reality view from the Mixed Reality display device.

instead of a graphical user interface (GUI). Section 5 describes future plans for the Phase 2 integration with other data sources and the SyncVis platform. Section 6 concludes the paper.

2   Related Work

ARES is a research and development (R&D) testbed for experimentation in battlespace visualization and decision-making [6]. Typically, ARES R&D focuses on human factors-related research in the areas of information visualization, multi-modal interaction, and human performance assessment. Garneau et al. [6], in a DEVCOM Army Research Laboratory technical report, discussed completed, ongoing, and planned research framing an overall strategy for future work with ARES as a R&D testbed. According to Garneau et al. [6], the predominant research question underlying all ARES research activities is "What improvements in battlespace visualization and decision-making aid in providing a common operating picture at the point of need and best meet user requirements?". Outcomes from our Friendly vs Hostile Decision Dynamics experiment will support and significantly contribute to Garneau's vision of ARES as an R&D testbed.

ARES software provides geospatial terrain information and map images allowing users to build or edit tactical mission plans and courses of action. On the ARES version of a traditional military sand table, the visualization uses a depth sensor device with the sand topography based on the user's physical interaction with the sand in real-time. ARES software also acts as a data server distributing the data to client applications that provide data to the users via one or more of the supported visualization modalities including Head-Mounted Display devices, web based interfaces, android table devices, and the mixed reality devices. Figure 2 shows the various modalities supported by the ARES battlespace visualization platform.

Fig. 2. ARES platform concept showing multiple visualization modalities.

Boyce et al. [7] research investigated military tactics comprehension using the ARES platform. Boyce's experiment assessed how displaying information onto different surfaces (flat vs. raised) influenced the performance, workload, and engagement of cadets answering questions on military tactics. Participant engagement was measured using a modified User Engagement Scale and the System Usability Scale; workload was measured by the NASA-TLX. The findings of the experiment indicated that a raised terrain surface led to reduced workload and increased engagement and time on task as compared to a flat terrain surface. ARES support of alternative display methods, in this case, demonstrated increased engagement by augmenting the instruction of the military tactical tasks. Boyce et al. [7] conclusions, based on empirical data, affirms the suitability of ARES as a testbed for our Friendly vs Hostile Decision Dynamics decision-making experimentation.

3   Implementation Details

The Friendly vs Hostile Decision Dynamics research investigates AI/ML approaches to decision-making in a MDO context. In Phase 1 of our research, we are investigating new computational and human decision-making principles such as decision-making under uncertainty with many near-optimal solutions in a complex decision space. As part of this research initiative, we designed a research platform with a new WMI to facilitate the understanding of how humans overcome complex decision-making challenges. The WMI will have a limited simulation capability inspired by Mission Command, which is a variation on the game Battleship [8]. Unlike previous AI games, our rules will be dynamic (e.g., unexpected new classes of L- and T- shaped battleships), and both friendly and hostile players must choose from a complex decision landscape with uncertainty.

In the decision dynamics component of the project, uncertainty may be titrated by limiting player visibility of the game scenario and the effectiveness of player actions. Dynamics can also be increased by asking opposing players to switch among several predefined strategies mid-game. This requires creating new algorithms to rapidly adapt to new strategies by forming flexible abstract representations tied to reward probabilities and by having mechanisms for both fast and slow learning. Our approach to developing these algorithmic capabilities is inspired by brain mechanisms for flexible memory and behavior-reward associations. We will leverage the ARES battlespace visualization platform as part of the research activities mentioned above including the development of the WMIs and the game scenarios.

3.1   Warfighter Machine Interfaces Design Using Augmented REality Sandtable Battlespace Visualization Platform

As described in the previous section, the ARES battlespace visualization platform allows users to build and edit tactical scenarios using one or more visualization modalities. In the Friendly vs Hostile MDO environment, the decision dynamics are visualized as a team-based wargaming scenario on a real-world terrain.

The ARES Table Manager allows users to specify a map of an area of operations based on available data from Google Maps, OpenStreetMaps, OpenTopoMap, and USGS, or from a user-uploaded map image. In the example scenario described below, cesium terrain tiles generate a high-resolution terrain of the area surrounding the Fort Irwin National Training Center located in northern San Bernardino County, California. The Mojave Desert's hills and the surrounding mountains provide an isolated area of over 1,000 square miles capacity for maneuver and ranges for conducting realistic joint and combined arms training [9].

After the terrain map is imported and loaded in the Table Manager, the terrain can be shared and displayed across 2D and 3D devices. Any number of scenarios can be created and overlaid on a terrain that can be saved, edited, shared, and exported. Here the ARES Tactical Web Planner application was used to build a simple tactical scenario using MIL-STD 2525C symbols [10] associated with the Friendly vs Hostile wargame (see Figs. 4 and 5).

The Web Tactical Planner provides the ability to run a web-based version of ARES in a browser on a desktop or laptop. The Web Tactical Planner has a 2D top-down view used for mission planning and a 3D viewer to provide a more immersive perspective of the terrain. Tactical symbols are added to the terrain using the Tactical Symbol Selection menu. There is also the capability to add the corresponding 3D model for the symbol using the Model Chooser panel with hierarchical filtering by Space, Air, Ground, Sea, and different types of Operations.

A visual prototype of the Friendly vs Hostile wargaming environment is overlaid on the terrain as a 10 by 10 grid as shown in Fig. 3. Currently, the wargame has two teams, Friendly and Hostile, and can be played with any combination of four human or AI (agent) players. There is a Land grid and a parallel and elevated Air grid. The grids, which are not visible to the players, assist in implementing game-related constraints.

Figure 4 shows a simple Friendly vs Hostile 2-player scenario created on the Fort Irwin terrain using the Web Tactical Planner's 2D view. Each team has 5 units: fixed wing Airborne Warning System (AEW), tank, cross-country truck, platoon of soldiers, and a mobile command post. The blue-colored symbols represent the Friendly team and the red-colored symbols represent the Hostile team. In Fig. 4, the Hostile team has taken control of a small fuel depot (right side) and situated their command post behind a fuel tank and small outbuilding. The Friendly team's position offers protection for a small isolated electric power plant (left side) located outside the main Fort Irwin area. Each team's AEW (symbols with "W") is scanning the opposing team's area of operations in an effort to locate their command post.

Figure 5 shows the Web Tactical Planner's 3D view offering a more realistic wargaming decision-making perspective. The 3D view visualizes spatial information of both the terrain and man-made features and the position of the units in relation to terrain features. This geospatial perspective enhances the ability of decision makers to make more informed decisions based on better perception of the terrain and more realistic presence of the units.

Figure 6 shows the mixed reality 3D view offering the most realistic wargaming decision-making perspective. The mixed reality 3D view also visualizes spatial information of both the terrain and man-made features and the position of the units in relation to those features. However, the mixed reality visualization platform offers the player a more natural interaction with the 3D environment. A player has the option to rotate, pan,

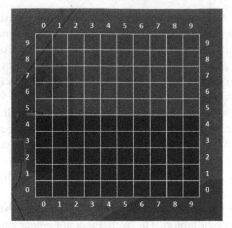

Fig. 3. Friendly vs Hostile wargaming 10 by 10 L and grid that implements 2-player game-related constrains but is not visible to players on the ARES Fort Irwin terrain. The blue-colored section represents Friendly team's initial unit placement area. The red-colored section represents Hostile team's initial unit placement area.

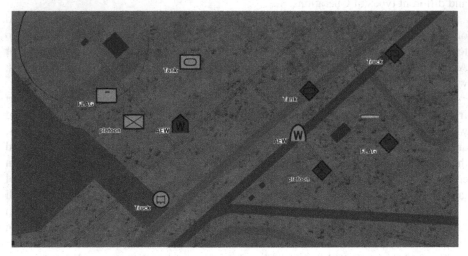

Fig. 4. ARES Tactical Web Planner 2D view of Friendly vs Hostile 2-player scenario created on the Fort Irwin terrain. Blue symbols (Friendly) protect a small electric power plant (left side); red symbols (Hostile) control a small fuel depot (right side).

and zoom into an area of interest on the terrain to investigate the wargaming decision-making alternatives in greater detail. The increased interactivity with the 3D environment together with the geospatial perspective further enhances the ability of decision makers to make more informed decisions compared to the other visualization modalities.

Fig. 5. ARES Tactical Web Planner 3D view of Friendly vs Hostile 2-player scenario created on the Fort Irwin terrain. 3D view offers a more realistic decision-making perspective, for example, showing elevation of the AEWs positioned over the opposing player's entities.

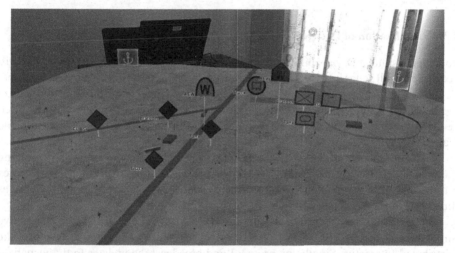

Fig. 6. ARES Mixed Reality 3D view of Friendly vs Hostile 2-player scenario created on the Fort Irwin terrain. Mixed Reality 3D view offers a more realistic decision-making perspective and a more immersive user interaction experience with the 3D environment.

3.2 Hardware and Software Environment

On the computational backend of the Friendly vs Hostile Decision Dynamics research, we are setting up the ARES battlespace visualization platform to run on the Persistence Services Framework deployed on high performance computing resources. Running on the Windows virtual machine, the ARES server pushes the scenario data to the connecting visualization modalities. The Web Tactical Planner running on the Secured Remote Desktop [11] on a high performance computing visualization node allows users to connect to the server running on the Persistence Services Framework.

Persistence Services Framework is a recently available distributed virtualization solution that can be leveraged to access or create non-traditional high performance computing services or workloads that utilizes a rich web front-end. Unlike traditional high performance computing computational nodes that are allocated to the users in batch mode for the time period requested, persistent services provide continuous access to data, databases, containerized toolsets, and frameworks. Unlike traditional batch mode where high performance computing resource are released back to the resource management system, these services and resources remain available to authorized users and processes as defined by the originator. Therefore, the ARES battlespace visualization platform would be able to take advantage of this type of high performance computing resources provisioning making available our Friendly vs Hostile tactical scenario data to any visualization modality connected to the data server from multiple users thus supporting collaborative visualization. Users using a head-mounted display will be able to collaborate with other users using the mixed reality display devices on the same tactical scenario.

3.3 Visualization of Decision Dynamics

To support simulation capabilities, we are implementing a simulation engine that will keep track of all states in a session of a Friendly vs Hostile Decision Dynamics wargame. Recording all decisions made by both human and AI players will allow us to analyze the decision-making behavior occurring during the game and then use the identified decision-making patterns and strategies to develop better AI players for tactical game play.

A key component of the ARES battlespace visualization platform is its messaging protocol that we can use to update our WMI described in Sect. 3.1 using the scenario states information from the simulation engine for a graphical representation of the scenario as illustrated in Figs. 4, 5 and 6.

One of the messaging protocols supported by ARES is the Distributed Interactive Simulation protocol (IEEE-1278.1). The data server can be configured to listen for the Distributed Interactive Simulation protocol and broadcast the updates to the visualization based on the data received. To implement the Distributed Interactive Simulation protocol in our simulation engine, we used an open-source implementation of the protocol, OpenDIS [12]. Since our simulation engine is implemented in Python, we were able to use the OpenDIS Python library in our simulation engine to send the scenario states to the ARES data server.

Additionally, the ARES platform has a native interface that can be used to send scenario updates to the data server. For our Phase 2 implementation, we plan to leverage the native interface that offers more features and is supported by the ARES visualization platform development team.

4 Discussion

The ARES-based visualization component of the Friendly vs Hostile decision dynamics research using the Fort Irwin terrain is currently under development. The AI/ML algorithm development component of the research uses a text-based user interface via a console window instead of a GUI or mixed reality interface of the battlespace. Command line interaction using a keyboard and text-based display is common when algorithm development is conducted on a high performance computing architecture, which is the case here. There are advantages and disadvantages to different types of user interaction. However, the goals of the visualization component of the Friendly vs Hostile decision dynamics research are to improve battlespace visualization, provide a user-defined common operating picture, and increase decision-making capabilities all of which are especially critical for success in a complex joint forces operation.

During our AI/ML algorithm testing with human players matched against one or more AI players, it became distinctly noticeable the lack of understanding, difficulty in interpretation, and general sustained confusion caused from using a text-based display of wargaming state space. Sometimes reading the unit position information from the text-based formatted table caused poor decision-making resulting in same team AEW collisions, friendly fire unit destruction, and friendly fire self-destroying projectiles. The presence of these erroneous decision making situations reaffirmed the critical need for embedding the human + AI game play within an advanced visualization platform such as ARES.

A text-based table or report, the more traditional form of distributing operation information, can be compared to Figs. 4, 5 and 6 where the Fort Irwin unit information is displayed geospatially using the ARES Tactical Web Planner and a HoloLens device. These advanced visualization modalities allow the players to interact with the visualization system using graphical elements such as windows, icons, menus, and images. For example, one click of the "view" icon in the Tactical Web Planner toggles between a 2D and 3D view of the terrain. Mouse buttons and the scroll wheel are used to zoom, pan, and rotate the terrain view. Players can select the type of unit, and unit symbol and corresponding 3D model from a series of menus and then place the unit on the terrain and drag the unit to new locations using a mouse. This type of interactive wargaming is visually intuitive and easy to understand accommodating a broader audience of user expertise. Additionally, the multimodal flexibility of the ARES platform enables user interaction with a wide range of electronic devices fulfilling specific user-defined requirements at their situated point of need. The mixed reality visualization modality of the ARES platform is especially apt at providing game players an accurate 3D visualization of the current state of the battlespace with capabilities for gesture-based system interaction with the units and terrain features in an immersive environment.

5 Future Work

In phase 2 of our Friendly vs Hostile Decision Dynamics research, we will begin expanding the effort to MDO-inspired problem spaces where human + AI teaming will support collaborative complex decision-making. We will examine how teams of humans + AI coordinate strategies and counter hostile strategies, e.g., AI aiding in strategy discovery and deception. In addition, we will investigate the effectiveness of certain actions that can be made contingent to other actions (e.g., key bricks in a Jenga tower) to better mimic the complex interdependencies in MDO decision-making. Phase 2 research will also include integration with MDO modeling and simulation tools to expand the breadth and MDO-relevance of the decision-making issues being investigated. This will include a tighter integration of the algorithm development and the ARES visualization platform, as well as assimilation of other information sources such as after-action reports and physiological signals while strengthening the focus on the foundational science of decision-making.

The integration effort with the ARES battlespace visualization platform will be expanded to leverage the use of SyncVis [13], a hybrid 2D and 3D data visualization platform, to investigate how problem solving occurs across an integrated or "synchronized" 2D and 3D problem space. Figure 7 shows using SyncVis to visualize 2D network devices connectivity status on a High-Resolution display device and visualizing the network connectivity between network devices in a 3D environment using a fully immersive Head-Mounted display device. In the context of the Friendly vs Hostile Decision Dynamics wargame, the 2D High-Resolution display system will visualize the unfolding of the complex AI neural network during game play while displaying the resulting MDO effects on a 3D mixed reality device.

Fig. 7. SyncVis, Hybrid 2D and 3D visualization platform supporting multiple synchronized views of the same problem space.

6 Conclusion

We overviewed the Phase 1 and future Phase 2 details of the Friendly vs Hostile Decision Dynamics investigation aimed at taking initial steps in bridging the gap between computer games and MDO wargaming. Currently, our AI/ML algorithm development and testing is conducted on high performance computing resources with game play displayed in a text-based format in a console window. Lack of understanding using the text-based display of game states during testing resulted in instances of poor decision making reaffirming the need for an advanced visualization platform such ARES. ARES multimodal capabilities are discussed in reference to a prototype battlespace terrain located at Fort Irwin National Training Center and an accompanying 2-team scenario. We plan to leverage the ARES battlespace visualization platform as an important component of the Friendly vs Hostile Decision Dynamics investigation.

References

1. Hung, C.P., Callahan-Flintoft, C., Fedele, P.D., Fluitt, K.F., et al.: Abrupt darkening under High Dynamic Range (HDR) luminance invokes facilitation for high contrast targets and grouping by luminance similarity. J. Vis. **20**(7), 9 (2020)
2. Hare, J.Z., Uribe, C.A., Kaplan, L.M., Jadbabaie, A.: Communication constrained learning with uncertain models. In: ICASSP 2020–2020 IEEE International Conference on Acoustics, Speech and Signal Processing (ICASSP), pp. 8609–8613 (2020).
3. Chen, J.Y., Lakhmani, S.G., Stowers, K., Selkowitz, A.R., et al.: Situation awareness-based agent transparency and human-autonomy teaming effectiveness. Theor. Issues Ergon. Sci. **19**, 259–282 (2018)
4. Rinderspacher, B.C.: Smooth constrained heuristic optimization of a combinatorial chemical space. ARL-TR-7294 (2015)
5. Amburn, C., Vey, N., Boyce, M., MAJ Mize, J.: The Augmented REality Sandtable (ARES). DEVCOM Army Research Laboratory Technical Publication ARL-SR-0340, October 2015
6. Garneau, C., Boyce, M., Shorter, P., Vey, N., Amburn, C.: The Augmented REality Sandtable (ARES) Research Strategy. DEVCOM Army Research Laboratory Technical Publication ARL-TN-0875, February 2018
7. Boyce, M., et al.: The impact of surface projection on military tactics comprehension. Mil. Psychol. **31**(1), 45–59 (2019). https://doi.org/10.1080/08995605.2018.1529487
8. Vanderlaken, P.: https://paulvanderlaken.com/2019/01/21/beating-battleships-with-algorithms-and-ai/. Accessed 8 Feb 2021
9. Wikipedia: Fort Irwin Training Center. https://en.wikipedia.org/wiki/Fort_Irwin_National_Training_Center. Accessed 8 Mar 2021
10. Department of Defense Interface Standard: Joint Military Symbology (MIL-STD-2525D). US Government, Washington, DC (2014)
11. DoD High Performance Computing Modernization Program, Data Analysis and Assessment Center. https://daac.hpc.mil/software/SRD/. Accessed 8 Mar 2021
12. Open DIS: An open-source implementation of the Distributed Interactive Simulation protocol (DIS), IEEE-1278.1. https://github.com/open-dis. Accessed 8 Mar 2021
13. Su, S., Perry, V., Dasari, V.: Hybrid 2D and 3D visual analytics of network simulation data. In: 2019 IEEE International Conference on Big Data (Big Data), Los Angeles, CA, USA, pp. 3992–3999 (2019). https://doi.org/10.1109/BigData47090.2019.9006235

Doing Versus Observing: Virtual Reality and 360-Degree Video for Training Manufacturing Tasks

Emily S. Wall[1]($\boxtimes$), Daniel Carruth[2] (iD), and Nicholas Harvel[2]

[1] Center for Advanced Vehicular Systems Extension, Mississippi State University, Starkville, MS, USA
ewall@cavse.msstate.edu

[2] Center for Advanced Vehicular Systems, Mississippi State University, Starkville, MS, USA

Abstract. Virtual reality is increasingly used for training workers manufacturing processes in a low-risk, realistic practice environment. Elements of the manufacturing process may be time-consuming or costly to implement accurately in simulation. The use of 360-degree video on its own or combined with interactive elements can bridge the gap between affordable VR capabilities and requirements for effective training. This paper discusses use of 360-degree video to create "learning by observing" and "learning by doing" VR training modules. The "learning by doing" module addresses work task training entirely with 360-degree videos embedded in an interactive training environment. In the "learning by doing" module, a hybrid approach successfully leverages 360-degree video to show complex task processes while implementing fully interactive elements when it was cost-effective to do so. Participants suggest "learning by observing" is effective while "learning by doing" is more engaging.

Keywords: Virtual reality · Workforce training · Immersive training

1 Introduction

1.1 VR Uses for Training

As research increasingly shows the advantages of using virtual reality (VR) as a process training tool, especially in medical and manufacturing environments, more organizations are wanting to implement this new technology in their training curriculum. Since "learning by doing" results in a 75% learning retention rate for users, VR applications help trainees to consume and retain vital information quicker than more traditional ways of teaching, such as lectures, which have been shown to have a much lower resulting learning retention rate [1]. VR training environments allow students to both observe and physically perform actions in a realistic environment. Both observing and doing tasks in VR provide trainees with the much-valued experience of "one-on-one" virtual instruction. However, it is theorized by this research team based on prior experience that as the level of VR interaction increases within VR training, then the level of information

J. Y. C. Chen and G. Fragomeni (Eds.): HCII 2021, LNCS 12770, pp. 556–568, 2021.
https://doi.org/10.1007/978-3-030-77599-5_38

retention should also increase. This paper will detail how two VR training modules, one leveraging "learning by observing" and one leveraging "learning by doing", were created for a tire manufacturing plant and relate the challenges faced and the lessons learned during the integration of different technologies and design approaches to produce an interactive and effective VR environment.

1.2 Technologies/Software/Hardware Used

There are many tools available to assist with the development of virtual training environments. In this study, the primary tool used to develop the VR environments was the Unity software. Unity software allowed for the easy combination of different media types (i.e. videos, audio files, 3D models) and supports popular VR headsets such as the HTC Vive, Oculus Rift, and Oculus Quest. Sketchup was used for creation of 3D models in the VR environment. Camtasia was used to compose and edit video and audio files. A high definition 360-degree video camera was used to record manufacturing processes. This recording served as the background of the training, both saving design time and providing a realistic view for the users. A ZCam stereoscopic VR video camera was used with its companion software WonderStitch which combined the data recorded from 4 separate lenses into a high quality 360-degree video.

2 Related Work

Virtual reality training systems has been shown to be effective in many, widely varying educational and training applications including, for example, manufacturing [2–4], construction [5], education [6], sports [7], and medicine [8]. VR provides realistic representations of workspaces that support active, experiential learning that is more engaging than traditional training [5–7]. Trainees are more engaged and more focused on the training in VR training environments even in video-based training [8]. VR training environments allow workers to practice working with new systems before they are installed [3]. The realistic recreation of equipment and workspaces in VR allows workers to gain expertise that effectively transfers to real-world expertise [4].

The development of effective VR training environments can be time-consuming and expensive [5]. Creating realistic, detailed, and interactive models of equipment and workspaces requires sophisticated technical skills from engineering, programming, and art [6]. It is challenging to create virtual models that fully replicate the environment and the worker's interactions with the environment [4]. There is an expectation that a certain level of physical fidelity is required to ensure effective transfer of skills from VR to real work tasks [4]. However, medium interaction fidelity may impair acceptance and performance with low-fidelity interactions and high fidelity interactions outperforming medium fidelity interactions [9, 10]. One approach is to focus on providing realism where it matters.

High fidelity interactions are preferred for object manipulation whereas moderate or low fidelity interactions are accepted (not necessarily preferred) for whole-body movements [11]. Preference for levels of fidelity in interactions may depend on the type of skill being developed. For example, learning an object manipulation task may require a high fidelity interaction, particularly if the object manipulation is unusual in some way [12]. If the intent of the training is to cognitive skills, low fidelity interactions are sufficient [10]. As an example, learning a procedure composed of detailed but common object manipulations (e.g., sequences of button presses, lever pulls, key turns, etc.) may not require high fidelity simulations of the interactions if the procedure is accurately modeled. A VR training environment can provide high fidelity interactions when there are significant motor components to the task and use lower fidelity, less expensive interactions in other parts of the task [4, 10]. In a VR tool designed to train patient positioning in radiography, the environment provides not only simulation of the patient positioning tasks but also interaction with the patient, a critical component of the overall procedure [13]. While it provides a high fidelity simulation of the patient positioning task and the user interface for the imaging tools, communication with the patient may be simulated by selecting dialog responses from a menu, a low fidelity but effective method for simulating a complex and technically challenging interaction.

Another approach to creating realistic environments for training is to use 360° video in place of virtual models. 360° videos are inexpensive to capture (compared to creating virtual models) and require fewer technical skills [4]. Video capture in VR can create far more realistic representations of workspaces and work tasks [4]. The videos can be augmented with interactive elements, 2D videos, and images to make them more engaging [4, 8].

In VR training environments, designers have considerable latitude in determining the level of interaction fidelity required to support knowledge and skill acquisition. Previous research has helped to identify some guidelines on when high fidelity interactions are preferred over low fidelity interactions and has considered the tradeoffs in time and cost between varying levels of fidelity [4, 9, 10]. In this paper, we use a systems engineering approach to leverage virtual modeling and 360° video to develop VR training environments for two manufacturing tasks. Challenges and lessons learned that expand on and emphasize findings of previous work are described in the following sections.

3 VR Training Applications

3.1 Background

A series of VR training tools were developed for a tire manufacturing company. The designers worked closely with the company's local management team to identify potential tasks for VR training. Initially, the company wanted to create a VR training module that would teach newly hired employees the steps in the rubber forming process. The company was motivated to pursue VR training for this process because it not only involved several complicated steps, but also led to quality issues when done incorrectly that led directly to lost time and money. To reduce the number of mistakes and the resultant quality issues, the VR tutorial would allow new employees to learn virtually in a risk-free virtual environment until they could competently complete the task without error.

The design team undertook a systems engineering process to develop the VR training tools in collaboration with the company. The classic systems engineering process begins with decomposition of the task and ends with realization of the product. The process begins with understanding the objective of the system and developing an initial concept. As the concept is developed, it can be decomposed into a set of functional requirements. Each functional requirement can be further decomposed into lower-level functions, interfaces to other functions, and integrated into an overall architecture. An analysis of the functional requirements can identify systems that require research and technical development to be fully defined and eventually realized in a working system.

After defining the general objective of the VR training tool, the design team visited the work site to observe the manufacturing process. Most of the steps in the process consisted of human-machine interactions that can be implemented in VR with some estimable amount of time and resources. However, a vital step in the process required the worker to manually adjust the raw material, thick sheets of rubber, to correct its placement on a shaping drum. Incorrect placement of the raw material leads directly to reduced quality in the final product. This extremely tactile step posed a problem for the research team. VR does not emulate tasks well where touch, feel, and the weight of an object is essential to preforming a task correctly. Before continuing with the implementation of the VR training tool, a technical feasibility study was done to investigate potential techniques for creating a high fidelity simulation of the worker's interaction with the flexible rubber in VR.

3.2 Technical Feasibility Study

After observing the manufacturing process, the research team immediately recognized that capturing the manual manipulation of the raw material would be a significant challenge in a VR training environment. Accurate placement of the material within narrow tolerances (± 1 cm) is critical to ensuring the quality of the final product. Teaching trainees the hand-poses and arm movements used to grip and manipulate the material accurately presented a significant challenge.

Fig. 1. A user manipulates a strand of cloth material in the prototype environment.

Prototype Environment. A simplified prototype environment was created in the Unity3D software for rapid implementation and evaluation of user input methods and material modeling. The VR environment consisted of an empty scene with a green floor and a simple cylinder represented the shaping drum (see Fig. 1). A simple texture was applied to the drum to test aligning the material with stripes on the drum. A narrow strip of material was used in the initial prototypes. In later prototypes, the material was replaced with a larger sheet of cloth that adhered to the drum unless manipulated by the user.

User Input. In the manufacturing task, the workers use varying hand poses, hand motions, and arm motions to manipulate the material. To fully simulate the task, trainees needed to be able to effortlessly grab, twist, stretch, and connect the materials in VR. Specifically, the trainee would need to grab the two ends of the material and move them together to remove the gap between the ends.

Hand-tracking methods have advanced significantly [14]. However, at the time of this work, accurate, fast, and detailed tracking of individual fingers in complex poses was not available in an open library. Accurately representing the complex interactions between the hands and the material at multiple points of contact would also be challenging even if the hand poses could be tracked.

Given the challenges with hand-tracking, we chose to iterate on a controller-based approach to manipulating the material. This phase of the prototyping effort used HTC Vive headsets with standard controllers. In the first iteration, the grips on the Vive controllers were used to allow the trainee to grab and manipulate the material similar to how they would grab the material in the manufacturing task. However, when gripping the controller, the focus of the gripping action is the center of the controller. In practice, it felt much more natural to grab with the tips of the controllers. Using the trigger on the controllers better matched the preferred grab position in VR even though it did not match the gripping action used in the field.

A common challenge that effects VR simulations is the inability for the virtual environment to apply force feedback to the user. In the manufacturing task, the material is resistant to movement and stretching. In the VR simulation, it was difficult to communicate the stiffness and strength of the simulated material to the trainee. A partial solution was to break the trainee's grip on the material if they moved too quickly implying a force that exceeded a certain level. However, this force check communicated only that the trainee had exceed the threshold and did not provide continuous feedback that would relate to the trainee how it would feel to manipulate the material.

Material Simulation. In our initial approach, the goal was to simulate the trainee's interactions with the material. The manufacturing process involved manipulation of relatively thin, large sheets of rubber material that could be lifted, twisted, bent, and stretched to move it into its proper position. Accurately representing the material in the work task required a dynamic simulation of the material.

ObiCloth is a commercial CPU-based real time engine for Unity that uses particle-based physics to simulate cloth and other deformable materials [15]. ObiCloth simulates thin material quite well. The API provides constraints that allow developers to alter the elasticity, flexibility, and overall malleability of materials. Each material vector allows for individual referencing of simulation parameters from external scripts. This allowed us to create a semi-adhesive cloth that would stick to the central cylinder and not slide off.

In early prototypes, the simulated material was limited to a small tube or strand. In later prototypes, the tube was replaced with a larger sheet of simulated material that more closely approximated the actual work material. The thicker material used in the manufacturing task was simulated in ObiCloth by defining a balloon-like material.

The larger sheets of material were given an internal pressure that helped model the resistance of the material. However, the mechanism created bloating on the larger faces. Although this bloating did not affect the physics simulation of the material, the effect on the visualization was unrealistic and was distracting to the user. A partial solution to the problem was to define additional cloth membranes inside the material to connect the larger faces together. This essentially stitched the layers together with the end result that the bloating was no longer noticeable.

Conclusion. Despite the successes in recreating some aspects of the material manipulation task, the final version of the prototype retained significant issues related to user input and material simulation. The result of the technical feasibility study indicated that creating a high fidelity interaction with the material was not possible within the time and resources available to the project.

3.3 "Learn by Observing" VR Training Module

After it was determined that the simulation of the raw material would not result in an accurate representation of the real process, the research team and the company put a hold on the manufacturing task and investigated a different task: the final inspection of a finished tire. Again, the research team undertook a systems engineering process that identified the overall objective and decomposed the task into functional requirements. In the tire inspection process, the worker inspects both sides of a newly formed tire and identifies any defects that can be seen or felt in the rubber. Any defects are then marked, and the bad tire is stopped from proceeding to the shipping department. Based on the review of the functional requirements for the task, it was determined that all steps of the training process could be implemented in VR.

In this case, a VR training environment was created that allowed trainees to "learn by observing" the steps of the inspection process. In order to speed production and reduce modeling costs, the inspection process was filmed using a 360-degree video camera. Two videos were collected on site: one video showed an experienced operator performing the tasks and a second video showed the workspace without the operator. The video footage was then edited using Camtasia to overlay task steps, audio, and visual instructions on the 3D environment. A frame of the video is shown in Fig. 2 below.

The first video, when embedded into the Unity3D software, allowed the trainee to closely watch the process as it was performed by an experienced team member. The second video then placed the final user into the shoes of the team member and allowed them to navigate through videos of the process steps at their own pace and prompting the software to advance to the next step once they were comfortable with what they had observed and done.

At the end of training, the trainees completed an interactive quiz in the VR environment to assess their knowledge. The trainees were presented with a series of defects in the VR environment and were asked to select the correct defect from multiple choices. This interactive quiz allowed for the research team and the company's management to gauge the effectiveness of the training. A quiz score was collected by the software and recorded for each user.

Fig. 2. Screenshot of 360 video with visual instructions

Trainee Performance and User Feedback. A group of 11 new hires were selected to test the "learn by observing" VR training module. While multiple headsets were used during the development of the VR environments, the Oculus Rift headset was used during the final testing of the VR environments because of its overall greater reliability. In this case, the Oculus Rift was considered more reliable because it did not use a battery to operate as it is powered via a cable connected to the computer running the VR environment.

All participants were able to complete the entire training. The participants scored 70% or better on the defect identification quiz. The high quiz scores indicated that the tutorial effectively taught the participants to perform the inspection. Overall, each participant reported that they enjoyed using the VR equipment and stated that they felt that this type of technology would be very helpful for new hires because it allows them to "see" the process in action and repeat the steps without incurring any quality risk or time loss.

The participants were also given two usability surveys and a simulation sickness survey after they completed the tutorial. These surveys, developed in-house, allowed the research team to gauge the overall reception of the tutorial, the VR environment, and the headset and handheld controllers. Overall, the results indicated that participants felt that their experience and ability to act in the VR environment was above average and that the visual display and controls were not detrimental to their ability to perform the required tasks (Table 1). The participants also reported that the VR training environment was easy to learn, good quality, and helpful for training (Table 2). There was some variability in responses to whether they felt they needed special training for using VR or would need technical assistance with the VR training environment. None of the participants reported any significant simulator sickness during the training (Table 3).

Table 1. Usability survey 1 results

	Q	Sample	1	2	3	4	5	6	7	8	9	10	11	Null Target	AVG
		Gender	F	M	M	F	M	M	F	F	F	M	F		
		Age range	36-45	26-35	36-45	46-55	26-35	26-45	26-35	46-55	36-45	46-55	46-55		
		Experience (months)	1	24	8	60	4	48	48	60	60	60	54		39
0 (None) 1 (Basic) 2 (Average) 4 (Expert)	1	How do you evaluate your knowledge in virtual reality technology?	4	2	2	2	1	3	1	2	3	4	3	2	2.42
	2	How would you rate yourself in regards to video game playing experience?	4	3	3	2	1	2	1	2	3	2	3	2	2.33
	3	How would you evaluate your knowledge on the process training prior to seeing the VR module?	2	2	2	3	2	2	3	2	4	3	3	2	2.50
	4	How helpful do you think the tutorial was?	4	4	4	4	3	3	4	4	4	4	4	4	3.83
	5	How much were you able to control events?	3	3	3	3	3	3	2	3	3	3	3	4	3.00
	6	How responsive was the environment to actions that you preformed?	4	3	3	2	3	3	3	3	4	4	3	4	3.25
	7	How natural did your interaction with the VR module seem?	4	4	3	2	3	3	2	3	4	4	4	4	3.33
	8	How natural was the mechanism which controlled movement in the VR environment?	4	4	2	4	3	3	3	3	4	4	4	4	3.50
	9	How much did your experiences in the VR environment seem consistent with your real-world experiences?	4	3	3	4	3	3	3	3	4	4	4	4	3.50
	10	How quickly did you adjust to the VR environment experience?	4	4	3	2	3	4	2	2	3	4	3	4	3.17
	11	How proficient in moving and interacting with the VR environment did you feel at the end of the experience?	4	3	3	4	4	3	3	3	4	4	4	4	3.58
	12	How much did the visual display quality interfere or distract you from preforming assigned tasks or required activities?	0	0	1	1	0	0	0	1	0	0	0	0	0.25
	13	How much did the control devices interfere with the performance of assigned tasks or with other activities?	0	0	1	0	1	0	2	0	2	0	0	0	0.50
	14	How well could you concentrate on the assigned tasks or required activates rather than on the mechanisms used to perform those tasks or activities?	4	3	3	3	3	2	3	3	3	4	4	4	3.25

Table 2. Usability survey 2 results

	Q														Average	Null Target
1 (Strongly Disagree) 2(Disagree) 3(Neutral) 4(Agree) 5(Strongly Agree)	1	I think that I would like to use the VR module to learn the work process.	5	5	5	5	5	5	5	5	5	5	5	5.0	5
	2	I would like to use VR for other trainings.	5	4	5	5	5	4	5	5	5	5	5	4.8	5
	3	I found this VR module easy to use.	5	5	4	5	4	5	4	5	5	5	5	4.7	5
	4	The VR modules helped me to establish the linkage between the written SOP and practice.	5	4	4	5	5	4	5	4	5	5	5	4.6	5
	5	I found the various functions (e.g. sound, pictures, controls) in this VR were well integrated.	5	4	5	4	5	5	5	5	5	5	5	4.8	5
	6	I thought there was too much inconsistency in the VR module.	1	1	1	1	1	2	1	1	3	1	1	1.3	1
	7	I would imagine that most people would learn to use this VR module very quickly.	5	4	3	5	4	5	4	4	5	5	5	4.5	4
	8	I think I would need the support of a technical person to use this VR module.	4	1	3	3	1	1	4	1	5	2	1	2.4	2
	9	I felt very confident using the VR module.	5	5	5	5	4	5	4	5	5	5	5	4.8	5
	10	I needed to learn a lot of VR related knowledge before I could get going with this VR module.	1	1	1	1	1	1	1	3	5	5	1	1.9	2

Design Challenges. Creating video content for the VR training tool was less time consuming and expensive than building a full 3D modeled scene but was still challenging. In the complex work environment, it was difficult to identify an acceptable location to film the process that would ensure that the stitch lines in the final rendering of the 360-degree video did not obscure or distort an important part of the process or the machinery. When using the video footage in a VR headset, the height of the video camera, when it

Table 3. Simulation sickness survey results

													Avg.	Null Target
	How do you feel when you wear a virtual reality headset?													
1	General discomfort	0	0	0	0	0	0	1	0	2	0	0	0	0
2	Fatigue	0	0	0	0	0	0	0	0	0	0	0	0	0
3	Headache	0	0	0	0	0	0	0	0	0	0	0	0	0
4	Eye Strain	0	0	0	0	0	1	0	0	1	0	0	0	0
5	Difficulty Focusing	0	0	0	0	0	1	1	0	0	0	0	0	0
6	Salivation Increasing	0	0	0	0	0	0	0	0	0	0	0	0	0
7	Sweating	0	0	0	0	0	0	0	0	1	0	0	0	0
8	Nausea	0	0	0	0	0	0	0	0	0	0	0	0	0
9	Difficulty Concentrating	0	0	0	0	0	0	0	0	0	0	0	0	0
10	Fullness of Head	0	0	0	0	0	0	0	0	0	0	0	0	0
11	Blurred Vision	0	0	0	0	1	1	1	0	3	0	0	1	0
12	Dizziness with Eyes Open	0	0	0	0	0	0	0	0	0	0	0	0	0
13	Dizziness with Eyes Closed	0	0	0	0	0	0	0	0	0	0	0	0	0
14	Vertigo	0	0	0	0	0	0	0	0	0	0	0	0	0
15	Stomach Awareness	0	0	0	0	0	0	0	0	0	0	0	0	0
16	Burping	0	0	0	0	0	0	0	0	0	0	0	0	0

(Left axis label: 0 (None) 1 (Slight) 2 (Moderate) 3 (Severe))

is recording, should be about the same height as the operator's eye level. This is done to ensure that the final product looks realistic when viewed in the VR headset. The 360-degree camera used for this experiment had four fish-eye lenses and simultaneously recorded both audio and video. Once the video footage was recorded the four separate video files from each lens were then stitched together to create the 360 effect. The areas in the video where these stitch lines occur, however, have a blurriness that is especially noticeable if over areas that have words, such as safety signs on a machine. Ensuring that vital areas of the environment have the needed video clarity by positioning a lens to directly face that area was a challenge when working in confined spaces or areas that have multiple focal points that are important to the training task process.

Lessons Learned. When creating the "learn by observing" VR training module, the most important lesson learned was to record many different takes of the process in action from multiple different viewpoints. As discussed in the design challenges section, ensuring that the video was capturing the process from a viewpoint that made the process clear to the observer without any stitch lines was a challenge. When capturing the tire inspection process, which took place in a small inspection cell, the operator was recorded from at least 4 different viewpoints as they performed the task. Having each of these viewpoints allowed for a more thorough look at the process in action. Camtasia easily allowed the researchers to cut from one viewpoint to another to quickly show the different tasks and areas of the machine as needed.

Despite using only 360-degree video for the VR training, the training tool was determined to be enjoyable and effective by the employees.

3.4 "Learn by Doing" VR Training Module

After the success of the "learn by observing" VR tutorial, the functional requirements for the tire manufacturing process were reexamined. While the material simulations and user input methods still had no immediate solution, the positive reception to the observation style videos was encouraging. While observing the critical step in the tire manufacturing process would not provide the preferred high-fidelity interaction with the material, the previous results suggested that video-based training was achievable and would be better than no training. For the tire building process, the revised approach was a "learn by doing" training module that combined observation style videos and more user interaction.

A 360-degree video was filmed to capture the overall work environment and the walls and roof surrounding the machinery. The video did not feature the work machine, workers, or the work process. Despite limiting the video to the area surrounding the machinery, the video brought additional realism to the overall tutorial and the time saved using video instead of creating a surrounding environment from scratch greatly outweighed any cost or time concerns with the filming and editing of the 360-video. A detailed SketchUp 3D model of the machinery was created and is shown in Fig. 3.

Fig. 3. Sketchup 3D model of machinery

The parts of the machinery that the user interacted with physically were created as separate models that could be manipulated by the user to allow for interaction with the virtual machinery using their hand-held Oculus controllers. Any animations needed to visualize the work process were also created. Creating the 3D models of the machinery was by far the most time-consuming part of the process.

For the steps in the process that could not be simulated in high fidelity, pop up video screens appeared in the virtual environment located near the operating areas of the machine. The videos would appear at appropriate times during the process and show the trainee how to perform those tasks that could not be emulated using the VR technology, e.g., the material manipulation step. Once the task was completed in the video, the pop-up screen would disappear, and the trainee would be prompted to continue on to the next task of the process. This hybrid approach allowed the users to work through the steps of the manufacturing process in VR at the overall pace of the task while showing a real-life perspective and allowing for repetition and practice of the process steps.

Design Challenges. Two challenges that presented itself to the research team included the creation of the 3D model of the machinery and maintaining a realistic pace in the virtual simulation of the process steps. The machinery used for this process was not only extremely large, but was also extremely complicated with several moving parts, input screens, and different locations that the user must move to throughout the process steps. Because of the user's movement to different locations around this machine, the use of a 360-degree video as the primary display method for the user was unacceptable since the user cannot move from their original location when using a video as the primary machinery display. A 3D model of the entire machine was necessary, even though it added a considerable amount of time to the overall project timeline. To aid in the overall time to model the machinery an additional technology of laser scanning the machine was proposed to speed up the modeling process. The research team used a Faro laser scanner to create a 3D point cloud model of the entire machine. This allowed for the research team to have a digital version of the machine on hand where accurate measurements could be taken from the point could model. The ability to use this digital version of the machine greatly reduced the amount of time to create a to-scale model that was easily integrated into Unity3D.

The second challenge was creating a realistic pace within the simulation that matched as closely as possible the actual machinery pace, but also allowed for the user to learn each step. Adding in start and stop buttons for the instructional videos aided in this effort. Not only did it give the user more interactions during the tutorial, but the videos, because they were of the real process, kept the simulation closer to the true process times, but also allowed the user time to process the information before moving on the next step since the user controlled when they started the next step. The start and stop buttons were only implemented during points in the process where the user, while doing the real process, would have some time flexibility. Thus, any additional time spent in the VR simulation before the user continued on the next step would be time that could be allowed in the real-life process such as time waiting for the machine to finish processing or time waiting for the team member to initiate the next task via a machine input. Any process steps that would trigger automatic responses from the machine were coded into the imbedded animations and, just as in real life, could not be altered by the user.

Lessons Learned. The primary lesson learned from first tutorial that was applied to the second "learn by doing" tutorial was that the observation only portion was largely unnecessary. Users felt that they paid more attention and learned the process steps faster when they were actively being prompted through the tutorial and was "doing" the process themselves. This learning style when repeated several times indicated to the research team the highest learning retention from the users.

Secondly, small design changes were observed and updated based on the survey results. Initially, the users were asked to turn on a laser selector with the hand-held controllers. However, when several of the design survey question responses fell below the target, it was determined that this extra step was confusing and unnecessary. The research team updated the tutorial and removed this toggle option so that the laser was always on for the user. This simple design change helped the user understand much quicker than before how to interact with the environmental buttons and elements.

4 Conclusion

There are major time tradeoffs between using 360-video style training versus 3D models that should be considered early in development of a VR training project. Whereas the 3D model approach allowed for many more user interactions and higher participant involvement, it nearly quadrupled the time required to design and create the VR tutorial in comparison to the "observing" 360-video training. Pursuing a fully detailed virtual model of the entire task would have required much more time and resulted in significant additional expense. The 360-videos were an effective and inexpensive solution for observing the inspection task. The hybrid approach effectively used 3D models where feasible and leveraged 360-video to present the elements of the task that could not be easily modeled. Overall both methods provided an immersive and interactive experience for the participants and the decision between which design style to create should be made with respect to time and cost restraints and the level of interaction needed to achieve the learning objectives of the training.

References

1. Norris, M., Spicer, K., Byrd, T.: Virtual reality: the new pathway for effective safety training. Prof. Saf. **64**(6), 36–39 (2019)
2. Shamsuzzoha, A., Toshev, R., Vu Tuan, V., Kankaanpaa, T., Helo, P., Digital factory – virtual reality environments for industrial training and maintenance. Interact. Learn. Environ. (2019)
3. Lin, F., Ye, L., Duffy, V., Su, C.-J.: Developing virtual environments for industrial training. Inf. Sci. **140**(1–2), 153–170 (2002)
4. Matsas, E., Vosniakos, G.-C.: Design of a virtual reality training system for human-robot collaboration in manufacturing tasks. Int. J. Interact. Des. Manuf. (IJIDeM) **11**, 139–153 (2017)
5. Eiris, R., Gheisari, M., Esmaeili, B.: PARS: using augmented 360-degree panoramas of reality for construction safety training. Int. J. Environ. Res. Public Health **15**, 2452 (2018)
6. Kavanagh, S., Luxton-Reilly, A., Wuensche, B., Plimmer, B.: Creating 360° educational video: a case study. In: Proceedings of the 28th Australian Conference on Computer-Human Interaction, pp. 34–39 (2016)
7. Kittel, A., Larkin, P., Elsworthy, N., Lindsay, R., Spittle, M.: Effectiveness of 360° virtual reality and match broadcast video to improve decision-making skill. Sci. Med. Football **4**, 255–262 (2020)
8. Harrington, C.M., et al.: 360° operative videos: a randomised cross-over study evaluating attentiveness and information retention. J. Surg. Educ. **75**(4), 993–1000 (2018)
9. McMahan, R.P., Bowman, D.A., Zielinski, D.J., Brady, R.B.: Evaluating display fidelity and interaction fidelity in a virtual reality game. IEEE Trans. Vis. Comput. Graph. **18**(4), 626–633 (2012)
10. Bhargava, A., Bertrand, J.W., Gramopadhye, A.K., Madathil, K.C., Babu, S.V.: Evaluating multiple levels of an interaction fidelity continuum on performance and learning in near-field training simulations. IEEE Trans. Vis. Comput. Graph. **24**(4), 1418–1427 (2018)
11. Rogers, K., Funke, J., Frommel, J., Stamm, S., Weber, M.: Exploring interaction fidelity in virtual reality: object manipulation and whole-body movements. In: CHI Conference on Human Factors in Computing Systems Proceedings (CHI 2019) (2019)
12. Levac, D.E., Huber, M.E. Sternad, D.: Learning and transfer of complex motor skills in virtual reality: a perspective review. J. NeuroEng. Rehabil. **16**(121) (2019)

13. Sapkaroski, D., Baird, M., McInerney, J., Dimmock, M.R.: The implementation of a haptic feedback virtual reality simulation clinic with dynamic patient interaction and communication for medical imaging students. J. Med. Radiat. Sci. **65**(3), 218–225 (2018)
14. Dennys Kuhnert. Hand Physics Lab: Holonautic. https://sidequestvr.com/app/750/hand-physics-lab
15. Virtual Method: ObiCloth. http://obi.virtualmethodstudio.com/

VAMR in Learning and Culture

Design and Research on the Virtual Simulation Teaching Platform of Shanghai Jade Carving Techniques Based on Unity 3D Technology

Beibei Dong[1], Shangshi Pan[2], and RongRong Fu[1(✉)]

[1] College of Art Design and Media, East China University of Science and Technology, 130 Meilong Road, Xuhui District, 200237 Shanghai, People's Republic of China
1756697404@qq.com
[2] Shanghai Art & Design Academy, Shanghai, China

Abstract. As one of the four major schools of Chinese jade carving, Shanghai style jade carving is a manifestation of Shanghai's unique regional culture and Shanghai style cultural spirit. And it has extremely high cultural and commercial value. However, in the teaching process of jade carving, there are problems such as high teaching cost, lack of teachers, and limited time and place. In order to solve these problems, we have designed a virtual teaching platform that combines Shanghai style jade carving skills with virtual simulation technology. We used Rhino and 3ds Max to model in a virtual environment. Based on Unity 3D development engine, we used C# scripting language to realize the human-computer interaction function of the system, and completed the design of teaching cognition, training of carving techniques, selection of carving tools, and teaching assessment. In addition, the research elaborates on the technical route, system framework and implementation process of the virtual teaching system in detail. Fifteen students of jade carving skills tested this system and verified the reliability and effectiveness of the system from their interviews. The system utilizes the immersive, interactive and imaginative functions of virtual technology. Therefore, it can effectively reduce the cost of jade carving training and improve learning efficiency, so that jade carving learners can't be limited by space, time, and materials. Moreover, it plays an important role in promoting the application of virtual reality technology in education and training.

Keywords: Unity 3D · Shanghai style jade sculpture · Virtual simulation · Intangible cultural heritage · Human-computer interaction

1 Introduction

As one of the most important traditional handicrafts in Shanghai, Shanghai style jade carving is a manifestation of unique regional culture and spirit. It possesses high cultural and business value, and therefore, it is of great significance to spare efforts to inherit jade carving [1]. However, due to long period of learning and complicated carving procedures, currently it is inevitable that some beginners do irreversible damage to raw materials in the practice of jade carving when they have not completely mastered the skills. This

© Springer Nature Switzerland AG 2021
J. Y. C. Chen and G. Fragomeni (Eds.): HCII 2021, LNCS 12770, pp. 571–581, 2021.
https://doi.org/10.1007/978-3-030-77599-5_39

results in unnecessary replacement of raw materials, not only consuming the practice time, but causing excessive loss of supplies.

At present, the teaching mode of Shanghai style jade carving is also very simple. Most of them are based on the traditional ways of "master leads apprentice, father leads child" or inheritance in studio. These modes would take a long time and have low efficiency, which has made Shanghai style jade carving encounter a bottleneck in development and inheritance. However, there is no denying that it is well recognized by the market. After realizing the huge talent gap in the jade carving industry, some companies and individuals actively meet market demand and establish vocational training schools in industrial areas, such as Shanghai Jade Carver Training Class. In addition, some local universities like Shanghai Art & Design Academy also focus on the cultivation and inheritance of jade carving skills. All of these provide market opportunities for the virtual simulation teaching system of Shanghai style jade carving [2].

Aiming at a series of practical problems in the inheritance and development of Shanghai style jade carving, this thesis designed and actualized a virtual simulation system based on the status quo of actual teaching mode. The immersive experience allows jade carving beginners to efficiently master the procedures without the restriction of space, time and material and thereby increasing the popularity of craft, pushing the sustainability of the talent training, and also serving as a reference for other intangible cultural teaching methods in China.

2 The Design of the Virtual Simulation Teaching System for the Craft of Shanghai Style Jade Carving

2.1 Shanghai Style Jade Carving Craft and Features

Shanghai style jade carving is an artistic style mainly based on Shanghai style but also developed from the characteristics of Suzhou, Yangzhou and court style, which can be described as "All rivers run into sea". Shanghai style jade carving is known for "fineness". Apart from fine carving, it also has vigorous and supple lines, and clear structures. Meanwhile, it is featured by the exquisiteness of furnace or bottle vessels and the vividness of characters or animals. Natural shape and color of jade can be well utilized. Now it has ranked in the four major jade carving art styles in China.

2.2 Functional Requirements Analysis of the Virtual Experience System

(1) The situations of material damage, collapse, and breakage that jade carving learners may face during the process are simulated, which boosts the users' learning efficiency and prevents the waste of materials.
(2) The technologies of VR, human-computer interaction application, etc. are used to break through the limitation of time and space, and enhance the authenticity and experience feeling in the jade carving practical training. The teaching procedures such as demonstration, prompting, and identification of jade carving are added to attract interest.

(3) The virtual simulation system is divided into three modules: teaching, training, and assessment. It allows experiencers to master the procedures, skills and precautions of identification, painting, carving, and grinding. During the assessment, the system automatically scores them, bringing the beginners an overall feeling of their own capability.

(4) In accordance with the characteristics of Shanghai style jade carving craft, the training of detailed model carving is added, so that the trainees can perceive its unique charm and features.

(5) There is a visualized data management center in the system maintenance module. The management platform can monitor the real-time dynamic data of the users' operation in the virtual environment. All data during the operation can be visualized in three dimensions. Users can view all of them by VR helmet.

2.3 Technology Roadmap of System Design

Field surveys were conducted to obtain the physical mapping drawings or design drawings of jade carving tools and jade materials. Rhino and 3DMax software were used for modeling and exporting the model in FBX format, and then importing the Unity3D engine to build a 3D virtual jade carving environment. Based on the know-how of operation tools, materials, techniques, etc., relevant expanded knowledge such as jade material identification was added to the system. Use Unity 3D to build scenes, integrate model resources, and use C# scripting language to realize human-computer interaction, including physical grabbing, rotation, zooming and other functions, to improve user experience, and finally release and test the program. The system development flow chart is shown in Fig. 1.

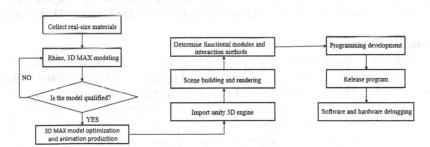

Fig. 1. The system development flowchart

2.4 System Frame Diagram

The system takes the production scene of Shanghai style jade carving as a prototype and uses Unity 3D technology to restore the carving production process. Four major modules are divided: system setting module, learning and cognition module, simulation training module and virtual assessment module. The core module is the simulation training, and

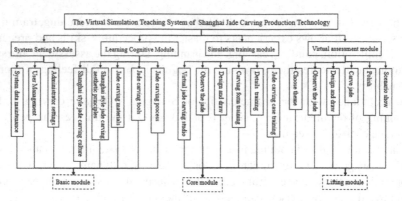

Fig. 2. The system framework

the promotion module is the virtual assessment. The system module controls user login and data maintenance, etc. The system framework is shown in Fig. 2.

Learning and Cognition Module

In learning and cognition module, the trainees aim to learn the process and tools of jade carving craft, etc. The learning modules include Shanghai style jade carving culture and aesthetic principles, jade carving materials, jade carving tools, etc., among which, tools are the most complex one. It includes mechanical tools, grinding head tools, grinding tools, polishing tools, etc. Trainees can refer to the graphics and texts of the interface to learn the selection and use of tools, the steps, evaluation criteria and key points of jade material identification. The learning module of Shanghai style jade carving culture and aesthetic principles is mainly pictures and texts, supplemented by case analysis. The jade carving production process is automatically played in the form of 3D animation.

Simulation Training Module

This module is a practical training course that simulates the actual jade carving production process, and the trainees aim to practice that process. According to the sequence of jade carving, this module is divided into jade identification training, drawing and sketching training, carving form training and case creation training. Virtual training can be carried out conveniently, and the system will provide tips on the operation steps in practical manipulation. In the case creation training, users can adjust the difficulty level on UI controller menu through VR handle to experience the complete process of jade carving works from identification, drafting, rough carving, fine carving to polishing. During this period, the system will give prompt to trainees for wrong operations. As Shanghai style jade carving keeps high demand for the carving of detailed models, a variety of fine techniques such as "hook", "push up" and "press" are added to the training module to clarify the details of the jade.

Virtual Assessment Module

In this module, trainees can make self-assessment of their learning process within a specified time. The system will no longer give any prompt about steps, so it is all relied on personal operation. Starting from material identification, trainees need to comprehensively sort the ten given jade materials by texture, gloss, and fineness. The system sets the ten jade materials with a grade difference, which is convenient for further grading. In the engraving stage, trainees choose the carving tools, parts and forms on their own, and the system will score based on their operations. In the virtual assessment, errors are allowed for each step but not allowed to exceed five times totally, otherwise the jade material will collapse and the trainee will fail the assessment. After the assessment, the system automatically demonstrates the results and operation reports, which can be viewed through the function menu "Score". For those who fail the assessment, the system automatically enters the repeated learning mode.

2.5 System Core Functions and Key Techniques

Scene Roaming of Virtual Jade Carving Studio

In order to enhance the on-site experience of jade carving craft, this system actualizes the scene roaming. It is mainly aimed at the virtual jade carving studio in the training module. The construction of the scene will improve the learning interest of the trainee and make the trainee interact with the scene and devices in the system in the first person. It is also controlled by the VR handle.

The virtual jade carving studio is divided into areas, including "working area", "tool area", "works show area", etc. Users can roam through each area on demand. This is shown in Fig. 3. Take "working area" as an example, after users enter the virtual studio and choose this area, they can enter the next virtual scene for carving techniques training. The buildings, props and other models are all created by 3DMAX and Rhino. During the process, the atmosphere of the jade carving studio is restored as much as possible, so that the trainee can get more authentic experience.

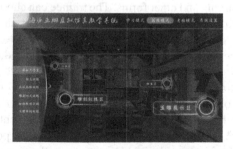

Fig. 3. Virtual jade carving studio system interface design rendering

The Display and Selection Module of Jade Carving Tools

Different tools can be selected through the UI controller menu in the display and selection module of jade carving tools. The first-level menu divides the tools into "mechanical tools", "grinding tools", "grinding head tools", "polishing tools", and " Other tools". The second-level menu includes "ball", "point needle", "hook mound" and other practical tools. In the tool display and selection area, VR handle is available to grasp, view, rotate, and zoom the tools, so as to further observe the three-dimensional tools in all directions. In order to enable every beginner to learn jade carving tools as soon as possible, the system provides a text introduction of the corresponding tool at the same time as each tool is displayed, including "brief introduction", "features", "main functions", "instruction", etc. The users can select different text introduction information through the VR handle to deepen the user's understanding of jade carving tools. In addition, after the user learns the tool, the system can conduct a small test on the user, and let the user choose the tool through voice questions. After the error is selected, the system will jump to the pop-up window to prompt the error, so as to consolidate the user's familiarity of the tool. The interface is shown in Fig. 4.

Fig. 4. Jade carving tool interface design rendering

Carving Technique Training Module

The carving technique training is set in the training mode of the system, which is divided into three-dimensional carving, semicircular carving, relief carving, openwork carving, hollow carving, line carving and other forms. The trainee can choose the "working area" in the "virtual jade carving studio" and choose different carving techniques with the equipped VR handle. As shown in Fig. 5 (a).

After choosing a technique, the trainee needs to select the needle in the "Jade Carving Tool Storage Box" according to the prompts, and then complete the installation of the needle and the operating handle. The system interface will prompt information such as the characteristics of the tool. As shown in Fig. 5 (b). After the installation is the training of carving techniques. To make the virtual environment closer to reality, the trainee can wear a VR helmet and then control and select the position point with the VR handle and optical orientation device. The system will give simple vibrate feedback according to different carving techniques. At the same time, the interface will display the application key points of different carving forms in practical operation. This training is designed to lead users to experience the procedures of different carving techniques. Since the system will prompt for operation, it is necessary to highlight the parts on the virtual simulation model. The details are shown in Fig. 5 (c). In the training mode, if the trainee operates improperly, the system will prompt an error with a pop-up dialog box for further corrections, as shown in Fig. 5 (d).

The detail carving training is designed for one feature of Shanghai style jade carving, namely "high quality in fineness". The trainee can observe the details through the "microscope" and adjust the parameters of size in unity3d software to achieve zooming. A variety of fine techniques such as "hook", "push up" and "press" can be learned to clarify the details of the jade. As shown in Fig. 5 (e). Through the training about detailed modeling, such as subtle patterns, hair of the characters, bird feather and dragon scale, etc., the trainee can understand the craft and characteristics of Shanghai style jade carving. As shown in Fig. 5 (f).

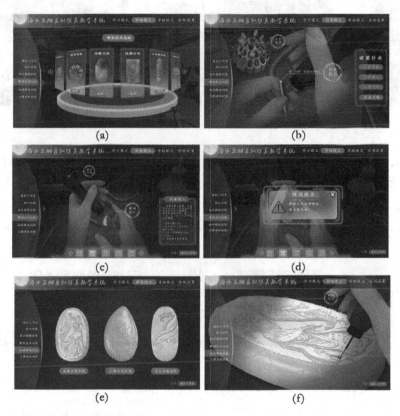

(a)   (b)

(c)   (d)

(e)   (f)

Fig. 5. Jade carving technique training system interface design renderings

3 System Evaluation

To evaluate the performance of the virtual jade carving teaching system, 15 students majoring in jade carving were invited for the system evaluation experiment. This experiment adopted the method of system experience test experiment combined with a Likert scale questionnaire. Before the experiment, it is necessary to explain the general process and requirements of the virtual teaching system to the participants. In the experiment, participants need to wear VR helmets, use VR handles for experience, grasping and observation, and perform according to the voice prompts. After the experiment, they need to fill in a questionnaire based on the 5-point Likert scale to evaluate the system performance.

During the experiment, though a few participants encountered some problems, the majority of participants successfully completed the entire process of virtual jade carving skill teaching, as shown in the Fig. 6 (Table 1).

Fig. 6. The experimental diagram of the virtual teaching experience

Table 1. Questionnaires and evaluation results of the experience of the Shanghai jade carving virtual teaching system

Purpose	Dimension	Number	Question	Score
Learning motivation	D1 attention	Q1	I think this way of learning jade carving skills is very interesting;	4.64
	D2 concentration	Q2	I can immerse myself in the experiment of the virtual jade carving teaching system and complete the experiment with full concentration;	4.36
	D3 confidence	Q3	I feel relaxed and confident in the virtual jade carving teaching system experiment;	4.36
System user experience	D4 System authenticity	Q4	I think this jade carving simulation experiment basically restores the scene of a jade carving studio or classroom. Through this experiment, you can understand the equipment, tools and operation steps required for jade carving;	4.14

(continued)

Table 1. (*continued*)

Purpose	Dimension	Number	Question	Score
	D5 System operability	Q5	I can easily grasp the system's UI interface, VR equipment and other operation methods, and I have not affected my learning because I can't operate it	4.36
System teaching effect	D6 Systematic learning modules	Q6	I can get a preliminary understanding of jade carving skills through the animation display and text description in the learning module;	4.29
	D7 Understanding of operating steps	Q7	The system operation steps are clear, and the error prompts are clear. I can complete the corresponding jade carving steps according to the system's prompts;	4.29
	D8 Explore after system operation	Q8	I have a certain grasp of the process and steps of jade carving, as well as the selected tools and jade texture;	3.86
		Q9	This system can help beginners have a preliminary understanding of the process and steps of jade carving skills;	4.43
		Q10	The system can help learners of jade carving to strengthen the process and steps of jade carving skills;	4.21
		Q11	I hope this system can be adopted by school teaching;	4.43
System feedback	D9 System feedback	Q12	What do you think are the shortcomings of the teaching system? What can be improved?	

The survey results show that the majority of students agree with the statements listed in the questionnaire. A small number of students believe that individual problems need to be further optimized. In addition, the students gave feedback on the deficiencies of this teaching system. The results are summarized in Table 2. The students put forward suggestions for improvement mainly from the software interface, interaction method and fluency, etc., which also provide a direction for the later iteration of the system.

Table 2. System feedback form

Main aspects	Problems
UI interface	Font design size and display slope issues
	The size of the prompt box
	Cumbersome switching between interfaces
Fluency	Lower resolution
	Slow response of operating equipment
Interaction method	Voice prompt interaction is not timely
	Insufficient guided interaction
	Grabbing and observing objects do not conform to human-machine

Main aspects Actual problems UI interface font design size and displayed slope The size of the prompt box Cumbersome switching between interfaces Fluency, lower resolution Slow response of operating equipment Fluency Voice prompt interaction is not timely Can add guided interaction Grabbing and observing objects do not conform to human-machine.

4   Conclusion

The virtual simulation teaching system of Shanghai style jade carving establishes virtual studios and tools, working platforms, jade, and other models by 3Dmax and Rhino. Then Unity 3D is adopted to develop the interactive functions in the system to achieve the following goals. 1. For amateurs and beginners in the field of jade carving, they can achieve an overall recognition of Shanghai style jade carving culture and production process; 2. In the tool learning module, they can learn about the characteristics, main functions and usages of different jade carving tools; 3. In the training of jade carving forms, they can master the skills and steps of different forms, as well as how to select tools; 4. In the training of jade material identification, they can distinguish the high or low quality of jade carving materials through standards like different gloss and transparency. This teaching system effectively improves the problems of time, space, consumables and teachers in the teaching application. It not only enhances the learning efficiency of jade carving beginners, but also provides reference for the teaching and inheritance of other traditional Chinese crafts.

References

1. Shen, Y., Fu, R.: Exploration of the training model of Shanghai-style jade carving talents. Enterp. Res. (04), 119–121+124 (2012)
2. Li, X.: The status quo, problems and countermeasures of Nanyang jade carving talent training. Nandu Xuetan **37**(01), 123–124 (2017)
3. Sun, J.: The historical development and intangible cultural heritage protection of Haipai jade carvings. Jilin University (2015)

4. Han, S.: Research on the style of Shanghai style jade carving. Anhui University of Finance and Economics (2014)
5. Li, B., Zhang, X., Wei, T., Huang, J., Wei, Y., Sun, Y.: Research on abdominal surgery simulation system based on virtual reality. Med. Health Equip. **41**(08), 19–24+44 (2020)
6. Sun, Y., Zhao, H., Sun, D.: Design of MTS virtual simulation experiment system based on Unity3D. Lab. Res. Explor. **39**(07), 98–100 (2020)
7. Zeng, Y.: Interaction design and implementation of Chu guqin based on Unity 3D. Wuhan Textile University (2020)
8. Zhao, R.: Design and implementation of game function module based on unity. Shandong University (2020)
9. Hu, F., et al.: The virtual simulation system of medicinal botany training based on Unity3D. Comput. Syst. Appl. **29**(01), 266–270 (2020)
10. Shi, H.: Development and design of ceramic VR display game based on Unity3D. Nanchang University (2019)
11. Liang, S.: The design and realization of the situational virtual experience system of the terracotta warriors and horses firing process. Tianjin University (2018)
12. Zhu, X.: The design and implementation of the coloring experience system of painted Qin figurines based on virtual reality technology. Tianjin University (2018)
13. Sun, Y., Yang, Q., Wang, X., Li, L., Chang, C.: Design and development of virtual simulation experiment system for rolling principle. Exp. Technol. Manag. **37**(08), 133–136 (2020)
14. Xiao, Z., Yuan, C., Jiao, H.: The virtual simulation system of Xinjiang Kazakh embroidery skills based on Unity3D. Mod. Electron. Technol. **42**(10), 179–181+186 (2019)
15. Xie, M.: Virtual museum roaming and virtual reality technology research based on Unity3D. Shanxi Normal University (2019)
16. Xu, X., Cheng, M., Shi, Y., Chen, L.: Design and implementation of virtual simulation based on Unity 3D mud movable type printing. J. Beijing Inst. Graph. Commun. **25**(02), 35–38 (2017)
17. Wang, D., Jiang, Y.: Ancient architecture three-dimensional virtual modeling and virtual-real interaction software realization. Comput. Appl. **37**(S2), 186–189 (2017)

IME^{VR}: An MVC Framework for Military Training VR Simulators

Romullo Girardi[1]([✉])(ID) and Jauvane C. de Oliveira[2](ID)

[1] Military Institute of Engineering (IME), Rio de Janeiro, Brazil
`romullogirardi@ime.eb.br`
[2] National Laboratory for Scientific Computing (LNCC), Petrópolis, Brazil
`jauvane@acm.org`

Abstract. In the military context, the traditional training methods based on field exercises have high costs, logistics complexity, spatial-temporal constraints, and safety risk. VR-based simulation environments can help address these drawbacks while serving as a platform for supplementing current training approaches, providing more convenience, accessibility, and flexibility. This paper identifies and discusses aspects that are crucial to a military training VR application and presents the first Brazilian Army VR framework (IME^{VR}), which seeks to facilitate the development and the reuse of solutions for common issues in different military training VR applications. The usage of the framework was validated by the development of the first Brazilian Army VR simulator for Army Artillery observer training (SAOA). Besides, this case study showed that the framework support provided savings of approximately one third in the application development effort (person-month).

Keywords: Virtual reality · Military training · MVC framework

1 Introduction

In recent years, the use of Virtual Reality (VR)-based simulators for training is becoming more widespread because traditional methods of training have some major drawbacks [12]. In the military context, these drawbacks related to traditional training methods based on field exercises are high costs, logistics complexity, and spatial-temporal constraints [13]. VR-based simulation environments can help address these drawbacks while serving as a platform for supplementing current training approaches [12]. Besides, computer simulations provide more convenience, accessibility, and flexibility [13].

Studies prove that computer-simulated environments can effectively help establish the link between theory and practice while providing a safe environment in which to acquire experience [8]. As safety is an important issue in the

Supported by Brazilian Army, Military Institute of Engineering (IME), and Brazilian National Council for Scientific and Technological Development (CNPq) through grant INCT-MACC CNPq 465586/2014-7.

© Springer Nature Switzerland AG 2021
J. Y. C. Chen and G. Fragomeni (Eds.): HCII 2021, LNCS 12770, pp. 582–594, 2021.
https://doi.org/10.1007/978-3-030-77599-5_40

military training context, Army Forces have seen an increased interest in using virtual environments for training purposes [22].

Even though there has been an increasing interest in using VR simulators that mock real scenarios and allow professionals to perform operations that previously would only be possible in a real environment [8], creating a VR application from scratch takes up a lot of time and research. Virtual Reality frameworks simplify this process of development by providing generic functions and features such as head and hand tracking, controller mapping, object manipulation, scene and task management, etc. These functions or features are reusable such that they can be used to any kind of VR application, and scalable such that customization can still be done depending on what the developer needs. Having a VR framework allows the developers to dedicate their time to the user interface (UI) and the 3D navigation/interaction systems rather than dealing with the core functionalities of a VR application [6]. This perception is very important because, according to [20], in a VR application, the key elements to offer a valuable experience to the end user are: virtual world, immersion, sensory feedback, and interactivity.

During the literature review, it was found that, although there is a lot of research related to the use of virtual reality in military training, there is not much emphasis on the use of frameworks to support the development of these applications. Considering this identified void, this paper discusses aspects that are crucial to a military training VR application and presents IME^{VR}, the first Brazilian Army VR framework, which seeks to facilitate the development and the reuse of solutions for common issues in different military training VR simulators.

2   Method

To achieve the objective proposed in the introduction, the study was structured in three phases:

1. Theoretical phase: a bibliographic review to identify the key aspects of military training VR simulators (Sect. 3).
2. Practical phase: a high-level view of the IME^{VR} framework's architecture, linking its components to the aspects identified in the theoretical phase (Sect. 4).
3. Test Phase: the usage of the framework in the implementation of SAOA, the first Brazilian Army VR simulator for Army Artillery observer training (Sect. 5).

3   Related Work

This section presents recent works (published in the last five years) linked to military training VR simulators.

According to these criteria, the following papers were chosen and analyzed: [1–5,7,9,11,14–17], and [18].

[1] discussed the virtual reality applied for enhanced education learning, military training, and sports.

[2] analyzed experiments and survey results of a VR application developed for Pakistani Army military physical training.

[3] showed a U.S. Navy VR simulator for training maintenance procedures.

[4] presented a 3D interactive virtual reality (VR) military system to train Chinese students in live firing.

[5] presented a study using VR simulation to assess performance in Canadian Navy emergency lifeboat launches.

[7] presented a Thai aircraft recognition training simulator using virtual reality.

[9] described a virtual reality soldier simulator with body area networks for Taiwanese Army team training.

[11] presented a study where virtual reality was used to train U.S. Army Landing Signal Officers (LSOs).

[14] presented a Chinese field operation rescue simulation system based on VR.

[15] described the design and usability evaluation of a mixed reality prototype to simulate the role of a U.S. Army tank platoon leader.

[16] investigated the impact of VR technology on 46 immersive gamified simulations with serious purposes. Military training applications were included in this set of simulators analyzed.

[17] analyzed the use of VR in the U.S. Air Force initial flight training.

[18] showed a VR simulator for Army Dismounted Soldier Training used by the Armies of the United States, Canada, and Denmark.

3.1 Key Aspects of Military Training VR Simulators

After analysing the related work, it was identified the following key aspects related to military training VR simulators:

1. Data model: considering roles and relationships, [2–4,9,11,14,15], and [18] implemented a data model based on an instructor evaluating a student during the execution of a training task.
2. Network: [2–4,9,11,14,15], and [18] presented a training workflow implemented by a communication protocol between simulator's terminals in a network-based application.
3. Game engine: the VR simulators were designed with Unity game engine in [2–4,11], and [15]. In the other papers, the game engine was not explicitly stated.
4. HMD: [2] used Samsung GearVR. [3,9,11], and [15] used Oculus Rift. [17] used HTC Vive. [16] analyzed simulators with different types of HMDs. In the other papers, the HMD was not explicitly stated.
5. Performance measurement: in all analyzed simulators, some type of performance measurement was considered (interactive feedback, report generation, etc.).

Table 1 summarizes the key aspects identified in the analyzed military training VR simulators.

Table 1. Key aspects of military training VR simulators

Key aspect	Considerations
Data model	An instructor evaluates a student during a training task
Network	Training workflow implemented by a communication protocol between simulator's terminals
Game engine	Unity is the most used solution
HMD	Different types of HMD should be available
Performance measurement	Some type of performance measurement should be used (interactive feedback, report generation, etc.)

4 Framework

Considering the key aspects identified in Sect. 3.1, this section details the framework specified, designed and tested in this work. The IME^{VR} framework is presented by two topics: solution specification and technologies used.

4.1 Solution Specification

Based on the instructor-student relationship presented in Sect. 3.1, it was specified that the framework should be composed of two terminals: the instructor terminal and the student terminal. These terminals are connected by a Wi-Fi network, as shown in Fig. 1.

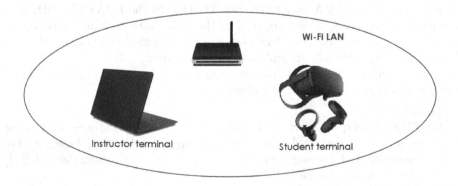

Fig. 1. General structure of the framework

In addition, based on the need to implement a communication protocol between terminals (presented in Sect. 3.1), the framework interaction diagram provides two base messages (task designation and finalization) and the necessary structure for the communication protocol messages implementation, as shown in Fig. 2.

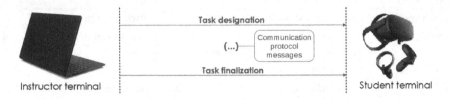

Fig. 2. Framework interaction diagram

As there are multiple ways to view and interact with data in a VR application, the framework uses the MVC (Model-View-Controller) architecture. This pattern is structured into three logical components that interact with each other. The Model component manages the system data and associated operations on that data. The View component defines and manages how the data is presented to the user. The Controller component manages user interaction (e.g., keypresses, mouse clicks, etc.) and passes these interactions to the View and the Model [21]. Following the MVC architecture, the framework specification was structured into two parts: Model and View-Controller.

Before detailing the MVC architecture of the framework, it is necessary to note that a framework is a generic structure that is extended to create a more specific subsystem or application [21]. To extend a framework, you cannot change its internal code. You must add concrete classes that inherit abstract class operations and/or define callbacks, methods that are called in response to events recognized by the framework. This feature of frameworks is known as inversion of control [19]. Based on the inversion of control, the framework specification includes two layers: FRAMEWORK and TO DO. In the FRAMEWORK layer are packages and classes that are part of the framework core and must not be modified by the user. In the TO DO layer are the packages and classes that can be edited, complemented, or implemented by the user.

Considering the key aspects presented in Sect. 3.1, as shown in Figs. 3 and 4, the framework was structured as follows:

1. Model
   (a) FRAMEWORK layer: data (data model, data persistence, and report generation), communication protocol (message handler, base/interface message, and message parser), and network (multithreaded TCP/IP client/server communication).
   (b) TO DO layer: data (definition of the task to be performed by the student), communication protocol (definition of the protocol messages related to the training task), and network (definition of the network parameters).

2. View-Controller
    (a) FRAMEWORK layer: application UI base structure and base controller
        for the integrated VR HMDs (Google Cardboard, Google Daydream, and
        Oculus Quest).
    (b) TO DO layer: user interface/interaction complementation.

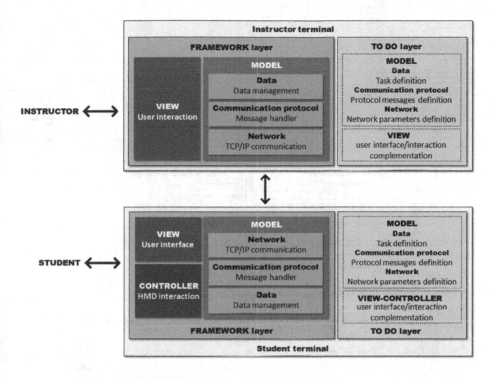

Fig. 3. Framework overview

4.2 Technologies Used

Table 2 presents the technologies used in the implementation of the IME^{VR}
framework.

About the VR HMDs, five candidates for the use in the framework were analyzed: Google Cardboard, Samsung GearVR, Google Daydream, Oculus Quest,
and HTC Vive (Table 3). Considering that the framework, in its initial version,
would include one HMD within each range of visual quality and cost, it was
integrated with Google HMDs (Google Cardboard and Google Daydream) and
Oculus Quest.

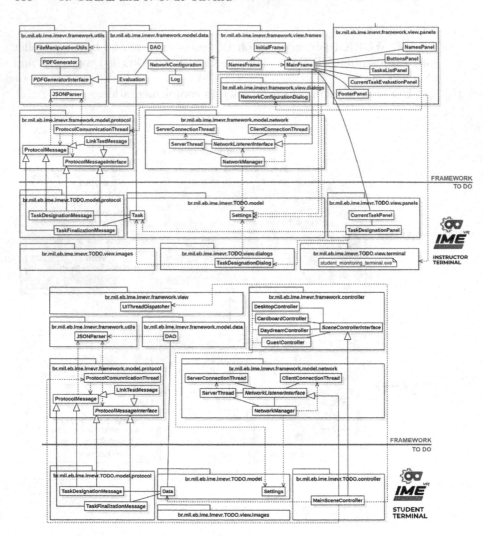

Fig. 4. Framework UML diagrams

Table 2. Technologies used in the IME^{VR} implementation

	Instructor terminal	Student terminal
Language	Java	C# (Unity)
Operating system	Cross-platform	Cross-platform
Communications	TCP/IP	TCP/IP
Hardware	Laptop or desktop with Java version 1.7 or higher installed in operating system	- Google Cardboard or Daydream with a compatible device OR - Oculus Quest

Table 3. VR HMDs analysis

	Cost	Visual quality	Mobile compatibility	Sensory capabilities
Google Cardboard	Low	Low	High	3-DOF with HMD button
Samsung GearVR	Medium	Medium	Low	3-DOF with HMD buttons
Google Daydream	Medium	Medium	Medium	3-DOF with controller
Oculus Quest	High	High	None	6-DOF with controllers
HTC Vive	High	High	None	6-DOF with controllers

5   Case Study

To validate the usage of the framework in the implementation of a military training VR simulator, an application for Army Artillery observer training called SAOA was developed. This simulator is detailed in [10]. The case study is presented considering 2 points of analysis: application and development effort.

5.1   Application Analysis

Figure 5 shows the main screen of the instructor terminal. Through this terminal, the instructor can create new assessment simulations, load previous assessment simulations, configure network-related data, manage training missions, and track observer's evaluation results on each of these missions.

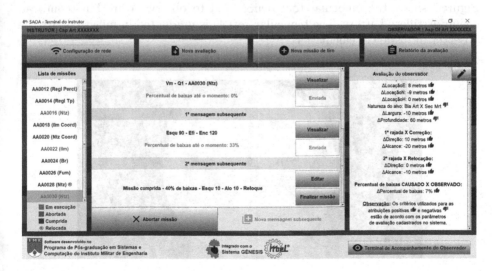

Fig. 5. Instructor terminal

In addition, the instructor terminal has a built-in copy of the observer terminal, called the observer monitoring terminal. This tool is very useful because it allows the instructor to follow, in real time, what is being visualized in the observer terminal. The observer's point of view is a 3-DOF rotational experience through which he or she can see the terrain and the targets/fires to be rendered. As shown in Fig. 6, to support the observation process, the system provides five auxiliary targets to be used as a reference for target location and correction adjustments.

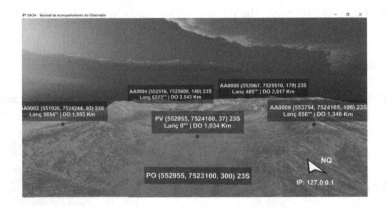

Fig. 6. Observer monitoring terminal (overview)

Another supporting feature provided to the observer is the binocular tool. Figure 7 shows the binocular tool being used to observe a fire burst onto an enemy Artillery battery. The binocular reticle is graduated in mils to assist the observer in distances calculation.

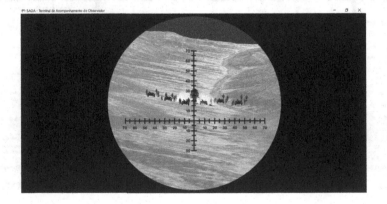

Fig. 7. Observer monitoring terminal (binocular tool)

Figure 8 shows a screenshot of the observer terminal version for Oculus Quest. Through this terminal, the observer can visualize all the objects involved in the simulation managed by the instructor terminal.

Fig. 8. Observer terminal

To perform the tests with this simulator, a sample of 13 users was used. All elements of the sample are Artillery officers formed by the Brazilian Army Military Academy and have extensive practical experience in observation. As shown in [10], the tests validated the simulator according to 2 parameters: sense of presence and effectiveness. The sense of presence analysis was based on the IPQ specification. The evaluation of effectiveness was made in terms of time and performance.

5.2   Development Effort Analysis

The software cost estimation model COCOMO was used to estimate the effort spent on developing the SAOA in 2 scenarios: from the scratch and using the IME^{VR} framework. Table 4 presents the data considering the application development from the scratch.

Considering the adjustment values related to communication, distribution, complexity, reuse, installation, and user interface, the function points calculated were 1493.42. Using the COCOMO formula, the development effort was estimated at 128.79 person-month.

Table 5 shows the data considering the application development using the IME^{VR} framework.

Adjusting the complexity values due to the support provided by the framework, the function points calculated were 1013.35. Using the COCOMO formula, the development effort was estimated at 85.92 person-month.

Table 4. SAOA development from the scratch

Measurement parameters	Instructor terminal	Student terminal
User inputs	496	9
User outputs	4	9
User inquiries	14	2
Files	3	1
External interfaces	5	2

Table 5. SAOA development using the IME^{VR} framework

Measurement parameters	Instructor terminal	Student terminal
User inputs	491	7
User outputs	2	7
User inquiries	6	2
Files	0	0
External interfaces	1	0

With this analysis, it was possible to estimate that the use of the IME^{VR} framework provided savings of 33.29% (approximately one third) in the SAOA development effort.

6   Discussions and Conclusion

In this paper, we presented the first Brazilian Army VR framework, IME^{VR}, an MVC framework for military training VR simulators. IME^{VR} seeks to facilitate the development and the reuse of solutions for common issues in different military training VR applications.

This framework was used in the implementation of SAOA, the first Brazilian Army VR simulator for Army Artillery observer training. The validation of this simulator proved the effectiveness and versatility of the framework in VR development. Besides, this case study showed that the use of the IME^{VR} framework provided savings of 33.29% (approximately one third) in the SAOA development effort.

Even though the framework provides some facilities, it is important to note that the final quality of a VR training application lies in the hands of those responsible for the design process. The proper use of the features and capabilities of the framework and the creation of a veritable environment are the responsibility of the developers.

As limitations, it can be pointed out that the framework does not include integration with haptic devices in addition to those included in the supported HMDs.

About future work, the following possibilities can be indicated:

- The usage of the IME^{VR} framework in the implementation of other military training VR simulators.
- The integration of other hardware into the framework (other HMDs, haptic devices, etc.).
- The evolution of the IME^{VR} framework to IME^{XR} through the inclusion of supporting components for the development of military training Augmented Reality (AR) applications.

References

1. Ahir, K., Govani, K., Gajera, R., Shah, M.: Application on virtual reality for enhanced education learning, military training and sports. Augment. Hum. Res. **5**(1), 1–9 (2019)
2. Ali, S., Azmat, S., Noor, A., Siddiqui, H., Noor, S.: Virtual reality as a tool for physical training. In: IEEE International Conference on Latest Trends in Electrical Engineering and Computing Technologies (INTELLECT), Karachi, Pakistan (2017)
3. Bailey, S.K., Johnson, C.I., Schroeder, B.L., Marraffino, M.D.: Using virtual reality for training maintenance procedures. In: Proceedings of the Interservice/Industry Training, Simulation and Education Conference (2017)
4. Bhagat, K., Liou, W., Chang, C.: A cost-effective interactive 3D virtual reality system applied to military live firing training. Virtual Reality **20**(2), 127–140 (2016). https://doi.org/10.1007/s10055-016-0284-x
5. Billard, R., Smith, J.: Using simulation to assess performance in emergency lifeboat launches. In: Proceedings of the Interservice/Industry Training, Simulation and Education Conference (2018)
6. Blonna, R., Tan, M.S., Tan, V., Mora, A.P., Atienza, R.: VREX: a framework for immersive virtual reality experiences. In: 2018 IEEE Region Ten Symposium (Tensymp), pp. 118–123 (2018)
7. Choensawat, W., Sookhanaphibarn, K.: Aircraft recognition training simulator using virtual reality. In: 2019 IEEE 8th Global Conference on Consumer Electronics (GCCE), pp. 47–48 (2019)
8. Dam, P., Prado, R., Radetic, D., Raposo, A., Dos Santos, I.H.F.: SimVR-Trei: a framework for developing VR-enhanced training. In: 2015 IEEE 8th Workshop on Software Engineering and Architectures for Realtime Interactive Systems (SEARIS), pp. 1–9 (2015)
9. Fan, Y.C., Wen, C.Y.: A virtual reality soldier simulator with body area networks for team training. Sensors **19**(3), 451 (2019)
10. Girardi, R., de Oliveira, J.C.: Virtual reality in army artillery observer training. In: 2019 21st Symposium on Virtual and Augmented Reality (SVR), pp. 25–33 (2019)
11. Greunke, L., Sadagic, A.: Taking immersive VR leap in training of landing signal officers. IEEE Trans. Visual Comput. Graphics **22**(4), 1482–1491 (2016)
12. Gupta, A., Cecil, J., Pirela-Cruz, M., Ramanathan, P.: A virtual reality enhanced cyber-human framework for orthopedic surgical training. IEEE Syst. J. **13**(3), 3501–3512 (2019)

13. Hill, R.R., Miller, J.O.: A history of united states military simulation. In: Proceedings of the 2017 Winter Simulation Conference. WSC 2017. IEEE Press (2017)
14. Huang, R., Mu, Z., Sun, S.: Analysis & design of field operation simulation system based on virtual reality. In: IEEE International Conference on Smart Grid and Electrical Automation (ICSGEA), Changsha, China, pp. 440–442. IEEE (2017)
15. Khooshabeh, P., Choromanski, I., Neubauer, C., Krum, D., Spicer, R., Campbell, J.: Mixed reality training for tank platoon leader communication skills. In: IEEE Virtual Reality (VR), Los Angeles, pp. 333–334. IEEE (2017)
16. Menin, A., Torchelsen, R., Nedel, L.: An analysis of VR technology used in immersive simulations with a serious game perspective. IEEE Comput. Graphics Appl. **38**(2), 57–73 (2018)
17. Pennington, E., Hafer, R., Nistler, E., Seech, T., Tossell, C.: Integration of advanced technology in initial flight training. In: 2019 Systems and Information Engineering Design Symposium (SIEDS), pp. 1–5 (2019)
18. Reitz, E., Seavey, K.: Virtual dismounted infantry training: requiem for a dream. In: Interservice/Industry Training, Simulation, and Education Conference (I/ITSEC), Orlando (2016)
19. Schmidt, D., Gokhale, A., Natarajan, B.: Leveraging application frameworks. ACM Queue **2**(5), 66–75 (2004)
20. Sherman, W., Craig, A.: Understanding Virtual Reality: Interface, Application and Design. Morgan Kaufmann Publishers Inc., San Francisco (2003)
21. Sommerville, I.: Software Engineering, 9th edn. Pearson Education Inc., Boston (2011)
22. Vaughan, N., Gabrys, B., Dubey, V.N.: An overview of self-adaptive technologies within virtual reality training. Comput. Sci. Rev. **22**, 65–87 (2016)

Extended Reality, Pedagogy, and Career Readiness: A Review of Literature

Patrick Guilbaud[1]([⊠]), T. Christa Guilbaud[2], and Dane Jennings[3]

[1] Graduate School and Learning Technology, Winthrop University, Rock Hill, USA
guilbaudp@winthrop.edu
[2] Learning Design and Technology, UNC at Charlotte, Charlotte, USA
tguilbau@uncc.edu
[3] Catapult Games, Schenectady, USA
DaneJ@CatapultGamesVR.com

Abstract. Recently, there has been a significant spike in the level of ideation with, and deployment of, extended reality (XR) tools and applications in many aspects of the digital workplace. It is also projected that acceptance and use of XR technology to improve work performance will continue to grow in the coming decade. However, there has not been a robust level of adoption and implementation of XR technology, to include augmented reality (AR), mixed-reality (MR), and virtual reality (VR) within academic institutions, training organizations, government agencies, business entities, and community or professional associations. This paper examines the current literature to determine how XR and related technologies have been explored, evaluated, or used in educational and training activities. As part of the literature review, we paid special attention on how XR tools, applications are being deployed to increase work and career readiness, performance, and resiliency of students, adult learners, and working professionals. Results from the study showed that XR applications are being used, often at pilot-testing levels, in disciplines such as medicine, nursing, and engineering. The data also show that many academic institutions and training organizations have yet to develop concrete plans for wholesale use and adoption of XR technologies to support teaching and learning activities.

Keywords: Extended reality · XR · Technology-enhanced learning · Affordance · Pedagogy · Skills development · Career readiness

1 Introduction

Considerable focus has been placed in the last few years on the importance and benefits of introducing new and advanced technology to support active and experiential learning activities within and outside the classroom environment [1–3]. As offered, by Ertmer [4] and many other authors [5–7] proper integration, use, and administration of education technology along with appropriate pedagogy such as active and experiential learning could facilitate greater student engagement, participation, and involvement in learning. Other researchers [8–10] have also offered that the use of technology along with hands-on

© Springer Nature Switzerland AG 2021
J. Y. C. Chen and G. Fragomeni (Eds.): HCII 2021, LNCS 12770, pp. 595–613, 2021.
https://doi.org/10.1007/978-3-030-77599-5_41

learning activities offer greater likelihood of knowledge retention, transfer and sharing. With the prevailing global knowledge economy, academic institutions from high school to colleges and universities continue to face the challenge of ensuring that their students will have the right combination of technical, professional, and socio-cultural skills to be ready for the workplace and for active citizenship upon graduation [11, 12]. As a result, it is critical for learning or training efforts, irrespective of the complexity level or delivery mode, to be designed and taught in a manner that allows the mastery of hard and soft skills and competencies. These include technical knowledge, numeracy, computer programming, critical thinking, decision-making, collaboration, and teamwork, all of which are in high demand by employers [13, 14].

Faculty and instructors strive to use the educational technology tools and applications that are available at their institutions to develop and offer stimulating and engaging learning opportunities for students. However, due to lack of time, resources, or other challenges, they often are unable to create and implement "hands-on" and "minds-on" activities that are designed to promote or reinforce the mastery of career readiness skills [15, 16]. Yet, given the acknowledged list of skills that are required for career and professional success in the 21st century workplace, learner-centered instruction -- whether delivered by face-to-face, distance education, or hybrid delivery modes -- must be organized to meet the educational needs and interests of students and be in sync with future employment opportunities [17]. Further, domain-general skills (i.e., time management, teamwork, or leadership) must be emphasized in all learning activities and assignments to assure knowledge transfer and utilization in postsecondary school environments and the workplace [18].

This paper examines how Extended Reality (XR) technology including Virtual Reality (VR), Augmented Reality (AR), and to a lesser extent Mixed Reality (MR), are being used or investigated for the purpose of career readiness and mobility. As part of that work, we conducted a systematic literature review (SLR) to: (a) Identify and interpret linkages and connections that exist between deployment of XR technologies and career training and readiness; and (b) Highlight and assess ground-breaking implementations, approaches, and practices of XR technologies that support the development or strengthening employment-related skills. In the next sections of the paper, we present an overview and a more recent perspective on the use of advanced technology to support learning inside and outside the classroom. We also highlight the aspects of learning and pedagogy that fit well with both the modern digital environments and skills development. We then note the results, findings, and conclusion from peer-reviewed articles, with a focus on the integration, implementation, or use of XR technologies to support career readiness and mobility.

2   Related Work

2.1   XR Technologies

XR is a catchall term for technologies such as VR, MR, and AR, all of which blend the real and virtual world to some degree [19, 20]. Further, XR-related tools and applications make use of devices such as desktop computers, tablet PCs, smart-phones, headsets with visual capabilities, or other multi-media devices to allow users to interact with virtual objects [20–28].

While VR is widely used to indicate the blending of realities, AR has recently gained greater acceptance and recognition by the general public with the successful introduction of the game Pokémon GO in 2016 [26]. The game, which is a location and AR-enhanced application, allows players to use their smartphones or other mobile computer devices equipped with Global-Positioning System (GPS) to search and capture pocket monsters (i.e. Pokémon).

There has been considerable debate regarding the nomenclature and taxonomy to be used for the different "realities" in the broader XR field. As part of that debate, Milgram et al. [28] offered a model called the reality–virtuality continuum to denote the different variations and compositions of real and virtual environments and objects. As shown in Fig. 1 below, that nomenclature or model starts with the real environment where people live and interact. Then it offers terminology where technology is used to blend that reality and virtual objects or create a fully immersive virtual environment.

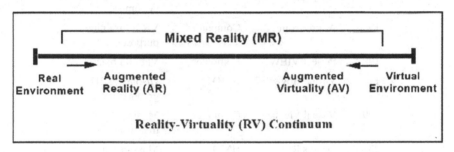

Fig. 1. Reality–virtuality continuum [23].

More recently, the term XR has been used as an umbrella term for all real and virtual environments [24–26]. AR, MR, and VR are now used to denote succeeding degrees of realities, generated by digital devices and wearables (body-borne portable personal computers) where interactions between people and virtual objects can take place. Although AR, MR, and VR are sometimes used interchangeably, they differ in the types and level of interactions they afford the user with virtual objects. VR, for example offers the user the possibility to have full immersion (i.e. 360°) in virtual worlds with the use of head-mounted displays (HMD) or CAVE (for Cave Automatic Virtual Environment) [27, 28]. In contrast, AR and MR are used in situations or contexts that blend the real and virtual worlds. Therefore, each technology affords a unique and targeted learning experience. Given the opportunity for engagement or interaction with the real and/or virtual world, both VR and AR technology can be leveraged in education and training situations that involve problem-solving, collaboration, and decision-making [21, 29, 30].

2.2 Evolution of XR Related Tools

Interest in VR tools and applications has been on the meteoric rise in the past 10 years with the introduction of Oculus VR headset and similar technologies that allow users to enter into a virtual world [31]. Yet, as shown in Table 1, the technology known today as XR really began in 1957 with the introduction of Sensorama, a simulator console created by Morton Heilig that offered users an interactive experience with virtual objects in an extended-reality space [32, 33].

Table 1. Key VR/AR related tools [34]

Year	Product	Display	Major achievement
1957	Sensorama	Kiosk	Interactive experience
1961	Headsight	Camera	Motion tracking system
1966	AForce Sim	Computer	VR for training purposes
1987	Project VIEW	Computer	Virtual objects
1995	Virtual Boy	HMD	Display of 3D graphics
1997	Virtual Vietnam	Computer	Medical treatment
2014	Oculus Rift	HMD	Mass product
2014	Cardboard	Smart Phone	Uses cell phones
2016	Playstation VR	HMD	Gaming console
2018	Oculus Go	HMD	Wireless and standalone
2019	Oculus Quest	HMD	Positional tracking

Other key advancements in the field include the use of motion tracking capabilities, and the use of the VR technology in training starting with the Air Force Simulation Project and other military-related endeavors [35, 36]. Thus, XR technologies are being used in a wide variety of fields and learning contexts for skills development, career improvement, and military/operational readiness [25, 36–38].

2.3 Current and Affordable XR Tools

Table 2 lists some of the VR and AR tools currently available on the market along with their prices. As shown, standalone VR/AR tools i.e. those that do not require a computer, can be purchased for as little as $299. High end systems either standalone or those that require a computer or a smartphone can run anywhere from $1,000 to $3,000 and higher.

Table 2. Affordable XR Tools and Systems (2021)

XR tool	TYPE	Cost	Set-up
Oculus Quest 2	VR	$299	Standalone
Oculus Rift S	VR	$299	Requires a PC
Valve Index	VR	$999	Requires a PC
HP Reverb G2	VR	$599	Requires a PC
HTC Vive Pro Eye	VR	$1,599	Requires a PC
MS Hololens 2	AR	$3,500	Standalone
Magic Leap One	AR	$2,295	Standalone
Vuzix M4000	AR	$2,499	Standalone
Vuzix Blade	AR	$899	Standalone/Right lens Display
Google Glass	AR	$1000	Standalone
Bose Frames	AR	$250	Standalone - Audio only

2.4 Career Readiness

Soft skills, including critical thinking and teamwork, are in high demand by employers [39, 40]. In fact, many employers now indicate that soft skills are more important than hard or technical skills as the latter can be taught in the workplace [41]. Google, for example, found that the top seven skills related to success in the company were "soft" or people-related ones [42]. Moreover, global and collaborative work teams are now the norm in business today as multinational businesses use technology to create and use virtual teams, international collaboration, and multi-national partnerships and other strategic global business arrangements to stay ahead of their competitors [43–46].

As a result, students and other learners must be provided the opportunity to strengthen their critical thinking, problem solving, and teamwork skills to be competitive in the global economy. As Barrows [47] and Hmelo-Silver [48] noted, students and working professionals need decision and work-related skills to find and maintain suitable employment and advance in their careers. Consequently, we argue that XR technologies can be used as a heuristic tool to help students and working professionals develop or strengthen their academic and career-oriented skills. More specifically, we note that XR tools and applications supported by sound pedagogy offer a means for enhancing the hard and soft skills that are critical for success in the 21st century workplace [11, 48].

2.5 Technology-Enhanced Learning

Technology has long been used to support a wide variety of teaching, learning and education activities [49–51]. Whereas in the past, technology was used mainly for vertical interaction or content delivery, e.g., from teacher to learner. The affordances that are available in current instructional tools and applications, offer faculty and instructional designers the means to implement horizontal interactions or learner-learner and learner-content activities [8, 9, 52].

Kennedy and Dunn [53] argue that one of the key strengths of using technology-enhanced learning (TEL) is the opportunity that it provides to keep students cognitively engaged. Other researchers have found that technology can be used to strengthen connection to educational content by both individual learners as well as collaborative learning teams [53, 54, 55]. Moreover, recent studies have placed focus on exploring how to best leverage the affordances and unique features of modern technology such as VR to improve skills and learning outcomes.

Starr [56], for example, found that TEL tools and applications such as gaming and simulation software allow the creation and implementation of hands-on and minds-on learning activities within the classroom. Thus, TEL allows students to have increased levels of interaction with their instructors and their classmates, leading to a greater level of retention and disposition to apply learning materials in a real-world setting.

2.6 Affordance and Pedagogy

Considerable debate exists regarding what is meant by the term affordance [56–59]. Some authors and researchers restrict the meaning to the original perspective offered by Gibson [59], who argues that the environment and animals have co-evolved and not necessarily people-constructed. Therefore, according to Gibson, objects in the environment afford or support certain capabilities, activities, interpretations that are totally independent of people. Other scholars such as Norman [60] have expanded upon the original definition of the term affordance to incorporate an aspect of utility or functionality to it.

More recently, there has been increased awareness that the affordances, which are imbedded in XR technologies, and sound pedagogy can help students gain both domain specific knowledge and interpersonal skills [see 25, 62–65]. Shin [64] notes that using technology such as VR in education and training helps keep students cognitively engaged. Other researchers are actively looking at how applications such as gaming, VR, and artificial intelligence can strengthen human learning [67, 68]. Therefore, educators and designers can use modern technology tools such as XR along with appropriate pedagogy to offer innovative learning experiences to students that are meaningful and relevant to their post-graduation lives [48, 69].

2.7 XR for Education and Skills Development

For the purpose of this paper, we look specifically at the impact of XR technologies (including VR and AR) on learning, since they are the tools that are most often used in education, and training environments [see 29, 70, 71, 72]. Below, we outline how both of these technologies are being leveraged to elicit the types of learner-focused activities that can help to strengthen skills that are relevant for academic and career readiness.

As previously noted, learning is most effective when people have the chance to engage in a meaningful way with the course or training content (e.g., through investigations, social interaction, problem-solving, and other active or experiential learning tasks) [73–75]. Moreover, we note that the integration of XR in education affords learners opportunities for open-ended and non-linear activities. Use of pedagogical approaches that are learner centered (e.g., active and experiential learning, which are highlighted in some of the previous sections of the paper) offer a greater likelihood for knowledge acquisition, retention, transfer, and sharing due to their strong focus and emphases on hands-on and practice-oriented activities [8, 76]. Therefore, by combining XR technology with sound pedagogy learners will gain the opportunity to test out the knowledge they have gained in new and unique situations and then receive immediate feedback with guidance for improvement or words of praise and encouragement [see 25, 36, 77, 78].

3 Methodology

3.1 Context

This research sought to explore how XR technology, and most specifically VR and AR, along with appropriate pedagogy are being used to facilitate the acquisition of skills that are in high demand in education programs and careers. We also wanted to gauge, from the current literature, the level and degree to which those technologies are being implemented for the purpose of facilitating or strengthening career readiness and mobility.

3.2 Research Approach

According to Dewey & Drahota [77] a SLR, identifies, selects, and then critically appraises research in order to answer a clearly formulated question. Moreover, the SLR needs to follow a clearly defined protocol or plan where the criteria is clearly stated before the review is conducted [78]. For this paper, we conducted a SLR on XR technologies, which included VR, AR, and MR, that are currently being used in the context of academic education, professional training, and research.

3.3 Research Questions

Our SLR study was guided by the following two key questions:

1. How have XR technologies been used or integrated in learning environments?
2. How can the XR interventions that been identified can best be classified in relation to their impact to academic and career readiness?

3.4 Data Collection

The literature search was conducted in November/December 2020 and in early January 2021 from two popular databases, JSTOR and ERIC through EBSCO host. We started the initial literature search through JSTOR focusing on 2010–2020 timeframe. The search keywords used were "Virtual, Augmented, Mixed, and Extended Reality plus Education and Career", which yielded 8,084 search results as shown in Fig. 2. The search result helped the researchers gain a preliminary idea of the scope and types of the research conducted in the field that are related to our research questions. We then excluded 6,089 articles from the data collected. These involved studies and research that were deemed too old e.g., no mention of AR, MR, and HMD. Grey literature (e.g., reports, theses, projects, conference papers, fact sheets, and similar documents that are not available through traditional bibliographic sources such as databases or indexes) was also excluded during this step.

We then removed 2,445 articles, which did not directly place focus on career-related issues. Exclusion criteria were studies involving K-8 that specifically did not involve pre-service or certified teacher training or professional development. High school-oriented papers were included in the data selected if it involved teacher preparation for career. The remaining 270 articles were closely examined by 2 reviewers to ascertain whether their titles, abstracts, and research questions were in congruence with the focus of the study. We then skimmed through the full-text articles to further evaluate the quality and eligibility of the studies. We deemed 60 journal articles to be relevant for further scrutiny. Discrepancies between the reviewers' findings were discussed and resolved. This resulted in 25 articles to include in our review. These were put in a spreadsheet along with the full reference, author, year, title, and abstract for detailed examination and evaluation.

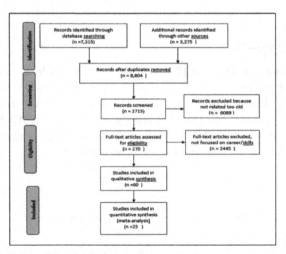

Fig. 2. From: Moher D, Liberati A, Tetzlaff J, Altman DG, The PRISMA Group (2009). Preferred Reporting Items for Systematic Reviews and Meta-Analyses: The PRISMA Statement. PLoS Med 6(6): e1000097. https://doi.org/10.1371/journal.pmed1000097. For more information, visit www.prisma-statement.org.

4   Results and Discussion

4.1   Dataset Categorization

The selected articles were analyzed, coded, and then categorized by the researchers according to their learning development aspect and field of focus. The first learning category developed for the data is Knowledge, Skills, and Abilities (KSA) development. Learning Domain was the second category that was determined for the study. Six sub-domain categories were identified. Further, we used two learning clusters for the articles to gauge whether the studies focused on school (A) or work related training (B). Table 3 below presents the Learning Domains and related clusters A, B, or A and B.

Table 3. Sub-domain Categories

Learning domain	Description	Cluster
Gen Ed	General Support and Readiness	A
LWD	Support for Learners With Disabilities	A
CPE	Continuing Professional Education (Non-Medical)	B
STEM	Science, Technology, Engineering, and Math (incl. Comp Science) Support and Readiness	A and B
Medical	Training of Physicians, Nurses, and other Healthcare Professionals	A and B
P/S/B Change	Personal, Social, and Behavioral Change	A and B

4.2 Literature Selected

Table 4 below presents the complete list of articles reviewed for the study along with the learning domains and KSA category for each of them. As shown, articles that met the selection criteria for the study range from 2017 to 2020. Further, the overwhelming majority of the selected articles (88%) were published in 2019 and 2020.

Table 4. Selected XR Articles

REF	LEARNING			XR	DATE
	DOMAIN	KSA	STUDY GOAL		
[81]	P/S/B Change	3	Enhance Behavior Intention	VR	2018
[82]	CPE	1, 3	Simulate marine battlefield	VR	2019
[83]	Sup of LWD	3, 5	VR and individuals with autism	VR	2017

(continued)

4.3 Question 1

Question 1 sought to gauge how XR technologies have been used or integrated in learning environments. To answer that question, we first identified sub-categories for KSA. This

Table 4. (*continued*)

REF	LEARNING			XR	DATE
	DOMAIN	KSA	STUDY GOAL		
[84]	STEM	4	Support problem-solving	VR	2020
[85]	STEM	2, 4, 5	Outdoor ecology	AR	2018
[86]	CPE	1–3	Enhance surgical education	XR	2020
[87]	P/S/B Change	2–4	Initial training of future teachers	AM	2020
[88]	CPE	2, 3	Computer animation affects	AR	2020
[89]	P/S/B Change	2, 3	Reduce sedentary behavior	AV	2020
[90]	Medical	1, 3	Telemedicine/COVID-19	AR	2020
[91]	CPE	2–4	Professional skill development	XR	2020
[92]	Medical	3, 4	Anatomical structure of heart	AR	2020
[93]	Gen Edu	3,4	Presentation and speaking skills	AR	2019
[94]	STEM	3	Learning Biochemistry concept	VR	2019
[95]	Gen Ed	3, 4	Improve critical thinking skills	AR	2019
[96]	STEM	3, 5	STEM efficacy for women	VR	2019
[97]	Sup of LWD	2, 4, 5	Accessibility/Design thinking	VR	2019
[98]	P/S/B Change	2–5	Preservice teacher self-efficacy	VR	2019
[99]	Gen Ed	3–5	Students' learning experiences	VR	2020
[100]	P/S/B Change	1–5	Classroom management	MR	2020
[101]	Sup of LWD	1,3,5	Supporting children with autism	MR	2019
[102]	Sup of LWD	1, 3, 5	Daily living skills disabilities	AR	2020
[103]	P/S/B Change	1, 3, 4	Nursing student motivation	MR	2020
[104]	CPE	1, 3, 4	Performance in welding practice	VR	2020
[105]	STEM	2–4	Complex chemistry concepts	VR	2019

was done via a careful review and examination by two authors of the paper of the research problems, background literature, and research objectives noted in the articles. Initial classifications were re-examined in case of divergence between the two authors. Final classification of determined upon agreement between the two authors. Figure 3 below presents the number of occurrences in the data for the KSA sub-category. As depicted, Self-Empowerment/Self-Efficacy (S EM/EF) had the highest level of focus. This was followed by Critical Thinking and Decision Making (CT/DM). The sub-categories of Technical Knowledge and Problem Solving (TK/PS) and Inclusive Excellence and Community of Practice (IE/CoP) both had 10 occurrences. Safety and Risk Reduction (S/R) had a total of 9 occurrences.

The studies reveal that XR technologies have strong potential to improve problem-solving and critical thinking skills [84]. For example, Syawaludin et al. [93] found that

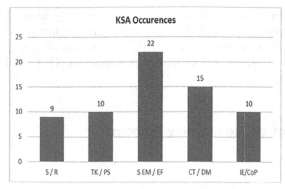

Legend:

S / R: Safety and Risk Reduction

TK / PS: Technical Knowledge and Problem Solving

S EM / EF: Self-Empowerment / Self-Efficacy

CT / DM: Critical Thinking and Decision Making

IE/CoP: Inclusive Excellence and Community of Practice

Note: *Articles were included under multiple sub-categories.*

Fig. 3. Learning category

augmented reality media in learning about earth and rock structures helped pre-service elementary school teachers develop their critical thinking skills as they actively engaged in learning activities (e.g. information gathering, analyzing, and solving problems). Further, Wu et al. [82] found that students studying electrical circuit design perceived a higher level of self-efficacy and increased sense of presence when using head-mounted displays (HMD) Netland et al. [97] posited that VR facilitates active learning and assists students in learning and remembering challenging concepts in operations management.

Several studies also showed that XR technologies are instrumental in supporting pre-professional training and professional skill development [99, 100, 103]. Wells and Miller [102], for example, discovered in a study about welding skill performance that VR can be beneficial for psychomotor skill development. Thus, XR can help facilitate skills development in situations where hand and body motions are necessary to operate power machinery or perform medical surgeries as well as in contexts in which repeated practice and skill refinement is imperative.

In summary, XR technologies are being used in a variety of education and training contexts. Moreover, VR and AR tools and applications are being used to help learners across education settings (i.e., K-12, college, workplace, continuing and professional education) develop both technical skill (e.g., decision-making, information management, problem solving and critical thinking) and soft skills (e.g., teamwork, collaboration, diversity, and intercultural). Additionally, XR allow users/students to perform repeated trials in a low-risk environment for mastery of academic and career related skills and competencies.

4.4   Question 2

Question 2 sought to understand ways in which the XR interventions that have been identified can best be classified in relation to their impact on academic and career readiness. Figure 4 below presents the distribution of XR and Learning Domains found and the percentage of their occurrence. STEM Support and Readiness (STEM) and Training of Physicians, Nursing, and Healthcare Professionals (Medical) were the two highest sub-categories represented in the literature. Continuing Professional Education (CPE) came in last at 8%.

Given that many science-oriented fields are widely considered to be early adopters of various advanced technology tools, life-like patient simulators, three-dimensional imaging, digital holography, and telehealth [see 92, 103, 106], it is not too surprising that both of STEM and Medical sub-categories are well represented in current XR-related training, implementation, and research.

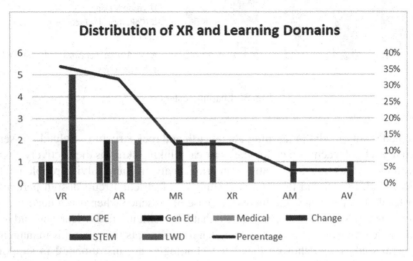

Fig. 4. Learning category

As shown in Table 5, 28% of the documents fell under the Academic cluster, 8% under Work-related and 64% under both clusters.

Table 5. Learning domains and focus

Domain	Focus*	%
General Support and Readiness	A	16%
Support for Learners With Disabilities	A	12%
Continuing Professional Education (Non-Medical)	B	8%
STEM Support and Readiness	A / B	24%
Training of Physician, Nursing, and Healthcare Professionals	A / B	24%
Personal, Social, and Behavioral Change	A / B	16%

A = Academic; B: Work-related

While most of the articles focused on both academic and work-related related endeavors, a few studies, particularly those in the exploratory or pilot-stage, targeted a specific learning domain cluster. For example, Wu et al. [82] explored the link between HMD and planning strategies for problem solving as part of an undergraduate engineering course.

In another study focused on preservice teacher preparation, Cooper, Park, Nasr, Thong & Johnson [96] found that VR showed promising results with regards to supporting classroom activities.

Research studies with a dual focus were mostly in the areas of medicine and health. For example, Liu et al. [88] explored how XR could be used in a telemedicine capacity to support COVID-19 interventions. Likewise, Abbas et al. [84] and Hauze & Marshall [103] investigated how XR could be used to improve physician training. In the work-related category, Netland et al. [97] explored how XR could be leveraged to strengthen operational improvements while Gallup & Serianni [81] looked at how XR could be used to support learners with disabilities, most specifically those with Autism Spectrum Disorder (ASD).

Researchers are exploring the use of XR in a broad range of learning domains and foci. The data suggest that perhaps STEM and health-related fields show promising uses of XR as an instructional method to avoid injuries and reduce risks. In regards to providing support to learners with disabilities, VR tools allow both pre-service and in-service teachers to practice communication scenarios and test out ideas prior to working with real children. Nevertheless, given recent developments in the STEM and medical fields to reduce equipment and training costs while gaining greater consumer interest, we also anticipate that fields such arts, ecology, engineering, history, travel and tourism, will be a stronger part of the XR literature in the future.

5 Conclusion

Widespread availability modern technology and significant decrease in the cost XR technologies have opened the door for designers to imbed increased user interaction in all types of learning, education, and training contexts [25, 31, 107, 108]. With changing perceptions regarding the use and integration of virtual objects in instruction, more focus will need to be placed on learner-centric pedagogy to help enhance the academic and career readiness of students and working professionals [109]. Moreover, as the market economy demands for a workforce that is prepared to think creatively, problem solve, and be adept with the most up to date technologies, educational institutions will need to adapt their methods and instructional delivery. Learning environments that leverage relevant aspects of XR technologies help facilitate multifaceted engagement and interactions (e.g., learner-learner, learner-contents, and learner-agent/avatar) as part of educational activities [110, 111, 112]. These interactions and exchanges will stand to surpass those that are encountered in traditional classroom settings and learning contexts. Faculty, teachers, instructors and related professionals across the education spectrum (K-12 schools, colleges/universities, private training organizations and other learning entities) will therefore need to rethink their approaches so they can allow students and leaners to become owners, collaborators, and constructors of their own knowledge. Through the advances in technology, XR will allow education to be offered and delivered for optimal engagement and interaction with learning contents. The new paradigm being led by XR in the education field will thus allow educators to present course and training to maximize knowledge acquisition, retention, and application by all learners.

References

1. Du Boulay, B.: Artificial intelligence as an effective classroom assistant. IEEE Intell. Syst. **31**(6), 76–81 (2016)
2. Magana, A.J.: Learning strategies and multimedia techniques for scaffolding size and scale cognition. Comput. Educ. **72**, 367–377 (2014)
3. Alexander, S., Sarrafzadeh, A., Hill, S.: Foundation of an affective tutoring system: learning how human tutors adapt to student emotion. Int. J. Intell. Syst. Technol. Appl. **4**(3), 335–367 (2008)
4. Ertmer, P.A.: Teacher pedagogical beliefs: the final frontier in our quest for technology integration? Educ. Technol. Res. Dev. **53**(4), 25–39 (2005). https://doi.org/10.1007/BF0250 4683
5. Atman, U.N., Usluel, Y.K.: Predicting technology integration based on a conceptual framework for ICT use in education. Technol. Pedagogy Educ. **28**(5), 517–531 (2019)
6. Chou, P.N., Feng, S.T.: Using a tablet computer application to advance high school students' laboratory learning experiences: a focus on electrical engineering education. Sustainability **11**, 1–14 (2019)
7. Goodson, I.F., Mangan, J.M.: Subject cultures and the introduction of classroom computers. Br. Educ. Res. J. **21**(5), 613–628 (1995)
8. Darin, A.: User experience of mobile virtual reality: experiment on changes in students' attitudes. Turk. Online J. Educ. Technol. **19**(3), 80–93 (2020)
9. Itin, C.M.: Reasserting the philosophy of experiential education as a vehicle for change in the 21st century. J. Exp. Educ. **22**(2), 91–98 (1999)
10. Kickul, J., Griffiths, M., Bacq, S.: The boundary-less classroom: extending social innovation and impact learning to the field. J. Small Bus. Enterp. Dev. **17**(4), 652–663 (2010)
11. Aggarwal, R.: Developing a global mindset: Integrating demographics, sustainability, technology, and globalization. J. Teach. Int. Bus. **22**(1), 51–69 (2011)
12. Nealy, C.: Integrating soft skills through active learning in the management classroom. J. Coll. Teach. Learn. **2**(4), 80–93 (2005)
13. Brynjolsson, E., McAfee, A.: The Second Machine Age: Work, Progress, and Prosperity in a Time of Brilliant Technologies. W. W. Norton & Co, New York (2014)
14. Strada Institute and Emsi, Robot-ready: Human, skills for the future of work (2018). https://www.economicmodeling.com/robot-ready-reports
15. L'Ecuyer, K.M., Pole, D., Leander, S.A.: The use of PBL in an interprofessional education course for health care professional students. Interdiscip. J. Probl. Based Learn. **9**(1), 6 (2015)
16. Llewellyn, A., Clarke, D.: How are CSU advertising students being prepared to be industry-ready graduates? J. Teach. Learn. Graduate Employab. **4**(1), 73–84 (2013)
17. Hart Research Associates: Takes more than a major: employer priorities for college learning and student success (2013). http://www.aacu.org/leap/documents/2013_EmployerSurvey.pdf
18. Robles, M.: Executive perception of the top 10 soft skills needed in today's workplace. Bus. Commun. Q. **75**(4), 453–465 (2012)
19. Haller, M., Landerl, F.: A mediated reality environment using a loose and sketchy rendering technique. In: Ismar: Proceedings of the 4th IEEE/ACM International Symposium on Mixed and Augmented Reality, Washington, DC, USA, pp. 184–185 (2005). https://doi.org/10.1109/ISMAR.2005.4
20. Maas, M.J., Hughes, J.: Virtual, augmented and mixed reality in K–12 education: a review of the literature. Technol. Pedagogy Educ. **29**, 231–249 (2020)
21. Mann, S., Furness, T., Yuan, Y., Iorio, J., Wang, Z.: All reality: virtual, augmented, mixed (X), mediated (X, Y), and multimediated reality. arXiv, abs/1804.08386 (2018)

22. Yang, K., Zhou, X., Radu, I.: XR-Ed framework: designing instruction-driven and learner-centered extended reality systems for education. arXiv, abs/2010.13779 (2020)
23. O'Callaghan, T., Harbin, A.: Truly immersive worlds? The pedagogical implications of extended reality. J. Interact. Technol. Pedagogy Spec. Issue Potential Ext. Reality (XR): Teach. Learn. Virtual Spaces **17** (2020)
24. Milgram, P., Takemura H., Utsumi A., Kishino F.: Augmented reality: a class of displays on the reality-virtuality continuum. In: Proceedings of Telemanipulator and Telepresence Technologies, pp. 2351–34 (1994)
25. Craig, A.: Understanding Augmented Reality: Concepts and Applications. Elsevier, Waltham (2013)
26. Flavián, C., Ibáñez-Sánchez, S., Orús, C.: The impact of virtual, augmented and mixed reality technologies on the customer experience. J. Bus. Res. **100**, 547–560 (2019)
27. Sivan, Y.: 3D3C real virtual worlds defined: the immense potential of merging 3D, community, creation, and commerce. J. Virtual Worlds Res. **1**(1), 1–32 (2008)
28. Okeil, A.: Hybrid design environments: immersive and non-immersive architectural design. J. Inf. Technol. Constr. (ITcon), **15**, 202–216 (2010). http://www.itcon.org/2010/16
29. Simon, A., Smith, R., Pawlicki, R.: OmniStereo for panoramic virtual environment display systems. In: Proceedings of IEEE Virtual Reality, pp. 67–74 (2004)
30. Alves, C., Luís Reis, J.: The intention to use E-commerce using augmented reality - the case of IKEA place. In: Rocha, Á., Ferrás, C., Montenegro Marin, C.E., Medina García, V.H. (eds.) ICITS 2020. AISC, vol. 1137, pp. 114–123. Springer, Cham (2020). https://doi.org/10.1007/978-3-030-40690-5_12
31. Shen, Y., Ong, S.K., Nee, A.Y.: Augmented reality for collaborative product design and development. Des. Stud. **31**, 118–145 (2010)
32. Cipresso, P., Giglioli, I.A.C., Raya, M.A., Riva, G.: The past, present, and future of virtual and augmented reality research: a network and cluster analysis of the literature. Front. Psychol. **9**, Article 2086 (2018). https://doi.org/10.3389/fpsyg.2018.02086
33. Laurel, B.: Computers as Theatre, pp. 49–65. Addison-Wesley, Reading (1993)
34. Sutherland, I.E.: A head-mounted three-dimensional display. In: Proceedings of the December 9–11, Fall Joint Computer Conference, Part I, pp. 757–764. ACM (1968)
35. Poetker, B.: The very real history of virtual reality (A Look Ahead). G2 Learning Hub (2019). https://learn.g2.com/history-of-virtual-reality
36. Pimentel, K., Teixeira, K.: Virtual Reality. McGraw-Hill, New York (1993). ISBN 978-0-8306-4065-2
37. Gračanin, D., Stewart, M., Duncan, T., Handosa, M., Schulze, H.: Mixed-reality and project based curriculum development: empowering STEM learners and educators in southwest virginia appalachian region. In: 2018 IEEE VR Third Workshop on K-12+ Embodied Learning Through Virtual & Augmented Reality (KELVAR 2018), Held as Part of IEEE Virtual Reality, Reutlingen, Germany. IEEE (2018)
38. Jenab, K., Moslehpour, S., Khoury, S.: Virtual maintenance, reality, and systems: a review. Int. J. Electr. Comput. Eng. **6**(6), 2698–2707 (2016)
39. Sarnoff, P.: The VR in the enterprise report: how retailers and brands are illustrating VR's potential in sales, employee training, and product development. BusinessInsider (2018). https://www.businessinsider.com/virtual-reality-for-enterprise-sales-employee-training-product-2018-12
40. Gray, K., Koncz, A.: The key attributes employers seek on students' Resumes (2017). https://www.naceweb.org/about-us/press/2017/the-key-attributes-employers-seek-on-students-resumes/
41. Mitchell, G., Skinner, L., White, B.: Essential soft skills for success in the twenty-first century workforce as perceived by business educators. Delta Pi Epsilon J. **52**(1), 43–53 (2010)

42. Davidson, K.: Employers find 'soft skills' like critical thinking in short supply. Wall Street J. (3) (2016)
43. Strauss, V.: The surprising thing google learned about its employees—and what it means for today's students. Washington Post (2017). www.washingtonpost.com/news/answer-sheet/wp/2017/12/20/the-surprising-thing-google-learned-about-its-employees-and-what-it-means-for-todays-students/
44. Badrinarayanan, V., Arnett, D.: Effective virtual new product development teams: an integrated framework. J. Bus. Ind. Mark. 23(4), 242–248 (2008). https://doi.org/10.1108/088 58620810865816
45. Jenster, N.P., Steiler, D.: Turning up the volume in inter-personal leadership: motivating and building cohesive global virtual teams during times of economic crisis. In: Mobley, W.H., Weldon, E. (eds.) Advances in Global Leadership. Emerald Group Publishing Ltd., Bradford, GBR (2011)
46. Levy, O., Beechler, S., Taylor, S., Boyacigiller, N.A.: What we talk about when we talk about "global mindset": managerial cognition in multinational corporations. J. Int. Bus. Stud. 38, 231–258 (2007)
47. Barrows, H.S.: Practice-Based Learning: Problem-Based Learning Applied to Medical Education. Southern Illinois University School of Medicine, Springfield (1994)
48. Hmelo-Silver, C.E.: Problem-based learning: What and how do students learn? Educ. Psychol. Rev. 16(3), 235–266 (2004). https://doi.org/10.1023/B:EDPR.0000034022.164 70.f3
49. Fabris, C.: College students think they're ready for the work force. Employers aren't so Sure. The Chronicle of Higher Education (2015). http://chronicle.com/article/College-Students-Think/151289/
50. Cuban, L.: Teachers and Machines: The Classroom Use of Technology Since 1920. Teachers College Press, New York (1986)
51. Foshee, C., Elliott, S.N., Atkinson, R.: Technology-enhanced learning in college mathematics remediation. Br. J. Educ. Technol. (2015)
52. Januszewski, A.: Educational Technology: The Development of a Concept. Libraries Unlimited (2001)
53. Kennedy, M., Dunn, T.: Improving the use of VLEs in higher education in the UK: A qualitative visualisation of students' views. Contemporary Educational Technology (2018)
54. Johnson, D.W., Johnson, F.: Joining Together: Group Theory and Group Skills, 9th edn. Allyn & Bacon, Boston (2006)
55. Henderson, M., Selwyn, N., Aston, R.: What Works and Why? Student perceptions of 'useful' digital technology in university teaching and learning. Stud. High. Educ. 42(8), 1567–1579 (2017). https://doi.org/10.1080/03075079.2015.1007946
56. Starr, L.: Integrating technology in the classroom: it takes more than just having computers (2011). http://www.educationworld.com/a_tech/tech/tech146.shtml
57. Steedman, M.: Formalizing affordance. In: Proceedings of the 24th Annual Meeting of the Cognitive Science Society, pp. 834–839 (2002)
58. Stoffregen, T.A.: Affordances as properties of the animal-Environment system. Ecol. Psychol. 15(2), 115–134 (2003). https://doi.org/10.1207/S15326969ECO1502_2
59. Gibson, J.J.: The Ecological Approach to Visual Perception. Houghton Mifflin (1979)
60. Norman, D.A.: The Psychology of Everyday Things. Basic Books, New York (1988)
61. Hussein, M., Nätterdal, C.: The Benefits of Virtual Reality in Education: A Comparison Study. University of Gothenburg, Chalmers University of Technology (2015). https://doi.org/10.1177/0011000003253155
62. Özgen, D.S., Afacan, Y., Sürer, E.: Usability of virtual reality for basic design education: a comparative study with paper-based design. Int. J. Technol. Des. Educ. 31(2), 357–377 (2019). https://doi.org/10.1007/s10798-019-09554-0

63. Ibáñez, M.B., Di Serio, A., Villarán, D., Kloos, C.D.: Experimenting with electromagnetism using augmented reality: impact on flow student experience and educational effectiveness. Comput. Educ. **71**, 1–13 (2014)
64. Shin, D.: The role of affordance in the experience of virtual reality learning: technological and affective affordances in virtual reality. Telematics Inform. (2017). https://doi.org/10.1016/j.tele.2017.05.013
65. Nye, B.D., Silverman, B.G.: Affordances in AI. In: Seel, N.M. (ed.) Encyclopedia of the Sciences of Learning, pp. 183–187. Springer, New York (2012). https://doi.org/10.1007/978-1-4419-1428-6_386
66. Montesano, L., Lopes, M., Bernardino, A., Santos-Victor, J.: Learning object affordances: from sensory motor maps to imitation. IEEE Trans. Robot. **24**(1) (2008)
67. Keengwe, J., Onchwari, G., Wachira, P.: The use of computer tools to support meaningful learning. AACE J. **16**(1), 77–92 (2008)
68. Bower, M., Howe, C., McCredie, N., Robinson, A., Grover, D.: Augmented reality in education–cases, places and potentials. Educ. Media Int. **51**, 1–15 (2014)
69. Engelbrecht, H., Lindeman, R., Hoermann, S.A.: SWOT analysis of the field of virtual reality for firefighter training. Front. Robot. AI **6**, 101 (2019)
70. Jensen, L.K.: A Review of the use of virtual reality head-mounted displays in education and training. Educ. Inf. Technol. **23**, 1515–1529 (2018)
71. Dewey, J.: Experience and Education. The Macmillan Company, New York (1938)
72. Kolb, D.A.: Learning Style Inventory. McBer & Company, Boston (1976)
73. Ord, J., Leather, M.M.: The substance beneath the labels of experiential learning: the importance of John Dewey for outdoor educators. J. Outdoor Environ. Educ. **15**, 13–23 (2011)
74. Yoder, J.D., Hochevar, C.M.: Encouraging active learning can improve students' performance on examinations. Teach. Psychol. **32**(2), 91–95 (2005)
75. Bacca, J., Baldiris, S., Fabregat, R., Graf, S., K.: Augmented reality trends in education: a systematic review of research and applications. J. Educ. Technol. Soc. **17**(4), 133–149 (2014)
76. Mikropoulos, T., Natsis, A.: Educational virtual environments: a ten-year review of empirical research (1999–2009). Comput. Educ. **56**(3), 769–780 (2011)
77. Dewey, A., Drahota, A.: Introduction to systematic reviews: Online learning module cochrane training (2016). https://training.cochrane.org/interactivelearning/module-1-introduction-conducting-systematic-reviews
78. MacKenzie, H., et al.: Systematic reviews: what they are, why they are important, and how to get involved. J. Clin. Prev. Cardiol. **1**(4), 193–202 (2012)
79. Wei-Che, H., Tseng, C., Kang, S.: Using exaggerated feedback in a virtual reality environment to enhance behavior intention of water-conservation. J. Educ. Technol. Soc. **21**(4), 187–203 (2018)
80. Li, D.: Application of 3D virtual ocean image simulation in ship vision. J. Coast. Res., 530–34 (2019). https://doi.org/10.2307/26853997
81. Gallup, J., Serianni, B.: Developing friendships and an awareness of emotions using video games: perceptions of four young adults with autism. Educ. Train. Autism Dev. Disabil. **52**(2), 20–131 (2017)
82. Wu, B., Hu, Y., Wang, M.: How do head-mounted displays and planning strategy influence problem-solving-based learning in introductory electrical circuit design? Educ. Technol. Soc. **23**(3), 40–52 (2020). https://doi.org/10.2307/26926425
83. Kamarainen, A., Reilly, J., Metcalf, S., Grotzer, T., Dede, C.: Using mobile location-based augmented reality to support outdoor learning in undergraduate ecology and environmental science courses. Bull. Ecol. Soc. Am. **99**(2), 259–276 (2018)

84. Abbas, J.R., Kenth, J.J., Bruce, I.A.: The role of virtual reality in the changing landscape of surgical training. J. Laryngol. Otol. **134**(10), 863–866 (2020). https://doi.org/10.1017/S00 22215120002078

85. Sáez-López, Cózar-Gutiérrez.: Augmented reality in higher education: An evaluation program in initial teacher training. Educ. Sci. **10**(2), 26 (2020)

86. Hiranyachattada, T., Kusirirat, K.: Using mobile augmented reality to enhancing students' conceptual understanding of physically-based rendering in 3D animation. Eur. J. Sci. Math. Educ. **8**(1), 1–5 (2020)

87. Vieira, E.R., et al.: Using augmented reality with older adults in the community to select design features for an age-friendly park: a pilot study. J. Aging Res. (2020). http://dx.doi. org.librarylink.uncc.edu/10.1155/2020/8341034

88. Liu, S., Xie, M., Ye, Z.: Combating COVID-19—how can AR telemedicine help doctors more effectively implement clinical work. J. Med. Syst. **44**(9), 1–2 (2020). https://doi.org/ 10.1007/s10916-020-01618-2

89. Vasilevski, N., Birt, J.: Analysing construction student experiences of mobile mixed reality enhanced learning in virtual and augmented reality environments. Assoc. Learn. Technol. J. Res. Learn. Technol. **28** (2020). http://dx.doi.org.librarylink.uncc.edu/10.25304/rlt.v28. 2329

90. Celik, C., Gokhan G., Nevin, K. C.: Integration of mobile augmented reality (MAR) applications into biology laboratory: anatomic structure of the heart. Assoc. Learn. Technol. J. Res. Learn. Technol. **28** (2020). http://dx.doi.org.librarylink.uncc.edu/10.25304/rlt.v28.2355

91. Damio, S.M., Ibrahim, Q.: Virtual reality speaking application utilisation in combatting presentation apprehension. Asian J. Univ. Educ. **15**(3), 235–244 (2019)

92. Kim, S., et al.: Virtual reality visualization model (VRVM) of the tricarboxylic acid (TCA) cycle of carbohydrate metabolism for medical biochemistry education. J. Sci. Educ. Technol. **28**(6), 602–612 (2019). http://dx.doi.org.librarylink.uncc.edu/10.1007/s10956-019-09790-y

93. Syawaludin, A., Gunarhadi, R., Peduk: Development of augmented reality-based interactive multimedia to improve critical thinking skills in science learning. Int. J. Instr. **12**(4), 331–344 (2019)

94. Starr, C.R., Anderson, B.R., Green, K.A.: I'm a computer scientist!: virtual reality experience influences stereotype threat and STEM motivation among undergraduate women. J. Sci. Educ. Technol. **28**(5), 493–507 (2019). http://dx.doi.org.librarylink.uncc.edu/10.1007/s10 956-019-09781-z

95. Calvert, P.: Virtual reality as a tool for teaching library design. Educ. Inf. **35**(4), 439–450 (2019). https://doi.org/10.3233/EFI-170150

96. Cooper, G., Park, H., Nasr, Z., Thong, L.P., Johnson, R.: Using virtual reality in the classroom: Preservice teachers' perceptions of its use as a teaching and learning tool. Educ. Media Int. **56**(1), 1–13 (2019)

97. Netland, T.H., Flaeschner, O., Maghazei, O., Brown, K.: Teaching operations management with virtual reality: bringing the factory to the students. J. Manag. Educ. **44**(3), 313–341 (2020). https://doi.org/10.1177/1052562919892028

98. Larson, K.E., Hirsch, S.E., McGraw, J.P., Bradshaw, C.P.: Preparing preservice teachers to manage behavior problems in the classroom: the feasibility and acceptability of using a mixed-reality simulator. J. Spec. Educ. Technol. **35**(2), 63–75 (2020). https://doi.org/10. 1177/0162643419836415

99. Fraser, D.W., Marder, T.J., deBettencourt, L.U., Myers, L.A., Kalymon, K.M., Harrell, R.M.: Using a mixed-reality environment to train special educators working with students with autism spectrum disorder to implement discrete trial teaching. Focus Autism Other Dev. Disabil. **35**(1), 3–14 (2020). https://doi.org/10.1177/1088357619844696

100. Bridges, S.A., Robinson, O.P., Stewart, E.W., Kwon, D., Mutua, K.: Augmented reality: teaching daily living skills to adults with intellectual disabilities. J. Spec. Educ. Technol. **35**(1), 3–14 (2020). https://doi.org/10.1177/0162643419836411
101. Hauze, S., Marshall, J.: Validation of the instructional materials motivation survey: measuring student motivation to learn via mixed reality nursing education simulation. Int. J. E-Learn. **19**(1), 49–64 (2020)
102. Wells, T., Miller, G.: The effect of virtual reality technology on welding skill performance. J. Agric. Educ. **61**(1), 152–171 (2020)
103. Bennie, S.J., et al.: Teaching enzyme catalysis using interactive molecular dynamics in virtual reality. J. Chem. Educ. **96**(11), 2488–2496 (2019). https://doi.org/10.1021/acs.jch emed.9b00181
104. Stuart, J., Rutherford, R.J.: Medical student concentration during lectures. Lancet **312**, 514–516 (1978). https://doi.org/10.1016/S0140-6736(78)92233-X
105. Yang, H., Tate, M.: Where are we at with cloud computing? A descriptive literature review [Paper presentation]. In: 20th Australasian Conference on Information Systems, pp. 807–819. AIS (2009). https://aisel.aisnet.org/acis2009/26/
106. Conole, G., Dyke, M.: What are the affordances of information and communication technologies? ALT-J **12**(2), 113–124 (2004)
107. Dalgarno, B., Lee, M.J.: What are the learning affordances of 3D virtual environments? Br. J. Edu. Technol. **41**(1), 10–32 (2010). https://doi.org/10.1111/j.1467-8535.2009.01038.x
108. Schild, J., Lerner, D., Misztal, S., Luiz, T.: EPICSAVE—enhancing vocational training for paramedics with multi-user virtual reality. In: 2018 IEEE 6th International Conference on Serious Games and Applications for Health (SeGAH), pp. 1–8. IEEE (2018)
109. Pereira, V., Matos, T., Rodrigues, R., Nóbrega., R., Jacob, J.: Extended reality framework for remote collaborative interactions in virtual environments. ICGI, Faro, Portugal, pp. 17–24 (2019). https://doi.org/10.1109/ICGI47575.2019.8955025
110. Cassard, A.M., Sloboda, B.W.: AI and AR: a copacetic approach in the new educational environment. In: Choi, D.H., Dailey-Hebert, A., Estes, J.S. (ed.) Current and Prospective Applications of Virtual Reality in Higher Education, pp. 216–231. IGI Global (2021). https://doi.org/10.4018/978-1-7998-4960-5.ch010

Development of an AR Training Construction System Using Embedded Information in a Real Environment

Yuki Harazono[1]([⊠])(iD), Taichi Tamura[1], Yusuke Omoto[1], Hirotake Ishii[1](iD), Hiroshi Shimoda[1](iD), Yoshiaki Tanaka[2], and Yoshiyuki Takahashi[2]

[1] Graduate School of Energy Science, Kyoto University, Kyoto, Japan
{harazono,tamura,omoto,hiotake,shimoda}@ei.energy.kyoto-u.ac.jp
[2] Institute for Integrated Radiation and Nuclear Science, Kyoto University, Kumatori, Japan
{tanaka.yoshiaki.2w,takahashi.yoshiyuki.7e}@kyoto-u.ac.jp

Abstract. In recent years, emergency drills have been held in important facilities such as nuclear facilities. The problem with these drills is that the number of emergency scenarios is limited. In this study, we have developed an augmented reality training system that allows users to easily create scenarios by simply assembling and placing blocks representing the components of the scenario in the real-world environment. The system is capable of simulating various scenarios, involving the interaction between the trainee and the real-world environment. A subjective experiment was conducted at a nuclear facility to evaluate the usability of the system and the flexibility about scenario creation. The results showed that the users can construct an AR training environment easily in a shorter time than the conventional text-based programming.

Keywords: Augmented reality · Training system · Authoring tool · Visual programming · Puzzle-like programming

1 Introduction

In recent years, trainings such as emergency drills have been held in nuclear facilities in order to improve the safety of these critical facilities and reduce damage when an accident occurs. In these trainings, there is a problem that the number of scenarios or roles which workers can experience is limited because many workers participate it all at once and the time that they can spend at the same time is limited. To solve this problem, it is supposed that trainings using augmented reality (AR) is effective to improve training efficiency [1,2]. In AR training system, the computer can play the role of characters in the training, such as other participants, intruders or police officers instead of actual humans. Therefore, many participants are not necessary to conduct the training at the same time. Thus, by using AR training system, users can conduct trainings easily with a few workers or alone and experience various scenarios and roles.

© Springer Nature Switzerland AG 2021
J. Y. C. Chen and G. Fragomeni (Eds.): HCII 2021, LNCS 12770, pp. 614–625, 2021.
https://doi.org/10.1007/978-3-030-77599-5_42

However, there are some problems when constructing AR training environments. For example, although it is desirable that workers themselves at nuclear facilities can create training scenarios, some information technology skills such as programming are required to develop AR training systems, so they are usually developed by software companies. However, the developers at the software companies are not familiar with nuclear facilities and actual training. The scenarios might become much different from ones required in the actual facilities. In addition, in order to create the effective scenarios, it is necessary to understand the situation of the field and create suitable scenarios. In conventional text-based programming, it is difficult to construct AR training environment and create its scenario with referring to the situation of the field where the training drills are held.

In this study, we have aimed to develop an AR training construction system that allows users to easily construct their own AR training environment without specialized knowledge or special skills such as programming. To achieve this purpose, we have developed "Program Block," which is a new real world oriented visual programming language.

2   Design and Development of AR Training Construction System

Figure 1 shows the overview of the AR training construction system. The AR training construction system consists of a training environment construction subsystem and a training experience subsystem. By using "Program Block," the users assemble the blocks to create "Scenario Blocks" which represent the actions and execution conditions of objects such as fire and water leakages in the scenario. Then, using the training environment construction subsystem, the users can design and create the entire training scenario by placing Scenario Blocks and scanning Scenario Blocks and environment. By taking pictures of the entire environment with a camera, the users can scan it. In the training experience subsystem, they can interactively experience the created training scenario by AR using a tablet PC.

2.1   Design and Development of Program Block

In this AR training construction system, the users can create interactive AR training scenarios using Program Block as shown in Fig. 2. In Program Block, each block represents an element of the training scenario, such as the content of the event and the condition when it happens. Program Block is designed to be assembled and placed like building blocks at the location where the event is to occur, so that the action set at that location is executed according to the movement of the user and the time elapsed. In this study, the training elements and types of blocks were chosen based on actual training scenarios conducted in nuclear facilities [3] in order to create the scenarios that look like they are actually held. The main drills actually conducted in nuclear facilities consist of

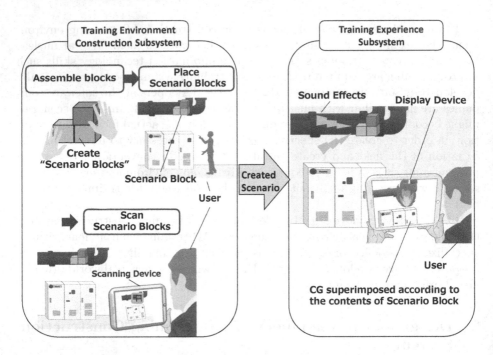

Fig. 1. Overview of AR training construction system.

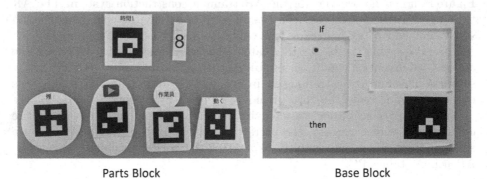

Parts Block   Base Block

Fig. 2. Developed program block.

disaster drills and counter-terrorism drills against illegal incidents assuming an act of terrorism. In the disaster drills, they are aiming to train how to respond to fire and water leakage in the facility. The counter-terrorism drills are conducted under the scenario that a suspicious person enters the facility from the outside, installs an explosive device, and causes an explosion in the building. As soon as calling the police, and police officers rush in to seize the intruder.

In the Program Block, the condition part that sets the condition and the processing part that is executed according to the condition are assembled to create one Scenario Block, which is one component of the scenario as shown in Fig. 2. The training scenarios can be written by attaching "part blocks" to "base block." About the setting of conditions, it is designed to set conditions related to distance or time, and the processing part is executed if its conditions are satisfied. Whether its conditions are satisfied or not is judged using the comparison operator such as "equal," "more than," and "less than." In the conditions related to distance, the distance between the user and the placed blocks is regarded to be the condition. In the conditions related to time, the elapsed time from one reference time is regarded to be the condition. About the elapsed time, multiple variables to set reference time are prepared so that the users can set them on various timings at the processing part. The value to compare with the elapsed time and the distance to the user can be set using part blocks that represent numbers ("0"–"9"). Distance can be set in meters, and time can be set in seconds. The shape of Program Block differs depending on their roles so that they can be assembled in only the correct combination to make it possible to follow the rules of description. The part block represents the training elements such as flames, water leakages, police officers, and the elements for conditions, and base block represents the grammar for writing scenarios such as "If A is B, then execute C."

When scanning the created Scenario Blocks in the training environment construction subsystem, by a tablet PC attached with a camera, it is necessary to scan the blocks and recognize them. In the Program Block, ArUco markers [4] are attached to each block in order to make it easy to recognize the kinds of blocks.

2.2   Design and Development of Training Environment Construction Subsystem

After describing the training scenario using the Program Block, the users scan the training area, and the locations and contents of the placed Scenario Blocks are recognized by the training environment construction subsystem. To scan the training environment and recognize the location of the placed blocks, it is necessary to identify the location of the user who is scanning (tracking). In the training environment construction subsystem, the tracking method using RGB-D camera which was originally developed by the authors [5] was adopted. In this subsystem, a tablet PC attached with an RGB-D camera is used as the scan device. The user scans the training environment and Scenario Blocks by the tablet PC. By scanning them, this subsystem makes a scenario file from scanned data. This subsystem has to recognize them with tracking in real time, and it is difficult for the poor-powered tablet PC to process them in real time. In the subsystem, therefore, the tablet PC sends the scanned data via wireless communication to a more powerful PC, and it processes the scanned data. In the recognition application, the recognized blocks are highlighted using AR while scanning in order to let the user know that blocks are being recognized correctly.

The hardware of the subsystem consists of a tablet PC, an RGB-D camera (Xtion Pro Live), and a laptop PC. The recognition application, tracking application, and communication application were developed by Visual Studio 2017, and the developed language was C++. To recognize the part blocks which represent numbers in recognize application, tesseract ocr [6] was adopted.

2.3 Design and Development of Training Experience Subsystem

In the training experience subsystem, based on the created scenario file, users can interactively experience the training scenario which was created by the training environment construction subsystem by using a tablet PC attached with an RGB-D camera. The training experience subsystem displays flames or water leakages following the user's situation and the progress of the scenario using AR with recognizing user's position and checking whether the current situation satisfies the described conditions in the created scenario. In order not to spoil the sense of reality, the presented image is displayed with considering the back-and-forth positional relationship between the superimposed CG and the real objects by using the depth image captured by the RGB-D camera. In addition, this subsystem also plays sound effects based on the scenario content. It has to display presented image to the user's situation and the progress of the scenario with tracking in real time as well as the training environment construction subsystem in order to recognize the user's situation. In this subsystem, therefore, the current camera view is transmitted via wireless communication to a more powerful PC, and it recognizes the current situation, generates presented image, and sends it back to the tablet PC.

The hardware of this subsystem consists of a tablet PC, an RGB-D camera (Xtion Pro Live), a laptop PC, and small Bluetooth speakers (EWA A109mini). The speakers are attached to Scenario Blocks placed in the environment. In this subsystem, the tablet PC executes the tracking application to estimate the user's location, the experience application to display the presented image on the tablet PC, and the communication application to send and receive images to the laptop PC. These applications were developed by Visual Studio 2017, and the developed language was C++. The laptop PC executes the communication application to send and receive images to the tablet PC and the rendering application to generate the presented images which is a composite image of camera image and CG. The communication application was also developed by Visual Studio 2017, and the developed language was C++. The rendering application was developed by Visual Studio 2017 and Unity 2017, and the developed language was C#. The CG such as the flames and water leakages and 3D models such as police officers were supplied from Unity Asset Store [7]. Mixamo [8] was used to make animation of 3D models such as the movement of police officers.

2.4 Operation Examples of AR Training Construction Subsystem

Figure 3 shows an example of assembling the Program Block and creating the Scenario Block that represents a fire accident. As shown in the figure, the user creates the Scenario Block by fitting the part blocks into the base block. Figure 4 shows an example of the screen that is displayed when a Scenario Block is scanned using the training environment construction subsystem. As shown in the figure, when a Scenario Block is correctly recognized, a green frame is superimposed around the block to show the user that it has been correctly recognized. Figure 5 shows an example of the screen that is displayed when the user experiences a fire accident using the training experience subsystem. The CG of the fire is superimposed at the location of the scanned Scenario Block.

Fig. 3. An example of creating Scenario Block using the Program Block.

3   Evaluation of AR Training Construction System

3.1   Purpose and Overview of the Evaluation

In this study, we aimed to design and develop the AR training construction system in order to construct the AR training environment easily without special knowledge or skills such as programming. In order to confirm that the systems are enough easy to operate and have enough flexibility to create various training scenarios, two subject experiments were conducted to evaluate easy operation (Easiness Evaluation) and flexibility (Flexibility Evaluation).

Seven staff members at Institute for Integrated Radiation and Nuclear Science, Kyoto University participated in the Easiness Evaluation, and two staff members also participated in the Flexibility Evaluation as evaluators. In each evaluation, the evaluators were asked to construct an AR training environment and then experience it using the AR training construction system. After that, questionnaires and interviews were conducted with evaluators to evaluate the easiness of this system and the flexibility of the training scenario.

Fig. 4. An example of scanning Scenario Block using the training environment construction subsystem.

Fig. 5. An example of experience AR training using the training experience subsystem.

3.2   Easiness Evaluation

Overview. In the Easiness Evaluation, it was evaluated that even a beginner user can easily understand how to use the AR training construction system and that the user can operate the AR training construction system as intended. In order to evaluate them in this evaluation, the evaluators were asked to do two "scenario creation tasks" so that all the functions of the AR training construction system would be used by them. In each scenario creation task, they were asked to create a designated scenario and then experience the scenario. The first scenario creation task (scenario creation task 1) was to create and experience the scenario that simulates indoor water leakage: "When the elapsed time from the start of the scenario reaches 6 s and 20 s, the CG of the water leakage will be played at two locations respectively, and when the elapsed time reaches 25 s and 30 s, they will stop." The second scenario creation task (scenario creation task 2) is: "An intruder breaks into the room and sets fire to the papers in the room. The fire spreads and an explosive object explodes. The user calls the police, and they arrive." Specifically, this task can be broken down to set up the following events: "an intruder enters, an intruder bends down to start a fire, an intruder leaves, a fire starts, a fire spreads, an explosion occurs, a user calls the police, and the police arrive one minute after the call."

Environment and Evaluators. This evaluation was conducted in a room at Institute for Integrated Radiation and Nuclear Science, Kyoto University. The top view of the room used for the evaluation is shown in Fig. 6. Figure 7 shows the scene during the evaluation. Seven staff members at Institute for Integrated Radiation and Nuclear Science, Kyoto University participated in the evaluation. All evaluators had experience in participating in actual emergency drills, and three of the evaluators had programming experience while the rest had no experience.

Procedure. The evaluation procedure is shown in Table 1. First, the experimenter explained the purpose and flow of this evaluation to the evaluators for about 3 min using a document, and then the evaluators watched a 2-min instructional video explaining how to use the AR training construction system. Next, the evaluators read an explanatory document for about 15 min, which showed an overview of the Program Block and examples of scenarios that could be created using the Program Block. Then, as a practice, the evaluators constructed a simple training environment as given in the explanatory document and experienced it.

Second, the evaluators were asked to work on the scenario describing task 1 and 2. For both tasks, the task was completed when the evaluators finished from starting to assemble the Program Block to completing experiencing the AR training. After the tasks, the evaluators were asked to answer a questionnaire about the easiness of the AR training construction system, and they were interviewed about the reasons for answering each questionnaire item. For each questionnaire item, the evaluators were asked to answer on a 5-point Likert scale. A part of the questionnaire items are shown in Table 2.

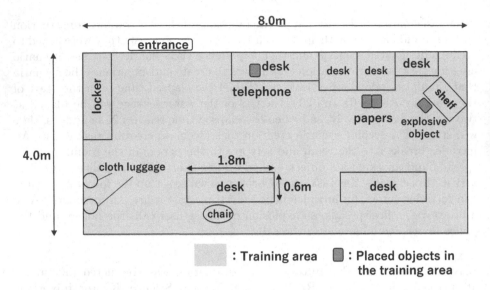

Fig. 6. Top view of the experimental room.

Fig. 7. Scenes during the evaluation.

Results and Discussion. Some of the questionnaire results, reasons and opinions are shown in Table 2. As shown in Table 2, for "You could understand which Part Block represents which function," all the evaluators gave a grade of 4 or more with a mean of 4.7. This showed that even a beginner user could easily understand the contents of the Program Block.

Table 1. Procedure of the Easiness Evaluation.

Procedure contents	Time length
Explanation of the Evaluation	3 min
Explanation of AR training construction system(with video)	17 min
Practice of AR training construction system	15 min
Scenario describing task 1	15 min
Scenario describing task 2	30 min
Questionnaires and interviews about easiness of operation	5 min

Table 2. Examples of the questionnaire items, results, and opinions in the Easiness Evaluation.

Questionnaire items	Grade average	Opinions
You could understand which Part Block represents which function	4.7	it would be better if the markers would be a design that can be understood by users
This system was easy to use even for beginners	3.4	It took time to learn
		It can be used with practice and reading manual

For "This system was easy to use even for beginners," only one evaluator gave a grade of 2 and the other evaluators gave a grade of 3 or higher with a mean of 3.4. In the interviews, we obtained the opinions that it took some time to learn and that it was difficult at first, but with practice and a explanatory document, it could be learned. Based on these results and opinions, it cannot be said that the AR training construction system is quite easy to use. However, comparing with the need to learn a programming language from scratch to construct an AR training environment in conventional methods such as text-based programming, it can be said that the AR training construction system is much easier to construct an AR training environment since it can be learned in about 30 min.

3.3 Flexibility Evaluation

Overview. In the Flexibility Evaluation, we evaluated whether it is possible to create training scenarios with the flexibility required in the actual training field with the AR training construction system. In the Flexibility Evaluation, the evaluators were asked to do "free-creation task". In free-creation task, at first, each evaluator was asked to consider a suitable AR training scenario. After that, they were asked to create their scenarios and experience them in the same way as the Easiness Evaluation.

Environment and Evaluators. This evaluation was conducted in the same room as the Easiness Evaluation. Two staff members who also joined the Easiness Evaluation participated in the evaluation.

Procedure. The evaluation procedure is shown in Table 3. In this evaluation, the evaluators were asked to do "free-creation task" . After the task, the evaluators were asked to answer a questionnaire about the flexibility of the AR training scenario, and they were also interviewed about the reasons for answering each questionnaire item. For each questionnaire item, the evaluators were asked to answer on a 5-point Likert scale as well as the Easiness Evaluation. Some examples of the questionnaire items are shown in Table 4.

Table 3. Procedure of flexibility evaluation.

Procedure contents	Time length
Free-creation task	30 min
Questionnaires and interviews about flexibility of the AR training scenario	5 min

Results and Discussion. Some examples of the questionnaire results, reasons and opinions are shown in Table 4. As shown in Table 4, for "This system has the CG for object actions needed to create the AR training scenario needed in actual

Table 4. Examples of the questionnaire items, results, and opinions in the flexibility evaluation.

Questionnaire items	Grades (two evaluators)	Opinions
This system has the CG for object actions needed to create the AR training scenario needed in actual training	4 and 2	I wanted to set the volume and strength of the CGs
		I wanted to display unvisible things like radiation
This system has the CG for person actions needed to create the AR training scenario needed in actual training	4 and 3	I wanted intruders with a variety of features like collapsed people

training," the evaluators gave grades of 4 and 2. For this questionnaire item, we obtained the following opinions: "I wanted to set the volume and strength of the CGs," and "I wanted to display invisible things like radiation." About the scale of CGs, this system can make it look like a large fire or water leakage by setting up multiple Scenario Blocks which represent fire and water leakage settings side by side, but it is not possible to reduce their scale or set their strength by the current system. These can be handled by preparing another kind of block which are set other scales. Visualizations of radiation can be also handled in the same way as CGs of fire and water leakages by creating a new part block which represents simulated radiation source.

For "This system has the CG for person actions needed to create the AR training scenario needed in actual training," they gave grades of 4 and 3. The opinion is: "I wanted intruders with a variety of features like collapsed people," it is expected that it will increase the flexibility of scenarios that users can create by adding part block, and with these levels of addition, it is supposed that the system would not be very complicated.

4 Conclusion

In this study, we developed the AR training construction system and Program Block in order that users can construct the AR training environment easily without expertise and skills such as programming. We evaluated the easiness of operation and its flexibility of created scenario by the staff members at the nuclear facility. From the results, it was found that users can construct an AR training environment easily. It was also found that the flexibility of training scenarios that can be created using the current Program Block is not sufficiently high. By adding some program blocks, however, it will be possible to create AR training scenarios that are required in the actual training.

References

1. Lee, K.: Augmented reality in education and training. TechTrends **56**(2), 13–21 (2012). https://doi.org/10.1007/s11528-012-0559-3
2. Itamiya, T., et al.: Augmented reality floods and smoke smartphone app disaster scope utilizing real-time occlusion. In: 2019 IEEE Conference on Virtual Reality and 3D User Interfaces (VR), p. 1397 (2019)
3. https://www.nsr.go.jp/data/000236041.pdf . Accessed 12 Feb 2021
4. Garrido-Jurado, S., et al.: Automatic generation and detection of highly reliable fiducial markers under occlusion. Pattern Recogn. **47**(6), 2280–2292 (2014)
5. Harazono, Y., et al.: Performance evaluation of scanning support system for constructing 3D reconstruction models. In: 2019 IEEE 5th International Conference on Computer and Communications (2019)
6. Tesseract-OCR library. https://github.com/tesseract-ocr/. Accessed 12 Feb 2021
7. Unity Asset Store. https://assetstore.unity.com/. Accessed 12 Feb 2021
8. Mixamo. https://www.mixamo.com/. Accessed 12 Feb 2021

LibrARy – Enriching the Cultural Physical Spaces with Collaborative AR Content

Andreea-Carmen Ifrim[(✉)], Florica Moldoveanu, Alin Moldoveanu,
and Alexandru Grădinaru

Faculty of Automatic Control and Computers, University POLITEHNICA of Bucharest,
Splaiul Independentei 313, Bucharest, Romania
andreea_carmen.ifrim@stud.acs.upb.ro

Abstract. In the last decade, technology has been rapidly evolving, making the humankind more dependent on digital devices than ever. We rely more and more on digitalization and we are excited to welcome emergent technologies like Augmented Reality (AR) into our everyday activities as they show great potential to enhance our standard of life. AR applications are becoming more popular every day and represent the future of human-computer interaction, by revolutionizing the way information is presented and transforming the surroundings into one broad user interface.

This paper aims to present the concept of LibrARy – an AR system that intends to create innovative collaborative environments where multiple users can interact simultaneously with computer-generated content. Its main objective is to improve cooperation by enabling co-located users to access a shared space populated with 3D virtual objects and to enrich collaboration between them through augmented interactions.

LibrARy will be developed as part of Lib2Life research project which addresses a topic of great importance – revitalizing cultural spaces in the context of recent technology advancements. In light of the research carried out for the Lib2Life project, a need for a more complex collaborative augmented environment has been identified. Therefore, we are now proposing LibrARy - an innovative component which has the potential to enhance the cooperation in multi-participant settings and provide unique interactive experiences.

This paper will present in more detail the concept and the functionalities of LibrARy. It will then analyze the possible use case scenarios and lastly discuss further development steps.

Keywords: Mixed reality and environments · Augmented Reality · Human-computer interaction · Collaborative applications · Collaborative environments

1 Introduction

1.1 Collaborative Augmented Reality

According to one of the most accepted definitions, Augmented Reality (AR) is generally envisioned as a variation of Virtual Reality (VR), acting as "a system that combines real

© Springer Nature Switzerland AG 2021
J. Y. C. Chen and G. Fragomeni (Eds.): HCII 2021, LNCS 12770, pp. 626–638, 2021.
https://doi.org/10.1007/978-3-030-77599-5_43

and virtual content, provides a real-time interactive environment, and registers in 3D". Unlike VR, AR supplements reality instead of completely replacing it, positioning itself on Milgram's Reality-Virtuality continuum [1] closer to the real environment than to the virtual one, but gaining potential from both worlds as shown in Fig. 1.

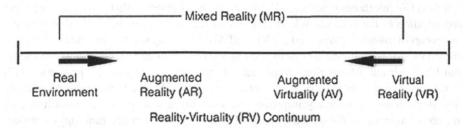

Fig. 1. Reality-Virtuality (RV) Continuum

Latest research [2–4] enhances this definition, describing AR as an enriched view of the physical environment, overlaid by computer-generated information. Moreover, as stated in most of the studies [5–7], it is generally accepted that any typical AR system should fulfil three main characteristics: 1) Combine real and virtual worlds, 2) Provide real time interaction and 3) Support 3D registration of virtual objects.

Once inaccessible and difficult to use, AR systems are promptly becoming popular and are regarded as the future of human-computer interaction, by shaping the real environment into one broad interactive user interface. But as M. Billinghurst et al. have noticed in their research [8], perhaps the greatest potential of AR technology lies in developing new types of collaborative platforms that focus on enhancing the communication and cooperation between participants in ways unreachable otherwise. Although still in its early days, collaborative augmented reality is currently thoroughly researched and can be successfully employed in a wide range of domains, including the educational, cultural, or artistic fields.

While single-user AR systems remain of great interest, Collaborative Augmented Reality (CAR) takes the technology one step further and promotes new types of interactions in an augmented environment. It allows co-located users to access simultaneously a shared space enriched with 3D content, thus strengthening collective interactions in day-to-day activities, and increasing their productivity. As the users remain grounded in their own physical environment, they can communicate through natural means (speech, gesture, etc.) and benefit directly from the supplemented interaction. This technique can prove itself extremely worthy in fields where social interaction between people situated in the same place is of crucial importance such as education [5], design [9] and cultural heritage [10].

Moreover, CAR can be successfully mixed with remote collaboration techniques in order to simulate a common working space for geographically distributed users. It provides unique capabilities that shape up distributed augmented spaces and support working together on different collaborative tasks. In particular, CAR systems can enrich cooperation in activities related to collaborative design [11, 12] and molecular modelling [13] or more often enable remote guidance and training. This technique is commonly referred to as "AR based coaching" [14] and allows experts to convey useful information or supervise remote users while performing a real-time task in their own environment [15].

In both scenarios, presenting virtual content is perhaps the most essential aspect of immersive technologies and, in order to support remote or face-to-face shared activities, collaborative interfaces make use of different types of displays that can ensure a proper visualization of the content. Bekele et al. identified in their research [16] five different categories of visual displays used for VR and AR, including see-through head-mounted-displays (HMDs), hand-held devices such as Samsung's Gear VR, or Spatial AR (SAR) that layers virtual information on the real environment either through projection [17] or through holographs. The evolution of technology and the advancement of tracking algorithms have considerably improved the usability and level of accessibility of all the above-mentioned AR-suited devices. Thus, most of them are nowadays compact and light-weighted while also providing high-resolution rendering, pose tracking, and natural interaction with virtual content. In addition, some of them are relatively affordable and already available for large-scale consumption such as Google Glasses, Microsoft's Hololens, DAQRI Smart Helmet, Zspace and HTC Vive.

Augmented Reality represents a way forward for developing new fundamentally different platforms that provide efficient face-to-face and remote collaboration. Through interactive interfaces combined with the user's environment, it promotes innovative and compelling experiences and founds new types of interactions. However, as Hayet Belghit et al. point out in their paper, there is still need for extensive research in the field in order to overcome several challenges related to performance, alignment, interaction, mobility and visualization [18, 19].

1.2 Collaborative Augmented Reality in Education and Art

The usage of AR technologies has been investigated and applied with great success across a wide range of fields, including medicine – for surgical planning [20] or training [4], videoconferencing [21], entertainment [22, 23], and sports [24, 25]. But, as pointed out by Bacca et al. in [26], in the recent years there has been an increased interest for researching the benefits of AR in the educational context. As shown by several studies [27], employing collaborative AR for educational purposes can increase a shared understanding of the scientific topics presented while supporting effective group interaction and cooperation. Moreover, it shows great appeal to younger generations as they are extremely proficient in handling AR-suited devices [28] and it has the ability to increase their motivation and engagement through interactive educational activities [29].

There have been already numerous successfully developed systems that promote cooperative learning and provide augmented face-to-face collaboration among teachers and students. Most of them have been shown to help scholars perform better in interest-driven classes that merge rigorous concepts from science, technology, engineering, and mathematics (STEM) where they can benefit from a collaborative "hands-on, minds-on" learning experience [30].

One such example is Meta-AR, an authoring platform for collaborative AR which provides students an unique opportunity of learning-while-making [31] and empowers them to become active agents in the learning process through a synergistic cooperation [32]. The system combines AR with the capabilities of cloud technology and introduces the pull-based collaborative model [33], a workflow to upload, share and download information that supports students to improve the learning content by adding their personal contributions to the original version. As concluded by the authors of the study, this approach can successfully spark creativity and curiosity amongst students during the learning process while leading to a considerable decrease in problem-solving errors. However, a great importance must be still placed on planning and structuring properly the STEM lessons as immersive technologies can overwhelm the students and reduce their ability to process information correctly [34].

Apart from the STEM educational context, CAR technologies are also gaining fast importance and popularity when it comes to humanities sciences, and in particular arts, as several studies point out that usage of new and combined media has the ability to also enhance cultural experiences [35]. Thus, in the recent years, there has been a great focus on the benefits that immersive technologies – a collective term for virtual-, augmented- and mixed-reality technologies - can bring to the Cultural Heritage (CH). As stated in [16], these technologies provide the means for user-centered experiences and make CH digitally available for a wide range of purposes, including education [36], exhibition enhancement [37, 38], exploration [39], reconstruction [40], and virtual museums [41].

One of the first systems to promote CH through collaborative-AR means is Virtuoso [42], an educational handheld application designed for studying the history of arts. In their studies, Wagner et al. [42] compared learning in a collaborative augmented environment enabled through PDAs (Personal Digital Assistant) to traditional PC interfaces. Even though Virtuoso represented only a prototype which struggled with technological limitations, such as a small screen and low audio quality, the results of their empirical research successfully prove that AR learning techniques are completely efficient also for untrained users, while representing an engaging and fun-factor in cultural environments. The same conclusion has been lately endorsed by Gurgalakos et al. in a study [43] that assesses an innovative approach which crosses the boundaries between schools and museums by allowing students to playfully learn while interacting with digital exhibitions. The paper claims that AR-aided cultural experiences provide significantly improved learning outcomes and can strongly increase students' curiosity and willingness to collaborate with the others.

Furtherly, extensive efforts have been made to provide more engaging and interactive experiences that support the exploration and full grasp of historical, cultural, and architectural details of the heritage places through novel AR visualization methods [35]. In [10] the authors introduce a distance-driven user interface (DUI) that enables collaborative exhibit viewing in an augmented reality museum. The platform grants different viewing privileges according to the users' distance to the physical exhibition and aims to promote AR cultural experiences without interfering with the existing artistic expositions. According to the authors' initial studies, the system has the potential to encourage users to explore more cultural galleries of their personal interests and share their experiences, while promoting collaboration in the AR museum.

Even though there are already a number successfully developed prototypes that prove the efficiency of an augmented approach to the diffusion, communication and exploitation of CH, furthers steps still need to be taken in order for them to reach a commercially distributable level. Multi-disciplinary research has to be carried out by experts in a wide range of fields ranging from the hardware infrastructure to social sciences such as tourism management and human behavior in order for AR applications to reach their highest potential. Moreover, as shown by the studies above, combining AR with collaboration techniques can achieve even better results when it comes to designing engaging and interactive experiences for the users in educational and cultural contexts.

2   LibrARy

2.1   General Description and Requirements

As pointed out by the studies referenced in the above section, AR technologies combined with new communication means have the potential to enhance the activities related to an extensive variety of areas in ways unreachable with traditional technology. We aim to explore their benefits in cultural and educational settings through LibrARy - an AR platform designed for creating innovative collaborative environments where multiple users can interact simultaneously with 3D virtual objects. Its main objective is to enrich and promote cooperation between co-located users by allowing them to freely share information in an augmented shared space.

The platform will be developed as part of Lib2Life research project [44, p. 2] which intends to revitalize cultural heritage, in particular libraries, through advanced technological means. Lib2Life intends to allow users to virtually explore 3D reconstructed libraries or directly access the physical spaces enriched with computer-generated content meant to boost their educational experience. Moreover, it will provide a means for remote collaboration, by virtually co-locating participants to a live cultural event organized in any previously defined location. The project aims to transcend cultural barriers through a more complex collaborative augmented platform – LibrARy – which can potentially influence the cooperation in any multi-participant setting and provide unique interactive experiences.

This section describes the main requirements of the LibrARy platform, divided in functional and non-functional, as listed below.

Functional Requirements

- **Collaborative interaction:** The AR platform should allow co-located users to simultaneously access, see and edit an augmented shared space.
- **Virtual content:** Each user should be able to enhance the collaborative environment by freely placing new 3D objects. Moreover, the platform should be integrated with an online 3D library and allow users to dynamically choose content from there.
- **Editing**: After being placed in the real environment, each virtual object should be editable; the platform should allow the users to perform a set of actions on the content related to its position, scale, or rotation.
- **Grouping:** Each virtual object can be independent or grouped together with others; this means that an action on one object triggers the same action on the rest of its group.

- **Sticky notes:** The platform should allow the users to use and place sticky notes in the collaborative scene as a particular type of virtual content; the sticky notes can be independent or associated with a pre-existing 3D object and will give the users the possibility to share information more easily amongst them; moreover, participants to the scene should be able to add replies to any sticky note, thus starting discussion threads on a topic of their choice.
- **Access rights:** Any user can grant different types of access to their own virtual content:

  - Viewing rights – the owner of a virtual object (the person who has initially placed the content in the collaborative scene) should be able to set up a list of users that are allowed to view the specific content.
  - Editing rights – the owner of a virtual object should be able to set up a list of users that are allowed to interact and modify the specific content.

- **Real-time collaboration:** Any change of the shared augmented scene should notify in real time all the connected client applications and be visible for all the users collaborating on the scene; this way, the system should ensure all the participants in the shared scene have the same view at all times.
- **Sign-up:** The platform should allow users to register either through creating new accounts or through connecting with an existing account for a social platform such as Facebook or Gmail. The accounts will be shared amongst all the modules of the Lib2Life project, thus granting users access to all the features of the system with one account.
- **Friends list:** The platform should allow users to define a custom friends list; the list can be either imported from a social platform and furtherly customized or newly created by adding participants via their username or email address. The predefined friends list can be furtherly used to grant different types of access for the owned virtual content.

Non-functional Requirements

- **Compatibility:** The system should be developed for smart devices such as smartphones and tablets that meet the minimum hardware requirements necessary for a satisfactory AR experience; a list of supported devices has been determined based on their quality of the camera, motion sensors, and design architecture in order to ensure each of them performs as expected and it's available on the official webpage of Google ARCore [45]. Furthermore, each device should have a powerful enough CPU in order to provide excellent performance and effective real-time calculations.
- **Operating System (OS):** According to the data analyzed and published by the International Data Corporation [46], the Android OS is currently leading the smartphone market with a share of almost 85% registered at the end the year 2020. Therefore, in order to ensure a large coverage of the user segment while maintaining compatibility with the latest AR development kits, the LibrARy component should be developed for Android devices running a 7.0 version or newer [45].

- **Accessibility:** The platform requires an active internet connection in order to ensure a proper synchronization amongst users and should be available 24/7.
- **AR experience:** The platform should allow any user to place a maximum of 30 virtual objects per minute that can be stored in the cloud and resolved across all client applications; this requirement is in line with Cloud Anchors quotas for request bandwidth which accept a maximum of 30 Anchor host requests per minute [47].
- **CAR experience:** The platform should allow any connected user to receive a maximum of 300 virtual objects newly placed or edited in the shared scene; this requirement is in line with Cloud Anchors quotas for request bandwidth which accept a maximum of 30 Anchor resolve requests per minute [47].

Designed and envisioned as a complex application with a multitude of features, LibrARy shows the potential to have a significant effect over the activities related to a great variety of areas. It can be employed in a diverse range of educational and cultural settings by bringing together the experiential learning and the emergent technology of AR – which offers the capability to superimpose virtual models over the physical surroundings and provide seamless interaction between the two worlds. Moreover, it can play an important role in collaboration and communication in day-to-day work activities, as AR interfaces can improve the conversational relationships amongst the subjects while increasing their shared understanding of the discussed topic.

2.2 System Design and Implementation

As stated above, the main functionality of LibrARy is allowing co-located users to simultaneously access a shared space, collaborate and dynamically enrich the scene with augmented content imported from online 3D collections. Even though in its initial phase, the system benefits from the latest technologies' advancements and successfully implements its main goal along with other complex features. This section will provide more insight into the application's design and present the significant implementation details.

Developed entirely in Unity, the system prototype is distributed in specific software components and relies on several external services and SDKs (Software Development Kits) as shown in the Component Diagram - Fig. 2. In order to create augmented environments and allow the users to freely place, see and interact with virtual content in their own real space, LibrARy employs the latest features from Google ARCore SDK and handles them through the ARCore Root component. The SDK offers access to native APIs (Application Programming Interface) which enable smart devices to sense the environment, understand and connect with it. It implements three fundamental AR features essential for integrating computer-generated objects with the real world as precepted through the device's camera [48]:

- motion tracking – ARCore can detect and track the device's position relative to the world, enabling thus an accurate placement of the virtual objects in the real environment.

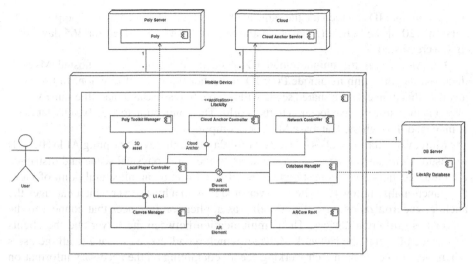

Fig. 2. Library's Component Diagram with external dependencies

- environment understanding – Using the phone's camera, ARCore API can detect the size and location of all surrounding surfaces: horizontal, vertical and even angled surfaces.
- light estimation – ARCore enables the phone to determine the environment's current lighting conditions; thus, the virtual objects can be artificially illuminated in order to fit best in their surroundings and appear as real as possible to the viewer.

Furtherly, the LibrARy system is integrated with Poly, an online collection of virtual content supported by Google [49]. The users can dynamically browse through thousands of 3D assets available in the virtual library, search by keywords, and choose the ones that fit best their individual needs. The connection with Poly is managed through the PolyToolKit Manager component which enables the application to download and import any asset at runtime. Therefore, once the user has selected a virtual object, they can instantly place it in the shared physical space and freely interact with it. However, according to the latest news, Poly library will be available only until June 30, 2021 and should be replaced in the further versions of the system with other online 3D collections such as Sketchfab [50].

The collaborative functionality of the application is supported by the concept of spatial anchors included in the ARCore SDK. According to the official documentation [51], an anchor describes a position and orientation relative to the world space and ensures that objects remain at the same location, maintaining thus the illusion of virtual objects placed in the real world. The Cloud Anchor API enables sharing an anchor from one smart device to another and synchronizing the location of the 3D objects across all the connected devices [47]. Once a user has placed a virtual object in the scene, the CloudAnchor Controller connects to the ARCore Cloud Anchor service to host its corresponding anchor and returns a unique identifier (ID) used to share the relative location of the content to all the participants. Afterwards, any participant to the scene with the unique ID can recreate the same anchor using the Cloud Anchor component. In version 1.20 of the SDK and newer, spatial anchors can be resolved for 365 days after they were hosted.

LibrARy stores the unique cloud ID of each object in a server-hosted MySQL database together with its unique Poly ID and other relevant information. In this way, any user that connects to a shared scene will be able to resolve and place the same virtual object at the same relative location to the world. The connection to the MySQL database is managed through the Database Manager component.

Moreover, LibrARy relies on Unity Multiplayer High Level Scripting API (HLAPI) to ensure simultaneous access of more users to the same physical scene and distribute the cloud anchors IDs amongst them in real time. From an architectural point of view, this functionality follows the client-server model, with a host server which manages the anchor synchronization, and clients acting as application instances that connect to the server from different devices. The communication between the server and the clients is managed through the Network Manager which broadcasts a message to all the users when there is a change in their working scene, containing all the necessary information for the objects to be resolved correctly.

3 Further Development Steps

As the next step of the LibrARy project, we intend to test the system in different use case scenarios in order to prove its usability and quantify the benefits it can bring to the collaboration and synergy amongst a group of co-located participants. Conceived and designed as a complex platform with broad and general CAR functionalities, LibrARy could be successfully employed in a wide range of cooperative contexts, including cultural and educational ones.

For the piloting phase of the project, we aim to assess and evaluate our project in a library where participants could visualize, interact and edit information in an interactive and engaging way. Moreover, with the help of the sticky notes functionality, they could also easily share knowledge and data with other co-located participants or leave messages for further visitors of the cultural space, aiding thus the communication between them.

Moreover, we want to appraise and determine the influence LibrARy can have in an educational setting, by testing our prototype in a university lecture at Faculty of Automatic Control and Computers, University Politehnica of Bucharest. Our main goal will be to prove that the system can increase shared understanding of the scientific topics presented while supporting effective group interaction and cooperation. Thus, LibrARy could have a significant impact in strengthening students' skills development and their learning interest by offering the possibility to better grasp abstract concepts and principles in science subjects.

When it comes to the prototype, we aim to improve its usability and reliability by focusing more on the human-computer interaction and graphical interface aspects. Moreover, currently intended to be used on smartphones, the system could be easily adapted for HoloLens or other head-mounted displays (HMDs) and smart glasses in the future.

4 Conclusions

Augmented reality represents a way forward for developing new fundamentally different platforms that provide efficient face-to-face and remote collaboration and could bring significant novelties in the future of human-computer interaction by transforming the surroundings into one broad user interface. Using edge technology, CAR systems can alter the dynamics of interaction in multi-participant settings and provide unique collaborative experiences, supporting advanced means of socialization and making working together straightforward and productive.

This article has presented the concept and the functionalities of LibrARy – an AR application designed for creating innovative collaborative environments where multiple users can interact simultaneously with computer-generated content. The prototype shows great potential to influence and enhance the activities related to an extended range of cooperative contexts and directly tested through pilot programs and redefined according to the observations and remarks.

References

1. Milgram, P., Kishino, F.: A taxonomy of mixed reality visual displays. IEICE Trans Inf. Syst. **E77-D**(12), 1321–1329 (1994)
2. Casella, G., Coelho, M.: Augmented heritage: situating augmented reality mobile apps in cultural heritage communication. In: Proceedings of the 2013 International Conference on Information Systems and Design of Communication, New York, NY, USA, pp. 138–140, July 2013. https://doi.org/10.1145/2503859.2503883
3. Haydar, M., Roussel, D., Maidi, M., Otmane, S., Mallem, M.: Virtual and augmented reality for cultural computing and heritage: a case study of virtual exploration of underwater archaeological sites (preprint). Virtual Real. **15**, 311–327 (2011). https://doi.org/10.1007/s10055-010-0176-4
4. Liarokapis, F., Greatbatch, I., Mountain, D., Gunesh, A., Brujic-Okretic, V., Raper, J.: Mobile augmented reality techniques for GeoVisualisation, vol. 2005, pp. 745–751, August 2005. https://doi.org/10.1109/IV.2005.79
5. Kaufmann, H.: Collaborative augmented reality in education. In: Proceeding of Imagina 2003 Conference, Monte Carlo, Monaco, pp. 1–4 (2003)
6. Höllerer, T.H., Feiner, S.K.: Mobile Augmented Reality. In: Karimi, H.A., Hammad, A. (eds.) Telegeoinformatics: Location-Based Computing and Services, pp. 392–421. CRC Press, Boca Raton (2004)
7. Azuma, R.T.: A survey of augmented reality. Presence Teleoperators Virtual Environ. **6**(4), 355–385 (1997). https://doi.org/10.1162/pres.1997.6.4.355
8. Billinghurst, M., Kato, H.: Collaborative augmented reality. Commun. ACM **45**(7), 64–70 (2002). https://doi.org/10.1145/514236.514265
9. Shin, J.G., Ng, G., Saakes, D.: Couples designing their living room together: a study with collaborative handheld augmented reality. In: Proceedings of the 9th Augmented Human International Conference, Seoul Republic of Korea, pp. 1–9, February 2018. https://doi.org/10.1145/3174910.3174930
10. Li, X., Chen, W., Wu, Y.: Distance-driven user interface for collaborative exhibit viewing in augmented reality museum. In: The Adjunct Publication of the 32nd Annual ACM Symposium on User Interface Software and Technology, New Orleans LA USA, pp. 42–43, October 2019. https://doi.org/10.1145/3332167.3357109

11. Wang, X., Dunston, P.S.: Tangible mixed reality for remote design review: a study under-standing user perception and acceptance. Vis. Eng. 1(1), 1–15 (2013). https://doi.org/10.1186/2213-7459-1-8
12. Wang, X., Dunston, P.S.: Comparative effectiveness of mixed reality-based virtual environ-ments in collaborative design. IEEE Trans. Syst. Man Cybern. Part C Appl. Rev. 41(3), 284–296 (2011). https://doi.org/10.1109/TSMCC.2010.2093573
13. Chastine, J.W., Zhu, Y., Preston, J.A.: A framework for inter-referential awareness in collab-orative environments. In: 2006 International Conference on Collaborative Computing: Net-working, Applications and Worksharing, pp. 1–5, November 2006. https://doi.org/10.1109/COLCOM.2006.361859
14. Kim, Y., Hong, S., Kim, G.J.: Augmented reality based remote coaching system. In: Pro-ceedings of the 22nd ACM Conference on Virtual Reality Software and Technology, Munich Germany, pp. 311–312, November 2016. https://doi.org/10.1145/2993369.2996301
15. Piumsomboon, T., Day, A., Ens, B., Lee, Y., Lee, G., Billinghurst, M.: Exploring enhance-ments for remote mixed reality collaboration. In: SIGGRAPH Asia 2017 Mobile Graphics & Interactive Applications, New York, NY, USA, pp. 1–5, November 2017. https://doi.org/10.1145/3132787.3139200
16. Bekele, M.K., Pierdicca, R., Frontoni, E., Malinverni, E.S.: A survey of augmented, virtual, and mixed reality for cultural heritage. J. Comput. Cult. Heritage 11(2), 36 (2018)
17. Carmigniani, J., Furht, B., Anisetti, M., Ceravolo, P., Damiani, E., Ivkovic, M.: Augmented reality technologies, systems and applications. Multimed. Tools Appl. 51(1), 341–377 (2011). https://doi.org/10.1007/s11042-010-0660-6
18. Belghit, H., Bellarbi, A., Zenati, N., Benbelkacem, S., Otmane, S.: Vision-based Collaborative & Mobile Augmented Reality, p. 4
19. Rabbi, I., Ullah , S.: A survey on augmented reality challenges and tracking. Acta Graph Znan. Časopis Za Tisk. Graf. Komun. 24(1–2), 29–46 (2013)
20. A Mixed-Reality System for Breast Surgical Planning. Body MRI Research Group (BMR). https://med.stanford.edu/bmrgroup/Publications/PublicationHighlights/HoloLensS urgicalPlanning.html. Accessed 07 Jan 2021
21. Spatial's collaborative AR platform is basically FaceTime in 3D | Engadget. https://www.eng adget.com/2018-10-24-spatial-augmented-reality-3d.html?guce_referrer=aHR0cHM6Ly93 d3cuZ29vZ2xlLmNvbS8&guce_referrer_sig=AQAAAJ2H_V9JiABSim5ySxgd1 (accessed Jan. 07, 2021).
22. Aal, K., Hauptmeier, H., Pokémon, G.O.: Collaboration and Information on the GO. In: The 17th European Conference on Computer-Supported Cooperative Work (2019). https://doi.org/10.18420/ECSCW2019_EP04
23. Calafiore, A., Rapp, A.: Gamifying the city: pervasive game elements in the urban environ-ment. In: Proceedings of the Workshop on Fictional Game Elements 2016 co-located with The ACM SIGCHI Annual Symposium on Computer-Human Interaction in Play (CHI PLAY 2016), vol. 1715, p. 6 (2016)
24. Daiber, F., Kosmalla, F., Kr, A.: BouldAR: using augmented reality to support collaborative boulder training. In: CHI 2013 Extended Abstracts on Human Factors in Computing Systems (CHI EA 2013), pp. 949–954 (2013)
25. Sargaana, U., Farahani, H.S., Lee, J.W., Ryu, J., Woo, W.: Collaborative billiARds: towards the ultimate gaming experience. In: Kishino, F., Kitamura, Y., Kato, H., Nagata, N. (eds.) ICEC 2005. LNCS, vol. 3711, pp. 357–367. Springer, Heidelberg (2005). https://doi.org/10.1007/11558651_35
26. Bacca, J., Baldiris, S., Fabregat, R., Graf, S., Kinshuk: Augmented reality trends in education: a systematic review of research and applications. J. Educ. Technol. Soc. 17, 133–149 (2014)

27. Virata, R.O., Castro, J.D.L.: Augmented reality in science classroom: perceived effects in education, visualization and information processing. In: Proceedings of the 10th International Conference on E-Education, E-Business, E-Management and E-Learning - IC4E 2019, Tokyo, Japan, pp. 85–92 (2019). https://doi.org/10.1145/3306500.3306556

28. López-FaicanFaican, L., Jaen, J.: EmoFindAR: evaluation of a mobile multiplayer augmented reality game for primary school children. Comput. Educ. **149**, 103814 (2020). https://doi.org/10.1016/j.compedu.2020.103814

29. Chang, G., Morreale, P., Medicherla, P.: Applications of augmented reality systems in education, pp. 1380–1385, March 2010. https://www.learntechlib.org/primary/p/33549/. Accessed 07 Jan 2021

30. Duran, M., Höft, M., Lawson, D.B., Medjahed, B., Orady, E.A.: Urban high school students' IT/STEM learning: findings from a collaborative inquiry - and design-based afterschool program. J. Sci. Educ. Technol. **23**(1), 116–137 (2013). https://doi.org/10.1007/s10956-013-9457-5

31. Brown, J., Brown, R., Merrill, C.: Science and technology educators' enacted curriculum: areas of possible collaboration for an integrative STEM approach in public schools. Technol. Eng. Teach. **71**(4), 30–34 (2012)

32. Villanueva, A., Zhu, Z., Liu, Z., Peppler, K., Redick, T., Ramani, K.: Meta-AR-app: an authoring platform for collaborative augmented reality in STEM classrooms. In: Proceedings of the 2020 CHI Conference on Human Factors in Computing Systems, Honolulu, HI, USA, pp. 1–14, April 2020. https://doi.org/10.1145/3313831.3376146

33. Gousios, G., Pinzger, M., van Deursen, A.: An exploratory study of the pull-based software development model. In: Proceedings of the 36th International Conference on Software Engineering, New York, NY, USA, pp. 345–355, May 2014. https://doi.org/10.1145/2568225.2568260

34. Makransky, G., Terkildsen, T., Mayer, R.: Adding immersive virtual reality to a science lab simulation causes more presence but less learning. Learn. Instr. **60** (2017). https://doi.org/10.1016/j.learninstruc.2017.12.007

35. Koo, S., Kim, J., Kim, C., Kim, J., Cha, H.S.: Development of an augmented reality tour guide for a cultural heritage site. J. Comput. Cult. Herit. **12**(4), 1–24 (2020). https://doi.org/10.1145/3317552

36. Matuk, C.: The learning affordances of augmented reality for museum exhibits on human health. Mus. Soc. Issues **11**, 73–87 (2016). https://doi.org/10.1080/15596893.2016.1142815

37. Mourkoussis, N., et al.: Virtual and augmented reality applied to educational and cultural heritage domains, undefined (2002). /paper/Virtual-and-Augmented-Reality-Applied-to-and-Mourkoussis-Liarokapis/a1d0722b924c03eabc8c861ae76c778337d4a2da. accessed 07 Jan 2021

38. Sdegno, A., Masserano, S., Mior, D., Cochelli, P., Gobbo, E.: Augmenting painted architectures for communicating cultural heritage. SCIRES-IT Sci. Res. Inf. Technol. **5** (2015). https://doi.org/10.2423/i22394303v5n1p93

39. Wiley, B., Schulze, P.: ArchAR - an archaeological augmented reality experience. Proc. SPIE - Int. Soc. Opt. Eng. **9392** (2015). https://doi.org/10.1117/12.2083449

40. Kang, J.: AR teleport: digital reconstruction of historical and cultural-heritage sites using mobile augmented reality. In: 2012 IEEE 11th International Conference on Trust, Security and Privacy in Computing and Communications, pp. 1666–1675, June 2012. https://doi.org/10.1109/TrustCom.2012.95

41. Vanoni, D., Seracini, M., Kuester, F.: ARtifact: tablet-based augmented reality for interactive analysis of cultural artifacts. In: 2012 IEEE International Symposium on Multimedia, pp. 44–49, December 2012. https://doi.org/10.1109/ISM.2012.17

42. Wagner, D., Schmalstieg, D., Billinghurst, M.: Handheld AR for collaborative edutainment. In: Pan, Z., Cheok, A., Haller, M., Lau, R.W.H., Saito, H., Liang, R. (eds.) ICAT 2006. LNCS, vol. 4282, pp. 85–96. Springer, Heidelberg (2006). https://doi.org/10.1007/11941354_10
43. Gargalakos, M., Giallouri, E., Lazoudis, A., Sotiriou, S., Bogner , F.: Assessing the impact of technology-enhanced field trips in science centers and museums. Adv. Sci. Lett. **4**, 3332–3341 (2011). https://doi.org/10.1166/asl.2011.2043
44. 'Lib2Life'. https://lib2life.ro/. Accessed 11 Jan 2021
45. ARCore supported devices. Google Developers. https://developers.google.com/ar/discover/supported-devices. Accessed 13 Jan 2021
46. IDC - Smartphone Market Share – OS. IDC: The premier global market intelligence company. https://www.idc.com/promo/smartphone-market-share. Accessed 13 Jan 2021
47. Cloud Anchors developer guide for Android I ARCore. Google Developers. https://developers.google.com/ar/develop/java/cloud-anchors/developer-guide-android. Accessed 11 Jan 2021
48. ARCore overview I Google Developers. https://developers.google.com/ar/discover. Accessed 13 Jan 2021
49. Poly, Google Developers. https://developers.google.com/poly/develop. Accessed 13 Jan 2021
50. Sketchfab - The best 3D viewer on the web. https://sketchfab.com/. Accessed 13 Jan 2021
51. Working with anchors I ARCore, Google Developers. https://developers.google.com/ar/develop/developer-guides/anchors. Accessed 13 Jan 2021

Supporting Embodied and Remote Collaboration in Shared Virtual Environments

Mark Manuel$^{(\boxtimes)}$ ⓘ, Poorvesh Dongre ⓘ, Abdulaziz Alhamadani,
and Denis Gračanin ⓘ

Virginia Tech, Blacksburg, VA 24060, USA
{mmark95,poorvesh,hamdani,gracanin}@vt.edu

Abstract. The COVID-19 pandemic has had a tremendous impact on businesses, educational institutions, and other organizations that require in-person gatherings. Physical gatherings such as conferences, classes, and other social activities have been greatly reduced in favor of virtual meetings on Zoom, Webex or similar video-conferencing platforms. However, video-conferencing is quite limited in its ability to create meeting spaces that capture the authentic feel of a real-world meeting. Without the aid of body language cues, meeting participants have a harder time paying attention and keeping themselves engaged in virtual meetings. Video-conferencing, as it currently stands, falls short of providing a familiar environment that fosters personal connection between meeting participants. This paper explores an alternative approach to virtual meetings through the use of extended reality (XR) and embodied interactions. We present an application that leverages the full-body tracking capabilities of the Azure Kinect and the immersive affordances of XR to create more vibrant and engaging remote meeting environments.

Keywords: Remote collaboration · Extended reality · Embodied interaction

1 Introduction

Less than a year into the COVID-19 pandemic and most of us already experience Zoom fatigue on a regular basis. This has been attributed to the added cognitive load of having to focus more intently during video-meetings, while struggling with the dissonance of performing work-related tasks in a contrary environment [21]. Other factors that make video-conferencing strenuous include increased self-awareness, frequency of meetings and the lack of body language cues. As a result of these factors, people find it difficult to stay focused and work productivity suffers. Therefore, there is a need to develop more engaging remote work tools that can capture and relay a shared sense of presence among colleagues.

© Springer Nature Switzerland AG 2021
J. Y. C. Chen and G. Fragomeni (Eds.): HCII 2021, LNCS 12770, pp. 639–652, 2021.
https://doi.org/10.1007/978-3-030-77599-5_44

Fig. 1. A body-tracked avatar of a remote collaborator in a shared virtual classroom environment (local user's POV).

Extended Reality (XR) can help address this challenge by creating immersive meeting spaces for users to remotely interact within. A shared virtual classroom environment for students and instructors, for example, can serve as a more engaging medium for learning to take place [4]. Virtual environments can transport users to faraway places (both familiar and unknown) where they can interact with 3D objects, spaces and each other. These environments can be modelled after real-world locations (like offices and classrooms) to give users a familiar space to collaborate in. Work artifacts can be visualized as 3D models that can be scaled, rotated and viewed from multiple angles. XR users can greatly benefit from all of the added affordances provided by immersive environments [15]. In addition to visual affordances, embodied interactions can provide users with a natural and intuitive way to interface with the shared virtual environment [16]. Embodied interactions can be used to promote engagement by enhancing a user's sense of presence in a virtual space [8] and can serve to compensate for the missing body language cues that make video-conferencing tedious (Fig. 1).

In this paper we present a novel approach to facilitating real-time remote collaboration in shared XR environments. Our approach leverages body-tracking, XR, and a lightweight communication platform to support telepresence among remote meeting participants. We describe the implementation of this approach and provide a case study. Our prototype implementation comprises of three components: 1) A body-tracking component that uses a peripheral depth sensor (Azure Kinect) to capture body frames and recognize user body joints. 2) A communication component that receives and relays captured joint data among connected client applications. 3) An XR component that comprises of a set of XR display devices that run an instance of a client Unity application for each remotely connected user.

Azure Kinect devices installed at each remote location continuously track each user's body-joint data which is then streamed to all other listening client applications. This data is used to rig virtual avatar representations of each user.

The avatars and their body movements are then rendered through the XR display device (client application). All communication between remote client applications is handled via the Message Queue Telemetry Transport (MQTT) messaging protocol (Fig. 2).

Each of the individual devices within all three system components can be easily switched out in favor of more accessible ones. For example, if XR headsets are unavailable to users, Web-based Unity applications can be substituted in for the XR component of the system. This approach makes the proposed system more accessible to remote users, while also opening up exciting new possibilities for platform-agnostic collaboration in shared virtual environments (i.e. MR-VR, MR-Web, Web-VR, etc.).

2   Related Work

The objective of this paper is to explore ways of enhancing the experience of remote collaboration. This aligns well with a large body of existing Computer-supported cooperative work (CSCW) research that envisions trends in remote collaboration and workplace team dynamics. Workplace practices and technology have been evolving rapidly over the last few decades, especially after the advent of computers. As a result, we now have various remote collaborative platforms that can help us better connect and work with people across the world. The importance of these technologies has increased exponentially with the advent of COVID-19. These work-from-home technologies typically exist as standalone applications and are not built to integrate with their user's surrounding environment.

However, workplace architecture can play an important role in determining local work practices. Streitz et al. [18] present an early conceptual framework into how data visualization can be better facilitated by workplace architecture, making the workplace environment a multi-modal interface to access relevant information. They leverage the ideas of ubiquitous computing [20] and invisible technology, stating that they will play an important role in making these adaptable architectural spaces a reality. Streitz et al. [17] argue that despite information and communication technologies having reshaped work processes, the design of work spaces have largely remained the same. To remedy this they propose the idea of *cooperative buildings*: "flexible and dynamic environments" capable of "supporting and augmenting human communication and collaboration".

Ladwig and Geiger [9] envision that the technology of the near future will allow us to create the "ultimate device" that will be capable of making the real world indistinguishable from the virtual world. Such a system would be capable of providing "realistic and complete embodied experiences" by utilizing multiple human senses including haptic, auditory, olfactory and even gustatory sensations.

XR is an effective tool that is bringing us closer to achieving Ladwig's vision. It also has great potential as a work-from-home tool. Zhao et al. discuss an approach that involves whole-body interaction with the Kinect, and responsive large-screen visualizations to support new forms of embodied interaction and collaborative learning. Their findings suggest that the pairing of physical interaction and visualization in a multi-user environment helps promote engagement and allows children to easily explore cause-and-effect relationships [23].

RGB-D sensors, like the Microsoft Kinect, can enhance a user's XR experience by providing them with embodied interactions [5]. Anderson et al. [1] developed an AR application "YouMove" that lets users train through various stages of a physical movement sequences. Task guidance and feedback was provided through an AR mirror. Handosa et al. [6] combined mixed reality with embodied interaction to create interactive training simulations for nursing students.

However, to connect two or more users in an immersive XR environment, an efficient communication platform is essential. Dasgupta et al. [3] developed an architecture for supporting context awareness in MR, enabling MR devices to scan and recognize workspace tools in real time using an MQTT broker, while also providing instructions on their use. We followed a similar approach and used MQTT as the communication back-end in our prototype implementation.

3   Approach

The COVID-19 pandemic has forced people to go about doing most of their daily activities from home. In-person meetings across the globe have been significantly reduced and almost all collaborative work has been moved online. However, the subsequent overuse of virtual videoconferencing platforms has resulted in what we now know as "Zoom Fatigue". Users reported feeling tired, anxious, and worried as a result of overusing these remote collaboration platforms [22]. A major reason for "Zoom Fatigue" is because videoconferencing tends to disrupt the regular communication practices that we are accustomed to [13]. Videoconferencing also deprives us of a significant amount of contextual information (through the loss of body language cues and micro expressions) due to the physical separation between meeting participants.

Current remote work practices suffer from several of the issues presented above. Given the inherent limitations of videoconferencing, our goal is to try and make remote meetings more engaging, life-like and immersive. Embodied interactions can help bridge the gap between virtual and in-person meetings. With the recent advances in XR infrastructure, motion-tracking sensors and network connectivity, it is possible to incorporate human body movement and gestures into meetings in virtual environments.

We describe an approach to designing collaborative virtual environments that can be used for a variety of purposes, including education and remote meetings. Our proposed system architecture consists of three components: Body Tracking, Communication, and XR Rendering. Each of these components are flexible and are not bound to specific hardware. Figure 2 depicts the use of these the components to create a shared XR space for two users. This system can be further expanded to support additional users. The three components are described in more detail below.

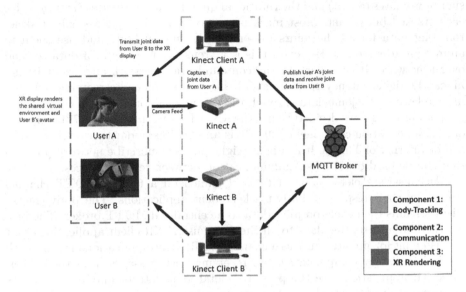

Fig. 2. System Architecture Diagram. 1) Component 1: Body Tracking—captures a local user's body frames and identifies joints. 2) Component 2: Communication—transfers the messages from the Kinect client to other remote user Unity client applications. 3) Component 3: XR Rendering—Renders each user's avatar at their respective positions in the virtual environment. The XR device allows the user to see and interact with other users and the shared environment.

3.1   Component 1: Body Tracking

Advancements in computer vision and object-recognition technology have led to the commercial availability of several body-tracking sensors. These sensors are capable of tracking human skeleton joints in real-time. Real-time tracking can be implemented via marker-based (Qualysis, OptiTrack) or markerless (Microsoft Kinect, Intel RealSense) techniques. While marker-based body trackers provide more robust tracking [19] and have larger coverage areas, they are not practical for personal use at home or in a workplace. Marker-less body trackers are smaller, portable and more cost-effective overall.

Our system design makes use of marker-less body trackers to capture user skeleton data. The skeleton joint data for user movements is repeatedly captured and used to rig virtual avatars that replicate their body movement in the XR application. Skeleton joint data for important body parts (head, arms, pelvis, legs, etc.) are continuously streamed to the XR applications of all the users in the meeting. This streaming is handled by our communication component.

3.2   Component 2: Communication

The skeleton joint data collected by the body tracking device includes the Cartesian coordinates (x, y, z) and the rotational quaternion coordinates (w, x, y, z) for each tracked body joint. Most marker-less body tracking devices collect skeleton joint data for all the joints present in the human body and use them to animate avatar models. However, this is a tremendous amount of data to send over a network. It can overload the communication network and result in significantly higher latency cost. To avoid this we recommend streaming only the most relevant user joint data through the communication channels.

For our design, we decided to use the MQTT network protocol [7] to support our communication component. MQTT is an OASIS standard messaging protocol for Internet of Things. It is a lightweight publish/subscribe network protocol that can be used to establish communication between remote devices.

Each user's skeleton joint data is streamed on a unique MQTT channel (topic) by their respective body-tracker client applications. The body-tracker client streams their skeleton joint data to a centralized MQTT broker. The broker then broadcasts this data to all the other users' XR client applications that are listening for updates on these channels. XR client applications run on each user's XR display component. Upon receiving new messages from the broker, these XR applications use the passed skeletal joint data to update each user's location within the shared remote meeting environment.

3.3   Component 3: XR Rendering

The XR component consists of an always-on application (developed on a game engine like Unity) that runs on the XR display hardware. This application displays the current state of shared virtual environment, along with the avatars of all remote meeting participants. Virtual environments can be designed to replicate traditional collaborative environments (classrooms, conference rooms, office spaces, etc.). The XR application is responsible for controlling everything that a user sees and does in the shared virtual environment. The application updates the user's position based on their movement.

It also registers any embodied interaction between the user and an environment object and sends this to a designated channel on the communication component. For instance, if the user moves a chair in shared virtual classroom environment, this movement is also propagated to the XR applications of each other remotely connected user. Finally, the XR application also receives streamed data from the communication component (other user body movements and environment object interactions) and updates the state of each of these entities in the environment.

4   Implementation

In this section, we describe our proof concept implementation based on the approach described in the previous section. Given the impact of COVID-19 and the switch to online modes of education, we decided to go with a virtual classroom scenario for our implementation prototype. We envisioned this to be a space where students can join in remotely to attend lectures, work on group projects and interact with faculty members.

4.1 Virtual Classroom Environment Overview

The first virtual classroom that we designed was inspired by a real classroom located in the Northern Virginia Center, a satellite campus of Virginia Tech. This virtual classroom was designed using the Unity game engine. Images of the real and virtual classrooms can be seen in Fig. 3.

Fig. 3. Left: The physical classroom at the Northern Virginia Center. Right: The virtual classroom environment Unity application.

After designing this classroom environment to closely resemble it's real-world counterpart, we re-configured its layout to allow users to interact in multiple environment settings. We created a total of four different classroom layouts:

- Small Classroom: The original classroom design from the Northern Virginia Center. This classroom environment is built to match the scale of its physical counterpart. It is best suited for small class sizes with more interpersonal engagement.
- Small Classroom post-COVID: This classroom environment was developed to reflect the"six-feet apart" social-distancing policy mandated at locations of in-person instruction, as a preventative measure against COVID-19.
- Conference Room: A modified classroom designed to resemble meeting rooms. The desks in this layout have been brought together to create a large table in the middle of the room.
- Large Classroom: This virtual environment was developed to seat a large number of students. This scenario is appropriate for lecture halls with minimal group-based discussions.

To speed up future development, we also created a script that would allow developers to automatically generate their desired classroom layouts by specifying their required layout parameters in the form of a JSON input file. A demo video highlighting the navigation and interaction aspects of our prototype implementation can be found here [11].

4.2   Application Components

As described in the Proposed Approach section, our implementation comprises of three major components:

Body-Tracking. We selected the Microsoft Azure Kinect as the body-tracking device for our implementation. Each remote user is equipped with a Kinect device and a dedicated client PC. Each user's Kinect captures their skeleton joints and updates the user's own avatar inside a Unity application running on the XR component. The joints tracked by the Kinect sensor are shown in Fig. 4. The Kinect client also streams the user's joint information to all other user's within the same shared virtual classroom environment (via the communication component). In our prototype implementation, we tested this out by having two remote users in the same virtual classroom environment at the same time.

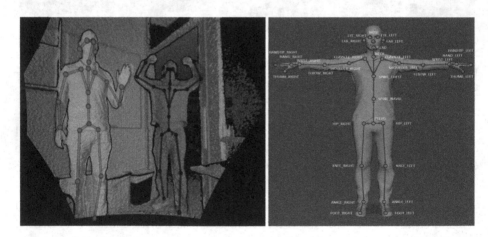

Fig. 4. Left: Two user skeleton joints tracked by the Kinect. Right: All joints capable of being tracked by the Azure Kinect sensor [12].

Communication. The communication component serves as the backbone of this implementation. Due to the high volume of messages that need to be sent over the network, picking an efficient, light-weight messaging protocol is imperative. We used the MQTT protocol as the communication back-end for our implementation. The MQTT protocol follows a publish-subscribe messaging pattern.

The MQTT broker is responsible for directing all of the shared virtual environment messages to their appropriate communication channels. A dedicated Raspberry Pi device served as our MQTT broker.

Kinect client PCs are always running an application that connects them to the MQTT broker and allows them to 'publish' (send) messages to specific communication channels. In our implementation, for example, coordinates for remote user A, were streamed to a channel called 'kinectCoords', while coordinates for user B were streamed to a channel called 'kinectCoords2'. Any device connected to the same MQTT broker can 'subscribe' (listen) to messages sent on these channels.

Whenever a user is tracked by the Kinect, their client PC applications publish their tracked skeletal joints along with the user's id to the MQTT broker on one of these channels. The broker in turn transmits these messages to all other devices that are listening to these channels. These include the XR applications running on each remote user's XR component that take the skeletal joint messages and update the corresponding user's avatar inside each user's local version of the shared virtual classroom environment.

XR Rendering. For each remotely connected user, the XR Rendering component is responsible for displaying the user's local view of the shared virtual environment. This component comprises of display hardware such as AR/VR/MR headsets. However, regular PC screens/displays can also be used to present the shared virtual environment (for improved accessibility). This component is always running a Unity application containing the current state of the shared virtual environment. The application is responsible for listening to messages sent via the MQTT broker and accurately updating the positions of all the users in the shared virtual environment. The positions of all interactable objects in the environment are also appropriately updated by this application. For our prototype application, the Kinect client PCs also ran the Unity XR application and displayed the local view of the shared environment for each remote user.

4.3 Performance Evaluation

To evaluate the suitability of our implementation for real-time remote collaboration, we conducted a few validation tests. Two remote users (A and B) met and interacted with each in our shared virtual classroom environment. The user's were made to perform simple actions like moving around and waving their hands (Fig. 5). The network latency for these interactions was measured for three remote user configurations. Equation 1 was used to calculate the travel time of 10000 MQTT messages between the Kinect client and XR applications of user A and user B. The round-trip travel time for the messages was computed and averaged in order to negate the effects of minor system clock time differences between each user's client PC. The results from running these latency tests are summarized in Table 1.

$$t_{Travel} = \frac{(t_{rec} - t_{sent})}{2} \tag{1}$$

where:

- t_{Travel} is the time taken to send a message from user A's Kinect client application to user B's XR application client over the internet using MQTT (one-way average network delay).
- t_{sent} is the timestamp of when user A's Kinect client application sent out a message to user B's XR application via MQTT.
- t_{rec} is the timestamp of when user A's Kinect client application receives confirmation of having received t_{sent} from user B's XR application.

Fig. 5. Left: The avatars of the two remote user's interacting. Right: The avatar of a remote user as seen from another user's point-of-view.

Table 1. Communication latency for different distances between locations.

Communication type	Distance (miles)	Communication time(s)
Same building, local area network	0	0.056
Short-distance, same town	3	0.060
Long-distance, different country	4710	0.120

In the first test configuration, both the users were located in separate rooms within the same building at our research lab facility (Virginia Tech, Blacksburg, VA, USA). As both of these users were on the same network, the latency of the communication component was a minimal 0.056s. As a result, avatar movements were updated very fast for both users.

In the second test configuration, user A was located at our lab facility, while user B joined the virtual classroom environment from the university library, three miles away from the lab. In this test, we noticed a delay of 0.06s, which also allowed for fast avatar position updates.

In our final test configuration, user A was located in Blacksburg, VA, USA, while user B joined the virtual classroom from Zagreb, Croatia. In this test, we noticed a larger delay of 0.120s per message. There was also more jitter in the avatar movements observed, but the movements of the avatars still matched the body movements of the users. Also, given the substantial physical distance between the two users (4710 mi), we believe this to be a tolerable amount of latency for real-time collaborative applications.

5   Discussion

Embodied cognition in shared virtual environments can be enhanced by ensuring that the latency between the movement of a user's body and their virtual avatar is minimal. In our evaluation, we measured the communication latency in updating avatars for two remote users in three scenarios. We observed that the communication time between updating user avatar positions corresponds to the physical distance between the users. We also noticed some jitter in the avatar movements, which was more pronounced in the case of large physical distance among users. This jitter could be attributed to packets of data containing user skeleton joints, not reaching user XR applications fast enough. This can be further optimized in future iterations of this implementation to improve the efficiency of the embodied experience.

Embodied cognition and interaction in remote collaboration can be of special relevance to online classrooms. Reportedly, many students are not able to pay as much attention in online classes as they could in physical classrooms. For students suffering from Attention deficit hyperactivity disorder (ADHD) focusing during online lectures is especially challenging. Research shows that ADHD is not simply a set of mental functions, but rather a range of bodily dynamics through which humans engage with their environment [10]. The embodied cognition of remote collaboration has the potential to significantly help students with attention disorders pay more in online classrooms.

Virtual-environment-based classroom sessions can also slowly be incorporated into existing Zoom-based online classrooms. During these sessions, students and the instructor can log into a shared virtual environment. The classroom can serve as a homeroom for the instructor to provide lesson overviews, introductions and set expectations for what students will encounter in that day's virtual environment. Virtual classroom sessions can range from simple sessions, where the instructor presents virtual models to the class, to transportation into completely virtual landscapes [14].

For example, the doors of the classroom could be made to be portals that teleport the students to Africa, where they can interact with local flora and fauna and gaze upon Mount Kilimanjaro. The students can use the doors/portals to move between classrooms for different subjects. Students can be allowed to dynamically interact with the objects in a room to change their state. Virtual objects can also be implemented to have textual and audio properties that play when a student interacts with them [2]. The interactive nature of virtual environments can captivate and hold student attention for much longer than in a typical lecture session. For this reason virtual environments can serve well as a supplement to existing online education.

However, a primary challenge to incorporating embodied interactions in shared virtual environments is making these environments accessible for all users. While VR, AR and MR headsets are slowly becoming commercially viable they are still a few years away from being used as personal devices for work (like laptops). Body-tracking sensors are also typically used for niche areas like for gaming, animation or research. The lack of commercial access to specific hardware can be a barrier to the widespread use of embodied interaction and XR.

A potential solution to this problem is democratize access by also making the shared virtual environments available as web-enabled experiences. Users would be able to open up a browser window and log into the virtual environment, just like they would to attend a Zoom meeting. Users would interact with the same virtual content through their browser as they would through an XR headset. The primary difference between the two being that XR users would experience the environment from a first-person perspective, while the online users would experience it in third-person. Both types of users can create custom avatars to represent themselves in the shared virtual environment. XR users could navigate and interact with the environment using their controller, while online users would use their keyboard and mouse to move their avatars around in a virtual environment. This kind of implementation would be accessible to a much wider range of users and can open up exciting new avenues for platform-agnostic collaboration in shared virtual environments.

6   Conclusion and Future Work

The objective of this study was to explore the scope for embodied interactions for remote meetings in shared virtual environments. The outbreak of COVID-19 has forced people to switch to video-conferencing platforms for remote work. The feeling of immersion, engagement, and presence in such video-conferencing platforms is low. This can result in reduced attention and increased fatigue among remote collaborators.

To address some of the challenges, we proposed and implemented an approach to conducting virtual meetings, while leveraging embodied interaction. These embodied interaction techniques can help facilitate better remote collaboration in shared virtual environments. Our approach comprises of a body tracking component, a communication component, and an XR rendering component. We developed a virtual classroom scenario as our prototype implementation and connected two locations, over 4000 mi apart. The maximum latency that we observed during our usability evaluation was 120 ms, suggesting the potential for this kind of approach in facilitating real-time remote collaboration.

Next steps will involve porting and testing the usability of the system with standalone XR headsets. We also intend to enhance our system design by exploring more efficient data management and communication protocols that can reduce jitter in avatar movements and allow several remote users to join the virtual environment. These additional components will be implemented and validated by a user study in our future work.

Acknowledgments. This work has been partially supported by a grant from the Virginia Tech Institute for Creativity, Art, and Technology.

References

1. Anderson, F., Grossman, T., Matejka, J., Fitzmaurice, G.: Youmove: enhancing movement training with an augmented reality mirror. In: Proceedings of the 26th Annual ACM Symposium on User Interface Software and Technology, pp. 311–320. ACM (2013)
2. Casu, A., Spano, L.D., Sorrentino, F., Scateni, R.: Riftart: bringing masterpieces in the classroom through immersive virtual reality. In: Proceedings of the Smart Tools and Apps for Graphics – Eurographics Italian Chapter Conference, pp. 77–84 (2015)
3. Dasgupta, A., Manuel, M., Mansur, R.S., Nowak, N., Gračanin, D.: Towards real time object recognition for context awareness in mixed reality: a machine learning approach. In: 2020 IEEE Conference on Virtual Reality and 3D User Interfaces Abstracts and Workshops (VRW), pp. 262–268 (2020)
4. Detyna, M., Kadiri, M.: Virtual reality in the he classroom: feasibility, and the potential to embed in the curriculum. J. Geogr. High. Educ. **44**(3), 474–485 (2020)
5. Fadzli, F., Kamson, M., Ismail, A., Aladin, M.: 3D telepresence for remote collaboration in extended reality (xR) application. In: IOP Conference Series: Materials Science and Engineering, vol. 979, November 2020
6. Handosa, M., Schulze, H., Gračanin, D., Tucker, M., Manuel, M.: Extending embodied interactions in mixed reality environments. In: Chen, J.Y.C., Fragomeni, G. (eds.) VAMR 2018. LNCS, vol. 10909, pp. 314–327. Springer, Cham (2018). https://doi.org/10.1007/978-3-319-91581-4_23
7. Hunkeler, U., Truong, H.L., Stanford-Clark, A.: MQTT-S–a publish/subscribe protocol for wireless sensor networks. In: Proceedings of the 3rd International Conference on Communication Systems Software and Middleware and Workshops (COMSWARE 2008), pp. 791–798. IEEE (2008)
8. Johnson-Glenberg, M.C.: Immersive VR and education: embodied design principles that include gesture and hand controls. Front. Robot. AI **5**, 81 (2018)
9. Ladwig, P., Geiger, C.: A literature review on collaboration in mixed reality. In: Auer, M.E., Langmann, R. (eds.) REV 2018. LNNS, vol. 47, pp. 591–600. Springer, Cham (2019). https://doi.org/10.1007/978-3-319-95678-7_65
10. Maiese, M.: Rethinking attention deficit hyperactivity disorder. Philos. Psychol. **25**(6), 893–916 (2012)
11. Manuel, M.: Video: Virtual classroom. https://youtu.be/XGzxcCI3RbA. Accessed 02 Sept 2021
12. Microsoft: Azure Kinect body tracking joints (2020). https://docs.microsoft.com/en-us/azure/kinect-dk/body-joints. Accessed 12 Feb 2021
13. Morris, B.: Why does Zoom exhaust you? Science has an answer. The Wall Street Journal, 27 May 2020
14. Sharma, S., Agada, R., Ruffin, J.: Virtual reality classroom as an constructivist approach. In: 2013 Proceedings of IEEE Southeastcon, pp. 1–5. IEEE (2013)
15. Shin, D.H.: The role of affordance in the experience of virtual reality learning: technological and affective affordances in virtual reality. Telematics Inform. **34**(8), 1826–1836 (2017)
16. Sra, M., Schmandt, C.: Metaspace II: object and full-body tracking for interaction and navigation in social VR (2015). arXiv:1512.02922 [cs.HC]
17. Streitz, N.A., Geißler, J., Holmer, T.: Roomware for cooperative buildings: integrated design of architectural spaces and information spaces. In: Streitz, N.A., Konomi, S., Burkhardt, H.-J. (eds.) CoBuild 1998. LNCS, vol. 1370, pp. 4–21. Springer, Heidelberg (1998). https://doi.org/10.1007/3-540-69706-3_3

18. Streitz, N.A., et al.: i-LAND: an interactive landscape for creativity and innovation. In: Proceedings of the SIGCHI Conference on Human Factors in Computing Systems, pp. 120–127. ACM, New York (1999)
19. van der Kruk, E., Reijne, M.M.: Accuracy of human motion capture systems for sport applications; state-of-the-art review. Eur. J. Sport Sci. **18**(6), 806–819 (2018)
20. Weiser, M.: Ubiquitous computing. Computer **26**(10), 71–72 (1993)
21. Wiederhold, B.K.: Connecting through technology during the coronavirus disease 2019 pandemic: avoiding "Zoom fatigue". Cyberpsychol. Behav. Soc. Netw. **23**(7), 437–438 (2020)
22. Wolf, C.R.: Virtual platforms are helpful tools but can add to our stress (2020). https://www.psychologytoday.com/ca/blog/the-desk-the-mental-health-lawyer/202005/virtual-platforms-are-helpful-tools-can-add-our-stress. Accessed 12 Feb 2021
23. Zhao, R., Wang, K., Divekar, R., Rouhani, R., Su, H., Ji, Q.: An immersive system with multi-modal human-computer interaction. In: Proceedings of the 13th IEEE International Conference on Automatic Face & Gesture Recognition (FG 2018), pp. 517–524. IEEE (2018)

A Survey on Applications of Augmented, Mixed and Virtual Reality for Nature and Environment

Jason Rambach[1]([✉])[ID], Gergana Lilligreen[2][ID], Alexander Schäfer[3][ID],
Ramya Bankanal[3], Alexander Wiebel[2][ID], and Didier Stricker[1,3][ID]

[1] Augmented Vision department, German Research Center for Artificial Intelligence,
Kaiserslautern, Germany
Jason.Rambach@dfki.de
[2] Hochschule Worms, UX-Vis Group, Worms, Germany
lilligreen@hs-worms.de
[3] University of Kaiserslautern, Kaiserslautern, Germany

Abstract. Augmented, virtual and mixed reality (AR/VR/MR) are technologies of great potential due to the engaging and enriching experiences they are capable of providing. However, the possibilities that AR/VR/MR offer in the area of environmental applications are not yet widely explored. In this paper we present the outcome of a survey meant to discover and classify existing AR/VR/MR applications that can benefit the environment or increase awareness on environmental issues. We performed an exhaustive search over several online publication access platforms and past proceedings of major conferences in the fields of AR/VR/MR. Identified relevant papers were filtered based on novelty, technical soundness, impact and topic relevance, and classified into different categories. Referring to the selected papers, we discuss how the applications of each category are contributing to environmental protection and awareness. We further analyze these approaches as well as possible future directions in the scope of existing and upcoming AR/VR/MR enabling technologies.

Keywords: Augmented reality · AR · Virtual reality · VR · Mixed reality · MR · Nature · Ecology · Environment · Survey

1 Introduction

Protecting and preserving the environment is necessary as natural resources are limited. The need for a change in paradigm has become apparent in the last years [84]. It is clear now that apart from the support of governments and industry, it is each individual's responsibility to make correct use of resources, conserve energy and adjust their lifestyle to support sustainability.

J. Rambach, G. Lilligreen and A. Schäfer—These authors contributed equally to this work.

© Springer Nature Switzerland AG 2021
J. Y. C. Chen and G. Fragomeni (Eds.): HCII 2021, LNCS 12770, pp. 653–675, 2021.
https://doi.org/10.1007/978-3-030-77599-5_45

When thinking of nature and the environment, digital content is not the first thing that comes to mind. Nevertheless, digitisation has also arrived in this area. New technologies such as augmented reality (AR), virtual reality (VR) and mixed reality (MR) can create fully virtual worlds (VR) or combine virtual elements with the real world (AR, MR). The enhancement of the real world environment by superimposing virtual content has the potential of providing enriching, interactive and captivating experiences. Highly interesting applications at a level of proof of concept systems or even commercial applications have been introduced in many diverse fields such as medicine and health care [28,63], education [24,46,49], entertainment [50,86], industrial maintenance [65] and many more. In this survey we investigate the use of AR, VR and MR in applications that relate to the preservation of the environment in a *direct* or *indirect* manner. It is apparent that such ecological applications are currently few in number, making this a topic that has not been explored extensively yet. Within this work we attempt to discover existing publications on the topic and to classify them. We look into applications that have a *direct* connection to ecology, but also into AR/VR/MR technologies that have the potential of contributing positively to the state of the environment in an *indirect* way, such as e.g. through the reduction of transportation needs for business purposes.

To the best of our knowledge, this is the first survey to cover the particular topic of AR/VR/MR for ecology and nature. Apart from listing existing work in the field, our survey investigates the topic and uncovers the potential opportunities that come with it. We look at the current state of AR/VR/MR in terms of existing technologies for tracking, display and scene understanding and make an initial evaluation of how upcoming advancements in these areas can contribute to the success of ecological AR/VR/MR topics. The rest of the paper is organized as follows: We start by describing the exact methodology (i.e. keywords, sources, selection criteria) we used for finding existing work relevant to this survey in Sect. 2. The classification structure that we propose is presented in Sect. 3 and the respective categories are explained. Statistics on the selected publications are provided in Sect. 4. In Sect. 5, we describe the main points of the most prominent work from each of the categories. In Sect. 6, we summarize our findings and also discuss the current state of AR/VR/MR and possible future developments. Concluding remarks are given in Sect. 7.

2   Search Methodology

We adopted an extensive search approach to discover as many existing publications as possible on the topics of interest. The search was performed using search queries in different data sources. Prominent data sources were Scopus (https://www.scopus.com), Google Scholar (https://scholar.google.com/) and IEEE Xplore (https://ieeexplore.ieee.org/). The search was performed by combining keywords that relate to AR/VR/MR ("augmented reality" OR "mixed reality" OR "virtual reality" OR "AR" OR "MR" OR "VR") with keywords relating to specific environmental topics to form regular expressions. A list of

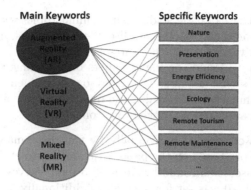

Fig. 1. Examples of keyword combinations used in our search.

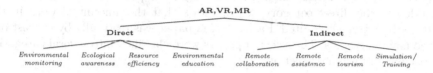

Fig. 2. Classification of augmented, virtual and mixed reality environmental applications.

several of the keywords used is shown in Fig. 1. All possible combinations of keywords from the left column with keywords from the right column were tested. An initially short list of keywords was expanded by the findings of the search. Through this iterative procedure, the search finally led to the initial identification of over 300 related publications. The literature search was performed between November 2019 and February 2020.

We decided to address the topic from both a more narrow and a broader perspective. Therefore the results of the search contained publications that explicitly focus and mention environmental issues (*direct* applications class; narrow) and publications that present applications that can have an environmental impact (based on the opinion of the surveyors) which is however not explicitly stated by the authors of the publication (*indirect* applications class; broad).

It became apparent at early stages of the search that topics covered in the indirect class have such a large extent of related publications that each topic would require a dedicated survey. This exceeds the scope of this survey. Thus, it has been decided to exhaustively search the direct area of environmental applications (narrow) only. For the indirect applications area, we present some key publications which from our point of view support the discussion on environmental perspectives. Next, we filtered the search results for further study and initiated the classification procedure. The main criteria for filtering were:

– **Relevance:** We graded the papers based on how closely the proposed work is related to the specific topic of environmental AR/VR/MR.

- **Originality:** In case of papers addressing similar topics with similar methodology, we kept the earlier paper and discarded later ones, unless they present an important advancement to the state-of-the-art.
- **Impact:** When we found too many papers on the same topic, we took the number of times that a paper was cited by subsequent publications as a measure of its impact. Additionally, the quality of the conference or journal where the work appeared was taken into consideration.

The publications were graded individually by the three main surveyors (score 0–10) in each category based on the paper title and abstract. The final selection was done after a discussion round between all 3 main surveyors. A threshold of an average score of 5.0 was set for selection. Additionally, a score below 2.5 in one of the categories led to direct exclusion. For the direct area of environmental AR/VR/MR publications this led to selecting 28 papers. Very few papers were excluded in the direct category, which shows that the amount of work in the field is still extremely limited. Each selected paper was read fully by at least one of the main surveyors. The selected papers were classified into several categories as discussed in the next section.

3   Classification

Our proposal for classification of environmental AR/VR/MR applications is presented in Fig. 2. Publications were first classified into the categories *direct* and *indirect* based on their type of relation to environmental topics. The category *direct* encompasses all applications and methodologies that are associated in a direct way with nature and ecology. On the other hand, the category *indirect* contains applications and methodologies with a looser connection to environmental issues. Applications from different domains that can have a clear impact on environmental issues like reduction of travel and its subsequent reduction of emissions are covered here. These approaches might not engage with the environment directly but help to reduce wasting of vital resources and pollution.

After searching and selecting the papers we classified them in subcategories based on similarity in the content, e.g. keywords (including synonyms) used in the papers. This lead, in the category *direct*, to subcategories like environmental education and ecological awareness, in which AR/VR/MR applications provide illustrations of characteristics and other related information about species that exist around us. As they learn more about nature and its problems, people can be encouraged to change their behavior and become more ecologically responsible. Environmental monitoring is another major category here. This category covers applications that visualize and monitor data on climate-related topics like air, water and soil. AR as an engaging tool, is capable of illustrating the negative influence of pollution, climate change etc. in order to make their effects fully tangible by humans. Finally, AR/VR/MR applications that support efficient usage of resources are placed under the resource efficiency category.

The category *indirect* involves subcategories like remote collaboration, remote assistance and remote tourism. In all applications from the subcategories there is an underlying potential of saving resources through the reduction of the need to travel for professional or entertainment reasons. AR/VR/MR as highly engaging techniques are able to create immersive remote experiences that help in achieving this. In the next section we look into each one of the categories individually.

4 Statistical Analysis

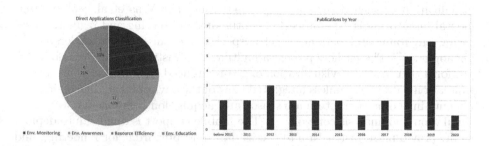

Fig. 3. Statistical analysis of publications cited in this survey in the *direct* environmental applications category. Left: Distribution by application class. Right: Distribution by year.

A statistical analysis of the publications mentioned in this survey is relevant only for the direct environmental application category which was researched in an exhaustive manner. A total number of 28 papers was selected in this category. In Fig. 3, we show a pie-chart of the distribution of selected papers over the four classification categories of direct applications on the left side. On the right side, we show the distribution of papers based on the year of publication. All years up to 2010 were summarized in one category. For 2020 the result is only partial as the search for papers ended in February 2020. Of the 28 papers, 12 (42.9%) were published as journal articles and 18 (57.1%) in conference proceedings. It is also worth mentioning that only 4 of the 28 publications appeared in dedicated AR/VR/MR journals or conferences.

We have also analyzed the number of citations of publications based on information from Google Scholar (https://scholar.google.com/) in August 2020. The average number of citations over the 28 selected publications is 10.42. The 5 most cited publications are [52](73), [85](40), [59](35), [32](26), [70](23). In citations per year the 5 most cited publications are: [52](24.33), [37](5.33), [85](5), [57](5), [59](3.5). The average number of citations for each classification category is as follows: environmental monitoring 9.86 (most cited [85](40)), ecological awareness 12.25 (most cited [52](73)), resource efficiency 10.83 (most cited [59](35)), environmental education 3.66 (most cited [45,77](5)).

5 Main Survey Insights

5.1 Direct Ecological Applications

This section presents a state-of-the-art analysis of AR/VR/MR applications with a direct connection to environment and nature for tasks such as monitoring, resource management or education.

Environmental Monitoring. Extreme changes in the environment fostered the development and usage of sensor networks for environmental data. The visualization of such data is an important issue. For Veas et al. [85] environmental monitoring is "the process of continuously observing and regularly measuring environmental parameters of a specific area in order to understand a phenomenon". The authors present a multilayer infrastructure and a mobile AR platform that leverages visualization of geo-referenced sensor measurements and simulation data in a seamless integrated view of the environment. The main components in the infrastructure are sensor and acquisition components, as well as simulation and analysis components. The mobile support is divided into deployment, providing infrastructure to access data and prepare it for rendering, and a run-time client, providing visualization and interaction capabilities. Two scenarios are chosen as case studies for the system - a snow science scenario in the context of snow avalanches and a hydrology scenario in the context of watershed modeling. AR shows a major value for presenting subsurface structures or different layers of "material" like soil, grass or snow. During workshops with experts, the authors noted a higher preference for 3D visualization in general, especially in unfamiliar environments. As an overall result the authors stated that on-site AR environmental monitoring can be regarded as a promising field.

Trees provide oxygen, conserve water, ameliorate quality of air by reducing amount of CO_2 and also preserve soil. Thus, reforesting helps in the fight against global warming and natural disasters while supporting wildlife as well. AR along with other technologies can be used for localization and monitoring of forests. In this context, West et al. [88] present work on visualizing and monitoring the urban forests using mobile AR. The authors' main aim is to provide an enriching experience to users and encourage the public to involve in tree planting and monitoring initiatives. They mention limitations of existing mechanisms such as remote sensing and field-based imaging and inventory and brief on how AR tries to overcome them. The prototype they present allows users to calibrate the tree location and then displays the dashboard presenting the diameter at breast height (DBH), height and other parameters of tree. In follow-up research [87] they investigate the integration of ground level rephotography with available LiDAR data, for creating a dynamic view of the urban forest, and its changes across various spatial and temporal scales. They explore the potential of overlaying augmentations within the picture taking process in a smartphone app for guiding persons to guarantee consistency in measurements over growing seasons.

In the PAN project [20] AR is used for environmental monitoring with smartphones in a different setting. Users located near points of interest (POI) can take photographs with an AR guidance application and act as citizen scientists. The photographs are processed to time-lapse videos and visualize the environmental changes and can be used for long term documentation. In their project the AR application is used in a limestone pit application case and for observing and documenting the progress of regularly flooded wetlands for the development of a valuable secondary biotope with many rare animal and plant species.

Fan et al. [37] provide a solution to accurately estimate the tree position, diameter at breast height (DBH) and height using a mobile phone with RGB-D-based Simultaneous Localisation and Mapping (SLAM). The measurements obtained are augmented on-screen using AR. This allows the users to easily observe whether estimated measurements are close to actual ones. The authors conclude that estimation of tree parameters with the proposed method gives accurate results.

A mobile AR application (PeakLens) for mountain exploration is discussed by Frajberg [38]. The application can be used to crowd-source mountain images for environmental purposes, such as the analysis of snow coverage for water availability prediction and the monitoring of plant diseases. Meta-data about mountain peaks is overlaid on the phone screen in real-time over relevant objects. For the AR module a computer vision algorithm, based on Deep Learning, is used for the extraction of the natural mountain skyline from the camera view of the mobile phone: "...such skyline is aligned with the skyline extracted from a virtual panorama, computed from the GPS position of the user, the orientation of the mobile phone view, and a Digital Elevation Model (DEM) of the Earth" [38].

A different viewpoint in the category environmental monitoring and AR is described by Studer et al. [78]. The art and science project flcabag uses data values from a biomonitoring system for river water quality. The data is analyzed and then transformed artistically, using AR, to expand the human perception through a sensually clear, visual and physical presence on the river side. For the visualization a symbolically shaped big 'water drop' is sculpted, offering an insight into the world of water fleas. On the back side of the transparent sculpture, a semi-transparent rear projection screen is embedded to project the animation. With good water quality, the 'good water particles' are floating and forming new patterns. The 'water fleas' (green colored) move in a 'relaxed' way through the pattern. With worse water quality the water fleas are colored in red and try to escape from the "bad" water particles, some of them disappear. Since art is used to attract the attention of people to water pollution level, this installation also raises ecological awareness, which is discussed in the following section.

Ecological Awareness. In recent times we have seen quickly rising pollution levels in many areas. The World Health Organisation states that "Between year 2030 and 2050, climate change is expected to cause approximately 250,000 additional deaths per year, from malnutrition, malaria, diarrhoea and heat stress" [19]. Thus it is essential to provide climate change information and its adverse effects to people in an understandable manner. Visualization of climate data with AR can be an effective approach due to AR's captivating nature.

The work of Ramachandran et al. [64] and Torres et al. [83] aims to contribute in this regard by developing applications with AR that visualize pollutants present in the air. Santos et al. have developed the application eVision [71]. In addition to gathering information about air quality, the application detects environmental threats like cars or factories. The users can "wipe" over these objects and the app than automatically displays objects that are environmental friendly, e.g. overlaying a car with a bicycle.

Environmental simulations allow a safe and easy way to acquire knowledge about hard-to-reach habitats. Taulien et al. [81] presented a MR simulation that enables users to convert a place like their living room into a maritime habitat, using the example of the Baltic Sea. The simulation system uses a HMD (Microsoft HoloLens) and the users can explore a virtual underwater world by walking in the real world. Animals, plants and stones are added and respond to users' actions. Through voice-over, additional information is provided when the users look at an object for a longer time, e.g. the oxygen production of a plant. A knowledge questionnaire for two groups - users using text vs. mixed-reality application - showed that both groups improved their knowledge, with a larger improvement using MR. Interestingly, some participants said that they were so fascinated by the MR simulation that they forgot to listen to the voice-over. Additional results show that the users of the mixed-reality application were more excited to experience the habitat.

To raise the awareness on energy consumption, a treasure hunt game where AR is used to visualize effects of energy waste and saving, is presented by Buehling et al. in [26]. The game content, including problem, solution, and clues, is presented through an AR phone application using markers. For example, AR is used to visualize energetic effects like the loss of heat when cooking with an open pot. Red arrows are overlaid on the open pot showing how energy is lost. In order to increase the motivation, the players' performance is visually presented as dynamic virtual gardens that change from poor to good status depending on the points collected in the quiz game. The use of markers generates serious restrictions for such as an application.

An AR underground visualization application is explained in [70]. Georeferenced information is used to augment virtual underground objects and monitor the water quality or the subsoil structure to locate infrastructures for public supply networks like water, sewage and telephone.

An interactive learning AR mobile application was developed for a botanical garden in [67]. A digital album allows the users to find the different species with their relevant information and visualized using AR (see Fig. 4).

Nim et al. [60] present a large-scale MR visualization of data about the Great Barrier Reef (GBR) and explore the impact of individual factors on the coral reef ecosystem. The visualization combines tiled displays and head-mounted displays, and dynamically presents individualized coral damage information grounded on viewers' footprint inputs. During a tour, users provide estimates of their water

Fig. 4. Fern visualized using AR on a mobile device (left) and list of its plant characteristics (right). Picture from [67] available via Creative Commons Attribution 3.0 Unported license (https://creativecommons.org/licenses/by/3.0/).

and carbon footprint, based on their own typical household activities like air travel or water use. They then can see an information of GBR bleaching and crown-of-thorn sea star (COTS) outbreak, supported by immersive technologies. The authors underline that "The aim of such interactive visualization application is to increase community understandings of the complex interplay of different factors for the reef's health" [60].

While the above mentioned works focus on techniques using AR, VR has also been used to promote ecological awareness. DeLeon and Berry [32] discuss an early (1998) attempt to create the illusion of "being there" with a projection-based 140-degree panoramic display. The installation allows spectators to navigate an airboat vehicle through a (at that time) highly realistic virtual landscape representation of the Everglades national park. Two decades later, promoting ecological awareness using VR is still a current topic as the discussion of immersive media for environmental awareness by McGinity [54] shows. Nelson et al. [58] describe the usage of 3D HMDs for showing 360° films about coral reefs and the importance of protecting them vs. showing a unidirectional film. They examine the effects of message framing (positive vs. negative) and VR on conservation behavior and emotions. The participants' behavior was measured using donations to a conservation charity organization. The authors emphasize that VR has the potential to raise ecological awareness and to attract more people to donate. Another current study [52] shows that immersive field trips into an underwater world, allowing users to experience the process and effects of rising sea water acidity, facilitates learning about climate change.

Resource Efficiency. Non-renewable energies like fossil fuels, coal and natural gas are being reduced day-by-day. They cannot be revitalized and their usage by-products and emissions are harmful to the environment. There is a clear need to reduce usage of these resources and also to promote the use of renewable sources such as bio fuels or solar and wind energy.

Informing people about their electrical power consumption can definitely make them more vigilant as discussed in [22]. Here, authors present a proof-of-concept where sensor nodes are installed between load and power socket supply. Electrical parameters from these sensor nodes are visualized in an AR environment through the communication layer based on Internet of Things (IoT). This allows consumers to visualize in AR the consumption of the appliances through the app, become aware of the situation and make more efficient use of this resource. Mylonas et al. [57] describe an IoT data AR energy visualization interface system used by students in a school laboratory. Various types of information like energy consumption, temperature, humidity and other real-time sensor data can be visualized. The authors claim that this educational activity using AR helps creating awareness among children about energy efficiency by making it tangible.

Lu [51] presents a system which provides eco-feedback via smart interconnected devices to remind users about their energy usage or waste. Their system synchronously visualizes the information of the physical environment with the virtual environment by using IoT enabled technologies. A 3D pet raising game rendered by a "Visualization Engine" module enables the continuous engagement of the users. The pet (an avatar) synchronizes with the activity of the user. "According to the contexts in this environment, an energy-gorging appliance will be incarnated by a monster to attack the pet. The player can turn off the energy-gorging appliance by beating the monster via the "User Interface" or by manually switching it off" [51]. Pre-processed sensor data make the system activity-aware. In a study, Lu found out that users prefer graphical to text-based visualization because the information is more comprehensive and agreeable. They also found game-based eco-feedback to be more motivating.

Chudikova et al. [30] reveal how VR and AR can help in planning, modelling and decision making in the selection of heat sources during the construction of buildings. Simulation of different heat sources can be evaluated against certain factors like price, lifespan etc. to decide upon it. Wind simulation in a 3D software or a VR walk through a complex machine room can help in the decision-making process for a suitable location for a wind turbine installation or for individual heating systems in a given space. The authors conclude that by using VR/AR technologies the heat source placement process can become clearer, easier and faster.

The production of renewable energy is getting more and more substantial around the world. For distant and isolated areas, where a demand for electricity is an everyday problem, photovoltaic systems and especially water pumping systems are a great value. Zenati et al. [89] propose a distributed e-maintenance platform enriched with AR functions for a photovoltaic pumping system. A remote expert sees the scene captured by the camera in the worker's device and proposes a maintenance procedure. The benefits that AR brings for remote assistance are further discussed in Sect. 5.2 of this paper.

All techniques supporting the construction of energy efficient products can also be considered as helping to reduce overall energy consumption. Construction tools, if designed for VR as presented by Neugebauer et al. [59], can be especially effective for this task. The authors show how a tool for understanding energy flows in a machine tool can be implemented in VR.

Environmental Education. The goal of environmental education is to increase people's understanding of nature and enabling them to attain a more ecological way of life [69]. Learning about environmental processes feeds into a person's appreciation for nature and into involvement in environmental protection.

Theodorou et al. [82] develop an AR based mobile application intended for teaching school students about climate change concepts and renewable energy resources. QR codes are scanned to view different learning topics. The authors conducted a test to measure knowledge gained by students before and after using the app. Results indicate that the increase in knowledge after using AR tool was higher compared to traditional teaching methods.

Huang et al. [45], describe a system that translates data of an ecological model into a high-fidelity 3D model in VR. The application can serve as an educational tool and the students can achieve knowledge about climate change in a virtual forest. The authors emphasize that "... creating an immersive experience of a future forest can shorten the psychological distance and increase the understanding of complex scientific data".

As a part of the EcoMOBILE project Dede et al. have created a mobile-based AR game consisting of multiple modules for students to use during their field visits [3]. The Atom Tracker Module enables students to follow a carbon or oxygen atom through their environment. It can help students better understand the cycling of matter in ecosystems, such as the processes of photosynthesis and respiration. Another AR module is the Water Quality Measurement AR experience, which invites students to explore a real pond or stream. It leads students to pick up environmental probes by visiting a water measurement "toolbox". Results indicate better understanding of basic concepts while using the AR app. The main reason is increased engagement due to the enriched experience that AR provides.

Srisuphab et al. [77] designed an application (ZooEduGuide) for motivating teenagers and children to learn about animals and wildlife and to raise their awareness for environmental preservation.

5.2   Indirect Application Areas

A large portion of the world-wide CO_2 emissions (about 20%) is created by the transport sector [14]. Apart from the transport of goods, these emissions are generated by travel either for professional (e.g. business meetings) or for personal reasons (e.g. tourism). Systems based on AR or VR that present the opportunity to do certain tasks remotely could have a positive impact in the reduction of emissions and pollution due to travel while training simulations can save resources. In this section we look deeper into some of these indirect ways in which AR/VR/MR can support the environment.

Remote Collaboration. Remote collaboration refers to working together, regardless of different geographic location. Remote collaboration systems have several potential impact factors on the environment. They can reduce the necessity of business travels and therefore help in a global reduction of carbon emissions. In addition, employees can be encouraged to work from home, thus reducing the total office space required, which in turn reduces the companies' environmental footprint. Various traditional video conferencing applications have been popular among people since a few decades but they lack the personal presence of a physical meeting. Advanced AR/VR/MR systems which create shared spaces that enable person embodiment and haptic interaction could become a more convincing alternative to travelling to distant conferences and meetings and help in reducing travel costs, time, carbon emissions and overall office space required.

We identify three main components in remote collaboration systems based on AR/VR/MR: *Environment, Avatars* and *Interaction*.

Environment. The virtual environment stimulates the sensory impressions of its users such as vision, hearing, touch or smell. While older systems experimented with the stimulation of many sensory impressions, more recent systems tend to rely on audiovisual stimuli only. As an example, Morton Heilig created an environment which featured 3D visuals, stereo sound, seat vibration, wind from fans and olfactory cues using aromas in the early sixties [1]. Marker based AR systems tend to have haptic feedback with tangible interfaces such as turntables [73,74] or a pen [75]. However, marker based systems are becoming obsolete due to the increasing maturity of AR tracking technology and therefore are developing a trend to use only audiovisual stimuli. The authors of [72] use multiple static panorama images to create a virtual meeting room where multiple people can participate simultaneously. It features simple presenting tools such as a virtual projector or TV. A live panorama video stream is used by Lee et al. [48] to create a wearable MR remote collaboration system.

Avatar. An avatar represents the user in virtual space (without necessarily resembling the appearance of the user) and is key to enabling communication to other users in a collaborative virtual environment. Monahan et al. [56] implemented a remote collaboration system for knowledge transfer, which allowed online lectures and students having online group meetings. The system featured avatars which could use gestures (e.g. raise hands) for communication besides audio and text chat. A system with an adaptive avatar was created by Piumsomboon et al. which featured a miniature avatar which was able to transmit nonverbal communication cues [62].

Interaction. The possibility to interact with the environment and other users is another important component of remote collaboration systems. Systems developed for product design such as [75,76] usually implement shared 3D object manipulation, including viewing, changing and annotation of 3D objects. Remote collaboration systems are also popular in architectural design, where systems usually integrate the viewing of houses, rooms and furniture while allowing the users to discuss either via audio or integrated tools such as drawing in the virtual environment [29,43,44]. Many professional remote collaboration systems such as [2,4,7,11,12,17] typically include screen sharing and media sharing as interaction possibilities.

Due to the COVID-19 outbreak, many events and conferences were held completely virtual. Some events utilized professional VR remote collaboration systems such as the IEEE VR 2020 conference. The organizing committee used a modified version of Mozilla Hubs [11] which is a professional social VR platform. During this event, the platform featured virtual rooms with up to 20 persons simultaneously in VR.

Another example is the Laval Virtual, an event usually attended by around 10,000 participants and 150 speakers with content covering three days. Due to the special circumstances during the COVID-19 outbreak, the 2020 event was held in VR (See Fig. 5). The professional platform used here was VirBELA [17], a platform specialized for large scale events in VR. Additionally to the meeting and design use cases there are remote collaboration systems which are used for remote assistance, which we address in the next section.

Fig. 5. The Laval Virtual 2020 held completely in VR. One of the authors took this screenshot while attending the event with the avatar that can be seen in the center of the image.

Remote Assistance. Remote assistance or remote support is one of the most heavily explored AR use-cases, especially in industrial scenarios [40]. The core idea of such applications is that a live connection can be established between an on-site user and a remote expert-maintainer. Using AR annotations and optionally audio or text, the expert can guide the user into performing a challenging task. Such processes have the potential of saving time and most importantly allow specialist maintainers of devices to avoid long-distance travel to perform on-site repairs. Apart from industrial maintenance use-cases the idea is also of interest for general customer support for home devices.

Early approaches relied on augmentations that are registered in 2D [53], but it soon became apparent that 3D registration of the target is needed for such systems. 3D object tracking of the maintenance target using an object model as reference is a viable option presented in [65]. Alternatively, the geometry of the environment needs to be reconstructed in real-time by a SLAM-based system in order to place annotations in 3D space [90].

Remote support is one of the most commercially advanced AR use-cases. Nowadays, several companies offer such services, either for see-through AR on head mounted displays (HMDs) or video see-through on mobile devices [15,16,18]. Despite the large investment, it is for now not clear to which extent such systems are already used in practice in industrial maintenance.

Currently, the more challenging task seems to be the capturing of the knowledge of the remote expert and its embedding in an intelligent system that is able to provide instructions for its maintenance or that of other systems. In the work of Petersen et al. [61], the focus is placed on automating knowledge capture from workflow videos, while Rambach et al. [66] present the idea of IoT objects that carry their own AR content that can be shared presented upon connecting to the objects. Furthermore, hand tracking for modelling the interaction of users with objects will be able to add value to maintenance applications [42], as well as recognizing objects and estimating their pose at different states [79].

Remote Tourism. Tourism beyond attraction destinations and entertainment also contributes to economic growth of a country by generating revenues, creating more employment opportunities and supporting the development of infrastructure. As an example, the tourism industry in Europe had around 1.5 billion nights spent at tourist accommodation establishments and over 200 billion euros spent by tourists in 2018 [5]. The relationship of tourism and the environment is complicated. It can be the cause of depletion of water and land resources and a source of pollution. Thus, tourism can gradually damage the environment which it depends on [80]. VR and AR technologies provide alternative forms of visiting famous destinations by bringing out the sense of presence without impacting the natural environment while also saving time, energy and costs.

In the work of Fritz et al. [39], authors illustrate a 3D visualization device developed using AR technologies and the tourist binoculars concept. With the help of this device users can view a remote place and obtain personalized multimedia information about it. Such devices can be used to get attractive and educative information about historical buildings, museums, art galleries and national parks. Another recent example is the work of [47] that offers a remote cultural heritage experience of the Jeju island in Korea through AR and VR. According to Moiseeva et al. [55], remote tourism using AR provides opportunities to disabled people to visit heritage sites, castles, museums and other inaccessible locations.

As an example, the Google Arts & Culture project [8] enables people from all over the world to experience an immersive world in AR and VR based on real locations. Many museums and galleries are already part of such projects and make their exhibited works available for preservation purposes. To mention one, the Chauvet Cave in Ardèche, France, is home to some of the oldest cave drawings in the world according to [27]. There are AR and VR applications to experience the cave in a completely virtual way. In AR, objects can be placed in the augmented world, such as pictures or parts of the cave with interesting wall paintings. A fully immersive experience in VR offers a full 3D reconstruction of the cave with interactive elements such as a torch to illuminate the cave and points of interest.

Although remote tourism can be a substitute for actual traveling, the work of Bogicevic et al. [23] suggests tourism brands to create VR platforms as marketing strategies. This turns VR in tourism into a double-edged sword. On the one hand, travel is prevented, but on the other hand the desire to travel can be awakened [33]. During the current travel-ban that most people are experiencing due to the COVID-19 pandemic, remote tourism can also be an opportunity for creating some revenue for touristic attractions that are not accessible.

Simulation/Training. Similarly to remote tourism, techniques that simulate certain environments and situations can also allow saving resources and reducing travel and emissions. Examples thereof are VR simulations of driving automobiles or aircrafts that can be used for training new drivers/pilots as in the work of Riegler et al. [68] and Bruguera et al. [25]. Simulations for other forms of training such as complex machinery or even training of personnel for critical situations is shown in the work of Gavish et al. [41] and Engelbrecht et al. [34].

The level of success of such applications depends highly on the quality of the simulation. While applications such as remote tourism mostly provide visualization with limited interaction, other simulation applications require much more detailed interaction and feedback mechanisms that rely on fully understanding body motion and interaction as well as haptic feedback.

Another example is VR for high risk training in particularly dangerous environments. For example, firefighters train in a nearly controlled environment, but those training conditions are still very dangerous since they must prepare for dangerous real life situations. This training is not only life threatening but also harmful to the environment. According to Evarts et al. [35] and Fahy et al. [36], there are over 8380 injuries and ten deaths from training accidents in the United States in 2017. These numbers promote virtual training scenarios. Companies that specialize in them, e.g. Flaim Systems [6] offer many realistic VR training scenarios for firefighters. In order to provide even more immersion, special hardware is also used for such training scenarios. For example a combination of real equipment like a firefighter suit, custom made hardware like a water hose trackable by VR and a heat west. The work of Engelbrecht et al. [34] gives a summary of VR training scenarios for firefighters.

Virtual training and simulation scenarios can also be used as marketing strategies whereby the environment benefits from these activities as well. In the home improvement sector, many people are not confident enough to do advanced or even simple tasks. Lowe (a large home improvement store in the USA) created *Holoroom How To* [9] and offers VR training in stores. The VR training includes mixing paint/cement, painting walls, tiling bathrooms and other use cases. Another example is *Holoroom Test Drive* [10] which is used as a try-before-you-buy model to enable customers to try out dangerous products like chainsaws or hedge trimmers in a safe, virtual space. It uses custom made hardware for a more educational and immersive experience. Simulations such as these help reducing the number of returned goods and thus also the ecological footprint.

The same applies to AR shopping apps. As an example, the IKEA Place app launched in September 2017 and has over 3.200 products in its portfolio according to Alves et al. [21]. One of the main advantages for customers is that they can see the real dimensions of products they want to buy and thus avoid unnecessary returns if the product does not fit as expected. Studies from Alves et al. [21] and Dacko et al. [31] have shown that users of AR placement apps feel greater confidence and greater purchasing convenience with an AR furniture placement app, which ultimately leads to less returned goods and thus less transportation as well.

6   Discussion

Examining the outcome of our search, we confirm our initial notion that ecological applications of AR/VR/MR are not yet widely researched or applied in products. Although this survey covers a considerable part of the existing literature, it was only possible to give an overview of the topics by focusing on important works and explaining their relevance to nature and the environment. For example, remote collaboration generally has a positive impact on the environment, regardless of the actual implementation details. To the best of our knowledge, there is no remote collaboration system which was developed for the sake of a positive impact on the environment.

In the category *direct* we identified papers that explicitly discussed applications for environmental education, monitoring, awareness and resource efficiency. Statistical analysis of these publications (Sect. 4) reveals some interesting insights even though the number of existing papers is limited to only 28. In the classification by topic (Fig. 3), environmental awareness appears to be significantly more popular than other categories. It is surprising that only 3 publications were found in the category environmental education when considering that education in general is arguably a heavily explored field of AR/VR/MR applications. The classification of publications by year shows an almost complete absence of related publications before 2011 as well as a possible developing trend in the last years (2018 and after). Finally, the fact that most publications were not published in dedicated AR/VR/MR conferences and journals shows that the topic has possibly not yet received significant attention by the AR/VR/MR community.

Looking more in detail at the publications we can draw further insights. Some of these works try to actively involve many users, as active participation is very important for learning, understanding, and engagement. This results in applications using common hardware such as smartphones and tablets. Therefore, many applications focus on technologies running on those devices. The usage of HMDs can be found more in applications for experts and in the industry field, which is also the main target group for the latest HMDs (e.g. Microsoft Hololens [13]). Nevertheless, it should be noted that the use of AR only for visualization or with limited interaction properties is a common pattern in this category. However, user studies performed show increased immersion or educational results in these cases. Many approaches still rely on tracking using markers as targets, a concept which is not fully scalable to all application scenarios. Efficient tracking and unknown scene understanding at a geometric as well as semantic level is still the main challenge that has to be overcome in order to facilitate AR applications in all covered areas. Although important steps in this direction have already been made in recent years (see for example Microsoft Hololens [13]), significant further advancement is expected in the future. Understanding dynamic scenes, human motion and hand gestures is additionally a current topic of importance.

It is also important to mention that the included publications mostly refer to augmenting the senses of sight and hearing while the other three - the sense of touch, taste and smell, are not considered. For example, the smell of fire could be very interesting for forest fire simulations as part of a climate change and for achieving better immersion. Although there is a small niche for some commercial products, most hardware for such applications is in a development phase, and the usage of our five senses in AR/VR/MR applications could be seen as a direction for the far future.

Some ideas for use cases in everyday life are discussed by McGinity [54]. He describes the usage of AR in a supermarket scenario for visually informing people about how far a product has travelled or how the choice of recycled products like paper towels could help protecting the forests. For these cases he suggests to visualize a forest regrow in AR. This type of AR usage is possible with the current state of the art and could be developed in the near future, perhaps to complement some other applications for products.

In the category *indirect* we covered the topics remote collaboration, remote assistance, remote tourism, and training with their respective applications. These applications have a positive impact on nature and the environment, but were developed and evaluated for other reasons. During the survey, we found that these applications have achieved different readiness levels. For example, basic remote support applications are less challenging and have been already integrated in commercial products, while remote collaboration systems based on AR/VR/MR have larger challenges that they need to overcome and are thus still at a research level. Especially during times when physical distancing is advised, the research in remote collaboration systems with AR, VR or MR technology will focus more on transferring nonverbal communication between users to substitute physical meetings.

During the COVID-19 outbreak which started in December 2019, a large part of the worldwide population has been required to remain at home as a protective measure. All remote collaboration systems and remote tourism scenarios thus have become even more important for the support of economies. This should be seen as a great opportunity to show how much can be achieved remotely and to reduce travel and emissions in the future and thus supporting the environment. Of course, not all human contact can or should be replaced by these technologies. They can however provide viable alternatives to some travels.

Other possible environmental application areas are training scenarios, which help to reduce the environmental destruction. An example described in Sect. 5.2 is the training of firefighters, where environmentally harmful resources are used by starting real fires and extinguishing these fires with chemicals. Virtual training scenarios are already quite advanced and often use custom hardware to support realism and immersion, making them a good substitute for real world training.

AR applications in the e-commerce sector can help the environment, reducing the ecological footprint of companies by minimizing return of goods. There are already many applications which let the user place objects (e.g. furniture in one's own home) and check if the color fits or measure the size of those objects to avoid mispurchases.

7   Conclusion

This survey explores AR/VR/MR applications and concepts that have a relation to nature, environment preservation and resource efficiency. Some work has been developed for direct impacts on nature. Other areas have an indirect impact on nature, such as remote collaboration systems, which are developed for the purpose of remote working or socializing together. These systems were primarily developed for knowledge transfer or virtual meetings, but they have an indirect impact on nature by reducing travel and office space. Therefore, the survey results are classified into applications that have a direct relation to ecology, and applications that can provide an indirect support on ecological goals. To the best of our knowledge there is no comparable survey with similar goals. Results of the survey confirmed that there is only a limited amount of work in AR/VR/MR with a direct ecological relation. After a further categorization, the benefits of AR/VR/MR across a wide variety of domains like education, energy consumption, ecological sensitization and remote collaboration are discussed. In retrospective, the main purpose of this survey was to explore an AR/VR/MR application topic that is not often considered, increase awareness in the scientific community, and create a direct reference to the existing work for the future. Considering the indirect cases in the classification, the search area has expanded considerably. This serves as an indicator that there is a real potential for environmental protection in the use of AR/VR/MR. For some applications this potential can be realized in the near future, while for others a significant advancement of enabling technologies is still required.

Acknowledgements. Parts of this work have been performed in the context of project SAARTE (Spatially-Aware Augmented Reality in Teaching and Education). SAARTE is supported by the European Union (EU) in the ERDF program P1-SZ2-7 and by the German federal state Rhineland-Palatinate (Antr.-Nr. 84002945). This work was also supported by the Bundesministerium für Bildung und Forschung (BMBF) in the context of ODPfalz under Grant 03IHS075B

References

1. Sensorama simulator (August 28 1962), US Patent 3,050,870
2. Breakroom. The social hub for remote teams. http://sine.space/breakroom. Accessed 15 July 2020
3. EcoMOBILE (Ecosystems Mobile Outdoor Blended Immersive Learning Environment). https://pz.harvard.edu/projects/ecomobile. Accessed 15 July 2020
4. EngageVR: Communicate, Teach, Learn. https://engagevr.io/. Accessed 15 July 2020
5. Eurostat annual data for tourism (last access 2020-07-15), https://ec.europa.eu/eurostat/web/tourism/data/database
6. Flaim Systems. https://www.flaimsystems.com/. Accessed 15 July 2020
7. Glue Universal Collaboration Platform. https://glue.work/. Accessed 15 July 2020
8. Google Arts & Culture Project. https://artsandculture.google.com. Accessed 15 July 2020
9. Holoroom How To. http://www.lowesinnovationlabs.com/holoroomhowto. Accessed 15 July 2020
10. Holoroom Test Drive. http://www.lowesinnovationlabs.com/testdrive. Accessed 15 July 2020
11. Hubs by Mozilla. https://hubs.mozilla.com/. Accessed 15 July 2020
12. MeetInVR. https://meetinvr.net/. Accessed 15 July 2020
13. Microsoft Hololens. https://www.microsoft.com/en-us/hololens/hardware. Accessed 15 July 2020
14. Our world in data. https://ourworldindata.org/co2-and-other-greenhouse-gas-emissions. Accessed 15 July 2020
15. Reflekt, https://www.re-flekt.com/reflekt-remote, https://www.re-flekt.com/reflekt-remote. Accessed 15 July 2020
16. ScopeAR. https://www.scopear.com/solutions/ar-remote-assistance/. Accessed 15 July 2020
17. VirBELA, The Future of Work. https://www.virbela.com/. Accessed 15 July 2020
18. Vuforia Chalk. https://chalk.vuforia.com/. Accessed 15 July 2020
19. WHO Facts. https://www.who.int/news-room/fact-sheets/detail/climate-change-and-health. Accessed 15 July 2020
20. Albers, B., Fuhrmann, B., Temmen, M.: Das PAN Projekt - Umweltmonitoring mit Smartphones und Augmented Reality. AGIT - Journal für Angewandte Geoinformatik 3–2017, July 2017
21. Alves, C., Luís Reis, J.: The intention to use e-commerce using augmented reality - the case of IKEA place. In: Rocha, Á., Ferrás, C., Montenegro Marin, C.E., Medina García, V.H. (eds.) ICITS 2020. AISC, vol. 1137, pp. 114–123. Springer, Cham (2020). https://doi.org/10.1007/978-3-030-40690-5_12
22. Angrisani, L., Bonavolontà, F., Liccardo, A., Schiano Lo Moriello, R., Serino, F.: Smart power meters in augmented reality environment for electricity consumption awareness. Energies 11(9), 2303 (2018)
23. Bogicevic, V., Seo, S., Kandampully, J.A., Liu, S.Q., Rudd, N.A.: Virtual reality presence as a preamble of tourism experience: the role of mental imagery. Tour. Manage. 74, 55–64 (2019)
24. Bower, M., Howe, C., McCredie, N., Robinson, A., Grover, D.: Augmented reality in education-cases, places and potentials. Educational Media Int. 51(1), 1–15 (2014)
25. Bruguera, M.B., Ilk, V., Ruber, S., Ewald, R.: Use of Virtual Reality for astronaut training in future space missions-Spacecraft piloting for the Lunar Orbital Platform-Gateway (LOP-G). In: 70th International Astronautical Congress (2019)

26. Bühling, R., Obaid, M., Hammer, S., André, E.: Mobile augmented reality and adaptive art: a game-based motivation for energy saving. In: International Conference on Mobile and Ubiquitous Multimedia. pp. 1–2 (2012)
27. Chauvet, J.M., Deschamps, E.B., Hillaire, C.: Chauvet cave: The discovery of the world's oldest paintings. Thames and Hudson (1996)
28. Chen, L., Day, T.W., Tang, W., John, N.W.: Recent developments and future challenges in medical mixed reality. In: IEEE International Symposium on Mixed and Augmented Reality (ISMAR), pp. 123–135. IEEE (2017)
29. Chowdhury, S., Schnabel, M.A.: Laypeople's collaborative immersive virtual reality design discourse in neighborhood design. Front. Robot. AI **6**, 97 (2019)
30. Chudikova, B., Faltejsek, M.: Advantages of using virtual reality and building information modelling when assessing suitability of various heat sources, including renewable energy sources. In: IOP Conference Series: Materials Science and Engineering. vol. 542, p. 012022. IOP Publishing (2019)
31. Dacko, S.G.: Enabling smart retail settings via mobile augmented reality shopping apps. Technol. Forecast. Soc. Chang. **124**, 243–256 (2017)
32. Deleon, V.J., Berry, H.R.: Virtual Florida everglades. In: International Conference on Virtual System and Multimedia VSSM98- FutureFusion Application Realities for Virtual Age, pp. 46–3 (1998)
33. Drengner, J., König, W., Wiebel, A.: Pervasive mobile Spiele und Virtual Reality als Instrumente der digitalen Ansprache von Veranstaltungsbesuchern: Auf schaz-Suche beim Rheinland-Pfalz-Tag 2018. Eventforschung. MB, pp. 227–245. Springer, Wiesbaden (2019). https://doi.org/10.1007/978-3-658-27652-2_13
34. Engelbrecht, H., Lindeman, R., Hoermann, S.: A SWOT analysis of the field of virtual reality for firefighter training. Front. Robot. AI **6**, 101 (2019)
35. Evarts, B., Molis, J.: United States firefighter injuries 2017. National Fire Protection Association (2018)
36. Fahy, R., LeBlanc, P., Molis, J.: Firefighter fatalities in the United States-2017, Quincy, pp. 1–33. National Fire Protection Association, MA (2018)
37. Fan, Y., Feng, Z., Mannan, A., Khan, T.U., Shen, C., Saeed, S.: Estimating tree position, diameter at breast height, and tree height in real-time using a mobile phone with RGB-D SLAM. Remote Sens. **10**(11), 1845 (2018)
38. Frajberg, D., Fraternali, P., Torres, R.N.: Heterogeneous information integration for mountain augmented reality mobile apps. In: IEEE International Conference on Data Science and Advanced Analytics (DSAA), pp. 313–322. IEEE (2017)
39. Fritz, F., Susperregui, A., Linaza, M.T.: Enhancing cultural tourism experiences with augmented reality technologies. In: International Symposium on Virtual Reality, Archaeology and Intelligent Cultural Heritage (2005)
40. Gallala, A., Hichri, B., Plapper, P.: Survey: the evolution of the usage of augmented reality in Industry 4.0. In: IOP Conference Series: Materials Science and Engineering, vol. 521, p. 012017. IOP Publishing (2019)
41. Gavish, N., et al.: Evaluating virtual reality and augmented reality training for industrial maintenance and assembly tasks. Interact. Learn. Environ. **23**(6), 778–798 (2015)
42. Hampali, S., Rad, M., Oberweger, M., Lepetit, V.: Honnotate: a method for 3D annotation of hand and object poses. In: Proceedings of the IEEE/CVF Conference on Computer Vision and Pattern Recognition, pp. 3196–3206 (2020)
43. Hong, S.W., El Antably, A., Kalay, Y.E.: Architectural design creativity in multi-user virtual environment: a comparative analysis between remote collaboration media. Environ. Plann. B: Urban Analyt. City Sci. **46**(5), 826–844 (2019)

44. Hsu, T.W., et al.: Design and initial evaluation of a VR based immersive and interactive architectural design discussion system. In: 2020 IEEE Conference on Virtual Reality and 3D User Interfaces. IEEE (2020)
45. Huang, J., Lucash, M.S., Scheller, R.M., Klippel, A.: Visualizing ecological data in virtual reality. In: IEEE Conference on Virtual Reality and 3D User Interfaces (VR), pp. 1311–1312. IEEE (2019)
46. Jensen, L., Konradsen, F.: A review of the use of virtual reality head-mounted displays in education and training. Educ. Inf. Technol. **23**(4), 1515–1529 (2018)
47. Jung, K., Nguyen, V.T., Piscarac, D., Yoo, S.C.: Meet the virtual jeju dol harubang-the mixed vr/ar application for cultural immersion in korea's main heritage. ISPRS Int. J. Geo Inf. **9**(6), 367 (2020)
48. Lee, G.A., Teo, T., Kim, S., Billinghurst, M.: Mixed reality collaboration through sharing a live panorama. In: SIGGRAPH Asia Mobile Graphics & Interactive Applications, pp. 1–4. ACM (2017)
49. Lilligreen, G., Keuchel, S., Wiebel, A.: Augmented reality in higher education: an active learning approach for a course in audiovisual production. In: EuroVR Conference (10 2019)
50. Liszio, S., Masuch, M.: Designing shared virtual reality gaming experiences in local multi-platform games. In: Wallner, G., Kriglstein, S., Hlavacs, H., Malaka, R., Lugmayr, A., Yang, H.-S. (eds.) ICEC 2016. LNCS, vol. 9926, pp. 235–240. Springer, Cham (2016). https://doi.org/10.1007/978-3-319-46100-7_23
51. Lu, C.H.: IoT-enhanced and bidirectionally interactive information visualization for context-aware home energy savings. In: IEEE International Symposium on Mixed and Augmented Reality-Media, Art, Social Science, Humanities and Design, pp. 15–20. IEEE (2015)
52. Markowitz, D.M., Laha, R., Perone, B.P., Pea, R.D., Bailenson, J.N.: Immersive virtual reality field trips facilitate learning about climate change. Front. Psychol. **9**, 2364 (2018)
53. Masoni, R., et al.: Supporting remote maintenance in industry 4.0 through augmented reality. Procedia Manuf **11**, 1296–1302 (2017)
54. McGinity, M.: Immersive media for environmental awareness. In: IEEE Workshop on Augmented and Virtual Realities for Good (VAR4Good), pp. 1–5. IEEE (2018)
55. Moiseeva, V., Lavrentyeva, A., Elokhina, A., Moiseev, V.: AR and VR technologies as a factor of developing an accessible urban environment in tourism: institutional limitations and opportunities. Int. J. Eng. Adv. Technol. **8**(6), 5313–5317 (2019)
56. Monahan, T., McArdle, G., Bertolotto, M.: Virtual reality for collaborative e-learning. Comput. Educ. **50**(4), 1339–1353 (2008)
57. Mylonas, G., Triantafyllis, C., Amaxilatis, D.: An augmented reality prototype for supporting IoT-based educational activities for energy-efficient school buildings. Electron. Not. Theor. Comput. Sci. **343**, 89–101 (2019)
58. Nelson, K.M., Anggraini, E., Schlüter, A.: Virtual reality as a tool for environmental conservation and fundraising. PLoS ONE **15**(4), e0223631 (2020)
59. Neugebauer, R., Wittstock, V., Meyer, A., Glänzel, J., Pätzold, M., Schumann, M.: VR tools for the development of energy-efficient products. CIRP J. Manuf. Sci. Technol. **4**(2), 208–215 (2011)
60. Nim, H.T., et al.: Communicating the effect of human behaviour on the great barrier reef via mixed reality visualisation. In: Big Data Visual Analytics (BDVA), pp. 1–6. IEEE (2016)
61. Petersen, N., Pagani, A., Stricker, D.: Real-time modeling and tracking manual workflows from first-person vision. In: IEEE International Symposium on Mixed and Augmented Reality (ISMAR), pp. 117–124. IEEE (2013)

62. Piumsomboon, T., et al.: Mini-me: an adaptive avatar for mixed reality remote collaboration. In: CHI Conference on Human Factors in Computing Systems, pp. 1–13 (2018)
63. Qian, K., Bai, J., Yang, X., Pan, J., Zhang, J.: Virtual reality based laparoscopic surgery simulation. In: ACM Symposium on Virtual Reality Software and Technology, pp. 69–78 (2015)
64. Ramachandran, G.S., et al.: An immersive visualization of micro-climatic data using USC AiR. In: International Conference on Mobile Systems, Applications, and Services, pp. 675–676 (2019)
65. Rambach, J., Pagani, A., Schneider, M., Artemenko, O., Stricker, D.: 6DoF object tracking based on 3D scans for augmented reality remote live support. Computers **7**(1), 6 (2018)
66. Rambach, J., Pagani, A., Stricker, D.: Augmented things: enhancing AR applications leveraging the internet of things and universal 3d object tracking. In: IEEE International Symposium on Mixed and Augmented Reality (ISMAR), pp. 103–108. IEEE (2017)
67. Rico-Bautista, D., et al.: Digital album with augmented reality: Francisco de Paula Santander Ocaña University botanic garden "Jorge Enrique Quintero Arenas". J. Phys. Conf. Ser. **1257**, p. 012009. IOP Publishing (2019). https://iopscience.iop.org/article/10.1088/1742-6596/1257/1/012009
68. Riegler, A., Riener, A., Holzmann, C.: AutoWSD: virtual reality automated driving simulator for rapid HCI prototyping. In: Mensch und Computer 2019, pp. 853–857. Association for Computing Machinery (2019)
69. Roczen, N., Kaiser, F.G., Bogner, F.X., Wilson, M.: A competence model for environmental education. Environ. Behav. **46**(8), 972–992 (2014)
70. Romão, T., et al.: Augmenting reality with geo-referenced information for environmental management. In: ACM International Symposium on Advances in Geographic Information Systems, pp. 175–180 (2002)
71. Santos, B., Romão, T., Dias, A.E., Centieiro, P., Teixeira, B.: Changing environmental behaviors through smartphone-based augmented experiences. In: Nijholt, A., Romão, T., Reidsma, D. (eds.) ACE 2012. LNCS, vol. 7624, pp. 553–556. Springer, Heidelberg (2012). https://doi.org/10.1007/978-3-642-34292-9_57
72. Schäfer, A., Reis, G., Stricker, D.: Towards collaborative photorealistic VR meeting rooms. In: Mensch und Computer 2019, pp. 599–603. ACM (2019)
73. Shen, Y., Ong, S., Nee, A.: A framework for multiple-view product representation using Augmented Reality. In: International Conference on Cyberworlds, pp. 157–164. IEEE (2006)
74. Shen, Y., Ong, S.K., Nee, A.Y.: Collaborative design in 3D space. In: ACM SIGGRAPH International Conference on Virtual-Reality Continuum and Its Applications in Industry, pp. 1–6 (2008)
75. Shen, Y., Ong, S.K., Nee, A.Y.: Product information visualization and augmentation in collaborative design. Comput. Aided Des. **40**(9), 963–974 (2008)
76. Shen, Y., Ong, S.K., Nee, A.Y.: Augmented reality for collaborative product design and development. Des. Stud. **31**(2), 118–145 (2010)
77. Srisuphab, A., Silapachote, P., Sirilertworakul, N., Utara, Y.: Integrated ZooEduGuide with multimedia and AR from the largest living classrooms to wildlife conservation awareness. In: TENCON IEEE Region 10 Conference, pp. 1–4. IEEE (2014)
78. Studer, C., Shave, J.: Water in augmented space. In: 2011 IEEE International Symposium on Mixed and Augmented Reality - Arts, Media, and Humanities, pp. 103–104 (2011)

79. Su, Y., Rambach, J., Minaskan, N., Lesur, P., Pagani, A., Stricker, D.: Deep Multi-state object pose estimation for augmented reality assembly. In: IEEE International Symposium on Mixed and Augmented Reality (ISMAR) Adjunct, pp. 222–227. IEEE (2019)

80. Sunlu, U., et al.: Environmental impacts of tourism. Options Méditerranéennes. Série A, Séminaires Méditerranéens **57**, 263–270 (2003)

81. Taulien, A., Paulsen, A., Streland, T., Jessen, B., Wittke, S., Teistler, M.: A mixed reality environmental simulation to support learning about maritime habitats: an approach to convey educational knowledge with a novel user experience. In: Mensch und Computer, pp. 921–925. ACM (2019)

82. Theodorou, P., Kydonakis, P., Botzori, M., Skanavis, C.: Augmented reality proves to be a breakthrough in Environmental Education. In: Protection and Restoration of the Environment XIV (2018)

83. Torres, N.G., Campbell, P.E.: Aire: visualize air quality. In: ACM SIGGRAPH Appy Hour, pp. 1–2. ACM (2019)

84. V Masson-Delmotte, E.A.E.: Global warming of 1.5° C. An IPCC special report on the impacts of global warming. Report (2018), https://www.ipcc.ch/sr15/

85. Veas, E., Grasset, R., Ferencik, I., Grünewald, T., Schmalstieg, D.: Mobile augmented reality for environmental monitoring. Pers. Ubiquit. Comput. **17**(7), 1515–1531 (2013)

86. Von Itzstein, G., Billinghurst, M., Smith, R., Thomas, B.: Augmented reality entertainment: taking gaming out of the box. In: Lee, N. (ed.) Encyclopedia of Computer Graphics and Games. Springer, Cham (2017). https://doi.org/10.1007/978-3-319-08234-9_81-1

87. West, R., Halley, A., O'Neil-Dunne, J., Gordon, D., Pless, R.: Collaborative imaging of urban forest dynamics: augmenting re-photography to visualize changes over time. In: The Engineering Reality of Virtual Reality. vol. 8649, p. 86490L. International Society for Optics and Photonics (2013)

88. West, R., Margolis, T., O'Neil-Dunne, J., Mendelowitz, E.: MetaTree: augmented reality narrative explorations of urban forests. In: The Engineering Reality of Virtual Reality, vol. 8289, p. 82890G. Int. Society for Optics and Photonics (2012)

89. Zenati, N., Hamidia, M., Bellarbi, A., Benbelkacem, S.: E-maintenance for photovoltaic power system in Algeria. In: IEEE International Conference on Industrial Technology (ICIT), pp. 2594–2599 (2015)

90. Zillner, J., Mendez, E., Wagner, D.: Augmented reality remote collaboration with dense reconstruction. In: IEEE International Symposium on Mixed and Augmented Reality Adjunct (ISMAR-Adjunct), pp. 38–39. IEEE (2018)

Flexible Low-Cost Digital Puppet System

Nanjie Rao[(✉)] [iD], Sharon Lynn Chu [iD], and Ranger Chenore [iD]

University of Florida, Gainesville, FL 32611, USA
{raon,slchu,rangerchenore}@ufl.edu

Abstract. Puppet-basedsystems have been developed to help children engage in storytelling and pretend play in much prior literature.Many different approaches have been proposed to implement suchpuppet-based storytelling systems, and new storytelling systems are stillroutinely published, indicating the continued interest in the topic across domains like child-computer interaction, learning technologies, and the broader HCI community. This paper firstpresents a detailed review of the different approaches that have been usedfor puppet-based storytelling system implementations, and then proposesaflexible low-cost approach to puppet-based storytelling system implementation that uses a combination of vision- and sensor-based tracking. We contribute a framework that will help the community to make sense of the myriad of puppet-based storytelling system implementation approaches in the literature, and discuss results from a perceptionstudy that evaluated the performance of the system output using our proposed implementation approach.

Keywords: Puppet storytelling system · Digital puppetry · Perception study

1 Introduction

Storytelling plays an important role in education. As an approach of nurturing storytelling, digital puppetry has been used to help people engage in storytelling and pretend play. It is a great way to encourage creativity in children through expressive storytelling activities [23], such as the free-form pretend play (also referred to in literature as fantasy play [21], make-believe play [4] or story enactment [3]). This paper addresses the design, implementation and evaluation of a puppet-based storytelling system.

Different kinds of media serve as feedback to tangible interaction in all tangible narratives [6]. To enable tangible interaction with a puppet system, the tracking system is the stepping-stone. It defines the limitation of movements of the puppets, hence it forms the interaction style between puppeteer and puppet system [5]. It also is impacted by the physical affordances of the puppet as an object, as

Supported by National Science Foundation Grant #1736225 *To Enact, To Tell, To Write: A Bridge to Expressive Writing through Digital Enactment.*

J. Y. C. Chen and G. Fragomeni (Eds.): HCII 2021, LNCS 12770, pp. 676–694, 2021.
https://doi.org/10.1007/978-3-030-77599-5_46

the tracking system could rely on characteristics of the puppets [8,10,17,22] or constrain the form of the puppets [1,2,18].

Puppet systems presented in the literature were either settled with fixed combinations of technology and certain physical affordances [5] or set up in a way to address concepts outside of storytelling [6], which call for a flexible low-cost digital puppet storytelling system. The novel approach for our proposed storytelling system implementation is that the six components in our system are designed and employed in ways that they can each make it convenient for each other to work and communicate seamlessly. Mazalek et al.'s work [17] on the Xperimental Puppetry Theater stated that smooth communication and continuous mapping from the puppet data to the virtual artwork is the most challenging part of the implementation of puppet-based storytelling systems. Furthermore, in our approach, the combination of these six components are flexible yet robust in the way that other researchers could easily substitute our components to the ones they prefer, including the physical affordances as a puppet and object, the vision-based position tracking system, the sensor-based rotation tracking system, the display system, the story creation interface, and the data communication system.

In Harley et al.'s framework [6], 21 existing tangible narrative systems were reviewed, and the systems target both adults and children. In our consideration, children's behaviors are more unpredictable, and we intend to include children as potential users for our puppet system. Hence, much of our design rationale took into account children's preferences and developmental needs. We developed our puppet storytelling system using 3D printed puppet and objects, YOLO real-time object detection, the Aimxy and the BBC:microbit sensors, and Unity. We present a study that evaluates the quality of the implementation. However, as time goes by and new technology emerges, researchers could update each component as they wish. For example, the YOLO vision tracking and sensors could be replaced by ultra-wideband radio technology so that position and rotation tracking can be implemented on a single microchip.

In summary, our contributions are: (1) a review of the existing approaches that have been usedfor puppet-based storytelling system implementations; (2) a flexible low-cost approach to puppet-based storytelling system implementation; (3) an online perception study demonstrating the perceived quality of the output of our puppet storytelling system.

2   Background and Related Work

2.1   Digital Puppetry and Tangible Narratives

The manipulation of digitally animated 2D or 3D characters and objects in a virtual environment is considered to be digital puppetry. Ferguson defines digital puppeteering as a reflection of human motions onto digital animations with possible abstraction [5]. The productions of digital puppetry were widely used for movies, television series, live theaters, and Disneylands (and other interactive theme parks). However, it is not uncommon that people without advanced animation skills want to create digital stories. These digital stories can be for purposes that include arts and performance, learning and education, self-expression, product prototyping, etc. With many existing storytelling systems, storytelling requires specific hardware and software systems, training on specific techniques and skills, and even the coordination of multiple people.

To enable low-cost and easy to learn digital puppetry, laborious, and time-consuming key-frame based animation techniques are unsuitable, especially for non-expert animators [11]. Stories created by reflecting the performer's movement in real life may be more suitable. Pricey high-end motion capture systems like Vicon and OptiTrack are adopted among the professional filmmaking industry [11]. However, with recent developments in computer vision, inertial motion unit (IMU) sensors, and mass production of related consumer electronics, many different kinds of low-cost approaches to motion tracking have emerged. Acceptable accuracy of tracking can be achieved without a high budget. Despite the large number of motion-tracking-based storytelling systems that have been proposed thus far, we still have little understanding of what approaches work best. We highlight two prior efforts that have attempted to make sense of existing approaches to storytelling systems.

Ferguson conducted studies using commercially available production from three companies [5]. The systems were evaluated as they were out of the box, including digital characters, software, rigs, constraints, relations, general setup, joystick control, data glove control, 6DOF magnetic sensor control, and microphone control. As intended for single person multimodal live operation systems, the experience and results from these existing systems were disappointing. Issues were identified by experts including inconsistent data stream, cumbersome setup, device limitation, erratic concept mapping, mismatch in perceptual-motor coordination, movement constraint, and operation fatigue.

Different from Ferguson's 2015 paper which focused on commercial systems, Harley et al. presented a framework for tangible narratives in 2016 [6]. Their framework isolated the characteristics resulting from the storytelling systems that utilized physical objects as media to map into virtual environments. Seven categories were identified and employed across 21 systems. The categories were "primary user, media, the narrative function of the tangible objects, diegetic tangibles, narrative creation, choice, and position", which defined the structure of the narrative. Regardless of the different categories, among all systems, the stories were pushed forward by tangible interaction. Interestingly, although there were many different stated motivations behind creating these tangible narrative systems, the story itself was never the main purpose.

2.2 Existing Puppet Storytelling Systems

Based on a review of existing approaches for puppet systems, we specified a framework for decomposing puppet-based storytelling systems. Each aspect of the framework corresponds to a component of the puppet system, shaping how the puppet system is created and utilized:

1. The physical affordances as a puppet and object;
2. The vision-based tracking system to get 3D position data of the objects;

3. The sensor-based tracking system to get the raw, pitch, yaw rotation data of the physical objects;
4. The display system to animate the tracked data into virtual avatar animations and movement
5. The story creation interface to scaffold the storyline;
6. The data communication system to deliver real-time tracking data from 2 and 3 to 4.

We summarize 17 puppet systems created between 2008 and 2019, using the framework described above. We abstain from discussing specific concepts in the systems outside of storytelling, focusing on how the puppetry is captured and how the interaction goes. Here are the variations of approaches found for each component across all the 17 systems reviewed:

- **Puppet and object**: 2D paper puppets [1,2]; 3D printed puppets [19]; traditional puppets with realistic fabric [9,16,17,20,24]; human skeleton [12]; human hands [11,13–15]; robot-like puppets [8,10,22], and VR controllers [9,18,20].
- **Vision-based tracking**: Marker-based tracking [1]; color detection [2], Kinect [12,19]; VR base station [9,18,20]; and Leap Motion [11,13–15].
- **Sensor-based tracking**: Sensors in the joints of robot-like puppets [8,10,17, 22]; IMU sensors (standalone module and inside VR controllers) [9,18–20].
- **Display system**: Unity engine [11–15,17,18]; non-Unity animator [1,2,8,10, 19,22]; actual physical puppets [9,16,20,24].
- **Story creation interface**: Special cultural themes [16,17,24]; close loop control as in games [14,15]; no systematic instruction [1,2,8–13,18–20,22].
- **Data communication**: Database and data feeding software [17].

Table 1 shows system characteristics of 17 tangible systems published from 2008 to 2019 using the sections defined above. Only one paper [17] described their data communication system in detail, so we didn't list this component.

Below, we selected 5 representative puppet storytelling systems from prior literature that illustrated different combinations of the various approaches in detail above for the 6 components. Although the intended audience of the systems may include either adults or children, children's preference and development need were discussed specifically because their behavior was more unpredictable.

FingAR: Marker-Based Tracking+2D Paper Puppets. Bai et al. [1] developed the FingAR Puppet system shown in Fig. 1. It's based on multiple open-source software. Their system framework used Microsoft XNA Game Studio 4.0, AR registration, and rendering used GoblinXNA 4.1, marker tracking used ALVAR2.0, and image processing used Emgu CV2.4. FingAR is a good example of puppet systems that majorly used computer vision to achieve tracking, and physical referents (shaped card boards) as the puppet design.

Due to the nature of vision-based tracking, the system would lose track of the object when the camera had a blur which happened frequently when the object

Table 1. System components of 17 puppet systems published from 2008 to 2019 using our framework. NB: sjr = sensors in the joint of robot-like puppets, clc = close loop control, and nsi = no systematic instruction.

System	Puppet and object	Vision tracking	Sensor tracking	Display	Story creation interface
FingAR [1]	2D paper puppets	Marker-based	n/a	non-Unity animator	nsi
Video Puppetry [2]	2D paper puppets	color detection	n/a	non-Unity animator	nsi
Jacobson et al.'s [8]	robot-like puppets	n/a	sjr	non-Unity animator	nsi
Kawahara et al.'s [9]	VR controllers	VR	IMU	actual physical puppets	nsi
Lamberti et al.'s [10]	robot-like puppets	n/a	sjr	non-Unity animator	nsi
Anim-Actor [12]	human skeleton	Kinect	n/a	Unity	nsi
Mani-Pull-Action [13]	human hands	Leap Motion	n/a	Unity	nsi
Virtual Marionette [11]	human hands	Leap Motion	n/a	Unity	nsi
Liang et al.'s 1st [14]	human hands	Leap Motion	n/a	Unity	clc
Liang et al.'s 2nd [15]	human hands	Leap Motion	n/a	Unity	clc
Liu et al.'s [16]	traditional puppets	n/a	IMU	actual physical puppets	special cultural themes
Mazalek et al.'s [17]	traditional puppets	n/a	IMU	Unity	special cultural themes
Nitsche et al.'s [18]	VR controllers	VR	IMU	Unity	nsi
Figurines [19]	3D printed puppets	Kinect	IMU	non-Unity animator	nsi
Sakashita et al.'s [20]	VR controllers	VR	IMU	actual physical puppets	nsi
Yoshizaki et al.'s [22]	robot-like puppets	n/a	sjr	non-Unity animator	nsi
Zhao et al.'s [24]	traditional puppets	n/a	IMU	actual physical puppets	special cultural themes

(a) Enact puppet   (b) Transform emotion   (c) Open-ended scenery objects   (d) Dramatic storyline

Fig. 1. FingAR puppet system overview in Bai et al.'s paper

was moving fast and the camera couldn't focus. It's relatively easy to implement because of the easy availability of open-source software and libraries including OpenCV and Aruco. It would be a "fast and dirty" solution for a puppet system that was meant to verify other concepts like emotions mentioned in Bai's work [1]. However, to achieve a puppet system that can support fluent and realistic storytelling where the focus is on the story creation, a higher tracking rate and a more robust system are required. And to bump the technical specs up, the cost would skyrocket. Also, there's no systematic instruction on storytelling creation in Bai et al.'s work.

Figurines: Fusion Tracking+3D Printed Puppets. Maxime Portaz et al. [19] proposed Figurines, adopted a hybrid system, using 2 RGB-D cameras and IMU sensors embedded figurines as vision-based and sensor-based tracking. They used 3D printed figurines and décor element as puppet design, and had 3d rendering offline after the recording of the narrative session. The designated area for puppet playing is the table shown in Fig. 2, sizing 70 cm × 70 cm. Obviously, taking advantage of RGB-D sensors and fusion tracking with IMU sensors made Figurines system more robust than the puppet systems that relied solely on vision-tracking. In fact, our framework was built on top of the fusion tracking framework since it combines the advantages of multiple techniques. It's incredible that some RGB-D sensors including Kinect and Intel RealSense are so commercially easily accessible at around 100 dollars. However, as we have tested, using RGB-D sensors had its own drawbacks. Firstly, it has a strict space limitation. This means that while holding the puppet, you cannot be too close or too far from the sensors. The IR sensor in this solution relies on the emission of the structured IR light pattern and the reflection it got back from the puppet. This also means that no mirror or other reflective material, including any smooth surface like a piece of paper, a side of a cabinet, or a cellphone screen should appear in the puppet playing space. This might be fine when the users are invited into a certain lab where the environments are strictly taken care of. But we demand more than a prototype in a lab environment. We want a truly robust and flexible puppet storytelling system so that we can bring it into a real elementary school where the children can freely enact stories on their own tables. Another important limitation of Maxime Portaz et al.'s puppet system is that the users cannot see their production on the digital display in real-time. And as it's been pointed out in the multiple works of Ferguson, Leite, and

Fig. 2. Figurines tangible storytelling system in Portaz et al.'s paper

Harley [5,7,11], it's important that the animation reflects the performer's movement in real life without post-processing. Also, there's no systematic instruction
on storytelling creation in Portaz et al.'s work.

Liang et al.'s System: Leap Motion+Human Hand. Liang et al. [15]
utilized the Leap Motion sensor to trigger pre-recorded animations of the crow
puppet. For the purpose of letting young children easily control, they mapped
different hand gestures to up, down, left and right, shown in Fig. 3.

This type of system has constrained degrees of freedom in mapping the real-
world movement to the digital puppet. Also, in our experience of using the
Leap Motion style sensor to capture the hand gesture, it felt more like using a
game controller instead of the free form storytelling we want. The command list
mapping might feel natural for a gamer, but it still differs from the original affordance of the physical puppet which all sorts of users could directly manipulate
the physical puppet to do storytelling freely [2].

Nitsche et al.'s System: VR Base Station+VR Controllers. Nitsche et al.
used 3 main sample mappings to exemplify different opportunities that open up
through bottom-up inclusion of puppetry principles in VR controls. Rod mapping

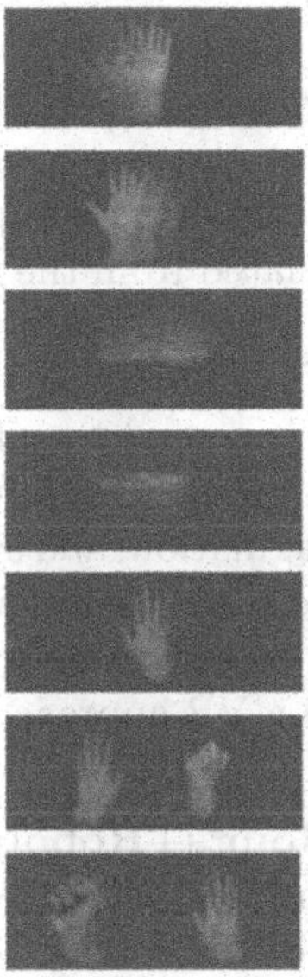

Hand gesture	Movement	Target action
	Move right	Fly to the right
	Move left	Fly to the left
	Move down	Fly down
	Move up	Fly up
	Stretch	Hover
	Stretch to grip	Grasp pebble/ stick
	Grip to stretch	Drop pebbles/ stick

Fig. 3. Hand gesture-based interactive puppetry system in Liang et al.'s paper

Fig. 4. VR marionette in Nitsche et al.'s paper

is an example of variable control schemes and emphasizes the relationship of the puppet to the environment. The marionette mapping is equally variable through a changing control mechanism and it offers a possible solution for a 3rd person VR control scheme that might allow higher mobility through spatial tracking of the Vive controllers, shown in Fig. 4. The hand puppet mapping demonstrates varying granularity where controls shift between different levels of "distance" as outlined by Kaplin.

The approaches in VR were considered to be cool for children in elementary school, but many individuals have glasses or motion sickness that are not compatible with VR applications. Also, an important element of the puppet storytelling system is social engagement, which is still in an early exploring phase for VR. While wearing HMD, the user is visually isolated from the rest of the world. The isolation might be good for some other applications, but not for puppet storytelling where research had stated that children's cognitive development in skills and judgment, as well as the appropriation of augmented tangible objects, were not sufficiently nurtured if isolated. During the open-ended puppet storytelling process, children exercise their cognitive skill, imagination, and symbolic transformation which are essential for their excellence and competence in their adulthood [1]. So we want an open space for the children to engage in open storytelling and social interactions instead of an isolated HMD in a VR approach.

Jacobson et al.'s System: Sensors in the Joints+Robot-Like Puppets.
Jacobson et al. [8] presented a tangible modular input device shown in Fig. 5. The sensors embedded in joints could infer the pose of the robot-like puppets. Since they adopted a modular design, the topology could be updated automatically with the alternation on the splitter parts. In terms of target acquisition and pose replication, robot-like puppets are preferred over mouse and keyboard.

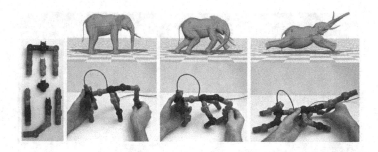

Fig. 5. Tangible and modular input device for character articulation in Jacobson et al.'s paper

Skeletal articulation made it accurate in terms of puppet limbs and action details, but it might still be a drag for a complete storyline where multiple scenes and characters would present. It's helpful for perfecting single poses, but the overall storyline was not addressed.

3   Goals for a New Flexible Low-Cost Digital Puppet Storytelling System

From our review of existing approaches, we can see that prior puppet-based storytelling systems have both strengths and limitations.

1. All the existing systems didn't focus on the story creation.
2. The systems usually required special setup and space, e.g., in the lab.
3. The operation for the systems required some expertise to use.
4. VR-based systems isolated the user from the real world.
5. The construction of the overall storyline was not scaffolded.
6. The systems would fail if any component didn't work.

To address the weaknesses identified, we propose six goals for a new flexible low-cost digital puppet storytelling system. The system should:

1. Support fluent storytelling where the focus is on the story creation.
2. Be robust enough to bring to an authentic classroom setting where children can freely enact stories on their own tables.
3. Be easy enough that persons of all ages and skill levels could readily engage.
4. Allow for social engagement.
5. Be able to support the overall storyline on top of enacting each scene.
6. Be modular enough such that each component is easily replaceable.

4   System Description

We developed a flexible low-cost puppet-based storytelling system that align with the six goals described above. Our proposed system can be described based on the six components of the framework specified in Sect. 2.2. Our system involves:

1. **Puppet and object**: 3D printed puppet and objects with the pattern for vision-based tracking and small slot left for sensor
2. **Vision-based tracking**: The YOLO vision tracking algorithm and training sets
3. **Sensor-based tracking**: The Aimxy and BBC:microbit
4. **Display system**: Self-created avatars and scripts inside Unity 3D
5. **Story creation interface**: A story creation interface inside Unity 3D
6. **Data communication**: UDP, Bluetooth, and shared memory mapping

The six components in our system are designed and employed so that they can each make it convenient for the other components to work and communicate seamlessly. For example, when we designed the 3D printed puppet and objects, we intentionally put in patterns on the base of puppet and object for better vision-based tracking and left small slots in the base for the sensor to be embedded, shown in Fig. 6. And the six components are so modular that other researchers could easily substitute our components for ones they prefer, including the physical puppet and object and supporting systems.

For better YOLO vision tracking results, we trained our own convolutional neural network using 148 picture samples marked by our researcher, shown in Fig. 7. The focus is on the base so that even if the 3D printed character and object change in other designs, the vision tracking would still work without training on the new set.

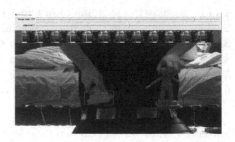

Fig. 6. Slot for sensor

Fig. 7. YOLO pattern selection on the base

The story creation interface was based on the work of Zarei et al. [23] shown in Fig. 8. A collection of story scenes can be planned and ordered chronologically to construct the storyline before enactment. This supports the overall storyline on top of enacting each scene. This also brings the focus back to the story creation. Different backgrounds, characters, and objects can be chosen as the user wishes before acting out the scene. Some examples were shown in the Fig. 9.

Fig. 8. Story creation interface

Fig. 9. Story backgrounds, characters and objects

Fig. 10. System setup

As mentioned in Mazalek et al.'s work [17], smooth communication, and continuous mapping from the puppet data to the virtual artwork was the most challenging part. The bridging software outside of Unity was also a crucial part of our puppet system. UDP (User Datagram Protocol) was used to broadcast the tracking data from the position tracking program to Unity, Bluetooth was used to send the rotation sensor data from the Aimxy and BBC:microbit to the receiving program on the computer, and shared memory mapping was used to send the received rotation data from the receiving program to Unity. As no fragile and expensive special devices were used, our system is both robust enough to bring to an authentic classroom setting and easy enough to use without expertise. Social engagement is also allowed because of no isolation of VR headset.

5   Evaluation of Our Puppet Storytelling System

Our research question for our evaluation study was as follows:

What is the perceived quality of the output of our proposed puppet storytelling system?

5.1   Evaluation Method

Due to the impact of COVID-19, no physical human subject study could be done. Instead, we conducted an online perceptionsurvey study to evaluate the performance of the system output using our proposed implementation approach. We recorded two stories with our system which were used in the evaluation. Both stories were enacted by the researcher. Both stories lasted less than three minutes. Story 1 was designed to be more complex as more "dramatic" movements were included by the researcher intentionally, while story 2 was simpler as the original storyline was created by a child in a previous full body enactment study. A sample physical set up of the system is shown in Fig. 10.

Our study had two independent variables: type of puppetry (IV1) and story design (IV2). Type of puppetry had 2 levels: Physical enactment; Virtual animation. Story design had 2 levels: Complex; Simple. For IV1, we were interested to see whether the virtual animation produced by the system faithfully represents the physical enactment of a story done by a user. Thus, we expected to see a replicated puppetry performance from physical puppetry to virtual animation (thus, no statistically significant difference between the 2 levels of the IV). An example of the physical puppetry and interface of virtual animation is shown in Fig. 11. From the raw footage (physical puppetry) and the system output (virtual animation), ratings from the participants were used as an evaluation of the puppet system. For IV2, complex stories were expected to be rated higher than simple stories, but we also expected an interaction between story designs (IV2) and the degree to which the virtual animation is perceived to faithfully represent the physical puppetry. Participants were expected to give their opinions in terms of the overall experience, appearance, clarity, degree of control, affective information, and importance of system components.

5.2 Study Participants and Study Protocol

We recruited workers on the Amazon Mechanical Turk crowdsourcing platform. Mturk workers were compensated via the Mturk platform as compensation. Out of 54 responses we collected, 23 of them (42.59%) were valid. Among these 23 Mturk workers, 13 (56.52%) of them are male, 10 (43.48%) of them are female.

Fig. 11. Comparisons between type of puppetry

Each participant would go through one story design and see videos for both types of puppetry (physical enactment and its corresponding virtual animation). The average time needed for valid responses made by the Mturk workers was 35 min. In our complete survey study flow, the participant would accept our task on Mturk, click on the survey link on the MTurk task page which will guide them to our web page. On our first web page, the participant would read the instructions and consent to participate in the study, which would direct the participant to one of four study flows. Two study flows addressed one story, and the other two study flows addressed the other story. For each story, since we are counterbalancing the order in which participants engaged with IV1 (the type of puppetry), there were 2 study flows. The study instructions informed the participant that the study involved them watching story videos generated from a puppet-based storytelling system that the researchers developed.

After answering a few demographic questions, the participant would be directed to watch a story video (Physical puppetry or virtual animation recording using our puppet system), answer questions about this specific video based on his/her opinions about the video. Upon finishing the questionnaire in the previous web page, he/she will then be directed to another video of the same story (still recorded with our system, with same narration but with different setup - if the previous video was the physical puppetry setup then this one would be the virtual animation). The same set of questions would be answered with regard to the video of the different setups. After answering the questions for the two videos of physical enactment and virtual animation separately, the participant would proceed to a page where he/she would be asked to make a direct comparison between the physical enactment video and the virtual animation video. Both videos he/she had seen in the previous web pages would be shown on the same web page for this comparison, see Fig. 12.

5.3   Study Measures

Our survey contains sections: overall experience, appearance, clarity, degree of control, affective information, importance of system components, and some open-ended questions. For most of our questionnaire items, the 7-point Likert scale was used for the participants to rate their perception from 1 (not at all) to 7 (Very much) since almost all the questions were started with "How." Ratings were given by the participants for physical enactment and virtual animation separately about the angle of rotation of the movement, the carried narration, storyline, story details, and affective information, which used question template "How X did you feeltheYpuppetry was?".

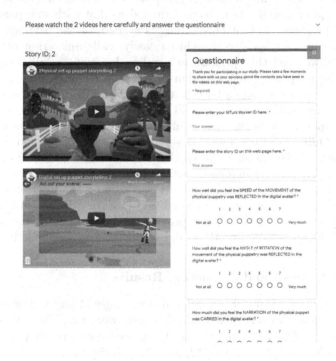

Fig. 12. The direct comparison web page in our evaluation

After separate ratings, participants were asked about direct comparison for speed of movement, angle of rotation of the movement, carried narration, storyline, story details, and affective information, which used question template "How well the virtual puppetry MATCH with the physical puppetry in terms of X?"

The participant would also describe their thought of the potential usage of the system, retell the story, and describe the details they observed between the physical and virtual animation. At the end of the questionnaires, the participant would be provided with a completion code that he/she need to enter in MTurk.

5.4   Response Validation

We ran a pilot test with the researcher observing the behavior of the pilot participants closely. Modifications were made to the parts where the participant felt
unclear. We also ran some pilot tests with the Mturk batch, and it turned out
that Mturk non-masters have a very high rate of not taking the survey carefully.
8 out of 9 (88.8%) pilot Mturk non-masters filled out invalid responses. A Mturk
Master Worker is identified by the platform as they did good jobs consistently
across different tasks assigned by multiple requesters. Thus, in the final iteration
of our study, we decided to only recruit MTurk Master workers.

Some considerations were implemented in our web pages so that the study for
the participants would involve less interruption and less invalid answers. On the
website, the questionnaire items were arranged so that each web page only contained four questions, so that no scrolling is needed for the participants. Hence
participants can refer back to the videos easily while answering the questions.
Furthermore, we used this question at random locations in all three questionnaires for the purpose of an attention check: "While watching the television,
how often have you ever had a fatal heart attack and died and were resurrected
by a puppet and said:'where's my UFO?'?" And there are five options in the
form of multiple-choice in the questionnaires, "Always, never, sometimes, rarely,
very often." Only one of them was considered to pass the attention check, which
was that "Never." The puppet and UFO were added into the question intentionally so unless the participants had read the contents of the questionnaire items,
they would not have noticed this question was serving as attention check.

Participant responses were considered invalid if they did not finish the study,
pass the attention check or did not provide quality entries to the open-ended
questions in the questionnaire. All invalid responses were excluded from analysis.

5.5   Data Analysis and Evaluation Results

For questions asked separately on different web pages of physical enactment and
virtual animation, two-way mixed ANOVA tests were run. There was no significant main effect of type of puppetry (IV1) on overall experience ($F(1, 21) = .42$,
$p = .52$), appearance ($F(1, 21) = .12$, $p = .74$), clarity ($F(1, 21) = .26$, $p = .61$),
degree of control ($F(1, 21) = .26$, $p = .61$), affective information ($F(1, 21) = .11$,
$p = .75$), and importance of system components ($F(1, 21) = .37$, $p = .55$).

In addition, there were significant main effects of story design (IV2) on
appearance ($F(1, 21) = 6.00$, $p < .05$), clarity ($F(1, 21) = 9.51$, $p < .05$), and
affective information ($F(1, 21) = 7.02$, $p < .05$) between the two stories. Descriptive statistics showed that for appearance, story 1 (mean = 4.05, SD = .36) has
higher ratings than story 2 (mean = 2.65, SD = .45); for clarity, story 1 (mean
= 4.63, SD = .30) has higher ratings than story 2 (mean = 3.13, SD = .38); for
affective information, story 1 (mean = 3.91, SD = .31) has higher ratings than
story 2 (mean = 2.59, SD = .39). No significant main effect was found for overall
experience ($F(1, 21) = 4.00$, $p = .06$), degree of control ($F(1, 21) = 0.00$, $p = .99$)
and importance of components ($F(1, 21) = 2.19$, $p = .15$).

For the interaction between IV1 and IV2, there was no significant interaction on appearance ($F(1, 21) = 1.79$, $p = .20$), clarity ($F(1, 21) = 3.12$, $p = .09$), degree of control ($F(1, 21) = 0.09$, $p = .77$), affective information ($F(1, 21) = 2.72$, $p = .11$), and importance of system components ($F(1, 21) = 2.14$, $p = .16$). There was a significant interaction on overall experience ($F(1, 21) = 11.18$, $p < .05$). Descriptive statistics showed that while for story 1, virtual animation (mean = 4.86, SD = .42) was higher than physical enactment (mean = 3.79, SD = .39); story 2 showed the opposite pattern, virtual animation (mean = 2.78, SD = .52) was lower than physical enactment (mean = 3.50, SD = .49).

Aside from separate ratings, for questions that prompted participants to give direct comparison for the speed of movement, the angle of rotation of the movement, the carried narration, storyline, story details and affective information, we got an array of matching degree for reflection from physical enactment to virtual animation. One-sample t-tests were run to examine if there exist statistically significant differences between matching degree and baseline (greater or equal than 5 out of 7). No statistically significant difference was found.

An open coding process was done on responses from open-ended questions.

6 Discussion

Two-way ANOVA tests showed no main effect of type of puppetry (IV1) on all the dependent variables. So users perceived similarly which meant the virtual animation was perceived to faithfully represent the physical puppetry. Future puppeteers would feel consistency between the virtual animation they created and the physical puppetry they used in their real-world performance.

For IV2 - story design, there were significant main effects on appearance, clarity, and affective information where story 1 was rated higher. When using our puppet system, the complex story was perceived as more appealing, clearer, and more emotional than the simple story. This met our expected outcome.

And no significant main effect was found for overall experience, degree of control and importance of components. This meant our puppet system was consistent regarding technical perception no matter the story was complex or simple.

The results from direct comparison questions showed good matching degrees for reflection from physical enactment to virtual animation.

Some interesting findings from open-ended questions regarding usage scenarios and differences between physical enactment and virtual animation were that almost every participant thought this system was designed for kids, and very few participants discovered a limitation of the system, which is when the puppet and object collide, the animation is not ideal enough.

The evaluation done in this study helped us to begin to understand the benefits and challenges of such connections and combinations of the technologies that scaffolded the new puppet storytelling system.

7   Conclusion and Future Work

This paper firstcovered approaches usedfor puppet-based storytelling system, and then proposedaflexible low-cost approach to puppet-based storytelling system using a combination of vision- and sensor-based tracking. The results showed the consistency of the technical perception of our puppet system for different story design. The virtual animation was perceived to faithfully represent the physical puppetry. And the complex story was perceived as more appealing, clearer, and more emotional than the simple story. The novelty of our approach does not rely on any single part of the system but exists in the connections that glue each and every part together and takes advantage of the strength of every part. This flexibility warrants easy upgrades of new technology into the system. This helps to open up the design and implementation space of future interactive narrative authoring tools.

For future work, one promising avenue is to take advantage of the flexibility of this puppet system framework and expand the usage scenario. For example, with the advancing cellphone-based VR/AR technology, such as Apple ARKit and Google ARCore, the vision-based tracking and sensor-based tracking are already combined. And developers could train their custom tracking models faster with Lidar. Because it measures distances by illuminating the target with laser light and measuring the reflection with a sensor, it excludes most of the noise from data before feeding it to train the model. If designed and employed properly, mobile-based puppet system could emancipate the creativity of users by allowing greater freedom.

Another exciting avenue is to support more types of interaction. The technical aspects and storytelling-oriented design of this puppet system framework can be extended to scaffold more types of narrative creations, such as tabletop miniatures games (e.g., Warhammer) and building blocks.

We will also carry out the physical study with kids once the pandemic is over.

Acknowledgments. This research is supported by National Science Foundation Grant #1736225 *To Enact, To Tell, To Write: A Bridge to Expressive Writing through Digital Enactment*. Thanks to Lara Disuanco, and Grace Nemanic, who helped in technical development of this project.

References

1. Bai, Z., Blackwell, A.F., Coulouris, G.: Exploring expressive augmented reality: the fingar puppet system for social pretend play. In: Proceedings of the 33rd Annual ACM Conference on Human Factors in Computing Systems, pp. 1035–1044 (2015)
2. Barnes, C., et al.: Video puppetry: a performative interface for cutout animation. In: ACM SIGGRAPH Asia 2008 papers, pp. 1–9 (2008)
3. Chu, S.L., Quek, F., Tanenbaum, J.: Performative authoring: nurturing storytelling in children through imaginative enactment. In: Koenitz, H., et al. (eds.) ICIDS 2013. LNCS, vol. 8230, pp. 144–155. Springer, Cham (2013). https://doi.org/10.1007/978-3-319-02756-2_18

4. Dias, M., Harris, P.L.: The effect of make-believe play on deductive reasoning. Br. J. Dev. Psychol. **6**(3), 207–221 (1988)

5. Ferguson, J.: Lessons from digital puppetry: updating a design framework for a perceptual user interface. In: 2015 IEEE International Conference on Computer and Information Technology; Ubiquitous Computing and Communications; Dependable, Autonomic and Secure Computing; Pervasive Intelligence and Computing, pp. 1590–1595. IEEE (2015)

6. Harley, D., Chu, J.H., Kwan, J., Mazalek, A.: Towards a framework for tangible narratives. In: Proceedings of the TEI 2016: Tenth International Conference on Tangible, Embedded, and Embodied Interaction, pp. 62–69 (2016)

7. Harley, D., Tarun, A.P., Germinario, D., Mazalek, A.: Tangible vr: diegetic tangible objects for virtual reality narratives. In: Proceedings of the 2017 Conference on Designing Interactive Systems, pp. 1253–1263 (2017)

8. Jacobson, A., Panozzo, D., Glauser, O., Pradalier, C., Hilliges, O., Sorkine-Hornung, O.: Tangible and modular input device for character articulation. ACM Trans. Graph. (TOG) **33**(4), 1–12 (2014)

9. Kawahara, K., Sakashita, M., Koike, A., Suzuki, I., Suzuki, K., Ochiai, Y.: Transformed human presence for puppetry. In: Proceedings of the 13th International Conference on Advances in Computer Entertainment Technology, pp. 1–6 (2016)

10. Lamberti, F., Paravati, G., Gatteschi, V., Cannavo, A., Montuschi, P.: Virtual character animation based on affordable motion capture and reconfigurable tangible interfaces. IEEE Trans. Vis. Comput. Graph. **24**(5), 1742–1755 (2017)

11. Leite, L.: Virtual marionette. In: Proceedings of the 2012 ACM International Conference on Intelligent User Interfaces, pp. 363–366 (2012)

12. Leite, L., Orvalho, V.: Anim-actor: understanding interaction with digital puppetry using low-cost motion capture. In: Proceedings of the 8th International Conference on Advances in Computer Entertainment Technology, pp. 1–2 (2011)

13. LEite, L., Orvalho, V.: Mani-pull-action: Hand-based digital puppetry. Proc. ACM Hum.-Comput. Interact. **1**(EICS), 1–16 (2017)

14. Liang, H., Chang, J., Deng, S., Chen, C., Tong, R., Zhang, J.J.: Exploitation of multiplayer interaction and development of virtual puppetry storytelling using gesture control and stereoscopic devices. Comput. Animation Vir. Worlds **28**(5), e1727 (2017)

15. Liang, H., Chang, J., Kazmi, I.K., Zhang, J.J., Jiao, P.: Hand gesture-based interactive puppetry system to assist storytelling for children. Vis. Comput. **33**(4), 517–531 (2016). https://doi.org/10.1007/s00371-016-1272-6

16. Liu, C.C., Liu, K.P., Wang, P.H., Chen, G.D., Su, M.C.: Applying tangible story avatars to enhance children's collaborative storytelling. Br. J. Educ. Technol. **43**(1), 39–51 (2012)

17. Mazalek, A., et al.: Pictures at an exhibition: design of a hybrid puppetry performance piece. In: Herrlich, M., Malaka, R., Masuch, M. (eds.) ICEC 2012. LNCS, vol. 7522, pp. 130–143. Springer, Heidelberg (2012). https://doi.org/10.1007/978-3-642-33542-6_12

18. Nitsche, M., McBride, P.: A character in your hand: puppetry to inform game controls. DiGRA (2018)

19. Portaz, M., et al.: Figurines, a multimodal framework for tangible storytelling. In: WOCCI 2017-6th Workshop on Child Computer Interaction at ICMI 2017-19th ACM International Conference on Multi-modal Interaction, pp. 52–57 (2017)

20. Sakashita, M., Minagawa, T., Koike, A., Suzuki, I., Kawahara, K., Ochiai, Y.: You as a puppet: evaluation of telepresence user interface for puppetry. In: Proceedings of the 30th Annual ACM Symposium on User Interface Software and Technology, pp. 217–228 (2017)
21. Seja, A.L., Russ, S.W.: Children's fantasy play and emotional understanding. J. Clin. Child Psychol. **28**(2), 269–277 (1999)
22. Yoshizaki, W., et al.: An actuated physical puppet as an input device for controlling a digital manikin. In: Proceedings of the SIGCHI Conference on Human Factors in Computing Systems, pp. 637–646 (2011)
23. Zarei, N., Chu, S.L., Quek, F., Rao, N., Brown, S.A.: Investigating the effects of self-avatars and story-relevant avatars on children's creative storytelling. In: Proceedings of the 2020 CHI Conference on Human Factors in Computing Systems, pp. 1–11 (2020)
24. Zhao, S., Kirk, D., Bowen, S., Chatting, D., Wright, P.: Supporting the cross-cultural appreciation of traditional Chinese puppetry through a digital gesture library. J. Comput. Cult. Heritage (JOCCH) **12**(4), 1–19 (2019)

Mixed Reality Technology Capabilities for Combat-Casualty Handoff Training

Ryan Schubert[1]([⊠])(iD), Gerd Bruder[1](iD), Alyssa Tanaka[2],
Francisco Guido-Sanz[1](iD), and Gregory F. Welch[1](iD)

[1] University of Central Florida, 4000 Central Florida Blvd, Orlando, FL 08544, USA
{ryan.schubert,bruder,frank.guido-sanz,welch}@ucf.edu
[2] Soar Technologies, Inc., 12124 High Tech Avenue #350, Orlando, FL 32817, USA
alyssa.tanaka@soartech.com

Abstract. Patient handoffs are a common, yet frequently error prone occurrence, particularly in complex or challenging battlefield situations. Specific protocols exist to help simplify and reinforce conveying of necessary information during a combat-casualty handoff, and training can both reinforce correct behavior and protocol usage while providing relatively safe initial exposure to many of the complexities and variabilities of real handoff situations, before a patient's life is at stake. Here we discuss a variety of mixed reality capabilities and training contexts that can manipulate many of these handoff complexities in a controlled manner. We finally discuss some future human-subject user study design considerations, including aspects of handoff training, evaluation or improvement of a specific handoff protocol, and how the same technology could be leveraged for operational use.

Keywords: Mixed reality · Handoff training · Combat casualty care

1 Introduction and Background

Problems with the transfer of a patient's care from one medical or non-medical individual, team, aircrew, or unit to another, referred to as a "handoff," can pose significant risks to patient safety. Patient handoffs, in particular under stressful situations, are error prone and have been shown to be frequently insufficient [5,22], leading to a national imperative to improve handoff training and practice. In particular, providing care to those wounded in combat from the point of injury through the continuum of care is a challenging process that requires a coordinated effort [1,2,14]. Hence, multiple agencies seek to improve and standardize handoff training and protocols.

At the narrowest scope, a handoff consists of three core roles:

- *Giver (G)*: The person who has had custody of the *patient* and needs to convey medically relevant information about the patient to the *receiver*.

© Springer Nature Switzerland AG 2021
J. Y. C. Chen and G. Fragomeni (Eds.): HCII 2021, LNCS 12770, pp. 695–711, 2021.
https://doi.org/10.1007/978-3-030-77599-5_47

- *Receiver (R)*: The person who is now assuming custody of the *patient* and needs to gather medically relevant information about the patient from the *giver*.

- *Patient (P)*: The injured person being transferred from the *giver* to the *receiver*.

In practice or during training, as we widen the scope we can include additional roles as well as important aspects of the context in which the handoff is being conducted:

- *Instructor (I)*: An expert who might be guiding, evaluating, or manipulating various aspects of the handoff within a training situation.

- *Observer (O)*: A person who, during a training or evaluation scenario, passively watches the handoff for the purposes of learning or reinforcing protocol knowledge or to evaluate the effectiveness or correctness of the handoff.

- *Companion (C)*: A non-medical, non-injured participant assisting with, providing knowledge about, providing support for, or otherwise comforting the *patient*; for example, in the case where the *patient* is a wounded warfighter, this could be another warfighter from the same unit, e.g., someone who has first-hand knowledge about the mechanism of the injury, the injury itself, symptoms of the injury, and any treatment thus far.

- *Environment (E)*: This broadly encompasses a wide range of contextually relevant aspects surrounding the handoff, from peripheral entities (e.g., people or vehicles nearby) to physical aspects of the location (e.g., terrain, climate, weather, etc.) to multi-sensory events or distractions taking place in the vicinity around the handoff (e.g., explosions, shouting, gunfire, or sirens).

For many of the above roles, there could also be multiple individuals occupying the same role during a handoff, such as handing off multiple patients (P_1 through P_n), having a group of passive observers (O_1 through O_n), etc. Additionally, in practice it is common for a patient to go through multiple handoffs in sequence, with altered parameters (physiological state, applied treatments, etc.) at each handoff event. Figure 1 illustrates the core roles and additional roles involved in a sequence of handoffs.

For handoffs between a *giver* and a *receiver*, a widely used verbal report format in the military is the *MIST report*. It is designed to present the most important information rapidly. The MIST report includes the following components:

- *Mechanism (M)*: a short description of the injury mechanism, e.g., gunshot wound or fire.
- *Injuries (I)*: a list of injuries, e.g., gunshot wound to the leg (often combined with *M*).

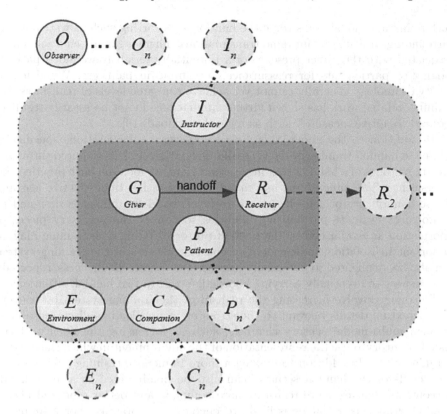

Fig. 1. Illustration of the roles involved in a handoff, including the core roles of a giver, a receiver, and a patient, which might occur in a sequence, plus additional roles of one or more instructors, observers, companions, and environmental aspects.

- *Signs/Symptoms (S)*: a description of signs or symptoms, e.g., related to the respiratory rate.
- *Treatment (T)*: a description of treatments performed on the patient, e.g., tourniquet.

There are many aspects related to the details and context of a specific handoff scenario that are independent of whether it is a real handoff or part of a training system. For example, the details of a handoff can directly cause or increase stress or cognitive load in different ways for various roles [8,12,27]. This is of particular interest in how it impacts the effectiveness or difficulty of the handoff itself as well as adhering to the desired protocol for the core roles of the *giver* and the *receiver*.

Stressors may include things such as (i) time constraints, e.g., because there is external pressure to move the patient quickly, (ii) emotional pressure from a present *companion*, or (iii) deteriorating patient physiology. In addition to general stress, a handoff participant may need to operate under increased cognitive load as a result of extraneous events or distractions or because they need to be performing additional tasks while the handoff is occurring such as watching the surroundings or listening for radio transmissions. There is further emotional load associated with the direct presence of a potentially seriously wounded patient, looking to participants for reassurance, screaming in pain, etc. While mixed reality technology generally cannot yet achieve the same levels of realism as live training, related work has shown virtual simulations do not necessarily result in reduced cognitive measures, such as mental workload [19].

In addition to the above, there are also several considerations specifically related to handoff training or the types of information or skills acquired through a specific instance of a handoff training system. Here, we focus on both practice and assessment *of the handoff and associated protocol* rather than effective learning of the handoff protocol itself. At a core level, handoff training is designed to reinforce or evaluate participants' abilities to convey the necessary pieces of information as established by the handoff protocol. While such training may be important in isolation, independent of context, aspects of the training system can also be augmented to potentially increase the overall effectiveness, especially with respect to eventually carrying knowledge over to real handoff situations.

This may involve increasing the realism of the training system by convey-ing contextual details relevant to the stress or mental load as discussed above, through multi-modal sensory channels, such as increasing the fidelity of the visual, auditory, or tactile representation of the environment in which the handoff is taking place. In addition to making a more immersive training environment, the details of the handoff scenario can also be manipulated to achieve hand-off contexts that are more realistic, more complex, and better represent actual handoff situations a trainee is likely to encounter in practice. For example, a handoff scenario could be designed to practice triage or prioritization in a case where there are multiple patients to handoff with varying physiological states, or could evaluate the effectiveness of adhering to the handoff protocol when one or more of the participants has less or no experience with the protocol.

The remainder of this paper is structured as following. In Sect. 2, we dis-cuss simulation asset technologies that can augment handoff complexities in a controlled manner. Section 3 discusses sensing of and feedback to trainees and instructors during handoff training. Section 4 focuses on use cases, link-ing training goals to infrastructures. Section 5, covers future human-subject user study design considerations, including aspects of handoff training, evaluation or improvement of a specific handoff protocol, and how the same technology could be leveraged for operational use. Section 6 concludes the paper.

2   Simulation Asset Technology

There is a variety of possible technology with which to augment a handoff train-ing system by supporting aspects of a simulated scenario context around the handoff itself. This includes many controllable aspects of the complexities of real handoffs.

2.1   Human Roles

Humans are an essential part of any handoff training, across the variety of roles described in Sect. 1, as a *giver*, a *receiver*, the *patient*, an *instructor*, an *observer*, or a *companion* to the patient. These human roles can be realized in a number of ways, depending on the availability of real people, specifics of any included medical training tasks, and the degree to which the parameters of the training objectives or scenario details should be controlled.

For example, a single user needing to train as both the giver and the receiver requires at least some manifestation for the opposite role, and potentially a patient being handed off. This manifestation could be as simple as an invisible proxy (e.g., handing off to a non-existent receiver), or a description (e.g., textual information about a patient), or could employ other real humans, such as another trainee (e.g., two trainees practicing handing off to each other with alternating roles $G_{i+1} = R_i$ and $G_i = R_i + 1$ for training trials $i = 1, .., n$) or a role player (e.g., a standardized patient actor or an instructor playing the role of the giver or the receiver).

While real humans can be very effective at capturing realistic behavior and evoking strong emotional load (e.g., as a patient role player or distressed companion), real humans also have several limitations. Perhaps most notably, real humans may not always be available; it is advantageous for a user to have the ability to train without needing any other people physically present. Additionally, real humans are limited when it comes to accurately conveying physical wounds or physiological symptoms or state. For this reason, moulage or mannequins are already frequently used. Another possible intermediate solution is the use of virtualized humans to replace one or more of the roles. Virtual participants in a handoff could be realized as anything from basic text or rendered imagery shown on a mobile phone or tablet all the way to an augmented reality lifesize three-dimensional manifestation that can interact with the trainee and the environment [6,7,9].

Such computer-controlled virtual participants can be realized with manipulable characteristics–verbal and non-verbal–some of which are directly implicit in the handoff interaction itself while others may only be indirectly relevant. The most obvious parameters are related to what the virtual character explicitly says, either verbally or via text. For example, specific vocabulary, phrases, or grammatical proficiency may be representative or expected in a given handoff scenario. Likewise, *which information* is given or requested and *the accuracy* of the information can be controlled and may directly affect the efficacy of the handoff. Other verbal cues may have a less direct effect on the protocol procedure, such as the volume, inflection, or rate of speech, all of which may make it harder or easier to understand the other person or correctly pick out necessary pieces of information. There are also many non-verbal characteristics of a given virtual participant. In particular, if the virtual character has a visual representation, his or her expression, attentiveness, and body language can all be manipulated. Likewise, passive aspects of the participant's appearance can also be altered, such as attire (e.g., wearing a specific military uniform or civilian clothing, etc.) or cleanliness that might provide indications for the mental and physical state or capabilities of the participant in cases where the scenario is not known a priori by the trainee. Such computer-controlled virtual participants have the potential to be shared as handoff training assets among trainers and trainees and improve the overall consistency and quality among handoff training instances together with opportunities in standardization or customization.

For example, the Virtual People Factory (VPF) is a widely used tool to create interactive virtual patients for medical education [16,23]. The VPF platform of the Virtual Patients Group (VPG, a consortium of North-American universities) was developed with support by the National Science Foundation and allows developers to create interactive scenarios between real trainees and virtual patients, relying on natural language interaction. The system implements on an interaction modeling approach called *human-centered distributed conversational modeling*, in which an interaction between end-users and virtual patients generates new verbal input such as questions or statements that are then evaluated by subject-matter experts to create new appropriate virtual patient responses [15].

An important aspect of actual handoffs is that the physiological condition of the patient is dynamic before, during, and after the handoff itself. This is, of course, part of the time pressure associated with the handoff. The more visceral the concern for patient safety, the more realistic the role of such stressors in the trainee experience. A simulated patient used for handoff training could be an advanced physical mannequin or a virtual representation [24]. In either case, the medically relevant state of the patient could be controlled using complex physiological simulation software, such as Pulse or BioGears [11]. Such simulations can dynamically adapt to external conditions, react to provided treatments, or allow for specific medical events (e.g., loss of consciousness, seizure, cardiac event, etc.) to be triggered at any specific point during a handoff. Such events could be planned in order to assess how a trainee or protocol handles rapidly shifting situational parameters or priorities, or be direct results of failures during one or more handoff (e.g., as a result of treatment or lack of treatment due to incorrect or missing information).

Such interactions with virtual participants could be automated and predefined or initiated *ad hoc* by an instructor. The instructor could be co-located with the trainee or be present remotely. For instance, the TeachLivE (TLE) system for education and training has a long history of relying on remote *telepresent* operators, who can embody one or multiple virtual participants during training sessions by observing the trainees via a live video stream [21]. In this approach, the expert instructors/operators can quickly switch from one training session to the next without the need for physical relocation. This provides a vista for the scalability of handoff training with respect to automated virtual participant behaviors and human instructors/operators.

2.2   Environment and Location

In addition to having control over any virtual participants and the physiological state of one or more patients involved in a specific handoff scenario, a training system could be expanded to also have control over aspects of the environment or the context within which the handoff is taking place. This can include affecting the perceived location. For example, a handoff performed on a battlefield under active gunfire has very different immediate concerns and priorities as compared to a similar handoff done on the deck of a ship or in a field tent, and none of those locations may match the conditions in which the training takes place. Associated with different locations are many possible contextual events, such as gunfire, sirens, other virtual humans (shouting, in pain, moving around, engaging in combat, etc.), or the proximity of vehicles or aircraft. To create a sense of being in varied rich environments, hardware devices can be utilized across a range of sensory modalities. Visually, the environmental context could use a visual augmented reality head-worn display (e.g., Microsoft HoloLens or Magic Leap One), projected imagery (e.g., CAVE immersive projection technologies), or a combination of the two. There are trade-offs between system cost, portability, configurability, and scalability between different possible realizations providing the visual display. Likewise, audio could come in the form of noise-cancelling headphones (in the case where one wants to more tightly control what the trainee can hear or if training in an inherently noisy area), open-ear headphone solutions such as bone conduction headphones (if multiple users may also need to communicate with each other), or from speakers positioned in the space around the user. Vibrotactile devices, e.g., a large low-frequency transducer attached to a simple platform on which the handoff takes place, can provide haptic sensations that correspond to environmental events such as a vehicle driving by or an explosion nearby [9,10]. Smaller haptic devices, potentially as simple as a vibrating mobile phone, could be worn or carried by a user. Olfactory scent delivery systems (e.g., MENA ScentPOP) can provide contextually relevant smells, e.g., gunpowder or burnt flesh, at a very low temporal resolution during a handoff interaction.

3   Sensing and Feedback

Automating analysis or evaluation of trainees during handoff training has the potential to provide feedback to trainees and instructors that is both more specific and immediate. Perhaps the most intuitive and general purpose interface for automated analysis during a handoff is parsing verbal statements made by one or more users [20]. This can be accomplished with minimal sensor requirements—essentially just a microphone. Such core functionality lends itself particularly well as a baseline that can then be augmented, scaled up, or specifically tailored to achieve training configurations able to support handoff scenarios that are more complex and realistic, depending on the available training environment and infrastructure as discussed in Sect. 2.

For extended trainee assessment, sensors for non-verbal metrics can be employed together with the verbal analysis system, such as head-worn eye trackers for gaze direction measurements (e.g., to measure eye contact [4] or mutual gaze [18]) or sensors that capture the trainee's body language (e.g., posture or gestures [26]). Capturing such non-verbal information could be as simple as placing a Microsoft Kinect sensor nearby or as rich as having a fully calibrated, multi-camera professional motion capture setup with body-worn tracked optical markers, depending on the training needs and available hardware. Additional physiological sensors such as the Empatica E4 wristband could provide additional feedback (e.g., stress levels) on the trainee's heart rate, temperature, and skin conductance.

In addition to providing a means for an instructor to control the context and details of a specific handoff scenario prior to and during a training session, a handoff training system may also provide an interface with distilled or visualized results from any automatic analysis that occurs from the training session. For instance, this could include seeing the fields in the MIST report filled in automatically from the verbal handoff speech, along with each corresponding audio clip, and a summary of detected key words or phrases. Such an instructor interface is useful *during* a training session (for flagging events, noticing possible trainee issues, and guiding dynamic adjustments to the simulation) and also *after* the training as part of an after-action review and feedback session between the instructor and the trainee.

Likewise, automated analysis can also be used as feedback to artificial intelligence systems designed to adapt the handoff simulation to user behavior and responses both in *real-time* (e.g., a virtual human "noticing" that a user appears to not be paying attention), and *collectively over time* to adjust simulation responses and events based on collective actual trainee behaviors accumulated over many training sessions.

4   Training Use Cases

For a given training instance, there is a bidirectional relationship between the *training goals* (i.e., what is important to learn or practice) and the *training infrastructure* (i.e., the available or required equipment, people, space, etc. able to be used for the training task). For example, if the most important training goal is to reinforce a single user's ability to verbally convey certain key pieces of information during a handoff, the corresponding required training infrastructure might consist of a single tablet-based application capable of automatically evaluating one side of a handoff procedure in whatever physical setting happens to be available for the user. A training goal of having users experience something closer to the actual chaos of a battlefield handoff under heavy stress and mental load likely requires more substantial training infrastructure, and perhaps even a dedicated installation. Similarly, the available infrastructure imposes certain restrictions on the possible types of handoff and training considerations that can be introduced as part of a training session. A small group of trainees in the field may not have access to a full projector-based muti-user immersive simulated environment, but may still be able to achieve some amount of additional simulation realism through a self-contained augmented or virtual reality head-worn display in combination with smartphones or tablets to provide information and record verbal communication, with comparable benefits to training efficacy [13]. A single user at home may only have access to his or her smartphone or tablet and therefore could not learn or practice training goals requiring an immersive handoff environment, although augmented and mixed reality is expected to continue becoming more prevalent, even in such situations [25].

The following three example use cases span a range of possible manipulable handoff and training considerations. These examples correspond to a baseline of relatively minimal technological capabilities, the Uniformed Services University of the Health Services (USUHS), and the simulation infrastructure at the Synthetic Reality Lab (SREAL) at the University of Central Florida (UCF).

1. *Asynchronous training* – Like the notion of asynchronous learning, *asynchronous training* is a trainee-centered approach to training, performance enhancement, and assessment without the constraints on time, place, and people. In the most basic manifestation, one or two trainees could, for example, utilize smartphones or tablets with speech recognition capabilities at a convenient location and time. By supporting ad hoc use that relies on a minimal set of relatively small, low-cost devices, this configuration has a few strong advantages: (i) it is likely that the necessary hardware is either already on hand or is easily attainable, (ii) the setup likely does not require an expert and initiating the training could be as simple as running an app on each device, and (iii) any convenient and available location can be used, as long as it meets some threshold for ambient noise that might interfere with automated voice recognition. On the other hand, this manifestation alone *cannot* capture fully realistic handoff factors such as environmental distractions, patient physiology, other roles, etc.

2. *Highly immersive training* – Towards the other end of the spectrum are specialized immersive training facilities. An example is the WAVE at USUHS [3], which supports large-scale combat casualty care training in an 8,000-square-foot area composed of two pods surrounded by circumferential 9 12-foot movie screens and a directional sound system (see the bottom-left insert in Fig. 2). Such a training setup can support group training with immersive environmental aspects (e.g., three-dimensional visual stimuli and spatial audio), using live standardized patients or advanced medical mannequins. Such facilities are very effective at providing a realistic context for a set of specific scenarios. However, they require some instrumentation of users (e.g., shutter glasses or immersive virtual reality head-mounted displays), require a substantial amount of dedicated space, and are very expensive and complex to setup and operate.

3. *Outdoor field training* – Instead of immersing users in a virtual training environment, portable augmented reality technologies such as head-worn displays and haptic feedback platforms, e.g., employed in our related outdoor training

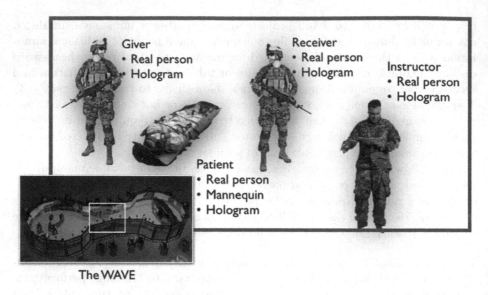

Fig. 2. Illustration of handoffs with different roles enabled by the technologies available in USUHS' highly immersive WAVE training facility, which features surrounding projected virtual imagery and audio feedback.

research, are able to embed virtual stimuli in the real environment, which is particularly effective if trainees are in a meaningful physical location such as on a field exercise. Such devices are significantly less expensive than a fully dedicated immersive simulation facility, and can support training in a variety of available locations, leveraging aspects of the existing physical environment where possible (e.g., making use of physical terrain, buildings, weather conditions, etc.). The use of augmented reality displays allows for any number of human roles to be occupied by real entities (e.g., live standardized patients, physical mannequins, or other human trainees) or highly controllable 3D virtual humans, depending on training goals. Although flexible, there are limitations on the spatial extent of a haptic platform (e.g., see Fig. 3) and users are required to wear head-worn displays that with current technology have a limited field of view for displaying virtual content.

Although the example use cases here are described largely as pertaining to training related applications, similar infrastructure could additionally or simultaneously allow for the possibility of testing a handoff *protocol* as well. For example, the same automated analysis technology discussed in Sect. 3 could be used to assess the robustness of the protocol itself rather than the user by identifying which specific aspects of the protocol break down under specific simulated contexts (e.g., in the presence of distractions, noise, or other more realistic conditions).

Fig. 3. Illustration of outdoor field training as researched at UCF, involving the use of augmented reality head-worn displays and visual stimuli involving virtual handoff participants as well as environmental effects.

5   Study Design and Evaluation Discussion

In light of the extensive range of possible manipulable aspects both explicit and implicit to handoffs in a training setting, we see a significant opportunity for evaluating the strengths and effectiveness of *specific* capabilities through human-subject user studies. The current COVID-19 pandemic presents a variety of challenges making in-person studies significantly more difficult logistically. In particular, even in addressing device disinfection, contact and proximity-limiting procedures, and more stringent Institutional Review Board (IRB) requirements, such user studies during pandemic conditions would likely have an additional psychological effect on participants. Participants may be (consciously or subconsciously) aware or concerned about personal safety with respect to being in shared, enclosed spaces, having extended physical contact with headsets or other equipment that could be perceived as potentially contaminated, adding additional confounds to any collected data or results.

In anticipation of being able to resume more normal human-subject studies, here we discuss some study design considerations. For example, SREAL's Human Surrogate Interaction Space (HuSIS) [17] provides a highly instrumented space for *simulating* a variety of field contexts within a much more controlled environment. Such an experiment testbed can allow for stable and predictable evaluation

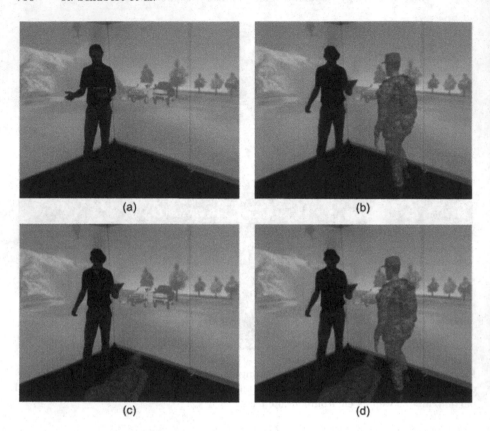

(a)   (b)

(c)   (d)

Fig. 4. Illustration of four mixed reality handoff training environments at UCF, showing different configurations of head-worn and projection-based displays, textual or full-body real or virtual representations of handoff participants and patients.

between technological realization or other factors of handoff training. For example, Fig. 4 shows an illustration of four potential study conditions comparing the manifestation (not present, textual only, or virtually present via an augmented reality headset) of both a *receiver* and/or a single *patient* within a hypothetical remote handoff location, with environmental context provided via the projection walls of the HuSIS, along with other multimodal stimuli, such as spatial background audio or haptic effects such as wind from a nearby helicopter.

Additionally, we discuss some interesting evaluation areas that may be initially less intuitive, such as the use of a handoff training system for improving the *protocol* itself, the *learning* of the protocol, and possible *operational use* opportunities that could also further guide and/or improve the training aspects.

5.1   Evaluation of Protocol/Education

Training use cases 1–3 in Sect. 4 are aimed at training individuals who have been educated in some way to use a particular protocol (e.g., MIST) in various handoff circumstances. However the same system technology could be used to evaluate the effectiveness of the protocol itself, or the educational process and tools used to learn the protocol.

For example, a particular protocol might be more or less able to accommodate secondary information from a companion (e.g., a fellow Soldier or Marine), might be more/less robust to language mismatches or spoken accents, more/less robust to time pressures, more/less robust to environmental distractions, and more/less robust to participant distractions. Also, a particular learning module or educational step might be more or less effective than another, or some variation.

The exact same technology used for training and assessing individuals could be used to assess *protocols* by holding the participant handoff skills constant, varying the participant or environment conditions, and measuring the effectiveness of the handoff. Protocol sensitivity analysis could be carried out much the same way sensitivity analysis is carried out for other systems: by choosing one parameter of interest, e.g., a particular wording or step of the protocol, then holding all other parameters constant while carrying out handoff instances and measuring the effectiveness of the handoff in the presence of small perturbations of the parameter of interest. This sort of differential analysis can provide insights into the fragility/robustness of the protocol. Whole new protocols or variations of protocols could be assessed in this way.

Similarly, the exact same technology used for training and assessing individuals could be used to assess *the process and tools used to learn* the protocols, by holding constant the participant handoff skills and the environment conditions for example, then varying the educational process or tools, and measuring the effectiveness of the handoff. Education sensitivity analysis could be carried out much the same way as protocol sensitivity analysis described above. Again, this sort of differential analysis can provide insights into the fragility/robustness of the education process or tools, and whole new educational modules or tools could be assessed in this way.

5.2   Evaluation of Operational Use

As depicted in Fig. 5 we recognize and envision that many of the technologies and insights discussed have promising potential for operational use as well. Real-time feedback provided to an instructor, such as automatically parsed and populated fields corresponding to MIST could instead be used as part of an operational system where an actual user could, for example, be given a visual indication of the automatically parsed speech, or detected type of information, serving as a passive checklist or reassurance to a user that nothing is erroneously omitted during an actual handoff. Taking it a step further, a system could provide active visual or auditory prompts for pieces of information that may have been skipped or that require clarification. Additionally, an operational use system could help with remembering specific details of what happened or what treatment steps have already been taken, potentially allowing the giver to provide a more accurate and detailed account during a subsequent handoff. Such visual and auditory feedback

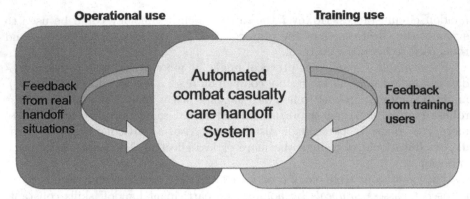

Fig. 5. Illustration of feedback mechanisms from operational or training use.

could be presented via something as simple as the user's existing communication radio output, or as complex as an integrated mixed reality display.

The inclusion of automated analysis in an operational context enables several novel possibilities related to the tracking and flow of data and information related to a patient, accumulated across a series of multiple handoffs of the same patient. This data could include patient physiology, both current state and accumulated history, verbal information as provided by the *patient*, previous *givers*, or a *companion* (e.g., accounts of what happened), as well as any treatments provided along the way. Such data could automatically transfer from person to person, associated with the patient, and provide a clearer and more complete timeline of events while detecting or reducing the risk of erroneous information or misunderstandings across multiple handoffs.

As with data collected during training, operational data could be aggregated across handoffs to bootstrap and adapt the system to be more effective both in continued operational use but also to provide more accurate training scenarios or to emphasize training related to aspects of the handoff that frequently cause the most critical issues in actual handoffs (see Fig. 5).

Operational data, including physiological measures, voice notes, etc. could be cached with/on a data device affixed to the patient, and uploaded to the cloud as the patient comes into range (edge) of the cloud, e.g., at a field hospital where Wi-Fi is available. Conversely, patient-specific cloud data could be downloaded to the patient device so that it is available off-line (when away from the cloud). Each access (input or output) would be logged with the ID of the individual, thus maintaining a complete chain of communication both for historical records and for operational needs, e.g., if more information is needed from one individual somewhere in the chain of handoffs. Synchronizing patient data between the cloud and the patient this way would provide the most reliable, timely, and useful access to the data, and the place and time where it is needed.

If the operational data is cached with/on a data device affixed to the patient as described above, and synchronized to the cloud when possible, this could help support *asynchronous handoff*. For example, if someone with knowledge about the mechanism of injury is able to convey information before the receiver is available, that information could be conveyed and then held until the appropriate receiver is available to receive it.

Finally, if asynchronous handoff is supported as described above, handoff involving future *robotic warfighter rescue devices* would be naturally supported. Warfighters at the point of access could provide information and immediately get back to the fight, while the wounded warrior and the critical handoff information is transported to an appropriate safe space. Mixed reality representations of a *receiver* (in the case of a warfighter asynchonously handing off "to" a robotic device) or *giver* (in the case of the person asynchronously receiving the casualty) could further assist in capturing and reproducing more natural handoff interactions, potentially increasing effectiveness or reducing errors.

6 Conclusion

In this paper we described technologies and use cases for combat-casualty handoff training with a view on the different roles involved in a handoff and related simulation asset technologies. We discussed a range of technological realizations for handoff training, with an emphasis on the significant benefits of integrating mixed reality capabilities for embodied three-dimensional virtual roles with the handoff context. Finally, we present some considerations for future human-subject studies to explore and evaluate many of the mixed reality handoff training combinations and parameters, including two closely related ideas of handoff protocol evaluation and how the same or similar technology could additionally be leveraged for or in combination with operational use situations.

Acknowledgment. This work is supported by the Defense Health Agency as part of the Defense Health Program under Contract No. W81XWH-19-C-0023; and the AdventHealth Endowed Chair in Healthcare Simulation (Prof. Welch). Any opinions, findings, conclusions, or recommendations expressed in this material are those of the authors and do not necessarily reflect the official views of the U.S. Government or Department of Defense.

References

1. Apker, J., et al.: Exploring emergency physician-hospitalist handoff interactions: development of the handoff communication assessment. Ann. Emerg. Med. **55**(2), 161–170 (2010)
2. Gakhar, B., Spencer, A.L.: Using direct observation, formal evaluation, and an interactive curriculum to improve the sign-out practices of internal medicine interns. Acad. Med. **85**(7), 1182–1188 (2010)
3. Goolsby, C., Vest, R., Goodwin, T.: New wide area virtual environment (wave) medical education. Mil. Med. **179**(1), 38–41 (2014)

4. Grillon, H., Thalmann, D.: Eye contact as trigger for modification of virtual character behavior. In: 2008 Virtual Rehabilitation, pp. 205–211. IEEE (2008)
5. Horwitz, L.I., Moin, T., Krumholz, H.M., Wang, L., Bradley, E.H.: Consequences of inadequate sign-out for patient care. Arch. Intern. Med. **168**(16), 1755–1760 (2008)
6. Kim, K., Maloney, D., Bruder, G., Bailenson, J.N., Welch, G.F.: The effects of virtual human's spatial and behavioral coherence with physical objects on social presence in AR. Comput. Anim. Virtual Worlds **28**(3–4), e1771 (2017)
7. Kim, K., et al.: A large-scale study of surrogate physicality and gesturing on human-surrogate interactions in a public space. Front. Robot. AI **4**, 32 (2017)
8. Laxmisan, A., Hakimzada, F., Sayan, O.R., Green, R.A., Zhang, J., Patel, V.L.: The multitasking clinician: decision-making and cognitive demand during and after team handoffs in emergency care. Int. J. Med. Inf. **76**(11–12), 801–811 (2007)
9. Lee, M., Bruder, G., Höllerer, T., Welch, G.: Effects of unaugmented periphery and vibrotactile feedback on proxemics with virtual humans in AR. IEEE Trans. Vis. Comput. Graph. **24**(4), 1525–1534 (2018)
10. Lee, M., Bruder, G., Welch, G.F.: Exploring the effect of vibrotactile feedback through the floor on social presence in an immersive virtual environment. In: 2017 IEEE Virtual Reality (VR), pp. 105–111. IEEE (2017)
11. Militello, L.G., Patterson, E.S., Sushereba, C.E., Wolf, S.P.: Principled design of an augmented reality trainer for medics. Technical Report, Unveil LLC Cancinnati United States (2018)
12. Novak, L.L., et al.: Understanding the information needs and context of trauma handoffs to design automated sensing clinical documentation technologies: qualitative mixed-method study of military and civilian cases. J. Med. Internet Res. **22**(9), e17978 (2020)
13. Reed, D., Maraj, C., Hurter, J., Eifert, L.: Simulations to train buried explosives detection: a pilot investigation. In: Proceedings of the Interservice/Industry Training, Simulation, and Education Conference (I/ITSEC) (2019)
14. Riesenberg, L.A.: Shift-to-shift handoff research: where do we go from here? J. Grad. Med. Educ. **4**(1), 4 (2012)
15. Rossen, B., Lind, S., Lok, B.: Human-centered distributed conversational modeling: efficient modeling of robust virtual human conversations. In: Ruttkay, Z., Kipp, M., Nijholt, A., Vilhjálmsson, H.H. (eds.) IVA 2009. LNCS (LNAI), vol. 5773, pp. 474–481. Springer, Heidelberg (2009). https://doi.org/10.1007/978-3-642-04380-2_52
16. Rossen, B., Lok, B.: A crowdsourcing method to develop virtual human conversational agents. Int. J. Human-Comput. Stud. **70**(4), 301–319 (2012)
17. Schubert, R., Welch, G., Daher, S., Raij, A.: HuSIS: a dedicated space for studying human interactions. IEEE Comput. Graph. Appl. **36**(6), 26–36 (2016)
18. Steptoe, W., et al.: Eye-tracking for avatar eye-gaze and interactional analysis in immersive collaborative virtual environments. In: Proceedings of the 2008 ACM Conference on Computer Supported Cooperative Work, pp. 197–200 (2008)
19. Stevens, J., Mondesire, S.C., Maraj, C.S., Badillo-Urquiola, K.A., Maxwell, D.B.: Workload analysis of virtual world simulation for military training. In: Proceedings of the MODSIM World, pp. 26–28, Virginia Beach, VA, USA (2016)
20. Tanaka, A., et al.: The development and implementation of speech understanding for medical handoff training. In: Interservice/Industry Training, Simulation, and Education Conference (I/ITSEC), Orlando, FL (2019)
21. TeachLivE: Center for Research in Education Simulation Technology (CREST). http://teachlive.org. Accessed 10 Feb 2021

22. Vidyarthi, A.R., Arora, V., Schnipper, J.L., Wall, S.D., Wachter, R.M.: Managing discontinuity in academic medical centers: strategies for a safe and effective resident sign-out. J. Hosp. Med. **1**(4), 257–266 (2006)
23. VPF: Virtual People Factory 2.0. http://www.virtualpeoplefactory.com. Accessed 10 Feb 2021
24. Welch, G.F.: Highlights of "Immersive Sciences" Research in the USA: Augmented/Virtual Reality and Human Surrogates (2016)
25. Welch, G.F., Bruder, G., Squire, P., Schubert, R.: Anticipating Widespread Augmented Reality: Insights from the 2018 AR Visioning Workshop (2019)
26. Xiao, Y., Yuan, J., Thalmann, D.: Human-virtual human interaction by upper body gesture understanding. In: Proceedings of the 19th ACM Symposium on Virtual Reality Software and Technology, pp. 133–142 (2013)
27. Young, J.Q., Ten Cate, O., O'Sullivan, P.S., Irby, D.M.: Unpacking the complexity of patient handoffs through the lens of cognitive load theory. Teach. Learn. Med. **28**(1), 88–96 (2016)

Author Index

Printed in the United States
by Baker & Taylor Publisher Services